ADVANCED FINANCIAL ACCOUNTING

Fifth Edition, Volume II
Chapters 9-16, Modules E-H

Ronald J. Huefner, PhD, CMA, CPA
DISTINGUISHED TEACHING PROFESSOR
STATE UNIVERSITY OF NEW YORK AT BUFFALO

James A. Largay III, PhD, CPA
ARTHUR ANDERSEN & CO. ALUMNI PROFESSOR OF ACCOUNTING
LEHIGH UNIVERSITY

Susan S. Hamlen, PhD, CFM, CMA
ASSOCIATE PROFESSOR OF ACCOUNTING
STATE UNIVERSITY OF NEW YORK AT BUFFALO

1999

DAME
PUBLICATIONS, INC.
HOUSTON, TX

| *Cover Design:* | Amanda Austin |
| | Andrea Leggett |

Cover Photo: © Corel Professional Photos. Images may have been combined and/or modified to produce final cover art.

| *Desktop Publishers:* | Sheryl New |
| | Raenelle Belch |

Graphic Artists:	Amanda Austin
	Naika Malveaux
	Andrea Leggett

| *Artist:* | Pam Porter |

© **DAME PUBLICATIONS, INC.–1998**
7800 Bissonnet–Suite 415
Houston, TX 77074
713/995-1000
713/995-9637–FAX
800/364-9757
E-mail: dame.publications@worldnet.att.net
Website: http://www.damepub.com

ISBN 0-87393-756-2

Library of Congress Card No. 98-70887

Printed in the United States of America.

Material from Uniform CPA Examination Questions and Unofficial Answers, copyright © 1994, 1992, 1989, 1988, 1987, 1983, 1982, 1981, 1980, 1979, 1978, 1977, 1976, 1975, 1974, 1973, 1972, 1971, 1970, 1969, 1968, 1967, 1966, 1965, 1964, 1963, 1962, 1961, 1960, 1959, 1958, 1957, 1954, 1953, 1951 by the American Institute of Certified Public Accountants, Inc., is reprinted (or adapted) with permission.

Material from the Certificate in Management Accounting Examinations, copyright © 1989, 1987, 1986, 1985, 1984, 1983, 1982, 1981, 1980, 1979, 1978, 1977, 1976, 1975, 1974, 1973 by the National Association of Accountants is reprinted (or adapted) with permission.

Exhibits 9.7, 9.9, 10.1, copyright © by Financial Accounting Standards Board, 401 Merritt 7, P.O. Box 5116, Norwalk, Connecticut, 06856-5116, U.S.A. Reprinted with permission. Copies of the complete document are available from the FASB.

Figure 13.1 copyright © by Governmental Accounting Standards Board, 401 Merritt 7, P.O. Box 5116, Norwalk, Connecticut, 06856-5116, U.S.A. Reprinted with permission. Copies of the complete document are available from the GASB.

TO OUR FAMILIES

For, as we know, there are three things needed by anyone who wishes to carry on business carefully.

The most important of these is cash or any equivalent, according to the saying *Unum aliquid necessarium est substantia*. Without this, business can hardly be carried on.

The second thing necessary in business is to be a good bookkeeper and ready mathematician . . .

The third and last thing is to arrange all transactions in such a systematic way that one may understand each one of them at a glance, i.e., by the debit (*debito*—owed to) and the credit (*credito*—owed by) method. This is very essential to merchants, because, without making the entries systematically, it would be impossible to conduct their business, for they would have no rest and their minds would be troubled.

—Luca Pacioli,
Double Entry Bookkeeping (1494)

PREFACE

This textbook is designed to serve, at either the undergraduate or graduate level, the course commonly known as **advanced accounting**. Throughout the five editions of this book, we use the title **Advanced Financial Accounting** to distinguish it from advanced textbooks in managerial accounting.

This book is written with three major objectives in mind. *First*, we seek to reflect the changing topical emphases and content in the advanced accounting course; coverage is completely updated for new developments concerning applicable reporting issues and requirements, including the newest FASB and GASB pronouncements and exposure drafts. *Second*, we write from the perspective of enhancing teachability; many of the topics in this course are complex and require careful explanation. We highlight the major issues in each topic and attempt to provide the student with the logical structure needed to analyze these issues, rather than merely explaining current practice. This view equips the student with the ability to analyze future reporting developments. Wherever possible, we also provide real life illustrations of reporting issues. Students often lack the business experience necessary to practically apply what they have learned. Illustrations of reporting by actual companies bring textbook concepts to life. *Third*, we identify a unifying theme—the **accounting entity**—underlying many of the apparently diverse advanced accounting topics and use it as a focal point throughout the text.

This edition modifies the organization adopted in the fourth edition. Although we still begin the book with the topics that receive the most emphasis in advanced accounting courses—business combinations and consolidated financial statements—we reorganized these and other topics into **16 core chapters and eight modules**. Modules are approximately half the length of a chapter. Some modules are used to separate out specialized topics related to core chapters; some instructors may wish to cover these topics, while others may not. Some modules cover short or emerging topics that do not require full chapter-length coverage. We believe that this new structure enhances flexibility for users.

Advanced accounting courses differ with respect to both the institution's curriculum and the instructor's interests. Virtually all courses are likely to use a substantial portion of Chapters 1-7, but we find that not all of the remaining chapters are covered in all courses. Organization by **core chapters** and **shorter modules** permits maximum instructor flexibility.

The first seven chapters of Volume I address business combination and consolidation topics in detail, followed by a chapter on corporate bankruptcy. Four modules of roughly half-chapter length covering consolidation-related topics complete Volume I.

Volume II begins with three chapters on international operations and derivative financial instruments. Translation of foreign currency statements and discussion of foreign currency forward contracts serves as a springboard for the analysis of derivative financial instruments. Our focus then shifts to entities other than the corporation; five chapters on governmental and not-for-profit entities and partnerships complete the 16 core chapters. Four more half-chapter length modules on a variety of topics round out Volume II.

TOPICAL COVERAGE

The first seven chapters address **business combinations and consolidated financial statements**, the major topic in advanced accounting. Chapter 1 discusses various forms of **merger and acquisition** transactions and introduces the purchase and pooling of interests methods of accounting. Chapter 2 extends the treatment of mergers and acquisitions by examining the accounting aspects of **junk-bond financing**, emergence of **leveraged buyout** transactions, the development of various **takeover defenses**, and approaches to corporate restructuring in the form of **spinoffs**. The next five chapters address **consolidated financial reporting**. Throughout these consolidation chapters, we discuss proposals made by the FASB in its 1995 *Exposure Draft*, "Consolidation Policy and Procedures." As this book goes to press, however, adoption of some or all of these proposals is uncertain. Commentary received by the FASB during the exposure period, turnover of Board members and the addition in 1996 of the business combinations project to the FASB's agenda have delayed final action on these proposals.

Chapter 3 introduces the **consolidation process**, focusing on consolidation immediately following acquisition, with emphasis on the balance sheet. Chapter 4 addresses consolidation at times subsequent to acquisition, introducing the equity method of accounting and the consolidated income statement. We use the **complete equity method** throughout the discussion of consolidation; the appendix to Chapter 4 explores consolidation when the cost method is used. The impact of **intercompany transactions** is studied in Chapters 5 and 6. Chapter 7 concludes our core chapter coverage of combinations and consolidation with consideration of various **special topics in consolidation**, including subsidiary preferred stock, changes in the parent's ownership, and indirect and mutual holdings. Chapter 8 addresses various aspects of corporate **bankruptcy and reorganization**, including reorganization and liquidation under bankruptcy law, and less formal means of restructuring, including **quasi-reorganization** and **troubled debt restructuring**. Modules A-D incorporate **optional consolidation topics** including conceptual issues, consolidated statement of cash flows, tax issues, consolidation of internal operations (also known as home office and branch accounting) and updated coverage of **segment reporting** based on FASB *Statement 131*.

The topic of consolidation leads us to a discussion of the **translation of foreign financial statements**, necessary when consolidating a foreign subsidiary. In this way we introduce the complex, and sometimes controversial, subject of **accounting for international operations.** We begin Chapter 9 by describing the international monetary system and the nature of exchange rates, and then discuss the alternative approaches to translating financial statements presented in currencies other than the U.S. dollar, as permitted by FASB *Statement 52.* Chapter 10 considers **international foreign currency transactions**—buying, selling, borrowing, and lending between a U.S. firm and a non-U.S. firm. We discuss the use of, and accounting for, **forward and option contracts** as a way of hedging exposure to risk due to exchange rate fluctuations.

The discussion of forward contracts leads naturally to a further examination of futures contracts and other **derivative financial instruments**. Chapter 11 covers **futures contracts, options, and financial swaps**, and includes discussion of the 1997 FASB *Draft Statement* on derivatives and hedging activities.

As this book goes to press, the FASB issued **SFAS 133**, "Derivative Financial Instruments and Hedging Activities" (1998). Its provisions are similar to those in the 1997 *Draft Statement* referenced throughout Chapters 10 and 11. Publishers' deadlines prohibited us from changing terminology and making further revisions in this edition.

The expanding role of **governmental and not-for-profit organizations** in our society requires extensive coverage of accounting and reporting issues related to these organizations. Chapter 12 introduces the basic principles of governmental accounting and applies them to the **routine activities** of state and local governmental units. Chapter 13 examines accounting and reporting for **nonroutine activities** of governments. External reporting requirements are also discussed, including coverage of the GASB's proposed reporting model, as described in its 1997 *Exposure*

Draft. Finally, Chapter 14 discusses accounting and reporting for various types of nongovernmental **not-for-profit organizations** and incorporates the requirements of FASB *Statements 116, 117* and *124*. Discussion in these chapters is highly applications-based, using extensive illustrations from actual financial statements and emphasizing key reporting issues occurring in practice.

The last two core chapters deal with **partnership accounting**. Partnerships are a common form of business organization, and their accounting and reporting practices differ somewhat from those used for the more familiar corporation. Chapter 15 addresses partnership formation, income determination, income allocation and expansion, and Chapter 16 discusses partnership contraction and liquidation, other partnership-type organizations and reporting alternatives to address **off-balance-sheet financing**. Tax aspects of partnerships are considered in the appendix to Chapter 15.

Modules E-H complete our topical coverage. Module E examines the **Securities and Exchange Commission (SEC)**, its role in financial accounting and reporting, and the principal SEC reporting and disclosure requirements. Module F introduces the emerging area of **environmental liabilities**. Module G focuses on the individual as an accounting entity and considers **personal financial statements**. These statements differ from business financial statements in that a *current value*, rather than historical cost, approach is used for the presentation of assets and liabilities. **Estate accounting**, involving reporting for fiduciary responsibility of the executor in managing and distributing a decedent's property, is studied in Module H. In addition to estate accounting and reporting, Module H introduces basic aspects of estate planning and taxation.

PEDAGOGICAL FEATURES

We wrote all text material carefully, and vigorously sought to simplify sentence construction and eliminate excess words. This is an ongoing effort that makes progress with each succeeding edition. All chapters include a **Chapter Preview**, one or more **Authors' Commentaries** in which we express our views on controversial issues, introduce emerging issues, or provide real life illustrations of reporting practice, and a **Summary of Key Concepts**.

Citations to professional pronouncements are included throughout the text. The original documents are identified as follows:

APBO: Accounting Principles Board Opinion
APBS: Accounting Principles Board Statement
ARB: Accounting Research Bulletin
ARS: Accounting Research Study
ASR: Accounting Series Release (SEC)
EITF: Emerging Issues Task Force Consensus
FRR: Financial Reporting Release (SEC)
IAS: International Accounting Standard
IFAS: Interpretation of Financial Accounting Standards
NCGA: National Council on Governmental Accounting
SAB: Staff Accounting Bulletin (SEC)
SFAC: Statement of Financial Accounting Concepts
SFAS: Statement of Financial Accounting Standards
SGAC: Statement of Governmental Accounting Concepts
SGAS: Statement of Governmental Accounting Standards
SOP: Statement of Position (AICPA)

Assignment Material. Each core chapter contains approximately 36 questions, exercises, and problems whereas each module has about half that number. Many of the questions are used to review topics in the chapter, while others are more thought-provoking and challenging. Exercises and problems, which also vary in level of difficulty, are sometimes designed to reinforce and deepen the student's understanding of a topic by introducing a new element or complexity beyond the examples in the text. Some possess user-oriented or interpretive elements. Numerous questions, exercises, and problems have been adapted from the Uniform CPA Examination and the Certified Management Accountant (CMA) Examination with the permission of the American Institute of Certified Public Accountants and the Institute of Certified Management Accountants, respectively. In many cases, these materials are modified to conform to our presentation of particular subjects.

MAJOR CHANGES IN THE FIFTH EDITION

We are pleased to have **Susan S. Hamlen** of the State University of New York at Buffalo as our co-author. A long-term user of the book and experienced advanced accounting instructor, Susan brings a fresh approach to governmental and not-for-profit accounting, as well as additional expertise in derivative financial instruments.

The entity-oriented theme of the first four editions remains unchanged but organizing the material into **16 core chapters** likely to be covered in most courses and **8 optional modules** is new. We updated the discussion throughout the text for the latest FASB and GASB developments and made numerous improvements intended to enhance clarity of presentation and teachability. Note that *SFAS 133*, "Derivative Financial Instruments and Hedging Activities" (1998) was released too late to be integrated into the text. The provisions of the 1997 FASB *Draft Statement* discussed in Chapters 10 and 11 are similar to those of *SFAS 133*. Major changes in the fifth edition include the following:

- Many chapters include new assignment items. Some of these items contain **user-oriented, interpretive scenarios** that require analysis of accounting information already prepared or application to decision situations.
- **Consolidation coverage** in Chapters 3 through 7 continues to focus on current practice, but includes discussion of proposals made in the FASB *Exposure Draft*, **"Consolidation Policy and Procedures" (1995)**. All tax material relating to business combinations and consolidated statements was removed from chapters and now appears in Module B.
- Chapter 2 on special topics in mergers and acquisitions contains a new section on **corporate spin-offs**.
- Translation of foreign statements in Chapter 9 now focuses exclusively on the current rate and temporal methods; coverage of non-GAAP translation methods is deleted.
- Chapter 10's treatment of **foreign currency transactions** explains how the 1997 FASB *Draft Statement* on derivatives applies to foreign currency forward and option contracts. Discussion of covered interest arbitrage is moved to an appendix.
- Chapter 11 on **derivative financial instruments** now includes discussions and illustrations of how the 1997 FASB *Draft Statement* applies to futures contracts, options contracts and financial swaps. Disclosure requirements are updated and moved to the end of the chapter, after the various instruments are discussed.
- Module D describes the new segment reporting requirements contained in FASB *Statement 131*, **"Disclosures about Segments of an Enterprise and Related Information" (1997)**.

- Chapters 12 and 13 on state and local governmental reporting have been completely revised to highlight the user perspective. While accounting and reporting procedures are covered extensively, a major focus is on the value of financial statements to interested readers. Actual reports of state and local governmental units augment topical coverage. The GASB's 1997 proposal for accrual-based external reporting fuels the debate concerning the strengths and weaknesses of current fund-based reporting.
- Chapter 14 on **not-for-profit organizations** is completely revised to focus on financial statement users and the reporting environment, emphasizing the external reporting requirements of FASB *Statements 116*, *117*, and *124*. Internal fund accounting is now in an appendix.
- An entirely new topic, accounting for **environmental costs** and **environmental liabilities**, has been added as Module F. The growing importance of environmental control and remediation laws leads to new accounting concerns for many companies. This module surveys the major laws, discusses the related accounting issues, and presents examples from company reports.
- The material in Module H on estate planning and taxation is updated.

INSTRUCTOR AND STUDENT SUPPORT MATERIALS

Two instructor support items are available. A **Solutions Manual** prepared by the authors contains detailed solutions to all end-of-chapter questions, exercises, and problems, along with a summary of the topics covered, level of difficulty, and estimated times required. It also includes carryback and carryforward tables referencing the problem material of the fifth edition to that of the fourth edition, and a checklist of key figures suitable for reproduction. A **Test Resource Manual**, prepared by Susan Hamlen, offers over 1,100 examination items, including true/false questions, multiple-choice questions, and problems. Many of these examination items are new for the fifth edition. For students, a **Study Guide**, prepared by Professor Richard File of the University of Nebraska at Omaha, provides chapter summaries and self-test materials.

ACKNOWLEDGMENTS

Many individuals helped us to develop this textbook. While we gratefully acknowledge their assistance, we accept responsibility for the errors that remain. In addition to our continuing appreciation for those who worked with us with the first four editions, we recognize, in alphabetical order, those who made helpful comments and suggestions during development of the fifth edition: Donald F. Arnold, Union College; Timothy Brezinsky, CPA, Bethlehem, PA; Ann B. Cohen, State University of New York at Buffalo; Eugene E. Comiskey, Georgia Institute of Technology; Michael L. Davis, Pepperdine University; and Richard G. File, University of Nebraska at Omaha.

Professor Largay owes special thanks to Robert S. Kay, New York University, for his constant encouragement and willingness to share his expert and voluminous class notes, and to Ronald J. Murray, Coopers & Lybrand LLP, for his careful review of Module E on the SEC.

Professor Hamlen's student assistant—Angela Gore—provided invaluable knowledge and advice for the governmental material. Janet Kiefer of the State University of New York at Buffalo and Janice Schaeffer of Lehigh University provided expert secretarial service. We are also thankful for the support, encouragement and superb technical work provided by Lisa Diemer, Sheryl New and Raenelle Belch of Dame Publications.

The permission granted by the AICPA, FASB, and GASB to quote from their documents is appreciated. Documents issued by the AICPA are copyright © by the American Institute of Certified Public Accountants, Inc. FASB documents are copyright © by the Financial Accounting Standards Board, Norwalk, Connecticut. GASB documents are copyright © by the Governmental Accounting Standards Board, Norwalk, Connecticut.

We express our appreciation for the support of the School of Management, State University of New York at Buffalo and the Department of Business, Lehigh University. Professor Largay also gratefully acknowledges the support that Arthur Andersen LLP provides for his work; it greatly facilitated preparation of the fifth edition.

Comments from users—both faculty and students—are encouraged. Our e-mail addresses are provided below.

Ronald J. Huefner (rhuefner@acsu.buffalo.edu)
James A. Largay III (jal3@lehigh.edu)
Susan S. Hamlen (hamlen@acsu.buffalo.edu)

ABOUT THE AUTHORS

Ronald J. Huefner, Ph.D. (Cornell University), CMA, CPA, is Distinguished Teaching Professor in the Department of Accounting & Law, State University of New York at Buffalo. He is a member of the American Accounting Association, the American Institute of Certified Public Accountants, the Institute of Management Accountants, and other professional organizations. Articles by Professor Huefner appeared in *The Accounting Review*, the *Journal of Accounting Research, Issues in Accounting Education, Management Accounting, Contemporary Accounting Research, The CPA Journal*, and other journals. He is coeditor of the *Accounting Literature Index*, and a contributor to the *Handbook of Modern Accounting*, the *Handbook of Cost Accounting*, and the *Management Accountant's Handbook*. He has been active in professional organizations, having served as President of the Buffalo Chapter of the New York State Society of CPAs, the Buffalo Chapter of the Institute of Management Accountants, and the Northeast Region of the American Accounting Association. Professor Huefner teaches undergraduate courses in financial and managerial accounting, and he has received the Chancellor's Award of the State University of New York for Excellence in Teaching.

James A. Largay III, Ph.D. (Cornell University), CPA, is Arthur Andersen & Co. Alumni Professor of Accounting in the Department of Business, Lehigh University. He is a member of the American Accounting Association, the American Institute of Certified Public Accountants and the Financial Executives Institute. Articles by Professor Largay appeared in *The Accounting Review*, the *Journal of Finance*, the *Journal of Political Economy, Accounting Horizons*, the *Journal of Accountancy*, and other journals. He is co-author of *Accounting for Changing Prices*, and a contributor to the *Handbook of Modern Accounting* and the *Handbook of Cost Accounting*. Professor Largay served as a co-editor of *Accounting Horizons*, as President of the Financial Accounting and Reporting Section of the American Accounting Association, and is a member of the FASB Task Force on Consolidations and Related Matters. He teaches undergraduate and graduate courses in financial accounting and statement analysis.

Susan S. Hamlen, Ph.D. (Purdue University), CFM, CMA is Associate Professor of Accounting in the Department of Accounting & Law, State University of New York at Buffalo. She is a member of the American Accounting Association and the Institute of Management Accountants, where she has served in various directorships. Articles by Professor Hamlen have appeared in *The Accounting Review*, the *Journal of Econometrics*, the *Southern Economic Journal* and other journals. Professor Hamlen has been active in executive education programs, and teaches undergraduate and graduate courses in financial and management accounting.

CONTENTS: VOLUME II

CHAPTER 11   DERIVATIVE FINANCIAL INSTRUMENTS: FUTURES, OPTIONS, AND FINANCIAL SWAPS   11-1

MODULE E   THE SEC AND ITS ROLE IN FINANCIAL REPORTING

MODULE F   ENVIRONMENTAL LIABILITIES

CHAPTER 9

TRANSLATING FOREIGN CURRENCY FINANCIAL STATEMENTS

CHAPTER PREVIEW

American companies with far-flung international operations must include those operations in financial statements issued to investors and creditors. To do so, however, requires that all such financial information be measured in U.S. dollars. The problem of **foreign currency translation**, or how best to convert the foreign currency financial statements of foreign entities into dollars, has vexed accountants for decades. When the FASB first ventured into this area with *SFAS 8* in 1975, it unleashed a storm of criticism which resulted in new accounting standards—*SFAS 52*—in 1981, barely six years later.

This chapter examines both general aspects of the foreign currency translation problem and the details of how current generally accepted accounting principles cope with it. To aid in understanding the financial environment within which currency translation occurs, the chapter also provides introductory discussions of foreign exchange rates and the international monetary system. The principal topics studied in this chapter are

- Introduction to foreign exchange rates and markets
- The international monetary system
- The multinational corporate entity
- Translating foreign currency financial statements
- Translation under *SFAS 52*
- Translation and financial statement analysis
- Other foreign currency translation matters
- Summary of foreign currency translation

The area of foreign currency translation is of considerable interest to corporate managers, professional accountants and academics. Its intrinsic appeal, as well as its ability to influence the content of financial statements, makes it a fascinating subject.

This is the first of two chapters that deal with the subject of accounting for international operations, concentrating on the need for U.S. companies to report their international operations in U.S. dollars. These chapters address the following two aspects of accounting for international operations.

First, Chapter 9 focuses on the complex reporting issues present when a U.S. company has business operations abroad. All foreign entities that are branches, divisions, or subsidiaries of U.S. firms maintain their books in units of foreign currency, not in dollars. *Translation of foreign currency financial statements* is therefore necessary for the financial affairs of these foreign entities to be reported in dollars as part of the U.S. parent company's financial statements.

Second, in Chapter 10 the appropriate accounting for the *foreign currency transactions* of U.S. firms is studied. These transactions include *import and export dealings* with foreign suppliers and customers, *borrowing and lending* in foreign currencies, and various *hedging* or *risk-neutralizing* transactions. The problem common to all such transactions—the fact that *their dollar equivalents change as the values of foreign currencies change*—is studied in detail in Chapter 10.

As an overall commentary on the importance of accounting for international operations, consider these excerpts from Note 1 to the 1993 consolidated financial statements of Air Products and Chemicals, Inc.

> **Foreign Currency Translation** The value of the U.S. dollar rises and falls day to day on foreign currency exchanges. Since the company does business in many foreign countries, these fluctuations affect the company's financial position and results of operations.
>
> Generally, foreign subsidiaries translate their assets and liabilities into U.S. dollars at current exchange rates. . . . The gains and losses that result from this process are shown in the cumulative translation adjustments account in the shareholders' equity section of the balance sheet.
>
> . . .
>
> Some transactions of the company and its subsidiaries are made in currencies different from their own. Gains and losses from these transactions are generally included in income as they occur. . . . Certain transactions . . . are sometimes used to hedge or protect the value of investments in certain foreign subsidiaries. . . . Additionally, foreign exchange contracts and foreign currency options are sometimes used to hedge firm commitments and certain anticipated export sales transactions.[1]

Accounting for, reporting, and analyzing the financial affairs of multinational corporations are complicated in two major ways:

■ the foreign subsidiaries, branches or divisions of the U.S.-based corporation maintain financial records in their local currency, and
■ accounting procedures follow the accounting principles of their country.

The financial statements of these units are usually consolidated with those of the parent company. For presentation in the U.S. parent's financial statements, it is necessary to both **restate** the foreign financial statements to U.S. generally accepted accounting principles, and **translate** them into U.S. dollars.

RESTATEMENT TO U.S. GAAP

Accounting standards differ widely among countries. For example, the pooling-of-interests method of recording a business combination is not accepted in most countries outside the U.S. The **International Accounting Standards Committee** (IASC) and the FASB are increasingly focusing on international standards, supporting greater harmonization and comparability of financial information among countries. For example, the IASC-U.S. Comparison Project is an ongoing joint effort among the IASC and the FASB which proposes to provide a basis for raising the quality of international standards, while increasing harmonization among countries. Details on differences

---

[1] Air Products and Chemicals, Inc., *Financial Review*, 1993, 11.

in standards among countries can be found in international accounting texts. For our purposes, we assume the financial statements of a foreign unit are already restated to U.S. GAAP.

CONVERSION TO U.S. DOLLARS

The financial records of a U.S. corporation's foreign units are not maintained in U.S. dollars. Just as Ford Motor Company's Jaguar subsidiary in the United Kingdom keeps its accounts in pounds sterling, the U.K. currency, Nissan's automobile assembly plant in Smyrna, Tennessee, records its transactions in U.S. dollars. Yet both Ford and Nissan must express their financial statements in a single currency, in order that the amounts reported are based on a common monetary measuring unit. Plans are underway in Europe for the adoption of a single currency (the Euro) by members of the European Union who meet certain conditions. However, at publication date, participation in this plan is limited—only seven countries were strongly committed to the plan— and the new currency is to be phased in over several years. It is very likely that the current system of multiple currencies will remain the norm for the foreseeable future. The process of translating foreign currency amounts into units of domestic currency employs *foreign exchange rates*. Foreign exchange rates are themselves the results of various forces operating within the *international monetary system*.

INTRODUCTION TO FOREIGN EXCHANGE RATES AND MARKETS

Foreign exchange rates are *prices*. They are not, however, prices for automobiles, television sets, or bananas. Rather,

> A **foreign exchange rate** is the price of a unit of one country's currency expressed in units of another country's currency.

Foreign currencies, such as the German deutsche mark and the Japanese yen, are traded in markets. Business transactions made with foreign companies by U.S. firms are often *denominated in the foreign currency*, meaning that these transactions must be *settled* in the foreign currency and not in dollars. In such situations, the U.S. firm must buy foreign currency in order to settle a bill due in that currency; the U.S. firm which receives foreign currency in settlement of amounts owed sells that currency for dollars. Foreign companies must in turn sell or purchase dollars to settle their dollar-denominated transactions with U.S. firms. Buyers and sellers of foreign currencies use **foreign exchange markets** for these purposes.

Similarly, assets owned and liabilities owed by foreign operations of U.S. companies are denominated in foreign currencies. Even if dollars are not exchanged for these currencies, the U.S. company uses market-determined foreign exchange rates to include the foreign currency account balances in U.S. dollar financial statements.

Each of the above situations demonstrates that an entity may conduct transactions across national boundaries, using various currencies. In addition, the fact that exchange rates move continuously, sometimes unpredictably, creates differences in the dollar equivalents of foreign currency balances at different points in time. These differences are called **exchange gains and losses**.

Foreign currencies are traded on *spot markets*, and *forward markets* or *futures markets*. Transactions involving *immediate delivery* of the foreign currency are executed at **spot rates**. In contrast, many business dealings require that foreign currency be delivered at some *later date*. One alternative is to buy or sell the currency in the spot market at the later date. Another alternative is to fix the future exchange rate now, in order to avoid an unfavorable spot rate in the future. Informal markets contracting for future delivery of foreign currencies are called **forward markets;** organized exchanges dealing in standardized contracts for future delivery of foreign currencies are known as **futures markets**.

To satisfy the need for foreign currency delivery at later dates, prices for future delivery—**forward rates**—in many foreign currencies are quoted along with spot rates. A typical quotation of both spot and forward foreign exchange rates is shown below. Readers should consult the financial pages of *The Wall Street Journal*, the *New York Times* and other major newspapers for current rate quotations.

Foreign Exchange Rates

France (Franc: F)	U.S. $ Price ($/F; Direct Form)	Foreign Currency Price per U.S. $ (F/$; Indirect Form)
Spot rate	$ .1703	F 5.8716
30-day forward	.1706	5.8610
90-day forward	.1712	5.8405
180-day forward	.1721	5.8117

The preceding foreign exchange rates are expressed in both the *direct and indirect forms*. The **direct form** gives the *dollar price of one unit of foreign currency* (the left-hand column), while the **indirect form** shows the *foreign currency price of one dollar* (the right-hand column). Consider first the spot rate for the French franc (F). At the time of this quotation, $.1703/F was the dollar price for immediate delivery of francs—the *direct* form. Similarly, F5.8716/$ was the franc price for immediate delivery of dollars—the *indirect* form. Because the *indirect rate is the reciprocal of the direct rate*, and vice versa, $.1703/F = $1/F5.8716. Forward rates are also listed for the French franc. In this case, the *direct* dollar price for delivery of francs in 180 days was $.1721/F. A discussion of the reasons for the differences that typically exist between spot and forward rates appears in the appendix to Chapter 10.

In the contemporary world economy, foreign exchange rates are generally the result of free market forces. Some of the underlying factors affecting exchange rates are relative rates of inflation, relative interest rates, and the terms of trade (or international commodity exchange ratios) between countries. As these conditions change, foreign exchange rates change. Economists refer to rates resulting from this system as **floating** or **flexible exchange rates**. Foreign exchange rates were not always this flexible. During much of the post-World War II period, exchange rates generally were fixed under the terms of an international agreement. The established set of exchange rates was maintained, or **pegged**, by central banks through their purchase and sale of foreign currencies in the foreign exchange markets.

We believe that the study of accounting for international operations is enriched by an understanding of the international monetary system, an important part of the international environment. Accordingly, the next section is devoted to a discussion of developments in the international monetary system.

THE INTERNATIONAL MONETARY SYSTEM

The growth in the world economy and the relative international economic stability experienced since World War II stemmed in large measure from negotiations undertaken near the end of the war. Determined to create an orderly international economic environment after the war, representatives of the Western allied powers met in 1944 at Bretton Woods, New Hampshire, to fashion the elements of a sound international monetary system. The USSR did not participate. Renowned British economist John Maynard Keynes played an important role at the conference.

The exchange rate instability experienced between World War I and World War II had been attributed, rightly or wrongly, to freely floating exchange rates and to the abuses perpetrated by international speculators. A desire for stability in the short run and flexibility in the long run led the Bretton Woods conferees to adopt what has been termed an **adjustable peg system**. Currency exchange rates were set, by agreement, in terms of the U.S. dollar. The value of the dollar, in turn, was tied to gold; the official price of gold was set at $35 per ounce. Discipline in the system was created by making the dollar freely convertible into gold. In other words, if the dollar became overvalued, making an ounce of gold worth more than $35, foreigners would convert their dollars into gold at the U.S. Treasury. This conversion would deplete the finite U.S. gold reserves, which is exactly what eventually happened.

The other countries that subscribed to the **Bretton Woods agreements** were to attempt to maintain the values of their currencies, in dollars, within 1 percent of the par or pegged exchange rate. Therefore, if the exchange rate for a particular country's currency began to move above or below the allowable 1-percent deviation, that country's central bank would be obliged to intervene in the foreign exchange market. To raise the exchange rate, the home currency is purchased with dollars or another acceptable international reserve, such as gold; to lower the exchange rate, the home currency is sold.

To assist countries facing temporary shortages of international reserves, the **International Monetary Fund (IMF)** was established as an integral part of the Bretton Woods agreements. Member countries were able to borrow specified quantities of international reserves from the IMF to tide them over in case of transitory deficits in international payments. The resources of the IMF were to consist of mandatory contributions made by member countries.

Flexibility in the system was to be achieved by permitting countries to change the official exchange rate by as much as 10 percent without IMF approval. Approval of the IMF was required for larger changes in the official rate. An *increase* in the direct form of the official peg was termed a **devaluation**, whereas a *decrease* implied **revaluation**. To understand this system, observe that by raising the *direct rate*—the price of a foreign currency in terms of the home currency—the home currency *loses value*; its purchasing power for world goods declines. That is, after the exchange rate is increased, the home currency is devalued because more units of it are needed to acquire the foreign currency. In the United States, the dollar is devalued by raising the dollar price of gold. Concurrently, a devaluation of one currency means that at least one other currency experiences a revaluation. In November 1967, the British pound sterling was devalued by the United Kingdom from $2.80 to $2.40. The effects of this action on the exchange rate between dollars and pounds were as follows:

	In New York ($/£)	In London (£/$)
Before the sterling devaluation	$ 2.80	£ .357
After the sterling devaluation	2.40	.417

Under the Bretton Woods agreements, the ability of a country to defend its currency in the face of a declining exchange rate was directly influenced by that country's supply of international reserves, including borrowing rights from the IMF. In contrast, the increase in international reserves caused by keeping the exchange rate from rising usually generated an expanding domestic money supply which created domestic inflationary pressures.

THE FATAL FLAW

The problem with an adjustable peg system is that when the exchange rate becomes more difficult to maintain through intervention, the direction of the forthcoming change in the official exchange rate is clear and "bear speculators are then presented with that rare, and greatly desired phenomenon, a 'sure thing'."[2] Under the Bretton Woods system, a large adjustment in the exchange rate occurred in a single discrete step. As the underlying economic conditions gradually changed, the exchange rate was not allowed to change accordingly. Eventually, as the central bank intervened more and more in the foreign exchange market, a forthcoming change in the official peg, usually a devaluation, was signalled. Speculators sold large amounts of the suspect currency and short sales increased. The central bank became the buyer of last resort for the currency expected to be devalued and often engaged in extremely costly counterspeculative policies. In connection with the devaluation of the British pound mentioned previously, on November 17, 1967, the Bank of England lost $250 million. This amount was expended to support the pound by purchasing it in the face of massive speculative sales of that currency.

To minimize the actions of speculators, and the resulting counterspeculative policies, deliberations regarding a devaluation were shrouded in secrecy, and announcements were made when markets were closed, typically on weekends or holidays. Unfortunately, this fundamental problem was aggravated by the general unwillingness of governments to adjust the peg frequently. Devaluations were seen as assaults on national pride. Hence, the crises, when they came, were massive and abrupt.

The requirement that central banks intervene in foreign exchange markets to support their currencies often created problems in domestic economic policy. Government intervention in the economy has grown in significance since World War II, so that the conflicting use of policy tools to achieve policy objectives was not forecast by the Bretton Woods conferees. As an example, suppose a particular country was confronted with both excessive domestic unemployment and an international deficit. Domestic monetary policy would likely be expansionary, leading to a larger money supply and lower interest rates to combat unemployment. Yet just the opposite is called for to cope with the international deficit. High interest rates, which worsen domestic unemployment, attract the foreign investment funds that help alleviate the international deficit. Such conflicts in economic policy were common under the adjustable peg system.

THE EVOLUTION OF FLEXIBLE EXCHANGE RATES

As time passed, changes in international economic relations simply outgrew the capability of the pegged exchange rate system to accommodate them.

---

[2] "Frank Graham, 'Achilles' Heels in Monetary Standards," *American Economic Review* (March 1940), 19.

It is not possible to date precisely the end of the international monetary system established at Bretton Woods in 1944. Different aspects of the system died at different times. And the basic principles of international financial cooperation on which the Bretton Woods system was based never died at all.

There is general agreement that the final end of the adjustable pegged par value exchange rate system established at Bretton Woods was marked by the initiation of generalized floating of exchange rates by the major industrial countries following the second devaluation of the dollar in early 1973. But many who viewed the gold convertibility of the dollar as the linchpin of the system would point to the formal termination of the convertibility of official dollar holdings into gold in August 1971 as the symbolic death date of the system. Still others would point out that, de facto, the unfettered gold convertibility of the dollar as envisioned at Bretton Woods had already ended years before.[3]

Essentially untouched by the devastation of World War II, the United States emerged as the major economic power in the free world. It had most of the free world's supply of gold, and its currency, the dollar, was in great demand worldwide as an international medium of payment. As various countries of the world were rebuilt, many with significant aid from the United States through such programs as the Marshall Plan, American economic dominance began to decline. The flow of dollars abroad became a flood in the late 1960s as, under pressure of the Vietnam War, the persistent balance of payments deficits which began in the late 1950s grew substantially larger.[4] The dollar shortage became a glut; conversion of dollars into gold at the official $35 price reduced the United States gold reserve to a low of $10.2 billion in 1971 from a high of $24.6 billion in 1949.

In August 1971, President Nixon reacted to the growing crisis of confidence in the dollar. Anticipating the record balance of payments deficit in 1971, which amounted to $29.7 billion on the official reserve transactions balance, the president unilaterally suspended convertibility of the dollar into gold as one of several economic policy initiatives announced on August 15, 1971. Subsequent appreciation of major foreign currencies led to an increase in the official price of gold to $38 per ounce in December 1971. A second devaluation of the dollar in February 1973 raised the official price of gold to $42 per ounce. In 1998 gold sells for about $295 per ounce.

Serious negotiations for the reform of the international monetary system began in earnest in 1972 and reached their culmination in Kingston, Jamaica, on January 7 and 8, 1976. At the Jamaica meetings, representatives of the 128 member nations of the International Monetary Fund ratified amendments to the IMF's Articles of Agreement, officially sanctioning flexible or floating exchange rates as the basis for our international monetary system. As Nobel laureate economist Milton Friedman suggested many years before,

Our problem is not to solve *a* balance of payments problem. It is to solve *the* balance of payments problem by adapting a mechanism that will enable free market forces to provide a prompt, effective, and automatic response to changes in conditions affecting international trade.[5]

This movement away from pegged exchange rates led to an international economic environment in which foreign exchange rates constantly fluctuate principally in response to market forces. The present-day system that eventually emerged from the Jamaica meetings, however, is

---

[3] Thomas D. Willett, *Floating Exchange Rates and International Monetary Reform* (Washington, DC: American Enterprise Institute for Public Policy Research, 1977), 1.

[4] The **balance of payments** refers to the net flow of funds in or out of a particular country. A deficit occurs when the quantity of funds flowing out exceeds the quantity flowing in.

[5] Milton Friedman, *Capitalism and Freedom* (Chicago: University of Chicago Press, 1962), 67.

not a pure floating-rate system. Some countries attempt to peg their currencies to the currency of an important trading partner, such as the U.S. dollar or the British pound. Occasionally central banks intervene in the foreign exchange markets to promote orderly markets, rather than to support specific currencies. News reports provide frequent reminders that this mixed system, often referred to as a *dirty float*, is still with us. Exchange rate movements in this economic environment affect the international operations of corporations and make the accounting for those operations more complex.

In the current system, exchange rates are determined primarily by economic and political factors such as inflation, interest rates, and the balance of payments. Changes in exchange rates are often described as a *strengthening* or *weakening* of one country's currency in relation to another country's currency. The currency that is **strengthening** can buy **more** units of another country's currency. The currency that is **weakening** can buy **fewer** units of another country's currency. For example, the Canadian dollar **weakened** against the U.S. dollar in the late 1990's. This means that one Canadian dollar could buy less U.S. currency. The Asian crisis, which began in 1997, led to a major weakening of such currencies as the Indonesian rupiah. Indonesian students in U.S. universities and colleges, who are supported by funds from home, found it difficult to remain in the U.S. as their currency lost purchasing power. On the flip side, the U.S. dollar **strengthened** against the Canadian dollar and the Indonesian rupiah. Americans visiting Canada or Indonesia were able to buy more goods in these countries with their U.S. dollars. When a currency is strengthening, the direct rate *decreases*. The $US/$Canadian declined substantially in recent years. The $US/rupiah declined even more. It took less in U.S. currency to buy one Canadian dollar or one rupiah.

THE MULTINATIONAL CORPORATE ENTITY

Import/export businesses, foreign manufacturing facilities, investments in foreign corporations, and obligations to foreign suppliers of capital are all indicative of the growing reliance of business on foreign markets. Although the expansion of world trade contributes to the current importance of international business activities, the structure of international flows of funds is also a significant factor. Whereas international operations were once characterized primarily by the import and export of *goods* among countries, international flows of *capital* now heavily influence relations among countries.

This changing character of the world economy meant new challenges for corporate managers, professional accountants, and financial analysts. These challenges increased as the multinational operations of domestic corporations grew and as the international monetary system evolved from a fixed exchange-rate regime to one essentially characterized by fluctuating exchange rates.

For a diversified conglomerate corporation headquartered in the United States, two major problems faced by management are (1) controlling wide-ranging, geographically diverse operations and (2) measuring the financial position and performance of the various divisions or subsidiaries included in the conglomerate. The fundamental managerial issue of centralization versus decentralization is familiar, as are accounting concerns involving transfer pricing, cost allocation techniques, and investment centers. Several other difficulties are also common to multinational operations:

■ Corporate headquarters located great distances from foreign operations.
■ Books of account maintained in units of various currencies.
■ Interest rates, inflation rates, and growth rates that vary widely across countries.

- Political conditions and economic institutions that differ among nations.
- Language and other cultural barriers to effective communication.
- Alternative sets of accounting principles and reporting standards around the globe.

Considering such obstacles to smooth operations, we can begin to grasp the dimensions of the problems in planning, organization, and control which confront top managements of multinational enterprises. Although further discussion of these problems is beyond the scope of this textbook, they must also be considered by the accountant who defines the boundaries of the reporting entity appropriate in a multinational enterprise and accumulates the financial information needed by decision makers inside and outside of the entity. Later in this chapter one aspect of these problems is discussed—the role of foreign currency translation in accumulating the financial information to be reported to users.

THE ENTITY CONCEPT IN MULTINATIONAL CORPORATIONS

We already indicated that many financial reporting and disclosure issues are tied to questions concerning which entity is appropriate for reporting in various circumstances. Many different entities can be involved in a given situation. For accounting purposes, *the entity theory holds that the corporation is separate from its shareholders*. In consolidated statements, treatment of noncontrolling interest often differs from that of the controlling interest. The segment reporting requirements in *SFAS 131* call for the entity known as *the enterprise* to identify its operating segments that individually appear to have the characteristics of a proper accounting entity.[6] Finally, we will see that governmental and nonprofit units consist of several accounting entities. What, then, is the appropriate entity or group of entities for accounting and reporting purposes of the multinational corporation?

The multinational corporation having foreign subsidiaries is a case in point. The Ford Motor Company manufactures and sells automobiles at numerous locations outside the United States. Currently, Ford issues worldwide consolidated financial statements. An alternative reporting posture would be for Ford not to consolidate its foreign subsidiaries and divisions but to report them as long-term investments and include their separate financial statements in the notes. Such a posture has an advantage: Ford's owners and creditors would have a better understanding of the financial status of the various pieces included in their ownership interest. At the same time, however, their view of the big picture with respect to Ford would be clouded. Ford stockholders have an interest in the totality of Ford's operations. Their interests are not divisible among the pieces of Ford spread around the world.

Therefore, the entity concept appropriate for reporting the status of the stockholders' and creditors' interests in multinational enterprises is generally one that includes the foreign operations of the enterprise. Moreover, this view is embraced by GAAP. As we shall see later in the chapter, however, certain circumstances create exceptions to this general rule. When effective control over the assets of domestically owned foreign subsidiaries is in jeopardy, a less inclusive entity definition may be warranted.

---

[6] Financial Accounting Standards Board, *Statement of Financial Accounting Standards No. 131*, "Disclosures about Segments of an Enterprise and Related Information," (Norwalk, CT: FASB, 1997).

TRANSLATING FOREIGN CURRENCY FINANCIAL STATEMENTS

We now turn to the accounting problems associated with translating foreign currency financial statements into financial statements based on the U.S. reporting currency, the dollar. The foreign currency statements to be considered report the assets, liabilities, revenues, and expenses of *foreign entities*—branches, divisions, and subsidiaries—*owned by U.S. companies*.

To introduce the translation concept, suppose a U.S. company establishes a foreign operation with the following initial balance sheet measured in the local currency (LC).

Cash	LC 10,000	Debt	LC 40,000
Other Assets	90,000	Equity	60,000
	LC 100,000		LC 100,000

If the direct exchange rate at that time is $1.20/LC, all account balances are multiplied by $1.20 to get the following foreign currency balance sheet translated into dollars:

Cash	$ 12,000	Debt	$ 48,000
Other Assets	108,000	Equity	72,000
	$ 120,000		$ 120,000

Because foreign exchange rates change as underlying relationships between supply and demand of various currencies change, ongoing and unpredictable fluctuations in exchange rates can quickly cause translated foreign account balances to become obsolete. The fact that the exchange rates used to translate foreign currency balances do move up *and* down differentiates this problem from a similar one caused by domestic inflation.

> As the exchange rate changes, the resulting translation to a current dollar equivalent produces an **exchange gain or loss**—the difference between the dollar equivalents of a constant foreign currency balance at two points in time.

One result of translation occurs when foreign exchange gains and losses resulting from the process are included in current income—excessive and unwarranted instability in reported earnings can occur. These exchange gains and losses are referred to as *translation gains and losses* (or *translation adjustments*). In Chapter 10, we see that exchange gains and losses, with different economic consequences, also arise from foreign currency *transactions*; those are labeled *transaction gains and losses* (or *transaction adjustments*).

TRANSLATION GAINS AND LOSSES

As foreign exchange rates vary, **translation gains and losses**—or **translation adjustments**—arise in financial statements because not all accounts in the financial statements are translated at the same exchange rate. Both *current* and *historical* rates are used.

> The **current exchange rate** is the spot rate at the end of the current reporting period. It is the rate in existence on the balance sheet date. A **historical exchange rate** is a past spot rate, in existence when a particular transaction occurred.

Those accounts translated at the *current rate* change in dollar equivalents, whereas those translated at *historical rates* remain fixed in dollar equivalents. Therefore a company's **exposure to translation gains and losses** comes from those accounts which are *translated at the current exchange rate*. To illustrate this important point, look at the following example. Suppose a company holds foreign inventory valued at LC10,000. If the direct exchange rate increases from $1.00 to $1.20, the U.S. dollar equivalent of this inventory balance increases from $10,000 to $12,000, if the inventory balance is translated at the current exchange rate. A gain of $2,000 is reported. However, assume that the inventory was acquired when the exchange rate was $1.00, and the historical rate is used to translate this balance. The U.S. dollar equivalent inventory balance remains at $10,000, regardless of changes in the current exchange rate, and no gain or loss is shown.

Translation gains and losses may have little economic significance. For example, suppose the London branch of a U.S. company purchases merchandise from a U.K. supplier on credit. The resulting payable will be liquidated with 10,000 pounds sterling (£) generated from business in the United Kingdom. Assuming that the direct exchange rate ($/£) *increases* by $.05, the dollar equivalent of the payable rises by $500, but the quantity of pounds required to discharge it does not change. Has the U.S. firm incurred a loss when this happens? Probably not.

A similar situation occurs when plant assets are acquired in a foreign country with foreign currency debt. The debt is to be retired with foreign currency generated in normal business operations. If the direct exchange rate ($/£) *falls* by, say, $.08, then $8,000 less is required to retire a £100,000 debt. Has the U.S. firm realized a gain? Probably not, as long as management does not intend to use dollars to retire the debt.

In cases such as these, there are neither actual nor intended conversions of dollars into foreign currency, and the U.S. firm is affected only indirectly, if at all. Such situations result in *translation* adjustments, often *paper gains and losses* with no immediate economic consequences. By contrast, when the U.S. firm uses dollars to liquidate foreign currency obligations, and purchases foreign currency to do so, the exchange gain or loss measures the change in the number of dollars to be paid. This type of exchange gain or loss involves actual money and is a *transaction* adjustment of the type to be examined in Chapter 10.

Thus, it seems that *translation* gains and losses may not have the same economic significance as *transaction* gains and losses. This point is embodied in the provisions set forth in current U.S. GAAP translation methods, that are intended to link accounting treatment of translation adjustments to their economic consequences.

Translation gains and losses arise because the generally accepted approaches to translating foreign currency financial statements translate some accounts at the current rate and other accounts at historical rates. Determining which accounts are to be translated at the current rate and which are to be translated at historical rates is the most controversial issue in accounting for international operations.

APPROACHES TO TRANSLATING FOREIGN CURRENCY STATEMENTS

Generally accepted accounting principles for translating the financial statements of foreign units are found in *SFAS 52*, "Foreign Currency Translation.[7]" Two methods are allowed: the **temporal** method, and the **current rate** method. *SFAS 52* provides specific guidelines as to when each method is appropriate. Before discussing the choice of method, however, we first go through the mechanics of both methods. Then you will better appreciate the implications of each choice.

Temporal Method

Under the temporal method, items measured at current money prices, such as cash, receivables, inventories carried at market value and most liabilities are translated at the current exchange rate. Items measured at historical prices, such as plant and equipment and inventories carried at cost, are translated at historical rates. The objective of the translation process is to show the financial statements **as if all transactions occurred in U.S. dollars**. Matching current rates to current prices and historical rates to historical prices achieves this objective. For example, if a foreign unit acquires land for LC100,000 when the direct exchange rate is $1.10, then if U.S. dollars are used to buy the land, $110,000 is needed.

With the temporal method, the accounts translated at the current exchange rate are the *assets and liabilities carried at current money prices*. Therefore, a company's **exposed position** is its *net assets measured at current money prices*. If a company holds assets such as cash and receivables, and the direct rate increases, the company shows a gain on the increased U.S. dollar equivalent of these balances. If a company holds liabilities such as accounts payable or long-term debt, the company shows a loss when the direct rate increases, since the U.S. dollar equivalent of these liabilities has increased. Companies with a positive position in net assets measured at current money prices show gains when the direct rate increases (U.S. currency weakens with respect to the foreign currency), and losses when the direct rate falls (U.S. currency strengthens). Companies with a negative position in net assets measured at current money prices—the more common situation—have the opposite result. When the temporal method of translation is used, the resulting translation gain or loss is reported as a component of the *income statement*. Thus fluctuations in the exchange rate directly impact a company's net income.

The concept of presenting foreign financial statements at the amounts resulting if U.S. dollars were used for each transaction was developed by Leonard Lorensen in *Accounting Research Study No. 12*.[8] This method is based on two fundamental principles:

- Translation changes the unit of measurement.
- Translation changes no other accounting principle.

Similar to the constant-dollar accounting method often advocated during periods of domestic inflation, foreign currency translation is viewed as an arithmetic technique designed to convert

---

[7] Financial Accounting Standards Board, *Statement of Financial Accounting Standards No. 52*, "Foreign Currency Translation" (Stamford, CT: FASB, 1981).

[8] Leonard Lorensen, *Accounting Research Study No. 12*, "Reporting Foreign Operations of U.S. Companies in U.S. Dollars" (New York: AICPA, 1972).

disparate measurement units to a common one. Valuation or other attributes of the items being translated are not, and should not be, affected by the translation process.

Lorensen established that the major attribute of assets and liabilities which accountants measure is the **money price**. *APB Statement No. 4* refers to money prices as "ratios at which money and other resources are or may be exchanged."[9] It follows that the *date* at which an item's foreign money price is measured should govern the date of the foreign exchange rate used to translate the item. This notion of dating the foreign money price measured and using the foreign exchange rate in effect on that date to translate the money price is known as the **temporal principle of translation**. Lorensen summarizes its meaning as follows:

> Under the **temporal method**, "money and receivables and payables measured at the amounts promised should be translated at the foreign exchange rate in effect at the balance sheet date. Assets and liabilities measured at money prices should be translated at the foreign exchange rates in effect at the dates to which the money prices pertain."[10]

Thus, all assets and liabilities valued at current prices, including cash, receivables and *securities or inventory carried at market*, are translated at the current rate. Those assets and liabilities valued at past prices, such as plant assets and *inventory carried at cost*, are translated at historical rates.

Current Rate Method

During the 1970s, professional societies of chartered accountants in England, Wales, and Scotland proposed the **current rate method**. Under the current rate method, all assets and liabilities are translated at the *current rate*. *Historical rates* are used to translate stockholders' equity accounts, and the *average rate* for the period is used to translate income statement accounts, including depreciation and cost of goods sold. The objective of the translation process is to **maintain the financial statement relationships as they exist in the local currency statements**. If all income statement balances are translated at the same (average) rate, profitability ratios such as the gross profit percentage will be the same whether calculated using local currency balances or translated U.S. dollar balances. If assets and liabilities are translated using the same (current) rate, liquidity ratios such as the current ratio will be the same in local currency as in U.S. dollars. However, measures which combine balance sheet and income statement numbers, such as return on assets (income divided by assets) are somewhat distorted by translation.

Since the current rate method requires that all assets and liabilities be translated at the current rate, a company's **exposed position** is its *net assets* (assets less liabilities). If the company has a positive net asset position—by far the most likely situation—and the direct rate increases, the company shows a gain on the increased U.S. dollar equivalent of the foreign net assets. Companies using the current rate method generally show a gain on translation when the U.S. dollar weakens and a loss when the U.S. dollar strengthens. Unlike the temporal method, however, this gain or loss is **not** shown as a component of income. Instead, it bypasses earnings and is accumulated in a *separate account in the stockholders' equity section of the balance sheet*.

---

[9] Accounting Principles Board, *Statement No. 4*, "Basic Concepts and Principles Underlying Financial Statements of Business Enterprises" (New York: AICPA, 1970), par. 70.
[10] Lorensen, 19.

CALCULATION OF THE TRANSLATION ADJUSTMENT

In the above discussion of the two translation methods, we referred to the translation gain or loss, or *translation adjustment*. Under the temporal method, this gain or loss is caused by holding assets and liabilities measured at current money prices while the exchange rate changes. Under the current rate method, this adjustment is caused by holding any assets and liabilities (net assets) while the exchange rate changes. In general, the translation adjustment is caused by a combination of the **exposed position**—those items translated at the current exchange rate—and **changes in the current exchange rate** over time.

> **Translation gains and losses** arise because the *ending exposed position* is translated at the *current rate,* while the *beginning exposed position* and *all changes* during the current year are translated at *historical* (or *average*) *rates.*

Effects of exchange rate movements on the exposed position during an accounting period generate the translation gain or loss, which is calculated at the end of the period. The exposed position at the *beginning* balance sheet date is translated at the beginning-of-period current rate. At the end of the period, this is a historical rate. Because of double entry accounting, increases and decreases in the exposed position occurring during the period just ended are also reflected in accounts which are translated at historical or average rates. The exposed position at the *ending* balance sheet date, which reflects increases and decreases during the period, is translated at the current rate. The general approach for computing the translation adjustment is presented in Exhibit 9.1.

General Approach

	FC	Exchange Rate ($/FC)	$	
Exposed Position, beginning of year	x	Rate at beginning of year: a . .	ax	
Plus Increases	y	Rate(s) when increases occurred: b	by	
Less Decreases	(z)	Rate(s) when decreases occurred: c	(cz)	(1)
Exposed Position, end of year	x + y – z		$ax + by - cz$	
		Current Rate end of year: d ⟶	$-d(x + y - z)$	(2)
Translation Adjustment (Gain if <0, Loss if >0)			(1) – (2)	

EXHIBIT 9.1   SCHEDULE TO COMPUTE THE TRANSLATION ADJUSTMENT

In examining Exhibit 9.1, note that a translation adjustment can occur in the absence of transactions. For example, if LC100 in cash is held for the entire year, and the direct rate falls (U.S. dollar strengthens with respect to the foreign currency) from $1.50 to $1.20, holding foreign cash will produce a translation *loss* of $30 [= ($1.20 - $1.50) X 100]. Here the cash balance did not change, but its dollar equivalent did.

COMPARING TRANSLATION APPROACHES

Exhibit 9.2 identifies the exchange rates used to translate various major balance sheet and income statement accounts under each of the two translation methods permitted in *SFAS 52*.

Balance Sheet	Temporal	Current Rate
Cash and Receivables	C	C
Inventory at Cost	H	C
Inventory at Market	C	C
Investments at Cost	H	C
Investments at Market	C	C
Plant Assets	H	C
Accounts Payable	C	C
Deferred Taxes	C	C
Long-Term Debt	C	C
Obligations under Warranties, Current (at current prices)	C	C
Capital Stock	H	H
Retained Earnings	a	a
Income Statement		
Sales Revenue	A	A
Cost of Goods Sold	H	A
Variable Expenses	A	A
Fixed Expenses	H, A[b]	A

Legend and Notes:

C = Current Rate; H = Historical Rate; A = Average rate during the year.

[a] "Translated" Retained Earnings is a residual.

[b] Fixed expenses such as depreciation and amortization are translated at the same historical rates as the related assets. Other fixed expenses which involve current outlays, such as rent and property taxes, are translated at the average rate during the year.

EXHIBIT 9.2   EXCHANGE RATES USED TO TRANSLATE SELECTED FINANCIAL STATEMENT ITEMS PER *SFAS 52*

Under the **temporal method**, balance sheet items measured at current money prices are translated using the current exchange rate. These include cash, receivables, and inventories and investments carried at market value. Accounts carried at cost, such as inventories and plant assets, are translated using historical rates. Capital stock is translated using the historical rate—when the stock was issued. Income statement accounts are translated at historical rates. Thus for most companies, use of historical rates to translate accounts such as sales revenue, wage expense and tax expense implies that the average rate is used, since these accounts represent inflows and outflows which occur evenly during the year. If this is not true, the average rate may not be appropriate. For example, if a company's sales occur only in December, the December exchange rate should be used to translate the sales revenue account. Use of historical rates to translate accounts such as cost of goods sold and depreciation expense requires using rates in effect when the related inventories or depreciable assets were acquired.

Under the **current rate method**, all assets and liabilities are translated using the current exchange rate. Capital stock is translated at the historical rate. All income statement balances are translated at the average rate. The timing of the actual transactions from which the balances are derived is not relevant to the choice of translation rate.

Development of Translated Financial Statements

To illustrate the temporal and current rate methods, we work through a simple example. Data for the example appear in Exhibit 9.3. In order to allow clear differentiation of the accounting results under each method, this example contains few transactions.

Multiple Methods, Inc.

Balance Sheet as of January 1, 19X1

		June 30, 19X1	**December 31, 19X1**
Cash	£ 50	Exchange Rate $1.60/£	$1.44/£
Inventory (2 Widgets @ £50) . .	100	Transactions	
Furniture (5-year life)	50	1. Sell 1 widget for £120.	1. Record straight-line depreciation on furniture, £10.
	£ 200	2. Replace widget for £80.	2. Close books and prepare financial statements. Assume FIFO for inventory.
Contributed Capital	£ 200	3. Pay other expenses of £30.	
		4. Accrue current warranty liability of	
Note: the exchange rate on January 1, 19X1, is $2.00/£.		estimated warranty service)[a]	£20 (current price of
			warranty service)

[a] The warranty liability pertains to services expected to be rendered during 19X2. As such, it is a current liability, and reflects the current cost of providing warranty service.

EXHIBIT 9.3   DATA FOR FOREIGN CURRENCY TRANSLATION ILLUSTRATION

Exhibit 9.4 shows the entries which Multiple Methods makes to record the events of 19X1, and the resulting balance sheet and income statement. Remember that these entries are denominated in pounds sterling.

It is now necessary to translate the financial statements presented in Exhibit 9.4, which are expressed in pounds sterling, into U.S. dollar financial statements.

Multiple Methods, Inc.

Entries made June 30, 19X1:

Cash	120		Other Expenses	30	
Sales		120	Cash		30

Cost of goods sold	50		Warranty Expense	20	
Inventory		50	Warranty Liability . .		20

Inventory	80	
Cash		80

Entry made December 31, 19X1:

Depreciation expense . . .	10	
Furniture		10

Balance Sheet at December 31, 19X1

Cash	£ 60
Inventory (1 widget @ 50, 1 widget @ 80)	130
Furniture, net	40
	£230
Warranty liability	£ 20
Contributed capital	200
Retained earnings	10
	£230

Income Statement for the year ended December 31, 19X1

Sales		£ 120
Cost of goods sold	£ 50	
Warranty expense	20	
Other expenses	30	
Depreciation expense . . .	10	110
Net income		£ 10

EXHIBIT 9.4 ENTRIES AND END-OF-YEAR FINANCIAL STATEMENTS FOR FOREIGN CURRENCY TRANSLATION ILLUSTRATION

Translation Using the Temporal Method

Calculation of exposure to translation gain or loss for Multiple Methods, Inc., using the temporal method, requires determination of the beginning and ending net assets carried at current money prices, and the transactions that affected these net assets during the year. In Multiple Methods' case, balances carried at current money prices are cash and the warranty liability. Look at the balance sheets for the beginning and end of the year to calculate these numbers. To determine the *changes* in net assets carried at current money prices during the year, look at the transactions that occurred and how they affected cash and warranty liabilities. The calculation of the translation loss for the year for Multiple Methods, Inc. appears in Panel a of Exhibit 9.5. In deciding whether the translation adjustment is a gain or loss, think clearly about the relationship between the ending exposed position translated at historical rates, $84.0, and the ending exposed position translated at the current rate, $57.6. The $84.0 represents net assets carried at current money prices, translated at historical rates. The $57.6 represents the same net asset position translated at the current rate, its current U.S. dollar value. Since the current value is *less than* the historical value, the company incurred a loss. Note that if the company's net assets carried at current money prices are *negative*, the same numbers would produce a *gain*—a reduction in a net liability position.

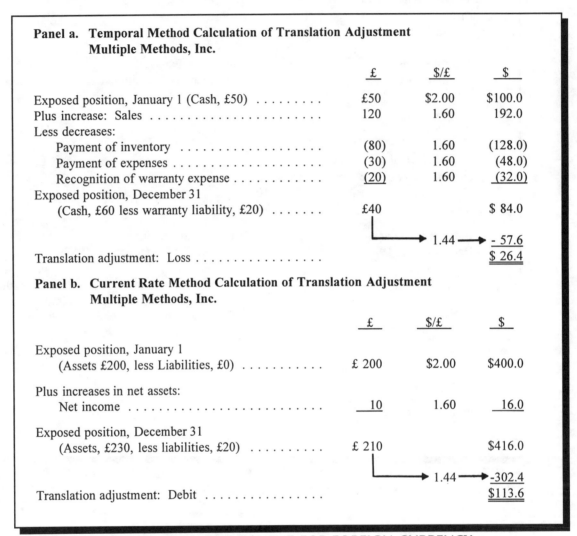

Panel a. Temporal Method Calculation of Translation Adjustment
Multiple Methods, Inc.

	£	$/£	$
Exposed position, January 1 (Cash, £50)	£50	$2.00	$100.0
Plus increase: Sales	120	1.60	192.0
Less decreases:			
Payment of inventory	(80)	1.60	(128.0)
Payment of expenses	(30)	1.60	(48.0)
Recognition of warranty expense	(20)	1.60	(32.0)
Exposed position, December 31			
(Cash, £60 less warranty liability, £20)	£40		$ 84.0
		1.44 →	- 57.6
Translation adjustment: Loss			$ 26.4

Panel b. Current Rate Method Calculation of Translation Adjustment
Multiple Methods, Inc.

	£	$/£	$
Exposed position, January 1			
(Assets £200, less Liabilities, £0)	£ 200	$2.00	$400.0
Plus increases in net assets:			
Net income	10	1.60	16.0
Exposed position, December 31			
(Assets, £230, less liabilities, £20)	£ 210		$416.0
		1.44 →	-302.4
Translation adjustment: Debit			$113.6

EXHIBIT 9.5   TRANSLATION ADJUSTMENT FOR FOREIGN CURRENCY TRANSLATION ILLUSTRATION

Translation of the year-end financial statements of Multiple Methods, Inc., using the temporal method, appears in Panel a of Exhibit 9.6. Note that the translation loss calculated in Panel a of Exhibit 9.5 is shown on the translated income statement. The translated retained earnings balance is determined from the translated income statement. Normally, the translated retained earnings balance is taken from the translated statement of retained earnings. However, for this illustration there is no beginning balance of retained earnings and no dividends were declared. Therefore, the ending retained earnings balance is the net income for the year. An example illustrating translation techniques for a more mature company appears later in this chapter.

**Panel a.   Temporal Method Translation of Financial Statements
                   Multiple Methods, Inc.**

Balance Sheet	£	$/£	$
Cash	£ 60	1.44	$ 86.4
Inventory, Unit 2	50	2.00	100.0
Inventory, Unit 3	80	1.60	128.0
Furniture, Net	40	2.00	80.0
Total Assets	£230		$394.4
Warranty Liability	£ 20	1.44	$ 28.8
Contributed Capital	200	2.00	400.0
Retained Earnings	10	see I/S	(34.4)
Total Liabilities and Equity	£230		$394.4

Income Statement			
Sales	£120	1.60	$192.0
Cost of Goods Sold	(50)	2.00	(100.0)
Warranty Expense	(20)	1.60	(32.0)
Other Expenses	(30)	1.60	(48.0)
Depreciation Expense	(10)	2.00	(20.0)
Translation Adjustment		see Exh. 9.5	(26.4)
Net Income (Loss)	£ 10		(34.4)

**Panel b.   Current Rate Method Translation of Financial Statements
                   Multiple Methods, Inc.**

Balance Sheet	£	$/£	$
Cash	£ 60	1.44	$ 86.4
Inventory, Unit 2	50	1.44	72.0
Inventory, Unit 3	80	1.44	115.2
Furniture, Net	40	1.44	57.6
Total Assets	£230		$331.2
Warranty Liability	£ 20	1.44	$ 28.8
Contributed Capital	200	2.00	400.0
Retained Earnings	10	see I/S	16.0
Cumulative Translation Adjustment		see Exh. 9.5	(113.6)
Total Liabilities and Equity	£230		$331.2

Income Statement			
Sales	£120	1.60	$192.0
Cost of Goods Sold	(50)	1.60	(80.0)
Warranty Expense	(20)	1.60	(32.0)
Other Expenses	(30)	1.60	(48.0)
Depreciation Expense	(10)	1.60	(16.0)
Net Income (Loss)	£ 10		16.0

**EXHIBIT 9.6   TRANSLATION OF FINANCIAL STATEMENTS FOR FOREIGN
CURRENCY TRANSACTION ILLUSTRATION**

Translation Using the Current Rate Method

Calculation of exposure to translation gain or loss for Multiple Methods, Inc., using the current rate method, requires determination of the beginning and ending net asset position (assets less liabilities, or equity), and the transactions that affected the net asset position during the year. Look at the balance sheets for the beginning and end of the year to calculate these numbers. To determine the *changes* in net asset position during the year, look at the events that affected equity. For Multiple Methods, the only change is net income. Other companies may also have other effects on equity during the year, such as dividends and capital stock transactions. Calculation of the translation adjustment for the year for Multiple Methods, Inc. appears in Panel b of Exhibit 9.5. In deciding whether the translation adjustment is a debit or credit, think clearly about the relationship between the ending exposed position translated at historical rates, $416.0, and the ending exposed position translated at the current rate, $302.4. The $416.0 represents the net asset position translated at historical rates. The $302.4 represents the net asset position translated at the current rate, its current U.S. dollar equivalent. Since the current amount is *less than* the historical amount, the company incurred a loss (debit).

Translation of the year-end financial statements of Multiple Methods, Inc. using the current rate method appears in Panel b of Exhibit 9.6. Note that the translation adjustment calculated in Panel b of Exhibit 9.5 is shown on the translated balance sheet. The translated retained earnings balance is determined from the translated income statement.

TRANSLATION UNDER *SFAS 52*

In December 1981, following three years of research, deliberations, and public hearings, the FASB issued *SFAS 52*, "Foreign Currency Translation." This statement superseded the controversial *SFAS 8*, which called for (1) translation by the temporal method in all situations and (2) inclusion of translation adjustments in periodic income. Many multinational companies objected to *SFAS 8* because it often produced translation adjustments having no economic significance. Further, when exchange rates were volatile, the translation adjustments caused reported earnings—especially quarterly earnings—to fluctuate wildly.

To address these criticisms, *SFAS 52* adopted a translation approach intended to be consistent with the objectives of foreign currency translation stated in paragraph 4 of the statement:

- Provide information that is generally compatible with the expected economic effects of a rate change on the enterprise's cash flow and equity.
- Reflect in consolidated statements the financial results and relationships of the individual consolidated entities as measured in their *functional currencies* in conformity with U.S. generally accepted accounting principles.

These objectives have a decision orientation in that they call for reported information to be consistent with the underlying economic developments that are of interest to decision makers. Thus, they agree with the general objectives of financial reporting given in the FASB's first *Concepts Statement*.[11]

---

[11] Financial Accounting Standards Board, *Statement of Financial Accounting Concepts No. 1* "Objectives of Financial Reporting by Business Enterprises" (Stamford, CT: FASB, 1978)

THE FUNCTIONAL CURRENCY

The specific translation methodology required by *SFAS 52* for a particular foreign entity follows from determination of that entity's *functional currency*.

> An entity's **functional currency** is the currency of the primary economic environment in which the entity operates and generates net cash flows.[12] It may be either (1) the foreign entity's local currency, (2) another foreign currency, or (3) the U.S. dollar.

A foreign entity's functional currency may or may not be its **reporting currency**—the currency in which its published financial statements are expressed. In the United States, the U.S. dollar is the reporting currency.

Appendix A of *SFAS 52* identifies several economic indicators to be considered individually and collectively when determining an entity's functional currency. Summarized in Exhibit 9.7, these indicators are used to assess the extent to which the foreign entity is relatively self-contained or is an extension of its U.S. parent. Another factor might be the hedging practices of the foreign entity. If the foreign entity regularly hedges its foreign currency commitments and positions in U.S. dollars, a case could be made for designating the dollar as the entity's functional currency.[13]

In the end, determination of the functional currency is essentially a matter of *fact*. The functional currency should be changed only when significant new economic facts and circumstances clearly indicate that a different functional currency is warranted. Because an entity's functional currency is not something to be manipulated, or "chosen," its selection is *not* considered to be a choice among alternative accounting principles. Thus, a change in the functional currency does *not* call for disclosure of the cumulative effect of the change in earnings as is otherwise required under *APBO 20*.[14]

After considering all relevant factors, **determination of the functional currency** can generally be summarized as follows:

- A foreign entity whose operations are relatively self-contained and integrated within the country in which it is located normally uses the *local currency* of that country as its functional currency.
- A foreign entity whose operations are a direct and integral component or extension of a U.S. parent company's operations normally uses the *U.S. dollar*, its reporting currency, as its functional currency.
- A foreign entity located in one foreign country but generating most of its cash flows in the *currency of another foreign country* normally uses the currency of the other foreign country as its functional currency.

---

[12] Financial Accounting Standards Board, *Statement No. 52*, par. 5.

[13] Deloitte Haskins & Sells, *Foreign Currency Translation—Issues and Answers* (New York: Deloitte Haskins & Sells, 1981), 3-4.

[14] Accounting Principles Board, *Opinion No. 20*, "Accounting Changes" (New York: AICPA, 1971).

	Functional Currency Probably Is:	
Economic Indicators	Local or Other Foreign Currency	Parent's Currency ($)
Cash Flow	Cash flows are primarily in the foreign currency and do not have a direct impact on the parent's cash flows.	Cash flows have an impact on parent's cash flows on a current basis and are readily available for remittance to the parent company.
Sales Price	Selling prices are determined primarily by local competition or governmental regulation, and not by short-term changes in exchange rates.	Selling prices are primarily determined by worldwide competition or international prices and respond to short-term changes in exchange rates.
Sales Market	Active sales market for the entity's products is primarily local.	Sales market for the entity's products is primarily in the parent's country or sales contracts are denominated in the parent's currency.
Expense	Costs of labor, materials, and so forth are primarily local costs.	Costs of labor, materials, and so forth are primarily costs for components obtained from the parent's country.
Financing	Financing is primarily denominated in the local currency and is serviced by foreign currency cash flows generated in the foreign country.	Financing is primarily from dollar-denominated obligations *or* parent company funds are needed to service debt obligations.
Intercompany Transactions and Arrangements	Volume of intercompany transactions is low, resulting in minimal relationship between the operations of the foreign entity and the parent	Volume of intercompany transactions is high, resulting in substantial relationship between the operations of the foreign entity and those of the parent.

Source: Financial Accounting Standards Board. *Statement of Financial Accounting Standards No. 52* (Stamford, CT: FASB, 1981), par. 42.

EXHIBIT 9.7   ECONOMIC INDICATORS WHICH INFLUENCE DETERMINATION OF THE FUNCTIONAL CURRENCY

An exception to the above arose when the FASB considered foreign entities located in the *highly inflationary economies* frequently found in countries such as Brazil, Peru, and Israel. Foreign inflation rates significantly higher than U.S. inflation rates can cause the direct $/LC rate to fall dramatically as the dollar strengthens and can result in severely distorted financial results and relationships. These considerations led the board to the following additional functional currency determination:

- A foreign entity located in a country with a **highly inflationary economy**—cumulative inflation of 100 percent or more over a three-year period—*must use the U.S. dollar* as its functional currency (*SFAS 52*, par. 11). The Board states in paragraph 107 of *SFAS 52* that this pragmatic decision was based on its belief that a local currency that "has largely lost its utility as a store of value cannot be a functional measuring unit."

TRANSLATION METHODOLOGIES

After the foreign entity's functional currency is determined, translating its local currency statements into U.S. dollars under *SFAS 52* is conceptually a two-step process:

1. **Remeasure** the entity's local currency (LC) statements into its functional currency (FC).
2. **Translate** the functional currency (FC) statements into the reporting currency, the U.S. dollar.

A diagram of this two-step process follows:

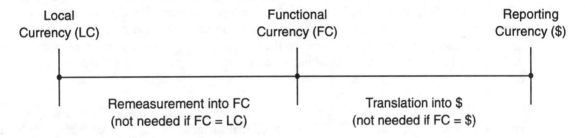

Note that *Step 1* above is *already complete* when the entity's functional currency is its *local currency* (LC), and *Step 2* is complete when the entity's functional currency is the *U.S. dollar*. Only when the entity's functional currency is neither its local currency nor the U.S. dollar are the numerical calculations in Steps 1 and 2 both required, as shown below:

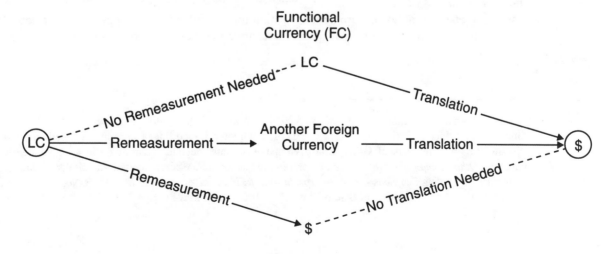

In each situation involving foreign currency translation, we must decide what translation method is to be used and how the translation adjustment is to be reported in the financial statements. Translation situations can be divided into three types:

Case 1. When the *foreign entity's functional currency is its local currency*, its accounts are *translated* into dollars by the *current rate method*. Because the resulting translation adjustments have little economic significance, they are *deferred* under *SFAS 52*; they bypass the income statement and are entered directly into a separate component of stockholders' equity.[15] We refer to this separate component as the *Cumulative Translation Adjustment*.

When the foreign entity is sold or liquidated, the accumulated translation adjustment—the balance in the Cumulative Translation Adjustment account—is recognized in earnings as part of the gain or loss from the sale or liquidation. In the event that *part* of the parent's ownership interest in the foreign entity is sold, a *pro rata* portion of the accumulated translation adjustment is recognized in measuring the gain or loss on the sale.[16]

Case 2. When the *foreign entity's functional currency is the U.S. dollar*, the entity's accounts are *remeasured* in the functional currency (the dollar) using the *temporal method*. Once the accounts are remeasured in dollars, functional currency and reporting currency measurements are identical. Thus, no further translation is necessary. In this case, because translation adjustments have economic significance—they result primarily from remeasuring foreign monetary items likely to be exchanged for dollars—they are included in consolidated net income under *SFAS 52*.

Case 3. When *the foreign entity's functional currency is another foreign currency*, the entity's accounts are first *remeasured* in the other foreign currency by the *temporal method*. The remeasured account balances are then *translated* into dollars using the *current rate method*. In this case the translation adjustment arising in the temporal remeasurement process is translated into dollars and included in consolidated net income, but the translation adjustment produced by the current rate translation process itself is carried directly to stockholders' equity.

Application of the above translation principles is summarized in Exhibit 9.8. When remeasurement is called for, *SFAS 52* requires that historical rates be used for certain accounts, following the temporal method. These accounts are listed in Exhibit 9.9. The current rate is used for other balance sheet accounts and the average rate for the year is used for other income statement accounts in the remeasurement process.

The relationships between the functional currency determination and the current rate and temporal methods follow from a basic objective of *SFAS 52*: *preservation of the foreign entity's financial results and relationships as expressed in its functional currency*. Lawrence Revsine observes that the functional currency determination "is intended to trigger a set of accounting mechanisms which result in reported foreign exchange numbers that correspond to the underlying

---

[15] Financial Accounting Standards Board, *Statement of Financial Accounting Standards No. 130*, "Reporting Comprehensive Income", (Norwalk, CT: FASB, 1997) requires reporting a current rate method translation adjustment as a component of **Other Comprehensive Income** (outside of earnings) in an expanded income statement. *Other comprehensive income* is then reported as a separate component of stockholders' equity.

[16] Financial Accounting Standards Board, *Interpretation of Financial Accounting Standards No. 37*, "Accounting for Translation Adjustments upon Sale of Part of an Investment in a Foreign Entity" (Stamford, CT: FASB, 1983), par. 2.

economics."[17] Thus a foreign subsidiary established primarily "as a conduit for transforming foreign currency transactions into dollar cash flows" should report translated data equivalent to those reported had the U.S. parent entered into those foreign currency transactions directly. *Temporal method remeasurement*, which simulates the foreign entity's transactions as if they had all taken place in dollars, accomplishes this objective.

Functional Currency of Foreign Entity	Input to Translation or Remeasurement Process	Translation or Remeasurement Method	Output of Translation of Remeasurement Process	Treatment of Translation Adjustment
Local foreign currency	Local currency units	Current rate method (translation)	U.S. dollars	Carried directly to Cumulative Translation Adjustment in stockholders' equity; bypasses income statement
U.S. dollar	Local currency units	Temporal method (remeasurement)	U.S. dollars	Included in consolidated or combined net income
Another foreign currency:				
Step 1	Local currency units	Temporal method (remeasurement)	Foreign functional currency units	Included in foreign functional currency income (input to Step 2)
Step 2	Foreign functional currency units	Current rate method (translation)	U.S. dollars	Translation adjustment from Step 1 (now measured in U.S. dollars) included in consolidated or combined net income; translation adjustment from Step 2 carried directly to Cumulative Translation Adjustment in stockholders' equity and bypasses income statement

EXHIBIT 9.8   TRANSLATION APPROACH UNDER *SFAS 52*

---

[17] Lawrence Revsine, "The Rationale Underlying the Functional Currency Choice," *The Accounting Review* (July, 1984), p. 509.

Marketable Securities Carried at Cost
Inventories Carried at Cost
Prepaid Expenses Such as Insurance, Advertising, and Rent
Property, Plant, and Equipment
Accumulated Depreciation on Property, Plant, and Equipment
Patents, Trademarks, Licenses, and Formulas (net)
Goodwill
Other Intangible Assets
Deferred Charges and Credits, except Deferred Income Taxes and Policy Acquisition
    Costs for Life Insurance Companies
Deferred Income
Common Stock
Preferred Stock Carried at Issuance Price
Revenues and Expenses Related to Nonmonetary Items, Such as:
    Cost of Goods Sold
    Depreciation of Property, Plant, and Equipment
    Amortization of Intangible Items Such as Goodwill, Patents, Licenses, etc.
    Amortization of Deferred Charges or Credits except Deferred Income Taxes and
        Policy Acquisition Costs for Life Insurance Companies.

Source: Financial Accounting Standards Board, *Statement of Financial Accounting Standards No. 52*,
    "Foreign Currency Translation" (Stamford, CT: FASB, 1981), Appendix B.

EXHIBIT 9.9   ACCOUNTS TO BE REMEASURED USING HISTORICAL EXCHANGE RATES

Alternatively, a foreign subsidiary established primarily as a self-contained business unit—buying, selling, investing and financing—in the foreign country in which "the eventual dollar impact of these . . . activities may not materialize for years," should report translated data equivalent to those reported in the local currency. Multiplying all assets and liabilities by one constant (the current rate) and revenues and expenses by another constant (the average rate), *current rate method translation* largely accomplishes this goal by preserving most local currency financial results and relationships.

Highly Inflationary Economies

The FASB's pragmatic decision to use the U.S. dollar as the functional currency of foreign entities located in *highly inflationary economies*, with remeasurement by the temporal method, was also intended to preserve local currency results and relationships. When the local currency is more inflationary than the dollar, the dollar strengthens and the direct rate falls. Use of a highly inflationary local currency as the functional currency produces translated foreign asset balances that dwindle to nominal amounts. Of particular concern is the **disappearing plant phenomenon** in which land, factories and other plant assets seem to disappear in translation. Because the local currency account balances and the plant assets themselves remain unimpaired, though, the translated balances are meaningless.

For example, consider a foreign entity located in a highly inflationary economy with plant assets of LC100,000,000 acquired when the exchange rate was $1/LC. With much lower inflation in the United States, the dollar strengthens and the direct exchange rate might drop to $.25/LC from $1/LC in a few years. Plant assets translated at the current rate under the current rate method would shrink to $25,000,000 from $100,000,000, suggesting that only 25% of the assets remained when in fact 100% of the physical assets are still intact. In contrast, continued translation at $1/LC, which becomes the historical rate used in the temporal method, preserves the reported plant assets at $100,000,000.

SFAS 52 TRANSLATION: ANOTHER ILLUSTRATION

We complete our discussion of *SFAS 52* translation methods by turning our attention to a foreign unit which has been in existence for more than one year. This example will illustrate the calculation of Retained Earnings and the Cumulative Translation Adjustment when translation occurs at some point after the foreign unit came into existence.

Some U.S. companies find that certain of their foreign entities have foreign functional currencies and others use the U.S. dollar as their functional currency. These companies use the current rate method for some of their foreign entities and the temporal method for others. The following example applies both translation methods to data for the same foreign company. In practice, though, this foreign company has only one functional currency and only one of the translation methods applies.

The Overseas Company: Background and Initial Balance Sheet

The opening balance sheet for the Overseas Company, our illustrative foreign entity, is given next. We assume that this company has been in existence for several years and that its accounts were remeasured by the temporal method in the past. All account balances are in *local currency (LC)* units.

Overseas Company
Balance Sheet at January 1, 19X1

Assets

Cash and Receivables	LC 1,000,000
Inventory and Plant Assets	3,000,000
Total Assets	LC 4,000,000

Liabilities and Stockholders' Equity

Liabilities	LC 2,000,000
Capital Stock	800,000
Retained Earnings	1,200,000
Total Liabilities and Stockholders' Equity	LC 4,000,000

Exhibit 9.10 shows the translation of this opening balance sheet. Two cases are provided. In *Case 1*, the functional currency is the local currency and the *current rate method* applies. In *Case 2*, the functional currency is the U.S. dollar and the *temporal method* applies. The current rate at January 1, 19X1, is assumed to be $2/LC. When applying the temporal method in Case 2, assume that Inventory and Plant Assets were acquired when the exchange rate was $1.90/LC and that

Capital Stock was issued when the exchange rate was $1.75/LC. In both cases, translated Retained Earnings is a plug.

Assets	LC		Current Rate Method (Functional Currency: LC)		Temporal Method (Functional Currency: $)	
		$/LC	$	$/LC	$	
Cash	LC 400,000	2.00	$ 800,000	2.00	$ 800,000	
Receivables	600,000	2.00	1,200,000	2.00	1,200,000	
Inventory	1,000,000	2.00	2,000,000	1.90	1,900,000	
Plant Assets	2,000,000	2.00	4,000,000	1.90	3,800,000	
Total Assets	LC 4,000,000		$ 8,000,000		$ 7,700,000	
Liabilities and Stockholders' Equity						
Accounts Payable	LC 660,000	2.00	$ 1,320,000	2.00	$ 1,320,000	
Long-Term Debt	1,340,000	2.00	2,680,000	2.00	2,680,000	
Capital Stock	800,000	1.75	1,400,000	1.75	1,400,000	
Retained Earnings	1,200,000	*	2,300,000	*	2,300,000	
Cumulative Translation Adjustment	—		300,000		—	
Total Liabilities and Stockholders' Equity	LC 4,000,000		$ 8,000,000		$ 7,700,000	

* Retained Earnings is a plug.

EXHIBIT 9.10 COMPARATIVE TRANSLATION TO DETERMINE THE INITIAL CUMULATIVE TRANSLATION ADJUSTMENT ACCOUNT AT JANUARY 1, 19X1, FOR THE OVERSEAS COMPANY

In Case 1, the assets and liabilities of Overseas at January 1, 19X1, are translated at the $2/LC current rate on January 1, 19X1; Capital Stock is translated at the $1.75/LC historical rate. In Case 2, Overseas Company's Cash and Receivables and Liabilities are remeasured at the current rate; Inventory and Plant Assets, and Capital Stock are remeasured at their respective historical rates.

We assume that this is the *first time* the current rate method is being applied to Overseas Company. Thus, the $300,000 difference between Case 1 *translated net assets*, $4,000,000 (= $8,000,000 − $4,000,000) and Case 2 *remeasured net assets*, $3,700,000 (= $7,700,000 − $4,000,000), is the *opening* balance in the *Cumulative Translation Adjustment*, shown in Exhibit 9.10. This separate component of stockholders' equity is used when the translation adjustment is deferred under the current rate method. No such account exists when the temporal method is used because translation adjustments flow through net income to retained earnings.

Once established, the balance in the Cumulative Translation Adjustment account increases (decreases) by the annual translation gain (loss) arising under the current rate method of translation in Case 1. In Case 2, there is no Cumulative Translation Adjustment account; rather, annual translation adjustments arising in the remeasurement process, which normally differ in sign and amount from those in Case 1, enter Retained Earnings as part of net income.

Translation of Income Statement and Balance Sheet at End of First Year

Continuing with our example of the Overseas Company, we now illustrate Case 1 translation and Case 2 remeasurement according to *SFAS 52* as of December 31, 19X1. Data related to the Overseas Company's operations during 19X1 are given in Exhibit 9.11.

Translation/remeasurement of the Overseas Company's 19X1 income statement and ending balance sheet and supporting schedules appears in Exhibit 9.12. As before, Case 1 illustrates *translation when the functional currency is the local currency* and the *current rate method* is used. Case 2 illustrates *remeasurement when the functional currency is the U.S. dollar* and the *temporal method* is used. You may wish to compare these translation processes to the previous illustration involving Multiple Methods, Inc., in Exhibits 9.3 through 9.6.

The Overseas example highlights the different exchange rates used in the current rate and temporal methods. Translated net income and assets differ from the remeasured amounts. The LC strengthened relative to the dollar as the direct rate rose. This event led to a $225,000 translation *gain* on a net asset exposed position in the current rate method that was carried directly to the Cumulative Translation Adjustment account. In the temporal method, the net liability exposed position led to an $80,000 translation *loss* that was included in net income.

Notice that translated net assets in Case 1, $4,620,000 (= $9,030,000 − $4,410,000), exceed Case 2 remeasured net assets, $4,145,000 (= $8,555,000 − $4,410,000), by $475,000. This difference may be reconciled as follows:

Balance in Cumulative Translation Adjustment Account, December 31, 19X1	$ 525,000
Plus Case 1 Translated Net Income	1,435,000
Minus Case 2 Remeasured Net Income	(1,485,000)
Difference in Net Assets between Methods	$ 475,000

Because the exchange rate rose to $2.10/LC from $2/LC during 19X1, the dollar weakened and the dollar equivalents of LC balances increased. The greater increase in translated net assets in Case 1, reflected in the Cumulative Translation Adjustment account, was partially offset by the higher Case 2 net income. Case 2 net income is $50,000 higher due to (1) $130,000 (= $5,330,000 − $5,200,000) less in cost of sales and depreciation from applying lower historical exchange rates for those items and (2) an $80,000 translation loss on the net monetary liabilities under the temporal method.

The Overseas Company
Statement of Income and Retained Earnings
for the Year Ended December 31, 19X1

Sales	LC	5,000,000
Cost of Sales		(2,250,000)
Depreciation		(350,000)
Current Operating Expenses		(1,700,000)
Net Income	LC	700,000
Retained Earnings, January 1		1,200,000
Dividends		(500,000)
Retained Earnings, December 31	LC	1,400,000

The Overseas Company
Balance Sheet at December 31, 19X1

Assets

Cash	LC	600,000
Receivables		600,000
Inventory		800,000
Plant Assets		2,300,000
Total Assets	LC	4,300,000

Liabilities and Stockholders' Equity

Accounts Payable	LC	840,000
Long-Term Debt		1,260,000
Capital Stock		800,000
Retained Earnings		1,400,000
Total Liabilities and Stockholders' Equity	LC	4,300,000

Additional information:

1. The exchange rate is $2.10/LC at December 31, 19X1. The weighted average exchange rate during 19X1 was $2.05/LC. Dividends were declared and paid when the exchange rate was $2.08/LC.
2. LC2,700,000 of inventory and plant assets were purchased during 19X1 at the average exchange rate of $2.05/LC. Cost of Sales and Depreciation are derived from some inventory and plant assets on hand at January 1, 19X1, and from some 19X1 purchases. The average historical exchange rate related to the inventory sold and to depreciation is $2.00/LC.

EXHIBIT 9.11 DATA RELATED TO APPLYING *SFAS 52* TO THE OVERSEAS COMPANY DURING 19X1

	Case 1: Current Rate Method (Functional Currency: LC)			Case 2: Temporal Method (Functional Currency: $)	

Statement of Income and Retained Earnings for the Year Ended December 31, 19X1

	LC	$/LC	$	$/LC	$
Sales	LC 5,000,000	$ 2.05	$ 10,250,000	$ 2.05	$ 10,250,000
Cost of Sales	(2,250,000)	2.05	(4,612,500)	2.00	(4,500,000)
Depreciation	(350,000)	2.05	(717,500)	2.00	(700,000)
Current Operating Expenses	(1,700,000)	2.05	(3,485,000)	2.05	(3,485,000)
Translation Loss	—	—	—	(2)[a]	(80,000)
Net Income	LC 700,000		$ 1,435,000		$ 1,485,000
Retained Earnings, January 1	1,200,000	—	2,300,000	—	2,300,000
Dividends	(500,000)	2.08	(1,040,000)	2.08	(1,040,000)
Retained Earnings, December 31	LC 1,400,000		$ 2,695,000		$ 2,745,000

Balance Sheet at December 31, 19X1

Assets					
Cash	LC 600,000	2.10	$ 1,260,000	2.10	$ 1,260,000
Receivables	600,000	2.10	1,260,000	2.10	1,260,000
Inventory	800,000	2.10	1,680,000	(3)[a]	1,602,500
Plant Assets	2,300,000	2.10	4,830,000	(3)[a]	4,432,500
Total Assets	LC 4,300,000		$ 9,030,000		$ 8,555,000
Liabilities and Stockholders' Equity					
Accounts Payable	LC 840,000	2.10	$ 1,764,000	2.10	$ 1,764,000
Long-Term Debt	1,260,000	2.10	2,646,000	2.10	2,646,000
Capital Stock	800,000	1.75	1,400,000	1.75	1,400,000
Retained Earnings	1,400,000	—	2,695,000	—	2,745,000
Cumulative Translation Adjustment	—	(1)[a]	525,000		—
Total Liabilities and Stockholders' Equity	LC 4,300,000		$ 9,030,000		$ 8,555,000

[a] The supporting schedule appears on the following page.

EXHIBIT 9.12 OVERSEAS COMPANY: TRANSLATION UNDER *SFAS 52* FOR THE YEAR ENDED DECEMBER 31, 19X1

(1) Analysis of Cumulative Translation Adjustment
(Current Rate Method)

	LC	$/LC	$
Balance, January 1, 19X1 (Exhibit 9.10)	—	—	$ (300,000)
19X1 Translation Adjustment:			
Exposed Position (Net Assets), January 1, 19X1	LC 2,000,000	$ 2.00	$ 4,000,000
Plus: Net Income in 19X1	700,000*	2.05	1,435,000
Less: Dividends Paid	(500,000)	2.08	(1,040,000)
Exposed Position (Net Assets), December 31, 19X1 . .	LC 2,200,000		$ 4,395,000
		2.10 →	−4,620,000
Net 19X1 Translation Adjustment (Gain)			$ (225,000)
Balance, December 31, 19X1			$ (525,000)

* The revenues and expenses which make up net income represent individual increases and decreases to the exposed position. Since they are all translated at the same average rate of $2.05/LC; a single entry for net income will suffice.

(2) Proof of Translation Loss (Temporal Method)

	LC	$/LC	$
Exposed Position, January 1, 19X1	LC (1,000,000)*	$ 2.00	$ (2,000,000)
Plus: Sales	5,000,000	2.05	10,250,000
Less: Purchase of Inventory	(2,050,000)	2.05	(4,202,500)
Less: Purchase of Plant Assets	(650,000)	2.05	(1,332,500)
Less: Payment of Current Operating Expenses	(1,700,000)	2.05	(3,485,000)
Less: Dividends Paid	(500,000)	2.08	(1,040,000)
Exposed Position, December 31, 19X1	LC (900,000)*		$ (1,810,000)
		2.10 →	−(1,890,000)
Translation Loss			$ 80,000

* The exposed position under the temporal method is Cash and Receivables minus Liabilities; at January 1, 19X1, it is (LC1,000,000) = LC1,000,000 − LC2,000,000 and at December 31, 19X1, it is (LC900,000) = (LC1,200,000 − LC2,100,000).

(3) Remeasurement of Inventory and Plant Assets (Temporal Method)

	LC	$/LC	$
Inventory, January 1, 19X1	LC 1,000,000	$ 1.90	$ 1,900,000
Amount Purchased	2,050,000	2.05	4,202,500
Amount Sold (Cost of Sales)	(2,250,000)	2.00	(4,500,000)
Inventory, December 31, 19X1	LC 800,000		$ 1,602,500
Plant Assets, January 1, 19X1	LC 2,000,000	1.90	$ 3,800,000
Amount Purchased	650,000	2.05	1,332,500
Depreciation Expense	(350,000)	2.00	(700,000)
Plant Assets, December 31, 19X1	LC 2,300,000		$ 4,432,500

EXHIBIT 9.12 *(Continued)*

Translation of Statement of Cash Flows at End of First Year

SFAS 95 requires companies to issue a **statement of cash flows** to state "the reporting currency equivalents of foreign currency cash flows using the exchange rates in effect at the time of the cash flows."[18] In the foreign currency context, the goal of the cash flow statement is therefore to report a foreign entity's cash transactions. Although translation adjustments accrue to all accounts that are translated or remeasured at the current rate, *only the portion of the translation adjustment affecting cash is to be disclosed separately in the statement of cash flows*. This approach allows reconciliation of the beginning and ending cash balances, but not of the beginning and ending balances in other accounts. The board concluded that since translation adjustments are not cash flows, translation adjustments affecting accounts other than Cash do not belong in a cash flow statement.

The translated statement of cash flows is obtained by either of two approaches:

1. Translating the statement prepared in local currency units into dollars at current period exchange rates.
2. Deriving the statement from the foreign entity's translated income statement, comparative balance sheets, and other information.

Alternative 1 is preferred because, except for the translation effect on cash, it avoids translation adjustments altogether.[19]

Regardless of the functional currency selected and translation method used, *the resulting statement of cash flows is exactly the same*. Even though the calculations in Alternative 2 depend on the translation method used, the *focus on cash transactions* ensures that the statement of cash flows is independent of the choice between the current rate and temporal methods of translation. Translating the foreign cash transactions proceeds as follows under both translation methods:

- *Repetitive cash transactions* are translated at the *average rate*.
- *Large, discrete cash transactions*, such as dividend payments or proceeds from issuing securities, are translated at the rate(s) in effect when they occurred.

The Overseas Company's statement of cash flows for the year ended December 31, 19X1, in local currency (LC) units and dollars ($), appears in Exhibit 9.13. Net income and depreciation expense are translated by the current rate method as shown in Case 1 in Exhibit 9.12. *Cash flow from operations is determined by the* **indirect method**, in which net income is adjusted for (1) those operating items included in net income that do not involve cash, and (2) those operating items *not* included in net income which *do* involve cash. All other cash flows and adjustments, except dividends, are assumed to have occurred evenly throughout the year and are translated at $2.05/LC, the average rate.

---

[18] Financial Accounting Standards Board, *Statement of Financial Accounting Standards No. 95*, "Statement of Cash Flows" (Stamford, CT: FASB, November 1987), par. 25.

[19] For further details, see Ronald J. Huefner, J. Edward Ketz, and James A. Largay III, "Foreign Currency Translation and the Cash Flow Statement," *Accounting Horizons* (June 1989), 66-75.

Overseas Company
Statement of Cash Flows for the Year Ended
December 31, 19X1 (Indirect Method)

	LC	$/LC	$
Cash Balance: January 1, 19X1	LC 400,000	2.00	$ 800,000
Operating Activities			
Net Income	LC 700,000	2.05	$ 1,435,000
Depreciation Expense	350,000	2.05	717,500
Decrease in Inventories	200,000	2.05	410,000
Increase in Accounts Payable	180,000	2.05	369,000
Cash Provided by Operating Activities	LC 1,430,000		$ 2,931,500
Investing Activities			
Acquisition of Plant Assets	LC (650,000)	2.05	$ (1,332,500)
Cash Used by Investing Activities	LC (650,000)		$ (1,332,500)
Financing Activities			
Retirement of Long-Term Debt	LC (80,000)	2.05	$ (164,000)
Dividends Paid	(500,000)	2.08	(1,040,000)
Cash Used by Financing Activities	LC (580,000)		$ (1,204,000)
Effect of Exchange Rate Changes on Cash	—		$ 65,000 *
Cash Balance: December 31, 19X1	LC 600,000		$ 1,260,000

$$* \text{ Translation Effect on Cash} = (\$2.10 - \$2.00)\ 400{,}000 + (\$2.10 - \$2.05)\ 700{,}000$$
$$- (\$2.10 - \$2.08)\ 500{,}000$$
$$= \$40{,}000 + \$35{,}000 - \$10{,}000$$
$$= \$65{,}000$$

EXHIBIT 9.13 OVERSEAS COMPANY: TRANSLATED STATEMENT OF CASH FLOWS

Note that the translation adjustment accruing to cash has three components. *First*, the $40,000 [= ($2.10 − $2.00) × 400,000] shows that the dollar equivalent of the beginning LC cash balance, held throughout the year, increased by $40,000 during 19X1 as the direct exchange rate rose and the LC strengthened. *Second*, the $35,000 [= ($2.10 − $2.05) × 700,000] indicates that the dollar equivalent of the net cash inflow occurring when the exchange rate was $2.05/LC increased by $35,000 by year-end. The LC700,000 consists of the operating inflow of LC1,430,000 less the LC650,000 investing outflow less the LC80,000 retirement of long-term debt. Thus, the first two components are *gains* from translation. *Third*, the $10,000 [= ($2.10 − $2.08) × 500,000] shows that the dividend *outflow* made when the exchange rate was $2.08/LC also rose in dollar equivalent by year-end and produced a translation *loss* of $10,000.

DISCLOSURES

Under *SFAS 52*, companies must disclose the aggregate *transaction gain or loss* reflected in net income for the period, plus any *translation gain or loss* produced by *remeasuring* foreign currency financial statements into the functional currency. In addition, an analysis of changes in the Cumulative Translation Adjustment account during the period shall be disclosed in a note to the financial statements, in a separate financial statement, or as part of a statement of changes in stockholders' equity. When a change in the exchange rate occurs after the balance sheet date but before the statements are issued, and has a significant effect on unsettled foreign currency transactions, the change and the magnitude of its effect also must be disclosed.

An example of one such disclosure appears in Note 14 to the financial statements in an annual report of CBS issued shortly after the adoption of *SFAS 52*. In the note, which is reproduced below, the reference to "gains and losses from certain hedges" in CBS's "Foreign Currency Fluctuations" account (its Cumulative Translation Adjustment account) relates to transaction adjustments accruing to *economic hedges of net investments in foreign entities*, which is discussed in Chapter 10.

---

14. FOREIGN CURRENCY TRANSLATION

The accounting for foreign currency translation conforms to Statement of Financial Accounting Standards No. 52. Generally, adjustments for currency exchange rate changes are excluded from net income for those fluctuations that do not have an impact on cash flow.

Net income included foreign currency losses of $15.9 million, $5.1 million and $5.4 million for 19X3, 19X2 and 19X1, respectively.

An analysis of the changes to the "Foreign Currency Fluctuations" component of shareholders' equity is as follows:

	Year Ended December 31		
	19X3	19X2	19X1
	(Dollars in Thousands)		
Balance at Beginning of Year	$ (50,795)	$ (15,456)	$ 10,940
Translation Adjustments, and Gains and Losses from Certain Hedges and Intercompany Balances, Net	(551)	(35,454)	(26,861)
Income Taxes Related to Hedges and Intercompany Balances Included Above . .	(64)	115	465
Balance at End of Year	$ (51,410)	$ (50,795)	$ (15,456)

TRANSLATION AND FINANCIAL STATEMENT ANALYSIS

Foreign currency translation affects analysis and interpretation of financial statements in pervasive ways. In the ensuing paragraphs we discuss the effects on ratio analysis and address the problem of interperiod comparisons when translated foreign currency data are present. Our discussion is aimed at helping the user of financial statements achieve the following objective:

To understand how a company's **reported performance** is affected by foreign currency translation methodologies.

In doing so, notice how the current rate and temporal methods impact components of financial statement data and influence ratios calculated with these data.

- Translated total assets under the current rate method are larger (smaller) than remeasured total assets under the temporal method when the exchange rate has been rising (falling) over time. This effect occurs because nonmonetary assets are remeasured at historical rates under the temporal method.
- Disregarding the translation adjustment, translated income is larger (smaller) than remeasured income when the exchange rate has been falling (rising) over time. This effect occurs because depreciation, amortization and cost of sales are remeasured at historical rates under the temporal method.
- Including the translation adjustment in income when the temporal method is used creates another difference between translated and remeasured income.

Measures of profitability, short-term liquidity and long-term solvency are all affected. We first examine the *DuPont Analysis*, a common approach to assessing profitability.

Effects on Profitability: The "DuPont Analysis"

The basic **DuPont Analysis**, named for the DuPont Corporation which developed it, disaggregates the *Return on Assets* (ROA) ratio into *Return on Sales* (ROS) and *Total Assets Turnover* (TATO) ratios as follows.

$$\text{Return on Assets} \quad = \quad \text{Return on Sales} \; \times \; \text{Total Assets Turnover}$$

$$\frac{\text{Income}}{\text{Average Total Assets}} = \frac{\text{Income}}{\text{Sales}} \times \frac{\text{Sales}}{\text{Average Total Assets}}$$

ROA measures the profitability of the firm's asset portfolio, **ROS** measures the profitability of sales and **TATO** measures efficiency—the ability of the firm's asset portfolio to generate sales.

Importance of Income Measure. Although various measures of income are used by different authors, we prefer either *aftertax operating income* (often approximated by net income + (1-t) interest expense) or *earnings before interest and taxes* (EBIT). Use of these income measures (before interest expense) rather than *net income* (after interest expense) enables measurement of profitability before considering interest payments to suppliers of capital. In this way, the firm's operating and investing decisions are separated from its financing decisions.

Illustration of Profitability Analysis. Relevant data from the Overseas Company example for 19X1 in Exhibits 9.10 through 9.12 are summarized below, followed by the profitability analysis calculations.

LC Financial Statement Data

		Relevant Exchange Rates	
Sales	LC 5,000,000	Average rate during 19X1 . .	$ 2.05/LC
Operating Income (= Net Income)	700,000	Rate on January 1, 19X1 . .	$ 2.00/LC
Average Total Assets	4,150,000	Rate on December 31, 19X1	$ 2.10/LC

Profitability Analysis

Currency	Return on Assets	=	Return on Sales	×	Total Assets Turnover
LC	$\dfrac{700,000}{4,150,000}$	=	$\dfrac{700,000}{5,000,000}$	×	$\dfrac{5,000,000}{4,150,000}$
	.17	=	.14	×	1.2
$ (current rate method)	$\dfrac{1,435,000}{8,515,000^1}$	=	$\dfrac{1,435,000}{10,250,000}$	×	$\dfrac{10,250,000}{8,515,000}$
	.17	=	.14	×	1.2
$ (temporal method)	$\dfrac{1,565,000^2}{8,128,000^3}$	=	$\dfrac{1,565,000}{10,250,000}$	×	$\dfrac{10,250,000}{8,128,000}$
	.19	=	.15	×	1.3

[1] Average total assets = (8,000,000 + 9,030,000)/2 [See Exhibits 9.10 and 9.12]
[2] 1,565,000 = 1,485,000 (net income) + 80,000 (translation loss)
[3] Average total assets = (7,700,000 + 8,555,000)/2 [See Exhibits 9.10 and 9.12]

The above calculations show that the temporal method presents a different picture of the foreign entity's profitability than the LC and current rate method measurements. The lower historical rates used in the temporal method to remeasure total assets and depreciation expense produce higher income and lower average total assets than the current rate method. Of course, the larger the difference between the current rate and applicable historical rates, the more the temporal method ratios diverge from the LC and current rate method ratios.

By adding the $80,000 temporal method translation loss to net income of $1,485,000, we obtained a measure of operating income uncontaminated by the translation adjustment. We excluded the translation adjustment because it is not an *operating item*; it arises from credit and payment decisions and is best viewed as financial revenue or expense, similar to interest. If one chooses to include the $80,000 translation loss in income, the ROA and ROS ratios in this example fall.

Effects on Short-Term Liquidity and Long-Term Solvency Analysis

Because the current rate and temporal methods generally lead to different translated asset balances, income, and stockholders' equity accounts, other ratios employing those translated amounts are also affected. For example, referring back to the Overseas Company's December 31, 19X1 data in Exhibits 9.11 and 9.12, we can make the following calculations:

Currency	Current Ratio	Total Liabilities/ Total Assets	Long-Term Debt/ Stockholders' Equity
LC	$\frac{2,000,000}{840,000} = 2.38$	$\frac{2,100,000}{4,300,000} = .488$	$\frac{1,260,000}{2,200,000} = .572$
$ (current rate method)	$\frac{4,200,000}{1,764,000} = 2.38$	$\frac{4,410,000}{9,030,000} = .488$	$\frac{2,646,000}{4,620,000} = .572$
$ (temporal method)	$\frac{4,122,500}{1,764,000} = 2.34$	$\frac{4,410,000}{8,555,000} = .515$	$\frac{2,646,000}{4,145,000} = .638$

In this example, the temporal method ratios portray liquidity and solvency less favorably than the LC data suggest; the lower historical rates used to remeasure inventory and plant assets depress the current ratio and raise the ratio of total liabilities to total assets (TL/TA). But when historical rates are higher than the current rate, temporal method remeasurement raises the current ratio and lowers the TL/TA ratio. Current rate method ratios preserve these particular LC relationships exactly—*both numerator and denominator measured in LC are multiplied by the same year-end current rate*.

Comments on the Ratio Analyses. *SFAS 52* justifies applying the current rate method to relatively self-contained and independent foreign entities by explaining that this method better preserves the financial results and relationships expressed in the entity's local currency. When the current rate method is used, the entity's functional currency is the local currency. The above ratio analyses indicate that the current rate method does a better job than the temporal method of preserving these local currency relationships.

Not *all* current rate method ratios, however, are identical to their LC counterparts. Significant changes in exchange rates and total assets cause ratios such as return on assets (ROA) to diverge. This occurs when the *average rate for the year used to translate income in the numerator does not equal the average of the beginning and ending rates used to translate average total assets in the denominator*. To see how this happens, carry the previous LC and current rate ROA and TATO calculations to more than two decimal places. Nevertheless, current rate method ratios avoid the potential large distortions that can occur when drastically different historical rates are used in the temporal method.

In contrast, the temporal method seeks to report the foreign transactions undertaken by the foreign entity in the same way that the domestic parent would report those transactions had the parent entered into them directly. Remeasuring those foreign transactions into dollars, at the exchange rates in effect when the transactions occurred, produces ratio values equal to those resulting if the parent transacted directly with foreign suppliers and customers. The *SFAS 52* functional currency concept indicates that preserving local currency results and relationships should be relatively unimportant when the foreign entity's functional currency is the dollar.

Interperiod Comparisons

Assessing changes in performance over time using translated or remeasured data is complicated by a factor over which the foreign entity has no control—*changes in exchange rates*. Comparative local currency data, desired by some financial analysts, are often not available to users of financial statements. Moreover, users of *consolidated statements* are not able to factor out an *individual foreign entity's* influence on those statements. Sufficient disaggregated data in dollars, either in the form of supplementary disclosures or internal breakdowns, are needed if an assessment is to be attempted.

One approach to judging year-to-year changes in a foreign entity's performance involves factoring out exchange rate changes and calculating data translated or remeasured with constant exchange rates. For example, suppose the following condensed income statement data and exchange rates pertain to a foreign entity.

	19X6	**19X5**
Sales	LC 1,000	LC 800
Costs and Expenses	(800)	(700)
Operating Income	LC 200	LC 100
Change in income (%)	100%	—

Average exchange rate for 19X6: $.90/LC   Average exchange rate for 19X5: $1.00/LC

Composite historical rates relating to Costs and Expenses:

19X6: $.95/LC   19X5: $1.05/LC

Comparative translated/remeasured data based on the above exchange rates are given next.

	Current Rate Method		Temporal Method	
	19X6	**19X5**	**19X6**	**19X5**
Sales	$ 900	$ 800	$ 900	$ 800
Costs and Expenses	(720)	(700)	(760)	(735)
Operating Income	$ 180	$ 100	$ 140	$ 65
Change in Income (%)	80%	—	115%	—

Note that the current rate method *understates* the percentage change in LC income by 20% (= 80% − 100%) and the temporal method *overstates* the percentage change in LC income by 15% (= 115% − 100%). Now we recalculate translated/remeasured income using the same 19X5 exchange rates in both 19X5 and 19X6.

	Current Rate Method		Temporal Method	
	19X6	**19X5**	**19X6**	**19X5**
Sales	$ 1,000	$ 800	$ 1,000	$ 800
Costs and Expenses	(800)	(700)	(840)	(735)
Operating Income	$ 200	$ 100	$ 160	$ 65
Change in Income (%)	100%	—	146%	—

Under the *current rate method*, 19X6 LC data are translated at the same rate used in 19X5—$1.00/LC—and the 100% change in translated income agrees with the 100% change in local currency income.

Unfortunately, the same cannot be said for the *temporal method*. Although the 19X5 rates of $1.00/LC and $1.05/LC were used to remeasure 19X6 local currency sales, and costs and expenses, respectively, the 146% change in remeasured income is greater than the 115% change observed when the 19X6 data were remeasured at 19X6 exchange rates. This occurs because LC sales increased by 25% whereas LC costs and expenses increased by only 14%. The effect on remeasured income of remeasuring the LC200 increase in 19X6 sales at $1.00/LC is much greater than the effect of remeasuring the LC100 increase in costs and expenses at $1.05/LC. Thus, whether use of 19X5 rates to remeasure 19X6 LC data under the temporal method parallels changes in LC results depends on both changes in the LC data and in exchange rates. To see this, refer to problem P9.4 at the end of the chapter. Data in that problem are such that use of the first year's rates to remeasure the second year's data under the temporal method more accurately reflects the percentage change in local currency income.

OTHER FOREIGN CURRENCY TRANSLATION MATTERS

The preceding section discussed and illustrated the principal concepts and methods underlying translation of foreign statements pursuant to *SFAS 52*. Additional issues are discussed below.

CHANGING THE FUNCTIONAL CURRENCY

Early in the chapter we remarked that determination of an entity's functional currency is a matter of *fact*, not a mere choice between accounting alternatives. But when facts and circumstances change, an entity's functional currency can also change. This section indicates how changes in functional currency are treated. All changes are accounted for *prospectively*, not by cumulative effect or prior period adjustments

Change from Local Currency to U.S. Dollar

Current rate method translated assets and liabilities at the end of the prior period are the beginning remeasured book values; last period's closing rate becomes the historical rate attached to nonmonetary items. The Cumulative Translation Adjustment is not removed from stockholders' equity.

Change from U.S. Dollar to Local Currency

Applying the current rate method to the Overseas Company at January 1, 19X1, earlier in the chapter illustrated the change from U.S. dollar to local currency in a non-highly inflationary economy. Assets and liabilities are translated at the current rate, creating an opening balance in the Cumulative Translation Adjustment, equal to the difference between net assets translated at the current rate and net assets translated according to the temporal method. Overseas' Company's opening credit balance when the current rate method was adopted on January 1, 19X1 was $300,000.

Highly Inflationary Economies

Recall the FASB's pragmatic decision to require entities located in highly inflationary economies to use the dollar as their functional currency. Even relatively self-contained entities that otherwise would have used the local currency as their functional currency had to use the dollar. As highly inflationary economies emerged from that dubious status, entities located therein began changing their functional currencies. EITF *Issue 92-4* addressed the accounting.[20]

The basic idea behind requiring the dollar as functional currency in highly inflationary economies, was to forestall the *disappearing plant phenomenon* by remeasuring historical book values of nonmonetary assets at historical exchange rates much higher than the current rate. Translating all nonmonetary assets at the (much lower) current rate, as normally is done when changing functional currency from the dollar to the local currency, produces that same disappearing plant phenomenon we sought to avoid. EITF *Issue 92-4* therefore creates *new local currency balances* by dividing existing *remeasured dollar balances* by the *current rate*.

To illustrate, suppose an entity had LC100,000 of land remeasured to $100,000 at the historical rate of $1/LC. If the current rate is now $.10/LC after years of high inflation, a balance of LC1,000,000 (100,000/.10) is needed to carry the $100,000 forward. All LC book values of nonmonetary items are recalculated in similar fashion when the functional currency is changed to the local currency upon cessation of high inflation.

BUSINESS COMBINATIONS

When a foreign entity's assets are acquired and its liabilities assumed in a business combination, these items must be translated into dollars for inclusion in the U.S. parent's financial statements. Both the foreign entity's functional currency *and* the method of accounting used by the parent—purchase or pooling of interests—are important in the translation process.

At date of business combination, all *purchase combinations* call for use of the *spot rate* in effect at date of business combination to translate *fair values* of assets acquired, liabilities assumed, and purchased goodwill. When needed, the *book value* of the foreign entity's stockholders' equity is also translated at the spot rate. In a *pooling* involving a foreign entity with a foreign functional currency, the *book values* of all assets, liabilities, and stockholders' equity accounts are translated at the *spot rate* at date of business combination. In contrast, when the functional currency is the U.S. dollar and the combination is accounted for as a pooling of interests, remeasurement is accomplished via the temporal method, and *historical rates* in

---

[20] EITF *Issue 92-4*, "Accounting for a Change in Functional Currency When an Economy Ceases to Be Considered Highly Inflationary," *EITF Abstracts* (Norwalk, CT: FASB, 1992), pp. 679-681.

existence prior to the business combination are used to translate assets acquired and liabilities assumed.

When consolidated statements are prepared *after date of business combination*, the *current rate method* applies to entities with *foreign functional currencies*. The *temporal method* is used when the entity's functional currency is the U.S. dollar. When the temporal method is applied in a purchase, the spot rate at date of business combination becomes the historical rate for purposes of remeasuring the entity's stockholders' equity in existence at date of business combination.

Translated *minority interest* in a partially owned foreign subsidiary is the minority's *pro rata* share of the subsidiary's stockholders' equity translated or remeasured as outlined in the preceding paragraph. It also includes the portion of the Cumulative Translation Adjustment attributable to the minority interest. The rules governing translation in business combinations are summarized in Exhibit 9.14.

EQUITY INVESTMENTS

Under the equity method explained in Chapter 4, an investor company records a percentage of an investee's annual net income. The financial statements of a foreign equity investee must therefore be translated or remeasured into dollars according to *SFAS 52* before the equity method income accrual is booked by the U.S. investor. When the *current rate method* is used, the portions of any purchase premium reflected in the original purchase price allocable to undervalued assets of the investee or to goodwill are to be translated at the *ending current rate*. The *weighted average current rate* for the period is used to translate the purchase premium amortization reflected in the equity method income accrual. In making the accrual, the investor also adjusts its investment account for its share of any changes in the investee's Cumulative Translation Adjustment account arising in translation, and includes its share in the Cumulative Translation Adjustment account appearing in the investor's U.S. financial statements.

Alternatively, when the investee's statements are *remeasured* using the *temporal method*, purchase premium amortization is based on the exchange rate when the shares were acquired. Moreover, the equity method income accrual includes the investor's share of the investee's translation gain or loss through its inclusion in the investee's remeasured net income.

CONSOLIDATION OF FOREIGN SUBSIDIARIES

Translation of foreign currency financial statements is required when the operations of foreign subsidiaries are to be included in the U.S. financial statements of the parent company. The foreign accounts are translated according to the rules presented in the previous sections. Issues related to reporting these foreign operations and including them in U.S. consolidated statements are discussed below.

Reporting on Foreign Operations

ARB 43 expresses concern over inclusion of translated foreign operations in U.S. company statements.[21] Given the inherent riskiness of foreign operations—distant geographical locations subject to foreign sovereign states—extreme care should be taken in reporting earnings in excess

---

[21] Committee on Accounting Procedure, *ARB 43*, Chapter 12.

Method of Accounting	Functional Currency	Translation Rate/Method		Accounting Basis to Be Translated
		Date of Business Combination	Subsequent to Business Combination	
Purchase	Foreign currency	Spot rate	Current rate method	Fair values of assets acquired, liabilities assumed, and purchased goodwill; book value of stockholders' equity
Pooling of Interests	Foreign currency	Spot rate	Current rate method	Book values of assets acquired, liabilities assumed, and stockholders' equity
Purchase	U.S. dollar	Spot rate	Temporal method utilizing spot rate at date of business combination as historical rate for those items in existence at date of business combination	Fair values of assets acquired, liabilities assumed, and purchased goodwill; book value of stockholders' equity
Pooling of Interests	U.S. dollar	Temporal method	Temporal method utilizing same historical rates used at date of business combination	Book values of assets acquired, liabilities assumed, and stockholders' equity

EXHIBIT 9.14 TRANSLATION OF ASSETS ACQUIRED, LIABILITIES ASSUMED, AND STOCKHOLDERS' EQUITY IN A BUSINESS COMBINATION

of amounts received in cash or available in cash for unrestricted transmission to the United States. Similarly, uncertainty with respect to the ultimate realization of other foreign assets is an issue to be resolved in determining the propriety of consolidated statements that include translated foreign assets and liabilities.

Translation of Intercompany Accounts

Preparation of consolidated financial statements requires that intercompany accounts and financial relationships be *eliminated*. **Intercompany accounts** are those that have equal and offsetting balances on the parent and subsidiary books. They arise out of the parent/subsidiary relationship or because transactions between the parent and subsidiary occurred. The simplest approach to translating intercompany accounts in the foreign statements is to use the dollar balances from the offsetting intercompany accounts on the parent company books as the translated balances.

Preparation of consolidated financial statements requires that the following intercompany accounts be eliminated:

- Investment in Subsidiary (Dr.) and Stockholders' Equity (Cr.)
- Intercompany Revenues (Cr.) and Expenses (Dr.)
- Intercompany Receivables (Dr.) and Payables (Cr.)

Intercompany accounts in the foreign subsidiary's statements are given translated balances equal to the dollar balances of the offsetting accounts on the parent's books. Where intercompany sales, purchases, receivables, and payables are concerned, the foreign subsidiary must inform the parent of the transactions it recorded. Only in this way can the parent reconcile the offsetting accounts without separately translating each entry made by the foreign subsidiary. The built-in check provided by offsetting dollar balances in the intercompany accounts of domestic affiliates becomes inoperable when a foreign affiliate is involved.

Preparation of Consolidated Statements

The basic consolidation procedure involves eliminating the investment account against the translated stockholders' equity of the foreign subsidiary. When the equity method is used by the parent, its share of the subsidiary's Cumulative Translation Adjustment account was already accrued. In this case, elimination of the subsidiary's translated stockholders' equity includes the Cumulative Translation Adjustment account. At *date of business combination*, the investment account reflects the parent's portion of the subsidiary's translated stockholders' equity, as well as a purchase premium or discount in purchase combinations. Once any purchase premium or discount is reclassified and allocated on the working paper, a clean elimination is possible.

For example, suppose that Domestic Corporation pays $4,200,000 cash for 80 percent of the common stock of the Overseas Company, the entity in Exhibits 9.10, 9.11, and 9.12. The Overseas Company's stockholders' equity at January 1, 19X1, translated at the $2/LC spot rate, is $4,000,000 [= $2(800,000 + 1,200,000)], and a *purchase premium* of $1,000,000 [= $4,200,000 − (.8 × $4,000,000)] results. If we also assume that the Overseas Company's inventory and plant assets have an estimated fair value of LC3,400,000 (their total book value is LC3,000,000), the purchase premium is allocated as follows:

Inventory and Plant Assets [.8 × $2(3,400,000 − 3,000,000)]	$ 640,000
Goodwill	360,000
Total Purchase Premium	$ 1,000,000

Following procedures developed in Chapter 3, preparation of a consolidated balance sheet at date of business combination—January 1, 19X1—requires the following working paper entries:

Consolidated Working Papers

Inventory and Plant Assets	640,000	
Goodwill	360,000	
Investment in Overseas Company		1,000,000
To reclassify and allocate the purchase premium.		
Capital Stock—Overseas Company ($2 × 800,000)	1,600,000	
Retained Earnings—Overseas Company ($2 × 1,200,000) . . .	2,400,000	
Investment in Overseas Company		3,200,000
Minority Interest in Overseas Company		800,000

To eliminate the investment account ($3,200,000 =
$4,200,000 − $1,000,000) against the stockholders'
equity of the Overseas Company and establish the
minority interest [800,000 = .2 × ($1,600,000
+ $2,400,000)], all as of January 1, 19X1.

At consolidation points *after date of business combination*, the procedures discussed in Chapters 4-7 are used. When the *equity method* is employed, the investment account is updated each year to reflect the parent's portion of the change in the translated book value of the subsidiary's stockholders' equity. Moreover, use of the current rate method of translation results in a currently translated unamortized purchase premium; the change in the translated amount is entered in the Cumulative Translation Adjustment account. When the parent employs the *cost method* to account for its investments in foreign subsidiaries, a working paper entry is necessary to adjust the investment account to the equity basis, as described in Chapter 4. In all cases, the Minority Interest in S reflects the minority's portion of the translated book value of the subsidiary's stockholders' equity, including the Cumulative Translation Adjustment, when reclassified on the working paper.

Continuing with the Overseas example, we work through consolidation at December 31, 19X1, one year after date of acquisition. Domestic Corporation uses the *equity method*. The Overseas Company's functional currency is assumed to be the *local currency in Case 1* and the *U.S. dollar in Case 2*.

First, consider Domestic's 19X1 *equity method income accrual*. Domestic's share of the Overseas Company's translated net income is reduced by purchase premium amortization. We assume that 25 percent of the original allocation to inventory and plant assets has been sold or depreciated and that goodwill is being amortized over ten years. The equity method income accrual is calculated in the schedule on the following page.

When applying the equity method, we first record Domestic's share of the Overseas Company's dividends, translated at the $2.08 rate assumed when the dividends were declared. We then record the 19X1 equity method income accrual and, in a separate entry under Case 1, adjust the investment account for Domestic's share of the change in the Overseas Company's Cumulative Translation Adjustment account. In this case, the change consists of the translation adjustment of $225,000 calculated under the current rate method in Exhibit 9.12.

Domestic Corporation
Schedule to Determine the Equity Method Income Accrual
for the Year Ended December 31, 19X1

	Case 1 (Current Rate Method)	Case 2 (Temporal Method)
Share of Overseas Company's Net Income (1)	$ 1,148,000	$ 1,188,000
Less Amortization of Purchase Premium:		
Cost of Sales and Depreciation (2) ...	$ 164,000	$ 160,000
Amortization of Goodwill (3)	36,900	36,000
	$ 200,900	$ 196,000
Equity Method Income Accrual for 19X1 ..	$ 947,100	$ 992,000

(1) These amounts are 80 percent of the respective translated net incomes calculated in Exhibit 9.12; $1,148,000 = .8 × $1,435,000; $1,188,000 = .8 × $1,485,000.

(2) These amounts reflect translation at the average rate of $2.05/LC and the historical rate of $2.00/LC, respectively; $164,000 = .8 × $2.05(3,400,000 − 3,000,000)/4; $160,000 = .8 × $2.00(3,400,000 − 3,000,000)/4.

(3) These amounts reflect translation at the average rate of $2.05/LC and the historical rate of $2.00/LC, respectively; goodwill in local currency is LC180,000 (= 360,000/2); $36,900 = $2.05 × 180,000/10; $36,000 = $2.00 × 180,000/10.

Books of Domestic Corporation

	Case 1 (Current Rate Method)		Case 2 (Temporal Method)	
Cash	832,000		832,000	
Investment in Overseas Company .		832,000		832,000
To record Domestic's share of Overseas Company's dividends; $832,000 = .8 × $2.08 × 500,000.				
Investment in Overseas Company	947,100		992,000	
Equity in Income of Overseas Company		947,100		992,000
To record Domestic's 19X1 equity method income accrual.				
Investment in Overseas Company	180,000		No entry	
Cumulative Translation Adjustment		180,000		
To record Domestic's share of the change in Overseas Company's Cumulative Translation Adjustment account; $180,000 = .8 × $225,000.				

We now turn to consolidation at the end of 19X1. Although the equity method entries are reversed, in Case 1 the entry for Domestic's share of the change in the Cumulative Translation Adjustment account is not reversed. Avoiding reversal of this entry is necessary so that the Cumulative Translation Adjustment account on the Overseas Company's translated balance sheet can be eliminated in consolidation. The working paper entries to reverse the current equity method entries, to allocate the purchase premium, and to eliminate the investment account are as follows:

Consolidated Working Papers

	Case 1 (Current Rate Method)		Case 2 (Temporal Method)	
Equity in Income of Overseas Company	947,100		992,000	
Dividends—Overseas Company		832,000		832,000
Investment in Overseas Company		115,100		160,000
To reverse the 19X1 equity method entries, thereby adjusting the Investment Account to its beginning-of-year balance, except for Domestic's share of the change in the Cumulative Translation Adjustment account.				
Inventory and Plant Assets	672,000		640,000	
Goodwill	378,000		360,000	
Investment in Overseas Company		1,000,000		1,000,000
Cumulative Translation Adjustment . . .		50,000		—
To reclassify and allocate the unamortized purchase premium as of January 1, 19X1.				

In Case 1, the unamortized amounts are translated at the December 31, 19X1, current rate. The effect of the changing exchange rate is entered in the Cumulative Translation Adjustment account; $50,000 = ($2.10 - $2.00)$ LC500,000, where LC500,000 [= $1,000,000/($2.00/LC)$] is the original purchase premium measured in units of foreign currency.

	Case 1 (Current Rate Method)		Case 2 (Temporal Method)	
Capital Stock—Overseas Company	1,600,000		1,600,000	
Retained Earnings, January 1, 19X1— Overseas Company	2,400,000		2,400,000	
Cumulative Translation Adjustment— Overseas Company	225,000		—	
Investment in Overseas Company		3,380,000		3,200,000
Minority Interest in Overseas Company		845,000		800,000
To eliminate the investment account against the stockholders' equity of the Overseas Company and establish the 20 percent minority interest.				

The eliminated balances of the investment account in the last working paper entry are determined as follows:

	Case 1	Case 2
Cost of the Investment, January 1, 19X1	$ 4,200,000	$ 4,200,000
19X1 Intercompany Dividends	(832,000)	(832,000)
19X1 Equity Method Income Accrual	947,100	992,000
19X1 Cumulative Translation Adjustment Entry	180,000	—
Balance per Books, December, 31 19X1	$ 4,495,100	$ 4,360,000
Reversal of Equity Method Entries	(115,100)	(160,000)
Reclassification of Purchase Premium	(1,000,000)	(1,000,000)
Eliminated Balances	$ 3,380,000	$ 3,200,000

Continuing with consolidation at December 31, 19X1, the working paper entries for the change in the minority interest and current purchase premium amortization are as follows:

Consolidated Working Papers

	Case 1 (Current Rate Method)		Case 2 (Temporal Method)	
Minority Interest in Net Income	287,000		297,000	
Dividends—Overseas Company		208,000		208,000
Minority Interest in Overseas				
Company		79,000		89,000

To record the change in the minority interest during 19X1. The minority's interest in the Overseas Company's net income is 20 percent of the respective translated amounts of $1,435,000 and $1,485,000 (see Exhibit 9.12).

	Case 1 (Current Rate Method)		Case 2 (Temporal Method)	
Cost of Sales and Depreciation	164,000		160,000	
Amortization Expense	36,900		36,000	
Cumulative Translation Adjustment	4,900		—	
Inventory and Plant Assets		168,000		160,000
Goodwill		37,800		36,000

To record purchase premium amortization for 19X1, as reflected in the schedule to determine the equity method income accrual.

In Case 1, the amortization is translated at the average rate of $2.05/LC, whereas the asset accounts are translated at the current rate of $2.10/LC; the difference is charged to the Cumulative Translation Adjustment account.

Intercompany Transactions. Transaction gains and losses on *foreign currency intercompany transactions* are usually included in net income. Under *SFAS 52*, however, if any intercompany transactions are deemed to be of a "long-term investment" nature in which settlement is not anticipated in the foreseeable future, the related transaction adjustments are *not* reported in income. Instead, they are carried directly to the Cumulative Translation Adjustment account and are included in the analysis of changes in that account.

Elimination of *unconfirmed intercompany profits* under *SFAS 52* is based on the exchange rates in effect when the intercompany transactions took place. Subsequent changes in the exchange rate do not affect the amount of intercompany profit to be eliminated. Instead, exchange gains and losses accrue on the consolidated balance of the unsold or unused items after removal of the dollar amount of intercompany profit determined when the transfer took place.

Statement of Cash Flows. As discussed earlier in the chapter, the foreign entity's translated or remeasured cash flow statement can be prepared directly from the local currency cash flow statement. The consolidated statement of cash flows, not illustrated here, is the sum of the U.S. dollar cash flow statements of the constituent companies, after any intercompany cash flows are removed.

Concluding Remarks. As the Overseas illustration demonstrates, consolidation of a foreign subsidiary can be complex when the current rate method is used. Not only must the foreign subsidiary's Cumulative Translation Adjustment account be dealt with, but the parent company also needs to consider the way in which the fluctuating exchange rate affects translation of purchase premium allocations and amortization. Thus, the *Cumulative Translation Adjustment* appearing in consolidated statements consists of (1) the parent's share of the foreign subsidiary's Cumulative Translation Adjustment account, (2) translation adjustments related to the purchase premium and its amortization, (3) transaction adjustments accrued on "long-term" intercompany transactions, and (4) transaction adjustments on "economic hedges of net investments in foreign entities."

SUMMARY OF FOREIGN CURRENCY TRANSLATION

SFAS 52 represented a major change in accounting for international operations when it was issued in 1981. In effect, it recognizes that the nature of a U.S. company's economic exposure to the risks of foreign operations depends in large measure on the nature of the foreign business activity. In certain situations, *SFAS 52* permits the current rate method to be used and translation adjustments to be excluded from periodic income. This method is applied when the parent's exposed position is best represented by its net investment in the foreign entity and its economic exposure is a direct function of the viability of the foreign entity's operations. The temporal method is used to account for foreign entities closely related to the U.S. parent and for situations in which the parent's economic exposure is more closely tied to the individual monetary assets and liabilities of the foreign entity.[22]

SFAS 52 offers another solution to a very complex fundamental problem. Fluctuating exchange rates are the result of many factors, and they contribute to the inherent difficulty of devising a reporting scheme which adequately reflects the economics of foreign operations. *SFAS 52* appears to be at least an acceptable solution to the problem. Unlike the much-maligned *SFAS 8*, there has been no clamor that *SFAS 52* be re-examined or repealed.

---

[22] For a critical evaluation of *SFAS 52*, see James A. Largay III, "*SFAS 52*: Expediency or Principle?," *Journal of Accounting, Auditing and Finance* (Fall 1983), 44-53.

AUTHORS' COMMENTARY

The fact that *SFAS 52* was approved by a bare 4-3 majority of the FASB indicated strong disagreement among board members on many provisions of the statement. This commentary identifies some of the statement's major accomplishments and some of its major problem areas.

Major Accomplishments of *SFAS 52*. The FASB's conceptual framework, embodied in *Statements of Financial Accounting Concepts (SFAC) 1-6*, was intended to provide a structure to guide board decisions on specific accounting issues. *SFAC 1* concluded that the principal objective of financial reporting is *usefulness to decision makers*, with particular emphasis on the role of financial information in assessing the amounts, timing, and uncertainty of future cash flows. Earlier in the chapter, we noted that paragraph 4 of *SFAS 52* calls for foreign currency translation to "provide information that is generally compatible with the expected economic effects of a rate change on the enterprise's cash flow and equity." Thus the board focused on decision usefulness in *SFAS 52*, not on an abstract theory that might be at odds with the world of affairs.

The *functional currency approach* seeks to match an entity's *economic exposure* to exchange rate movements with the *accounting exposure* that produces translation adjustments. When a foreign entity's economic exposure is best measured by the viability of the entity's operations, the exposed position of the current rate method (net assets) applies. In contrast, when the entity's economic exposure relates to specific monetary assets and liabilities, an exposed position focusing on those items leads to translation adjustments under the temporal method.

It was alleged that under *SFAS 8*,[23] companies used economic resources to neutralize the income effect of translation adjustments produced by their accounting exposure. U.S. companies with relatively independent, self-contained foreign subsidiaries no longer need to waste resources in this way. Under the current rate method, translation adjustments bypass earnings and are carried directly to stockholders' equity.

Problem Areas. Views of the three board members who dissented from *SFAS 52* were published in the statement. On the whole, they felt that the functional currency approach of *SFAS 52* contradicted long-standing accounting principles. Specifically, the dissenters made the following arguments:

- *SFAS 52*'s multiple perspectives and multiple units of measure contaminate consolidated statements traditionally based on the single perspective and measuring unit of the parent company.
- The direct entries to stockholders' equity permitted under the current rate method conflict with previous pronouncements and with an *SFAC 3* passage that refers to gains and losses (not equity adjustments) being created by exchange rate movements.

---

[23] Financial Accounting Standards Board, *Statement of Financial Accounting Standards No. 8*, "Accounting for the Translation of Foreign Currency Transactions and Foreign Currency Financial Statements" (Stamford, CT: FASB, 1975).

Although financial statement users may applaud the decision usefulness embraced by *SFAS 52*, they may have some difficulty working with the translated data. First, as we saw earlier in the chapter, ratios such as the return on assets can produce inappropriate signals when based on data translated by the current rate method. Second, when nonmonetary assets are translated at the current rate, their meaning in U.S. dollars becomes unclear. They are neither historical dollar measures of historical cost nor current dollar measures of current value.

Perhaps the most interesting observation of all, however, is that in explaining the conclusions reached in *SFAS 52*, the FASB rejected conclusions it had accepted only six years earlier in *SFAS 8* and accepted conclusions it had rejected in *SFAS 8*.

SUMMARY OF KEY CONCEPTS

The price of one currency in terms of another is called a **foreign exchange rate**. The **spot rate** is the price for immediate delivery of the foreign currency. Delivery at a specified time in the future can be contracted at the appropriate **forward** or **futures rate** with a foreign exchange broker or dealer.

Corporations do business abroad within the context of an international monetary system characterized by **flexible** or **floating exchange rates**. These constantly changing exchange rates make the tasks of accounting and reporting foreign operations more difficult.

Domestic corporations with branches, divisions, and subsidiaries abroad must **translate** the accounts of those business units into dollars for inclusion in the U.S. financial statements. Methods devised to accomplish this translation use the **current exchange rate** at the balance sheet date to translate some accounts and **historical exchange rates** to translate other accounts.

Translation rules are found in *SFAS 52*, which prescribes either the **temporal** or **current rate method**. Choice of method depends on the foreign entity's **functional currency**—the currency of the principal economic environment in which the entity generates net cash flows.

The **current rate method** is used when the functional currency is a **foreign currency**; the **temporal method** is used when the functional currency is the **U.S. dollar**. Each method defines an exposed position consisting of accounts to be translated at the current rate; other accounts are translated at historical rates.

Fluctuating exchange rates produce a **translation gain or loss** which normally differs according to which translation method is used. This **translation adjustment** arises because the **exposed position**—accounts translated at the current rate—is translated at the current rate, although changes in the exposed position are translated at historical rates.

The **translation adjustment** is carried directly to a separate component of stockholders' equity—the **Cumulative Translation Adjustment account**—when the functional currency is a **foreign currency** (the current rate method is used). In contrast, the translation gain or loss is included in **current earnings** when the functional currency is the **U.S. dollar** (the temporal method is used).

The **translated statement of cash flows** is best prepared directly from the foreign entity's local currency cash flow statement. The **U.S. dollar equivalents of foreign currency cash flows** are reported along with the **portion of the translation adjustment** related to **cash**.

Analysis of translated/remeasured foreign currency statements must contend with the **accounting effects** of the translation method used. **Intertemporal comparisons** are similarly affected and complicated by **year-to-year changes in exchange rates.**

Translation of a foreign subsidiary's assets and liabilities in a **business combination** differs under the **purchase** and **pooling-of-interests** methods. When **purchase accounting** is used, the **spot rate at date of business combination** is used to translate the subsidiary's assets and liabilities in existence at date of business combination. The **original spot rate** is also used under **pooling** when the functional currency is a **foreign currency**. When the functional currency is the **U.S. dollar**, the book values of the subsidiary's accounts at date of business combination are **remeasured** at whatever historical rates existed when those balances arose.

The **dollar balances of parent intercompany accounts** are generally used as the translated balances of the **offsetting intercompany accounts** at foreign subsidiaries.

When consolidated financial statements are prepared, the resulting dollar amounts will depend upon whether the foreign entity's accounts have been **translated** or **remeasured**.

QUESTIONS

Q9.1   What is the major change that took place in the International Monetary System during the 1970s? Briefly explain why this change occurred.

Q9.2   Briefly discuss the nature of the financial accounting problems peculiar to multinational corporations.

Q9.3   Explain why any translation methodology inevitably produces translation adjustments.

Q9.4   The size of the translation adjustment and whether it is a gain or loss is influenced by the entity's *exposed position.* Give an example of how an entity can report a translation gain under one translation method and a translation loss under another method.

Q9.5   Compare the effect on the translation gain or loss associated with translation of inventory at the current rate (under the current method) and at the historical rate (under the temporal method) when exchange rates are (1) rising and (2) falling.

Q9.6   What is an entity's "functional currency"? Explain the role of functional currency in the translation process under *SFAS 52*.

Q9.7   Distinguish between *remeasurement* and *translation*. How is the exchange gain or loss produced by remeasurement and translation reported in the financial statements of a U.S. company?

Q9.8 Suppose a foreign entity records the same local currency sales, expenses and net income in two consecutive years. The average direct rate declines by 50% from year one to year two. What will be the effect on translated net income in the two years? On the *return on sales* ratio? Assume the local currency is the functional currency.

Q9.9 What is the nature of the "disappearing plant" phenomenon for a domestic company's foreign subsidiary located in a highly inflationary economy? Explain how *SFAS 52* deals with this phenomenon.

Q9.10 Explain the approach and rationale for translating the assets and liabilities of foreign subsidiaries for inclusion in consolidated financial statements when the business combination was accounted for (1) as a purchase and (2) as a pooling of interests.

Q9.11 Explain why, in a translated statement of cash flows, only the portion of the translation adjustment pertaining to cash is disclosed.

EXERCISES

E9.1 Translation of Inventory, Plant Assets and Depreciation Consider the following independent situations:

1. On January 1, 19X8, the Ben Company formed a foreign subsidiary. On February 15, 19X8, Ben's subsidiary purchased 100,000 local currency (LC) units of inventory. LC25,000 of the original inventory purchased on February 15, 19X8, made up the entire inventory on December 31, 19X8. The exchange rates were LC2.2 to $1 from January 1, 19X8, to June 30, 19X8, and LC2 to $1 from July 1, 19X8, to December 31, 19X8.

2. The France Company owns a foreign subsidiary with LC2,400,000 of property, plant, and equipment before accumulated depreciation at December 31, 19X8. Of this amount, LC1,500,000 were acquired on January 1, 19X6, when the rate of exchange was LC1.5 to $1, and LC900,000 were acquired on January 1, 19X7, when the rate of exchange was LC1.6 to $1. The rate of exchange in effect at December 31, 19X8, was LC1.9 to $1. The weighted average of exchange rates in effect during 19X8 was LC1.8 to $1.

REQUIRED:

1. For Case 1, calculate the translated inventory balance of Ben's foreign subsidiary at December 31, 19X8, under (a) the current rate method and (b) the temporal method.

2. In Case 2, assume that the property, plant, and equipment are depreciated using the straight-line method over a ten-year period with no salvage value. How much depreciation expense relating to the foreign subsidiary's property, plant, and equipment should be charged in France's income statement for 19X8? Calculate the translated balances of property, plant, and equipment and accumulated depreciation at December 31, 19X8, under (a) the current rate method and (b) the temporal method.

E9.2 Translation Adjustment Calculations On September 10, 19X6, the Globe Trading Company advanced $30,000 to its representative in Bogota, Colombia, to establish a small sales office. The representative, Mr. Moreno, converted the $30,000 into 1,000,000 pesos (P) and opened a bank account in Bogota. No formal accounting system is established in Bogota. At December 31, 19X6, Mr. Moreno submitted the following report to Globe:

	Pesos
Funds Received on September 10, 19X6	1,000,000
Payments:	
Purchase of Equipment on September 10	270,000
Office Rent	70,000
Secretary's Salary	120,000
Telephone and Other Expenses	100,000
Total Payments	560,000
Cash (Pesos) on Hand, December 31, 19X6	440,000

The exchange rate was $.033/P on December 31, 19X6, and averaged $.031/P during the period from September 10 to December 31, 19X6.

REQUIRED:

1. Assuming the functional currency is the U.S. dollar, prepare a schedule to compute the translation gain or loss related to the Bogota sales office in 19X6.
2. Repeat No. 1 but assume the functional currency is the peso.
3. Suppose Globe treats the $30,000 as an advance. Give the journal entries which would be made by Globe on September 10 and on December 31, when Globe's books are closed and the accounts of the Bogota branch are included in Globe's financial statements. Consider both functional currency alternatives.

E9.3 Translation of Account Balances: Temporal Method U.S. Industries has a subsidiary in Switzerland. The subsidiary's financial statements are maintained in Swiss francs (SF). Exchange rates ($/SF) for selected dates are as follows:

Jan. 1, 19X4	$ .75		Jan. 1, 19X6	$ .68
Jan. 1, 19X5	.70		Dec. 31, 19X6	.65

REQUIRED: Assuming the functional currency of the Swiss subsidiary is the U.S. dollar, calculate the correct dollar amount for each of the following items appearing in the subsidiary's trial balance at December 31, 19X6:

1. Cash in Bank, SF400,000.
2. Inventory on LIFO basis, SF300,000. The inventory cost consists of SF100,000 acquired in January 19X4 and SF200,000 acquired in January 19X6.
3. Machinery and Equipment, SF1,100,000. A review of the records indicates that the company bought equipment costing SF500,000 in January 19X4 (20 percent of this was sold in January 19X6) and additional equipment costing SF700,000 in January 19X5. Ignore accumulated depreciation.

4. Depreciation Expense on machinery and equipment, SF110,000 (depreciated over ten years, straight-line basis).

E9.4 **Translation Adjustment Calculations** The following data relate to Sterling, Limited, located in the city of Liverpool, England. Sterling is controlled by a U.S. company.

Net Monetary Assets (Liabilities), January 1, 19X1	£ 70,000
Acquisition of Plant Assets for Debt, February 15, 19X1	100,000
Purchase of Inventory Made Evenly during 19X1	350,000
Collection of Receivables Outstanding at January 1, 19X1	270,000
Sales Made Evenly during 19X1	600,000
Cost of Goods Sold	330,000
Depreciation of Assets Acquired When the Exchange Rate was $1.80/£ .	40,000
Current Operating Expenses (Excluding Depreciation and Amortization),	
Incurred Evenly during 19X1	120,000
Refinancing or "Rollover" of Commercial Paper	80,000

Exchange rates ($/£) during 19X1 were as follows:

Jan. 1, 19X1	$ 1.90	Average for 19X1 . . .	$ 1.97
Feb. 15, 19X1	1.95	Dec. 31, 19X1	2.01

REQUIRED:

1. Assuming Sterling's functional currency is the U.S. dollar, prepare a schedule to compute the translation adjustment for Sterling during 19X1.
2. Repeat No. 1 but assume that Sterling's functional currency is the pound and that net assets on January 1, 19X1, amounted to £120,000.

E9.5 **Translation Adjustments, Cumulative Translation Adjustment Analysis** The following transactions were recorded by the Larson Company's subsidiary in Finland during 19X3. The Finnish currency is the markka (M).

	Amount (M)	Exchange Rate ($/M)
Purchase of Inventory	4,000,000	$ .30
Proceeds from Sale of Land	500,000	.31
Book Value of Land Sold	350,000	.47 (1)
Sales	5,000,000	.33 (2)
Cost of Sales	3,000,000	.41 (1)
Cash Operating Expenses	900,000	.33 (2)
Issue of Bonds Payable for Cash	1,000,000	.35
Amortization of Prepayments	100,000	.34 (1)

(1) Exchange rates when assets sold or amortized were acquired by the Finnish subsidiary.
(2) The weighted average exchange rate during 19X3.

The exchange rate at January 1, 19X3 was $.45/M; at December 31, 19X3 it was $.36/M.

REQUIRED:

1. Assuming the functional currency is the U.S. dollar, prepare a schedule to compute the 19X3 translation adjustment. Net monetary assets (liabilities) amounted to (M6,000,000) at January 1, 19X3.
2. Assuming the functional currency is the markka, prepare a schedule to analyze the change in Larson's cumulative translation adjustment during 19X3, including computation of the 19X3 translation adjustment. Net assets amounted to M4,500,000 at January 1, 19X3. Using historical rates, translated net assets on January 1, 19X3 amounted to $2,300,000.

E9.6 Effect of Translation Methods on Ratios The following data relate to the Bainbridge Company's South African subsidiary, which maintains its records in the South Africa Rand (R), its local currency.

	R	Translated Amounts in $ when Functional Currency is	
	R	**$**	**R**
Sales	R 5,000,000	$ 2,000,000	$ 2,000,000
Operating Income	1,000,000	320,000	400,000
Average Total Assets	8,000,000	4,800,000	3,400,000

REQUIRED:

1. Using the "DuPont Analysis," compute and disaggregate the subsidiary's Return on Assets into its Return on Sales and Total Asset Turnover components under the three alternatives shown.
2. Explain whether the exchange rate ($/R) has been increasing or decreasing and how that change might affect the usefulness of these ratios.

E9.7 Remeasured Financial Statements On January 2, 19X9, Maddox Corporation, headquartered in the United States, opened a branch in Mexico City. An initial investment of $100,000 was made on that date; the exchange rate was $.10/peso. During 19X9, the following cash transactions occurred at the Mexico City branch. All amounts are in pesos (P).

Legal Expenses of Organizing the Branch (Jan. 2; 5-Year Life) . . .	30,000
Purchase of Office Equipment (Apr. 1; 10-Year Life)	100,000
Sales	1,200,000
Merchandise Purchases	900,000
Operating Expenses	300,000

The exchange rate was $.11/P in April when the office equipment and P200,000 of merchandise were purchased. Sales, other merchandise purchases, and operating expenses were assumed to have been made or incurred at an average exchange rate of $.12/P. At year-end, the exchange rate had risen to $.15/P and the ending inventory (LIFO) amounted to P200,000. All depreciation and amortization is straight-line.

REQUIRED: Prepare a balance sheet and income statement for the Mexico City branch as of December 31, 19X9, in dollars, the branch's functional currency. Show all calculations, especially those supporting the translation gain or loss.

E9.8 **Cumulative Translation Adjustment Analysis** Oliver Corporation decided on January 1, 19X2, that its subsidiary's functional currency is the foreign currency rather than the U.S. dollar. On that date, the net assets of its foreign subsidiary amounted to FC20,000,000 and to $15,000,000 when translated according to the temporal method; the exchange rate was $.80/FC. During 19X2, the foreign subsidiary reported net income of FC2,500,000 and paid dividends of FC1,000,000. No other changes in owners' equity occurred.

REQUIRED: Prepare an analysis of the Cumulative Translation Adjustment account for 19X2. Relevant exchange rates were $.78/FC (average); $.765/FC (dividend declaration date); $.76/FC (December 31, 19X2).

E9.9 **Translated/Remeasured Financial Statements** The Thode Company established a branch in Saudi Arabia on January 1, 19X6, when the exchange rate was $.28/riyal (R). Of Thode's initial $5,000,000 investment, $2,800,000 was used to acquire plant assets (ten-year life) and $1,400,000 was used to acquire inventory. The remaining amount was initially held as cash by the branch.

During 19X6, the branch reported net income of R2,000,000. It remitted R4,000,000 to Thode's home office in the United States on September 30, when the exchange rate was $.255/R. No other transactions occurred between the branch and the home office. The branch's condensed income statement appears below:

Sales	R 8,500,000
Cost of Goods Sold	(4,000,000) (1)
Depreciation Expense	(1,000,000) (2)
Other Expenses	(1,500,000)
Net Income	R 2,000,000

(1) R3,000,000 was from original inventory; the balance had been acquired evenly throughout the year from local sources.
(2) Relates solely to plant assets acquired on Jan. 1, 19X6.

The average exchange rate during the year was $.265/R. On the balance sheet date, it was $.25/R.

REQUIRED:

1. Assuming the functional currency is the riyal, translate the branch's income statement into dollars and prepare an analysis of the branch's Cumulative Translation Adjustment account during 19X6.
2. Assuming the functional currency is the U.S. dollar, remeasure the branch's income statement into dollars. Disregard the translation adjustment.

E9.10   Exchange Rate Changes and Return on Assets Murdock Company has a foreign subsidiary whose functional currency is the local currency (LC). Relevant translated data for the subsidiary appear below.

	Total Assets	Operating Income	Exchange Rate
1/1/X7	$ 105,000,000	—	$ 1.40/LC
19X7	—	$ 12,000,000	1.20/LC*
12/31/X7	90,000,000	—	1.00/LC
19X8	—	10,890,000	.90/LC*
12/31/X8	90,000,000	—	1.00/LC

* Average Rate

REQUIRED:

1. Calculate the Return on Assets (ROA) ratio for 19X7 and 19X8 using both translated ($) and LC data.
2. Explain whether translation has distorted the foreign subsidiary's performance in 19X8 compared with 19X7. If so, explain how changes in the exchange rate contributed to the distortion.

E9.11   Simple Cash Flow Statement Translation The Luh company's 19X6 cash flow statement appears below in its functional currency, Taiwan dollars ($T).

The Luh Company
Statement of Cash Flows
For the Year Ended December 31, 19X6

Operating Activities

Net Income	$T100,000,000
Depreciation and Amortization Expense	45,000,000
Gain on Sale of Long-Term Investments	(4,000,000)
Decrease in Other Current Operating Assets	24,000,000
Decrease in Current Operating Liabilities	(32,000,000)
Cash Provided by Operating Activities	$T133,000,000

Investing Activities

Acquisition of Plant Assets	$T (85,000,000)
Sale of Long-Term Investments	50,000,000
Cash Used in Investing Activities	$T (35,000,000)

Financing Activities

Retirement of Long-Term Debt	$T (98,000,000)
Issuance of Common Stock	170,000,000
Dividends Paid	(65,000,000)
Cash Provided by Financing Activities	$T 7,000,000
Increase In Cash	$T 105,000,000
Cash Balance, January 1, 19X6	210,000,000
Cash Balance, December 31, 19X6	$T 315,000,000

Additional information:

1. Exchange rates: 1/1X6: $.042/$T; 12/31/X6: $.039/$T; 19X6 weighted average: $.04/$T
2. Changes in current operating assets and liabilities and dividend payments occurred at the weighted average rate.
3. Common stock was issued and plant assets were acquired when the rate was $.0423/$T.
4. The long-term investments were sold and the long-term debt was retired when the rate was $.0394/$T.

REQUIRED: Translate the above statement of cash flows into dollars. Include a computation of the effect of exchange rate changes on cash.

E9.12 **Consolidation at Acquisition Date: Purchase and Pooling** Following is the condensed balance sheet of the Cheung Company at September 15, 19X8. On that date, Wint Corporation, headquartered in Chicago, acquired 90 percent of Cheung's outstanding stock in exchange for its own stock valued at $2,000,000. Both book value and fair value data are given in units of foreign currency (FC).

Assets	Book Value (FC)	Fair Value (FC)
Current Assets	3,000,000	3,400,000
Noncurrent Assets	5,000,000	6,000,000
Total Assets	8,000,000	
Liabilities and Stockholders' Equity		
Current Liabilities	2,000,000	2,000,000
Noncurrent Liabilities	2,000,000	2,600,000
Stockholders' Equity	4,000,000	—
Total Liabilities and Stockholders' Equity . . .	8,000,000	

The exchange rate at September 15, 19X8, is $.40/FC. The noncurrent assets and noncurrent liabilities (mostly long-term debt) were acquired (incurred) at average exchange rates of $.45 and $.50, respectively. Cheung's current assets and liabilities are monetary items except for inventory of FC1,000,000, acquired when the exchange rate was $.42. Capital stock of FC2,000,000 was issued when the exchange rate was $.45.

REQUIRED:

1. Assuming that the purchase method of accounting is used and that Cheung's functional currency is the foreign currency, give the eliminating entries made on a consolidated balance sheet working paper prepared at September 15, 19X8. Show all calculations.
2. Assuming that the pooling-of-interests method of accounting is used and that Cheung's functional currency is the U.S. dollar, repeat No. 1.

PROBLEMS

P9.1 Remeasuring a Condensed Trial Balance—Equity Method Income Accrual The trial balance of Valiant Corporation, a small Swedish company, is given below. Its functional currency is the U.S. dollar. The account balances are for the year ended December 31, 19X4, and are measured in krone (K), the Swedish currency.

Account	Amount (K) Dr. (Cr.)
Cash	240,000
Accounts Receivable	400,000
Allowance for Uncollectible Accounts	(40,000)
Plant and Equipment, Net	2,000,000
Accounts Payable	(200,000)
Notes Payable	(600,000)
Capital Stock	(400,000)
Retained Earnings, January 1, 19X4	(1,160,000)
Sales	(1,200,000)
Depreciation Expense	320,000
Other Expenses	640,000
	0

Valiant Corporation was formed, and its stock issued, when the exchange rate was $.20/K. The plant assets were acquired and the notes payable executed when the exchange rate was $.25/K. Sales and Other Expenses occurred evenly during 19X4. The remeasured balance of Valiant's January 1 retained earnings is $272,000. Exchange rates in 19X4 were as follows:

Time	Rate ($/K)
Jan. 1, 19X4	$ .30
Average for 19X4	.33
Dec. 31, 19X4	.35

REQUIRED:

1. Remeasure Valiant's trial balance into dollars.
2. Prepare a remeasured income statement and balance sheet for Valiant.
3. If Domestic Corporation, a U.S. firm, owns 70 percent of Valiant's outstanding stock, prepare the journal entry made by Domestic to record the equity method income accrual at December 31, 19X4. There were no intercompany transactions and no purchase premium or discount.

P9.2 Translating a Condensed Trial Balance—Equity Method Income Accrual Refer to Problem P9.1. Repeat the requirements of P9.1, assuming the krone (K) is the functional currency and that the translated balance of Valiant's January 1 retained earnings is $150,000. In No. 2, also prepare an analysis of the Cumulative Translation Adjustment account.

P9.3 **Translating Selected Accounts** On January 1, 19X1, the Franklin Company formed a foreign subsidiary which issued all of its currently outstanding common stock on that date. Selected captions from the balance sheets, all of which are shown in units of local currency (LC), are as follows:

	December 31	
	19X2	**19X1**
Accounts Receivable		
(Net of Allowance for Uncollectible Accounts of LC2,200		
at Dec. 31, 19X2, and LC2,000 at Dec. 31, 19X1) . . .	LC 40,000	LC 35,000
Inventories, at Cost	80,000	75,000
Property, Plant, and Equipment		
(Net of Accumulated Depreciation of LC31,000 at		
Dec. 31, 19X2, and LC14,000 at Dec. 31, 19X1)	163,000	150,000
Long-Term Debt	100,000	120,000
Common Stock		
Authorized 10,000 Shares, Par Value LC10 per share,		
issued and outstanding 5,000 shares at		
Dec. 31, 19X2 and Dec. 31, 19X1	50,000	50,000

Additional information:

1. Exchange rates are as follows:

	LC/$
Jan. 1, 19X1—July 31, 19X1	2.0
Aug. 1, 19X1—Oct. 31, 19X1	1.8
Nov. 1, 19X1—June 30, 19X2	1.7
July 1, 19X2—Dec. 31, 19X2	1.5
Average Monthly Rate for 19X1	1.9
Average Monthly Rate for 19X2	1.6

2. An analysis of the accounts receivable balance is as follows:

	19X2	**19X1**
Accounts Receivable		
Balance at Beginning of Year	LC 37,000	—
Sales (LC36,000 per month in 19X2 and		
LC 31,000 per month in 19X1)	432,000	LC 372,000
Collections	(423,600)	(334,000)
Write-Offs (May 19X2 and Dec. 19X1)	(3,200)	(1,000)
Balance at Year-End	LC 42,200	LC 37,000

	19X2	**19X1**
Allowance for Uncollectible Accounts		
Balance at Beginning of Year	LC 2,000	—
Provision for Uncollectible Accounts	3,400	LC 3,000
Write-Offs (May 19X2 and Dec. 19X1)	(3,200)	(1,000)
Balance at Year-End	LC 2,200	LC 2,000

3. An analysis of inventories, for which the FIFO inventory method is used, is as follows:

	19X2	19X1
Inventory at Beginning of Year	LC 75,000	—
Purchases (June 19X2 and June 19X1)	335,000	LC 375,000
Goods Available for Sale	LC 410,000	LC 375,000
Inventory at Year-End	80,000	75,000
Cost of Goods Sold	LC 330,000	LC 300,000

4. On January 1, 19X1, Franklin's foreign subsidiary purchased land for LC24,000 and plant and equipment for LC140,000. On July 4, 19X2, additional equipment was purchased for LC30,000. Plant and equipment is being depreciated on a straight-line basis over a ten-year period with no salvage value. A full year's depreciation is taken in the year of purchase.

5. On January 15, 19X1, 7 percent bonds with a face value of LC120,000 were sold. These bonds mature on January 15, 19X7, and interest is paid semiannually on July 15 and January 15. Bonds with a face value of LC20,000 were retired on January 14, 19X2.

   REQUIRED: Prepare a schedule remeasuring the selected captions above into U.S. dollars (the functional currency) at December 31, 19X2, and December 31, 19X1, respectively. Show supporting computations in good form.
   (AICPA adapted)

P9.4 **Translation and Performance Evaluation** Management compensation is often based on reported profits. What profit measurement is appropriate for top management to use in judging the performance of a foreign subsidiary of a U.S. company? Consider a Dutch subsidiary that reported the following results in guilders (G) for two consecutive years.

	19X2	19X1
Sales	G 2,400	G 2,000
Cost of Sales	1,320	1,200
Gross Margin	G 1,080	G 800
Other Operating Expenses	230	200
Profit Before Taxes	G 850	G 600
Income Tax Expense	255	180
Net Income	G 595	G 420

Exchange Rates:

Average for 19X2: $.55/G   Average for 19X1: $.67/G

Composite historical rates relating to Cost of Sales and Other Operating Expenses (including depreciation):

19X2: $.59/G   19X1: $.69/G

REQUIRED:

1. Considering the above comparative income statements, assess the Dutch subsidiary's performance, in guilders, and in dollars under both the current rate and temporal approaches (ignore the remeasurement adjustment). Support your assessment with calculations.
2. How "comparable" are the "comparative" data you worked with in 1? Apply a computational adjustment to enhance comparability to these data. Comment on the results.

P9.5 Translation under *SFAS 52* and Ratio Analysis On January 1, 19X2, the Webster Company established a foreign subsidiary having the following condensed balance sheet in units of its functional currency, the foreign currency (FC):

Assets		Liabilities and Stockholders' Equity	
Cash	FC 100,000	Liabilities	FC 200,000
Plant Assets, Net	300,000	Capital Stock	200,000
		Total Liabilities and	
Total Assets	FC 400,000	Stockholders' Equity . .	FC 400,000

At December 31, 19X2, the subsidiary reported the following condensed trial balance:

	Amount Dr. (Cr.)
Cash	FC 210,000
Plant Assets, Net	250,000
Liabilities	(220,000)
Capital Stock	(200,000)
Sales	(500,000)
Expenses	460,000
	FC 0

No dividends were declared or paid. Relevant exchange rates are as follows:

	$/FC
January 1, 19X2	$ 2.00
Average for 19X2	1.80
December 31, 19X2	1.60

REQUIRED:

1. Prepare translated financial statements for the foreign subsidiary as of December 31, 19X2, using the current rate method of *SFAS 52*. Include an analysis of the Cumulative Translation Adjustment account.
2. Assume that the Expenses account includes FC50,000 of depreciation on the original plant assets. Compute the ratios of operating income/sales and operating income/total assets at December 31, 19X2, using the foreign currency data and dollars translated according to the current rate and temporal methods. Comment on the results.

3. Suppose the foreign currency continues to weaken ($/FC continues to decrease) in subsequent years. What will happen to the ratios computed in No. 2? Do the signals they provide indicate improving or deteriorating performance? Should Webster's management use the ratios as justification for additional investments in the foreign subsidiary?

P9.6 Translating Cash Flow Statement Comparative balance sheets and the intervening statement of income and retained earnings for the Trippeer Company's foreign subsidiary appear below.

Foreign Subsidiary
Comparative Balance Sheets

	12/31/X8		12/31/X7	
Assets	**FC**	**$**	**FC**	**$**
Cash	120	156	100	120
Other Current Operating Assets	730	949	700	840
Plant Assets, Net	990	1,287	900	1,080
Total Assets	1,840	2,392	1,700	2,040
Liabilities and Stockholders' Equity				
Accounts Payable and Accruals	340	442	310	372
Income Taxes Payable	100	130	105	126
Long-Term Debt	650	845	600	720
Total Liabilities	1,090	1,417	1,015	1,218
Capital Stock	200	200	200	200
Retained Earnings	550	615	485	534
Cumulative Translation Adjustment	—	160	—	88
Total Stockholders' Equity	750	975	685	822
Total Liabilities and Stockholders' Equity	1,840	2,392	1,700	2,040

Foreign Subsidiary
Statement of Income and Retained Earnings
For the Year Ended December 31, 19X8

	FC	$
Sales	2,000	2,500.00
Cost of Goods Sold	(1,200)	(1,500.00)
Operating Expenses	(510)	(637.50)
Depreciation Expense	(90)	(112.50)
Income Tax Expense	(60)	(75.00)
Net Income	140	175.00
Retained Earnings, December 31, 19X7	485	534.00
Dividends Paid	(75)	(93.75)
Retained Earnings, December 31, 19X8	550	615.25

REQUIRED:

1. Prepare a statement of cash flows (indirect approach) in FC and $ for 19X8 and a computation of the effect of exchange rate changes on cash.
2. Prepare an analysis of the cumulative translation adjustment for 19X8.
3. How would the translated cash flow statement differ if the other translation method allowed by *SFAS 52* is used? Explain.

P9.7 Acquisition of Foreign Subsidiary Peller Corporation plans to acquire Mexco, a Mexican company, and maintain it as a foreign subsidiary. Mexco's functional currency is the peso (P). The recent price of Mexco's common stock on a Mexican stock exchange is P3,200. Peller's stock trades in the U.S. at $60. Both companies have similar risk and return profiles although the price of Mexco's stock can vary widely due to stock market conditions in Mexico. Peller plans a stock swap and prefers to use the pooling-of-interests method of accounting.

Mexco's condensed balance sheet in pesos, restated to conform with U.S. generally accepted accounting principles, appears below, along with fair values that differ from book values.

	Book Value	Fair Value
Cash and Receivables	P 50,000,000	
Inventories (FIFO)	80,000,000	P 100,000,000
Plant Assets, Net (10-year life)	100,000,000	150,000,000
	P 230,000,000	
Current Liabilities	P 70,000,000	
Long-Term Debt (10% coupon; 30-year life)	80,000,000	140,000,000
Stockholders' Equity	80,000,000	
	P 230,000,000	

Mexco's inventories and plant assets were acquired when the exchange rate averaged $.012/P and $.015/P, respectively. Mexco's common stock was issued when the exchange rate was $.02/P.

REQUIRED:

1. Given the variability of Mexco's stock price, what concession might Peller demand that would preclude use of the pooling-of-interests method of accounting?
2. Assume the companies agree to a stock swap in which Peller acquires all 50,000 of Mexco's P1,000 par value outstanding shares. Calculate the stock exchange ratio (number of shares of Mexco received by Peller per share of Peller stock surrendered) assuming a current exchange rate of $.01/P.
3. Peller's long-term debt/equity (D/E) ratio is .8 (= $32,000,000/$40,000,000). Mexco's remeasured retained earnings is $500,000. Calculate the consolidated D/E ratio assuming (a) pooling-of-interests accounting and (b) purchase accounting.
4. Peller exchanges 26,667 shares of its common stock for all of the Mexco stock and expects the exchange rate to remain close to $.01/P during the next year. Calculate

the differential effect on next year's pretax earnings under purchase accounting compared with pooling of interests. Goodwill will be amortized over 20 years.

P9.8   Translated/Remeasured Trial Balances; Translation Adjustment Calculations On January 1, 19X3, the U.K. branch of U.S. International Corporation had the following condensed balance sheet, in pounds (£):

Assets		Liabilities and Owners' Equity	
Cash and Receivables	£ 2,000	Accounts Payable	£ 2,100
Inventory (LIFO)	2,200	Long-Term Debt	1,200
Plant Assets	1,600	Home Office	2,100
Accumulated Depreciation .	(400)		
	£ 5,400		£ 5,400

The exchange rate on January 1, 19X3, was $2/£. Inventory and Plant Assets at January 1 were acquired when the exchange rate was $1.80/£. Plant assets costing £200 were purchased during the year when the exchange rate was $2.15/£. No depreciation was taken on these assets in 19X3, and no transactions between the home office and branch occurred during 19X3. At the end of 19X3, the branch reported the following trial balance, in pounds:

Account	Dr. (Cr.)
Cash and Receivables	£ 2,660
Inventory (LIFO)	2,500
Plant Assets	1,800
Accumulated Depreciation	(560)
Accounts Payable	(2,200)
Long-Term Debt	(1,100)
Home Office	(2,100)
Sales	(4,000)
Cost of Goods Sold	2,000
Depreciation Expense	160
Other Operating Expenses	840
	£ 0

The exchange rate when the new LIFO layer was acquired was $2.05/£. Merchandise sold was purchased at an average exchange rate of $2.12/£. Sales and Other Operating Expenses occurred evenly over the year. At year-end, the exchange rate stood at $2.20/£; the average for the year was $2.10/£.

REQUIRED:

1. Remeasure the trial balance in accordance with the temporal method (functional currency is the U.S. dollar). The remeasured balance of "Home Office" on January 1, 19X3, was $3,520. The "Home Office" account represents U.S. International Corporation's equity in the branch.
2. Repeat No. 1 using the current rate method (functional currency is the pound) and assuming that the translated balance of "Home Office" at January 1, 19X3, is $4,200.

3. Prepare a schedule to calculate the translation adjustment arising in No. 1. Describe the accounting treatment of this item.
4. Repeat No. 3 for the translation adjustment arising in No. 2.

P9.9   **Remeasuring Branch Accounts and Preparing Combined Trial Balance Working Paper** The Copra Trading Company established a foreign branch office in Arpoc Cay in 19X0 to purchase local products for resale by the home office and to sell company products. The branch's functional currency is the U.S. dollar.

You were engaged to examine the company's financial statements for the year ended December 31, 19X7, and you engaged a chartered professional accountant in Arpoc to examine the branch office accounts. He reported that the branch accounts were fairly stated in pesos, the local currency, except for a franchise fee, and that any possible adjustments required by home office accounting procedures were not recorded. Trial balances for both the branch office and home office appear in Exhibit 9.15.

Your examination disclosed the following information:

1. The peso was devalued on July 1, 19X7, from 4 pesos per $1 to 5 pesos per $1. The former rate of exchange had been in effect for ten years. Branch ending inventory and prepaid expenses were acquired after the devaluation.
2. Sales to the branch are marked up 33⅓ percent and shipped F.O.B. home office. The *Sales to Branch* account is carried at home office cost and the mark-up is recorded in *Overevaluation of Branch Inventory*, which also includes the mark-up in the branch's beginning inventory. Branch sales to the home office are made at branch cost.
3. The branch had a beginning and ending inventory on hand valued at 80,000 pesos, of which one-half at each date had been purchased from the home office. The home office had an inventory at December 31, 19X7, valued at $520,000.
4. The Deferred Marketing Research account is the unamortized portion of a $15,000 fee paid in January 19X6 to a U.S. firm for continuing marketing research for the branch. Currency restrictions prevented the branch from paying the fee, which was paid by the home office. The home office charges the branch $3,000 annually during the five-year amortization period, and the branch records the expense.
5. The branch incurred its long-term indebtedness in 19X2 to finance its most recent purchase of fixed assets.
6. The government of Arpoc imposes a franchise fee of 10 pesos per 100 pesos of net income of the branch in exchange for certain exclusive trading rights granted. The fee is payable each May 1 for the preceding calendar year's trading rights and had not been recorded by the branch at December 31, 19X7.
7. Two "intercompany" accounts—*Branch Current* and *Home Office Current*—represent, respectively, the home office's investment in the branch (at equity) and the branch's owners equity (home office is the owner).

REQUIRED: Prepare a combined trial balance working paper for Copra and its foreign branch office with all amounts stated in U.S. dollars. Your working paper should have captions for Branch Trial Balance (pesos), Translation Rate, Branch Trial Balance (dollars), Home Office Trial Balance, Adjustments and Eliminations, and Combined Trial Balance. Ending inventories must be included and supporting computations must be in good form. Number the working paper adjusting and eliminating entries.
(AICPA adapted)

Copra Trading Company and Branch Office
Trial Balances
at December 31, 19X7

Debits	Branch Office (In Pesos)	Home Office (In Dollars)
Cash	P 110,000	$ 90,000
Trade Accounts Receivable	140,000	160,000
Branch Current	—	10,000
Inventory, January 1	80,000	510,000
Prepaid Expenses	10,000	18,000
Fixed Assets	1,000,000	750,000
Deferred Marketing Research	—	12,000
Purchases	488,889	3,010,000
Purchases from Home	711,111	—
Purchases from Branch	—	140,000
Operating and General Expenses	190,000	680,000
Depreciation Expense	100,000	50,000
Total Debits	P 2,830,000	$ 5,430,000
Credits		
Accumulated Depreciation	P 650,000	$ 350,000
Current Liabilities	220,000	240,000
Home Office Current	50,000	—
Long-Term Debt	230,000	200,000
Capital Stock	—	300,000
Retained Earnings, January 1	—	142,500
Sales	1,057,778	4,035,000
Sales to Branch	—	120,000
Sales to Home	622,222	—
Overvaluation of Branch Inventory	—	42,500
Total Credits	P 2,830,000	$ 5,430,000

EXHIBIT 9.15 TRIAL BALANCE DATA TO BE USED IN P9.9

P9.10 Translating Financial Statements under *SFAS 52* The SA Company was organized in Mexico on December 31, 19X1, with a capital stock issue that yielded 1,000,000 pesos (P). The exchange rate was $.10/P. Transactions engaged in during 19X2 and the relevant exchange rates are shown below.

	January 5, 19X2	**June 30, 19X2**	**December 31, 19X2**
Exchange Rate:	$.10/P	$.12/P	$.15/P

Transactions:

1. Buy 2,000 wood carvings at P200 each.

2. Purchase office equipment (ten-year life) for P200,000.

1. Sell 1,000 carvings for P300,000.

2. Buy 1,500 carvings for P360,000.

3. Pay rent of P30,000.

1. Record straight-line depreciation on office equipment.

2. Write-down the carvings bought on June 30 to market of P320,000.

3. Close books and prepare financial statements.

REQUIRED: Using schedules like those presented in Exhibit 9.5 and 9.6, prepare translated balance sheets and income statements under the temporal and current rate translation methods. Show the calculation of the translation adjustment for each method separately. Assume FIFO for inventory.

P9.11 Preparing Consolidated Financial Statements with Purchased Foreign Subsidiary
On January 1, 19X4, the Phillips Company acquired 80 percent of the outstanding shares of Standard, Ltd., a U.K. firm, for $10,000,000 cash. At the end of 19X4, the two companies presented the condensed financial statements appearing in Exhibit 9.16.

At date of acquisition, the exchange rate was $2/£. Standard's inventory and buildings were undervalued by £100,000 and £500,000, respectively. All of the undervalued inventory was sold during the year, and the buildings are being depreciated over a 20-year life. Other relevant information is as follows:

1. The exchange rate at December 31, 19X4, was $2.30/£.
2. Standard's sales and other operating expenses occurred evenly during the year. The average exchange rate was $2.15/£.
3. Standard's inventory and goods sold were acquired when the exchange rate was $2.10/£.
4. Standard's plant assets were acquired when the exchange rate was $1.80/£.
5. Phillips' policy is to amortize intangibles over 40 years.
6. Phillips carries its Investment in Standard at equity. However, the equity method income accrual for 19X4 has not been booked and can be disregarded in this problem. Intercompany dividends, paid when the exchange rate was $2.10, were credited to the investment account.

REQUIRED: Assuming the pound is the functional currency, prepare a consolidated balance sheet and a consolidated statement of income and retained earnings for Phillips and Standard. Neither a working paper nor formal working paper entries are required. All supporting computations should be in good form.

Balance Sheets

Assets	Phillips ($)	Standard (£)
Cash and Receivables	$ 7,680,000	£ 3,000,000
Inventory	4,000,000	3,000,000
Property, Plant, and Equipment, Net	12,000,000	5,000,000
Investment in Standard	8,320,000	—
Total Assets	$ 32,000,000	£ 11,000,000
Liabilities and Stockholders' Equity		
Current Liabilities	$ 8,000,000	£ 4,000,000
Long-Term Debt	4,000,000	1,000,000
Capital Stock	10,000,000	2,000,000
Retained Earnings	10,000,000	4,000,000
Total Liabilities and Stockholders' Equity	$ 32,000,000	£ 11,000,000

Statements of Income and Retained Earnings

	Phillips ($)	Standard (£)
Sales	$ 30,000,000	£ 10,000,000
Cost of Goods Sold	$ 20,000,000	£ 6,000,000
Depreciation	1,000,000	500,000
Other Operating Expenses	5,000,000	2,000,000
	$ 26,000,000	£ 8,500,000
Net Income	$ 4,000,000	£ 1,500,000
Dividends Declared and Paid	(2,000,000)	(1,000,000)
Increase in Retained Earnings	$ 2,000,000	£ 500,000

EXHIBIT 9.16 PHILLIPS COMPANY AND STANDARD, LTD.: CONDENSED FINANCIAL STATEMENTS TO BE USED IN P9.11

P9.12 **Translating Postcombination Balance Sheets under Pooling and Purchase; Analysis of Cumulative Translation Adjustment** Marcus Corporation acquired all of the outstanding stock of Blatt, Ltd., a U.K. company, on December 31, 19X4, for stock worth $1,200,000. On that date, the exchange rate was $2.00/£. Blatt's condensed balance sheet as of December 31, 19X4, is given below:

Assets		Liabilities and Stockholders' Equity	
Cash and Receivables ..	£ 600,000	Current Liabilities	£ 400,000
Inventory (FIFO)	250,000	Long-Term Debt	300,000
Plant Assets, Net	350,000	Capital Stock	200,000
Patents	100,000	Retained Earnings	400,000
	£1,300,000		£1,300,000

Blatt was organized on June 15, 19X1, when the exchange rate was $2.10/£. The capital stock was issued and £200,000 (net) of plant assets were acquired on that date. The remaining net plant assets were acquired and the long-term debt issued when the exchange rate was $2.05/£. Blatt acquired the patents when the exchange rate was $1.90/£.

REQUIRED:

1. Translate Blatt's condensed balance sheet into dollars for inclusion in Marcus's consolidated statements on December 31, 19X4. Assume that the combination was accounted for as a *pooling of interests* and that the U.S. dollar is the functional currency.
2. Repeat No. 1 assuming that the combination was accounted for as a *purchase* and that the pound is the functional currency.
3. Blatt reported net income of £100,000 and paid dividends of £60,000 during 19X5. There were no other changes in Blatt's stockholders' equity. The average exchange rate during 19X5 was $2.10/£ and the dividends were declared when the exchange rate was $2.06/£. Prepare an analysis of the Cumulative Translation Adjustment account during 19X5 assuming that the acquisition of Blatt had been accounted for by the purchase method, that the exchange rate on December 31, 19X5, is $2.02/£, and that the pound is the functional currency.

P9.13 **Analysis of Cumulative Translation Adjustment Disclosure** Ford Motor Company's 1993 Annual Report includes the following excerpt from the Consolidated Statement of Stockholders' Equity.

Consolidated Statement of Stockholders' Equity
For the Years Ended December 31, 1993 and 1992 (in millions)

	1993	1992
Foreign Currency Translation Adjustments and Other (Note 1)		
Balance at beginning of year	**(62)**	838
Translation adjustments during year	**(508)**	(975)
Minimum pension liability adjustment	**(400)**	—
Other	**(108)**	75
Balance at end of year	**(1,078)**	(62)

REQUIRED:

1. Explain what this disclosure indicates about the functional currencies of at least some of Ford's foreign operations and how those operations are reported in Ford's consolidated statements.
2. If Ford had used the alternative approach allowed under *SFAS 52* to report those foreign operations, explain whether Ford's 1992 and 1993 earnings would have been higher or lower than reported earnings. Clearly state any assumptions made.

CHAPTER 10

ACCOUNTING FOR FOREIGN CURRENCY TRANSACTIONS

CHAPTER PREVIEW

Participation of American companies in the globalized marketplace of today encompasses more than establishing business operations abroad. The volume of foreign trade and the well-known "trade deficit" frequently reported in the news indicate the vast number of business transactions involving U.S. companies, foreign customers and suppliers, and foreign currencies. When transactions such as these must be settled in foreign currencies rather than dollars, the cash flows of domestic companies are exposed to the risks of adverse movements in foreign exchange rates. Certain financial instruments enable companies to *hedge* or *neutralize* these risks.

This chapter considers several common classes of foreign currency transactions and the use of forward and option contracts to hedge the risk created by fluctuating exchange rates. Major topics examined in this chapter are as follows:

- The nature of foreign currency transactions
- Accounting for import/export transactions
- Hedging foreign exchange exposures
- Using forward contracts to hedge import and export transactions
- Using forward contracts to hedge firm foreign currency commitments
- Using forward contracts to hedge forecasted transactions
- Decisions involving hedging
- Foreign lending and borrowing transactions
- Economic hedge of a net investment in a foreign entity
- Use of forward contracts for speculation
- The structure of foreign exchange rates (appendix)

This study of accounting for foreign currency transactions will round out your background in accounting for international operations. Moreover, the emphasis on forward contracts provides important background for the further study of financial instruments available in Chapter 11.

THE NATURE OF FOREIGN CURRENCY TRANSACTIONS

In this chapter, we look at transactions between U.S. companies and foreign suppliers or customers, and ways to manage the resulting foreign exchange risk caused by changes in exchange rates. A U.S. company may be an **exporter**, selling its products to customers in other countries. Or the U.S. company may be an **importer**, purchasing products from suppliers in other countries. When the payment from the foreign customer to the U.S. exporter is in U.S. dollars, the export sale is accounted for the same as a domestic sale. Similarly, when the U.S. company pays its foreign supplier in U.S. dollars, the accounting for the import purchase is identical to a domestic purchase. However, when the amount received from the foreign customer or paid to a foreign supplier is denominated in a foreign currency, there are new risks and accounting issues involved.

Recall from Chapter 9 that foreign exchange rates are *prices*.

> A **foreign exchange rate** is the price of a unit of one country's currency expressed in units of another country's currency.

These prices can be expressed in two ways: the amount of foreign currency which can be acquired per unit of domestic currency (**the indirect rate**), or the amount of domestic currency needed to acquire one unit of foreign currency (**the direct rate**). In the case of a U.S. company, the indirect rate is the foreign currency per U.S. dollar, such as the number of yen per dollar, or the number of francs per dollar. For example, an indirect rate of 6.0827 francs/U.S. dollar means that each U.S. dollar can be exchanged for 6.0827 francs. The direct rate is the number of U.S. dollars that can be purchased for one yen or franc. For example, if the direct rate is $.1644/franc, it takes $.1644 to buy one franc. Notice that the direct rate is the reciprocal of the indirect rate. When accounting for a U.S. company's foreign transactions, the direct rate is used to express foreign currency amounts in U.S. dollars.

Foreign currencies are traded on both **spot markets** and **forward markets** or **futures markets**. Transactions involving *immediate delivery* of the foreign currency are executed at **spot rates**. Transactions involving delivery of the foreign currency at some *later date* are executed at **forward rates**. A discussion of the structure of foreign exchange rates appears in the appendix to this chapter.

In this chapter, we address issues involved if a U.S. company engages in transactions which are **denominated** (must be settled) in a foreign currency. If a U.S. exporter sells goods to a customer in Japan, and payment will be received in yen, how should the sale be recorded on the books of the exporter? If the customer is extended credit, and makes payment on the sale at some future time, how is the U.S. dollar equivalent of the sale affected if the foreign exchange rate changes between the time the sale is made and the payment is received in yen?

When a U.S. exporter sells to a foreign customer on credit, the U.S. company expects to receive foreign currency at some future date. The U.S. company is exposed to *foreign exchange risk*, because it takes the chance that the U.S. dollar equivalent of this future cash receipt will *decline* due to changes in the foreign exchange rate. Similarly, a U.S. importer may purchase goods from a foreign supplier on credit. The U.S. importer is exposed to foreign exchange risk because it is possible that the U.S. dollar equivalent of this future cash payment will *increase* due to changes in the foreign exchange rate. Of course, changing exchange rates can be an advantage as well. The U.S. dollar equivalent of a customer's payment may *increase*, and the U.S. dollar equivalent of a payment to a supplier may *decrease*. The U.S. importer or exporter can utilize financial instruments designed to neutralize the risks caused by changing exchange rates. In the next sections, we discuss the accounting for import purchases and export sales, and the accounting for investments to neutralize, or **hedge**, foreign exchange risk using financial instruments.

ACCOUNTING FOR IMPORT/EXPORT TRANSACTIONS

Import/export transactions—purchases from foreign suppliers and sales to foreign customers—present no particular accounting problem *if* all sales, purchases, payments, and receipts are made in dollars. Such an unlikely situation means, however, that our international customers and suppliers do business in terms of the dollar, a currency foreign to *them*. The basic problem caused by the need to transact in a foreign currency may be summarized as follows:

> When a transaction is **denominated in a foreign currency**, its value in dollars is affected by the appropriate foreign exchange rate. The *passage of time* between inception of a transaction and its ultimate settlement with cash *allows the dollar value of the unsettled balance to change as the foreign exchange rate changes.*

Therefore, when a U.S. company makes a credit sale abroad and the transaction price is stated in units of foreign currency, the dollar value of the account receivable may change before payment is received in the foreign currency and converted into dollars. Similarly, when a U.S. company purchases goods from abroad on account at a price denominated in foreign currency units, the dollar amount owed may change before dollars are converted into the foreign currency and payment is made. These changes in the dollar value of receivables and payables generate *exchange gains and losses* to the U.S. firm that must be recognized at settlement and at intervening balance sheet dates. Because the ultimate settlement of these receivables and payables requires other transactions to *convert* dollars into foreign currency or foreign currency into dollars, we describe these exchange gains and losses as **transaction gains or losses** or **transaction adjustments**. As one of two general types of exchange gain or loss, the transaction gain or loss has clear economic significance because it involves an increase or decrease in actual money. The other type, the translation adjustment discussed in Chapter 9, generally has less economic significance. It arises when foreign currency financial statements are translated into dollars and does not involve an increase or decrease in actual money.

> In sum, a **transaction gain or loss** indicates that there was, or will be, an actual currency conversion. In a **translation gain or loss**, there is no actual currency conversion, just a restatement of accounting balances.

Generally accepted accounting principles for import and export transactions denominated in a foreign currency are found in *SFAS 8*, "Accounting for the Translation of Foreign Currency Transactions and Foreign Currency Financial Statements," and *SFAS 52*, "Foreign Currency Translation." The initial sale or purchase transaction is recorded at the U.S. dollar equivalent, using the foreign exchange spot rate in effect at the time of the transaction. Any *changes* in the U.S. dollar equivalent of the resulting receivable or payable are treated separately as **transaction gains or losses**, with no effect on the original U.S. dollar value of the sale or purchase. The following summarizes the accounting procedures to be used in accounting for import or export transactions:

1. Restate the foreign currency invoice price into dollars using the appropriate foreign exchange spot rate.
2. Record the transaction in dollars.
3. Record a transaction gain or loss when the transaction is settled if the number of dollars received or paid differs from that originally recorded in step No. 2.
4. If the transaction is not settled at a balance sheet date, record a transaction gain or loss on the existing receivable or payable by adjusting it to the dollar equivalent implied by the spot rate at the balance sheet date.

Observe the two objectives of these procedures. *First*, recognition is given to changes in the value of receivables and payables attributable to movements in the exchange rate. *Second*, this recognition is based on accrual accounting and is not deferred until eventual settlement if a balance sheet date occurs prior to settlement.

The following example illustrates the accounting for import and export transactions.

1. On October 16, 19X1, Acme International purchased lamb's wool at an invoice price of 17,000 New Zealand dollars ($NZ17,000) from a New Zealand rancher. The exchange rate was $.62/$NZ. Payment was to be made on December 16, 19X1.

October 16, 19X1

Purchases or Inventory	10,540	
Accounts Payable		10,540

To record the purchase of wool from New Zealand; $10,540 = $.62 × 17,000.

2. On December 16, 19X1, Acme purchased $NZ17,000 at an exchange rate of $.63/$NZ and transmitted them to the rancher's bank in New Zealand.

December 16, 19X1

Transaction Loss	170	
Accounts Payable		170

To recognize the transaction loss on the account payable; $170 = ($.63 − $.62) 17,000.

Foreign Currency	10,710	
Cash		10,710

To purchase sufficient foreign currency to pay off the New Zealand rancher; $10,710 = $.63 × 17,000.

Accounts Payable	10,710	
Foreign Currency		10,710

To record payment of the liability to the New Zealand rancher; $10,710 = $10,540 + $170.

Consider the transaction loss recorded in Event 2. Acme had a liability to the New Zealand rancher denominated in New Zealand dollars. Because the exchange rate had risen, so that it took more U.S. dollars to purchase New Zealand dollars, the dollar value of the liability increased, and Acme incurred a transaction loss.

3. On December 20, 19X1, Acme purchased wool fabrics from a British mill for £40,000, when the exchange rate was $2/£. Payment is due on January 20, 19X2.

December 20, 19X1

Purchases or Inventory	80,000	
Accounts Payable		80,000

To record the purchase of wool fabric from Great Britain; $80,000 = $2 × 40,000.

4. On December 22, 19X1, Acme sold a quantity of deluxe wool blankets to a Canadian concern for 9,800 Canadian dollars ($CN9,800). The exchange rate was $.67/$CN. Acme's terms are 60 days, net.

December 22, 19X1

Accounts Receivable	6,566	
Sales		6,566

To record the sale of blankets to Canada; $6,566 = $.67 × 9,800.

5. On December 29, 19X1, Acme purchased buttons costing 10,000 pesos (P10,000) from a Mexican manufacturer. The exchange rate was $.05/P; a check was mailed immediately.

December 29, 19X1

Purchases or Inventory	500	
Cash		500

To record the cash purchase of buttons from Mexico; $500 = $.05 × 10,000.

Note that because no time lapsed between the accrual-based recording of the transaction and time of payment in Event 5, there can be *no exchange gain or loss*.

6. Financial statements were prepared at December 31, 19X1, and the following adjusting entries were made. Exchange rates were $1.96/£ and $.685/$CN at December 31, 19X1.

December 31, 19X1

Accounts Payable	1,600	
Transaction Gain		1,600

To record the transaction gain accrued on the liability to the British mill; $1,600 = ($2.00 − $1.96) 40,000. The dollar value of this liability decreased to $78,400 (= $1.96 × 40,000).

Accounts Receivable	147	
Transaction Gain		147

To record the transaction gain accrued on the receivable from Canada; $147 = ($.685 − $.67) 9,800. The dollar value of this asset increased to $6,713 (= $.685 × 9,800).

Contrast the two transaction gains accrued at December 31, 19X1, in Event 6. Because the exchange rate for pounds sterling declined, the dollar value of Acme's liability declined too, so a transaction gain resulted. Although the exchange rate of Canadian dollars rose by year-end, it also produced a transaction gain. The gain resulted because Acme had a receivable denominated in Canadian dollars. As the value of Canadian dollars rose, so did the U.S. dollar value of Acme's receivable from the Canadian firm.

7. Acme paid its obligation to the British mill on January 20, 19X2. The exchange rate was $1.93/£.

January 20, 19X2

Accounts Payable	1,200	
Transaction Gain		1,200
To recognize the transaction gain on the account payable; $1,200 = ($1.96 − $1.93) 40,000.		
Foreign Currency	77,200	
Cash		77,200
To record the purchase of foreign currency to pay the British mill; $77,200 = $1.93 × 40,000.		
Accounts Payable	77,200	
Foreign Currency		77,200
To record payment of the liability to Great Britain; $77,200 = $80,000 − $1,600 − $1,200.		

8. On February 20, 19X2, payment was received from the Canadian customer on the sale of the blankets. The exchange rate was $.65/$CN.

February 20, 19X2

Transaction Loss	343	
Accounts Receivable		343
To recognize the transaction loss on the receivable; $343 = ($.685 − $.65) 9,800.		
Foreign Currency	6,370	
Accounts Receivable		6,370
To record receipt of foreign currency from Canada in payment of the receivable; $6,370 = $.65 × 9,800 = $6,566 + $147 − $343.		
Cash	6,370	
Foreign Currency		6,370
To record sale of the Canadian currency for U.S. dollars.		

To summarize, accounts receivable and accounts payable arising in international transactions are often denominated in a foreign currency and are recorded at the dollar equivalent of a fixed quantity of foreign currency. Because these receivables and payables are *exposed* to exchange rate risk, as the exchange rate changes their dollar equivalents also change. The effects of changing exchange rates on the dollar equivalents of these exposed accounts and the resulting transaction gains and losses are as follows:

Effects of Changing Exchange Rates on Exposed Receivables and Payables Denominated in Foreign Currencies

	Transaction Gains and Losses Due to Changes in Direct Exchange Rate ($/FC)	
	Increase	Decrease
Exposed Account	**($ Weakens)**	**($ Strengthens)**
Accounts Receivable (A/R)	A/R increases; gain	A/R decreases; loss
Accounts Payable (A/P)	A/P increases; loss	A/P decreases; gain

---

The accounting for import and export transactions specified by *SFAS 8* and reaffirmed in *SFAS 52* is referred to as the **two-transaction approach**. Under this approach, the U.S. dollar valuation of the inventories purchased from foreign suppliers or the sales revenue on sales made to foreign customers is unaffected by changes in the foreign exchange rate between the time the purchase or sale is made and the foreign currency is paid or collected. For example, Acme's purchase of lamb's wool on October 16, 19X1 is valued at $10,540, even though Acme ends up actually paying $10,710 to settle the transaction. The transaction loss of $170 is shown separately on the income statement. The alternative **single-transaction approach** views a sale or purchase denominated in a foreign currency as incomplete until settled. Under this alternative, any intervening transaction gain or loss is used to adjust the dollar basis of the initial transaction and is not reported separately. Using the single-transaction approach, Acme's purchase of lamb's wool on October 16, 19X1 is initially valued at $10,540, but since Acme must pay $170 more to settle the debt, this additional payment is added to the cost of the inventory purchased.

The FASB specifically rejected the single-transaction view by observing that "the exchange exposure in a purchase or sale transaction whose price is denominated in a foreign currency stems not from the purchase or sale itself but from a delay in the payment or receipt of the equivalent dollars."[1] The FASB's position on this issue is an example of the traditional separation of operating transactions from financing transactions—for example, if a building is financed by a mortgage, the interest on the mortgage is not included as a cost of the building. In the case of an importer, the cost of the inventory purchased is not affected by the manner in which the purchase is financed.

HEDGING FOREIGN EXCHANGE EXPOSURES

At the beginning of this chapter, we discussed how importers or exporters are exposed to *foreign exchange risk*. In the case of an importer, there is the danger that the direct exchange rate will *rise* between the time the importer makes the purchase and the time the foreign currency obligation for the purchase is made, requiring the importer to use more U.S. dollars to purchase the foreign

---

[1] Financial Accounting Standards Board, *Statement No. 8*, Par. 114.

currency necessary to pay the obligation. In the case of an exporter, there is the risk that the exchange rate will *fall* between the time the exporter makes the sale and the time the foreign currency is received from the customer, causing the exporter to receive fewer U.S. dollars on conversion of the foreign currency received from the customer. There is also the chance that rates will move in the U.S. company's favor.

FORWARD CONTRACTS

Importers and exporters can **hedge**, or neutralize foreign exchange risks by trading in the forward or futures markets. In this case, hedging involves covering a foreign currency exposure by contracting in the forward market to purchase or sell foreign currency at a specified time in the future for a fixed price. In this way, managers neutralize the impact of changing exchange rates on the exposure by removing the uncertainty involved in not knowing how many U.S. dollars will be paid or received.

Contracting for future delivery of a foreign currency can involve either **forward contracts**—individual contracts negotiated with dealers—or **futures contracts**—standardized contracts traded on organized exchanges that generally require margin deposits. Futures contracts are discussed in detail in Chapter 11. *SFAS 52* prescribes the same accounting treatment for forward *and* futures contracts in *foreign currencies*. We concentrate here on forward contracts because forwards are the most basic hedging instrument and are the easiest to understand. Other foreign currency transactions, such as foreign loans and investments in foreign debt securities, can also function as hedges. When they do, accounting for the exchange gains or losses on such transactions parallels the forward contract case.

As an example of hedging using a forward contract, look at the illustration in the previous section. On October 16, 19X1, Acme International agrees to pay a New Zealand rancher $NZ17,000 on December 16, 19X1 for the lamb's wool. The current exchange rate is $.62/$NZ, but there is the risk that the exchange rate will increase by the time payment is to be made. Acme can remove this uncertainty by contracting with a foreign exchange broker on October 16, 19X1 to buy $NZ17,000 in 60 days at a fixed price. This contract is called a **forward contract**. Prices for future delivery of currency are called **forward rates**. Assume the forward rate for delivery of New Zealand dollars in 60 days is $.61. Acme is no longer affected by the uncertainty of the future exchange rate; it is now known with certainty that $10,370 ($.61 × 17,000) will be paid for the merchandise. In hindsight, this arrangement was beneficial for Acme, since without the forward contract $10,710 would have been paid on December 16, 19X1. Note carefully, however, that hedging neutralizes both the potential *losses* and the potential *gains* from changes in the exchange rate. If the spot rate *fell* to $.58 on December 16, Acme is still required to fulfill the forward contract and pay $10,370 for the $NZ17,000 necessary to pay the obligation, even though without the forward contract only $9,860 ($.58 × 17,000) is paid for the needed currency on the spot market. The forward contract removes the uncertainty of decreases as well as increases in the exchange rate—thus both potential gains and potential losses are neutralized.

GRAPHICAL INTERPRETATION OF FORWARD CONTRACTS

Hedging with a forward contract involves neutralizing an underlying exposure—exchange gains/losses on the forward contract offset the exchange losses/gains accruing on the foreign currency receivables and payables. These relationships are diagrammed in Figure 10.1. For example, the *downward-sloping diagonal* line in Panel A of Figure 10.1 links the exchange gain/loss (vertical axis) arising on an exposed liability (payable) to changes in the exchange rate (horizontal axis). Movements in the exchange rate occur along the horizontal axis to either side of the spot rate at the origin. Because settlement of the payable in foreign currency units requires that the foreign currency be purchased, exchange losses/gains occur as the cost of purchasing that foreign currency rises/falls.

Panel B shows how the dollar equivalent of a *forward purchase contract*, entered to obtain the currency when needed, changes in response to movements in the exchange rate. As the exchange rate moves along the horizontal axis to either side of the origin, the dollar value of the foreign currency to be received changes. The *upward-sloping* diagonal line in Panel B links these exchange rate movements to exchange gains/losses on the vertical axis. Combining the diagonals in Panels A and B produces the horizontal line in Panel C, indicating no net gain/loss from a changing exchange rate.

Numerical Illustration of Panels A and B in Figure 10.1

The general principles behind these graphs can be further amplified with a numerical illustration. Refer again to Panels A and B where an exchange rate of $.50/FC is assumed to lie at the origin of both panels. Suppose a company incurs an account payable denominated in foreign currency units (FC)—FC1,000—when the exchange rate is $.50/FC; the initial dollar balance is $500.

In *Panel A*, visualize moving to the right of the origin on the horizontal axis as the exchange rate rises above $.50/FC. If the exchange rate increases to $.56/FC, the company must pay $560 (= $.56 × 1,000) for the foreign currency needed to liquidate the payable. This extra $60 (= $560 − $500) is a *transaction loss on the account payable*. If these numbers were on the axes in Panel A, we would see that a vertical line drawn from the horizontal (exchange rate) axis to the *downward-sloping* diagonal line in the lower right-hand quadrant connects with a horizontal line drawn to the vertical (gain/loss) axis at the point indicating a $60 loss.

Now turn to *Panel B* and assume the company enters a forward purchase contract to buy FC1,000 at $.52/FC. Regardless of what the exchange rate does, the company will pay $520 to obtain FC1,000 to liquidate its account payable. However, the value of the foreign currency to be received when the contract matures varies with the exchange rate. Again assume the exchange rate increases to $.56/FC. The company experiences a $60 *transaction gain* on the forward contract as the FC1,000 to be received when the contract matures are now worth $560. Visualize a vertical line drawn from the right of the origin on the horizontal (exchange rate) axis at $.56 to the *upward-sloping* diagonal line in the upper right-hand quadrant in Panel A. This line connects with a horizontal line drawn to the point on the vertical (gain/loss) axis indicating a $60 gain.

Thus the gain on the forward purchase contract exactly offsets the loss on the account payable—a **perfect hedge.** The company has successfully neutralized the effect of exchange rate changes and fixed the FC1,000 account payable at $520, the rate specified in the forward contract.

OPTION CONTRACTS

Foreign exchange **options** are a way to hedge against the "downside risk" of foreign exchange transaction *losses*, without also losing the chance to experience foreign exchange transaction *gains*. The option holder has the right—but not the obligation—to buy or sell the contracted amount of foreign currency at a specified exchange rate called the **exercise price** or **strike price**. Options that give the holder the right to *buy* currency at a fixed price are called **call** options. Options that

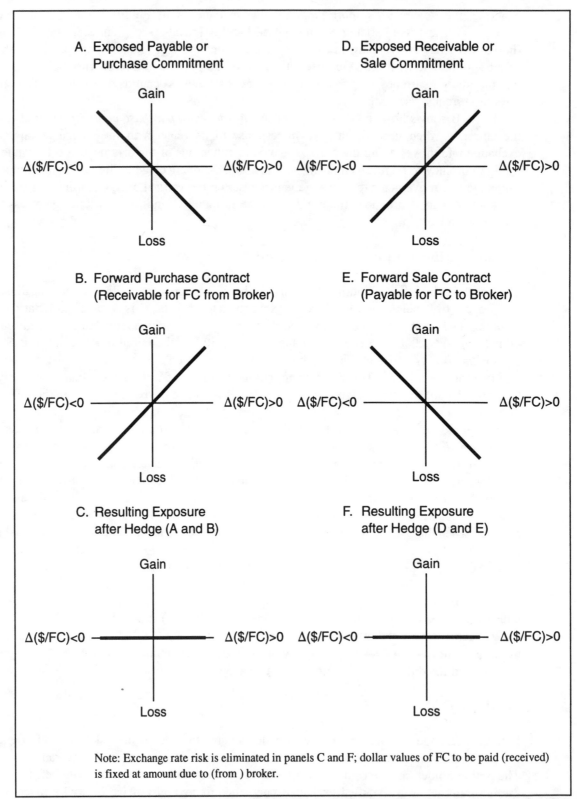

Note: Exchange rate risk is eliminated in panels C and F; dollar values of FC to be paid (received) is fixed at amount due to (from) broker.

FIGURE 10.1   PAYOFF PROFILES OF FOREIGN CURRENCY (FC) EXPOSURES, FORWARD CONTRACTS, AND THE EFFECTS OF HEDGING

give the holder the right to *sell* currency at a fixed price are called **put** options. The option writer must follow through with selling or buying the currency if the option is exercised by the option holder. However, if it is not favorable to the option holder to exercise the option, the holder can let the option expire. Notice that the option writer incurs the risk of potential loss on the contract. For this reason, the option writer charges the holder a fee or **premium** as compensation for the risk undertaken.

As an example of hedging using an option contract, look again at Acme International's purchase of lamb's wool on October 16, 19X1, with payment of $NZ17,000 to be made on December 16, 19X1. Acme can hedge the risk that the exchange rate will increase during this time interval by investing in a 60-day call option giving Acme the right to buy $NZ at a fixed price. Let's assume the option's strike price is $.61, and the option costs Acme $400. If the spot rate on December 16, 19X1 is above $.61, Acme exercises the option and pays $10,370 ($.61 × 17,000) for the currency necessary to pay the obligation. If the spot rate is below $.61, Acme lets the option expire and buys the currency on the spot market.

TYPES OF FOREIGN EXCHANGE RISK

In the previous section, we concentrated on the risk associated with holding a receivable or payable denominated in a foreign currency. There are a number of other ways in which a company can be exposed to foreign exchange risk. The company may use hedging instruments to manage these risks as well.

- In addition to the accounts receivable of an exporter and the accounts payable of an importer, a company may borrow or lend abroad. The resulting loans or notes payable or receivable, denominated in the foreign currency, expose the company to foreign exchange risk.

- A company may hold an investment in a foreign subsidiary or division. Recall from Chapter 9 that the financial statements of a foreign subsidiary may be translated using either the temporal or current rate method, depending on the functional currency of the subsidiary. Exposure to foreign exchange risk is defined in terms of the balances translated at *current exchange rates*. This is the subsidiary's *net asset* position when the current rate method is used, and the subsidiary's *net balances measured at current money prices* when the temporal method is used.

- A company may enter into a firm *agreement* to buy merchandise from a foreign supplier or sell merchandise to a foreign customer. In this case, the exposure to foreign exchange risk is in the future. This situation is referred to as a **firm foreign currency commitment**.

- A company may regularly buy from foreign suppliers or sell to foreign customers. Although the anticipated transactions may not be in the form of specific firm commitments, the risk associated with the expectation of holding accounts receivable or payable denominated in a foreign currency is just as real. These expected events are known as **forecasted transactions**.

The accounting for these situations and related hedging activities is covered later in this chapter.

REPORTING FORWARD AND OPTION CONTRACTS IN FINANCIAL STATEMENTS

Forward and option contracts are recorded when entered, although no money may change hands until the contracts are settled. If the company must pay some cash upon inception of the contract, it is reported in the current asset section of the company's balance sheet. *Gross amounts of forward and option contracts are not reported in financial statements.* Rather, their components—indicated in the ensuing sections—are *netted*. As these net amounts are likely to be small, they usually are not reported separately and are included with other items in a caption under Current Assets or Current Liabilities.

Because forward contracts are *derivative financial instruments* and can themselves expose an entity to exchange rate risk, they are subject to the disclosure requirements of *SFAS 105* (1990)[2] and *SFAS 107* (1991).[3] A 1994 FASB *Statement—SFAS 119*—deals specifically with derivative financial instruments and imposes additional disclosure requirements.[4] A FASB *Draft Statement*[5] scheduled to become final in 1998, also addresses disclosure requirements for derivatives. These matters are discussed in more detail within Chapter 11's broader discussion of derivative financial instruments. For now, though, think of a **derivative financial instrument** as a financial instrument whose value is tied to or *derived from* the value of some underlying or reference item. A foreign currency forward or option contract's value is derived from the value of the currency referenced in the contract based on the spot exchange rate.

Generally accepted accounting principles for investments used to hedge foreign currency risk are found in *SFAS 52*, "Foreign Currency Translation," and the FASB 1996 *Exposure Draft*, "Accounting for Derivative and Similar Financial Instruments and for Hedging Activities," which evolved into the 1997 *Draft Statement*. At this writing, the *Draft Statement* recommendations are not yet effective, but the FASB plans to issue a final *Statement* in 1998, effective for fiscal years beginning after June 15, 1999. In cases where the *Draft Statement* amends *SFAS 52* requirements, both accounting methods are discussed.

We can see from the discussion above on the nature of hedging contracts that the purpose of these contracts is to neutralize the gains and losses—or just the losses in the case of an option contract—on holding accounts receivable or payable denominated in a foreign currency. In accounting for the foreign exchange exposure and the hedge instrument, it is important that recognition of the gains or losses on the exposure be **matched** with the offsetting losses or gains on the hedge instrument. If recognition of the gain or loss on the exposure is delayed to a future period, recognition of the loss or gain on the hedge should also be delayed. If the gain or loss on the exposure is recognized as exchange rates change, recognition of the loss or gain on the hedge should also be recognized as the exchange rates change.

---

[2] Financial Accounting Standards Board, *Statement of Financial Accounting Standards No. 105*, "Disclosure of Information about Financial Instruments with Off-Balance-Sheet Risk and Financial Instruments with Concentrations of Credit Risk" (Norwalk, CT: FASB, 1990).

[3] Financial Accounting Standards Board, *Statement of Financial Accounting Standards No. 107*, "Disclosures about Fair Value of Financial Instruments" (Norwalk, CT: FASB, 1991).

[4] Financial Accounting Standards Board, *Statement of Financial Accounting Standards No. 119*, "Disclosure about Derivative Financial Instruments and Fair Value of Financial Instruments" (Norwalk, CT: FASB, 1994).

[5] Financial Accounting Standards Board *Draft Statement*, "Accounting for Derivative Instruments and Hedging Activities" (Norwalk, CT: FASB, 1997).

USING FORWARD CONTRACTS TO HEDGE IMPORT AND EXPORT TRANSACTIONS

In this section, accounting for *forward contracts* is illustrated in detail. The accounting for foreign exchange *option contracts* parallels the accounting for option contracts in the commodities and financial markets. Accounting for option contracts is covered in Chapter 11.

ACCOUNTING FOR FORWARD PURCHASE CONTRACTS

A **forward purchase contract** gives its holder the obligation to purchase foreign currency at a specified time in the future for a known price. An **importer** enters into a *forward purchase contract* so that, when an obligation to a foreign supplier comes due, the needed amount of foreign currency is available at a price agreed upon in advance. For accounting purposes, three components of a forward purchase transaction are important:

1. The **forward purchase contract** (debit), representing the *right to receive foreign currency*. It is recorded at the current value of the foreign currency to be purchased; that is, the quantity of foreign currency translated at the *spot rate*. This asset is *denominated in units of the foreign currency* and is based upon the current translated value of the foreign currency. *Its dollar value changes with the spot rate* and transaction gains and losses accrue on it.
2. The **liability to the foreign exchange broker** (credit), denoted *Due to Exchange Broker*. It is recorded at the agreed-upon dollar value of the foreign currency to be purchased; that is, the quantity of foreign currency translated at the applicable *forward rate*. Because the rate is fixed by the contract, *this liability is denominated in dollars*. It is unaffected by changes in the exchange rate and generates no transaction gain or loss.
3. The **premium or discount on the forward purchase contract** (debit or credit), the difference between the current and future values of the foreign currency to be purchased. A premium exists when the forward rate exceeds the spot rate; a discount arises when the forward rate is less than the spot rate. This difference is considered a financing revenue or expense to the firm. Amortization of this premium or discount is accounted for separately from any transaction gain or loss on the forward purchase contract.

Forward Purchase Contract Illustration

As an example, suppose that goods costing £1,000 are purchased from a British supplier on October 1 when the spot rate is $2.10/£. Payment in pounds is due in 30 days. Because the liability (account payable) is denominated in pounds, it is exposed to risk of exchange rate movements. To hedge this **exposed liability** to the British supplier, a *forward purchase contract* calling for the broker to deliver £1,000 in 30 days is entered on October 1. If the 30-day forward rate is $2.20/£, the *liability to the exchange broker* is fixed at $2,200 (= $2.20 × 1,000) and is not affected by subsequent movements in the exchange rate. Thus the £1,000 needed to pay the British supplier will be purchased for $2,200. Translating the £1,000 at the spot rate of $2.10 gives us the current value of the right to receive the foreign currency, $2,100 (= $2.10 × 2,000), which we call the forward purchase contract. Because the foreign currency was purchased in the forward market for *more* than the current spot rate, a *premium on the forward purchase contract* of $100 [= ($2.20 − $2.10) 1,000] results. Entries recording (1) the purchase of goods and (2) the forward purchase contract on October 1 are given below:

October 1

Purchases	2,100	
Accounts Payable		2,100
To record the purchase of goods from Britain;		
$2,100 = $2.10 × 1,000.		

Forward Purchase Contract ($2.10 × 1,000)	2,100	
Premium on Forward Contract [($2.20 − $2.10) 1,000]	100	
Due to Exchange Broker ($2.20 × 1,000)		2,200
To record the forward purchase contract entered to hedge		
the payable to the British supplier.		

On October 31, when the forward contract is settled and the British supplier is paid with the £1,000 received from the broker, the spot rate is $2.14/£. The following entries made on October 31 show the accrual of the transaction gain on the forward purchase contract and the settlement of the contract:

October 31

Forward Purchase Contract	40	
Transaction Gain		40
To accrue the transaction gain on the forward contract;		
$40 = ($2.14 − $2.10) 1,000.		

Due to Exchange Broker	2,200	
Cash		2,200
To record payment to the foreign exchange broker.		

Foreign Currency	2,140	
Forward Purchase Contract		2,140
To record receipt of the foreign currency from the broker;		
$2,140 = $2.14 × 1,000 = $2,100 + $40.		

Expense—Premium Amortization	100	
Premium on Forward Contract		100
To amortize the premium on the forward contract.		

At this point, the forward contract is settled, the importer has the £1,000 from the broker, and the premium is expensed. We now recognize the transaction loss on the account payable and record payment of the £1,000 to the British supplier:

October 31

Transaction Loss	40	
Accounts Payable		40
To recognize the transaction loss accrued on the		
account payable; $40 = ($2.14 − $2.10) 1,000.		

Accounts Payable 2,140
    Foreign Currency 2,140
    To record payment of the liability to the British
    supplier; $2,140 = $2.14 × 1,000 = $2,100 + $40.

The transaction gain on the forward contract exactly offsets the transaction loss on the account payable. In retrospect, however, the hedge was not profitable. Even though the transaction loss of $40 was avoided, a premium of $100 was paid to do so. In other words, $2,200 was paid for £1,000 which could have been purchased on October 31 for $2,140, or purchased on October 1 for $2,100. Although these numbers illustrate a point, the implicit interest cost of almost *5 percent for 30 days*, shown by the premium on the forward contract (.05 ≈ $100/$2,100), is quite high. The importer might have been better off purchasing the £1,000 for $2,100 on October 1.

ACCOUNTING FOR FORWARD SALE CONTRACTS

A **forward sale contract** gives the holder the obligation to sell foreign currency at a specified time in the future for a known price. An **exporter** enters into a *forward sale contract* so that when foreign customers remit payments in foreign currency to the exporter, the foreign currency can be sold for prearranged quantities of dollars. These contracts also have three components of importance for accounting.

1. The **receivable from the foreign exchange broker** (debit), designated *Due from Exchange Broker*. It consists of the agreed-upon dollar value of the foreign currency to be sold. This is the quantity of foreign currency translated at the applicable *forward rate*. This *receivable is denominated in dollars*, is unaffected by any change in the exchange rate, and generates no transaction gain or loss.
2. The **forward sale contract** (credit), representing the obligation to deliver the foreign currency. It is *denominated in units of the foreign currency* and is recorded at the current dollar equivalent of the currency to be sold; its dollar value changes with the *spot rate*, and transaction gains and losses accrue on it.
3. The **premium or discount on the forward contract** (credit or debit), the difference between the current and future values of the currency to be sold. As before, this is generally attributable to interest rate differentials or expected exchange rate changes and is accounted for separately from any transaction adjustment on the forward sale contract.

Forward Sale Contract Illustration

As an example of a forward sales contract, suppose that goods were *sold* to a British customer on December 1 at a price stated in pounds, £1,000, when the spot rate is $2.10/£. Payment in pounds will be received in 30 days. Because the account receivable is denominated in pounds, it is exposed to risk of exchange rate movements. To hedge this **exposed asset**, the receivable from the British customer, a forward sale contract calling for delivery of £1,000 to the broker in 30 days, is entered on December 1. If the 30-day forward rate is $2.20/£, the *receivable from the exchange broker* is fixed at $2,200 (= $2.20 × 1,000) and is not affected by subsequent movements in the exchange rate. Thus the £1,000 received from the British customer will be sold for $2,200. Translating the £1,000 at the spot rate of $2.10 gives us the current value of the obligation to deliver the foreign currency, $2,100 (= $2.10 × 1,000), which we call the *forward* *sale contract.* Because the foreign currency was sold in the forward market for *more* than the current spot rate, a *premium on the forward sale contract* of $100 [= ($2.20 − $2.10) 1,000] results. The entries recording (1) the sale of goods and (2) the forward sale contract on December 1 are given below:

December 1

Accounts Receivable 2,100
     Sales 2,100
    To record the sale of goods to the British customer;
    $2,100 = $2.10 × 1,000.

Due from Exchange Broker ($2.20 × 1,000) 2,200
    Premium on Forward Contract [($2.20 − $2.10) 1,000] . . 100
    Forward Sale Contract ($2.10 × 1,000) 2,100
    To record the forward sale contract entered to hedge the
    receivable from the British customer.

On December 31, the British customer pays the £1,000, which is then delivered to the broker in settlement of the forward contract. The spot rate rose to $2.14/£. Because the receivable must be collected before the forward contract can be settled in this case, the first two entries made on December 31 relate to the transaction gain on the account receivable and the collection of the receivable:

December 31

Accounts Receivable 40
    Transaction Gain 40
    To recognize the transaction gain accrued on the
    account receivable; $40 = ($2.14 − $2.10) 1,000.

Foreign Currency 2,140
    Accounts Receivable 2,140
    To record collection of the receivable from the
    British customer; $2,140 = $2.14 × 1,000 = $2,100 + $40.

Now that the receivable is collected, £1,000 is available for delivery to the broker. We accrue the transaction loss on the forward contract and settle the contract:

December 31

Transaction Loss 40
    Forward Sale Contract 40
    To recognize the transaction loss accrued on the
    forward contract; $40 = ($2.14 − $2.10) 1,000.

Forward Sale Contract 2,140
    Foreign Currency 2,140
    To record delivery of the foreign currency to the
    broker; $2,140 = $2.14 × 1,000 = $2,100 + $40.

Cash 2,200
        Due from Exchange Broker 2,200
     To record the $2,200 received from the broker.

Premium on Forward Contract 100
        Revenue—Premium Amortization 100
     To amortize the premium on the forward contract.

The same exchange rates were used in the purchase and sale illustrations just presented to aid in comparison. Just as the transaction adjustments were offsetting in the purchase case, the transaction loss on the forward sale contract exactly offsets the transaction gain on the account receivable in the sale case; both cases represent perfect hedges. Unlike the purchase hedge, however, the sale hedge did turn out to be profitable. Even though the transaction gain of $40 was negated, a premium of $100 over the original spot rate was received. That is, $2,200 was received for £1,000, which could have been sold on December 31 for only $2,140. In the purchase case, $2,200 was paid for £1,000, which could have been bought on December 31 for $2,140. Those entities selling pounds sterling benefited from the structure of exchange rates during this time period whereas those entities purchasing pounds sterling did not.

DETERMINING WHETHER A DISCOUNT OR PREMIUM EXISTS ON A FORWARD CONTRACT

A premium on a forward contract exists when the forward rate exceeds the spot rate; a discount exists when the forward rate is less than the spot rate. To assist in accounting for a premium or discount on a forward contract, the following rules may be used:

		Income Effects of Discounts and Premiums on Forward Contracts		
Case	Type of Contract	Forward Rate (FR) $\geq$ Spot Rate(SR)	Discount/ Premium	Income Statement Effect
1	Forward sale	FR<SR	Discount (Dr)	Expense
2	Forward Purchase	FR<SR	Discount (Cr)	Revenue
3	Forward sale	FR>SR	Premium (Cr)	Revenue
4	Forward purchase	FR>SR	Premium (Dr)	Expense

As an alternative to the above, one may think of these discounts and premiums in terms of **differentials**. For example, when the foreign currency is sold forward and the forward rate is *less than* the current spot rate as in Case 1, a **debit differential** arises. Similarly, if the foreign currency is purchased forward and the forward rate is *greater than* the current spot rate as in Case 4, a debit differential also arises.

USING FORWARD CONTRACTS TO HEDGE FIRM FOREIGN CURRENCY COMMITMENTS

Many transactions are preceded by the issuance of purchase orders or other contractual agreements. Known as **executory contracts**, these are contracts in which performance has not occurred. Forward contracts may therefore be entered when a purchase order is issued but before the underlying transaction occurs and is recorded. Indeed, a forward contract is itself an executory contract. For this reason, only the net premium or discount on forward contracts is reported in financial statements.

If a forward contract is entered into *before* a transaction denominated in the foreign currency is recorded, and meets the conditions described below, it is considered a **hedge of a firm foreign currency commitment.** Should the contract remain in effect, or be entered into, *after* a payable or receivable transaction denominated in the foreign currency is recorded, it is then treated as a **hedge of an exposed asset or liability position.** These situations are depicted as follows for a *forward purchase contract*:

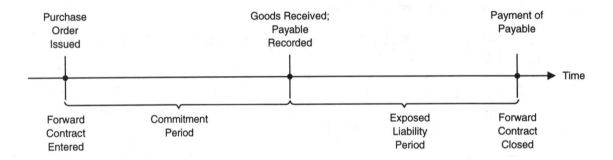

A forward contract serves as a *hedge of a firm foreign currency commitment* when the following conditions are met:

- The contract is designated as, and is effective as, a hedge of a foreign currency commitment. An **effective hedge** is one that achieves its stated risk-neutralizing purpose.
- The foreign currency commitment is firm.

Because the FASB did not define "firm" in *SFAS 52*, questions arose whether particular commitments were sufficiently firm to justify hedge accounting for the hedge instrument. A definition appears in *SFAS 80*, discussed in Chapter 11, indicating that a **firm commitment** must be legally enforceable and possess more than a nominal penalty for nonperformance.[6] The FASB 1997 *Draft Statement* defines a firm commitment as "an agreement with an unrelated third party, usually legally enforceable, under which performance is probable because of a sufficiently large disincentive for nonperformance."[7]

---

[6] Financial Accounting Standards Board, *Statement of Financial Accounting Standards No. 80*, "Accounting for Futures Contracts" (Norwalk, CT: FASB, 1984).

[7] 1997 *Draft Statement*, "Accounting for Derivative Instruments and Hedging Activities," Appendix D.

The forward contract need not be in the currency being committed. Under *SFAS 52*, contracts in currencies *economically linked to* (that is, moving in tandem with) the currency being committed can function as hedges so long as the conditions above are satisfied. Moreover, other foreign currency transactions such as loans or investments can serve as hedges of identifiable foreign currency commitments when they satisfy the above conditions. Treatment of exchange gains and losses on such other transactions parallels the forward contract case. Functioning as an *effective hedge* means that the transaction gain or loss accruing on the hedge is opposite from the transaction gain or loss accruing on the foreign currency position or commitment being hedged. For example, when the foreign currency position being hedged produces a transaction *loss* and the hedge produces a transaction *gain*, the hedge is *effective*.

In the case of a firm foreign currency commitment, a company may enter into a hedge investment *prior to* booking the exposure: the account receivable or account payable. Gains or losses on the hedging instrument are therefore incurred before the exposure occurs, causing difficulties in matching the hedge gains and losses against the hedged item's losses and gains. The accounting for a hedge of an identifiable foreign currency commitment, prescribed in *SFAS 52*, differs from that provided by the 1997 FASB *Draft Statement*. Both accounting treatments are presented below.

SFAS 52 ACCOUNTING FOR FOREIGN CURRENCY COMMITMENTS

SFAS 52 specifies that transaction adjustments accruing on the forward contract during the commitment period are *deferred* and are used to adjust the dollar basis of the purchase or sale when it occurs.

> A forward contract serving as a **hedge of a firm foreign currency commitment** is viewed as an *integral part of the purchase or sale transaction* to which the commitment relates.

When the hedge is entered, it fixes the dollar equivalent of the transaction, subject to slight modification depending on the accounting treatment of the premium or discount on the forward contract. If the forward contract is of sufficient duration to also hedge the exposed asset or liability arising when the transaction is recorded, it also fixes the number of dollars ultimately to be paid or received. The examples that follow illustrate these points.

Hedging a Foreign Currency Purchase Commitment

For the importer, *a firm foreign currency commitment* is based on a purchase order issued prior to actual receipt of the goods. As mentioned, a forward contract entered when the purchase order is issued is viewed as an integral part of the purchase transaction. Any *transaction gain or loss* accruing on the forward contract during the commitment period is *deferred* until the payable to the foreign supplier is booked. At the time the purchase is recorded, the deferred transaction gain or loss is included in the dollar basis of the purchase transaction. After this, transaction gains and losses accruing on both the forward contract and the payable are recorded but are offsetting. The *premium or discount* may either be :

- deferred until the transaction is recorded or
- amortized proportionately over the life of the contract.

When the premium or discount is deferred until the transaction is recorded, the portion pertaining to the commitment period is used to adjust the dollar basis of the transaction, as entered in the Purchases (or Inventory) account.

To illustrate a purchase commitment hedge, assume that on August 10, 19X2, Acme International issues a purchase order to Queens, Ltd., a U.K. exporter, to purchase fabric valued at £100,000; the spot rate is $1.80/£. Delivery of the fabric in the United States is expected on November 30, 19X2, and payment is due on January 10, 19X3. This future payment of £100,000 is a firm foreign currency commitment, and Acme elects to hedge it by purchasing £100,000 for delivery on January 10, 19X3. The **commitment period** runs from August 10, 19X2, to November 30, 19X2, a period of 3⅔ months. With a 5-month forward rate of $1.83/£, the forward contract results in a premium of $3,000, which Acme elects to defer. The time line for this sequence of events is shown below.

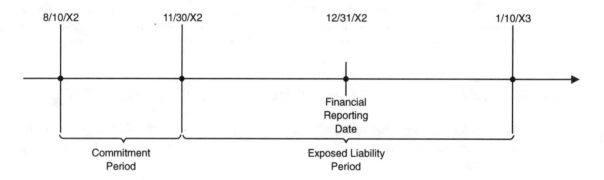

Hedging During the Purchase Commitment Period. Because the purchase order for the fabric does not generate an accounting entry, the only entry made during the *commitment period* recognizes the forward contract at its inception, as shown below:

August 10, 19X2

Forward Purchase Contract ($1.80 × 100,000)	180,000	
Premium on Forward Contract [($1.83 − $1.80) 100,000] . . .	3,000	
Due to Exchange Broker ($1.83 × 100,000)		183,000
To record the forward purchase contract engaged in to hedge		
the firm foreign currency commitment to Queens, Ltd.		

The commitment period expires once the fabric is received and the purchase transaction is recorded. After the purchase and related payable are recorded, the forward contract acts as a **hedge of an exposed liability**—the account payable. Because the payable is denominated in pounds, its dollar value changes as the $/£ exchange rate changes. Thus the payable is *exposed* to foreign exchange rate risk.

At the time the purchase and related payable are recorded, the accountant must also record the deferred transaction adjustment accrued on the forward purchase contract during the commitment period. Then, Purchases must be adjusted by (1) the deferred transaction adjustment on the forward purchase contract and (2) the portion of the premium on the forward purchase contract pertaining to the commitment period. (The company had elected to defer, rather than amortize, the premium during the commitment period.) The spot rate at November 30, 19X2, is $1.82/£. The entries are as follows:

November 30, 19X2

Forward Purchase Contract   2,000

    Deferred Transaction Gain   2,000

    To record as *deferred* the transaction gain accrued on the
forward purchase contract during the commitment period;
$2,000 = ($1.82 − $1.80) 100,000.

Purchases or Inventory   182,000

    Accounts Payable   182,000

    To record the purchase of fabric from Queens, Ltd.,
in the United Kingdom; $182,000 = $1.82 × 100,000.

Deferred Transaction Gain   2,000

    Purchases or Inventory   2,000

    To adjust the dollar basis of Purchases recorded by the
accrued transaction gain on the forward exchange contract
during the commitment period.

In the last entry, Purchases is decreased by the deferred transaction gain of $2,000 that accrued on the forward purchase contract during the commitment period. At this point, Purchases has a balance of $180,000 (= $182,000 − $2,000), the amount originally recorded as Forward Purchase Contract on August 10. As mentioned, though, treatment of the premium can cause Purchases to differ from $180,000. This is illustrated in the next entry.

Purchases or Inventory   2,200

    Premium on Forward Contract   2,200

    To adjust the dollar basis of Purchases recorded by
the portion of the premium on the forward contract
pertaining to the commitment period.

The entry above shows how *deferral* of the premium can affect recorded Purchases. Recall that the commitment period covered 3⅔ months of the 5-month forward purchase contract, so that $2,200 [= [((3⅔)/5) × $3,000] is recorded as an increase in Purchases. If the premium was *amortized*—charged to income at financial reporting dates—Purchases would remain at $180,000.

Hedge of Exposed Liability at Balance Sheet Date. At December 31, 19X2, a financial reporting date, both the payable to Queens, Ltd., and the forward purchase contract are still outstanding. The forward purchase contract is now hedging an exposed liability position. The spot rate rose to $1.84/£ at December 31 from $1.82/£ on November 30. In the next two entries, the transaction adjustments on these items are accrued.

December 31, 19X2

Transaction Loss   2,000

    Accounts Payable   2,000

    To record the transaction loss accrued on the liability
to Queens, Ltd.; $2,000 = ($1.84 − $1.82) 100,000.

| Forward Purchase Contract . . . . | 2,000 | |
| Transaction Gain . . . . | | 2,000 |

To record the transaction gain accrued on the
forward purchase contract for £100,000;
$2,000 = ($1.84 − $1.82) 100,000.

Note that the transaction loss on the account payable is offset by the transaction gain on the forward purchase contract. Amortization of the premium for December, 19X2 is as follows:

December 31, 19X2

| Expense—Premium Amortization . . . . | 600 | |
| Premium on Forward Contract . . . . | | 600 |

To amortize the one-fifth of the premium related to
December 19X2; $600 = .2 × $3,000.

Balance Sheet Reporting. When we introduced forward contracts as hedging instruments, we noted that *forward contracts are reported at net* in the balance sheet. Acme International's forward *purchase* contract in this example is reported on the December 31, 19X2 balance sheet as a current asset with a *debit balance of $1,200*, determined as follows:

Forward purchase contract ($180,000 + $2,000 + $2,000)	$ 184,000
Unamortized premium on forward contract ($3,000 − $2,200 − $600)	200
Due to exchange broker	(183,000)
Net *debit balance* at December 31, 19X2	$ 1,200

Settlement of Payable and Forward Contract. On January 10, 19X3, the forward purchase contract matures, and the payable to Queens, Ltd., becomes due. The spot rate is $1.835/£. The next six entries record the closing out of the forward purchase contract, amortization of the remaining premium, disbursement of the foreign currency to Queens, Ltd., and accrual of the offsetting transaction loss and gain on the forward purchase contract and the account payable.

January 10, 19X3

| Transaction Loss . . . . | 500 | |
| Forward Purchase Contract . . . . | | 500 |

To recognize the transaction loss accrued on the forward
purchase contract since December 31, 19X2;
$500 = ($1.84 − $1.835) 100,000.

| Due to Exchange Broker . . . . | 183,000 | |
| Cash . . . . | | 183,000 |

To record payment to the foreign exchange broker.

| Foreign Currency . . . . | 183,500 | |
| Forward Purchase Contract . . . . | | 183,500 |

To record receipt of the foreign currency from the
broker; $183,500 = $1.835 × 100,000.

Expense—Premium Amortization	200	
Premium on Forward Contract		200

To expense the remaining premium on the forward
contract; $200 = $3,000 − ($2,200 + $600).

Accounts Payable	500	
Transaction Gain		500

To recognize the transaction gain accrued on the
account payable since December 31, 19X2;
$500 = ($1.84 − $1.835) 100,000.

Accounts Payable	183,500	
Foreign Currency		183,500

To record payment of the liability to Queens, Ltd.;
$183,500 = $180,000 + $2,000 + $2,000 − $500.

To summarize, the importer uses the hedging process to fix the dollar amount of the liability to the foreign supplier at $183,000. Of the $3,000 premium, $2,200 went to increase Purchases and the other $800 was expensed. Had the hedging not taken place in the above example, Acme would lose $3,500 [= ($1.835 − $1.80) 100,000] due to the adverse exchange rate movement from the time the purchase was negotiated in November to final payment the following January. Because it paid a premium of $3,000 to avoid this loss, the hedging saved Acme $500 (= $3,500 − $3,000).

Hedging a Foreign Currency Sale Commitment

In the sale case, the exporter will receive foreign currency and contracts in the forward market to sell it for dollars to a broker at a specified time in the future for a given price. When the contract is entered before the exporter records the foreign sale and the conditions specified in *SFAS 52* are met, we have a hedge of a firm foreign currency commitment. Any transaction gain or loss that accrues during the commitment period is deferred and generates an adjustment to the dollar basis of the sale transaction. The premium or discount is either amortized proportionately over the life of the forward contract or deferred. When the premium or discount is deferred, that portion relating to the commitment period is used to adjust the dollar basis of the sale transaction. When the contract remains in force after the sale and receivable are recorded, it becomes a *hedge of an exposed asset*—in this case, the receivable. During this time, the remaining premium or discount is amortized. Any transaction gain or loss accruing on the forward sale contract is now recognized at a financial reporting date and is not deferred. The commitment period and the exposed asset period for a forward sale contract are depicted below:

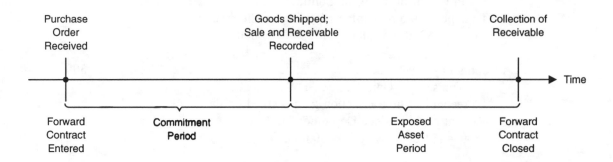

We illustrate the accounting for a forward sale contract used to hedge a foreign sale commitment with an example in which the sale transaction, collection, and settlement of the forward contract take place simultaneously. Therefore, the forward sale contract is hedging *only* the foreign currency commitment; there is *no* exposed asset to be hedged following the sale.

Suppose that Acme International negotiated a sale of wool coats to Corsin, a Canadian retailer, on October 21, 19X2. Corsin is to pay on January 19, 19X3, when the coats are delivered and the sale is recorded. The sale price was stated in Canadian dollars ($CN) and amounted to $CN50,000. On October 21, 19X2, the spot rate was $.70/$CN. Concurrently, Acme sold $CN50,000 for future delivery on January 19, 19X3, at a forward rate of $.68/$CN. Acme elects to *amortize* the discount of $1,000 over the life of the contract. Because the discount is not deferred, no portion of it is used to adjust the dollar value of the sale transaction. The time line for this example appears below.

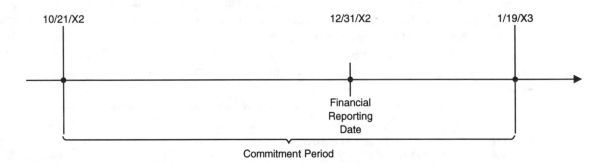

Subsequent spot rates were $.705/$CN on December 31, 19X2, and $.67/$CN on January 19, 19X3. Note that the balance sheet date of December 31, 19X2, falls during the commitment period, after 71 days of the 90-day commitment period expired. The entries recording events in the example follow:

October 21, 19X2

Due from Exchange Broker ($.68 × 50,000)	34,000	
Discount on Forward Contract [($.70 − $.68) 50,000]	1,000	
Forward Sale Contract ($.70 × 50,000)		35,000
To record the forward sale contract engaged in to hedge		
the firm foreign currency commitment with Corsin.		

December 31, 19X2

Deferred Transaction Loss	250	
Forward Sale Contract		250
To record the transaction loss accrued on the forward		
sale contract for $CN50,000 between October 21 and		
December 31; $250 = ($.705 − $.70) 50,000.		

Expense—Discount Amortization	789	
Discount on Forward Contract		789
To amortize the portion of the discount relating to		
19X2; $789 = (71/90) $1,000.		

Thus at the end of 19X2, the forward sale contract is restated to $35,250 and the resulting $250 transaction loss is deferred pending completion of the sale to Corsin. Because Corsin elected *not* to defer the discount on the forward contract, the $789 portion of the discount pertaining to 19X2 is expensed via amortization.

Balance Sheet Reporting. Acme International's forward *sale* contract in this example is reported on the December 31, 19X2 balance sheet as a current liability with a *credit balance of $1,039*, determined as follows:

Forward sale contract ($48,000 + $250)	$(35,250)
Unamortized discount on forward contract ($1,000 − $789)	211
Deferred Transaction Loss	250
Due from exchange broker	34,000
Net *credit balance* at December 31, 19X2	$ (789)

Recognition of Sale and Settlement of Forward Contract. When the commitment period ends and the sale is made on January 19, 19X3, foreign currency is collected from Corsin and exchanged for dollars with the broker to settle the forward contract. Note also that the Sales account is increased by the net deferred transaction adjustment on the forward contract at January 19, a $1,500 gain.

January 19, 19X3

Foreign Currency	33,500	
Sales		33,500
To record sale of wool coats to Corsin of Canada		
and receipt of foreign currency from Corsin;		
$33,500 = $.67 × $CN50,000.		

Forward Sale Contract	1,750	
Deferred Transaction Gain		1,750

To recognize the deferred transaction gain accrued
on the forward sale contract between December 31, 19X2
and January 19, 19X3; $1,750 = ($.705 − $.67) 50,000.

Forward Sale Contract	33,500	
Foreign Currency		33,500

To record disbursement of the foreign currency to
the broker; $33,500 = $35,000 + $250 − $1,750.

Cash	34,000	
Due from Exchange Broker		34,000

To record payment received from the foreign exchange
broker.

Deferred Transaction Gain	1,750	
Deferred Transaction Loss		250
Sales		1,500

To adjust the dollar basis of recorded sales by the net
deferred transaction gain accrued on the forward contract
during the commitment period; $1,500 = $1,750 − $250.

Expense—Discount Amortization	211	
Discount on Forward Contract		211

To expense the remaining discount on the forward
contract in 19X3; $211 = (19/90) $1,000.

Here the exporter used the hedging process to fix the dollar amount to be received from the foreign customer at $34,000. If hedging was not undertaken, Acme would lose $1,500 [= ($.70 − $.67) × 50,000]. Because this loss was avoided, Acme actually saved $500 (= $1,500 − $1,000 discount) by using the forward market. Sales are recorded at $35,000 (= $33,500 + $1,500 net deferred transaction gain). The $1,000 discount was amortized and expensed, $789 in 19X2 and $211 in 19X3. Had the discount been deferred and used to adjust Sales, the amount recorded as Sales equals $34,000 (= $35,000 − $1,000).

In this example, the forward contract expired when the transaction was recorded at the end of the commitment period. The foreign currency was collected immediately and delivered to the broker, so there was no exposed asset to be hedged. If the receivable was not collected immediately and the forward sale contract extended beyond the transaction date, offsetting transaction gains and losses would accrue. Additionally, the remaining period of the forward sale contract absorbs a portion of the discount amortization.

FASB *DRAFT STATEMENT* ACCOUNTING FOR FOREIGN CURRENCY COMMITMENTS

Under the 1997 *Draft Statement*, gains and losses on the hedging instrument are **not** deferred, but are instead recognized in earnings as exchange rates change. Losses or gains on the hedged item—the sales or purchase order—are also recognized in earnings as exchange rates change. The accounting procedures are illustrated using Acme's hedge of a foreign currency sale commitment.

The original entry on October 21, 19X2 is the same as under *SFAS 52*.

October 21, 19X2

Due from Exchange Broker	34,000	
Discount on Forward Contract	1,000	
Forward Sale Contract		35,000

To record the forward sale contract engaged in to hedge the firm foreign currency commitment with Corsin.

However, on the December 31, 19X2 balance sheet date, the following adjusting entries are made:

December 31, 19X2

Transaction Loss	250	
Forward Sale Contract		250

To record the transaction loss accrued on the forward sale contract for $CN50,000 between October 21 and December 31; $250 = ($.705 - $.70) 50,000.

Foreign Exchange Receivable	250	
Transaction Gain		250

To record the transaction gain accrued on the sale commitment for the period October 21 to December 31, 19X2.

Note that the transaction gain is recognized, but there is no existing account against which to offset the gain since the commitment has not yet been booked. Therefore a "Foreign Exchange Receivable" is recognized, which will be offset against Sales when the commitment is recognized as a sale. Both the gain and the loss appear on Acme's income statement for 19X2. Amortization of the discount on the forward contract is the same as under *SFAS 52*.

Expense-Discount Amortization	789	
Discount on Forward Contract		789

To amortize the portion of the discount relating to 19X2; $789 = (71/90)$1,000.

On January 19, 19X3, the following entries are made:

January 19, 19X3

Forward Sale Contract	1,750	
Transaction Gain		1,750

To recognize the transaction gain accrued on the forward sale contract between December 31, 19X2 and January 19, 19X3; $1,750 = ($.705 - $.67) 50,000.

Transaction Loss 1,750
     Foreign Exchange Payable 1,750
To recognize the transaction loss accrued on the sale
commitment for the period December 31, 19X2
to January 19, 19X3. Again, the "Foreign
Exchange Payable" will be offset against Sales
when the sales revenue is recognized.

Expense-Discount Amortization 211
     Discount on Forward Contract 211
To expense the remaining discount on the
forward contract in 19X3; $211 = (19/90) $1,000.

Foreign Currency 33,500
     Sales 33,500
To record sale of wool coats to Corsin of Canada
and receipt of foreign currency from Corsin; $33,500
= $.67 × $CN50,000.

Foreign Exchange Payable 1,750
     Foreign Exchange Receivable 250
     Sales 1,500
To adjust the dollar basis of recorded sales by
the net transaction gain accrued on the
forward contract during the commitment period;
$1,500 = $1,750 - $250.

Forward Sale Contract 33,500
     Foreign Currency 33,500
To record disbursement of the foreign currency
to the broker; $33,500 = $35,000 + $250 - $1,750.

Cash 34,000
     Due from Exchange Broker 34,000
To record payment received from the foreign
exchange broker.

Note that the net effect is the same as under *SFAS 52*; although the gains and losses on the hedge are recognized currently rather than deferred, they cancel each other out on the income statement. The net position in the hedge investment is then offset against the hedged item, in this case Sales, which is the same as netting the gains and losses on the hedge against the hedged item's carrying value.

USING FORWARD CONTRACTS TO HEDGE FORECASTED TRANSACTIONS

Under *SFAS 52*, hedge accounting does not apply to forecasted, planned or anticipated transactions which are not firm commitments. However, it is common practice for companies to hedge planned transactions, even though there is no firm commitment involved. *SFAS 52* treats hedges of forecasted transactions as if they are speculative contracts, with gains and losses recognized in income currently—see coverage of speculative contracts later in the chapter. The FASB *Draft Statement* corrects this deficiency by specifying accounting for hedges of forecasted transactions. The *Draft Statement* allows for **deferral** of exchange gains and losses on hedges of forecasted transactions, as a component of comprehensive income, outside of earnings. These gains and losses are recognized in earnings when the hedged forecasted transaction impacts earnings, thereby matching the income effect of the hedge instrument against the income effect of the hedged item.

Forecasted transactions must meet stringent criteria in order to qualify for delayed recognition of gains and losses accruing to the hedge instrument. These criteria include:

- The forecasted transaction must be identified, probable, part of an established business activity, and expose the company to exchange risk.
- There is formal documentation of the hedging relationship and the entity's risk management strategy for undertaking the hedge.
- The hedging relationship is expected to be highly effective and is assessed on a regular basis.
- The forecasted transaction involves an exchange with a third party external to the reporting entity.

If these criteria are not met, the hedge instrument is accounted for as if it is speculative.

The following illustrates the proposed accounting for forecasted transactions. A company plans to purchase merchandise at the end of July, 19X5, from a supplier in France for 1,000,000 francs. To hedge against a possible weakening of the U.S. dollar against the franc, the company enters a forward contract on June 2, 19X5, for delivery of 1,000,000 francs on July 31 at a forward rate of $.17.

Under the *Draft Statement*, the forward purchase contract is valued at its market value, without separating out the premium or discount. Since no cash changes hands initially, the company probably does not make a formal entry to record the initial agreement. However, for illustrative purposes it is clearer to show the following entry:

June 2, 19X5

Forward Purchase Contract	170,000	
Due to Exchange Broker		170,000
To record the forward contract; $170,000 =		
$.17 × 1,000,000.		

On June 30, 19X5, the company's balance sheet date, assume that the forward rate for delivery on July 31, 19X5 is $.172. The forward contract's market value has therefore increased by ($.172 - $.17) × 1,000,000 = $2,000.

June 30, 19X5

Forward Purchase Contract	2,000	
Unrealized Gain (comprehensive income item)		2,000

To record the increase in the market value of the
forward contract for the period June 2 to
June 30, 19X5; $2,000 = ($.172 - $.17) × 1,000,000.

On July 31, 19X5, the company buys the foreign currency using the forward purchase contract and makes the forecasted purchase. Assume the spot rate is now $.182, so the value of the forward purchase contract increased by ($.182 - $.17) × 1,000,000 = $12,000 less the $2,000 gain recognized on June 30.

July 31, 19X5

Forward Purchase Contract	10,000	
Unrealized Gain (comprehensive income item)		10,000

To record the increase in the market value of the forward
contract for the period June 30 to July 31, 19X5;
$10,000 = ($.182 - $.172) × 1,000,000.

Due to Exchange Broker	170,000	
Cash		170,000

To record payment to the foreign exchange broker.

Foreign Currency	182,000	
Forward Purchase Contract		182,000

To record receipt of the foreign currency from the broker;
$182,000 = $.182 × 1,000,000.

Inventory	182,000	
Foreign Currency		182,000

To record acquisition of the inventory under the purchase
commitment.

The gain on the hedge instrument, the forward purchase contract, is deferred until the forecasted transaction impacts earnings. In this case, the transaction gain is deferred until the inventory is sold. Assume the inventory is sold on August 21, 19X5. The entries are as follows:

August 21, 19X5

Cost of Goods Sold	182,000	
Inventory		182,000

To record sale of the inventory.

Unrealized Gain (comprehensive income item)	12,000	
Transaction Gain		12,000

To record recognition of the deferred gain in
current earnings; $12,000 = $2,000 + $10,000.

DECISIONS INVOLVING HEDGING

The use of forward contracts for hedging was examined extensively in the preceding sections. Although the hedges discussed were effective, firms still must decide whether hedging is the best way to neutralize exchange rate risk. On several occasions we contrasted the effects of hedging versus not hedging by comparing, *ex post*, the forward rate paid (received) at inception of the forward contract with the spot rate existing when settlement is made. For example, if the forward rate in a purchase contract was $1.00/FC and the spot rate is $1.10/FC when the firm liquidates its payable, the firm gained $.10/FC by hedging in addition to neutralizing the exchange rate risk. But if the spot rate is $.95/FC at settlement, the firm lost $.05/FC by hedging. An obvious alternative to hedging involves purchasing the foreign currency up front.

A firm could *avoid exchange rate risk by purchasing the foreign currency up front* and either paying immediately or holding the currency until payment is due. In the latter case, a large-enough amount of foreign currency could probably be placed in a foreign short-term interest-bearing investment.

To illustrate, suppose the Knutson Company has a FC1,000,000 payable due in 60 days; the current spot rate is $1.00/FC and the 60-day forward rate is $1.01/FC.

Case 1: Forward Contract. If Knutson enters a 60-day forward purchase contract, $1,010,000 (= $1.01 × 1,000,000) is required when the contract matures to purchase FC1,000,000 from the broker and liquidate the payable.

Case 2: Purchase FC Now. By purchasing FC1,000,000 now and holding the currency for 60 days (or paying now), Knutson liquidates the payable for $1,000,000, a saving of $10,000 over the forward contract. However, interest is a relevant cost or benefit in this analysis. Knutson may be able to earn interest on the FC1,000,000 by investing it in a foreign short-term interest-bearing instrument. On the other hand, by investing $1,000,000 in foreign currency now, Knutson may give up interest on possible alternative investments of the $1,000,000. If Knutson must borrow to acquire the foreign currency, the interest expense on the loan must be taken into account. In summary, the $10,000 savings on acquiring the FC1,000,000 now represents only one part of the larger economic picture. Knutson must consider all effects—additional interest revenue, interest expense, or interest lost—in evaluating the choice between a forward contract and purchasing the foreign currency now.

In sum, a firm may be able to neutralize exchange rate risk with a strategy that does not involve hedging. Be sure to consider all relevant costs when analyzing such situations.

FOREIGN LENDING AND BORROWING TRANSACTIONS

Growth in the volume of international capital flows indicates that substantial investment funds move across national boundaries. U.S. companies engage in the following investment transactions requiring foreign currency conversions:

- Investment in securities of foreign companies, banks, and governments.
- Borrowing from foreign lenders.
- Direct investment in branches and subsidiaries abroad.

Loans and investments in securities of foreign entities often require the U.S. firm to convert dollars into foreign currency to acquire the security and then to convert the foreign currency into dollars when the security matures or is sold. Similarly, borrowing from abroad may mean that the U.S. firm borrows a quantity of foreign currency, converts it into dollars for use domestically, and later purchases sufficient foreign currency to repay the amount borrowed. Direct investment in branches and subsidiaries abroad usually involves setting up a business operation, acquiring assets, and incurring debts in the foreign country. The problems associated with translation of these items for inclusion in U.S. company financial statements were addressed in Chapter 9.

When an interest-bearing investment or note payable is denominated in a foreign currency, what exchange rate should the U.S. firm use to translate the foreign interest income or expense? Theoretically, the average exchange rate in effect while the foreign interest is accruing should be used. Yet the receivable, payable, or collection or disbursement of cash when the accrued interest is recorded is translated at the current exchange rate. Taken together, these practices result in a discrepancy between the revenue or expense and the asset or liability when exchange rates are fluctuating. We avoid this by *translating accrued interest income and expense at the current spot rate when the interest is recorded*. When interest receivable and interest payable are recorded, they are subject to transaction gains or losses caused by subsequent movements in the exchange rate.

Because all such transactions expose the U.S. firm to the risk of changes in the exchange rate, they may either (1) require a hedge, such as a forward contract, to offset the risk or (2) serve as a hedge to offset the risk on another foreign currency transaction. Note that a forward contract could be entered to hedge an exposed asset or liability represented by a single transaction, such as a foreign investment, trade receivable, or trade payable. Alternatively, a forward contract could be entered to hedge an *exposed net asset or liability position* comprised of the firm's **net monetary assets or liabilities**—cash, claims to receive cash, and obligations to disburse cash—denominated in foreign currencies. These **monetary items** represent *fixed* quantities of foreign currency and are not susceptible to price changes; only movements in the exchange rate cause their dollar equivalents to change. In either case, the following accounting treatment is required for foreign contracts that hedge exposed assets or liabilities in foreign currencies:

- Accrued transaction gains or losses are to be recognized currently in income and not deferred. Current recognition offsets the transaction gain or loss on the items being hedged.
- A premium or discount on a forward contract must be amortized to income over the life of the contract.

ILLUSTRATION OF A FOREIGN LENDING TRANSACTION

As an example, we consider a U.S. investment in a foreign bank certificate of deposit (CD). On August 15, 19X2, Acme International purchases a 90-day CD from a Swiss bank. The certificate has a face value of 1,000,000 Swiss francs (SF1,000,000), costs $600,000 (the spot rate is $.60/SF), and pays interest at an annual rate of 10 percent. The entry to record purchase of the CD is:

August 15, 19X2

Temporary Investments	600,000	
Cash		600,000
To record purchase of a Swiss CD with face value of		
SF1,000,000.		

On November 13, 19X2, the certificate of deposit matures and Acme receives principal and interest of SF1,025,000 [= SF1,000,000 +.1(SF1,000,000)/4]; the spot rate is $.59/SF. The following three entries record the transaction adjustment on the certificate, recognize receipt of the foreign currency from the Swiss bank, including interest earned; and record the conversion of the Swiss francs into dollars.

November 13, 19X2

Transaction Loss	10,000	
Temporary Investments		10,000

To recognize the transaction loss accrued on the certificate of deposit; $10,000 = ($.60 − $.59) 1,000,000.

Foreign Currency ($.59 × 1,025,000)	604,750	
Temporary Investments ($600,000 − $10,000)		590,000
Interest Income ($.59 × 25,000)		14,750

To record foreign currency received at maturity of the CD and record the interest income translated at the current spot rate.

Cash	604,750	
Foreign Currency		604,750

To record the exchange of SF1,025,000 for $604,750.

Borrowing and lending transactions of the type just illustrated present no particular accounting problems. When they are used to hedge a firm foreign currency commitment, forecasted transaction, or exposed position, accounting treatment of their transaction gains and losses follows that prescribed for forward contracts.

ECONOMIC HEDGE OF A NET INVESTMENT IN A FOREIGN ENTITY

In addition to the hedges already mentioned, *SFAS 52* also recognizes as hedges those forward contracts or other foreign currency transactions undertaken to neutralize the effect of exchange rate movements on a U.S. firm's investment in a foreign branch, an equity investee, or a subsidiary. If a hedge is so designated and is effective, it is viewed as an **economic hedge of a net investment in a foreign entity**. Accounting treatment of the transaction gain or loss on such "economic hedges" depends on the **functional currency** of the foreign entity (the currency in which the foreign entity generates most of its net cash flows), a concept discussed in Chapter 9.

Recall that when the *functional currency* of the foreign entity is the *U.S. dollar*, the *translation* adjustment is included in net income; a *transaction* adjustment accruing on the hedge of the net investment in such an entity is also included in net income. When a forward contract is used as the hedge, any premium or discount is amortized over the life of the contract.

In contrast, when the *functional currency* of the foreign entity is the *foreign currency* of the entity's home country, the *translation* adjustment is carried directly to a separate component of stockholders' equity—the Cumulative Translation Adjustment account—and bypasses periodic net income although it appears as a component of comprehensive income. A *transaction* adjustment accruing on the hedge of the net investment in such an entity also affects the Cumulative Translation Adjustment account. When a forward contract is used to hedge the net investment in this type of entity, any premium or discount is either amortized over the life of the contract *or* carried directly to the Cumulative Translation Adjustment account.

USE OF FORWARD CONTRACTS FOR SPECULATION

Forward contracts entered for hedging purposes represent defensive measures to protect against adverse effects of exchange rate movements. In contrast, firms may sell or purchase foreign currency forward for **speculative purposes**—to gain from anticipated changes in the exchange rate.

To return to the Acme example, suppose that the 180-day forward rate at the time the CD was purchased was $.63/SF. Perhaps Acme's management believed that, despite the 180-day forward rate of $.63/SF, the spot rate for Swiss francs will be $.57/SF in 180 days. To speculate on that eventuality, Acme could sell 5,000,000 Swiss francs forward for delivery in 180 days. Such a contract is for $3,150,000 (= $.63 × 5,000,000). If Acme is correct, in 180 days it will purchase SF5,000,000 for $2,850,000 (= $.57 × 5,000,000) to cover the forward sale and realize a gain of $300,000 (= $3,150,000 − $2,850,000). Should the spot rate in 180 days be above $.63/SF, of course, Acme incurs a loss. *SFAS 52* provides the following accounting rules for such **speculative forward contracts:**

- *Both* the amount due to or from the exchange broker and the forward exchange contract are recorded at the *forward* rate. As a result, neither discount nor premium is separately measured.
- Transaction gains and losses are to be based on the *difference between the forward rate specified in the contract and the forward rate for the period remaining until settlement* and are to be recorded currently.

Note the contrast with the accounting rules governing hedges. Forward exchange contracts used for hedging are measured using the current spot rate; speculative contracts are measured using the forward rate for the remaining period in the contract. Transaction gains and losses for hedges are due to movements in the spot rate; for speculations, they are caused by movements in the forward rate. Finally, any discount or premium is accounted for explicitly in the hedge and implicitly in the speculative contract.

SPECULATIVE FORWARD CONTRACT ILLUSTRATION

As an example, suppose Acme decides to speculate in the Dutch guilder (G) by purchasing, on November 1, 19X2, G8,000,000 for delivery in 90 days. Acme will cover the contract by selling the guilders received when the forward contract matures on January 29, 19X3, in the spot market. December 31, 19X2 is a financial reporting date. Relevant direct exchange rates ($/G) are as follows:

Date	Spot Rate	Forward Rate
November 1, 19X2	$ .500	$.470 (90-day)
December 31, 19X2	.495	.465 (30-day)
January 29, 19X3	.462	—

Acme records the events relating to this speculative forward contract, including sale of the guilders received from the forward contract, as follows:

November 1, 19X2

Forward Purchase Contract	3,760,000	
Due to Exchange Broker		3,760,000

To record a forward purchase contract calling for delivery
of G8,000,000 in 90 days at the forward rate of $.47/G;
$3,760,000 = $.47 × 8,000,000.

December 31, 19X2

Transaction Loss	40,000	
Forward Purchase Contract		40,000

To recognize the transaction loss accrued on the
forward contract, using the 30-day forward rate;
$40,000 = ($.47 − $.465) 8,000,000.

Acme's 12/31/X2 balance sheet reports the net credit balance of this speculative forward contract as a current liability. The ($40,000) amount equals the difference between the ($3,760,000) Due to Exchange Broker and the Forward Purchase Contract of $3,720,000 (= $3,760,000 − $40,000).

January 29, 19X3

Transaction Loss	24,000	
Forward Purchase Contract		24,000

To recognize the transaction loss accrued on the
forward contract since December 31, 19X2;
$24,000 = ($.465 − $.462) 8,000,000.

Foreign Currency	3,696,000	
Forward Purchase Contract		3,696,000

To record receipt of the foreign currency from the broker;
$3,696,000 = $.462 × 8,000,000 = $3,760,000 − $40,000
− $24,000.

Due to Exchange Broker	3,760,000	
Cash		3,760,000

To record payment to the broker.

Cash	3,696,000	
Foreign Currency		3,696,000

To record sale of the G8,000,000 in the spot market at
$.462/G.

We can see clearly that the total transaction loss recognized in the accounts, $64,000 (= $40,000 + $24,000), equals the net cash loss of $64,000 (= $3,760,000 − $3,696,000) from the speculative activity. The speculative contract results in a loss of $64,000 because Acme must purchase G8,000,000 under the contract for $.47, and then sell the foreign currency on the spot market for $.462.

SUMMARY OF ACCOUNTING FOR FORWARD CONTRACTS

In all forward contracts, the account *Due to (from) Exchange Broker* is denominated in dollars. It fixes the number of dollars to be paid to, or received from, the exchange broker based on the appropriate forward rate when the contract is signed. Consequently, it does not move with the exchange rate and does not generate transaction gains and losses. It is the *Forward Purchase (Sale) Contract* account that is denominated in the foreign currency. Its dollar value does change with the exchange rate, and transaction gains and losses accrue to it. In published financial statements, these two accounts are offset against each other and any unamortized premium or discount. Only the net amount is shown as a current asset or liability in the balance sheet. The accounting treatments prescribed for forward exchange contracts by *SFAS 52* are summarized in Exhibit 10.1. The accounting treatments prescribed for forward exchange contracts by the FASB *Draft Statement* are summarized in Exhibit 10.2.

CONCLUDING REMARKS

This completes our discussion of accounting for foreign currency transactions. These transactions produce assets or liabilities on the U.S. company's books denominated in foreign currencies. Although some variations apply to certain forward contracts, the general accounting for foreign currency transactions is summarized as follows:

- Record the asset or liability when it arises, restating the foreign currency amount to dollars at the spot rate.
- Adjust the carrying value of the asset or liability to its current dollar equivalent when it is settled and at any intervening balance sheet dates. A transaction gain or loss results.
- Recognize the transaction gain or loss in current income, except in the case of certain hedges.

Purpose of Contract	Balance Sheet Valuation		Treatment of Transaction Gain or Loss	Treatment of Discount or Premium
	Amount Due to (from) Broker	Forward Purchase (Sale) Contract		
To hedge a firm foreign currency commitment.	Fixed at the dollar equivalent of the foreign currency translated at the forward rate.	Varies with the dollar equivalent of the foreign currency translated at the spot rate.	Deferred during the commitment period until the transaction is recorded;[a] used to adjust the dollar basis of the recorded transaction.	Deferred during the commitment period or amortized over the life of the contract. If deferred, the portion pertaining to the commitment period is used to adjust the dollar basis of the recorded transaction. Any remaining amount is amortized over the contract's remaining life
To hedge an exposed net asset or net liability position.	Fixed at the dollar equivalent of the foreign currency translated at the forward rate.	Varies with the dollar equivalent of the foreign currency translated at the spot rate.	Recognized in income currently as it accrues; not deferred.	Amortized over the life of the contract.
Economic hedge of a net investment in a foreign entity.	Fixed at the dollar equivalent of the foreign currency translated at the forward rate.	Varies with the dollar equivalent of the foreign currency translated at the spot rate.	Recognized in income currently as it accrues if functional currency is U.S. dollar; component of comprehensive income if functional currency is a foreign currency.	Amortized over the life of the contract if functional currency is U.S. dollar; amortized over the life of the contract *or* component of comprehensive income if functional currency is a foreign currency.
Speculation.	Fixed at the dollar equivalent of the foreign currency translated at the forward rate.	Varies with the dollar equivalent of the foreign currency translated at the forward rate for the remaining life of the contract.	Recognized in income currently as it accrues; not deferred.	Included as part of gain or loss but not recognized separately.

[a] Paragraph 21 of *SFAS 52* states that deferral of transaction losses on forward contracts is not appropriate if deferral could lead to recognition of losses in subsequent periods. For example, if the loss exceeds the expected gross profit (less costs of sale or disposal) on a sale transaction that has been hedged, the loss should *not* be deferred until that sale transaction is complete.

Source: Financial Accounting Standards Board, *Statement of Financial Accounting Standards No. 52*, "Foreign Currency Translation" (Stamford, CT: FASB, 1981), pars. 17–21.

EXHIBIT 10.1 SUMMARY OF *SFAS 52* ACCOUNTING FOR FORWARD EXCHANGE CONTRACTS

Purpose of Contract	Treatment of Transaction Gain or Loss	Comparison to *SFAS 52* Treatment
To hedge a firm foreign currency commitment.	Both the gain or loss on the commitment and the loss or gain on the hedge instrument are recognized in earnings as exchange rates change; used to adjust the dollar basis of the recorded transaction.	*SFAS 52* defers recognition of the loss or gain on the hedge instrument until the sale or purchase is booked; no gain or loss on the commitment is recognized.
To hedge a forecasted foreign currency transaction.	Shown as a component of comprehensive income until the forecasted transaction impacts earnings.	Hedges of forecasted transactions are treated as speculative.
To hedge an exposed net asset or net liability position.	Recognized in income currently as is accrues; not deferred.	Same as *SFAS 52*.
Economic hedge of a net investment in a foreign entity.	Recognized in income currently as it accrues if functional currency is the U.S. dollar; component of comprehensive income if functional currency is a foreign currency.	Same as *SFAS 52*.
Speculation	Recognized in income currently as it accrues; not deferred.	Same as *SFAS 52*.

EXHIBIT 10.2 SUMMARY OF FASB *DRAFT STATEMENT* ACCOUNTING FOR FORWARD EXCHANGE CONTRACTS

AUTHORS' COMMENTARY

Grappling with foreign currency forward contracts often becomes a "mind expanding" exercise. Unlike most of the accounting transactions with which we are familiar, the nature of forward contracts appears shadowy. The contracts themselves seem like phantom transactions. In fact, if the principal purpose of forward contracts were investment or speculation, how such contracts produce gain or loss might be easier to grasp. The gain or loss arises because the dollar value of the currency to be sold or purchased when the forward contract matures differs from the dollar amount to be paid to or received from the broker as stated in the contract. Once hedging is introduced as the major use of forward contracts, though, the contracts' link to the items being hedged clouds developments affecting the contracts themselves.

Rationale for Forward Contract Accounting Procedures. Although the rules governing the accounting for forward contracts are complex, the underlying rationale appears reasonable. Because the forward contract that hedges a firm foreign currency commitment is an integral part of the transaction resulting from the commitment, it is appropriate to defer transaction gains and losses on the forward contract until the transaction is recorded per *SFAS 52*, or recognize both the loss (gain) on the forward contract and the gain (loss) on the commitment on the income statement as rates change, per the FASB *Draft Statement*. The gain or loss on the forward contract offsets the effect of a changing exchange rate on the dollar value of the commitment. A similar logic applies to the treatment of gains and losses on hedges of forecasted transactions, per the FASB *Draft Statement*.

Other forward contract hedges may not be related to specific transactions and may contain an element of speculation. Hence the transaction gains and losses on these other hedges are recognized currently. Such current recognition offsets the currently recognized transaction losses and gains on the foreign currency denominated assets and liabilities being hedged. The premium or discount is viewed as a financing item and is separately amortized to income over the contract's life. Finally, the main product of speculative forward contracts is the generation of gains or losses from movements in exchange rates. Unlike hedges, speculative forward contracts are separate instruments unrelated to underlying assets or liabilities. Transaction gains and losses on speculative contracts are recognized currently as they occur, with no deferral. Moreover, the premium or discount on a speculative contract is not viewed as a financing item and is not accounted for separately.

Time spent on understanding forward contracts, particularly their hedging capability, is well spent. Other financial instruments, such as futures contracts and currency swaps, have similar characteristics.

SUMMARY OF KEY CONCEPTS

The price of one currency in terms of another is called a **foreign exchange rate**. The **spot rate** is the price for immediate delivery of the foreign currency. Delivery at a specified time in the future can be contracted at the appropriate **forward** or **futures** rate with a foreign exchange broker or dealer.

Import/export transactions and borrowing and lending abroad by domestic companies often generate **receivables and payables denominated in a foreign currency**. As the exchange rate rises (falls), the number of dollars ultimately to be received or paid increases (decreases). These changes in the dollar equivalents of receivables and payables generate **transaction gains and losses** (or **transaction adjustments**) that are recognized by the domestic company as they occur.

Forward exchange contracts and other foreign currency transactions are often used to **hedge** the risk of gain or loss from movements in the exchange rate. A contract may be used to hedge a forecasted transaction. When the contract is entered after a transaction has been negotiated but before it is recorded, it hedges a **firm foreign currency commitment**. If the contract remains in effect after the transaction is recorded, it hedges an **exposed asset (liability) position**. Many forward contracts cover both the commitment and exposed periods.

When the forward rate is greater than (less than) the current spot rate, there is a premium (discount) on the forward contract. This **premium or discount** is either **deferred during the commitment period** or **amortized over the entire life of the contract**. The amount deferred during the commitment period should be proportional to the total life of the contract and is used to adjust the dollar basis of the transaction. The balance is amortized over the remaining life of the contract.

Transaction gains and losses accrue to the **forward purchase (sale) contract**, not to the amount due to (from) the exchange broker. The net transaction adjustment accruing during the **commitment period** is deferred and is used to adjust the dollar basis of the transaction per *SFAS 52* or is recognized in income currently along with the change in value of the commitment, per the FASB draft *Statement*. **Once the transaction is recorded**, an exposed liability or asset position results. **Further** transaction gains or losses accruing to the forward contract are **recognized as they occur.**

A forward contract or other foreign currency transaction may serve as an **economic hedge of a net investment in a foreign entity**. When the foreign entity's **functional currency is the U.S. dollar**, transaction gains and losses on the hedge are recognized in **income currently**; any **premium or discount** on a forward contract is **amortized**. When the **functional currency is the currency of the foreign entity's home country**, transaction adjustments on the hedge are included in comprehensive income, outside of earnings; any premium or discount on a forward contract may be included in comprehensive income or be **amortized**.

A forward purchase (sale) contract may be entered solely in anticipation of an increase (decrease) in the spot rate; that is, for **speculative reasons**. In such cases, there is **no hedging**, no separate measurement of premium or discount, and all transaction gains and losses are recognized currently in income.

THE STRUCTURE OF FOREIGN EXCHANGE RATES

Forward rates differ from spot rates for two reasons:

1. Market-makers expect the spot rate to change in the future, perhaps because of economic forecasts or upcoming political developments. Suppose, for example, that the U.S. demand for Japanese products is expected to decrease and the value of the dollar relative to the Japanese yen is expected to increase. Both of these factors should reduce the demand for yen in the future, and the forward rate for yen may be lower than the spot rate.
2. Investors observe that interest rates and expected rates of inflation differ between countries and, through the practice of *covered interest arbitrage*, cause the observed difference between spot and forward foreign exchange rates.

Covered Interest Arbitrage

The phenomenon of **covered interest arbitrage** takes place when investors (1) react to higher interest rates abroad by purchasing foreign investments and (2) protect themselves against adverse exchange rate movements by covering their foreign investments with forward contracts to sell the foreign currency when the investments mature. This practice is the major reason why some currencies sell at a premium and others at a discount in the forward market.

Suppose that interest rates on 6-month certificates of deposit are 4 percent per 6-month period in the United States and 5 percent in Germany. In a free market, American investors in search of a higher yield will move their funds from dollars into deutsche marks (DM) and purchase certificates of deposit issued by banks in Germany. To hedge against the foreign exchange risk associated with converting DM back into the dollars American investors eventually want, the investors will *cover their investments*, now *denominated in DM*, by selling DM forward for dollars with delivery in 6 months. These forward sales of DM exert downward pressure on the direct 6-month forward rate for DM so that DM will cost less and dollars will cost more. These changes continue until the **discount** (= *spot rate − forward rate*) on DM sold forward 6 months approximately equals the interest rate differential of 1 percent. At this point, U.S. investors stop moving their funds from dollars into DM because the German interest rate advantage has been offset by a decline in the dollar value of DM when the investments mature in 6 months. Therefore, in New York the price for DM sold six months forward reflects a discount of approximately 1 percent from the spot rate, while in Frankfurt the price for dollars sold six months forward reflects a premium of approximately 1 percent.

Consistent with **covered interest arbitrage**, when the *foreign interest rate exceeds the U.S. interest rate*, the direct forward rate is *lower* than the direct spot rate, and forward contracts sell at a *discount* from the spot rate. Similarly, when the *foreign interest rate is below the U.S. interest rate*, the direct forward rate is *higher* than the direct spot rate, and forward contracts sell for a *premium* over the spot rate.

To illustrate the interplay between spot and forward exchange rates and interest rate differentials, consider the investment of $10,000 in Exhibit 10.3.

Foreign Exchange Rates   **Interest Rates Per 6-Month Period**

	Spot	6-Month Forward	6-Month Certificates of Deposit (CD)	
New York	$.5/DM	$.4952/DM	4%	Differential = 1%
Frankfurt	DM2/$	DM2.0194/$	5%	

Case 1: Domestic Investment

Time 0

Investor in New York invests $10,000 in a 6-month CD.

Six Months Later

CD matures, producing $10,400 (= 1.04 × $10,000).

Case 2: Foreign Investment Covered with a Forward Contract

Time 0

a. Investor in New York converts $10,000 into DM20,000 (= $10,000/$.5) and invests in a 6-month CD.

b. Investor in New York enters a 6-month forward contract to convert DM into dollars (at $.4952/DM) when the German CD matures.

Six Months Later

a. CD matures, producing DM21,000 (= 1.05 × DM20,000).

b. Forward contract matures and the DM21,000 from the CD are converted into $10,400 (= 21,000 × $.4952).

Conclusion

In both cases, the investor ends up with $10,400. The fact that the 6-month forward rate of $.4952 is approximately 1 percent lower than the spot rate offsets the fact that 6-month CD rates in Frankfurt are 1 percent higher than in New York.

EXHIBIT 10.3 THE EFFECTS OF COVERED INTEREST ARBITRAGE

Covered interest arbitragers act upon the interest rate differential of 1 percent to create the necessary equilibrating discount in the forward rate for deutsche marks in New York and premium in the forward rate for dollars in Frankfurt. Investing the $10,000 in a U.S. certificate of deposit generates $10,400 (= 1.04 × $10,000) in six months. Converting dollars to deutsche marks at the spot rate of $.5/DM permits an investment of DM20,000 (= $10,000/$.5) in Germany. This investment provides DM21,000 (= 1.05 × DM20,000) in six months. If deutsche marks were sold forward to hedge the foreign currency conversion, the DM21,000 provided by the investment is also worth $10,400 (= DM21,000/ DM2.0194).

These relationships may be formalized into the following equation:

$$R_{f,t} = R_s(1+I_{US,t})/(1+I_{FN,t}), \text{ where}$$
$$R_{f,t} = \text{Forward rate for delivery at time } t$$
$$R_s = \text{Spot rate}$$
$$I_{US,t} = \text{U.S. interest rate for period ending at time } t$$
$$I_{FN,t} = \text{Foreign interest rate for period ending at time } t$$

Substituting the data from Exhibit 10.3 into the above equation, we have:

$$R_{f,6} = .5(1.04)/(1.05)$$
$$R_{f,6} = .4952$$

Thus the formula expressed in this equation can be used to solve for the forward rate consistent with covered interest arbitrage or for any of the other variables as long as three of the variables are known.

Maintaining Consistency among Foreign Exchange Rates

The structure of foreign exchange rates is brought into equilibrium by traders known as **arbitragers**. When inconsistencies in the structure of exchange rates appear, the prospect of immediate and risk-free gains will motivate arbitragers to buy and sell the appropriate currencies until the inconsistencies are removed. For example, **two-point arbitrage** removes any difference between the exchange rates for the same currency on two different markets. Suppose that in New York the rate $/£ = $2.000 and in London $/£ = $2.006. Arbitragers would quickly purchase pounds with dollars in New York and sell the pounds for dollars in London until both rates equalize and the arbitrage gains disappear.

A more intricate scheme involves **three-point arbitrage**. This technique exploits inconsistencies existing among the exchange rates of three currencies and, by so doing, removes them. To illustrate this process, consider the following set of foreign exchange quotations:

In New York	In Tokyo
$/£ = $ 2.000	Yen/£ = Y 410
$/Yen = $ .005	

Alert traders would observe that a pound could be bought for $2 in New York and exchanged for 410 yen in Tokyo. The 410 yen could each be sold for $.005 in New York for a total of $2.05, a gain of $.05 per pound purchased. Holding the rate in Tokyo constant, arbitragers in New York might purchase pounds with dollars and thereby cause the dollar price of pounds to rise gradually, perhaps to $2.0295. At the same time, the arbitragers could sell yen for dollars in New York until the dollar price of yen fell to $.00495, thereby eliminating any further gains from arbitraging ($2.0295 = 410 × $.00495). Alternatively, the same result would be achieved by bidding up the dollar price of pounds to $2.05, holding the other rates constant. Whatever new exchange rates result, however, arbitragers will keep them in equilibrium with the rates in other markets and for other currencies.

QUESTIONS

Q10.1 This text has drawn a distinction between *transaction* gains and losses and *translation* gains and losses. What is the basis for the distinction? As a financial statement user, would you prefer separate disclosure of both types of exchange gains and losses? Explain.

Q10.2 In *SFAS 52* the FASB adopted the *two-transaction approach* to account for many foreign currency transactions. Compared with the *single-transaction approach*, explain how the two-transaction approach affects the amount, timing and character of reported income.

Q10.3 The Barber Corporation is considering developing some overseas markets for its products. Credit and payment policies for overseas customers are two of several matters being considered. You have been engaged by Barber to explain the accounting implications of export transactions as well as to give general advice on the subject to Barber's controller. What special risks would be faced by Barber in overseas markets? What kinds of general information should be considered in formulating credit and payment policies for foreign customers?

Q10.4 Describe the *hedging* process and identify its costs and benefits.

Q10.5 Briefly explain why a foreign currency forward contract is known as a *derivative financial instrument*.

Q10.6 If a forward contract is entered to hedge an identifiable foreign currency commitment, transaction gains and losses accruing during the commitment period are deferred and used to adjust the dollar basis of the transaction. What is the logic behind this rule?

Q10.7 The Armen Company has outstanding receivables, denominated in pounds sterling (£), of £1,000,000. If Armen sells £1,000,000 forward for delivery in 30 days when the receivables are to be collected, is this likely to be an *effective hedge*? Why or why not?

Q10.8 Explain how forward contracts are reported in a company's balance sheet.

Q10.9 *SFAS 52* requires that the premium or discount on a forward contract entered to hedge an exposed asset or liability position be amortized to operations over the life of the contract. Comment on the propriety of this treatment.

Q10.10 Although this text has concentrated on the use of foreign currency forward contracts to hedge against exchange rate risk, briefly describe two other foreign currency transactions that could be used as hedges.

Q10.11 *SFAS 52* introduced the concept of a foreign currency transaction entered into to serve as an "economic hedge of a net investment in a foreign entity." Explain this concept and indicate how transaction adjustments accruing to such hedges are treated.

Q10.12 (Appendix) Suppose that interest rates on six-month certificates of deposit are 12 percent in the United States and 10 percent in the United Kingdom. Based on this information alone, would you expect pounds sterling to be delivered in six months to sell at a premium over or discount from the spot rate? Explain.

EXERCISES

E10.1 **Recording Import Transactions** The Eastern Merchandise Company imports a variety of items for resale to U.S. retailers. During one month it made the following purchases (on credit) and payments:

Country	Amount	Currency	Spot rate at Purchase	Spot Rate at Payment
Australia	15,000	Australian Dollar	$ 1.100	$ 1.130
Finland	42,000	Markka	.260	.250
Indonesia	730,000	Rupiah	.002	.003
Turkey	80,000	Lira	.060	.060

REQUIRED: Give the journal entries made by Eastern to record the above purchase and payment transactions.

E10.2 **Recording Export Transactions** Western Exports sells many different items abroad. During one month it made the following sales (on credit) and collections:

Country	Amount	Currency	Spot rate at Sale	Spot Rate at Collection
Austria	25,000	Schilling	$ .074	$ .082
Greece	400,000	Drachma	.028	.025
Iraq	300,000	Dinar	.014	.017
South Africa	10,000	Rand	1.150	1.140

REQUIRED: Give the journal entries made by Western to record the above sale and collection transactions.

E10.3 **Recording Import and Export Transactions** Walsh Corporation imports raw materials from foreign countries and exports finished goods to customers throughout the world. Information regarding four such transactions, all denominated in units of foreign currency (FC), is given below:

Transaction	Amount (FC)	Spot Rate at Transaction Date	Spot Rate at Payment Date
1. (Import)	30,000	$ 1.10	$ 1.15
2. (Import)	100,000	.30	.28
3. (Export)	50,000	.97	.93
4. (Export)	40,000	.16	.17

REQUIRED: Prepare the journal entries made by Walsh to record the above on the transaction date and on the payment date.

E10.4 **Hedging Purchase Commitment and Exposed Liability** On September 15, 19X3, the Haskell Corporation agreed to purchase 5,000 radios from a South Korean company for a total invoice price of 12,000,000 won (W). The radios are received on October 15 and payment made on November 14. Concurrently, on September 15, 19X3, Haskell purchased W12,000,000 for delivery on November 14, 19X3. Haskell's accounting practice is to defer a premium or discount on a forward contract during the commitment period. Relevant exchange rates ($/W) are as follows:

	9/15/X3	10/15/X3	11/14/X3
Spot Rate	$ .002	$ .0021	$ .0022
Sixty-Day Forward Rate	.00185	—	—

REQUIRED: Prepare the journal entries made by Haskell on September 15, 19X3, October 15, 19X3, and November 14, 19X3, per (a) *SFAS 52*, and (b) the 1997 FASB *Draft Statement*.

E10.5 **Hedging Exposed Liability** On March 15, 19X3, Schaeffer Corporation purchased goods from a South Korean company at an invoice price of 20,000,000 won (W); payment is due on April 14, 19X3. Concurrently, Schaeffer purchased W20,000,000 for delivery in 30 days at a forward rate of $.0019/W. The spot rate is $.002/W on March 15 and rises to $.0021/W on April 14.

REQUIRED:

1. Prepare the journal entries made by Schaeffer on March 15 and April 14.
2. Calculate the cash gain or loss realized by Schaeffer by hedging compared with not hedging.

E10.6 **Hedging Exposed Asset** On September 1, 19X6, Ruhf Company sold coffee-roasting equipment which it manufactured to a Brazilian customer. The invoice price is 40,000,000 cruzeiros (C); the customer pays on September 30, 19X6. Concurrently, Ruhf sold C40,000,000 for delivery in 30 days at a forward rate of $.072/C. The spot rate is $.07/C on September 1 and falls to $.069 on September 30.

REQUIRED:

1. Prepare the journal entries made by Ruhf on September 1 and September 30.
2. Calculate the cash gain or loss realized by Ruhf by hedging compared with not hedging.

E10.7 **Hedging Sale Commitment and Exposed Asset** The Livingstone Company, a calendar-year corporation, manufactures various kinds of filter materials. On April 15, 19X4, Livingstone received an order from a diamond-mining company in South Africa for a large quantity of reusable filters to be used in the dust masks of diamond miners. The total price in rands (R) was R12,000. Livingstone planned on shipping the filters on April 30, 19X4, and payment is to be received in rands on May 15, 19X4. Upon receipt of the purchase order, Livingstone immediately sells R12,000 for delivery in 30 days. The firm's practice is to amortize any premium or discount on a forward contract over the life of the contract. Relevant exchange rates ($/R) are shown below:

	4/15/X4	4/30/X4	5/15/X4
Spot Rate	$1.15	$1.16	$1.19
Thirty-Day Forward Rate	1.18	—	—

REQUIRED: Prepare the journal entries made by Livingstone on April 15, 19X4, April 30, 19X4, and May 15, 19X4, per (a) *SFAS 52*, and (b) the FASB *Draft Statement*.

E10.8 **Adjusting Entry at Balance Sheet Date** The Carolina Company's books reflected the following receivables (payables) denominated in foreign currency (FC) units prior to closing on December 31. The spot rates at December 31 are also given.

Item	Amount		Spot Rate
	$	FC	($/FC)
1	$ 100,000	FC 1,000,000	$ .09
2	180,000	225,000	.82
3	(500,000)	(400,000)	1.30
4	(50,000)	(200,000)	.24

REQUIRED: Prepare the adjusting entry recorded by Carolina at December 31. Show all calculations.

E10.9 **Recording Foreign Investment** To take advantage of high short-term interest rates. Carlton Enterprises purchased a 1,000,000 deutsche mark (DM) six-month certificate of deposit from a German bank for $500,000 on October 1, 19X8. The annual interest rate is 15 percent. Exchange rates ($/DM) at December 31, 19X8, and March 31, 19X9, are $.52 and $.465, respectively.

REQUIRED:

1. Prepare the journal entries recorded by Carlton on October 1, 19X8, December 31, 19X8, and March 31, 19X9.
2. Was this a good investment? Explain with calculations.

E10.10 **Hedge of Net Investment** The Williams Company has a wholly owned subsidiary in Uruguay. The subsidiary's net assets in *new pesos* (NP, the currency of Uruguay) amount to NP35,000,000. At a time when the spot rate is $.02/NP, Williams wishes to hedge its investment in this foreign entity.

REQUIRED:

1. For the hedge to be effective, should Williams borrow NP (or sell NP forward) or invest in NP (or purchase NP forward)? Why?
2. Assume Williams undertakes such a hedge by entering into a forward contract at $.019/NP calling for delivery of NP20,000,000 in 90 days. Prepare the journal entry to record the forward contract as an effective hedge.
3. If the books are closed in 45 days when the spot rate is $.0194/NP, calculate the transaction adjustment and indicate the accounting treatment for it and for the discount on the forward contract.

E10.11 **Speculative Forward Contracts** Levy Corporation makes markets in several foreign currencies. Although it tries to hedge its various positions, on December 16, 19X8, Levy finds itself with the following unhedged forward contracts:

- Agreement to purchase 10,000,000 Hong Kong dollars ($H) in 30 days at $.13/$H.
- Agreement to sell 10,000,000 Singapore dollars ($S) in 30 days at $.32/$S.

Relevant exchange rates are:

30-day forward rates at December 16, 19X8	$.128/$H	$.317/$S
15-day forward rates at December 31, 19X8	$.125/$H	$.321/$S
Spot rates at January 15, 19X9	$.131/$H	$.318/$S

REQUIRED: Prepare the journal entries made by Levy on December 31, 19X8, and January 15, 19X9, assuming that the balances of the forward contracts are properly stated at December 16, 19X8.

E10.12 **Covered Interest Arbitrage (Appendix)** An investor seeking high returns worldwide invests $120,000 in a 6-month foreign investment denominated in local currency units (LC). The investment pays 6% interest and is made when the exchange rate = $.60/LC.

REQUIRED:

1. If the 6-month forward rate is $.63/LC, calculate the 6-month interest rate on dollar-denominated securities of comparable risk.
2. The investor concurrently enters a 6-month forward contract at $.63/LC to hedge the principal amount of the foreign investment. Calculate the net number of dollars received when the investment matures if the spot rate is $.61/LC at that time.
3. If the 6-month interest rate on dollar-denominated securities of comparable risk is 4%, calculate the 6-month forward rate expected to prevail under the theory of covered interest arbitrage.

PROBLEMS

P10.1 **Accounting for Forward Contracts—Hedging and Speculation** Futura Corporation, a calendar-year corporation, is an active trader in foreign exchange, both for purposes of hedging its international activities and for outright speculation. In particular, it had several transactions in the forward market for rands (R), the currency of South Africa, during 19X7. Relevant exchange rates ($/R) are shown below.

	11/1/X7	12/31/X7	1/29/X8
Spot Rate	$ 1.15	$ 1.17	$ 1.19
Thirty-Day Forward	1.13	1.16	1.20
Sixty-Day Forward	1.11	1.15	1.21
Ninety-Day Forward	1.09	1.14	1.22

On November 1, 19X7, Futura entered into the following forward contracts. The contracts were settled on January 29, 19X8.

1. Sold R100,000 forward to hedge a forthcoming sale to a South African firm; the sale price of R100,000 has been negotiated although delivery and collection will not take place until January 29, 19X8.
2. Purchased R200,000 forward to hedge the exposed net liability position of its South African branch.
3. Sold R100,000 forward in anticipation of a fall in the spot rate.

REQUIRED:

1. Following *SFAS 52*, prepare the journal entries made by Futura on November 1, 19X7, December 31, 19X7, and January 29, 19X8. Assume that Futura defers the premium or discount on a forward contract when permitted to do so under *SFAS 52*.
2. Comment on the specific use of the forward market by Futura in the problem.

P10.2 **Computation of Exchange Gain or Loss** Wheelstick Corporation, incorporated in the state of Delaware, is active in the import/export business. An analysis of Wheelstick's receivables, payables, and other assets (liabilities) prior to adjustment at December 31, 19X2, disclosed the following:

Receivables

U.S. Customers	$ 100,000
Belgian Customers (300,000 Francs)	9,000
Indian Customers (120,000 Rupees)	14,400
Saudi Arabian Customers (90,000 Riyal)	27,000
Exchange Broker (Forward Sale Contract for 300,000 Francs)	9,300
Total Receivables	$ 159,700

Payables

U.S. Suppliers	$ (47,000)
Ecuadorian Suppliers (600,000 Sucre)	(24,000)
Mexican Suppliers (500,000 Pesos)	(19,000)
Exchange Broker (Forward Purchase Contract for 500,000 Pesos)	(20,000)
Total Payables	$ (110,000)

Other Assets (Liabilities)

Trademarks	$ 75,000
Forward Purchase Contract (500,000 Pesos)	19,000
Forward Sale Contract (300,000 Francs)	(9,000)
Total Other Assets (Liabilities)	$ 85,000

Spot rates for the above currencies at December 31, 19X2, are:

Currency	Exchange Rate
Belgian Francs	$ .036
Rupees	.125
Riyal	.287
Sucre	.042
Mexican Pesos	.035

REQUIRED: Prepare a schedule to compute the exchange gain or loss recognized by Wheelstick in 19X2. Record the needed adjusting entries.

P10.3 **Journal Entries for Hedged Import Commitment, Import and Export Transactions**
The following international transactions were entered into during 19X5 by CONNCO, an American Corporation:

1. June 15, 19X5: Entered into a firm commitment to purchase goods from Italy which will be resold in the United States. The invoice price is 40,000,000 lira (LI), and delivery and payment are to be made in 60 days. The spot rate is $.0014/LI. Concurrently, LI40,000,000 are purchased in the forward market for delivery in 60 days at the forward rate of $.0012. The goods are received, payment is made, and the forward contract is settled on August 14, 19X5, when the spot rate is $.0015/LI.
2. September 1, 19X5: Agricultural products priced at 30,000 riyal (RI) are sold to a concern in Iraq when the spot rate is $3.44/RI. Payment is received on November 3, 19X5, and the RI are converted to dollars at the spot rate of $3.47/RI.

REQUIRED:
(a) Prepare the 19X5 journal entries made by CONNCO relating to the above, per *SFAS 52*. Amortize the discount or premium on the forward contract.
(b) Prepare the 19X5 journal entries following the FASB *Draft Statement*.

P10.4 **Hedging, Leverage, Return On Assets** The ABC Corporation's 12/31/X1 balance sheet shows total liabilities of $700 and total assets of $1,000; measured financial leverage is therefore .7. Included in current liabilities is $400 (FC1,000) payable to a foreign supplier. Assuming that ABC's management always seeks to portray the most positive financial picture possible, assess the effects of the following actions. Disregard income taxes.

REQUIRED:

1. On January 1, 19X2, management enters into a 90-day forward purchase contract costing $440 as it expects an exchange rate of $.43/FC to prevail on March 31 and on April 1 when the forward contract matures and payment must be made to the foreign supplier. Compute the economic gain or loss from hedging compared with not hedging. Assuming total assets and liabilities are unchanged, except as indicated by exchange rate movements, analyze how the hedge affects ABC's financial leverage when first quarter 19X2 interim financial statements are issued.

2. If ABC can borrow domestically at 12% per annum, evaluate the wisdom of using the forward contract to neutralize the exchange rate risk.

3. ABC's operating income for 19X1 was $152; its annual return on average total assets (ROA) in 19X1 was .16. ABC projects the same relationship for 19X2 at current exchange rates. Suppose the exchange rate is expected to rise to $.43/FC on March 31, 19X2 when interim financial statements are prepared and on April 1, 19X2 when the above-mentioned payable is due. Management considers purchasing FC1,000 on January 1, 19X2 for delivery in 90 days for $425 to hedge the payable to the foreign supplier. ABC projects total assets of $1,200 at March 31, 19X2. Holding March 31, 19X2 assets constant at $1,200, analyze how hedging the payable, compared with not hedging, would affect the first quarter ROA. Recall that amortization of the forward contract premium is interest expense and assume for this exercise that transaction adjustments enter operating income.

P10.5 **Transaction Exposure and Credit Analysis** You were recently hired as a credit analyst at a large financial institution. As you savor your fresh-ground morning coffee, visualizing Michael Caine in an early scene of "The Ipcress File," you begin scanning the contents of the "Poole Corporation" manila folder on your desk. After two cups of steaming hot coffee, you have assembled the following information for Poole.

Poole Corporation
Balance Sheet
December 31, 19X4

Cash and Receivables	$ 450,000
Inventory	300,000
Plant Assets, Net	500,000
Total Assets	$1,250,000
Current Liabilities	$ 400,000
Long-Term Liabilities	475,000
Stockholders' Equity	375,000
Total Liabilities and Stockholders' Equity	$1,250,000

Additional information:

1. Net income reported for 19X4 was $150,000.
2. Depreciation expense was $50,000.
3. Noncash working capital increased by $40,000, including $25,000 of unrealized transaction gains accruing on foreign currency denominated current assets ($11,000) and liabilities ($14,000).
4. Unrealized transaction gains on long-term debt, $22,000.
5. Inventory includes $100,000 in items normally sold to foreign customers for FC500,000; estimated sales value at the current spot rate of $.35/FC is $175,000.
6. Poole's various disclosures indicate no hedging of foreign currency exposures.

REQUIRED:

1. One dimension of earnings quality is nearness to cash. Using the information given, calculate cash flow from operations to assess this dimension of earnings quality.
2. Sales to foreign customers are denominated in a highly volatile foreign currency. The dollar is forecast to strengthen relative to this currency during 19X5, with the spot rate possibly falling to $.20/FC. Discuss the likely effect of this development on Poole's cash flow, using an analysis suggested by the above data.
3. Describe the measures you would like to see Poole undertake to raise your level of comfort before making a loan to the company.

P10.6 **Hedging a Foreign Currency Commitment—Effects on Income** On October 1, 19X2, Ellis Corporation agreed to sell 50,000 electric motors to a Swiss customer for 500,000 Swiss francs (SF). Delivery is to be made on November 30, 19X2, and payment is to be received on January 31, 19X3. Concurrently, Ellis sold SF500,000 forward for delivery on January 31, 19X3, for a total contract price of $249,000. Ellis closes its books annually on December 31.

REQUIRED:

1. Prepare all dated journal entries relative to the sale and the forward contract during 19X2 and 19X3, per *SFAS 52*. Ellis elects to defer any premiums or discounts on forward contracts during the commitment period. Relevant spot rates are as follows:

	Spot Rate ($/SF)
October 1, 19X2	$ .45
November 30, 19X2	.48
December 31, 19X2	.47
January 31, 19X3	.51

2. Suppose Ellis had elected to amortize the premium or discount on the forward contract during the commitment period. How would Ellis's income be affected in 19X2? In 19X3? Explain.

P10.7 **Recording a Hedged Foreign Loan** The Roderick Company borrowed 50,000 pounds (£) from a London bank on December 16, 19X1. The £50,000 were immediately converted to dollars for use in the United States and are scheduled to be repaid with interest of £500 on January 15, 19X2. To hedge the risk of an unfavorable change in the exchange rate, Roderick purchased £50,500 for delivery on January 15, 19X2. Roderick's accounting period ends on December 31, 19X1. Exchange rates ($/£) on the various dates are as follows:

	12/16/X1	12/31/X1	1/15/X2
Spot Rate	$2.10	$2.08	$2.05
Thirty-day Forward Rate	2.13	—	—

REQUIRED: Prepare the journal entries made by Roderick on December 16, 19X1, December 31, 19X1, and January 15, 19X2.

P10.8 **Analyzing the Performance of an Import/Export Department** William Johnston manages the import/export department of Bush Specialty Products. Because of the complexities of foreign currency transactions and the continual changes in exchange rates, Bush's management is having difficulty determining exactly how Johnston's operation is performing. You have been called in as a consultant to give advice on this performance-evaluation task.

Import Transactions

Quantity—Part No.	Unit Cost (FC)	Spot Rate When Purchased	Spot Rate When Paid	Unit Selling Price
2,000—K14	6.4	$ .83	$ .80	$ 7.75
17,000—KR08	10.0	.49	.58	6.00
5,000—L16	8.2	1.13	1.22	10.00
10,000—M290	25.2	.37	.32	9.20

Export Transactions

Quantity—Part No.	Unit Selling Price (FC)	Spot Rate When Sold	Spot Rate When Collected	Unit Cost
14,000—A24	8.4	$ .27	$ .29	$ 1.98
6,000—DD2	12.5	2.00	1.92	24.00
20,000—A27	10.0	1.10	1.16	8.90
1,000—B23	14.6	.63	.58	8.50

Forward Contracts

Quantity of FC Purchased (Sold)	Average Spot Rate at Inception	Average Forward Rate at Inception	Average Spot Rate at Maturity	Purpose of Contract
210,000	$ .57	$ .62	$ .59	Hedge
(300,000)	.88	.90	.87	Hedge
1,000,000	.28	.25	.22	Speculation
(1,000,000)	.75	.74	.85	Speculation

EXHIBIT 10.4 BUSH SPECIALTY PRODUCTS: SUMMARY OF IMPORT/ EXPORT DEPARTMENT ACTIVITIES TO BE USED IN P10.8.

After you discuss the problem with Mr. Johnston, he produces the summary of his department's activities shown in Exhibit 10.4. The letters FC identify foreign currency units, and exchange rates are defined as $/FC. Premiums and discounts on forward contracts are always amortized over the contracts' lives, never deferred.

REQUIRED:

1. Prepare, in good form, schedules to calculate the profit contribution or loss realized by the import/export department.
2. Write a short memorandum to top management regarding your findings. Should Mr. Johnston be fired? Explain.

P10.9 **Adjusting Entries at Balance Sheet Date** You have been engaged to audit the books of Warner Corporation as of December 31, 19X7. Because assets and liabilities recorded by Warner but denominated in foreign currencies have required extensive audit adjustments in the past, you look sharply at the schedule prepared by Warner's controller. It appears in Exhibit 10.5.

Accounts Receivable

Domestic Customers	$ 25,000,000
Australian Customers (2,000,000 Australian Dollars)	2,280,000
Norwegian Customers (5,000,000 Krone)	1,000,000
Peruvian Customers	1,900,000
Spanish Customers (10,000,000 Pesetas)	200,000
ABC Foreign Exchange Specialists (10,000,000 Drachma)	300,000
Union Bank Foreign Exchange Department (10,000,000 Pesetas)	210,000
Total Accounts Receivable	$ 30,890,000

Accounts Payable

Domestic Suppliers	$ (15,000,000)
Brazilian Suppliers (4,000,000 Cruzeiros)	(200,000)
Colombian Suppliers (6,000,000 Pesos)	(180,000)
Dutch Suppliers (10,000,000 Guilders)	(5,000,000)
Swedish Suppliers	(800,000)
BR Foreign Exchange Service (5,000,000 Rupees)	(500,000)
Union Bank Foreign Exchange Department (10,000,000 Guilders)	(5,500,000)
Total Accounts Payable	$ (27,180,000)

Other Assets (Liabilities)

Note Payable, Nippon Bank, Japan (200,000,000 Yen)	$ (1,000,000)
Forward Purchase Contract (5,000,000 Rupees)	500,000
Forward Purchase Contract (10,000,000 Guilders)	4,800,000
Forward Sale Contract (10,000,000 Drachma)	(300,000)
Forward Sale Contract (10,000,000 Pesetas)	(190,000)
Total Other Assets (Liabilities)	$ 3,810,000

EXHIBIT 10.5 SCHEDULE OF WARNER CORPORATION'S ASSETS AND LIABILITIES TO BE USED IN P10.9

Spot rates at December 31, 19X7, are as follows:

Currency	Rate	Currency	Rate
Australian Dollar ...	$ 1.200	Pesetas	$ .020
Cruzeiro	.060	Pesos	.032
Drachma	.028[a]	Rupees	.102[a]
Guilder	.490	Yen	.006
Krone	.190		

[a] Forward rates for remaining terms of speculative contracts are $.025 and $.11 for drachma and rupees, respectively.

REQUIRED: Prepare the necessary adjusting entries for Warner Corporation as of December 31, 19X7. Support with calculations in good form.

P10.10 **Taxes, Hedging and Pricing International Transfers** Recall that intercompany sales/purchases and unconfirmed intercompany profits are eliminated when consolidated financial statements are prepared. When intercompany transfers are sold externally, though, the intercompany profits are deemed confirmed and are not eliminated, thereby producing a particular allocation of the total profit among the controlling and minority interests.

The allocation resulting from intercompany transfer pricing policy is important to multinational firms—it can influence the significance of exchange rate movements on profit and can lead to charges of "dumping." Moreover, it may affect worldwide income tax liabilities when tax rates differ across national boundaries. When related corporations do *not* file a consolidated income tax return, transfer pricing schemes can have a dramatic effect on tax liabilities. There is no "equity method" in the U.S. tax code. Thus, by not declaring intercompany dividends, the parent's share of the income from a subsidiary in a low-tax foreign jurisdiction may be sheltered from U.S. taxes.

Suppose the income tax rate is 40% in the U.S. and 15% in the fictional Pacific Rim republic of Sarkhan. A product that costs FC250 ($25 at the current exchange rate of $.10/FC) to manufacture in a U.S. company's Sarkhan subsidiary can be sold in the U.S. for $108.

REQUIRED:

1. Calculate the dollar transfer price that minimizes the company's worldwide income tax liability, assuming no limits on the company's ability to set the transfer price reported for tax purposes other than the fact that reporting a gross margin of less than 20% on cost is generally deemed indefensible.
2. Transfer prices defensible for tax purposes should reflect arm's-length market prices between unrelated parties. Discuss the likely extent to which this requirement inhibits U.S.-based multinationals from manipulating transfer prices to minimize their worldwide income tax liability.
3. Suppose the transfer price is denominated in FC, say at FC900, rather than in $. Experts predict that the dollar will strengthen relative to the FC, perhaps by as much as 20%. Using calculations as needed, explain the advantages and disadvantages of hedging to lock in a high dollar transfer price.
4. What must the U.S. company do to make sure a forward purchase contract qualifies as a hedge of its anticipated purchases from the subsidiary?

P10.11 Evaluation of Domestic and Foreign Investments The treasurer of Enormo Corporation is always on the lookout for short-term, high-yielding investments. Six-month low-risk domestic investments currently yield 12 percent per annum. Two foreign investments of comparable risk are presented:

1. A six-month certificate of deposit issued by the Bank of England has a coupon rate of 14 percent per annum. Spot and six-month forward exchange rates are $2.00 and $2.03, respectively.
2. A six-month certificate of deposit issued by the Bundesbank in Germany carries a coupon rate of 8 percent per annum. Spot and six-month forward rates are $.50 and $.55, respectively.

REQUIRED:

Assuming that Enormo has $1,000,000 to invest, cannot tolerate exchange rate risk, and wants to maximize the number of dollars at the end of six months, analyze the three alternative investments and make a recommendation. Support your analysis with calculations.

P10.12 Purchase Alternatives and Cash Flow Analysis (Appendix) On April 1, 19X3, the Wyatt Company contracted with a British firm to purchase components periodically over the next six months. Although the total payment of £600,000 is due on September 30, 19X3, the British firm offers a 2% discount for payment of the entire amount by April 10. The current spot rate is $1.40/£ and is expected to vary about 10% above and below $1.40 during the next six months. Wyatt's management asks your advice on paying for this purchase.

Additional information:

1. The current annual U.S. interest/discount rate is 8%; 6-month rate is 4%.
2. The forward rate for 180-day delivery of £ is $1.44/£.
3. A domestic firm offered to supply similar components, with a slightly higher failure rate, for $800,000 payable on September 30. If the domestic supplier is used, additional warranty costs of $50,000 will be incurred in the Spring of 19X4.

REQUIRED:

1. Calculate the payment to be made under each of the following scenarios, converting all cash flows to their present value on April 1.
   a. Full payment on April 1.
   b. Hedging with a forward contract entered on April 1.
   c. Investing in a 6-month £-denominated fixed income security
      (HINT: Compute the applicable U.K. interest rate using the formula in the chapter). This investment is *not* designated as a hedge.
   d. Purchase from the domestic firm according to the terms outlined above.
2. Make a recommendation to management accompanied by the potential advantages and disadvantages of your recommendation. Explain whether any of the payment scenarios will affect earnings volatility over the next six months.

CHAPTER 11

DERIVATIVE FINANCIAL INSTRUMENTS: FUTURES, OPTIONS AND FINANCIAL SWAPS

CHAPTER PREVIEW

The growth of international capital markets and the increasing sophistication of market participants have produced new financial instruments and innovative uses for some traditional financial instruments. Many of these instruments are used in international transactions. Accountants have been hard-pressed to develop sound accounting principles for some of the financial instruments emerging in this rapidly changing environment. Disclosure requirements were promulgated by the FASB when *SFAS 105* (1990) and *SFAS 107* (1991) were issued. *SFAS 119* (1994) expands the scope of previous requirements and provides for additional disclosures about *derivative financial instruments*. On the horizon is a 1997 FASB *Draft Statement* specifying uniform accounting standards for derivatives.

The purpose of this chapter is to introduce and illustrate three of the more common derivative financial instruments used in domestic and international operations not studied in previous accounting courses. Although many readers will have some familiarity with futures contracts, options and financial swaps, the related accounting issues can be challenging and, in some cases, are unsettled. Principal topics studied in this chapter are:

- What are derivative financial instruments?
- New developments affecting derivatives
- Futures contracts
- Options
- Introduction to financial swaps
- Currency swaps
- Interest rate swaps
- Disclosure requirements

We believe that financial markets are becoming more complex. We also believe that the knowledge of forward contracts provided in Chapter 10 facilitates the study of financial instruments offered in this chapter. The FASB is in the midst of a long-term project on accounting for financial instruments. *SFAS 105*, *SFAS 107* and *SFAS 119* are the first pronouncements to come out of that project. An understanding of the financial instruments discussed here will help readers work with and interpret subsequent pronouncements as they are issued.

As discussed in Chapter 10, accounting for derivatives called foreign currency forward contracts is a natural component of foreign currency transactions. In addition, there is dramatic growth in the use of other derivative financial instruments—futures, options, and swaps—in international and other contexts. How these other financial instruments function can often be explained in terms of forward contracts. Moreover, futures, options, and financial swaps frequently have applications in international financial management and give rise to similar accounting issues.

As this book goes to press, the major FASB project on **"Financial Instruments and Off-Balance-Sheet Financing Issues,"** begun in 1986, is still underway. The three phases of the project deal with (1) disclosure, (2) recognition and measurement, and (3) distinguishing between liabilities and equity. The FASB's work on the disclosure phase resulted in:

- *SFAS 105*, "Disclosure of Information about Financial Instruments with Off-Balance-Sheet Risk and Financial Instruments with Concentrations of Credit Risk" (1990).[1]
- *SFAS 107*, "Disclosures about Fair Value of Financial Instruments" (1991).[2]
- *SFAS 119*, "Disclosure about Derivative Financial Instruments and Fair Value of Financial Instruments" (1994).[3]

Work on the recognition and measurement phase produced a 1996 *Exposure Draft,* revised as a:

- 1997 *Draft Statement*, "Accounting for Derivative Instruments and Hedging Activities."

We discuss the *Draft Statement* as we examine the principal types of derivative financial instruments, contrasting the *Draft Statement's* provisions with current practice. Disclosure requirements of *SFAS 105, 107* and *119* are summarized and illustrated near the end of the chapter. Readers should be alert for further developments as the financial instruments project progresses.[4]

WHAT ARE DERIVATIVE FINANCIAL INSTRUMENTS?

In general, a **derivative financial instrument** is a financial instrument whose value is tied to or derived from the value of a reference asset, financial instrument or index. Two important characteristics of *derivatives* are:

1. They are tied to one or more **underlyings**—an interest rate, per share price, foreign exchange rate, commodity price and the like—that is subject to price changes. An underlying is a *variable,* such as the price of an asset, but not the asset itself.
2. They are based on a **contractual** or **notional amount**—face value of debt, number of shares, quantity of currency, number of bushels and the like—stated in the instrument's contract.

Thus, a *derivative's cash flows* = the price change in the underlying × the notional amount.

> *SFAS 119* specifies that "a **derivative financial instrument** is a futures, forward, swap or option contract, or other financial instrument with similar characteristics."

---

[1] Financial Accounting Standards Board, *Statement of Financial Accounting Standards No. 105*, "Disclosure of Information about Financial Instruments with Off-Balance-Sheet Risk and Financial Instruments with Concentrations of Credit Risk" (Norwalk, CT: FASB, 1990).

[2] Financial Accounting Standards Board, *Statement of Financial Accounting Standards No. 107*, "Disclosures about Fair Value of Financial Instruments" (Norwalk, CT: FASB, 1991).

[3] Financial Accounting Standards Board, *Statement of Financial Accounting Standards No. 119*, "Disclosure about Derivative Financial Instruments and Fair Value of Financial Instruments" (Norwalk, CT: FASB, 1994).

[4] As to the liability/equity part of the project, see the FASB *Discussion Memorandum*, "Distinguishing between Liability and Equity Instruments and Accounting for Instruments with Characteristics of Both" (Norwalk, CT: FASB, 1990).

Before beginning our study of futures contracts, options and financial swaps, and the accounting and reporting of them, we offer an overview of key aspects of the 1997 FASB *Draft Statement.* When finalized, this document will significantly affect accounting for some derivatives while leaving the accounting for others mostly unchanged.

NEW DEVELOPMENTS AFFECTING DERIVATIVES

In June, 1996, the FASB issued two *Exposure Drafts* affecting accounting and reporting for derivative financial instruments. One of these was later finalized as *SFAS 130,* "Reporting Comprehensive Income" (1997). The other dealt with derivative and similar financial instruments and hedging activities. Retitled "Accounting for Derivative Instruments and Hedging Activities," a complete revision dated September 12, 1997, is now available and is subject to further modifications as this book goes to press. Because this document was not reissued as a revised *Exposure Draft,* we refer to it here, and in Chapter 10, as a **Draft Statement.** This section summarizes the major provisions of this *Draft Statement;* later sections apply its provisions to illustrations of the futures contracts, option contracts and financial swaps studied in this chapter.

Before examining the 1997 *Draft Statement* in detail, we briefly review *SFAS 130.* Building on concepts developed in FASB *Concepts Statements 5* and *6, SFAS 130* prescribes how the components of **comprehensive income**—all changes in owners' equity other than those resulting from transactions with owners—are to be reported in an expanded income statement or elsewhere in the financial statements or notes. *Other* **comprehensive income** refers to components other than those reported in net income. These components currently include (1) *SFAS 52* foreign currency translation adjustments arising when the *current rate method* is used and (2) *SFAS 115* unrealized gains and losses on *available-for-sale securities* that currently bypass the income statement and are carried directly to stockholders' equity. The *Draft Statement* adds a new component—gains and losses on derivatives used in certain hedging situations.[5]

1997 FASB *DRAFT STATEMENT* ON DERIVATIVES

The 1997 *Draft Statement* was developed and is being modified in an atmosphere of sometimes intense criticism by financial and nonfinancial companies and Federal Reserve Board Chairman Alan Greenspan. Congressional initiatives seek to overturn the proposed new rules and/or to remove accounting standard setting from the private sector. However, the FASB is committed to this project and has the support of the SEC. As we go to press, the Board intends to issue a final statement later in 1998, effective for fiscal years beginning after June 15, 1999. The FASB states that the *Draft Statement* incorporates four important principles:

- **Derivatives are assets and liabilities** and should be recognized in the financial statements, not only as footnote disclosures.
- **Fair value** is the only relevant valuation basis for derivatives.
- **Only assets and liabilities** should be reported in the balance sheet.
- **Special accounting for hedge instruments and hedged items** should be restricted to qualifying transactions, based primarily on an assessment of offsetting changes in fair values or cash flows.

---

[5] For further discussion of these issues, see L. Todd Johnson and Robert J. Swieringa, "Derivatives, Hedging and Comprehensive Income," *Accounting Horizons* (December, 1996), 109-122.

ACCOUNTING FOR CHANGES IN FAIR VALUE

Accounting for changes in the fair value of a derivative depends on why it is held. Fair value changes are reported in earnings *unless* the derivative qualifies as a hedge and is designated as a hedging instrument. Either all or a part of a derivative may be designated as the hedge instrument. The rules are summarized next:

- **Derivatives *not* designated as hedges:** value changes are reported in current earnings.
- **Derivatives designated as hedges:** how value changes are reported varies with the type of exposure being hedged, as follows:
  - *Fair value hedges:* for hedges of exposure to changes in fair value of *existing assets, liabilities or firm commitments,* the gain or loss due to a change in fair value of the derivative is reported in earnings concurrently with the change in the fair value of the hedged item. When *firm commitments* are hedged items, an asset or liability that represents the fair value of the financial instrument aspect of the commitment is recognized.
  - *Cash flow hedges:* for hedges of the variable cash flows of a *forecasted transaction,* the gain or loss due to a change in the fair value of the derivative is initially reported in *other comprehensive income* (outside of earnings) and then in earnings during the period(s) in which the forecasted transaction affects earnings.
  - *Foreign currency hedges:* these hedges include both derivative *and* designated nonderivative financial instruments, such as a foreign currency denominated loan. Fair value and cash flow foreign currency hedges are accounted for as above, *except* that the gain or loss on the hedge of a foreign available-for-sale security is recorded in earnings together with the gain or loss on the hedged available-for-sale security. (Under *SFAS 115*, gains/losses on available-for-sale securities are otherwise reported in other comprehensive income). A *transaction adjustment* on a hedge of a net investment in a foreign entity is reported the same way as the *translation adjustment* on the foreign entity. Both enter the cumulative translation adjustment component of *other comprehensive income* when the current rate method of translation is used. Any other value change in the hedge is reported in earnings.

Fair Value Hedges

When the hedged item is an *existing asset or liability*, whether carried at cost or fair value, the gain or loss attributable to the hedged risk is reported in earnings and adjusts the carrying value of the asset or liability. The offsetting gain or loss on the hedge instrument is concurrently reported in earnings. Thus if the hedged item is carried at fair value and value changes are otherwise reported in other comprehensive income, the value change now enters current earnings to offset the value change of the hedge. The adjusted carrying value of the hedged item enters earnings when the asset is sold or the liability is liquidated.

When the hedged item is a *firm commitment,* there is no asset or liability to be adjusted to market to offset the gain or loss on the hedge instrument. Therefore, the offset to the gain or loss is itself recognized as creating a new asset or liability. This was illustrated in Chapter 10 for foreign currency firm commitments. In these situations, the hedge has no net effect on current earnings—offsetting gains/losses are both reported—and the reported amount of sales or purchases is adjusted by closing the newly-created asset or liability to sales or purchases.

Example 1: Foreign Currency Fair Value Hedge. Suppose a U.S. company enters a foreign currency forward sale contract to hedge investments in yen denominated debt securities, classified as available-for-sale under *SFAS 115*. These securities increase in value by $25,000, assumed equal to the transaction loss on the forward sale contract as the $/yen rate increases. This transaction loss is reported in earnings. Under *SFAS 115,* the $25,000 gain on the securities, hedged or not, is reported in other comprehensive income, net of tax. In contrast, the *Draft Statement* reports the $25,000 gain on the *hedged* securities in earnings to offset the $25,000 transaction loss on the forward sale contract, the hedging instrument.

Cash Flow Hedges

These hedges relate to forecasted or anticipated transactions, *not* firm commitments. When such forecasted transactions are denominated in foreign currency units, *SFAS 52* treats instruments used to hedge foreign currency risk on forecasted transactions as *speculative*. Thus *SFAS 52* prohibits deferral of value changes in the hedging instrument, instead reporting them in earnings. Moreover, because *SFAS 52* was enacted prior to *SFAS 130* on comprehensive income, there was no place "outside" of current earnings to report the gain or loss. Thus, if the forward sale contract in Example 1 is instead hedging a forecasted foreign currency sale transaction, the $25,000 transaction loss is reported in other comprehensive income until the forecasted foreign currency sale transaction occurs. At that time the loss is released from other comprehensive income and enters earnings.

Foreign Currency Hedges

Foreign currency fair value and cash flow hedges are examined in the above paragraphs. To explain how hedges of net investments in foreign entities are treated, we offer this example.

Example 2. Now assume a U.S. company *issued* foreign currency denominated debt securities to hedge its net investment in a foreign operation. When the direct rate falls, the dollar strengthens and creates a transaction gain on the foreign debt. At the same time, the net assets of the foreign operation decline in dollar equivalent, creating a translation loss. Further assume that this translation loss is $25 million but that the fair value of the foreign currency debt decreased by $35 million. This $35 million includes a $25 million transaction gain and another $10 million gain due to credit conditions in the foreign country. The *Draft Statement* reports the foregoing as follows:

- Translation loss on foreign investment—$25 million charged to other comprehensive income under the current rate method of translation
- Transaction gain on foreign debt—$25 million credited to other comprehensive income
- Additional gain on foreign debt—$10 million credited to current earnings

Although the ensuing discussions of accounting for derivatives emphasizes current practice, we note how the 1997 *Draft Statement* affects current practice and apply it to selected illustrations in the chapter.

FUTURES CONTRACTS

Although discussion of hedging foreign currency transactions in Chapter 10 focused on *forward contracts* used for these purposes, accounting for *foreign currency futures contracts*—standardized contracts for future delivery as discussed below—is also prescribed by *SFAS 52*. We now turn to *other* types of futures contracts, such as *commodity futures, interest rate futures, and stock index futures*, and the accounting standards developed for them in *SFAS 80*, "Accounting for Futures Contracts."

INTRODUCTION TO FUTURES CONTRACTS

The FASB defines a **futures contract** as follows:

> A legal agreement between a buyer or seller and the clearinghouse of a futures exchange . . . in the United States and . . . in other countries . . . (a) They obligate the purchaser (seller) to accept (make) delivery of a standardized quantity of a commodity or financial instrument at a specified date or during a specified period, or they provide for cash settlement rather than delivery, (b) they effectively can be canceled before the delivery date by entering into an offsetting contract for the same commodity or financial instrument, and (c) all changes in value of open contracts are settled on a regular basis, usually daily.[6]

From this definition we see that traders in futures contracts have agreements with a *clearinghouse*, or clearing corporation, not with other traders. Changes in market value are usually settled in cash with the clearinghouse on a daily basis. Contracts can be effectively closed out by entering an identical but offsetting contract. Although actual delivery pursuant to a futures contract is rarely contemplated—overall delivery rates approximate only 3 percent—it does vary between type of contract, with delivery occurring more frequently where financial instruments are involved. No delivery mechanism exists for Treasury Bill futures, for *index futures*—futures contracts for stock market and other market indexes—or for *Eurodollar futures*—futures for dollar balances on deposit outside the United States; instead, cash settlements are made. Futures contracts are traded on the Chicago Board of Trade, the New York Mercantile Exchange, the London International Financial Futures Exchange, and other exchanges.

Futures and Forward Contracts Compared

Both forward contracts and futures contracts are *derivative financial instruments*—their values are *derived* from the prices of the items deliverable under the contracts. To illustrate transacting in a foreign currency futures contract, as opposed to a forward contract, consider an importer that requires a steady supply of pounds sterling at known prices. The company purchases a *foreign currency futures contract*, traded on a futures exchange, for a desired quantity of the needed pounds sterling. The futures price is $1.20/£. As the futures contract approaches maturity, its price moves in tandem with the spot price. If the spot price increases by $.12/£ at maturity, the futures price rises to about $1.32/£. Even though the company purchases the currency on the spot market,

---

[6] Financial Accounting Standards Board, *Statement of Financial Accounting Standards No. 80*, "Accounting for Futures Contracts" (Stamford, CT: FASB, 1984), par. 15.

the spot price paid is reduced by the gain on the futures contract, which was realized daily as the futures price moves up. Thus the company pays a net of $1.20/£ (= $1.32/£ − $.12/£).

In contrast, *foreign currency forward contracts* are usually made with dealers in foreign exchange and are tailored to fit the needs of the transacting entity. Delivery of the subject currency is intended and does occur. Changes in the market value of a forward contract constitute accounting events, but cash is not actually transferred until the contract matures and the currency is delivered.

Graphical Interpretation of Futures Contracts

Because a futures contract is analytically similar to a standardized forward contract, the payoff profiles of futures and their ability to hedge underlying exposures mirror those same characteristics of forward contracts. These characteristics are diagrammed in Figure 11.1, which is similar to Figure 10.1. Note that the horizontal axes in the Figure 11.1 diagrams reflect a more general measure of price change (ΔP) than the exchange rate change used for forward contracts in the last chapter. This notation accommodates the need here, and in other similar diagrams throughout this chapter, for price changes to refer to commodity prices, stock prices, foreign currency prices (exchange rates), bond prices, or interest rates. In interpreting Figure 11.1, note that the top two panels—A and D—refer only to the futures contracts. If the futures contracts serve as hedges, panels B and E graph the underlying exposure to be hedged. Panels C and F show the net result of using a futures contract as a perfect hedge of the underlying exposure.

Consider Panels A, B, and C in Figure 11.1. Recall that a forward purchase contract may be used to hedge a liability or other commitment to be settled in units of foreign currency. It does so by fixing the dollar price of the foreign currency to be purchased to settle the foreign currency liability. In the more general futures context, one purchases a futures contract (goes *long*; Panel A) in order to hedge, or fix the price of, items to be purchased which will be delivered to settle a liability or similar commitment (the underlying exposure; Panel B). Whether or not delivery under the terms of the futures contract occurs, the long futures position must be closed out with the clearinghouse. The gain (loss) realized when the futures position is closed out offsets the loss (gain) resulting from the change in price of the needed item on the spot market. Thus the net cost of the item approximates the futures price when the futures contract was initially purchased. When delivery does occur, the final futures price, which is close to the spot price, generally serves as the transaction price.

The underlying exposure and the hedge produce offsetting gains and losses so that in Panel C we see that risk of both loss *and* gain is eliminated. Similarly, to hedge or neutralize the effects of price changes on assets held for sale (Panel E), one sells a futures contract (goes *short*; panel D). If the price falls and produces a loss on the asset, the short futures contract can be closed out at a gain by purchasing a long position at the lower price. When the asset's price rises, however, the gain on the asset is offset by a loss on the futures contract. Panel F shows that the net effect of hedging is to remove the chance of both loss and gain.

Numerical Example of Panels D, E and F in Figure 11.1. Suppose a farmer owns 100,000 bushels of a particular commodity expected to be sold in 90 days. The current spot price is $4.00/bushel. Panel E shows the farmer's exposure. Assume that $4.00/bushel is the spot price at the origin. If the spot price falls to $3.80/bushel in 90 days—to the left of the origin—the farmer incurs a loss of $.20/bushel, indicated by the *upward-sloping* diagonal line in the *lower* left quadrant of Panel E.

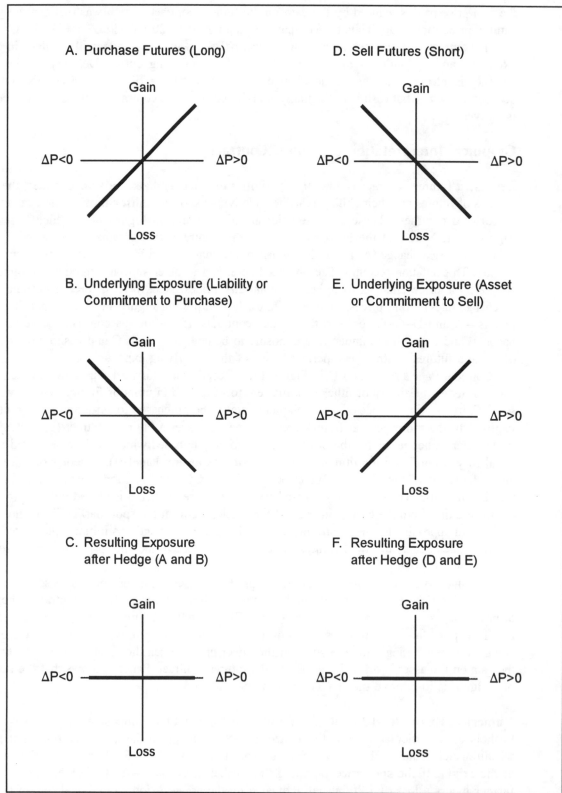

FIGURE 11.1   PAYOFF PROFILES OF FUTURES CONTRACTS, UNDERLYING
EXPOSURES AND RESULTING EXPOSURES

To hedge this exposure, the farmer sells futures for 100,000 bushels; Panel D shows the exposure created by the futures contract alone. Ignoring basis, the $.20/bushel decrease in the spot price creates a gain on the futures contract, indicated by the *downward-sloping* diagonal line in the *upper* left quadrant of Panel D. When the futures contract is closed by purchasing futures for $3.80 and the commodity inventory is sold, the original $4.00/bushel price is maintained:

Original value of commodities owned (100,000 × $4.00)	$400,000
Loss on commodities owned [($3.80 − $4.00)100,000]	(20,000)
Net proceeds from sale of commodity inventory	$380,000
Gain on futures contract [($4.00 − $3.80)100,000]	20,000
Net proceeds to farmer	$400,000

Thus the exposure in Panel E and the hedge in Panel D create Panel F in which the possibility of loss *and* gain is removed.

Commodity futures, which involve contracting for future delivery of specified fungible commodities such as agricultural products and precious metals, have existed for well over 100 years. **Interest rate futures,** however, developed within the last 20-25 years. "An interest rate futures contract is a contract to make or take delivery of a certain type of interest-bearing security at some future time. The price that will be received (or paid) is based on the price of the particular futures contract when a trade is executed."[7] That is, the price of the futures contract, when entered, fixes the price to be received or paid for the securities. Although delivery of the securities bought or sold in an interest rate futures contract rarely occurs, value changes in the futures contract preserve the price when the trade was executed. Prices of interest rate futures are normally stated as an index, a percentage of 100 or face value, which reflects annual yield. Thus if the futures price is 89, the designated securities will be delivered at a discount yield of 11 percent (= 100 − 89).

Among the most common interest rate futures are futures contracts on *U.S. Treasury securities* and *Eurodollar deposits* of varying maturities. The **Eurodollar market** is a market for U.S. dollar-denominated loans and time deposits of varying maturities made by banks outside the U.S.—foreign banks and foreign branches of U.S. banks. This market started with a group of European banks in the 1960s; today it is a widely diversified international market. Such banks often operate in jurisdictions less regulated than the U.S. and can offer more favorable interest rates to depositors and borrowers.

The Eurodollar market is one component of the **Eurocurrency market**, the international market for bank time deposits and loans denominated in currencies other than the bank's home currency. *Euroyen* and *Eurodeutschemarks* are examples.

Just as we shall see that U.S. Treasury bill futures can be used to hedge against changes in U.S. interest rates, Eurodollar futures can be used to hedge against changes in interest rates on Eurodollar deposits. Indeed, the linkages between domestic interest rates on Treasury securities and Eurodollar interest rates produce nearly identical performance in Treasury bill futures and Eurodollar futures.

Transacting in Futures Contracts

Futures contracts rarely result in actual delivery. Rather, an entity transacting in the futures markets settles or closes its futures position at some time during the term of the contract by

---

[7] Larry M. Walther, "Commodity Futures: What the Accountant Should Know," *Journal of Accountancy* (March, 1982), 78.

entering an offsetting futures position. Actual sale and delivery of commodities or securities for which futures contracts exist occur in cash or spot markets. Because spot prices and futures prices usually move together, any gain or loss realized on the futures contract usually offsets the loss or gain resulting from movements in spot prices of the commodities or securities of concern.

Even though spot prices and futures prices tend to move together, they *differ* by an amount called *basis*.

> **Basis** refers to the difference between an item's spot price and the corresponding futures price.

For *commodities*, basis is the difference between the spot price in a particular locality and the futures price for delivery in the nearest futures delivery month. To illustrate, when the cash (spot) price of soybean meal in Decatur, Illinois, is $167 per ton in June and the futures price for July delivery is $174 per ton, the July basis is said to be "$7 under." For *foreign currencies* such as the British pound, when the spot price (exchange rate) of the British pound in July is $1.546/£ and the September futures price is $1.544/£, the September basis is said to be "$.002 over." Because basis fluctuates over time due to changing supply/demand conditions in futures and spot markets, and across locations, spot and futures prices do not always move in perfect tandem. Unanticipated changes in basis mean that hedging rarely results in a "perfect wash".[8]

Accounting Events in Futures Trading

An entity using futures contracts traded on an organized exchange encounters two types of accounting events prior to settlement of the contract:

1. An **initial margin deposit**—cash or government securities—must be paid to the broker upon inception of the contract. The margin deposit ranges from less than 1 percent of face value on some interest rate futures contracts to over 10 percent on some commodity futures. This is not a commission or transaction cost; rather, it represents a performance bond.

2. At the end of each trading day, the clearinghouse values each outstanding contract at the closing price. The contract is thereby **marked to market** and the entity must either deposit additional funds with the broker—a realized loss—or receive cash or a credit to its account from the broker—a realized gain—for the change in the value of the contract. The amount deposited, however, cannot fall below the applicable *maintenance margin* required by the clearinghouse.

If the entity has a *long* position (it is a *purchaser* of futures), an increase in price produces a gain and a decrease in price produces a loss. The entity could choose to close out its long position and lock in the realized gain or loss by selling its long contract. Similarly, if the entity has a *short* position (it is a *seller* of futures), an increase in price produces a loss and a decrease in price produces a gain. Here the entity could close out its short position by purchasing a long

---

[8] For more on *basis*, see *Understanding Basis: The Economics of Where and When*, prepared by the Chicago Board of Trade Clearing Corporation and Fred Bailey (n.d.).

contract, again locking in the realized gain or loss. Both long and short positions in futures are illustrated next.

'Long' Example. Suppose an entity purchases commodity futures (goes *long*) for 100,000 units at $7.50 per unit. At the close of the next trading day, the commodity futures are selling at $7.60 per unit. The entity realizes a *gain* of $10,000 [= ($7.60 − $7.50) 100,000] on the commodity futures because it would receive an additional $.10 per unit if it sold the contracts for $7.60 per unit to close out its long position.

'Short' Example. Suppose an entity sells (goes *short*) $1,000,000 face value interest rate futures (91-day Treasury bills) at 88. At the close of the next trading day, the interest rate futures have increased to 88.5. The entity realizes a *loss* of $5,000 [= (.88 − .885) $1,000,000] on the interest rate futures; it would have to pay an additional $.005 per dollar if it purchased long futures contracts at 88.5 to close out its short position.

The examples just presented refer to Panels A and D of Figure 11.1; that is, to the futures contracts only. Without underlying exposures—as in Panels B and E—the futures are entered for speculative purposes. When the futures contracts in the above examples serve as hedges, the gain on the commodity futures is approximately offset by the rising cost of purchasing the needed commodities, and the loss on the interest rate futures offsets the gain from lower interest cost when short-term notes are issued.

ACCOUNTING STANDARDS FOR FUTURES CONTRACTS

With the basic economics in mind, we now consider the fundamental accounting issue relating to treatment of the realized gain or loss on a futures contract: Should it be recognized in income immediately or should it be deferred? Although *SFAS 80* provides generally for *immediate recognition in income*, the gain or loss is *deferred* when the contract is an *effective hedge* of one of the following:

- An **existing exposure**—ownership of or liability to deliver the commodity.
- A **firm commitment**—legally enforceable obligation to make or accept delivery of the commodity.[9]
- An **anticipated transaction**—intended and expected performance that is not legally enforceable.

An **effective hedge** arises if the item to be hedged exposes the entity to price or interest rate risk and the futures contract reduces that exposure and is designated as a hedge.[10] The entity must expect high correlation between the market value of the futures contract and the fair value or interest rate on the hedged item. In evaluating hedges, *SFAS 80* generally calls for the futures contract to reduce the exposure of the *enterprise* to risk. By comparison, an *SFAS 52* hedge requires that a foreign currency forward/futures contract reduce the more narrow exposure of a

---

[9] The notion of a *firm commitment* was further amplified in EITF (Emerging Issues Task Force) *Issue 91-1*. The EITF agreed that a **firm commitment** requires the presence of sufficiently large disincentives for nonperformance, such as fiduciary responsibilities to lenders, government regulations or large economic penalties.
[10] *SFAS 80*, par. 4.

transaction to risk.[11] Even with effective hedges, however, *when the hedged item is carried at market*, with concurrent recognition of changes in market values in income as gains or losses, changes in the market value of the futures contract serving as the hedge are also *recognized currently in income.*

If the futures contract is entered without the underlying exposure needed for hedge accounting, it becomes an **investment** or **speculative** instrument. Realized gains and losses on such instruments are recognized in income immediately.

Accounting treatment of realized gains and losses on **hedges** of items **not carried at market value** may be summarized as follows:

- *Existing exposure*: Gain or loss adjusts the carrying value of the hedged item, whether carried at cost or lower of cost or market.
- *Firm commitment*: Gain or loss is deferred and adjusts the dollar basis of the transaction occurring when the commitment is fulfilled.
- *Anticipated transaction*: Gain or loss is deferred and adjusts the dollar basis of the related subsequent transaction when it occurs.

Although the accounting for Cases 2 and 3 above is identical (both are similar to the hedge of an identifiable foreign currency commitment discussed in Chapter 10), Case 3 represents a rather broad hedging concept and is the subject of controversy. Indeed, *SFAS 52* requires that a firm commitment—and *not* an anticipated transaction, no matter how probable—exist if hedge accounting is to be used in the foreign currency context. Paragraph 9 of *SFAS 80* discusses two conditions, both of which must be met if a futures contract related to an anticipated transaction is to be treated as a hedge with concurrent deferral of realized gains and losses. These conditions specify (1) that the significant characteristics and expected terms of the anticipated transaction be identified and (2) that it be probable that the anticipated transaction will occur.

At inception, when the futures contract is initially entered, *SFAS 80* requires only that the margin deposit be recorded; this deposit is subsequently marked to market as daily cash settlements are made with the clearinghouse. The adjusted margin deposit is disclosed on the entity's balance sheet at financial reporting dates.

Impact of the 1997 FASB *Draft Statement*

When finalized, the *Draft Statement* supersedes *SFAS 80*. Although the value changes in futures contracts used for investment or speculative purposes continue to be reported in current earnings, the following changes will occur:

- *Fair value hedges* encompass *SFAS 80's* hedges of *existing exposures* and *firm commitments;* value changes in *both* the futures contract and the hedged item will be reported in current earnings. When hedging a firm commitment, the gain/loss on the futures contract is accompanied by a change in cash or the margin deposit. This realization feature of futures contracts means that the value change in the commitment

---

[11] See John E. Stewart, "The Challenges of Hedge Accounting," *Journal of Accountancy* (November 1989), 48-56, for a discussion of hedging issues related to forward contracts, futures contracts, options, and financial swaps.

does not require separate asset/liability recognition, as it does in forward contracts. Thus deferred gains/losses on futures contracts will no longer be recognized.

■ *Cash flow hedges* encompass *SFAS 80's* hedges of *anticipated transactions;* the value change in the futures contract will be reported in other comprehensive income pending completion of the anticipated/forecasted transaction. Deferred gains/losses on futures contracts will no longer be recognized.

ILLUSTRATIONS OF ACCOUNTING FOR FUTURES CONTRACTS

The following examples demonstrates how the provisions of *SFAS 80* are applied. In each example, the futures contract is closed out prior to delivery. Daily mark-to-market is ignored for convenience; instead, total realized gain or loss is recognized when each futures contract is closed. Brokerage commissions and other transaction costs are ignored.

Example 1: Hedge of an Exposed Asset Position

An entity owns 100,000 units of a commodity carried in inventory at cost, $800,000. The commodity will be sold in the normal course of business in 90 days, and the entity wishes to guarantee the current 90-day futures price of $900,000. Thus it sells commodity futures (goes *short*) for delivery in 90 days for $900,000. A margin deposit of $60,000 is recorded as follows:

Margin Deposit	60,000	
Cash		60,000
To record the initial margin deposit on the sale of $900,000 in commodity futures.		

By the end of the next accounting period, the futures price decreased to $850,000 and the company decides to close out its position. To do so, the company purchases a futures contract at the current price of $850,000 and locks in the realized gain of $50,000 (= $900,000 − $850,000), adding it to the deposit account at the brokerage. Because this is a hedge of an *existing exposure*, the realized gain *reduces the carrying value of the hedged inventory*. When the inventory is sold, the reduced carrying value is charged to Cost of Goods Sold and the gain is recognized as a component of gross profit.

Margin Deposit	50,000	
Inventory		50,000
To mark the futures contract and the hedged inventory to market.		

Cash	110,000	
Margin Deposit		110,000
To record receipt of cash from the broker, including the $60,000 initial margin, when the futures contract is closed out.		

In this example, the entity wished to lock in profit of $100,000 (= $900,000 − $800,000). If the inventory is sold at this point for $850,000, the anticipated profit is achieved. The $50,000 gain on the futures contract reduces the carrying value of the inventory to $750,000, and profit of $100,000 (= $850,000 − $750,000) results. Without hedging, profit on sale of the inventory is only $50,000 (= $850,000 − $800,000).

Draft Statement **Application.** To illustrate how the 1997 FASB *Draft Statement* is applied to futures contracts, the $50,000 value change is recorded under the *Draft Statement* as follows:

Margin Deposit	50,000	
Gain on Futures Contract (Earnings)		50,000
To record in earnings the gain on the futures contract		
hedging inventory, an existing asset.		

Unrealized Loss (Earnings)	50,000	
Inventory		50,000
To record in earnings the decrease in fair value		
of the hedged inventory.		

Thus under the *Draft Statement,* the effects on earnings in both timing and amount do not change, and the hedged inventory is marked to market as it was under *SFAS 80.* However, the offsetting gain on the futures contract and loss on the inventory *both* appear in earnings; neither was reported under *SFAS 80.*

Example 2: Hedge of a Firm Liability Commitment

An entity contracts with a financing syndicate to roll over a $1,000,000 floating rate term loan every 91 days. The current annual interest rate on such loans is 12 percent; on U.S. Treasury bills it is 10.5 percent. Assume that the yield on Treasury bills is highly correlated with the yield on the entity's floating rate term loans. To hedge against the possibility that interest rates will rise in 91 days, the entity sells (goes *short*) $1,000,000 face value of 91-day Treasury bill (interest rate) futures at 89.5 (= 100 − annual discount yield of 10.5 percent) and deposits $2,500 cash with the broker as margin:

Margin Deposit	2,500	
Cash		2,500
To record the initial margin deposit on the sale of		
$1,000,000 face value 91-day Treasury bill futures.		

At the end of the 91-day period, the futures price has risen to 92.3 and the entity realized a loss of $7,000 [= (.895 − .923) $1,000,000/4]. Although these are 91-day Treasury bills, the futures price reflects *annual* yields, not 91-day yields. The entity now closes out its short futures position, transferring an additional $7,000 to the broker to cover the loss and retrieving the original margin deposit.

Deferred Loss on Futures Contract	7,000	
Cash		7,000
To record the realized loss on the futures contract,		
deferring it pending completion of the new loan,		
and transfer $7,000 cash to the broker.		

Cash	2,500	
Margin Deposit		2,500
To record receipt of the initial margin deposit from		
the broker when the futures contract is closed out.		

At this point the futures contract is closed out. The original $2,500 deposited when the short position was entered at 89.5 is returned. In effect, the additional $7,000 transferred to the broker, and not returned, is the incremental cost of offsetting the short position entered at 89.5 with a long position entered at 92.3. Now the loan is rolled over.

Short-Term Loan Payable (Old)	1,000,000	
Short-Term Loan Payable (New)		1,000,000
To roll over the floating rate term loan.		

Discount on Short-Term Loan Payable (New)	7,000	
Deferred Loss on Futures Contract		7,000
To reclassify the deferred loss on the futures contract		
entered to hedge the new loan payable as a *discount*		
on that new loan payable.		

In addition to coupon interest on the new short-term loan, the $7,000 discount on the loan will be amortized to interest expense over the 91-day term of the new loan. Note that at 92.3, Treasury bills have an annual yield of 7.7 percent (= 100 − 92.3). Assuming that the 1.5 percent (= 12 percent − 10.5 percent) spread between the entity's short-term loans and Treasury bills still holds, the new loan pays interest at the rate of 9.2 percent (= 7.7 percent + 1.5 percent). The $7,000 loss on the futures contract is exactly offset by the reduced interest on the new loan, $7,000 [= (.12 − .092) $1,000,000/4]. Effectively, the old 12 percent rate is maintained for another 91-day period. Had the hedge *not* been undertaken, however, the interest cost on the loan is only 9.2 percent. Although the hedge could be criticized, it was effective; that is, it locked in the previous interest cost and extended it to the new financing.

In contrast, if interest rates rise, the futures price decreases. This decline in the futures price produces a gain on the short futures contract that is offset by the increased interest the entity must pay on the new loan. Although this was the situation the company was hedging against, an effective hedge works regardless of whether the price of the hedged item rises or falls, and neutralizes both loss *and* gain.

Example 3: Hedge of an Anticipated Purchase

A jewelry manufacturer is planning its silver requirements over the next several months. The entity anticipates an increase in the demand for silver jewelry with a concurrent upward movement in the price of silver. Although it is not contractually required to supply silver jewelry to its customers, the entity expects to do so because it fears loss of customers if it does not supply the jewelry ordered at competitive prices. Therefore, to guarantee a supply of silver at relatively favorable prices, the entity purchases (goes *long*) 20,000 ounces of silver bullion for delivery in 90 days at $7.70 per ounce and makes a margin deposit of $20,000 cash:

Margin Deposit	20,000	
Cash		20,000
To record the initial margin deposit of $20,000 on the		
purchase of $154,000 (= $7.70 × 20,000) of silver futures.		

Over the next three months, the futures price increases to $7.90 per ounce, as the entity predicted. A gain of $4,000 [= ($7.90 − $7.70) 20,000] is realized. The entity closes out its long position and, several days later, purchases the silver it needs on the spot market for $7.88 per ounce. These events are recorded as follows:

Margin Deposit	4,000	
Deferred Gain on Futures Contract		4,000

To record the gain on the futures contract, which
increases the deposit with the broker, and defer
it pending completion of the anticipated transaction.

Cash	24,000	
Margin Deposit		24,000

To record receipt of cash from the broker, including
the initial $20,000 deposit, when the futures contract
is closed out.

Inventory	157,600	
Cash		157,600

To record the purchase of 20,000 ounces of silver
billion at $7.88 per ounce on the spot market.

Deferred Gain on Futures Contract	4,000	
Inventory		4,000

To adjust the carrying value of the silver bullion just
purchased—the anticipated transaction occurred—by
the deferred gain on the futures contract.

Note that the hedge effectively locked in the desired price of $7.70 per ounce. Even though a $4,000 gain was realized on the futures contract, it was offset by the higher current cost of silver on the spot market. When the silver was acquired on the spot market at $7.88 per ounce, its net cost, considering the hedge, was $7.68 [= ($157,600 − $4,000)/20,000] per ounce.

Example 4: Using Futures in an Investment Portfolio

Money managers and individual investors with large diversified portfolios are using futures in an attempt to reduce risk.[12] The basic idea is to invest some portion of a portfolio in stock and bond index futures and commodity futures (go *long*) instead of purchasing the securities or commodities themselves. Money equal to the value of the futures contracts desired is set aside; the amount not used for margin requirements is invested in liquid low-risk securities.

Suppose $520,000 is available to invest. A Standard & Poor (S&P) 500 Index futures contract sells for 500 times the value of the Index. Such a contract maturing in March 19X9 sells for about $130,000 in September, 19X8. Four of these contracts absorb the $520,000. Assuming a 15 percent margin requirement, a $78,000 (= 4 × .15 × $130,000) margin deposit is required when the four contracts are purchased. The remaining $442,000 (= $520,000 − $78,000) is invested in Treasury bills yielding 7 percent annually to soften the swings on what is essentially a $520,000 investment in equities. A money manager using this strategy records the following:

---

[12] Stanley W. Angrist, "Futures Can Reduce Risk, Some Contend," *The Wall Street Journal*, September 2, 1988, 25.

Margin Deposit	78,000	
Investment in Treasury Bills	442,000	
Cash		520,000

To record the initial margin deposit on four March,
19X9, S&P 500 Index futures contracts and the
purchase of Treasury bills for $442,000.

Three months later, at the end of December 19X8, the S&P 500 Index futures price declined by 1 percent and the contracts are closed out by selling them when their current value is $514,800. A loss of $5,200—1 percent of the contracts' original value in September—is realized and cash is deposited accordingly. This loss is recognized currently because the futures are used for speculation, not for hedging. Originally bought at a discount, the Treasury bills increased in price, providing interest income of $7,735 (= .07 × $442,000/4), which is now accrued.

Loss on Futures Contracts	5,200	
Cash		5,200

To record the loss on the futures contracts and the
additional cash deposit to cover it.

Cash	78,000	
Margin Deposit		78,000

To record receipt of the initial margin deposit once
the contracts are closed out.

Investment in Treasury Bills	7,735	
Interest Income		7,735

To accrue the interest income of $7,735 on the
Treasury bills.

The net result of this strategy is that the low margin requirement on futures contracts allows a full investment in $520,000 of diversified equities *and* a $442,000 short-term risk-free investment. Because the equities were not actually purchased, though, dividends declared on them are foregone. In this case, the interest income turned the $5,200 loss on the equities, excluding the foregone dividends, into a net gain of $2,535 (= $7,735 − $5,200).

OPTIONS

Like futures contracts, **options** represent a way to protect against, or take advantage of, developments occurring at a later time. Options (like futures) are *derivative financial instruments*—their values are *derived* from the prices of the optioned items or from expectations about those prices. Unlike futures contracts, however, *options are one-sided* and require performance by only one of the parties. Options on individual equity securities and various indexes, such as the S&P 500, Value Line, and Gold/Silver indexes, are traded on the Chicago Board Options Exchange, the American Stock Exchange, the Philadelphia Stock Exchange, and other exchanges. Option traders execute agreements with the clearing corporations of those exchanges, not with each other as individuals. There are also many *over-the-counter* options having *nonstandardized* terms which are not traded on exchanges. Options on many futures contracts—**futures options**—are traded on several exchanges. In this latter case, the optioned item is a *futures contract on a commodity, currency, or financial instrument*, rather than the commodity, currency, or financial instrument itself. Following is a good working definition of an option:

> An **option** is a contract *allowing*, but *not requiring*, its holder to buy (*call*) or sell (*put*) a *specific* or *standard* commodity or equity security or other financial instrument at a *specified price* during a *specified time period* or on a *specified date*.[13]

As stated above, whereas futures contracts obligate *both* the long trader and the short trader to perform, an option is *one-sided*. The option obligates *only* the writer—the individual or entity granting the option—to perform; it *allows* the holder to demand performance from the writer. Whether performance will be demanded, however, depends upon the terms of the option and the current market price of the optioned item.

AUTHORS' COMMENTARY

Strategies involving futures contracts and options can be very complex* and often involve combinations of long and short positions as well as various types of hedging and speculative activities. Similarly, the accounting for such transactions can also be complex. Moreover, application of accounting standards is unsettled in several areas. Controversy still swirls around what constitutes an anticipated transaction for which *hedge accounting* is appropriate, the applicability of hedge accounting to complex hedging strategies, and measurement of correlation between the hedge instrument and the hedged item.

Hedge Accounting. Hedge accounting refers to accounting treatments used to implement the notion that a hedge instrument is an integral part of the hedged item. Because the economic purpose of the hedge is to neutralize gain/loss on the hedged item, accounting should report that result. In most cases, historical cost accounting recognizes gain/loss only when *realized*. For this reason, exceptions must frequently be made in hedge accounting so that offsetting income effects of the hedge instrument and the hedged item are reported in the same accounting period. Futures contracts are an obvious example. By definition, the cash transfer made under daily *mark-to-market* represents *realized* gain/loss on the futures.

Under the **deferral approach,** prevalent in current practice, the realized gain/loss on the hedge instrument is *deferred* pending recognition of gain/loss on the hedged item, either by adjusting the carrying value of existing exposed assets/liabilities or by holding the deferred amount in suspense pending completion of qualifying future transactions. Under the **mark-to-market approach,** favored by the 1997 FASB *Draft Statement*, both the hedged item and the hedge instrument are measured at fair value; value changes in both items are *recognized* in income in the periods in which they occur.

---

[13] Arthur Andersen & Co., *Accounting for Options* (Chicago: Arthur Andersen & Co., 1986), p. 24 (emphasis added).

Application of Hedge Accounting. The problem in applying hedge accounting in current practice involves the inconsistent criteria currently governing when this type of accounting is applied to different hedge instruments. We saw that *SFAS 52* and *SFAS 80* have different requirements for hedge accounting applied to almost identical hedge instruments. Applicability of hedge accounting to instruments discussed in the remainder of the chapter—options and financial swaps—and to other instruments not studied here is not adequately covered by current authoritative guidance. When finalized, the 1997 FASB *Draft Statement* should resolve this problem. Although we cannot, in this space, solve the problem of when hedge accounting is appropriate, we urge the reader to appreciate its seriousness. *Hedge accounting often results in shifting reported gain/loss to a period other than the period in which the economic gain/loss occurred*; extreme care should be taken to specify when such shifting is permitted.

---

* For further reading, see Harold Bierman, Jr., L. Todd Johnson and D. Scott Peterson, *Hedge Accounting: An Exploratory Study of the Underlying Issues*, A FASB *Research Report* (Norwalk, CT: FASB, 1991); Robert H. Herz, "Hedge Accounting, Derivatives, and Synthetics: The FASB Starts Rethinking the Rules," *Journal of Corporate Accounting and Finance* (Spring, 1994), 323-335; L. Todd Johnson, Halsey G. Bullen and Victoria W. Kern, "Hedge Accounting: Is Deferral the Only Option?" *Journal of Accountancy* (January, 1994), 53-56, 58; and Keith Wishon, "Futures Contracts: Guidance on Applying Statement 80," *Highlights of Financial Reporting Issues* (Stamford, CT: FASB, June, 1985).

DEFINITIONS

The two basic types of options are commonly referred to as *puts* and *calls*. A **put**, also known as an *option to sell*, allows the *holder* to *sell* the optioned item to the *writer*, who is obligated to pay the agreed-upon price during the agreed-upon time period. The put writer who sold the optioned item short is said to be **covered** because exercise of the put provides the writer with the item to cover the short sale. Otherwise the put writer is **naked.**

In contrast, a **call**, also known as an *option to buy*, allows the *holder* to *purchase* the optioned item from the *writer*, who is obligated to accept the agreed-upon price during the agreed-upon time period. A *covered* call writer is one who owns the optioned item, which can be delivered if the call is exercised. Otherwise the call writer is *naked*. Consider the individual who owns 100 shares of IBM stock and writes a call on IBM. If the call is exercised, the writer delivers the shares owned, and does not have to get the cash needed to first purchase IBM shares in the market at their current price.

As a simple illustration, suppose A sells to B a *call option* for 100 shares of stock, exercisable at the stock's current market price of $60 per share and expiring in 90 days. A receives $120 for the call. If the price of the stock does not rise above $60 during the 90 days, B does not exercise the right to buy and allows the call to expire. In this case, A made $120 from writing the call and B lost $120. Should the stock rise above $60, say to $62, B either exercises the call by paying $6,000 to A for 100 shares of stock worth $6,200 or sells the call. The call's price is at least $200 [= ($62 − $60)100], reflecting the increase in the stock's price *above* $60.

In contrast, if A had instead written and sold to B a *put option* with the above terms, B will exercise or sell the put only if the stock's price falls below $60. If the stock's price falls to $57,

B can exercise the put by selling stock worth $5,700 to A for $6,000. Similarly, the put could be sold at a price reflecting the $300 [= ($60 − $57)100] decrease in the stock's price *below* $60.

The *agreed-upon price* is referred to as the **strike price** or **exercise price**, and the *agreed-upon time period* is bounded by the expiration date. An **American option** can be exercised at any time during the agreed-upon time period, whereas a **European option** can be exercised only on the *expiration date*. Only American options are discussed in this text.

An option is **in the money** when it is more profitable for the holder to exercise the option instead of transacting directly in the optioned item. Otherwise the option is **out of the money** or, when the current market price of the optioned item equals the strike price, the option is **at the money**. A *put* is in the money when the strike price *exceeds* the current market price of the optioned item; a *call* is in the money when the strike price is *less than* the current market price of the optioned item.

For example, suppose that stock in Apple Computer is selling for $45.50 a share in the stock market. A *call option* on Apple Computer stock with a strike price of $50 is *out of the money* because the holder could purchase the stock directly in the stock market for $45.50, less than the strike price of $50 it would cost to exercise the call and purchase the stock from the writer. In contrast, a *put option* at $50 is *in the money*, because the holder could sell the stock to the writer for $50, more than the $45.50 it would bring from sale in the stock market. These relationships are summarized below.

Price Relationship	In, Out or At the Money	
	Puts	Calls
Strike Price > Price of Optioned Item	In	Out
Strike Price < Price of Optioned Item	Out	In
Strike Price = Price of Optioned Item	At	At

The price of an option is referred to as its **premium**. The premium is composed of the option's **intrinsic value**—the amount that the option is *in the money*—and its **time value**—the excess of the premium over the option's intrinsic value. Because the probability that the option will be in the money increases as the expiration date grows more distant, the time value component of the premium is positively related to the time remaining to expiration. For the hedger, the time value is the *cost of protection* and is a type of insurance cost.[14]

Consider the above options on Apple Computer stock with a $50 strike price. The stock is currently priced at $45.50. Under "Listed Options Quotations" in the financial press, we see that a *call option* on one share of Apple Computer stock expiring in 40 days, even though out of the money, commands a premium (time value) of $.44. The premium (time value) on a call option expiring in 100 days is $1.38. A *put option* expiring in 40 days, in the money by $4.50 (= $50.00 − $45.50), trades at a premium of $4.63, indicating a time value of $.13. The same put expiring in 100 days has a premium of $5.25, which includes a time value of $.75. In general, the time value cannot be negative and reflects market participants' expectations regarding anticipated

---

[14] Controversy over the use of stock options for executive compensation produced FASB *Statement 123*, "Accounting for Stock-Based Compensation" (1995). Because executive stock options are usually *out of the money* when granted, firms recognized no compensation expense when granting these options to employees. Under *SFAS 123*, on the grant date firms either (1) charge the estimated fair value (i.e., *time value)* of such options to earnings or (2) provide footnote disclosure of the effect on earnings.

movements in the market price of the optioned item, which in this case is stock in Apple Computer.

APPLICATIONS: EFFECTS ON WRITER AND HOLDER

As with the other financial instruments discussed in this chapter, options are used for hedging and speculative purposes. One clear advantage to the holder of options is the one-sided ability to benefit from constructive ownership of large quantities of Apple stock with a minimal investment, although any dividends or interest paid on an optioned security are not received by the option holder. Purchase of one call contract—a standard option contract is for 100 shares—on Apple Computer stock with a $50 exercise price that expires in 100 days costs about $138. This compares with a $4,550 outlay to buy 100 shares of Apple, or perhaps half that amount if the shares are bought on margin. If Apple stock increases to $54.25 per share before the option expires, the option goes in the money by $4.25. Thus the holder's investment—covering 100 shares—more than triples [$425 > (3 × $138)] but any dividends declared by Apple during the option period are foregone.

In contrast, the *writer* of the call is assuming the risk that Apple Computer stock will rise; the time value component of the premium is the writer's compensation. While the option writer may be thought of as a speculator, many option writers take offsetting speculative positions to substantially hedge their aggregate risk.

Changes in the optioned item's price affect the option's intrinsic value only when the option is *at* or *in* the money. How such changes affect the holder and writer depends in turn on whether the option is a put or a call. The gain/loss effects are clearest when the option is in a neutral position—*at the money*.

	Holder		Writer	
Price of Optioned Item	**Puts**	**Calls**	**Puts**	**Calls**
Increases	—*	Gain	—*	Loss
Decreases	Gain	—*	Loss	—*

* The holder's potential loss and writer's potential gain are limited to the initial premium.

Graphical Interpretation of Options

Figure 11.2 depicts the payoff profiles of put and call options and, when these options are used as hedges, the resulting exposure considering the payoff profiles of the underlying hedged assets or liabilities.

The diagrams in Figure 11.2 assume that the options are *at the money* at the origin. Thus the put holder in Panel A (solid line) gains as the price of the optioned item falls (the put goes *in the money*). The holder can still sell the item to the writer at the price existing at the origin, perhaps after purchasing it at the lower market price. Similarly, the call writer in Panel D (dashed line) loses as the price of the optioned item rises (the call goes *in the money*). The writer is obligated to sell the item to the holder at the price existing at the origin while the holder may immediately resell it at the higher market price.

Using options as hedges removes potential losses, but not potential gains (recall that when hedging with futures contracts, *both* potential losses *and* gains are negated). The cost to the holder of negating potential losses is the option's *premium*. If premiums are considered in Figure 11.2,

A. Purchase Put (Solid Line),
Write Put (Dashed Line)

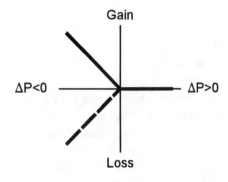

D. Purchase Call (Solid Line),
Write Call (Dashed Line)

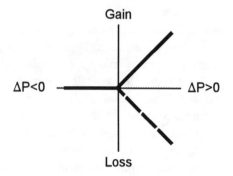

B. Underlying Exposure (Asset
or Commitment to Sell)

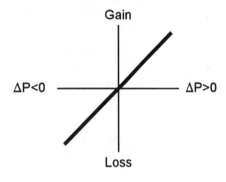

E. Underlying Exposure (Liability or
Commitment to Purchase)

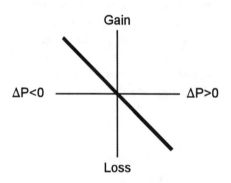

C. Resulting Exposure after Hedge
(Purchase Put from A and B)

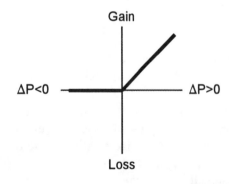

F. Resulting Exposure after Hedge
(Purchase Call from D and E)

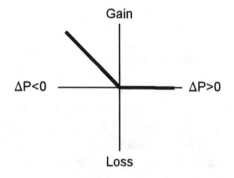

Note: Premiums on options are ignored here.

**FIGURE 11.2 PAYOFF PROFILES OF PUTS AND CALLS, UNDERLYING EXPOSURES
AND RESULTING EXPOSURES**

the solid *gain lines* in Panels A and D would shift *down* by the amount of the premium; the premium creates an initial cost and reduces the potential gain. The option writer, of course, benefits as the dashed *loss lines* in Panels A and D shift *up* by the amount of the premium; the premium creates a potential gain and reduces the potential loss. Consequently, the payoff profiles of the hedges in Panels C and F shift down by the amount of the premium.

Numerical Illustration of Panels D, E and F in Figure 11.2. We begin with Panel E which we assume relates to a liability denominated in foreign currency—FC100,000. The current spot rate at the origin is $.50/FC. If the rate rises to $.54/FC by moving to the right on the horizontal axis, the cost to liquidate the liability grows to $54,000 and a $4,000 [= ($.54 − $.50)100,000] transaction loss occurs. If $.54/FC appears on the horizontal axis, a vertical line drawn to the *downward-sloping* diagonal line in the lower right-hand quadrant connects with a horizontal line drawn to the vertical axis at a loss of ($.04).

To protect against this loss we would buy currency calls as shown in Panel D. Suppose currency calls on FC at the money with a strike price of $.50/FC are selling for $.01/FC. Thus the cost of using options to neutralize this loss (the *premium*, not shown on the graph) is $1,000 (= $.01 × 100,000). The right-hand *upward-sloping* diagonal line, kinked at the origin, indicates that the calls can produce gains for the holder but not losses, excluding the premium. Unlike forwards and futures, which permit both gain and loss and have no explicit cost, purchased options permit gain and avoid loss but at a specific cost, the premium.

Now, as the exchange rate rises to $.54/FC, the calls go *in the money* and the *upward-sloping* diagonal line in the upper *right*-hand quadrant tracks the gain of $.04 on each FC currency call. The calls must sell for at least $.04 else purchase and exercise of the call for less than $.54 and sale of the FC at $.54 allows immediate risk-free profit, a condition arbitragers do not permit to exist. The total $4,000 gain [= ($.54 − $.50)100,000] on the calls offsets the $4,000 transaction loss on the liability.

Thus we wind up with Panel F. The gain on the calls offsets the transaction loss on the liability, as shown by the horizontal line for exchange rates to the right of the origin. However, the *upward-sloping* diagonal line in the upper *left*-hand quadrant reflects the availability of transaction gains on the liability if the exchange rate drops *below* $.50/FC.

In general, one can use puts and calls to produce effects similar to those of a futures contract or an equivalent forward contract. For example, one who buys a futures contract stands to gain when the futures price rises and to lose when it falls. Purchasing a call and writing a put on the same item with the same strike price and expiration date also produce a gain when the optioned item's price rises and a loss when the optioned item's price falls. The accounting for such a combination of puts and calls, also known as a **synthetic futures contract**, generally should follow *SFAS 80*; when foreign currencies are involved, however, *SFAS 52* governs. Creation of a synthetic futures contract using options *at the money* is diagrammed in Figure 11.3.

To explain the impact of option premiums on Figure 11.3, note that the premiums on puts and calls with the same strike price are not likely to be equal. When the put is in the money and the premium has intrinsic value, the call is out of the money, and vice-versa. Even if both are at the money, as in Figure 11.3, the time value components of the two premiums generally differ due to market expectations regarding the price of the optioned item. Thus the payoff profiles in Panels C and F generally pass above or below the origin by the net premium amount.

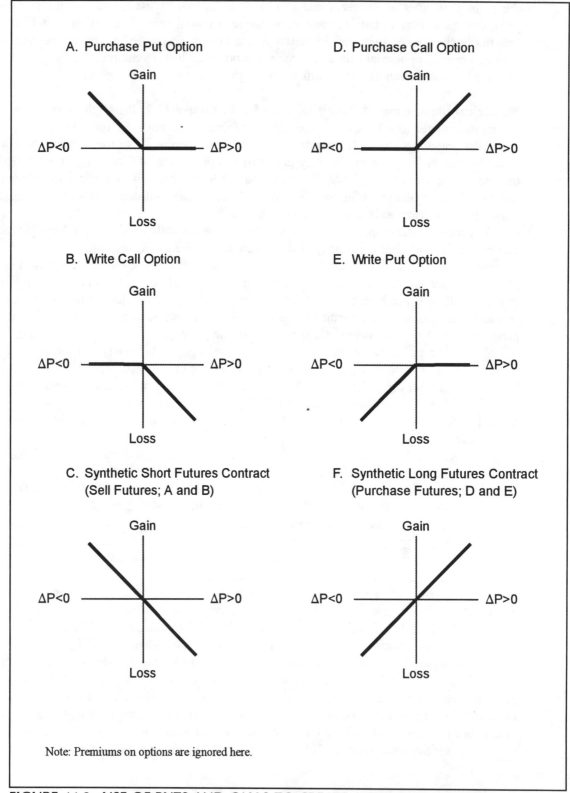

Note: Premiums on options are ignored here.

**FIGURE 11.3 USE OF PUTS AND CALLS TO CREATE SYNTHETIC FUTURES
CONTRACTS**

PRINCIPAL ACCOUNTING ISSUES

The two principal issues in accounting for options are accounting for the option's *premium* and accounting for any *gain or loss* on the option due to movements in its price. Timing of recognition is determined by whether the option qualifies as a hedge. When the option serves as a hedge, it becomes an integral part of the item or transaction being hedged. As with futures contracts, options may be used as hedges of *existing exposures, firm commitments*, and probable *anticipated transactions* if the options reduce price or interest rate risk and are designated as hedges.

It is important to keep in mind that accounting for options is still being developed and that variations will appear in practice. Concrete accounting guidance from analogous situations is not always available. For example, *SFAS 80* permits hedge accounting for futures contracts used to hedge probable anticipated transactions. Yet *SFAS 52* does not permit hedge accounting when foreign currency futures or forward contracts are entered to hedge anticipated transactions; it does not specifically address foreign currency options. Even so, we have developed a sensible approach to these accounting issues which we believe is consistent with overall GAAP.[15]

Accounting for Premiums Paid and Received

Premiums paid on purchased options are initially recorded as assets. Premiums received on written options are initially recorded as liabilities. Because the *time value* component of the premium on a *purchased option* qualifying as a *hedge* represents a type of insurance cost, the time value should generally be accounted for separately from the option's intrinsic value. The time value should be amortized to income over the life of the option. As with the premium or discount on foreign currency forward contracts, though, an entity may choose to defer the portion of an option's time value relating to the commitment or "anticipation" period and adjust the transaction accordingly when it occurs. The intrinsic value is adjusted as the option's market value changes. Whether *written options* (as opposed to *purchased options*) can serve as hedges is an unresolved issue. Because option writers assume risk, rather than protect against it, we believe that written options are rarely intended to be hedges. The SEC staff appears to concur with this view and "will object to deferral of losses with respect to written foreign currency options because they do not reduce but increase risk.[16]

The time value component of a premium paid or received on an option serving as a *speculative* transaction should not be accounted for separately and amortized as it does not relate to "insurance." Instead, the entire premium serves as the starting point for subsequent realization of gains and losses resulting from changes in the option's market value.

Accounting for Gains and Losses

The accounting for gains and losses on options—changes in the options' *intrinsic value*—is similar to that used for futures contracts. Recall that with futures a *mark-to-market* system is used based

---

[15] For more detailed discussion of these accounting issues, see Arthur Andersen & Co., *Accounting for Options* (Chicago: Arthur Andersen & Co., 1986), and Accounting Standards Division Task Force on Options, "Accounting for Options," *Issues Paper* (New York: AICPA, 1986).

[16] See discussion regarding EITF *Issue 91-4*, "Hedging Foreign Currency Risks with Complex Options and Similar Transactions," *EITF Abstracts* (Norwalk, CT: FASB, 1992), p. 653.

on the daily cash settlement with the futures exchange resulting from changes in futures prices. The movement of cash in the futures case means that the gains and losses are *realized* currently; their *recognition* depends on two factors: (1) whether the contract qualifies as a hedge and (2) if a hedge, whether the hedged item is carried at market or at other than market.[17] With options, though, changes in value are *not* settled in cash prior to exercise or expiration; these changes are *unrealized*.

Most options are *marked to market*. The occasional entity that accounts for its short-term investments using the lower-of-cost-or-market (LCM) method, however, will use LCM to account for its investment or speculative positions in options.[18] Recognition of unrealized gains and losses on options, whether from mark-to-market or LCM accounting, proceeds as follows.

- *Gains and losses are recognized currently* when the option is *not* serving as a hedge or when the option is hedging an existing asset or liability exposure being carried at *market*. In the latter case, the recognized gains/losses on the option offset the recognized losses/gains due to changes in the market value of the optioned item. However, following *SFAS 115* (below), not all recognized gains/losses on hedges impact current earnings.
- *Gains and losses on all other hedge options are initially deferred*. At reporting dates, the deferred gains and losses adjust the carrying amount of hedged assets and liabilities carried at other than market, such as at cost, amortized cost, or LCM. Deferred gains and losses on options that hedge firm commitments and probable anticipated transactions are carried forward and adjust the dollar measurements of these transactions when they occur.

In the absence of specialized industry practices, companies account for options on individual securities according to *SFAS 115*, "Accounting for Certain Investments in Debt and Equity Securities,"[19] which prescribes the accounting for the securities themselves. *SFAS 115* calls for companies to classify their holdings of marketable equity securities and debt securities and account for them as follows:

1. *Debt securities held to maturity*: amortized cost.
2. *Trading securities*: mark to market; report value changes in current earnings.
3. *Securities available for sale*: mark to market; report value changes outside of earnings, in *other comprehensive income*, pursuant to *SFAS 130*.

Category 1 includes only debt securities. Debt *and* equity securities are included in Categories 2 and 3. Thus changes in value of options owned on Category 2 securities are included in current earnings and changes in value of options owned on Category 3 securities are reported in *other comprehensive income*.

---

[17] Under *SFAS 52*, gain or loss on a foreign currency forward or futures contract used to hedge an economic investment in a foreign entity is entered directly into stockholders' equity when the translation adjustment on the foreign entity is so entered under the current rate method of translation. Presumably this same treatment would apply when foreign currency options are used for this purpose.

[18] The SEC requires that *speculative foreign currency options* be accounted for at *market*. See Appendix D-16 in *EITF Abstracts* (Norwalk, CT: FASB, 1992), p. 4973.

[19] Financial Accounting Standards Board, *Statement of Financial Accounting Standards No. 115*, "Accounting for Certain Investments in Debt and Equity Securities" (Norwalk, CT: FASB, 1993).

Impact of the 1997 FASB *Draft Statement*

When finalized, the *Draft Statement* provides new authoritative guidance that supersedes prior practice. As with futures contracts, value changes on options used for investment or speculative purposes continue to be reported in current earnings. Prior practice will be revised as follows:

- *Separating the premium* into time value and intrinsic value on options used as hedges will *not* occur. The process of marking to market will incorporate the entire value change in the option, not just the intrinsic value portion revalued in current practice. In effect, amortization of the time value component is reflected in value changes as it moves toward zero at expiration date. This pseudo-amortization will not be straight-line, however, and could actually be negative as the time value component could temporarily increase prior to expiration.

- Value changes on options used as *hedges* generally follow the same rules as futures contracts, with value changes on options hedging forecasted transactions being reported in other comprehensive income pending completion of the forecasted transaction. However, when value changes in options are not accompanied by cash settlement, hedges of firm commitments require that an asset or liability be established for the financial instrument aspect of the commitment, as in forward contracts, so that no "deferred gain or loss" is recorded.

ILLUSTRATIONS OF ACCOUNTING FOR OPTIONS

A group of common options applications and suggested accounting treatments follows. Brokerage commissions and other transaction costs are ignored.

Example 1: Hedge of an Exposed Asset Carried at Cost

On March 30, 19X8, a firm owns $3,000,000 face value 9.125-percent U.S. Treasury bonds due in 20Y8. They were purchased at face value and are carried at that amount in the "held to maturity" category, pursuant to *SFAS 115*. These bonds currently sell for 97 and yield about 9.33 percent. Concerned about forecast increases in interest rates and concurrent decreases in Treasury bond prices, the firm purchases September 19X8 *put options* on these bonds with a strike price of 100. The puts, which allow the firm to sell the bonds for 100, are designated as an effective hedge of the bonds owned. The premium is $3.04 per $100 of bonds, $91,200 [= $3.04 (3,000,000/100)] in total. Because the 100 strike price exceeds the bonds' current price of 97, the puts are *in the money* by $3.00; $90,000 of the total premium is intrinsic value and $1,200 is time value. The following entry records purchase of the Treasury bond puts.

Options Owned (Intrinsic Value)	90,000	
Options Owned (Time Value)	1,200	
Cash		91,200
To record the purchase of put options to hedge Treasury bonds owned.		

On June 30, 19X8, when the firm's books are closed, the bonds are selling for 98 and the puts for $2.24. The loss of $1 (= 97 − 98) in the option's intrinsic value, $30,000 [= (.98 − .97)

$3,000,000] in total, is deferred by adding it to the carrying value of the bonds and considering it to be a premium on the bond investment. This premium is amortized to interest income over the remaining life of the bonds (not illustrated here). One-half of the original $1,200 time value covering the period from April to June is amortized now; the current increase in the time value component of the put's premium is not recognized at this time.

Premium/Discount on Treasury Bonds	30,000	
Options Owned (Intrinsic Value)		30,000
To recognize the decline in the puts' intrinsic value by		
adjusting the carrying value of the hedged bonds.		
Other Expense/Revenue	600	
Options Owned (Time Value)		600
To amortize half of the original time value component		
of the premium.		

We now assume that as of September 1, 19X8, the price of the firm's Treasury bonds decreased to 95 and the firm decides to close out the hedge by selling the put options for their current premium of $5.19. Each put is now in the money by $5.00. Total proceeds amount to $155,700 [= $5.19 (3,000,000/100)], of which the time value is $5,700. The carrying value of the bonds is adjusted by the subsequent change in the options' intrinsic value, and the time value component of the current premium—now realized—is offset against the unamortized portion of the original time value; $5,100 = $5,700 − $600.

Options Owned (Intrinsic Value)	90,000	
Premium/Discount on Treasury Bonds		90,000
To recognize the increase in the puts' intrinsic value		
by adjusting the carrying value of the hedged bonds.		
Other Expense/Revenue	600	
Options Owned (Time Value)		600
To amortize the last half of the original time		
value component of the premium.		
Cash	155,700	
Options Owned (Intrinsic Value)		150,000
Other Expense/Revenue		5,700
To record sale of the puts for an amount higher than their		
intrinsic value; $150,000 = $90,000 − $30,000 + $90,000.		

Note that the overall *gain* of $60,000 on the puts due to an increase in their intrinsic value from $3 to $5 offsets the decline in current value of the bonds by $60,000 [= (.97 − .95) $3,000,000]. In sum, after the puts are sold, the company netted $64,500 in cash (= $155,700 proceeds − $91,200 cost). Of this amount, $60,000 (= $30,000 premium recorded on June 30 − $90,000 discount recorded on September 1) is credited to the bond investment, reducing its carrying amount to $2,940,000 from $3,000,000. The remaining $4,500, the difference between the $5,100 (= $5,700 − $600) increase in the unamortized time value and the $600 of time value amortized on June 30, is recorded as revenue.

Example 2: Hedge of an Exposed Liability Carried at Market

In this example, on September 1, 19X2, a U.S. company has a note payable to an Australian company denominated in Australian dollars ($A). The amount is $A5,000,000. As a foreign currency transaction, this liability is carried at market value of $4,050,000; the direct exchange rate is $.81/$A. To protect itself against a decline in the $ before the note is to be paid in four months, the U.S. company buys December 19X2 *call options* for $A5,000,000 with a strike price of $.82/$A for a premium of $.0105.[20] The calls allow the U.S. firm to purchase $A for $.82, thereby limiting the amount the U.S. firm has to pay for $A to settle the note to $.82. With purchased calls, the fact that the strike price exceeds the current exchange rate means that the calls are *out of the money*. The calls therefore have no intrinsic value and the entire premium of $52,500 (= $.0105 × 5,000,000) is time value.

Options Owned (Time Value)	52,500	
Cash		52,500
To record the purchase of call options to hedge a note payable denominated in $A.		

When the books are closed on September 30, the direct exchange rate rose to $.83/$A, indicating that the $ weakened. The calls, which now are $.01 *in the money*, are selling for $.019, so the time value component is currently $.009. The U.S. company must now recognize the transaction loss on the note payable (carried at market), as well as the partially offsetting transaction gain due to the increase in intrinsic value of the call options, and must amortize one-fourth of the original time value.

Transaction Loss	100,000	
Note Payable		100,000
To record the transaction loss accruing to the note payable; 100,000 = ($.83 − $.81) × 5,000,000.		

Options Owned (Intrinsic Value)	50,000	
Other Expense/Revenue	13,125	
Transaction Gain		50,000
Options Owned (Time Value)		13,125
To record the increase in the options' intrinsic value caused by the exchange rate change and amortize one-fourth of the time value; $13,125 = $52,500/4.		

By December, when the note comes due, the $ weakened further and the direct exchange rate is $.84/$A. The company could elect to exercise the call options and acquire $A5,000,000 for

---

[20] EITF *Issue 90-17* indicates that purchased foreign currency options with little or no intrinsic value are valid hedging instruments for exposed positions and firm commitments (*SFAS 52* hedging criteria) and probable anticipated transactions (*SFAS 80* hedging criteria). EITF *Issue 91-1* extends this guidance to intercompany transactions. Hedging with complex options is discussed in EITF *Issue 91-4*. Although no EITF consensus was reached, the SEC staff objects to deferral of gains and losses on complex options and similar transactions used to hedge anticipated transactions.

$4,100,000, a saving of $100,000 over the current spot price. Instead, the company decides to close out the calls by selling them at their current price of $.02 (no time value remains this close to expiration date) and to purchase the $A separately a few days later. This provides the company with another $50,000 [= ($.84 − $.83) × 5,000,000] transaction gain which, when added to the $50,000 recognized in September, equals the saving of $100,000. Also, the transaction loss of $50,000 that accrued on the note payable must be recorded.

Transaction Loss	50,000	
Note Payable		50,000
To record the transaction loss on the note payable;		
$50,000 = ($.84 − $.83) × 5,000,000.		

Cash	100,000	
Other Expense/Revenue	39,375	
Options Owned (Intrinsic Value)		50,000
Options Owned (Time Value)		39,375
Transaction Gain		50,000
To record the sale of the call options for $.02/$A,		
amortize the remaining time value, and recognize the		
transaction gain accruing on the options prior to sale.		

In summary, the company experienced the following:

Loss on note payable: ($.84 − $.81) 5,000,000	$ 150,000
Gain on option (intrinsic value): ($.84 − $.82) 5,000,000	(100,000)
Initial premium (time value; the insurance cost)	52,500
Net loss	$ 102,500

Thus the net gain on the hedge is $47,500 (= $100,000 − $52,500), and the company is that amount better off than it would have been without hedging.

***Draft Statement* Application.** To illustrate how the 1997 FASB *Draft Statement* is applied to options, the first entry records the $52,500 option cost as Options Owned without the "Time Value" designation.

Options Owned	52,500	
Cash		52,500
To record the purchase of call options to hedge a note		
payable denominated in $A.		

On September 30, the fair value of the options increased to $95,000 (= $.019 × 5,000,000) and we record a gain of $42,500 (= $95,000 − $52,500), disaggregated below.

Increase in intrinsic value ($.01 × 5,000,000)	$50,000
Decrease in time value [($.009 − $.0105) 5,000,000]	(7,500)
Net gain	$42,500

Although the *Draft Statement* does not explicitly consider the time value, we see that the gain reflects implicit time value amortization of $7,500.

Options Owned   42,500
   Gain on Options (Earnings)   42,500
   To record in earnings the gain on the options hedging
   a foreign currency note payable.

Comparing the $42,500 gain on the options and the $100,000 transaction loss on the note payable, recorded separately, we see that the options hedge some but not all of that $100,000 loss. This results because (1) the options were out of the money when acquired and (2) the time value decreased.

In December the note payable comes due and a $50,000 transaction loss is recorded separately. Also, the options are sold for $100,000 (= $.02 × 5,000,000), producing a further gain of $5,000 (= $100,000 − $95,000) that is recorded next.

Cash   100,000
   Options Owned   95,000
   Gain on Options   5,000
   To record sale of the call options for $.02/$A;
   $95,000 = $52,500 + $42,500.

Even though the accounting for the options differs from current practice, the company still incurs a net loss of $102,500, shown below, and the company is still better off by the net gain on the hedge of $47,500 (= $42,500 + $5,000).

Loss on note payable ($.84 − $.81) 5,000,000 . . . . $150,000
Gain on options . . . .   (47,500)
Net loss $102,500

Example 3: Hedging with an Interest Rate Cap

Companies often purchase an **interest rate cap** to protect against rising interest rates on their variable rate borrowings. Effectively a call option, an interest rate cap goes in the money when the variable rate rises above the cap's strike price—the rate specified in the cap agreement. Once in the money, the writer of the cap is obligated to pay the holder the difference between the holder's variable rate interest and the cap.

To illustrate, assume that on January 2, 19X6, Stewart, Inc. borrows $10 million from its bank for five years at prime plus 2 percent, a variable rate adjusted quarterly. Although prime currently stands at 9 percent, it has been rising, and Stewart buys a five-year, 12 percent interest rate cap from another bank for .5 percent per year to be paid in full immediately. The cap is out of the money [strike price (12 percent) > current variable rate (11 percent = 9 percent + 2 percent)], so the entire premium is time value. When the cap is in the money, the writer reimburses Stewart each quarter.

Interest Rate Cap Owned (Time Value)   250,000

    Cash   250,000

    To record the premium paid on a five-year 12 percent

    interest rate cap; $250,000 = .005 × $10,000,000 × 5.

Ten months later, prime increased to 11 percent, forcing Stewart's variable rate to 13 percent during the last quarter of 19X6, and the interest rate cap is now in the money. On December 31, 19X6, Stewart's end-of-period entries include the following:

Interest Expense   325,000

    Cash   325,000

    To record interest paid to the bank for the last quarter

    of 19X6; $325,000 = .13 × $10,000,000/4.

Interest Rate Cap Owned (Intrinsic Value)   25,000

    Interest Expense   25,000

    To record the gain on the option (the excess interest);

    $25,000 = (.13 − .12) × $10,000,000/4.

Other Expense/Revenue   50,000

    Interest Rate Cap Owned (Time Value)   50,000

    To amortize, for 19X6, one-fifth of the total $250,000

    time value premium for five years.

Subsequently, when the writer of the cap reimburses Stewart for the excess interest in the fourth quarter, Stewart's entry is as follows:

Cash   25,000

    Interest Rate Cap Owned (Intrinsic Value)   25,000

    To record collection of excess interest due under the

    interest rate cap agreement.

Entries similar to the above will be made during the next four years to record the quarterly events occurring pursuant to the loan and the rate cap. To summarize, the company received $25,000 under the cap agreement to reduce interest costs and amortized $50,000 of the premium paid, for a net loss of $25,000 in 19X6. Whether the entire transaction is profitable depends on what the prime rate does over the next four years. If prime remains at 11 percent, the company collects an additional $400,000 [= (.13 − .12) × $10,000,000 × 4] under the rate cap, which exceeds the unamortized premium by $200,000 [= $400,000 − ($250,000 − $50,000)]. In these circumstances, the company realizes an overall gain of $175,000 (= $200,000 − $25,000 loss in 19X6) over the entire five-year period.

Example 4: Speculating in Options

In a **straddle**, the option trader anticipates either (1) a substantial movement in the price of a stock or (2) no substantial movement. The *buyer* of a straddle *purchases both a put and a call* on the same stock with the same strike price and expiration date. Suppose, for a stock selling for $60, a call costs $2 and a put costs $3, with both options specifying a $60 strike price. The buyer makes a profit when the stock rises above $65 (sell or exercise the call) or falls below $55 (sell or exercise the put). The buyer recovers part of the $5 premium cost when the price (1) rises but stays below $65 or (2) falls but stays above $55.

In contrast, the *writer* of such a straddle, expecting the stock's price to not deviate far from $60, *sells the above put and call* for a total premium of $5. The writer generally earns a profit when the stock price (1) rises but stays below $65 or (2) falls but stays above $55. Although either the put *or* the call could be exercised, only when the stock is highly volatile are *both* exercised. Of course, the writer can lose and the buyer can gain on both ends of the straddle when the stock's price moves *both* below $55 *and* above $65 prior to expiration, because both the put *and* the call will probably be exercised. The positions of the purchaser and writer of the above straddle are diagrammed in Figure 11.4.

Consider now the accounting by the writer of a straddle involving offsetting puts and calls written on 1,000 shares of Honeywell Corp. stock. Assume that on August 31, 19X8, Honeywell Corp. stock closed at $58.75; calls with a strike price of $60 and an October 19X8 expiration date closed at $1.75. Parallel puts closed at $2.75. A firm that neither owns nor sold short Honeywell stock (the firm is a naked option writer) writes and sells 1,000 of these calls and puts. Mark-to-market accounting is used because the options are *trading securities*, pursuant to *SFAS 115*. The following entry records the written straddle:

Cash	4,500	
Options Written (Calls)		1,750
Options Written (Puts)		2,750
To record a **straddle** written on 1,000 shares of Honeywell		
stock. The Options Written accounts are liabilities.		

Honeywell stock falls to $54 on September 30, 19X8, and the writer closes out the puts at $6.75 before they are exercised. Also, because the firm follows mark-to-market accounting, the firm adjusts the calls to their current market price of $.25 when its books are closed.

Options Written (Puts)	2,750	
Realized Loss on Options Trading	4,000	
Cash		6,750
To record closing out of 1,000 puts.		

Options Written (Calls)	1,500	
Unrealized Gain on Options Trading		1,500
To mark the outstanding written calls to market and recognize		
the unrealized gain; $1,500 = 1,000 ($1.75 − $.25).		

Over the next few weeks, Honeywell stock drifts in the high $50s and the calls expire without being exercised. The writer now recognizes the remaining $250 (= $1,750 − $1,500) premium received as income.

Options Written (Calls)	250	
Realized Gain on Options Trading		250
To recognize expiration of the calls and the related		
premium income.		

A. Purchase Put Option

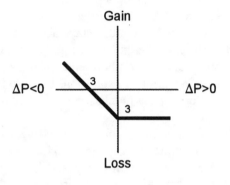

B. Purchase Call Option

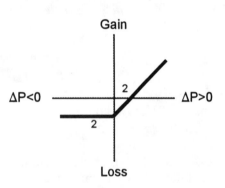

C. Combine the Put in *A* and the Call in *B* into a Straddle

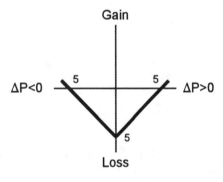

D. Write Put Option

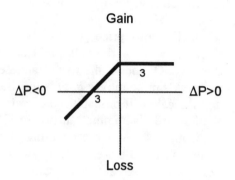

E. Write Call Option

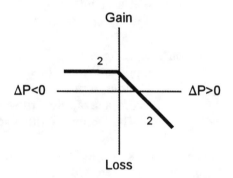

F. Combine the Put in *D* and the Call in *E* into a Straddle

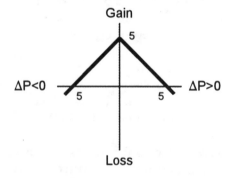

Note: All options have same strike price: $60 at origin; premium on put is $3, premium on call is $2.

FIGURE 11.4 USING PUTS AND CALLS TO CREATE STRADDLES

In the above example, the writer of the straddle incurs a net cash loss of $2,250 (= $4,500 − 6,750). A purchaser of this straddle realizes a cash gain of $2,250, assuming the puts were sold when their price was $6.75 and the calls were allowed to expire unexercised.

This completes our discussion of accounting for options. We have not illustrated options used to hedge *probable anticipated transactions*. The treatment is identical to that provided by *SFAS 80* for futures contracts entered before the hedged transaction actually occurs, except for the presence of a premium in the option case. Any gains and losses accruing to the options are deferred and are used to adjust the dollar basis of the anticipated transaction when it is recorded.

INTRODUCTION TO FINANCIAL SWAPS

Financial swaps comprise another group of *derivative financial instruments* used primarily to lower financing costs and hedge risk, as well as for speculative purposes. These instruments involve "an exchange of cash flows over time between two parties (generally referred to as *counterparties*)."[21] Their values are *derived* from the values of the swapped cash flows. Although the variety of swaps found in practice is expanding, we focus here on two types used quite frequently today: **currency swaps** and **interest rate swaps**. A variation on this theme is a **commodity swap,** not discussed in detail here, in which the exchange of cash flows is based on the price of a commodity, such as oil.[22]

DEFINITIONS AND COMPARISON WITH FUTURES AND OPTIONS

In a financial swap, two end-users, or **counterparties**, negotiate a contract to exchange a series of cash flows at specified times and at specified prices. Typically there will be an **intermediary** that links the counterparties and that may assume obligations with the counterparties. That is, the counterparties may deal with each other directly or through an intermediary, such as a bank. The **principal amount** is the amount on which the swapped flows are calculated and often consists of assets or liabilities of the counterparties. When the principal itself is not exchanged, it is called the **notional amount**.

A swap is equivalent to a series of forward contracts[23] and has many analytical similarities to forwards, futures, and options. But there are some important practical differences. Like a forward contract, a swap permits accurate matching of the cash flows of underlying assets and liabilities, whereas the standardized nature of futures and exchange-traded option contracts does not. Swaps and forwards are generally tailor-made to users' specifications and, unlike futures and options, swaps are not currently traded on organized exchanges. This absence of a secondary market means that the relative liquidity of forwards and swaps is lower than that of futures and exchange-traded options.

Another important difference between swaps and certain other financial instruments is **credit risk** or **default risk**. A typical forward contract of the type discussed in Chapter 10 has relatively high credit risk—compared to futures—in that there is no settlement prior to maturity. Futures contracts have virtually no credit risk, since traders are required to settle up daily with the futures

---

[21] Clifford W. Smith, Jr., Charles W. Smithson and Lee Macdonald Wakeman, "The Evolving Market for Swaps," *Midland Corporate Finance Journal* (Winter, 1986), 20.

[22] Stanley W. Angrist, "Big-Stakes Hedge Starts Branching Out: Commodity Swaps Grow for Oil, Metal," *The Wall Street Journal*, September 26, 1989, C-1, C-14.

[23] The article by Smith et al provides a good discussion on this point, and on others in this section.

exchange. The credit risk of swaps lies between these two extremes when there are intermediate settlement dates prior to expiration of the swap. Moreover, in some swap agreements, a missed payment by one counterparty voids the corresponding obligation by the other counterparty. Indeed, often only the net payment between the counterparties actually changes hands. An intermediary, however, must worry about the entire stream of payments because a default by one counterparty does not necessarily terminate the intermediary's obligation to the other counterparty. Penalty provisions in the standardized swap contract developed by the International Association of Swap Dealers define the impact of a default.

CURRENCY SWAPS

In a **currency swap**, the two counterparties exchange currencies at time 0 and reverse the exchange at some subsequent time T. The parties usually agree on the exchange rates to be used at inception and completion of the swap. Intermediate payments in the foreign currency, usually made during the swap period, are based on agreed-upon exchange rates. Although gross amounts are sometimes exchanged, usually the only cash flows that actually change hands are net amounts, structured as fees or based on interest rate/exchange rate differentials. Currency swaps are made for two basic reasons.[24]

1. To provide **long-date cover** by hedging or covering the exchange rate risk associated with foreign currency flows occurring over longer terms than those for which forward contracts are available. Existing markets in foreign currency futures and forwards are not sufficient to create hedges for many configurations of foreign currency cash flows. Examples are foreign currency flows from recurring international transactions, from foreign loans and investments, or both.
2. To use **arbitrage** to reduce financing costs by taking advantage of interest rate, tax, and regulatory differences across countries and markets. For example, favorable tax treatment of zero coupon bonds in one country could be exploited to lower borrowing costs by a firm in another country with less favorable tax laws.

Because a currency swap is an **executory contract**—its execution is contingent upon subsequent events—it does not currently require liability recognition. The gross cash flows from a typical currency swap are diagrammed in Figure 11.5.

---

[24] See Carl R. Beidleman, *Interest Rate Swaps* (Homewood, IL: Business One-Irwin, 1990) and Carl R. Beidleman Ed., *Cross Currency Swaps* (Homewood, IL: Business One-Irwin, 1992) for detailed discussion and illustrations of swaps.

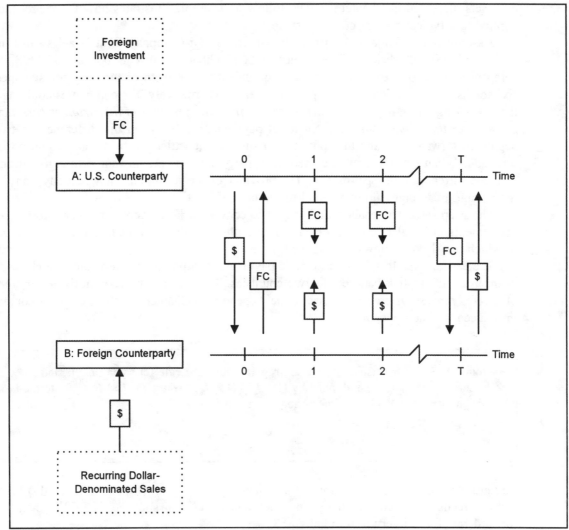

FIGURE 11.5   CASH FLOWS IN A TYPICAL CURRENCY SWAP

Figure 11.5 shows the two counterparties: *A* is a U.S. firm and *B* is a foreign firm. Counterparty A has foreign investments which generate periodic foreign currency (FC) cash flows. Because A wants dollars, it agrees to swap the intermediate FC flows from its foreign investments to B. For its part, B makes periodic export sales to U.S. customers denominated in dollars. Because it wants FC, B agrees to swap the intermediate dollar flows from its U.S. customers to A. The exchange and re-exchange of principal amounts at times *0* and *T* may or may not take place. If they do occur, each counterparty has the option of immediately converting the unwanted foreign currency into its home currency; if they do not occur, the principal amount becomes *notional*.

ACCOUNTING FOR CURRENCY SWAPS

Paragraph 17 of *SFAS 52* states that currency swaps are equivalent to a series of foreign currency forward contracts. Accordingly, accounting for currency swaps follows the procedures for forward contracts discussed in Chapter 10. The following example illustrates how those procedures are applied to a typical foreign currency swap.

Assume that Company A in the United States and Company B in Israel swap a notional amount of 1,000,000 shekels (S), equivalent to $600,000 at the current spot rate of $.6/S. The two companies agree to re-exchange amounts equivalent to one-tenth of the currency swapped every six months and to terminate the swap in five years. Alternatively, the companies could agree that the re-exchanges take the form of *net payments from the provider of the stronger currency to the provider of the weaker currency*. Such net payments are based on the differences between the negotiated forward rates and the spot rates at subsequent settlement times, and could go in either direction. When net payments are used, each party converts the unwanted foreign currency into its home currency on the spot market. The provider of the strong currency actually transfers only the amount of foreign currency equal to the net payment.

The swap agreement enables Company A to convert shekels received regularly from fixed-rate investments in Israel into dollars every six months. It effectively hedges the exchange rate risk to which the shekel inflows are exposed.

The parties agree that the intermediate payments incorporate forward rates which result from interest rate differentials between the two countries. These concepts were motivated by the forces of *covered interest arbitrage* discussed in the Appendix to Chapter 10; the following equation was introduced in that Appendix.

> From a U.S. dollar perspective, the **appropriate forward rate** for some time period t, $R_{f,t}$ equals the current spot rate, R_s, multiplied by $(1 + I_{us,t})/(1 + I_{fn,t})$, where $I_{us,t}$ and $I_{fn,t}$ refer to the U.S. and foreign interest rates for the time period being considered:
>
> $$R_{f,t} = R_s(1 + I_{us,t})/(1 + I_{fn,t})$$

To illustrate, when 6-month government securities yield 4 percent (8 percent annually) in the U.S. and 6 percent (12 percent annually) in Israel, and the current spot rate is $.60/S, then the direct forward rate for delivery in 6 months is:

$$R_{f,6} = \$.6(1.04)/(1.06) = \$.5887/S.$$

Once we have both the spot rate and the forward rate, Company A records the initial forward contract implicit in the swap as follows:

Due from Company B	58,870	
Discount on Forward Contract	1,130	
Forward Sale Contract		60,000

    To record the obligation to swap S100,000 in six months
    at the agreed-upon rate of $.5887/S as a forward sale
    contract measured at $.60/S, the current spot rate.

From A's perspective, the swap serves as a hedge of a firm commitment—the coupons on the fixed-rate shekel investment—and the discount is recorded separately and amortized.

Let us assume that at the end of the first 6-month period, the dollar weakened, the shekel strengthened, and the spot rate is $.65/S (or S1.5385/$). Company A in the U.S. transfers

S100,000 worth $65,000 to Company B in Israel, receiving $58,870 in return. Company A records the re-exchange as follows:

Transaction Loss	5,000	
Forward Sale Contract		5,000
To recognize the transaction loss accrued on the forward sale contract; $5,000 = ($.65 − $.60)100,000.		
Forward Sale Contract	65,000	
Foreign Currency		65,000
To record delivery of the S100,000 to the Israeli firm, Company B.		
Cash	58,870	
Due From Company B		58,870
To record the $58,870 received from Company B.		
Expense—Discount Amortization	1,130	
Discount on Forward Contract		1,130
To expense the discount on the forward sale contract (had the books been closed during the 6-month period, a portion would have been amortized at that time).		

Use of a net payment instead of the gross transfer just mentioned produces the following results: the provider of the *stronger currency*, in this case the U.S. company A which is providing shekels, settles the initial re-exchange by transferring shekels worth $6,130 [= ($.65 − $.5887) × 100,000] to Company B, the provider of the weaker currency. Because the 100,000 shekels to be transferred are currently worth $65,000, more than their agreed-upon forward value of $58,870, the $6,130 compensates the Israeli firm, which holds dollars received from its dollar-denominated international sales, for the decline in value of those dollars in terms of shekels. This net payment is represented by the original discount of $1,130 and the transaction loss on the forward sale contract of $5,000.

This currency swap is treated as a series of six-month forward contracts, each of which will be recorded at inception and termination in a manner similar to the above entries. Only the net amount is disclosed on an intervening balance sheet. Also be aware that we have recorded the swap only from the perspective of the U.S. firm and that we have not dealt explicitly with the hedged item. In particular, the transaction loss on the swap during the first six months effectively offsets the transaction gain accruing to the fixed-rate shekel-denominated investments owned by the U.S. firm. The situation could reverse in subsequent periods.

Currency swaps developed to replace a technique known as a *parallel loan*. In a **parallel loan**, firms in different countries make offsetting loans in their own currencies to each other. During the terms of the loans, each firm makes payments in the currency borrowed—the foreign currency. Although parallel loans successfully achieved their objectives, the loans appear as debt on the parties' balance sheets and increase measured financial leverage. Because of their executory nature, currency swap arrangements are not currently recognized as balance-sheet liabilities.

Impact of the 1997 FASB *Draft Statement*

As previously stated, the *Draft Statement* changes the accounting for forward contracts that hedge firm commitments and permits hedge accounting when forward contracts hedge forecasted (anticipated) transactions. These matters are discussed and illustrated in Chapter 10. In the currency swap example, the *Draft Statement* changes neither the accounting nor the result. The text example records the transaction loss on the forward contract as it accrues. This $5,000 loss, together with the $1,130 discount, measures the overall loss incurred by Company A for agreeing in advance to surrender S100,000 for $58,870 at a time when the S100,000 were actually worth $65,000.

INTEREST RATE SWAPS

Interest rate swaps involve an exchange of interest payment obligations on existing or new debt. Because the principal amount of the debt itself is not exchanged, it is *notional*. These are currently the most widely used type of financial swap and typically call for exchanging a floating rate interest obligation for a fixed rate interest obligation, both on debt denominated in the same currency. In this way, floating rate debt is effectively converted to fixed rate debt, and vice versa. Other versions include **basis** (or **basis rate**) **swaps** and **currency coupon swaps** (also known as a **circus**—combined interest rate and currency swap).

We illustrate here the simplest single-currency, fixed-for-variable interest rate swap, called a **plain vanilla swap**.[25] Again, hedging and speculation provide the motives for these swaps. A company wishing to avoid the risk of rising interest rates may swap its floating rate obligations for fixed rate obligations. Another company which already has fixed rate investments, such as mortgages, may seek to convert its floating rate debt into fixed rate debt. Or a company which can borrow fixed rate debt only at high rates may swap its floating rate obligations to a counterparty able to borrow at low fixed rates. And a company speculating on a decline in interest rates may swap its fixed rate obligation for a floating rate obligation.

It is common for the floating rate to be tied to an interest rate index. The **London Interbank Offered Rate (LIBOR)**—a fluctuating free-market rate for Eurodollar deposits—or a Treasury bill rate is frequently used. The positions of the parties and the movements of the swapped cash flows in a plain vanilla interest rate swap are shown in Figure 11.6.

Let us assume the following facts about the swap diagrammed in Figure 11.6. When the swap is entered, LIBOR stands at 8 percent or 800 *basis points*. A **basis point (bp)** is 1/100 of a percent in interest or .0001.

- AA has $200 million of existing debt with a floating rate equal to LIBOR + 60 basis points (currently 8.6 percent). It wants to protect against increases in interest rates but cannot borrow directly at a fixed rate of less than 10 percent.
- BB also has $200 million of debt, but its debt carries a fixed coupon of 9.5 percent. Moreover, BB has $200 million of floating rate investments. It seeks to protect against decreases in interest rates which would cause its floating rate revenues to decline and its fixed rate expenses to become more onerous.
- Intermediary proposes the following swap: it offers AA floating rate payments at LIBOR + 60 basis points in exchange for fixed rate payments from AA at 9.7 percent;

---

[25] See Keith Wishon and Lorin S. Chevalier, "Interest Rate Swaps—Your Rate or Mine?" *Journal of Accountancy* (September 1985), 64; this excellent article (pp. 63-84) discusses interest rate swap arrangements, including terminology and accounting issues.

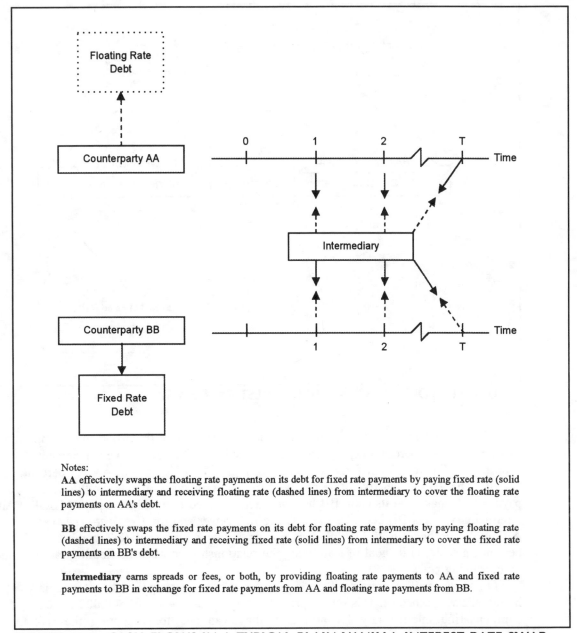

FIGURE 11.6   CASH FLOWS IN A TYPICAL PLAIN VANILLA INTEREST RATE SWAP

it offers BB fixed rate payments at 9.5 percent in exchange for floating payments from BB at LIBOR + 80 basis points. All payments are to be calculated on a notional amount of \$200 million. Terms of the proposed swap and positions of the parties are depicted in Figure 11.7. The effects on the parties to the swap are summarized next.

AA: Because AA pays LIBOR + 60 bp on its debt and receives LIBOR + 60 bp from intermediary, its net outflow is the 9.7 percent fixed payment to intermediary. AA therefore becomes the *fixed rate payer* and the *floating rate receiver* in the swap. AA has an annual opportunity gain of \$600,000 [= (.10 − .097) × \$200M] because the swap enables it to borrow

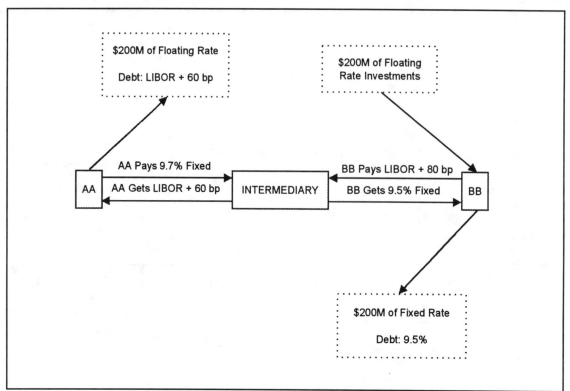

FIGURE 11.7   DETAILS OF AA/BB INTEREST RATE SWAP

fixed at 9.7 percent—30 bp or .3 percent below its best direct fixed borrowing opportunity. By locking in this 9.7 percent rate, AA benefits directly if LIBOR goes above 9.1 percent (9.1 percent + 60 bp = 9.7 percent) but forgoes interest savings if LIBOR stays below 9.1 percent.

BB: The 9.5 percent fixed rate payment from intermediary offsets the 9.5 percent fixed rate payment BB makes on its debt. BB has *unlocked* its fixed rate and now pays LIBOR + 80 bp to intermediary. Thus BB becomes the *floating rate payer* and the *fixed rate receiver* in the swap. Although BB benefits if LIBOR does not go above 8.7 percent (8.7 percent + 80 bp = 9.5 percent), it achieved its goal of stabilizing the relationship between its floating rate revenues and its borrowing costs.

Intermediary: The swap produces a net spread of 40 basis points to intermediary, as shown in the following schedule. This spread provides annual cash flow of $800,000 (= .004 × $200M), compensating intermediary for arranging the swap and for accepting the risk that either counterparty might default.

Fixed payment received from AA	.097
Fixed payment made to BB	(.095)
Floating payment received from BB, net of LIBOR	.008
Floating payment paid to AA, net of LIBOR	(.006)
Net Spread to Intermediary	.004

In this example, BB can obtain 9.5 percent fixed rate financing lower than AA's 10 percent. Conversely, AA can obtain LIBOR + 60 bp floating rate financing lower than BB's LIBOR + 80 bp available from intermediary. As stated, BB becomes the floating rate payer and AA becomes the fixed rate payer. Note, however, that even when BB can obtain lower fixed rate financing *and* lower floating rate financing than AA, a swap can still occur.

To illustrate, suppose BB can obtain 50 bp lower fixed rate financing *and* 30 bp lower floating rate financing than AA. If BB wants the floating rate financing, BB can swap its lower fixed rate payments to AA for AA's higher floating rate payments *and* an additional payment (or higher rate) from AA so that both BB and AA benefit. If AA pays another 40 bp to BB, then AA is 10 bp (= 50 bp − 40 bp) better off and BB is 10 bp (= 40 bp − 30 bp) better off.

PRINCIPAL ACCOUNTING ISSUES

Although accounting standards for interest rate swaps are still being developed, *SFAS 52, SFAS 80*, and *SFAS 91*[26] provide some guidance. Articles by Nair *et al.*,[27] Wishon and Chevalier,[28] and Bierman[29] provide thorough discussions of the issues and offer some tentative conclusions. Our views on the principal accounting issues generally coincide with what Nair et al. refer to as the **synthetic instruments approach**. In this approach, swaps are considered not as separate financial instruments, but as devices which change a fixed or variable rate instrument into a synthetic variable or fixed rate instrument. Thus a matched swap changes a variable rate bank loan into a synthetic fixed rate loan. The accounting recognizes the incremental effects the swap has on the underlying matched asset or liability, rather than account for the swap separately as a distinct instrument in its own right. There is general agreement that the important accounting issues which affect the parties to a swap include the following:

- Accounting for fees paid/received
- Differential interest and asset/liability effects
- Gain/loss recognition upon termination

Accounting for Fees Received/Paid

When a swap requires an up-front origination or other fee to be paid by a counterparty to the intermediary, its accounting likely follows GAAP covering analogous situations. The primary recognition issue pertains to fees received by intermediaries. Paragraph 5 of *SFAS 91* requires that lenders, such as banks and mortgage companies, defer loan origination fees and amortize them to interest income over the life of the loans. This adjusts the yield on the loan over its life.

Although fees received by intermediaries arranging swaps are similar to loan origination fees, current practice only partially follows *SFAS 91*. Intermediaries recognize a portion of the fee as up-front income and defer the balance to offset credit risk and administrative costs of servicing swaps. Intermediaries then carry the swaps as trading instruments and mark them to market.

---

[26] Financial Accounting Standards Board, *Statement of Financial Accounting Standards No. 91*, "Accounting for Nonrefundable Fees and Costs Associated with Originating or Acquiring Loans and Initial Direct Costs of Leases" (Stamford, CT: FASB, 1986).

[27] R.D. Nair, Larry E. Rittenberg and Jerry J. Weygandt, "Accounting for Interest Rate Swaps—A Critical Evaluation," *Accounting Horizons* (September 1990), 20-30.

[28] Wishon and Chevalier, "Interest Rate Swaps."

[29] Harold Bierman, Jr., "Accounting for Interest Rate Swaps," *Journal of Accounting, Auditing and Finance* (Fall 1987), 396-408.

The counterparty that pays the fee should consider it to be a debt issuance cost and should amortize it as an adjustment to interest expense over the life of the swap. Although effective-interest amortization is required, straight-line amortization can be used if the result is not materially different.

Differential Interest and Asset/Liability Effects

A swap is an executory contract that modifies the total obligation relating to existing debt, without affecting the counterparty's obligations to its debtholders. Viewed as a **synthetic instrument**, the swap neither creates nor extinguishes debt, although it does modify each counterparty's effective periodic interest expense. The net payments between each counterparty and the intermediary serve to adjust each counterparty's periodic interest revenue and expense. The intermediary records the net payments from the counterparties as gains realized in marking the swap to market. Because the floating rate in each succeeding period is not known in advance, the interest adjustments occur one period at a time. In the example just discussed, with LIBOR at 8 percent, AA's interest expense in the first year of the swap *increases* by $2,200,000 [= (.097 − .086) × $200M] and BB's interest expense *decreases* by $1,400,000 [= (.088 − .095) × $200M]. These events are recorded by the parties to the swap as follows:

Books of AA

Interest Expense	2,200,000	
Cash		2,200,000

To record cash paid to intermediary to settle additional interest under the terms of the swap.

Books of BB

Cash	1,400,000	
Interest Expense		1,400,000

To record cash received from intermediary to reduce interest expense under the terms of the swap.

Books of Intermediary

Cash	800,000	
Realized Gain on Interest Rate Swap		800,000

To record gain realized on the swap; $800,000 = [(.097 − .086) + (.088 − .095)] × $200,000,000.

Recognition by the counterparties of the present value of all expected future interest adjustments as assets or liabilities at inception of the swap is currently not appropriate; synthetic instruments are not presently given accounting recognition because they are *executory*. Consequently, the only asset/liability effects of swaps on the counterparties relate to the incremental interest receivable/payable that accrues under the terms of the swap and the deferral of unamortized fee balances.

Swap Valuation and Marking to Market

Valuation of financial swaps is common today for trading, accounting, and financial reporting purposes. When available, market quotations are the preferred basis for valuing swaps. In the absence of such quotations, fair value may be estimated using the present value approach discussed next.

Swap Valuation. Each swap can be thought of as having a *fixed side* and a *variable side*. In an *interest rate swap*, one side has fixed interest payments and a notional "payment" at maturity. *Like a bond*, the present value (PV) of these payments changes as market interest rates change. The other side has variable interest payments and a notional "payment" at maturity. The present value (PV) of these payments equals the notional principal amount and does *not* change because the discount rate is the same market rate used to determine the variable payments. Because this statement is not strictly true when valuations are made between dates at which the interest rate is reset, we assume that *valuations occur at the same date(s) that the variable interest rate is reset.*[30]

A swap's fair value can be expressed in the familiar accounting equation and in T-account form. Consider *counterparty BB's* side of the *interest rate swap* in the example *at inception*. To simplify the calculations, assume that the swap is for two years and LIBOR, initially at 8%, is reset annually.

$$
\begin{aligned}
\text{BB's asset} &= \text{PV of fixed 9.5\% payments from intermediary} \\
&\quad + \text{PV of \$200M principal} \\
&= \$19,000,000/1.095 + \$19,000,000/(1.095)^2 + \\
&\quad \$200,000,000/(1.095)^2 \\
&= \$17,351,598 + \$15,846,208 + \$166,802,194 \\
&= \$200,000,000
\end{aligned}
$$

$$
\begin{aligned}
\text{BB's liability} &= \text{PV of floating LIBOR} + 80 \text{ bp payments to} \\
&\quad \text{intermediary} \\
&= \$17,600,000/1.088 + \$17,600,000/(1.088)^2 + \\
&\quad \$200,000,000/(1.088)^2 \\
&= \$16,176,471 + \$14,868,079 + \$168,955,450 \\
&= \$200,000,000
\end{aligned}
$$

$$
\begin{aligned}
\text{BB's swap value} &= \text{BB's asset} - \text{BB's liability} \\
&= \text{"net worth" of swap} \\
&= \$0 \text{ at inception}
\end{aligned}
$$

The PV of the floating side remains at $200,000,000—a change in the floating rate affects *both* the floating payments *and* the discount rate used when the floating rate changes. However, when rates change and the discount rate applied to the fixed side changes, the PV changes: a positive (negative) value indicates a net asset (liability). Next we visualize this process in a T-

---

[30] The computational problem arising when valuing interest rate swaps *between reset dates* occurs because the mid-period discount rate will have changed whereas the period's variable interest payment is fixed. Thus the present value of the variable payments will change during the period between reset dates and the present value of *both* fixed and variable interest payments must be calculated in the valuation process.

account, starting at inception and revaluing the fixed side one year later when the swap has one year to go and the discount rate applied to the fixed side *decreases* to 9%.

BB's Interest Rate Swap Asset (Liability)

PV of fixed 9.5% payments from intermediary	PV of floating LIBOR + 80 bp payments to intermediary
At inception: 200,000,000	200,000,000
1 year later: 200,917,431*	200,000,000
Net asset 1 year later 917,431	

$$* \ 200,917,431 \ = \ 19,000,000/1.09 + 2,000,000/1.09$$
$$= \ 17,431,193 + 183,486,238$$

Similarly, in a *currency swap*, one side has payments denominated in dollars, fixed because they do not change with changes in the exchange rate. The other side has foreign currency-denominated payments; their dollar equivalent varies with changes in the exchange rate. Note the difference between interest rate and currency swaps. In the former, the present value of the fixed payments changes; in the latter the variable dollar value of the foreign currency payments changes. Consider *Company A's* side of the *currency swap* illustrated previously in the text *at inception*.

$$\text{A's asset} = \text{Dollars due from B} + \text{unamortized discount}$$
$$= \$58,870 + \$1,130$$
$$= \$60,000$$

$$\text{A's liability} = \text{Dollar value of shekels due to B}$$
$$= \$60,000$$

$$\text{A's swap value} = \text{A's asset} - \text{A's liability}$$
$$= \text{"net worth" of swap}$$
$$= \$0 \text{ at inception}$$

Next we visualize this process in a T-account, starting at inception and revaluing the variable side three months later at an assumed balance sheet date when the exchange rate is $.62/S and one-half of the discount is amortized.

A's Currency Swap Asset (Liability)

Dollars due from B + unamortized discount	Dollar value of shekels due to B
At inception: 60,000	60,000
3 months later: 59,435*	62,000+
Net liability 3 months later	2,565

$$* \ \ 59,435 = \ 58,870 + 1,130/2 \qquad + \ 62,000 = .62 \times 100,000$$

Marking to Market. For financial reporting purposes, swaps are marked to market (1) for disclosure under *SFAS 107* and *SFAS 119* or (2) for recognition in the balance sheet when they are viewed as separate financial instruments, as hedges of assets or liabilities carried at market, or as speculation (there is no underlying asset or liability to be hedged). If BB is marking its *interest rate swap* to market, the following journal entry is made on BB's books.

Books of BB (Interest Rate Swap)

Investment in Swaps	917,431	
Gain on Swaps		917,431

    To mark interest rate swap to market; record
    gain due to interest rate decrease.

The *currency swap* is, of course, a foreign currency forward contract governed by *SFAS 52*. Chapter 10 indicated that forward contracts are revalued at financial statement dates and reported at net as shown next for this example.

Books of A (Currency Swap)

Transaction Loss	2,000	
Other Expense	565	
Forward Sale Contract		2,565

    To mark currency swap (forward contract) to market;
    record exchange loss and discount amortization.

Because the forward contract had a net balance of zero at inception, this entry recognizes in the financial statements the $2,565 net liability under *SFAS 52*. The new forward contracts entered at the ends of successive 6-month periods will be revalued similarly at subsequent balance sheet dates.

Impact of the 1997 FASB *Draft Statement*

The preceding section on marking to market illustrates how the *Draft Statement* works with financial swaps. Because the $2,565 net liability for the forward contract is the same under the *Draft Statement* as under *SFAS 52,* we examine the interest rate swap in more depth.

Current practice does not mark to market those interest rate swaps qualifying as hedges. Instead, only the net cash payments are recorded by the counterparties as adjustments to their own interest expense. The *Draft Statement* changes this by requiring that the swap be reported at market and, since it is hedging an existing liability, that liability is also revalued to market. In the example given, one year after inception of the swap, both the debt and the swap are marked to market by BB. The gain on the swap and the loss on the debt are both reported in current earnings.

Investment in Swaps	917,431	
Gain on Swaps		917,431

    To mark interest rate swap to market and record the
    gain produced by the decrease in interest rates.

Unrealized Loss   917,431
    Long-Term Debt   917,431
To mark hedged fixed-rate debt to market and record
the loss produced by the decrease in interest rates.

The decline in the market rate of interest on this fixed-rate debt means that all remaining fixed interest and principal payments now have a higher present value. This fact is recognized both in the increase in present value of the net payments coming from intermediary (the swap) and in the increase in the amount borrowed at the current market interest rate (the debt). In other words, if the 9.5% coupon fixed-rate debt is issued today, with one year to maturity, when the market is demanding only 9%, the debt issuance proceeds are greater by $917,431.

Gain/Loss Recognition Upon Termination

Swaps may be terminated voluntarily by mutual agreement between two or more of the parties or if one or more parties default. This textbook considers *voluntary termination* only. In our example, AA may wish to terminate the swap if interest rates fall enough so that AA can borrow directly at a fixed rate below the 9.7 percent it currently pays intermediary. In the absence of contractual provisions governing swap termination, AA must negotiate a *termination payment* to intermediary to compensate the latter for its lost income and increased risk from having an unmatched swap with BB. Note that a decline in LIBOR adversely affects intermediary's separate swap with BB. Intermediary's fixed 9.5 percent payments to BB could be much greater than the floating payments it receives. Indeed, intermediary might then seek to terminate its swap with BB or otherwise hedge its exposure. The accounting results of voluntary termination on the counterparties of swaps used as hedges follow the guidance provided in EITF *Issue 84-7*, "Termination of Interest Rate Swaps".[31]

- AA is using the swap as a hedge against the interest rate risk inherent in its floating rate debt. Because interest rates declined, the termination payment is made to intermediary to avoid higher outlays required by the swap in future periods. This payment is capitalized and amortized by AA, typically over the remaining life of the swap. The periodic amortization is offset against the periodic gains resulting from lower interest on AA's floating rate debt.
- The same treatment applies if BB voluntarily terminated its swap with intermediary because BB also uses the swap as a hedge to neutralize fluctuations in revenue from its floating rate investments.

Voluntary termination of a naked speculative swap is *not* viewed as a synthetic early extinguishment of debt with extraordinary gain or loss. Instead, the payment is offset against the carrying value of the swap in calculating the ordinary gain or loss to be recognized in the period of termination.

---

[31] EITF *Issue 84-7*, "Termination of Interest Rate Swaps," *EITF Abstracts* (Norwalk, CT: FASB, 1992), pp. 15-16.

DISCLOSURE REQUIREMENTS

This section summarizes the principal disclosure requirements of *SFAS 105, SFAS 107* and *SFAS 119*. Note 12 to The Walt Disney Company's 1996 consolidated financial statements illustrates how companies comply with these disclosure requirements. Although some requirements also relate to nonderivative financial instruments, we examine the derivatives disclosures in the Disney report.

DISCLOSURE REQUIREMENTS OF *SFAS 105*

Financial instruments are pervasive throughout business. We encountered many of them, such as cash, receivables, bonds, shares of stock, and foreign currency forward contracts, in this textbook and in previous accounting courses. *SFAS 105* provides a definition of a financial instrument broad enough to encompass financial instruments currently in existence as well as those that will emerge in the future. This definition appears in paragraph 6 of *SFAS 105*.

> A **financial instrument** is cash, evidence of an ownership interest in an entity, or a contract that both:
>
> a. Imposes on one entity a contractual obligation (1) to deliver cash or another financial instrument to a second entity or (2) to exchange financial instruments on potentially unfavorable terms with the second entity.
>
> b. Conveys to that second entity a contractual right (1) to receive cash or another financial instrument from the first entity or (2) to exchange other financial instruments on potentially favorable terms with the first entity.

Notice that familiar items such as *accounts payable* and *accounts receivable* fit the contractual obligation/right to deliver/receive cash in the definition. *Convertible bonds* illustrate the "potentially unfavorable" aspect of the definition. When one entity redeems a convertible bond, common stock often worth many times the original price received by the second entity that issued the bond must be given to the first entity. In this chapter we use our knowledge of forward exchange contracts as a basis for studying less-familiar financial instruments—futures contracts, options, and financial swaps—which are examples of *contracts* that incorporate Parts *a* and *b* in this definition.

The principal thrust of *SFAS 105* is to require entities to *disclose information about financial instruments* that have *off-balance-sheet risk* or *concentrations of credit risk*. This requirement addresses concern over the **risk of accounting loss,** the loss that might occur if (1) another party to a contract involving the entity fails to perform (credit risk) or (2) changes in market prices impair the value of the financial instrument (market risk). When a customer defaults on an account receivable, accounting loss is measured by the carrying value of the receivable on the entity's balance sheet; the risk of loss is therefore not off-balance-sheet.

> **Off-balance-sheet risk** refers to the *risk of accounting loss* that exceeds the amount currently recognized as an asset or liability in the balance sheet.

As an example of *off-balance-sheet risk*, recall from Chapter 10 that *foreign currency forward contracts* are only reported at net in the balance sheet. For this reason, a speculative forward purchase (sale) contract—an unrecorded asset (liability)—has potential for loss beyond what is shown in the balance sheet if the exchange rate falls (rises).

To illustrate how a speculative forward contract produces off-balance-sheet risk, suppose that when the spot rate is $1.10/LC, an entity purchases LC100,000 for delivery in 90 days at the forward rate of $1.20/LC. Because the entity plans to sell the LC100,000 in 90 days in the spot market, and not to liquidate an underlying commitment or liability to a foreign supplier, the forward purchase contract is *not a hedge*. Although the entity hopes the LC will strengthen, and the spot rate will rise, suppose the spot rate falls to $.95/LC in 90 days. Now the LC100,000, to be purchased from the foreign exchange broker for $120,000, can be sold for only $95,000. Prior to *SFAS 105*, the forward contract that exposed the entity to the off-balance-sheet risk of losing this $25,000 [= ($.95 − $1.20)100,000], or more if the exchange rate dropped further, need not be disclosed when the contract is entered. The instruments studied in this chapter, and many others, also possess off-balance-sheet risk.

SFAS 105 prescribes the following kinds of disclosures, in the financial statements or notes, about the entity's *financial instruments with off-balance-sheet risk* (paragraphs 17, 18):

- The face, contract, or notional amount.
- The nature, terms, credit and market risk, cash requirements and the method of accounting used.
- Amount of accounting loss from any party's failure to perform, assuming collateral is worthless (off-balance-sheet credit risk instruments).
- Policy for requiring collateral, access to it, and description of it (off-balance-sheet credit risk instruments).

In addition to disclosures of off-balance-sheet risk, *SFAS 105* also requires disclosure of *concentrations of credit risk*.

> **Concentrations of credit risk** exist when the *risk of credit loss* from financial instruments, both on-balance-sheet and off-balance-sheet, is concentrated in particular geographic regions, industries, or customer groups that are exposed to common adverse economic developments.

Many examples of concentrations of credit risk are familiar. These include an entity's significant receivables from customers in a particular geographic region or loans to individuals and entities dependent upon the agricultural sector. In both of these cases, adverse developments affecting the subject geographic region or the agricultural sector expose the entity to concentrated losses from failure of the affected customers to repay their debts to the entity.

Disclosures regarding *concentrations of credit risk* are specified in paragraph 20 of *SFAS 105*:

- Description of the concentration—activity, geographic region or economic characteristic.
- Amount of accounting loss due to credit risk if parties comprising the concentration fail to perform, assuming collateral is worthless.
- Policy for requiring collateral, access to it, and description of it.

DISCLOSURE REQUIREMENTS OF *SFAS 107*

SFAS 107 calls for disclosures about "fair value of all financial instruments, both assets and liabilities recognized and not recognized in the statement of financial position" (par. 2). Quoted market prices are preferred but, if not available, pricing models may be used. Exclusions are discussed in par. 8 and include employers' obligations for pension benefits, most insurance policies, equity investments and other items. Par. 13 excludes separate disclosure of trade receivables and payables when their carrying amounts approximate fair value. Moreover, fair value estimates are not required when it is not *practicable* (i.e., when it is *too costly*) to do so. Disclosures shall include:

- Methods and assumptions used to estimate fair value.
- Estimates of the fair value of deposit liabilities by *financial institutions*, excluding ". . . the value of long-term relationships with depositors, commonly known as *core deposit intangibles*, which are separate intangible assets, not financial instruments." (par. 12)

DISCLOSURE REQUIREMENTS OF *SFAS 119*

SFAS 119 is the FASB's initial response to certain criticisms of previous disclosures and the growing demand for information about companies' use of derivatives. It imposes the following principal disclosure requirements by category of financial instrument:

- Information about derivatives that do *not* have off-balance-sheet risk, expanding the scope of *SFAS 105*. This information shall distinguish between derivatives held or issued for (1) *trading purposes* and (2) *purposes other than trading* (such as hedging).
  - Face, contract or notional amount.
  - Discussion of credit and market risk and cash requirements.
- Fair values and net trading revenue (loss) of derivatives held or issued for *trading purposes*.
- Descriptions of the entity's objectives, financial reporting policies and hedging activities, including amount of deferred gains and losses, for derivatives held or issued for *purposes other than trading*.
- Presentation of information in more user-friendly ways than currently provided for in *SFAS 107*, including a summary table cross-referenced to related disclosures in other footnotes and a clear distinction between assets and liabilities in the fair value disclosures.

News articles indicating losses sustained by large companies, such as Air Products & Chemicals and Procter & Gamble, on derivatives held or issued by them indicate that these companies, and users of their financial statements, may have been unaware of the risks involved.[32] The *SFAS 119* disclosure requirements are therefore timely and should be helpful in assessing companies' exposure to loss from their activities in derivatives.

---

[32] James P. Miller, "Air Products Takes a Charge of $60 Million," *The Wall Street Journal* (May 12, 1994, p. A3); "Did Procter & Gamble Play with Fire?" *Business Week* (April 25, 1994, p. 38); Larry M. Greenberg, "Bank of Montreal's Harris Unit Records $51.3 Million Loss from Derivatives," *The Wall Street Journal* (June 27, 1994, p. A4).

THE 1996 WALT DISNEY COMPANY DISCLOSURES

Exhibit 11.1 contains excerpts from Note 12 to The Walt Disney Company's 1996 consolidated financial statements. We deleted material not clearly related to derivatives, removed most 1995 references and disclosures, and offer brief comments on the developments in 1996. The first four bullets following Exhibit 11.1 comprise *SFAS 107, SFAS 119* and some *SFAS 105* disclosures. The last bullet relates specifically to *SFAS 105*.

Note 12: Financial Instruments

Financial Risk Management

The Company is exposed to the impact of interest rate changes. The Company's objective is to manage the impact of interest rate changes on earnings and cash flows and on the market value of its investments and borrowings. The Company maintains fixed rate debt as a percentage of its net debt between a minimum and maximum percentage, which is set by policy.

The Company transacts business in virtually every part of the world and is subject to risks associated with changing foreign exchange rates. The Company's objective is to reduce earnings and cash flow volatility associated with foreign exchange rate changes to allow management to focus its attention on its core business issues and challenges. Accordingly, the Company enters into various contracts which change in value as foreign exchange rates change to protect the value of its existing foreign currency assets and liabilities, commitments and anticipated foreign currency revenues. By policy, the Company maintains hedge coverage between minimum and maximum percentages of its anticipated foreign exchange exposures for each of the next five years. The gains and losses on these contracts offset changes in the value of the related exposures.

It is the Company's policy to enter into foreign currency and interest rate transactions only to the extent considered necessary to meet its objectives as stated above. The Company does not enter into foreign currency or interest rate transactions for speculative purposes.

Interest Rate Risk Management

The Company uses interest rate swaps and other instruments to manage net exposure to interest rate changes related to its portfolio of borrowings and investments and to lower its overall borrowing costs. Significant interest rate risk management instruments held by the Company at September 31, 1996 are described below.

Interest Rate Risk Management—Borrowings

At September 30, 1996, the Company had outstanding interest rate swaps on its borrowings with notional amounts totaling $900 million, which effectively converted floating rate commercial paper to fixed rate instruments. At September 30, 1996, the Company had outstanding interest rate swaps on its borrowings with notional amounts totaling $1,520 million, which effectively converted medium-term notes to commercial paper of LIBOR-based variable rate instruments. These swap agreements expire in two to 15 years.

Interest Rate Risk Management—Investment Transactions

At September 30, 1995, the Company had outstanding $154 million notional amount of interest rate swaps designated as hedges of investments, and $225 million of options, futures and forward contracts. These swaps and contracts were terminated during 1996 and the realized gains and losses are included in earnings.

EXHIBIT 11.1 DERIVATIVES DISCLOSURES OF WALT DISNEY COMPANY

Note 12: Financial Instruments *Continued*

Interest Rate Risk Management—Summary of Transactions

The following table reflects incremental changes in the notional or contractual amounts of the Company's interest rate contracts during 1996 and 1995. Activity representing renewal of existing positions is excluded.

	Balance at September 30, 1995	Additions	Maturities/ Expirations	Terminations	Balance at September 30, 1996
Pay floating swaps	$ 719	$1,195	$(115)	$ (279)	$1,520
Pay fixed swaps	4,680	1,460	—	(5,240)	900
Forward contracts	—	93	(93)	—	—
Futures contracts	123	6	—	(129)	—
Option contracts	102	12	(40)	(74)	—
	$5,624	$2,766	$(248)	$(5,722)	$2,420

The impact of interest rate risk management activities on income in 1996 and the amount of deferred gains and losses from interest rate risk management transactions at September 30, 1996 were not material.

Foreign Exchange Risk Management

The Company primarily uses option strategies which provide for the sale of foreign currencies to hedge probable, but not firmly committed, revenues. While these hedging instruments are subject to fluctuations in value, such fluctuations are offset by changes in the value of the underlying exposures being hedged. The principal currencies hedged are the Japanese yen, French franc, German mark, British pound, Canadian dollar, Italian lira and Spanish peseta.

Foreign Exchange Risk Management Transactions

The Company uses options contracts to hedge anticipated foreign currency revenues. The Company also uses forward contracts to hedge foreign currency assets, liabilities and foreign currency payments the Company is committed to make in connection with the construction of two cruise ships. Cross-currency swaps are used to hedge foreign currency-denominated borrowings.

At September 30, 1996, the notional amounts of the Company's foreign exchange risk management contracts, net of notional amounts of contracts with counterparties against which the Company has a legal right of offset, the related exposures hedged and the contract maturities are as follows:

	1996		
	Notional Amount	Exposures Hedged	Fiscal Year Maturity
Option contracts	$5,563	$3,386	1997-1999
Forward contracts	1,981	1,174	1997-1999
Cross-currency swaps	2,308	2,536	1997-2001
	$9,852	$7,096	

EXHIBIT 11.1 *CONTINUED*

Note 12: Financial Instruments *Continued*

Gains and losses on contracts hedging anticipated foreign currency revenues and foreign currency commitments are deferred until such revenues are recognized or such commitments are met, and offset changes in the value of the foreign currency revenues and commitments. At September 30, 1996, the Company had net deferred gains of $28 million related to foreign currency hedge transactions, which will be recognized in income over the next three years. Amounts recognizable in any one year are not material and will be substantially offset by gains and losses in the value of the related hedged transactions.

The impact of foreign exchange risk management activities on income in 1996 and 1995 was not material.

Fair Value of Financial Instruments

At September 30, 1996, the Company's financial instruments included cash, cash equivalents, investments, receivables, accounts payable, borrowings and interest rate and foreign exchange risk management contracts.

At September 30, 1996, the fair values of cash and cash equivalents, receivables, accounts payable, commercial paper and securities sold under agreements to repurchase approximated carrying values because of the short-term nature of these instruments. The estimated fair values of other financial instruments subject to fair value disclosures, determined based on broker quotes or quoted market prices or rates for the same or similar instruments, and the related carrying amounts are as follows:

	1996	
	Carrying Amount	Fair Value
Investments	$ 41	$ 41
Borrowings	(12,342)	(12,270)
Risk management contracts	466	460
	$(11,835)	$(11,769)

Credit Concentrations

The Company continually monitors its positions with, and the credit quality of, the financial institutions which are counterparties to its financial instruments and does not anticipate nonperformance by the counterparties. The Company would not realize a material loss as of September 30, 1996 in the event of nonperformance by any one counterparty. The Company enters into transactions only with financial institution counterparties which have a credit rating of A- or better. The Company's current policy in agreements with financial institution counterparties is generally to require collateral in the event aggregate exposures exceed limits as defined by contract. In addition, the Company limits the amount of credit exposure with any one institution. At September 30, 1996, financial institution counterparties posted collateral of $201 million to the Company, and the Company was not required to collateralize its financial instrument obligations.

The Company's trade receivables and investments do not represent significant concentrations of credit risk at September 30, 1996, due to the wide variety of customers and markets into which the Company's products are sold, their dispersion across many geographic areas, and the diversification of the Company's portfolio among instruments and issuers.

EXHIBIT 11.1 *CONTINUED*

- Note 12 begins with an overview of its **financial risk management** practices and states that "The Company does not enter into foreign currency or interest rate transactions for speculative purposes."

- Disney's **interest rate risk management** practices are described next followed by a tabular summary. Interest rate swaps are by far the largest component of the Company's derivatives used for hedging interest rate risk. The overall notional amount fell by almost 60% in 1996; it increased by 180% in 1995, indicating great fluctuation in amounts being hedged.

- A discussion of **foreign exchange risk management** follows. The tabular summary indicates that options are most widely used for this purpose although forwards and currency swaps are also important. One wonders why, if Disney does not speculate in foreign currencies, derivatives' notional amounts are so much larger than exposures hedged. As expected, the Company defers transaction adjustments on hedges of foreign currency commitments and anticipated revenues.
- **Fair values** of all of Disney's financial instruments are described and then shown in the third tabular display. Note how minuscule the total carrying amount/fair value of risk management contracts is compared to the total notional amount. This indicates that these instruments' off-balance-sheet risk greatly exceeds the amount on balance sheet.
- The last item refers to the *SFAS 105* **concentrations of credit risk.** Disney monitors these matters closely and believes its credit risks are widely diversified.

CONCLUDING REMARKS

This concludes our discussion of some of the more common derivative financial instruments. They all represent the attempts of market participants to increase the adequacy or completeness of exchange arrangements in the market in terms of fulfilling investors' and issuers' needs. And there are some commonalities among these instruments: the executory aspect of many of them, their forward- looking nature, and the notion that, when serving as hedges, they become integral parts of the hedged items. Moreover, by combining the basic payoff profiles of the various instruments in creative ways, a wide variety of exposure/payoff profiles can be constructed.[33]

The accounting for some of these instruments is unsettled and continues to evolve. When finalized, the 1997 FASB *Draft Statement* will resolve many of these issues, including extending accounting recognition to an expanded set of executory contracts.

SUMMARY OF KEY CONCEPTS

Financial instruments include cash, ownership interest in an entity, and contracts (1) obligating an entity to deliver cash or financial instruments to a second entity on potentially unfavorable terms, and (2) entitling the second entity to receive cash or financial instruments on potentially favorable terms from the first entity.

Derivative financial instruments are financial instruments whose value is tied to or derived from the value of a reference asset, financial instrument or index. They are linked to **underlyings**— prices and interest rates subject to change—and are based on a **contractual** or **notional amount**—face value of debt, quantity of currency and the like—stated in the instrument's contract.

Because many financial instruments are **executory contracts**, not fully recognized in an entity's financial statements, *SFAS 105* requires disclosure of **off-balance-sheet risk**, including **market risk** and **credit risk**, pertaining to such financial instruments. Information on **concentrations of credit risk** must be disclosed for all financial instruments. *SFAS 107* requires disclosures about

---

[33] Charles W. Smithson, "A LEGO Approach to Financial Engineering: An Introduction to Forwards, Futures, Swaps, and Options," *Midland Corporate Finance Journal* (Winter, 1987), 16-28.

fair value of all financial instruments and *SFAS 119* requires information about **derivative financial instruments**.

A buyer (seller) of a **futures contract** is **required** to accept (make) delivery of a standardized quantity of a commodity or financial instrument from (to) the clearinghouse of a futures exchange at a specified date or enter into an offsetting contract. Changes in value of open contracts are settled in cash with the clearinghouse, generally on a daily basis.

Accounting for most **futures contracts** is prescribed by *SFAS 80*; foreign currency futures follow *SFAS 52*. Contracts are **marked to market** as settlement is made with the clearinghouse. Gains and losses due to changes in futures prices are recognized in income unless the futures contract functions as an **effective hedge** and the hedged item is not carried at market.

Gains and losses on futures contracts that hedge an **existing exposure**, a **firm commitment**, or an **anticipated transaction** are not recognized in income currently unless the hedged item is carried at market. Gains and losses adjust the carrying value of existing exposures; they are deferred and adjust the dollar basis of transactions recorded when firm commitments are fulfilled and anticipated transactions occur.

An **option** is a contract **allowing** but **not requiring** the holder to **buy (call)** or **sell (put)** the optioned commodity or financial instrument at a **specified price (strike price)** during a **specified time period**.

An option is **in the money** when exercise of the option profits the holder more than transacting directly in the optioned item. Otherwise the option is **out of the money**; a point of indifference indicates that the option is **at the money**.

Accounting for options is evolving. When an option is used as a **hedge**, the **time value** component of the option's cost or **premium** is generally **amortized** over the life of the option. Publicly traded options are **marked to market** daily; accounting for the resulting gains and losses closely parallels that for futures contracts. Gains and losses are not recognized currently unless the option is hedging an existing exposure carried at market or is speculative.

Financial swaps involve an exchange of cash flows over time between **counterparties** which are often linked by a bank or other **intermediary**. Common examples are **currency swaps, interest rate swaps** and **commodity swaps**. The swapped flows are based on a principal amount which, when not exchanged itself, is called the **notional amount**. Swaps are not yet traded on organized exchanges.

Because swaps are **executory contracts**, even more so than futures and options, accounting issues and practices are evolving. **Currency swaps** follow the accounting prescribed in *SFAS 52* for foreign currency forward contracts. **Interest rate swaps** are typically viewed as **synthetic instruments**. Like forwards, futures and options, **interest rate swaps are derivative financial instruments** whose value is tied to or derived from an underlying asset, financial instrument or other reference item. **Disclosure** and the propriety of **marking to market** are important issues.

For interest rate swaps, **differential interest effects are recognized** and **fees paid/received** are generally amortized to income/expense over the swap's life. **Valuation of interest rate swaps** generally involves calculating the change in the present value of the fixed payment side of the swap as the present value of the floating payment side normally remains constant.

The **1997 FASB** *Draft Statement,* when finalized, will standardize accounting and reporting for most derivative financial instruments. It calls for recognizing **more value changes in earnings,** for **more marking to market,** and utilizes the **comprehensive income** reporting framework of *SFAS 130*.

QUESTIONS

Q11.1   As if FASB *Statements 105* and *107* were not enough, the FASB required additional disclosures for financial instruments in *SFAS 119*. What, in your opinion, is the overriding reason for these increased disclosure requirements?

Q11.2   *SFAS 105* provides a formal definition of financial instruments. Explain how the two provisions in part *b.* of that definition relate to the holder of *callable convertible preferred stock.*

Q11.3   Explain to what extent you believe that *off-balance-sheet risk* and *off-balance-sheet financing* are related concerns in financial reporting.

Q11.4   What is the general meaning of *derivative financial instrument*? Why should users of financial statements be interested in the extent and nature of an entity's involvement in derivatives?

Q11.5   "Even though futures contracts can reduce risk of loss, the use of futures contracts can also increase risk." Briefly comment on this statement.

Q11.6   What is meant by hedge accounting? Briefly discuss when the use of hedge accounting is proper.

Q11.7   Briefly describe how options differ from both futures and forward contracts.

Q11.8   What is meant by a naked option writer? A covered option writer? Explain the risk assumed by the writer in each of these circumstances.

Q11.9   What movement in interest rates can a put option on bonds be used to hedge against?

Q11.10   What is the most significant risk assumed by counterparties engaging in an interest rate swap? How can it be avoided?

Q11.11   In a plain vanilla interest rate swap, one counterparty is the fixed rate payer and the other is the floating rate payer. Describe the nature of the obligation—fixed or floating— swapped by each of the above counterparties. What motivates the counterparties to enter interest rate swaps?

Q11.12 The notion of valuing a swap implies that the swap can be viewed as a separate financial instrument. Briefly describe the approach to valuing swaps. How do you know whether the value computed is an asset or liability to the entity valuing the swap?

EXERCISES

E11.1 **Commodity Futures (Short) Entries, Profit Calculation** Marcelino Co. manufactures several varieties of pasta. The price of pasta is very sensitive to the cost of certain commodities. On January 1, 19X6, the company had excess commodity inventories carried at acquisition cost of $150,000. The commodities might be manufactured into pasta later in the year or might be sold by Marcelino. To hedge against possible declines in the value of its commodities inventory, on January 6 Marcelino sold commodity futures (went short), obligating the company to deliver the commodities in February for $160,000. The futures exchange requires a $10,000 "good faith" deposit. On February 19, the futures price has increased to $171,000 and the company closes out its futures contracts. Spot prices continue to rise and Marcelino sells its inventory for $173,500 on March 2.

REQUIRED:

1. Following *SFAS 80*, prepare the journal entries related to Marcelino's futures contract and sale of commodities inventory. Assume a perpetual inventory system.
2. By how much would Marcelino's profit increase if the hedge was *not* undertaken?
3. Repeat *1.* according to the 1997 FASB *Draft Statement*.

E11.2 **Multiple Choice: Interest Rate Futures** Petren Corporation, a fabric retailer in Clark, N.J., purchases all its stock from various manufacturers throughout the country. The company buys 300,000 yards of cloth every 3 months at an average price of $3.00 per yard. To finance these purchases, at the end of every quarter the company sells the necessary number of $1,000 Treasury bonds from its investment portfolio. The bonds are presently carried at 90, their current market value.

REQUIRED: Select the best answer to each of the following multiple choice questions.

1. Petren sells Treasury bond futures (goes short) at 90 on enough bonds to finance the next quarter's purchases and closes out the contract at 92 in three months. Considering both the futures contract and sale of the company's own Treasury bonds to finance purchases, the foregoing results in:
   a. an unrealized gain of $20,000.   d. a cash loss of $40,000.
   b. a realized gain of $40,000.   e. neither gain nor loss.
   c. an unrealized loss of $20,000.

2. Petren buys Treasury bond futures (goes long) at 90 on enough bonds to finance the next quarter's purchases and closes out the contact at 93 in three months. Considering both the futures contract and sale of the company's own Treasury bonds to finance purchases, the foregoing results in:
   a. a realized gain of $60,000.   d. a realized loss of $60,000.
   b. an unrealized gain of $60,000.   e. neither gain nor loss.
   c. an opportunity loss of $30,000.

E11.3 **Commodity Futures (Long) Journal Entries** Daley, Inc., engages in futures trading on a regular basis. Its books are closed on June 30 of each year. On June 1, 19X6, it enters a futures contract and makes an initial margin deposit of $10,000. Under the contract, Daley purchases 10,000 units of commodity futures at $10 per unit, specifying delivery in 90 days. Daley has a liability, recorded as Deferred Revenue, to supply the commodity (which it plans to purchase on the spot market) in 90 days to a customer. The customer has already paid the full $150,000 selling price.

REQUIRED:

1. Prepare the journal entries made on June 1, on June 30 when the futures are selling at $11 per unit, and on August 29 when the long position is closed out at $11.50 per unit, following *SFAS 80*.
2. Repeat *1.* according to the 1997 FASB *Draft Statement*.
3. Explain why Daley purchased commodity futures when it intends to purchase the commodity on the spot market. How much did Daley save by hedging as opposed to not hedging?

E11.4 **Commodity Futures (Short) Journal Entries** On June 1, 19X2, Keister, Inc. sells 100,000 units of commodity futures at $5 per unit for delivery in 120 days, making an initial margin deposit of $10,000 in the process. Keister has a firm commitment to purchase the commodity from a supplier in 90 days and to resell it 30 days later. Keister's fiscal year ends on June 30.

REQUIRED: Prepare the journal entries made on June 1, on June 30 when the futures are selling at $4.80 per unit, on August 29 when the futures are selling for $4.75 per unit and the commodity is purchased at a total cost of $460,000, and on September 28 when the short position is closed out at $4.77 per unit.

E11.5 **Economics of Hedging with Futures; Hedge Accounting** McVeigh Company buys 100,000 units of commodity futures at $5.50 per unit to cover a firm commitment to deliver 100,000 units (which McVeigh does not own) to a customer at a fixed price. Spot and futures prices for this commodity are equal (basis is ignored here) and generally fluctuate between $4 and $6 per unit.

REQUIRED:

1. Use calculations to show that, regardless of whether McVeigh eventually purchases the commodity for as little as $4 or as much as $6, hedging with futures fixes the net cost to McVeigh at $5.50 per unit.
2. Suppose McVeigh grows the commodity on its own farms and will not need to purchase it on the spot market. Explain whether *SFAS 80* permits hedge accounting treatment for the 100,000 units of commodity futures purchased by McVeigh.

E11.6 **Economics of Hedging with Options; Hedge Accounting** Refer to the data in E11.5. Instead of purchasing futures, McVeigh purchases 100,000 commodity call options with a strike price of $5.50/unit at the money for $45,000.

REQUIRED:

1. Use calculations to show that, regardless of whether McVeigh eventually purchases the commodity for as little as $4 or as much as $6, hedging with options limits the cost to a range between $4.45 and $5.95 per unit.
2. Give an argument *against* the use of hedge accounting for options of the type described here.

E11.7   Interest Rate Cap: Journal Entries On July 1, 19X1, Molson Corporation borrowed $3 million for two years with interest paid semi-annually based on LIBOR adjusted semi-annually. On that date, LIBOR is 7 percent per annum, and the company expects interest rates to fall. However, an increase in LIBOR would weaken the ability of the company to service its debt. Thus, to hedge against a possible rise in interest rates, on July 2 Molson bought a two-year 7.1 percent interest rate cap for .3 percent per year, payable in full immediately. At the end of 19X1, LIBOR fell to 6.9 percent, but during the first half of 19X2 it increased to 7.3 percent. Molson closes its books on December 31 and June 30.

REQUIRED: Prepare all journal entries related to the loan interest and the interest rate cap on December 31, 19X1, and June 30, 19X2.

E11.8   Put Options: Journal Entries In January, 19X1, Combo Corporation purchased $200,000 of 9 percent government bonds at par. By late February, the bonds were selling at 98. To hedge against a further price decrease on these bonds, on March 1, 19X1, Combo purchased March 19X2 put options on these bonds at 101 for a premium of $3.10 per $100 of bonds. By June 30, 19X1, the company's fiscal year-end, the bonds are selling at 100 and the puts for $2.30. On December 31, 19X1, when the bonds are selling at 97, Combo decides not to exercise the put options. Instead, Combo closes out its position by selling the puts for $5.30.

REQUIRED:

1. Prepare the journal entries related to the puts made by Combo Corporation during 19X1, following current practice.
2. Repeat *1.* according to the 1997 FASB *Draft Statement.*

E11.9   Currency Calls: Journal Entries Taking advantage of lower interest rates in the United Kingdom, Carlton Inc., a U.S. manufacturer, borrowed £2,000,000 on July 1, 19X1, to be repaid in one year. When the transaction occurred, the exchange rate was $1.50/£. To hedge against possible appreciation of the British pound, Carlton bought July 19X2 call options on £2,000,000, with a strike price of $1.49/£, at a premium of $0.014/£. On December 31, 19X1, when Carlton's books are closed, the exchange rate is $1.55/£, and the calls are selling for $0.069/£. On July 1, 19X2, Carlton decides to close out the calls by selling them for $0.12/£. The exchange rate at that time is $1.61/£.

REQUIRED:

1. Prepare the journal entries made by Carlton in connection with the calls. Ignore any transaction adjustments relating to the loan payable. Follow current practice.
2. Repeat *1.* according to the 1997 FASB *Draft Statement.*

E11.10 **Straddle: Journal Entries and Profit Calculation** Suavo, Inc. trades put and call options on common stock. Acting on a tip, on January 31, 19X4, Suavo wrote calls and puts expiring on March 31—a straddle—on 5,000 shares of Montclair Corporation stock. Montclair stock was selling for $42 a share; March 19X4 calls with a strike price of $45 closed at $2; puts with the same terms closed at $3.10. On February 28, when the price of Montclair stock rose to $49, Suavo closed the calls at $4.20; the puts were selling for $0.80 on that day. On March 31, Montclair stock fell to $47 and the puts expired without being exercised.

REQUIRED:

1. Prepare journal entries to record writing the puts and calls and any other related accounting events including expiration of the puts. The books are closed monthly.
2. Calculate Suavo's cash gain or loss on the straddle.

E11.11 **Currency Swap: Journal Entries** On October 1, 19X2, Moderno Corporation, a U.S. company, and Sidney, Inc., an Australian corporation, swap a notional amount of $A8,000,000, equivalent to $6,400,000 at the current spot rate of $.80/$A. The agreement calls for the two companies to re-exchange one-eighth of the currency swapped at the end of every three months. At inception of the swap, one-year government securities in the United States yield 12 percent, while similar securities in Australia yield 10 percent. By the end of 19X2, the $ had appreciated in value and the spot rate was $.75/$A. On December 31, 19X2, Moderno transferred $A1,000,000 to Sidney, Inc. and received $ in return.

REQUIRED:

1. Compute the direct forward rate for delivery on December 31, 19X2.
2. Show the journal entries for the transactions on Moderno's books starting at the inception of the swap up to and including the transfer at the end of 19X2.

E11.12 **Benefits of Interest Rate Swap** The following information relates to an interest rate swap between Apricot, Inc. and Pear, Inc. Apricot, Inc. borrowed $2 million one year ago at a floating rate of LIBOR + 30 bp. Apricot prefers fixed rate financing but was unable to get fixed rate financing at less than 11 percent due to its low credit rating. Pear, Inc. has an AAA credit rating and pays 9.2 percent fixed on its $2 million debt. In addition, because it has investments that generate floating rate earnings, Pear, Inc. is ripe for an arrangement that would enable it to hedge its interest rate risk. Nectar Interbank offers Apricot, Inc. floating rate payments at LIBOR + 30 in exchange for fixed rate payments of 9.5 percent. The notional amount is $2 million. Concurrently, Nectar offers Pear, Inc. fixed payments of 9.2 percent on its $2 million debt in exchange for floating rate payments of LIBOR + 50.

REQUIRED: Assuming the three parties agree to the swap, compute the annual interest rate advantage to Apricot, Inc. and Pear, Inc., given their preferred alternatives, as well as the annual net interest rate spread Nectar Interbank will enjoy. Use a LIBOR rate of 8 percent.

E11.13 **Interest Rate Swap: Profit and Default** On July 1, 19X8, Queen Corp. and Prince, Inc. entered into an interest rate swap on a notional amount of $1 million. With T representing the Treasury bill rate, they accepted the following offer of Meno Bank, an intermediary:

To Meno Bank from Queen	LIBOR + 30 (floating)
To Meno Bank from Prince	T + 40 (fixed)
To Queen from Meno Bank	T + 30 (fixed)
To Prince from Meno Bank	LIBOR + 20 (floating)

At inception of the swap, T = 6 percent and LIBOR = 6.3 percent. Due to an increase of 20 bp in the floating interest rate at the end of September, Queen Corp. defaulted and Meno Bank honored its commitment to Prince, Inc. by continuing with the swap.

REQUIRED:

1. What monthly profit, if any, was Meno Bank making on the swap before default?
2. Is Meno Bank losing money after the default? If so, how much?

E11.14 **Interest Rate Swap: Journal Entries** Refer to the data in E11.13. Assume that the floating rate is adjusted on October 1 and that default did *not* occur.

REQUIRED: Prepare the journal entries made by Queen, Prince and Meno Bank on September 30, 19X8 when the first payments pursuant to the swap are made.

E11.15 **Multiple Choice: Effects of Interest Rate Swap Default on Intermediary** Lima Bank is an intermediary in a plain vanilla interest rate swap.

REQUIRED: Select the best answer(s) to the following multiple choice questions relating to the bank's exposure to risk when a certain event occurs.

1. The floating interest rate has risen sharply and the floating rate payer defaults. Which of the following are necessarily true?
   a. The bank is exposed to a loss.
   b. The bank is presently losing money on the transaction.
   c. The bank must pay a lower interest rate to a new fixed rate receiver.
   d. The bank will pay a higher interest rate to a new floating rate receiver.
2. The fixed rate payer defaults while the floating rate is rising sharply. Which of the following are necessarily true?
   a. The bank is exposed to a loss.
   b. The bank is not exposed to a loss.
   c. The bank will receive a higher interest rate from the new fixed rate payer.
   d. The bank will receive a lower interest rate from the new fixed rate payer.

PROBLEMS

P11.1 Commodity Futures (Short) Entries, Gain/Loss Calculations The Davis Company grows soybeans and processes them into soybean meal for eventual sale to a variety of manufacturing concerns. The company currently owns 10,000 tons of soybean meal, carried in inventory at cost of $1,100,000. Soybean meal is currently trading on the spot markets for $150 per ton; three-month futures are selling for $163 per ton. Davis expects to sell the 10,000 tons in 90 days. On August 1, 19X5, Davis sells 10,000 tons of soybean meal futures to be delivered on October 30, 19X5, at the $163 price. The price of Davis' futures contracts has advanced to $167 on September 30, when the books are closed for interim reporting purposes. Davis closes out its short position on October 28, 19X5, when the price is $161 per ton.

REQUIRED:

1. Assuming that Davis deposits $75,000 margin with the broker on August 1, prepare the journal entries it makes on August 1, on September 30, and on October 28.
2. If Davis sells the soybean meal in the spot market on November 2, 19X5, for $158.50 per ton, calculate its net cash gain or loss from the sale, taking into account the hedging transaction.
3. Suppose instead that Davis *purchased* the 10,000 tons of soybean futures on August 1, 19X5, closing the long position on October 28, 19X5. Calculate the net cash gain or loss on the long futures position and compare its accounting treatment with the gain or loss on the short futures position in *1*. above at October 28, 19X5.

P11.2 Interest Rate Futures Entries and Analysis As part of its cash management activities, Greenstein Corp. regularly invests in 91-day Treasury bills. It purchased $1,000,000 face value of these bills on June 1 and, fearing lower interest rates when it "rolls over" these short-term investments, Greenstein purchases $1,000,000 face value Treasury bill futures at 90 to be delivered in 91 days and makes a $10,000 margin deposit.

REQUIRED:

1. Prepare the journal entries made on June 1, on June 30 when the Treasury bill futures are selling at 91, and on August 30 when the old Treasury bills mature and the new ones are delivered. On August 30, Greenstein's futures contract is selling at 91.5.
2. Assume the new Treasury bills cost $978,750. Use calculations to show how the hedge enables Greenstein to report a 10% annualized return on the new Treasury bills even though they are currently selling to yield 8.5% annually.

P11.3 Transaction Risk Versus Enterprise Risk You read in the text that an effective hedge arises under *SFAS 52* when the hedge reduces or neutralizes the risk on a transaction or net asset position. In contrast, *SFAS 80* requires that an effective hedge reduce or neutralize *enterprise risk*. Although accounting for both foreign currency forward and futures contracts is covered by *SFAS 52*, assume for purposes of this question that *SFAS 80* governs foreign currency futures but not forwards.

REQUIRED:

1. Give an example of an effective hedge under *SFAS 52* deemed *not* effective under *SFAS 80*.
2. Give an example of an effective hedge under *SFAS 80* deemed *not* effective under *SFAS 52*.
3. Suppose an entity had the following receivables (payables) denominated in foreign currencies:

FC	$
£1,000,000	1,600,000
FF10,000,000	2,000,000
¥500,000,000	517,000
¥(300,000,000)	(310,200)

   Assume movements of all three currencies are uncorrelated and that the entity seeks to hedge the yen (¥) receivables with forward or futures contracts. What is the maximum amount of hedged yen receivables that hedge accounting could apply to under *SFAS 52*? Under *SFAS 80*?
4. Repeat *3.* for yen payables.
5. Assume the British pound sterling (£) and the French franc (FF) move in tandem, but opposite to the Japanese yen (¥), and the entity seek to hedge the sterling and franc receivables with forward or futures contracts. What is the maximum amount of hedged sterling and franc receivables that hedge accounting could apply to under *SFAS 52*? Under *SFAS 80*?

P11.4 **Evaluating Hedging With Futures Contracts** A large farming company likes to firm up prices for the agricultural products it will be harvesting over the next year. It anticipates harvesting 1,000,000 bushels of a particular commodity in six months. Constant news reports and changes in forecasts cause fluctuations in the spot price for this commodity.

The current spot price is $5.00 per bushel. Futures contracts are available at $4.75 per bushel and six-month put option contracts with an exercise price of $5.00 per bushel are available for $.35. A noninterest-bearing margin deposit of $200,000 will be required if futures contracts covering the entire 1,000,000 bushels are sold. The company's current cost of money is 8% per annum.

REQUIRED:

1. Explain the advantages and disadvantages of hedging the expected harvest with futures contracts.
2. Calculate the spot price six months hence at which the company would have been indifferent between not hedging and hedging with futures contracts.
3. Assume the spot price stands at $5.25 per bushel when 1,000,000 bushels of the commodity are harvested (not sold) and that commodity inventories are carried at market. Explain, using calculations as needed, how the company's financial statements will differ without hedging compared to hedging with futures contracts.

P11.5 Evaluating Hedging With Option Contracts Refer to the data in P11.4.

REQUIRED:

1. Explain the advantages and disadvantages of hedging the expected harvest with option contracts.
2. Calculate the spot price 6 months hence at which the company would have been indifferent between not hedging and hedging with option contracts.
3. Assume the spot price stands at $4.75 per bushel when the commodity is harvested (not sold) and that commodity inventories are carried at market. Explain, using calculations as needed, how the company's financial statements will differ without hedging compared to hedging with option contracts.

P11.6 Multiple Choice: Currency Options The following multiple choice questions relate to the use of options as a means of protecting against or taking advantage of exchange rate fluctuations.

REQUIRED: Circle the best answer(s)—there may be more than one.

1. Mega Shoes Co. is a U.S. importer of soccer shoes. Its British supplier sets prices when an order is received and requires payment in British pounds. Mega Shoes pays for the shoes one month after they are delivered. Mega fears that the dollar will depreciate in value. To hedge against potential losses caused by the weakening of the dollar, Mega could
   a. buy a put option to sell U.S. dollars for British pounds.
   b. write a put option to sell U.S. dollars for British pounds.
   c. buy a call option to purchase British pounds with U.S. dollars.
   d. write a call option to purchase British pounds with U.S. dollars.
2. Riba Corporation, a Mexican importer of washers and dryers, has recently entered into a contract with a U.S. firm at a time when the exchange rate was 100 pesos (P)/$. It is expected that when payment on the merchandise is due, the exchange rate will be P200/$. Payment is denominated in U.S. dollars. Riba Corporation can take advantage of the anticipated weakening of the peso (and strengthening of the dollar) by
   a. buying an option to sell pesos for dollars.
   b. buying an option to purchase pesos with dollars.
   c. writing an option to purchase pesos with dollars.
   d. writing an option to sell pesos for dollars.
3. Garden Construction, Inc. is a U.S. company that is building a football stadium in Italy. All Garden's costs are incurred in Italian lira, but the Italian suppliers require payment in U.S. dollars. The exchange rate between the dollar and the lira is unstable. In order to hedge against exchange losses, Garden Construction, Inc. should
   a. do nothing.
   b. write an option to purchase lira with dollars.
   c. buy an option to purchase dollars with lira.
   d. buy an option to purchase lira with dollars.
4. Due to higher interest rates in the United Kingdom, South Valley Bank in California decided on January 1, 19X1, to invest the equivalent of £20 million there for 12 months. Presently, the relevant interest rate is 9 percent and the exchange rate is

$.6667/£. The bank's financial advisor recommends writing a December 19X1 call at the money on the interest of £180,000; the premium is $.1111/£. The U.S. dollar is expected to appreciate in value. If the exchange rate at the end of the year is $.625/£ and South Valley wrote the recommended call,

 a. the call will be exercised.

 b. the call will expire unexercised.

 c. the call will increase the company's net return.

 d. the call will decrease the company's net return.

5. North Mountain Corp., a U.S. company, borrowed the equivalent of DM2,000,000 from a German bank, taking advantage of the low 8 percent interest rate in Germany. At the time the money was borrowed the exchange rate was $1.4/DM. The mark has been appreciating lately and North Mountain fears that any further appreciation of the mark would eliminate the interest rate advantage the firm had by borrowing in Germany. North Mountain Corp. now decides to hedge the first year's interest payment and buys an option to purchase DM160,000 at the money at $1.43/DM; the premium is $.03125/DM. If at year end the exchange rate is $1.45/DM, then

 a. North Mountain will have exercised the call or sold the call for a gain.

 b. North Mountain will not have exercised the call.

 c. compared with not hedging, the call decreased North Mountain's financing cost.

 d. compared with not hedging, the call increased North Mountain's financing cost.

P11.7 **Analysis of Interest Rate Cap** At July 1, 19X6, Comiskey Company has $10,000,000 of debt due in four years with interest floating at prime. The rate is adjusted annually each July 1 and interest for the preceding year is payable on June 30. Comiskey closes its books on June 30 and December 31 of each year. Prime currently stands at 8% annually and is expected to fluctuate between 6% and 12% over the next four years. On July 1, 19X6, a bank offers Comiskey a 4-year interest rate cap with a strike price of 9% for $400,000 payable immediately.

REQUIRED:

1. Suppose the prime rate is expected to be 10% on July 1, 19X7, 12% on July 1, 19X8, and stay at 12% for the remaining two years. Use a present value analysis to determine whether purchasing the cap is a good economic decision in this set of circumstances. *Hint*: let the applicable prime rate(s) when the interest changes occur be the discount rate(s).

2. Suppose instead that the prime rate drops to 6% on July 1, 19X7, and stays at 6% for the remaining three years. Use a present value analysis to determine whether the savings in interest cost would offset the cost of the cap.

3. Assume the cap is purchased and prime rises to 10% on July 1, 19X7. Prepare the journal entries made by Comiskey to account for the periodic interest expense and the cap at December 31, 19X7 and June 30, 19X8.

P11.8 **Hedging Exposed Assets with Put Options** Gupta Company has a large portfolio of marketable equity securities held as short-term investments. To protect against declines in the value of certain securities, on November 1, 19X5, Gupta purchased 90-day put options for $35,000 on the 10,000 shares of ABC Corp. it had purchased at $40. The exercise price is $40 and the shares are selling for $38 each.

Gupta classifies the ABC Corp. shares as "securities available for sale." According to *SFAS 115*, securities held "available for sale" are carried at market; the net unrealized gain or loss is accumulated in a separate component of stockholders' equity (other comprehensive income) and recognized as gain or loss when the securities are sold.

REQUIRED:

1. Prepare journal entries to record purchase of the puts and events to be recorded when the books are closed 60 days later at 12/31/X5 and the stock is selling for $35.50.
2. Thirty days after the closing in *1.*, Gupta decides to sell both the 10,000 shares of ABC Corp. for $32 each and the put options. Calculate the net cash gain or loss realized on these sale transactions.
3. How much of this net cash gain or loss is recognized in 19X5 income? In 19X6 income?

P11.9 Economics of Interest Rate Swaps Assume that two companies wish to enter a mutually advantageous interest rate swap. In many cases, the company with the lower floating rate will simply swap that rate to the company having the lower fixed rate.

In other cases, one company may have access to *both* lower floating rate and fixed rate financing. For a swap to occur in these latter situations, the parties negotiate to enable both to benefit. For example, suppose A obtains fixed rate financing 20 bp lower and floating rate financing 50 bp lower than B can obtain. If B wants floating rate financing and A is indifferent, B offers to swap its 20 bp higher fixed rate financing for A's 50 bp lower floating rate financing.

To accept this swap, A will require B to pay the floating rate financing at, say, 18 bp (*not* 50 bp) lower than B could get. Thus B gains an 18 bp advantage and becomes the floating rate payer (to A) at 32 bp (= 50 bp − 18 bp) above A's floating rate. A becomes the fixed rate payer (to B) at 20 bp higher than A's fixed rate financing but obtains from B a floating payment 32 bp higher than A's own floating rate financing. A's advantage is therefore 12 bp (= 32 bp from B − 20 bp to B).

REQUIRED: In each of the following situations, *pre-swap* financing alternatives are presented. If a swap occurs, determine which of the two parties is likely to be the fixed rate payer in the swap and which is likely to be the floating rate payer in the swap.

1. Axle Co. can get fixed rate financing at 9% and floating rate financing at LIBOR + 90 bp. Boda Co. can get fixed rate financing at 8.7% and floating rate financing at LIBOR + 130 bp.
2. Cino Co. can get fixed rate financing at 8% and floating rate financing at LIBOR + 30 bp. Dana Co. can get fixed rate financing at 8.2% and floating rate financing at LIBOR + 80 bp.
3. Eske Co. can get fixed rate financing at 9.5% and floating rate financing at LIBOR + 40 bp. Fox Co. can get fixed rate financing at 9.3% and floating rate financing at LIBOR + 20 bp.
4. Gary Co. can get fixed rate financing at 7.8% and floating rate financing at LIBOR + 70 bp. Hawk Co. can get fixed rate financing at 7.3% and floating rate financing at LIBOR + 30 bp.

P11.10 **Currency Swap: Entries and Comparison with Options** King International Corporation is a U.S. construction company that has recently entered into a contract to build the Nicosia shopping center in Cyprus. King will be paid in local currency which it will convert to $. Soupi Ltd. is a Cyprus exporter to the U.S. and will need to convert the $ it receives from its U.S. customers into local currency. To hedge against exchange rate fluctuations, on July 1, 19X1, King and Soupi agree to swap 14 million Cyprus pounds (CP), equivalent to $28,000,000 at the current spot rate of $2/CP. The currency swap provides for both companies to re-exchange one-fourth of the currency swapped every six months. On July 1, the 6-month yield on Cyprus government securities is 5.1 percent and the 6-month yield on equivalent U.S. securities is 3.5 percent. At December 31, 19X1, when King and Soupi transferred the agreed-upon amount of money, the Cyprus pound had appreciated and the spot rate stood at $2.1/CP.

REQUIRED:

1. Compute the direct forward rate governing delivery by the two counterparties on December 31, 19X1, and prepare all entries made by King relating to the currency swap through December 31, 19X1.
2. Suppose that, instead of swapping CP3,500,000 for the 6-month period ending on December 31, 19X1, King International purchases currency options at the money to cover the CP3,500,000. Identify whether King will purchase puts or calls and the maximum premium King could have paid on July 1, 19X1 without being worse off than under the original swap.

P11.11 **Interest Rate Swap: Entries and Mark to Market** Johnson Company has $10,000,000 of floating rate debt, with interest at LIBOR + 120 bp adjusted quarterly, and an equivalent amount of 2-year fixed rate investments yielding 10% annually. In order to match fixed rate financing with its fixed rate investments, Johnson swaps 9% fixed payments to intermediary in exchange for LIBOR + 120 bp on the notional amount of $10,000,000. LIBOR currently stands at 7.8% annually.

REQUIRED:

1. After the swap has been in effect one quarter, LIBOR rises to 8.3% and the fixed rate increases to 9.5%. Prepare the entries made by Johnson at the end of the *second quarter* to record net interest expense under the swap.
2. Assume that the swap is a separate financial instrument which Johnson marks to market at the end of the second quarter. Prepare the entry to mark the swap to market; include all supporting calculations.
3. Prepare the entries to revalue the swap and the hedged investments at the end of the second quarter, according to the 1997 FASB *Draft Statement*. Assume a value change of $65,000 (not the correct amount).

P11.12 **Critique Proposed Currency/Interest Rate Swap Arrangement** On June 25, 19X6, Reno Company, a U.S. firm, will be taking out a £10,000,000 loan, due in three years and carrying an annual interest rate of LIBOR + 80 bp. In anticipation of the loan, a spot rate of $1.6/£ and LIBOR of 8%, Reno negotiates a currency swap and interest rate swap with Sterling Benteen, Ltd. (SB), a British firm. SB recently negotiated a fixed-rate dollar-denominated loan. Proceeds from both loans will be converted into the home currency and used to finance projects in each company's home country. The two counterparties propose the following.

- On June 25, 19X6, Reno will receive £10,000,000 from SB in exchange for $16,000,000.
- On June 24, 19X9, Reno will receive $16,000,000 from SB in exchange for £10,000,000.
- On June 24, 19X7, 19X8 and 19X9, SB will pay Reno $1,440,000 (fixed at 9% annually) in exchange for sufficient £ to cover the annual interest on Reno's £10,000,000 floating rate loan.

Despite hours of staff work and pages of elegant computer printouts, you sense that this deal does not pass the "smell test." You wonder whether you are becoming a harbinger of doom. Surely the fate of George Armstrong Custer at the Little Bighorn, so vividly depicted by Errol Flynn in the classic film, "They Died with Their Boots On," can easily make one skeptical of forecasts and analyses of conditions performed by others.

REQUIRED:

1. What is wrong with the above arrangements? Recast them into swaps sensible for Reno and SB.
2. After you recast the arrangements into sensible swaps, suppose throughout the year ended June 24, 19X9, LIBOR is 10% and the spot rate is $1.50. For that year only, calculate the undiscounted number of dollars that Reno saved (lost) by entering these swaps as opposed to not entering them.

ACCOUNTING AND REPORTING FOR ROUTINE ACTIVITIES OF STATE AND LOCAL GOVERNMENT

CHAPTER PREVIEW

This chapter is the first of two chapters examining accounting procedures and disclosures for state and local governments. These procedures and disclosures are quite different from what you have seen before, because governmental organizations operate in a different environment and have different goals and restrictions than businesses.

Chapter 12 introduces accounting and reporting by state and local governmental entities, provides an overview of their operating environment, introduces the major accounting structure, and discusses in detail the accounting for routine operating activities. Chapter 13 covers the accounting for other governmental activities, the current requirements for external reporting, and new standards for external reporting proposed by the Governmental Accounting Standards Board.

The following major topics are studied in this chapter:

- The nature of governmental activities
- Sources of GAAP for state and local governments
- Objectives of financial reporting
- The fund structure
- Nature of accounting and reporting by funds
- Accounting for the general fund
- Financial statements for the general fund
- Accounting for fixed assets and long-term debt
- Comprehensive illustration of general fund accounting

THE NATURE OF GOVERNMENTAL ACTIVITIES

Government at all levels is an increasingly important segment of the economy. As the scope and diversity of governmental services and programs expand, so too does the importance of governmental accounting and reporting. The internal and external structure of accounting and reporting for state and local governments has been determined by the operating environment, legal constraints, and goals of these governments. Because a government differs on all these dimensions from a business, the accounting and reporting policies are very different.

Major factors differentiating a state or local government from a business include the following:

■ Resources are derived from such sources as taxes, fees, and fines. The government has a legal right to collect taxes, which comprise the major source of resources.
■ There are no ownership interests in a governmental unit.
■ A governmental unit must adhere to a legal budget. Expenditures cannot exceed amounts provided in this budget.
■ Financial inflows are often earmarked for a particular activity. For example, a bond issue for construction of a building must be used for that purpose. Citizens may be assessed a special tax to finance a city water project.
■ The main purpose of the governmental unit is to provide services to citizens, usually on a nonprofit basis. Expenditures do not necessarily match with revenues, since revenue recognition is generally not based on services provided. Profit is not a valid measure of performance for most governmental activities.
■ Users of governmental financial statements are:
  ■ credit market representatives, who determine bond ratings, provide bond insurance guaranteeing bond payments, and provide investment banking services
  ■ elected and appointed officials of the government
  ■ citizens, typically from citizen budget advisory groups.
  Credit market representatives are the most frequent users of the financial statements.
■ The **Governmental Accounting Standards Board** (GASB), rather than the FASB, sets accounting requirements for governmental external reporting. Many governments are legally required to follow GAAP and issue audited financial statements.

Activities of a governmental unit can be divided into three major categories: governmental, proprietary, and fiduciary. As we will see later in the chapter, the accounting structure is also divided in this manner. *Governmental activities* consist of primary services to citizens, such as health and safety, education and legislative services. These activities typically do not generate inflows of resources, but are funded by tax levies. *Proprietary activities* are similar to the activities of a business, in that goods and services are primarily financed by user fees, where the users are either citizens or other governmental units. User fees are usually set to approximate the cost of the goods or services provided. Examples are parking and recreational facilities, and utilities. *Fiduciary activities* are those where the government acts as an agent for someone else. For example, the local government may collect sales taxes for the state. A citizen may donate money to a town, with income earned on investment of that money to be used to finance maintenance of a town park. A municipality may fund and manage a pension plan for its employees.

AUTHORS' COMMENTARY

Credit market representatives use municipal financial statements to evaluate the credit worthiness of the governmental unit. The major forms of municipal debt obligations are bonds, notes, and leases. There are legal restrictions on the amount and types of debt a municipality may issue.

There are two basic types of bonds—*general obligation* and *revenue bonds*. **General obligation bonds** are secured by the full faith, credit, and general taxing powers of the municipality. Investors generally consider this form of debt to be the most secure. **Revenue bonds** are secured by the pledge of specific revenues and, unlike general obligation bonds, usually contain bond covenants or restrictions. As an example, water revenue bonds, issued to finance the construction of a water treatment plant, are revenue bonds. A portion of the connection fees and charges paid by users of the water system is pledged to pay the principal and interest on the bonds. Bond restrictions may include a requirement that the construction be completed, and that rates be sufficient to pay all costs, including bond debt service.

Hybrid bond securities have characteristics of both general obligation and revenue debt, or possess other unique features. A common example is **guaranteed revenue bonds**, revenue debt also backed by the full faith and credit of the municipality. If pledged revenues are insufficient to repay the debt, it is repaid through the municipality's general revenues. Other types of bonds may be backed by insurance, earmarked tax revenues, or letters of credit. For example, **insured bonds** are guaranteed by insurance policies written by commercial insurance companies.

A municipality may issue **notes**, typically outstanding for periods of less than three years. Examples are tax, revenue, grant, and bond anticipation notes, as well as tax-exempt commercial paper. These notes are issued in *anticipation* of collecting expected taxes, revenue, grant revenue, or bond proceeds. For example, a **bond anticipation note** is issued to finance the start-up costs of a project for which the bonds cannot be issued immediately. These notes are repaid from the subsequent bond issue proceeds.

Leasing is a common form of borrowing used to finance capital equipment. An advantage to some municipalities of leasing over other forms of borrowing is that the use of noncapitalized operating leases may circumvent statutory debt limitations.

In general, the classification of debt is important because it determines which regulations and limitations apply. Both federal and state laws regulate the issuance and trading of municipal debt securities. For example, although nontaxable municipal bonds are exempt from the federal regulatory requirements of the 1933 and 1934 securities acts (see Module E in this textbook), they are not exempt from the antifraud provisions. State laws may limit the amounts and/or types of debt financing allowed by local governments. Some states only allow the issuance of revenue bonds, whereas others allow only general obligation bonds. State law may limit the amount of debt issued, and limits can vary depending on the type of debt. For example, the state of Pennsylvania limits the amount of nonelectoral debt—debt that does not need voter approval—but not the amount of electoral debt.

EXTERNAL USERS OF GOVERNMENTAL FINANCIAL STATEMENTS

External users of governmental financial statements include credit market representatives, elected officials, and citizens. The GASB, as part of its current project on developing a new financial reporting model, collected information from statement users on what they look for in analyzing financial reports of state and local governments.

Credit Market Representatives

Organizations that provide funding to the government, in the form of bonds and loans, are interested in its ability to generate resources to make required interest and principal payments. Important factors in this assessment include:

- sources of revenues and expenditures by function and program
- funding information on pensions and related liabilities
- changes in all liabilities, including pending litigation and contingent liabilities
- future financing plans
- extent to which revenues from one program subsidize costs of another program
- individual program or activity surpluses or deficits
- material departures from GAAP
- whether financial statements are audited on a timely basis
- liquidity and flexibility of the governmental unit
- evidence of management's performance
- economic factors

Elected Officials and Citizens

Citizens, legislators and oversight officials are concerned with how much money a government has available to spend, how tax dollars are used, how much governmental services cost, sources of funding for various programs, and how current activities and plans affect future taxes and future ability to provide services. Financial information on these issues includes:

- where a government's money comes from and goes
- how much in resources a government has available to spend
- budget allocations for major programs
- comparison of actual results to the original budget
- detailed capital improvement plans
- costs of services in detail
- percentage of total expenditures financed by taxes
- impact of current performance on future tax rates and services

SOURCES OF GAAP FOR STATE AND LOCAL GOVERNMENTS

As is the case with business accounting, current accounting principles for governments developed from several sources and in response to user needs. Although many principles and procedures evolved from practice over the years, formal pronouncements currently play an increasingly important role. A sense of how GAAP developed is valuable background for understanding current requirements.

In the late 1800s, misuse of funds was prevalent in many large cities. As a result, accounting and financial reporting recommendations, developed by the National Municipal League, were adopted by some cities. In 1904, New York was the first state to require standardized financial reporting by cities. In the depression years of the 1930s, new demands for services were placed on governments while resources diminished. The Municipal Finance Officers Association (MFOA) formed a committee to develop accounting and financial reporting standards. The MFOA was the first in a series of organizations which issued standards. None of these were of the status of "authoritative pronouncements," however.

In the 1970s, many cities were near bankruptcy, due largely to high interest rates and heavy expenditures on social and economic programs. Popular sentiment was that governmental accounting and reporting methods were at least partly to blame by hiding the true financial condition of troubled governments, and that these deficiencies were not being adequately addressed by the National Council on Governmental Accounting (NCGA), the organization which at that time issued prevailing standards. Lack of confidence in this organization led to formation of the Governmental Accounting Standards Board (GASB) in 1984. The GASB is appointed by the Financial Accounting Foundation, which also oversees the FASB. The GASB goes through the same types of procedures in establishing standards as the FASB. Current GAAP for state and local government is established by the GASB. The Government Finance Officers Association (GFOA), formerly known as the MFOA, sponsored the NCGA and still publishes a widely used source of nonauthoritative guidance on the application of GAAP: the GAAFR—*Governmental Accounting, Auditing and Financial Reporting*.

GOVERNMENTAL ACCOUNTING STANDARDS BOARD

The GASB issues authoritative standards on accounting and financial reporting by state and local governmental entities, including not-for-profit entities owned by or related to the government, such as state colleges and universities and public hospitals. The FASB issues authoritative standards for all other entities, including *nongovernmental* not-for-profit entities, studied in Chapter 14 of this textbook. The Governmental Accounting Standards Board (GASB) does *not* establish GAAP for the *federal* government. Standards for federal government units are developed by the Office of Management and Budgets (OMB), the General Accounting Office (GAO), and the Treasury Department.

Not all states require that local governments follow GAAP. Also, some states do not require that their own financial statements follow GAAP, as they are exempt from federal financial disclosure regulations. According to the National Association of State Auditors, Comptrollers and Treasurers (NASACT), 26 states currently require their local governments to follow GAAP.[1] There is considerable diversity in the financial reporting practices of individual states; some conform more closely to GAAP than others.

As of April 1998, the GASB has issued 32 *Statements of Governmental Accounting Standards (SGAS)*, two *Statements of Governmental Accounting Concepts (SGAC)*, and several *Interpretations* and *Technical Bulletins*. Current accounting principles deemed authoritative by the GASB are organized into a book titled *Codification of Governmental Accounting and Financial Reporting Standards*[2], similar to the FASB's *Accounting Standards—Current Text*. The *Codification* is updated periodically.

The GASB issued an *Exposure Draft* in 1997 that proposes to change the external financial reporting of state and local governments in fundamental ways.[3] This proposal would supersede

---

[1] National Association of State Auditors, Comptrollers and Treasurers, *NASACT's State Comptrollers: Technical Activities and Functions* (Lexington, KY: NASACT, 1996).

[2] Governmental Accounting Standards Board, *Codification of Governmental Accounting and Financial Reporting Standards* (Norwalk, CT: GASB, 1995).

[3] Governmental Accounting Standards Board, *Exposure Draft*, "Basic Financial Statements—and Management's Discussion and Analysis—for State and Local Governments" (Norwalk, CT: GASB, 1997).

many current pronouncements and changes both the measurement focus and the external presentation of governmental financial statements. The *Exposure Draft* is discussed in detail in Chapter 13.

THE GAAP HIERARCHY IN GOVERNMENT ACCOUNTING

The GASB is *the* source of authoritative governmental accounting principles today. However, pronouncements of other standard-setting bodies and guidance of professional organizations may be relevant as well. Certain publications by the NCGA and the American Institute of Certified Public Accountants were embraced by the GASB in *SGAS 1*. The FASB has standards covering issues on which the GASB is silent. To advise governmental reporting entities of the sources of accounting principles to be followed and their authoritative ranking, the *Codification* (p. xvi) establishes the following **GAAP hierarchy**.

    a. GASB *Statements* and *Interpretations,* including FASB and AICPA pronouncements adopted by the GASB.

    b. GASB *Technical Bulletins* and applicable AICPA *Industry Audit and Accounting Guides* and *Statements of Position* cleared by the GASB.

    c. Applicable AICPA *AcSec Practice Bulletins* cleared by the GASB and consensus positions of groups of accountants organized by the GASB from time to time.

    d. GASB staff *Implementation Guides* and practices commonly found in state and local government.

    e. Other accounting literature, such as GASB *Concepts Statements,* and AICPA and FASB pronouncements not specifically dealing with state and local governmental accounting.

Items *a* and *e* above indicate that the FASB continues to play a role in governmental accounting, although many of its pronouncements are viewed as advisory. Until recently, though, standards issued by the FASB had to be followed in the absence of GASB standards. Clearly, the relationship between the GASB and the FASB, which was established about ten years before the GASB, has not always been smooth and is still evolving. For example, in August 1987 the FASB issued *SFAS 93*, requiring not-for-profit organizations—including private *and* governmental colleges and universities—to recognize depreciation in their accounts. Shortly thereafter, in January 1988, the GASB released *SGAS 8*, which denied the applicability of *SFAS 93* to governmental colleges and universities.

Recognizing the possibility of two sets of accounting standards for colleges and universities, depending upon whether they are public or private, the FASB used *SFAS 99* (September 1988) to postpone the effective date of *SFAS 93* until 1990. This jurisdictional dispute was addressed by the Financial Accounting Foundation (FAF), the oversight body for both standard-setting boards.

A report issued in January 1989 by the Committee to Review Structure for Governmental Accounting Standards discussed this and other issues related to operations of the GASB.[4] Most of the report's recommendations were accepted by the FAF. The jurisdictional dispute, however, was only partially resolved. The original GASB jurisdiction over not-for-profits owned by or

---

[4] Committee to Review Structure for Governmental Accounting Standards, *The Structure for Establishing Governmental Accounting Standards* (Norwalk, CT: Financial Accounting Foundation/Governmental Accounting Standards Advisory Council, 1989).

related to the government was retained, but the GASB is now responsible for evaluating the need for comparability with private-sector not-for-profits subject to FASB standards. In addition, the FAF revised the "GAAP Hierarchy." This revision was subsequently modified to the form given above by *Statement of Auditing Standards No. 69.*

Major outcomes of the GASB's evaluation of the current reporting model for governments and its lack of comparability with the reporting requirements for private-sector not-for-profits are two 1997 *Exposure Drafts*: "Basic Financial Statements—and Management's Discussion and Analysis—for State and Local Governments," and "Basic Financial Statements—and Management's Discussion and Analysis—for Public Colleges and Universities." Both *Exposure Drafts* follow a reporting model similar to that required by the FASB for private not-for-profit organizations.

OBJECTIVES OF FINANCIAL REPORTING

A formal statement of the objectives of financial reporting by state and local governments was made in 1987 by the GASB in *SGAC 1*, "Objectives of Financial Reporting."[5] *SGAC 1* states that governmental financial reports should respond to the needs of the citizenry, their representatives (either elected or appointed members of oversight boards), and investors and creditors involved in the lending process. Paragraph 32 of *SGAC 1* lists four specific **uses of financial reports** in making economic, social and political decisions, and in evaluating accountability:

1. Comparing actual financial results with the legally adopted budget.
2. Assessing financial condition and results of operations.
3. Assisting in determining compliance with finance-related laws, rules and regulations.
4. Assisting in evaluating efficiency and effectiveness.

Note the stress on **accountability** in Items 1 and 3, in terms of fulfilling the budgetary plan and in complying with relevant laws, such as those specifying taxing and debt limits. These matters are simply not within the domain of information required by users of financial reports of business enterprises. Indeed, in paragraph 56 of *SGAC 1*, the board states that "Accountability is the cornerstone of all financial reporting in government. . . . Accountability requires governments to answer to the citizenry—to justify the raising of public resources and the purposes for which they are to be used." Another key concept identified by the board is **interperiod equity**, a balanced-budget notion stressing the need for users of governmental financial reports to "assess whether current-year revenues are sufficient to pay for the services provided that year and whether future taxpayers will be required to assume burdens for services previously provided." (par 60) The board believes that little difference exists between the financial reporting objectives of governmental and business-related activities.

The *Concepts Statement* goes on to specify the **objectives of financial reporting** in the governmental context, as follows:

■ Financial reporting should assist in fulfilling the government's duty to be publicly accountable and should enable users to assess that accountability (par. 77):

---

[5] Governmental Accounting Standards Board, *Statement of Governmental Accounting Concepts No. 1*, "Objectives of Financial Reporting" (Stamford, CT: GASB, 1987).

- Financial reporting should provide information to determine whether current-year revenues were sufficient to pay for current-year services.
- Financial reporting should demonstrate whether resources were obtained and used in accordance with the entity's legally adopted budget; it should also demonstrate compliance with other finance-related legal or contractual requirements.
- Financial reporting should provide information to assist users in assessing the service efforts, costs and accomplishments of the governmental entity.
- Financial reporting should assist users in evaluating the operating results of the governmental entity for the year (par. 78):
  - Financial reporting should provide information about sources and uses of financial resources.
  - Financial reporting should provide information about how the governmental entity financed its activities and met its cash requirements.
  - Financial reporting should provide information necessary to determine whether the entity's financial position improved or deteriorated as a result of the year's operations.
- Financial reporting should assist users in assessing the level of services that can be provided by the governmental entity and its ability to meet its obligations as they become due (par. 79):
  - Financial reporting should provide information about the financial position and condition of a governmental entity.
  - Financial reporting should provide information about a governmental entity's physical and other nonfinancial resources having useful lives that extend beyond the current year, including information that can be used to assess the service potential of those resources.
  - Financial reporting should disclose legal or contractual restrictions on resources and risks of potential loss of resources.

IDENTIFYING THE REPORTING ENTITY

In this chapter the term **governmental unit** refers to a state or local governmental unit. The accounting concepts and procedures discussed apply equally to states, towns, cities, counties, school districts, water districts, fire protection districts, and other governmental units. For financial reporting purposes, however, the appropriate reporting entity—which can consist of several governmental units—must be determined.

Although a governmental unit such as a town, which is a separate legal entity, may appear to be the reporting entity, other entities also may need to be considered. Additional legal entities often exist within a governmental unit or overlap it. For example, a school district may be a legally separate entity from a city or town, and the two may or may not geographically coincide. A municipality may contain **special districts**—legally separate entities that provide a particular service such as sewers, sidewalks, street lighting, or fire protection to a particular area. Each of these units—the city, the town, the school district, the fire district—constitutes a separate legal entity. And each is likely to have its own taxing authority, ability to issue debt, and other powers.

Even though we initially focus on the legal entity as the one whose activities must be accounted for and reported to the taxpayers or other constituencies, the concept of economic entity dominates in external financial reporting. In corporate accounting, the entity concept led to presentation of consolidated financial statements (one economic entity) for several corporations (separate legal entities). Conversely, following the economic entity concept in governmental accounting may lead to (1) to division of one legal entity—the governmental unit—into several economic entities called *funds* or (2) inclusion of more than one legal entity into an appropriate economic entity for which financial reports are issued.

The notion of an economic entity differs for business and local government. In the corporate context, the presence of common managerial control over the affairs of several corporate entities leads to the conclusion that one economic entity exists for financial reporting purposes. In the context of local government, however, the GASB concluded in *SGAS 14* that "The concept underlying the definition of the financial reporting entity is that elected officials are **accountable** to their constituents for their actions." (par. 10) The nucleus of a governmental financial reporting entity is a **primary government** that has a separate governing body elected by the citizenry. A state government, a general purpose local government—city, county, township, etc.—and a special purpose government such as a school district are primary governments as long as they satisfy all three conditions in par. 13 of *SGAS 14*.

1. It has a **separately elected** governing body.
2. It is **legally separate.**
3. It is **fiscally independent** of other state and local governments.

Organizationally, a primary government includes all funds, agencies, departments and bureaus that make up its legal entity. Using this central concept, the GASB concluded in par. 12 that:

> The **financial reporting entity** consists of (a) the primary government and (b) its **component units:** organizations for which the primary government is **financially accountable,** and **other organizations** for which the nature and significance of their relationship with the primary government are such that exclusion would cause the reporting entity's financial statements to be misleading or incomplete.[6]

A primary government has **financial accountability** for a legally separate organization when it controls appointment of a voting majority of that organization's governing body and can **impose its will** on the organization's operations. Financial accountability also exists when the primary government can derive financial benefits or financial obligations from the component organization.

Although professional judgment is required to assess the treatment of other closely-related "significant" organizations as component units, *SGAS 14* cites the following examples:

1. An authority with a state-appointed board that provides temporary financial assistance to a local government could be a component unit "if the authority issues debt on behalf of the local government and serves as a conduit for . . . repayment of the debt" (par. 40).
2. "An example of an affiliated organization that may be evaluated for inclusion [as a component unit] is a nonprofit corporation whose purpose is to benefit a governmental university by soliciting contributions and managing those funds." (par. 41).

Implications of the foregoing for financial reporting call for both an overview of the units for which the primary government is financially accountable as well as discrete presentation of the financial results of the primary government and its individual component units. Some individual

---

[6] Governmental Accounting Standards Board, *Statement of Governmental Accounting Standards No. 14*, "The Financial Reporting Entity" (Norwalk, CT: GASB, 1991), par. 12.

component units are so closely related to the primary government that their financial results are included or **blended** with those of the primary government.

THE FUND STRUCTURE

A key aspect of accounting and reporting for state and local government is the use of different reporting entities to account for resources subject to different restrictions, and separate listings of the fixed assets and long-term debt of several of the fund types. This structure is considerably different from that encountered in business and can often require multiple journal entries to record a single transaction.

A typical governmental unit engages in most or all of the three types of activities discussed above: governmental, proprietary, and fiduciary. Legislation and regulations often define the purposes for which resources may be used. It may be stipulated that resources derived from local property taxes be spent in certain ways, resources derived from a bond issue in other ways, and resources received from federal programs in yet other ways. One of the responsibilities of state and local government management is to ensure that resources are spent in the legally prescribed manner. This responsibility is often referred to as **stewardship**, meaning that management is entrusted with these resources by the community and must carry out certain specified responsibilities with respect to their use.

Typical activities of a state or local government are as follows:

Governmental activities:

- Collection of taxes, fees and fines
- Issuance of bonds and repayment of bond principal and interest
- Primary services for which no user fees are collected, such as education, public safety, social and judicial services, administration
- Acquisition, construction, and disposition of long-term assets, financed either by general resources, by special assessments or by long-term debt

Proprietary activities:

- Services for which a cost-based fee is collected from the public, such as utilities, public transportation, parking facilities, recreational facilities
- Services provided to other governmental units at cost by, for example, a central motor pool or central supplies activity

Fiduciary activities:

- Financial resources held in trust, such as pensions
- Financial resources collected for another governmental unit, such as state sales taxes collected by the county

Because of the need to adhere to legal requirements concerning the source and use of resources, and the large number and diversity of governmental activities, the financial reporting system of a single governmental entity is likely to be organized into several accounting entities, called *funds*.

> A **fund** is defined as a fiscal and accounting entity with a self-balancing set of accounts recording cash and other financial resources, together with all related liabilities and residual equities or balances, and changes therein, which are segregated for the purpose of carrying on specific activities or attaining certain objectives in accordance with special regulations, restrictions, or limitations.[7]

Instead of being treated as one entity with one set of books, the governmental unit is divided up into several entities, or funds. Each fund has its own set of books and financial statements, and is self-balancing. As we see in Chapter 13, the current external reporting model retains the fund structure when reporting for the governmental entity as a whole. The reporting model proposed in the GASB's 1997 *Exposure Draft* requires disclosure on both an full *entity* basis and on a *fund basis*.

Essentially, funds are **accounting segregations of financial resources**, with the purpose of achieving accountability and stewardship over resources. Assets are resources of the various governmental funds based on the purposes for which they are to be used, liabilities are obligations of the funds from which they are to be paid, and the difference between fund assets and liabilities is **fund equity**. Because a government has no owners, no stockholders' equity accounts are present in fund accounting. The fund equity balance measures the difference between a fund's assets and liabilities, or its **net financial resources**. Portions of fund equity are often *reserved* to signify restriction on the spending of resources. Total fund equity therefore consists of (1) an *unreserved portion*, indicating that financial resources are available for spending, and (2) one or more *reserved portions*, signifying that these amounts are not available for expenditure or are legally segregated for specific future uses. As will be seen in later sections of this chapter, fund equity is called **fund balance** in funds that account for governmental-type activities such as collection of taxes and provision of primary services.

An important focus of governmental financial reporting is demonstrating fiscal compliance. Operating statements report on whether financial resources received during a period are sufficient to cover expenditures and whether spending in particular areas is in compliance with approved budgets. Consequently, division of resources into funds, each dedicated to spending for particular purposes, is used as a control technique. Each fund is a self-balancing set of accounts used to keep track of the flows of financial resources dedicated to specific activities. Financial reporting on fund activities should reveal whether uses of financial resources were within restrictions imposed by law or by third parties. This leads to the presentation of multiple sets of financial statements for a single governmental reporting entity.

THE SEVEN STANDARD FUNDS

Under current GAAP, the financial affairs of a governmental unit are organized into as many as seven types of fund entities, each of which is used for certain governmental activities. In any local governmental unit, some or all of these seven standard funds exist. Each of these seven fund types belongs to one of the following groups:

- **Governmental** or **expendable** funds account for most traditional governmental functions.
- **Proprietary** or **nonexpendable funds** account for a government's ongoing businesslike activities similar to those found in the private sector.

---

[7] GASB, *Codification*, par. 1100.102.

■ **Fiduciary funds** account for assets held by the governmental unit in a trustee or agency capacity on behalf of individuals or other organizations.

The following example uses the case of a city government to describe each of these fund types in terms of the source of its resources and the activities and purposes for which its resources are used.

Governmental Funds

1. **General fund**—Accounts for the basic services provided by city government, through the use of general revenue, that are not required to be accounted for in another fund.
   a. Resources are derived from property taxes, sales taxes, general state aid, fees, fines, and so on.
   b. Resources are used for city administration, police, fire protection, courts, streets, parks, sanitation, etc.
2. **Special revenue funds**—Account for specified activities of the city, funded from revenue restricted to those activities.
   a. Resources are derived from state or federal aid for specific purposes (for example, resources from federal programs to be used in activities such as public safety); taxes levied for certain purposes, grants, etc.
   b. Resources are used for the particular operations specified by the revenue source, as indicated above.
3. **Capital projects funds**—Account for the construction or acquisition of major capital assets not accounted for in enterprise, internal service, and trust funds, including those financed by special assessments on property owners.
   a. Resources are derived primarily from proceeds of bond issues for specific projects; other sources include state or federal aid, or allocation of general revenues from the general fund.
   b. Resources are used for construction or acquisition of buildings, major equipment, and public improvements—commonly known as **infrastructure**—such as roads, bridges, and sewer systems.
4. **Debt service funds**—Account for the accumulation and payment of resources for principal and interest on the general long-term debt of the city.
   a. Resources are generally derived from transfers from other funds, such as the general fund or the capital projects fund, from certain special assessment levies and from interest earned on investments.
   b. Resources are used for payment of interest and principal; in some cases, resources are accumulated and invested to provide for future debt service payments.

Proprietary Funds

5. **Enterprise funds**—Account for certain business-type activities of a city in which goods or services are sold on a continuing basis to the public, such as a city water department or a municipal golf course.
   a. Resources are derived from amounts charged to customers on a cost recovery basis, and from financing sources.
   b. Resources are used for the activity's operating expenses, capital expenditures and financing payments.
6. **Internal service funds**—Account for central services provided to other departments of the city on a cost-reimbursement basis; for example, a central supply unit that buys supplies in large quantities and issues them to various departments, a central vehicle maintenance shop, or a central computer facility.
   a. Resources are derived from charges to other city departments, that is, transfers from other funds, and from financing sources.
   b. Resources are used for operating expenses of the central service activities, capital expenditures, and financing payments.

Fiduciary Funds

7. **Trust and agency funds**—Account for resources collected by the city on behalf of another entity and resources held by the city under a trust agreement.
   a. Resources are derived from collections on behalf of other entities, such as income taxes withheld from employees and certain special assessment levies (*agency funds*), and from amounts received to be held in trust and used for a specific purpose, such as an endowment for the public library (*expendable trust funds* for assets or earnings to be spent currently, *nonexpendable trust funds* for principal to be held intact).
   b. Resources are used for transmittal of amounts collected to other entities and for service of certain special assessment levies (*agency funds*), for expenditures in accord with trust agreements (*expendable trust funds*), and for maintenance of principal (*nonexpendable trust funds*; earnings are transferred to an expendable trust fund when permitted by the trust agreement).

A comparison of the seven fund types with the list of governmental activities presented above reveals that these funds encompass all the activities of a city government. *One*, and *only one*, general fund always exists. In the case of each of the other fund types, none, one, or several exist. For example, if a city has no construction projects underway, there are no capital projects funds. On the other hand, if three projects are currently under construction, the city may use three capital projects funds or combine all three projects in one capital projects fund.

To further illustrate how sources and uses of resources for governmental activities are structured into these seven fund types, Exhibit 12.1 presents the fund structure of a typical school district. As noted earlier, some governmental units do not need all seven funds. There is, however, always a general fund; this fund accounts for the basic operations of the governmental unit.

Sample financial statements for the general fund of a county appear in Exhibit 12.2.

Fund	Resources Derived from	Resources Used for
General	School tax; local, state, and federal aid; fees.	Administration, instruction, transportation, maintenance, debt service.
Special Revenue	Special state or federal aid (for example, Head Start Program).	Instruction and other costs related to specified program.
Capital Projects	Bond issues, state or federal aid, or transfers from general fund.	Construction, acquisition, or renovation of school buildings; major equipment purchases (for example, fleet of buses).
Debt Service	Transfers from general or capital projects funds.	Payment of principal and interest.
Enterprise	Charges to customers of cafeteria, bookstore, and other enterprises; may be supplemented from other sources (for example, state aid for school lunch program).	Operating expenses of cafeteria, bookstore, or other enterprises.
Internal Service	Transfers from other funds for central services.	Costs of central services.
Trust and Agency	Collections for others (for example, taxes withheld); gifts for specified purposes (for example, scholarship funds).	Transmittal of amounts collected; payment of scholarships.

EXHIBIT 12.1 FUND STRUCTURE OF A SCHOOL DISTRICT

Sample County
Balance Sheet
December 31, 20X0

Assets		**Liabilities and Fund Balance**	
Cash	$ XX	Vouchers Payable	$ XX
Certificates of Deposit	XX	Fund Balance	
Property Taxes Receivable	XX	Reserved for Encumbrances.	XX
Due from Other Funds	XX	Unreserved	XX
Total Assets	$ XX	Total Liabilities and Fund Balance	$ XX

Sample County
Statement of Revenues, Expenditures, and Other Changes in Fund Balance
for the Fiscal Year Ended December 31, 20X0

Revenues

Property Taxes	$ XX
Fines, Licenses, Permits	XX
Total Revenues	$ XX

Expenditures

Public Safety	$ XX
General Government	XX
Sanitation	XX
Highways and Streets	XX
Total Expenditures	$ XX

Other Financing Sources (Uses)

Transfers to and from Other Funds	$ XX
Bond Proceeds	XX
Total Other Financing Sources (Uses)	$ XX
Excess of Revenues and Other Sources Over	
Expenditures and Other Uses	$ XX
Beginning fund balance	XX
Ending fund balance	$ XX

EXHIBIT 12.2 SAMPLE GENERAL FUND FINANCIAL STATEMENTS

Sample County
Statement of Revenues, Expenditures, and Other Changes
in Fund Balance—Budget and Actual—General Fund
for the Fiscal Year Ended December 31, 20X0

Revenues	Budget	Actual	Variance
Property Taxes	$ XX	$ XX	$ XX
Fines, Licenses, Permits	XX	XX	XX
Total Revenues	$ XX	$ XX	$ XX
Expenditures			
Public Safety	$ XX	$ XX	$ XX
General Government	XX	XX	XX
Sanitation	XX	XX	XX
Highways and Streets	XX	XX	XX
Total Expenditures	$ XX	$ XX	$ XX
Excess of Revenues over (under)			
Expenditures	$ XX	$ XX	$ XX
Other Financing Sources (Uses)			
Transfers to and from Other Funds	$ XX	$ XX	$ XX
Bond Proceeds	XX	XX	XX
Total Other Financing Sources (Uses)	$ XX	$ XX	$ XX
Excess of Revenues and Other Sources Over			
Expenditures and Other Uses	$ XX	$ XX	$ XX
Beginning fund balance	XX	XX	XX
Ending fund balance	$ XX	$ XX	$ XX

EXHIBIT 12.2 *(Continued)*

THE TWO STANDARD ACCOUNT GROUPS

Note in the example above that the general fund does not show long-term assets or long-term liabilities on its balance sheet. This is true of all governmental-type funds. Outlays for long-term assets appear as *expenditures* on the Statement of Revenues, Expenditures, and Other Changes in Fund Balance, and ultimately reduce fund equity, rather than increasing assets. Inflows of resources from issuing long-term debt appear as *financing sources* on the Statement of Revenues, Expenditures, and Other Changes in Fund Balance, and ultimately increase fund equity, rather than increasing liabilities. These and other deviations from business accounting are discussed in the next section. Because long-term assets and long-term debt of governmental funds are not recognized as assets and liabilities in the funds themselves, current GAAP call for two **account groups** to establish control and accountability for the *fixed assets* and *long-term capital debt* attributable to governmental funds. These account groups are not funds, because they have no resources available for expenditure or use, but are merely self-balancing accounting records of fixed assets and long-term liabilities. Each account group merely *inventories* the fixed assets and long-term liabilities attributable to each of the governmental funds.

1. **General fixed assets account group**—Accounts for the fixed assets acquired by purchase or capitalized lease or donated to activities accounted for in *governmental funds*. No financial resources are received or expended by this account group.
2. **General long-term debt account group**—Accounts for the long-term capital debt, including bonds, notes, capitalized lease obligations, etc., which are not specific liabilities of proprietary or trust funds. No financial resources are received or expended by this account group.

Additional details on accounting for fixed assets and long-term debt in local government appear later in this chapter and in Chapter 13.

SPECIAL ASSESSMENT ACTIVITIES

In addition to the activities mentioned above, local governments also engage in projects funded by **special assessment levies** on property owners in limited geographic areas. Such activities benefit a limited number of property owners rather than the general citizenry and are paid for, either in whole or in part, by the benefitted property owners.

Service-type activities funded by special assessments, such as snow removal, are accounted for in the general or special revenue funds. Construction of capital improvements funded by special assessments, such as sidewalks and storm sewers, is accounted for in capital projects funds. Transactions related to special assessment levies and debt are accounted for in an agency fund if the government has no liability for the debt. Otherwise, the debt is recorded in the General Long-Term Debt Account Group, and payment of interest and principal thereon is accounted for in a debt service fund, as is collection of the special assessment levies. In all cases, fixed assets funded by special assessments are recorded in the General Fixed Assets Account Group.

NATURE OF ACCOUNTING AND REPORTING BY FUNDS

The following discussion considers the general accounting principles applicable to the fund entities discussed above, and introduces the typical financial statements issued by the governmental unit.

ACCOUNTING FOR PROPRIETARY FUNDS

For the **proprietary funds**—enterprise and internal service funds—the concepts of revenue recognition and matching of expenses against revenues are appropriate, because the operations of these funds are similar to those of private sector businesses. It is important to know the costs of providing services, because the fees charged to users—whether citizens or other governmental units—are expected to cover those costs. Normal **accrual accounting** is used. Revenues are recognized when earned and measurable, and expenses are matched with revenues as product costs or recognized with the passage of time as period costs. Outlays for buildings and equipment are capitalized as assets and charged to depreciation expense over their useful lives. Amounts borrowed through loans or bond issues are shown as liabilities and interest expense is accrued as owed. Standard statements for these funds are the **Statement of Revenues and Expenses and Changes in Retained Earnings**, the **Cash Flow Statement**, and the **Balance Sheet**. Fund equity on the balance sheet consists of **contributed capital** and **retained earnings**. Proprietary funds are studied in Chapter 13, and essentially follow the familiar procedures of business accounting.

ACCOUNTING FOR GOVERNMENTAL FUNDS

For **governmental funds**—general fund, special revenue funds, capital projects funds, or debt service funds—the *modified accrual basis* of accounting is used. The measurement focus is on accountability and the flow of financial resources. The GASB defines the flow of resources as **the flow of current financial resources—cash, receivables, prepaid items, consumable goods such as supplies, and related current liabilities**. This means that any transaction affecting *current financial resources* is shown on the operating statement of a governmental fund. This statement is called the **Statement of Revenues, Expenditures, and Changes in Fund Balance**. Fund equity on the balance sheet of a governmental fund is called **fund balance**.

The **modified accrual basis of accounting** has the following reporting implications:

- Revenues are defined as *inflows of current financial resources*, excluding borrowings and most transfers from other funds. There is no requirement that revenues be earned. Instead, revenues are recognized when they are **measurable** and **available to finance expenditures of the current period**. Property taxes, routine fees, intergovernmental grants, and sales and income taxes are accrued as receivables and therefore recognized as revenue before the cash is collected, if there is a reasonable way to estimate the uncollectible portion, and amounts collected are expected to be available to liquidate current period obligations.[8] Note that inflows of current financial resources from the sale of long-lived assets meet the definition of revenues.
- Borrowings and transfers from other funds are shown on the Statement of Revenues, Expenditures and Other Changes in Fund Balance, in a category separate from revenues. Note that inflows of resources from long-term financing appear on this Statement and eventually increase Fund Balance. They are **not** shown as liabilities.
- Expenditures are recognized when they are **measurable** and the **related liability is incurred**, regardless of when paid. However, remember that expenditures are defined as outflows of **current financial resources**. Although most expenditures are recognized on the same basis as under accrual accounting, there are two notable exceptions:
  - Payments of current financial resources for long-lived assets are considered to be expenditures. This implies that long-term assets are not capitalized in governmental funds, and no depreciation is recognized since it is not an outflow of current resources, and there is no capitalized asset to depreciate.
  - Interest on long-term debt is not accrued over time, but only in the period when it is expected to be paid—it is not an outflow of current resources until the period when paid.
- Payments on long-term debt and transfers to other funds appear on the Statement of Revenue, Expenditures and Changes in Fund Balance in a separate category from expenditures, but eventually reduce the fund balance.
- An excess of revenues over expenditures is not profit; it instead reduces the need to levy taxes next year. Similarly, expenditures in excess of revenues burden taxpayers or reduce services in future years. The concept of **interperiod equity** focuses on the degree to which services provided to citizens today result in reduced services to taxpayers in the future. An example at the federal level is the continuing discussion regarding the viability of the Social Security system for future generations.

---

[8] GASB, *Codification*, Section P70.101-109, and pars. 1600.110-111.

- Resource inflows from short-term borrowings and other current liabilities, and resource outflows to repay those liabilities are *not* recorded in the statement of revenues, expenditures, and changes in fund balance, but are recorded as increases and decreases in current liabilities. Care must be taken to distinguish between fund *transfers*, that are included as other financing sources and affect fund balance, from resource flows between funds where *repayment is expected*. If repayment is expected, such flows are reported as receivables and payables, typically labelled "due from" or "due to" a specific fund.

The concepts identified above for governmental funds are explained and illustrated more fully in the next section, where accounting for the general fund is studied in detail. The *governmental fund measurement focus* is on determination of current financial position and changes in current financial position—sources, uses, and balances of financial resources—rather than upon net income determination. The statement of revenues, expenditures, and changes in fund balance is the primary governmental fund operating statement, and it compares inflows and outflows of current financial resources. It may be supported or supplemented by more detailed schedules of revenues, expenditures, transfers, and other changes in fund balance. Standard statements for governmental funds are the **Statement of Revenues and Expenditures and Changes in Fund Balance**, the **Balance Sheet**, and the **Budgetary Comparison Statement**, which compares budgeted and actual revenues, expenditures and other changes in fund balance.

The 1997 GASB *Exposure Draft* retains the current measurement focus for governmental funds, but also requires entity-wide reporting on a *full accrual basis*. Discussion of this *Exposure Draft* and the motivation for the new requirements appear in Chapter 13.

ACCOUNTING FOR FIDUCIARY FUNDS

Fiduciary funds account for governmental activities where resources are held in trust, or the governmental unit collects resources for another governmental unit. Fiduciary funds are classified as either **trust funds** or **agency funds**.

Accounting for Trust Funds

A **trust fund** is used when a governmental unit holds, manages, and spends resources under terms of a trust agreement. The measurement focus depends on whether the fund is an **expendable trust** or a **nonexpendable trust**. An *expendable* trust fund accounts for trusts where all resources in the fund may be spent for the specified purpose. For example, a citizen may donate $1,000,000 to be used to purchase artwork for display in county public libraries. Here there is no need to distinguish between the principal of the donation and any income earned thereon, and **the modified accrual basis of accounting** is used. A *nonexpendable* trust fund accounts for trusts where the principal is to be left intact, with only the income to be spent for the specified purpose. If the citizen donates $1,000,000, specifying that the principal remain intact and only the income earned on investment of the principal be used for art acquisitions, it is necessary to use **fiduciary accounting** to determine which portion of fund resources consists of income and which is principal. Fiduciary accounting is used in the business setting in accounting for estates and trusts, and is studied in Module H of this textbook. Trust fund accounting for state and local governments is studied in Chapter 13.

Accounting for Agency Funds

Agency funds accumulate resources held for disbursement to other entities. An example is a county fund used to collect and remit state sales taxes. The accounting for an agency fund is simple: resources accumulated are liabilities, and payments of these resources to the appropriate entity are reductions in liabilities. Agency funds therefore have no fund equity or revenues and expenses. Agency fund accounting is studied in Chapter 13.

ACCOUNTING FOR THE GENERAL FUND

Most governmental activities are recorded in the general fund, which handles routine operating activities of the governmental unit. This section explains accounting procedures for the general fund.

BUDGETARY ACCOUNTS

Accounting serves an important control function in state and local government—namely, to aid in ensuring that resources are spent in compliance with legal requirements. Legal restrictions on spending are usually expressed in the form of a **budget**, which prescribes both the total amount of spending allowed and the amounts in each expense category. A budget may be adopted by legislative/executive action (for example, passage by a city council and acceptance by a mayor) or by popular vote, as is the case with many school district budgets. Typically, any change in the total budget must be approved in the same way, whereas changes within the budget—transfers among budget components—usually require less formal approval. For example, a school board may approve budget transfers without outside approval.

In fund accounting *the budget is recorded in the accounts* to aid in control of revenues and expenditures. At the beginning of the year, the budgeted revenues and budgeted expenditures are entered in **budgetary accounts**. As actual revenues are received and resources are expended during the year, comparison with the budget is made regularly by management. This comparison helps to ensure that, in each category of the budget, actual spending does not exceed the authorized amount. Recording budget data in the accounts is one of the key aspects of fund accounting and one of the major ways in which governmental accounting differs from business accounting. In government, the budget is more than a managerial plan; it is a legal constraint. The budget establishes legal spending limits, which must not be exceeded.

Budget Entry

Like fund accounting in general, budgetary accounts are a means to facilitate accountability and control over resources. This is important in a government, as expenditures are legally limited to approved budgeted amounts. A budget has two elements: planned revenues and planned expenditures. In state and local government, the account for the former is **Estimated Revenues**; for the latter it is **Appropriations**, meaning budgeted expenditures. When the budget entry is made, Estimated Revenues is debited because it represents the expected inflow of resources to the fund, roughly analogous to receivables. Similarly, Appropriations is credited because it represents the expected outflow of resources from the fund, roughly analogous to payables. To illustrate, assume that expenditures of $800,000 are budgeted, and revenues are also expected to be $800,000, so that the budget is balanced. The budget entry is as follows:

Estimated Revenues   800,000
    Appropriations   800,000
     To record budget for the year.

It is not necessary that the budget be balanced in a particular fiscal period, although the concept of *interperiod equity*—whether current year revenues are sufficient to pay for current period services—calls for overall balance during consecutive fiscal periods. A local government may plan to spend less than its anticipated revenue and thus to increase the net financial resources of the fund, represented by **Fund Balance—Unreserved**. In this circumstance, the budget entry shows a credit to the unreserved fund balance, signifying a planned increase in net financial resources for the period.

Continuing the example, if revenues are expected to amount to $810,000, and expenditures are budgeted at $800,000, the unit is planning to spend less than it receives and to increase its unreserved fund balance by $10,000. The budget entry follows:

Estimated Revenues   810,000
    Appropriations   800,000
    Fund Balance—Unreserved   10,000
     To record budget for the year and planned increase in
     fund balance.

Alternatively, a local government may plan to spend more than its anticipated revenue, using resources accumulated in previous periods. The budget entry in this case debits the Fund Balance—Unreserved. If revenues are expected to amount to only $785,000, and expenditures are budgeted at $800,000, the unit is planning to decrease its unreserved fund balance by spending more than it receives this year. The following budget entry is made:

Estimated Revenues   785,000
Fund Balance—Unreserved   15,000
    Appropriations   800,000
     To record budget for the year and planned decrease in
     fund balance.

Note that after the budget is recorded, the fund balance account shows the **expected year-end balance**. In the preceding example, where budgeted revenues were $785,000 and budgeted expenditures were $800,000, assume that the fund balance at the beginning of the year was $105,000. After the budget is recorded, the fund balance is $90,000. If the budgeted figures are achieved, the amount of the actual fund balance at the end of the year will also be $90,000.

RECORDING PROPERTY TAX REVENUES

Under the modified accrual approach used in fund accounting, some revenues are recorded on the accrual basis, while others are recorded on the cash basis. When revenues are recorded, note that the Revenues account signifies the actual amount of revenues, as distinct from the budgeted amount recorded in the Estimated Revenues account.

In our presentation, and in practice, control accounts are generally used for revenues and expenditures. All revenue transactions in the fund are credited to the Revenues account. A subsidiary ledger, containing accounts for each type of revenue, is also maintained. The total of the detailed accounts in the subsidiary ledger must equal the balance in the Revenues control account. Expenditures, discussed in the next section, are handled in the same manner.

Property tax revenue is an important illustration of use of the accrual basis, because the amount of revenue can be estimated with reasonable accuracy and the probability of collection on a timely basis is very high. The amount of the tax levy, less an appropriate allowance for uncollectibles, is recorded as revenue. Even though the gross amount of the levy is recorded as Taxes Receivable—Current, the amount credited to Revenues is the **net** amount that the local government expects to collect. This amount reflects the financial resources expected to be available for expenditure during the current period. This procedure is a deviation from business accounting, where revenues are recorded gross and bad debt expense is recorded separately. Remember that in fund accounting, expenditures are outflows of current financial resources. Bad debt expense does not meet this definition.

Property tax *collections*, a major source of financial resources for most local governments, may not occur until a few months after they are levied. To provide operating cash for the period between levy and collection, local governments often issue **tax anticipation notes**. These notes are **short-term borrowings** that are repaid from tax collections and are *not* considered as revenues.

After a period of time, often by the end of the fiscal period, the status of any uncollected taxes changes from current to delinquent. These taxes receivable should be reclassified to a Taxes Receivable—Delinquent account with a corresponding Allowance for Uncollectible Taxes—Delinquent. Although not required by GASB standards, it is common to **fully reserve** delinquent taxes because they are not expected to be collected. To do so, the amount of the allowance for uncollectibles is set equal to the amount of delinquent taxes receivable; it may be necessary to adjust the original estimate of uncollectible taxes to bring it into agreement with the delinquent amount. Revenues are then adjusted downward or upward by the amount needed to increase or decrease the allowance for uncollectible taxes.

To illustrate the accounting for property tax transactions, assume that a city levies a property tax of $3,000,000, which is expected to be 95-percent collectible. The following entry is made to record the property tax levy:

Taxes Receivable—Current	3,000,000	
Allowance for Uncollectible Taxes—Current		150,000
Revenues		2,850,000
To record tax levy.		

Subsequent collection of $2,800,000, declaration of unpaid amounts as delinquent, and *fully reserving* the delinquent taxes are recorded as follows:

Cash	2,800,000	
Taxes Receivable—Current		2,800,000
To record collection of property taxes.		
Taxes Receivable—Delinquent	200,000	
Taxes Receivable—Current		200,000
To reclassify unpaid taxes as delinquent.		
Allowance for Uncollectible Taxes—Current	150,000	
Revenues	50,000	
Allowance for Uncollectible Taxes—Delinquent		200,000
To reclassify allowance for uncollectible taxes and increase		
it to $200,000 in order to fully reserve the delinquent taxes.		

Note that to fully reserve the delinquent taxes, we adjust the allowance so that it equals the amount of delinquent taxes and reclassify it as Allowance for Uncollectible Taxes—Delinquent. The allowance is increased (credited) by $50,000 to $200,000 and Revenues—originally recorded as $2,850,000—are decreased (debited) by $50,000 accordingly. This adjustment corrects the original entry made to record the tax levy, so that the amounts actually collected are recorded as revenues. Similarly, the allowance for uncollectible delinquent taxes balance now equals the amount of delinquent taxes receivable. Had the collections exceeded the amount originally entered as revenues, resulting in delinquent taxes being less than the allowance for uncollectible taxes, the adjusting entry would increase (credit) revenues and decrease (debit) the allowance.

When delinquent taxes are fully reserved, no revenue from these particular tax levies is anticipated. The criteria for accrual of revenue require that collection occur within a short time and that the degree of collectibility be capable of reasonable estimation. These criteria are generally not met in the case of delinquent taxes. The collection process may take a long time, and its success is highly uncertain. As a result, revenue from delinquent taxes is not accrued. Subsequent collections of delinquent taxes are recorded as revenues, on the cash basis, at time of collection. For example, a $10,000 collection of fully-reserved delinquent taxes is recorded as follows:

Cash	10,000	
Allowance for Uncollectible Taxes—Delinquent	10,000	
Taxes Receivable—Delinquent		10,000
Revenues		10,000
To record collection of delinquent taxes.		

After additional time passes, delinquent taxes may become tax liens. **Tax liens** are legal claims against the taxed property, which may be satisfied by forcing sale of the property. Reclassification to a Tax Liens Receivable account, with a corresponding allowance for uncollectibles, should be made. It is common practice also to fully reserve tax liens. The entries are similar to those illustrated above for reclassifying taxes receivable from current to delinquent.

PURCHASE OF GOODS AND SERVICES

The acquisition of goods and services by a governmental unit typically involves three steps: (1) a purchase order or contract is issued, (2) the goods or services are received, and (3) payment is made. In business accounting, only steps (2) and (3) are formally recorded in the accounting records. However, unlike a business, a governmental unit has legal limits on its spending authority. Because of these legal restrictions, it is important at a given time to know not only the amount actually spent to date and the amount of unpaid bills, but also the amount of outstanding spending commitments. If no formal record is kept of purchase orders, the danger exists that the government will overcommit itself and exceed the legal spending authority. Any commitment to spend is a potential charge against the budget; to aid in the control of expenditures, spending commitments, known as **encumbrances**, are recorded in the accounts.

Recording Purchase Orders

Accounting for placement of a purchase order requires the following:

- A debit to *Encumbrances* representing the potential charge against the fund's limited spending authority; encumbrances become expenditures when the goods or services ordered are delivered.
- A credit to *Fund Balance—Reserved for Encumbrances* signifying restriction of a portion of the fund balance to the items ordered. It signifies that, because of this commitment, these financial resources are set aside for a specific future use.

Recording encumbrances does not create liabilities because the goods and services have not been delivered. Encumbrance entries are temporary. Encumbrances are recorded when purchase orders are issued and reversed when the goods or services are delivered.

As an example of the purchase of goods and services by local government, assume that a city places an order for repair services on March 18, with the expected cost of the services being $18,500. To formally record this commitment, an encumbrance entry is made on March 18.

Encumbrances	18,500	
Fund Balance—Reserved for Encumbrances		18,500
To record purchase order for repair services.		

This entry signifies that $18,500 of the repair services budget is committed. Suppose that the repair services budget is $42,000 and that $8,000 was previously spent. Recording the encumbrance of $18,500 on March 18 tells city management that only $15,500 of the repair services budget is still uncommitted and available for use during the current period. This uncommitted balance is often referred to as **available funds**.

Original Budget for Repair Services	$ 42,000
Expended to Date	8,000
Unexpended Balance	$ 34,000
Outstanding Purchase Order	18,500
Uncommitted Balance (*Available Funds*)	$ 15,500

Recording Receipt of Goods and Services

Receipt of goods or services by the governmental unit, and concurrent acknowledgment of the liability for payment, call for *expenditures* to be recorded, following the modified accrual approach. If an encumbrance was previously recorded when these goods or services were ordered, we first reverse the amount originally encumbered. This reversal signifies that the purchase order is no longer outstanding. The expenditure is then recorded.

Recall that *expenditures* in fund accounting signify outflows of financial resources. This is different from the concept of *expenses* used in business accounting, which measure consumption of resources in the process of earning revenue. To illustrate the difference, in fund accounting an expenditure is recorded when financial resources are used to acquire office equipment; periodic depreciation expense is not recorded. In business accounting, however, resources used to acquire the office equipment are capitalized; consumption of that equipment over time is recognized through periodic depreciation expense.

Expenditures is a control account; individual accounts for particular expenditure items are maintained in a subsidiary ledger. Also, the term **vouchers payable** is commonly used in fund accounting to indicate the liability for payment, rather than the term *accounts payable* used in business accounting.

Continuing the example presented above, assume that by April 3 the repair services ordered on March 18 are provided, accompanied by an invoice for $18,650. Two entries are required: (1) the previously recorded encumbrance is reversed, and (2) the expenditure is recorded.

Fund Balance—Reserved for Encumbrances	18,500	
Encumbrances		18,500
To reverse encumbrance entry; services performed.		
Expenditures	18,650	
Vouchers Payable		18,650
To record cost of repair services.		

The amount of the encumbrance and the amount of the expenditure need not be equal. At the time the purchase order was placed, the exact cost of the goods or services may not have been known, and an estimate was used. Note that the reversing entry is based on the amount *previously encumbered*, $18,500, while the expenditure entry is based on the *actual cost* of $18,650.

Two special problems with respect to accounting for materials and supplies in local government merit further discussion. One is the presence of inventories, discussed below; the other is the existence of outstanding purchase orders at year-end, discussed in a later section.

INVENTORIES

Two methods of expenditure accounting for supplies inventories (and other prepayments) in governmental funds have traditionally existed: the *consumption method*, which treats inventory items as expenditures when *used*, and the *purchases method*, which treats inventory items as expenditures when *purchased*. Because both methods are currently permitted and used in practice, we illustrate both.

The **consumption method** treats inventory as a financial resource, a spendable or consumable asset, similar to cash. Consequently, Supplies Inventory is debited when supplies are purchased, and Expenditures is debited when the supplies are used. To illustrate the consumption method, suppose that $210,000 of supplies are acquired during the year. Encumbrances are recorded when supplies are ordered and are reversed upon delivery. Receipt of the supplies is recorded as follows:

Supplies Inventory	210,000	
Vouchers Payable		210,000
To record purchase of supplies under the		
consumption method.		

Suppose further that supplies costing $177,000 were consumed during the year so that ending inventory is $33,000 (= $210,000 − $177,000). The following entry summarizes the year's expenditures for the supplies consumed.

Expenditures	177,000	
Supplies Inventory		177,000
To record supplies used under the *consumption method*.		

Alternatively, Expenditures is debited when the supplies are received and the inventory established at year-end. When this procedure is followed, the following two entries are used:

Expenditures	210,000	
Vouchers Payable		210,000
To record purchase of supplies under the *consumption method*.		

Supplies Inventory	33,000	
Expenditures		33,000
To record supplies on hand at year-end under the *consumption method*.		

Regardless of which procedure is followed, the *consumption method* reports Expenditures for supplies used of $177,000 and Supplies Inventory of $33,000.

Under the **purchases method,** the cost of materials and supplies is charged to Expenditures as the items are purchased, without regard to whether they are consumed during the current period. The method is based on the view that once materials and supplies are purchased, spending authority is used. Whether the materials or supplies are currently consumed is of little importance insofar as spending authority is concerned.

The purchases method recognizes no inventories of materials and supplies in the accounts. If significant physical levels of inventory are on hand at year-end, the GASB *Codification* requires that this inventory be reported on the balance sheet. To avoid changing the expenditure already recorded, the following entry is made:

Supplies Inventory	XX	
Fund Balance—Reserved for Supplies Inventory		XX
To record supplies inventory at year-end.		

This entry does not change either reported expenditures or unreserved fund balance, but merely discloses the supplies inventory balance on the balance sheet.

To illustrate the *purchases method*, the supplies acquired at a cost of $210,000 in the previous example are recorded as an expenditure when delivered:

Expenditures	210,000	
Vouchers Payable		210,000
To record purchase of supplies under the *purchases method*.		

To report supplies that cost $33,000 which remain in inventory, the following year-end entry is made:

Supplies Inventory	33,000	
Fund Balance—Reserved for Supplies Inventory		33,000
To record inventory of supplies at year-end under the *purchases method*.		

In subsequent years, changes in the amount of supplies on hand are recognized in the purchases method by either using or reversing the above entry to record the changes. Suppose that by the end of the following year, the supplies inventory decreased to $28,000. At year-end the following adjusting entry reduces the inventory balance and the corresponding reserve by $5,000.

Fund Balance—Reserved for Supplies Inventory	5,000	
Supplies Inventory		5,000

      To adjust inventory to current year-end balance of $28,000 under the *purchases method*.

The **consumption method** is the same as regular business accounting—inventory is an asset when purchased and an expenditure when used up. Since expenditures are defined in fund accounting as *outflows of current financial resources*—cash, receivables and payables, if the consumption method is used, inventories must be defined as current financial resources. Purchase of inventories does not involve outflows of net current financial resources—instead, we merely trade one current financial resource for another. Using the **purchases method**, current financial resources do **not** include inventories. Purchase of inventory is therefore a use of current financial resources and is recorded as an expenditure.

Either the consumption or purchases method can currently be used in a governmental unit's external financial statements. The 1997 proposed accounting model for external reporting by state and local governments requires reporting on a fund basis *and* on an entity basis, using full accrual accounting. Under this proposal, the consumption method is required for the entity basis statements.

AUTHORS' COMMENTARY

If the purchases method is used, an additional entry to recognize the actual inventory on hand is recorded if significant amounts of inventory exist at year-end, since it is felt that no recognition of inventory on hand on the balance sheet is misleading. When inventory is recognized under the purchases method, *total* fund balance—reserved and unreserved—is the *same* regardless of whether the purchases or consumption method is used. However, the *unreserved* fund balance differs between the two methods. Under the consumption method, unreserved fund balance is reduced only when the inventory is used up. Under the purchases method, unreserved fund balance is reduced when the inventory is purchased. Choice between the two methods depends on one's interpretation of what the "unreserved fund balance" represents. Is it resources available to spend, including resources tied up in inventory (consumption method), or resources available to spend after deducting resources tied up in inventory (purchases method)?

INTERFUND TRANSACTIONS

Transactions among funds—**interfund transactions**—are common in state and local government. These transactions are of five general types, each with its own accounting treatment as indicated below. Because of their intragovernmental nature, interfund transactions are not accounted for as revenues or expenditures by the transacting funds, except as noted.

Loans or advances are temporary transfers from one fund to another, with authorization by statute or ordinance often required and repayment expected. These transfers are recorded as receivables or payables by the funds involved. Special account titles are used: *Due from Fund* and *Due to Fund*. Temporary interfund transfers may be used to provide initial financing for a particular activity. For example, suppose a federal grant is awarded to a city to support a project to be accounted for in a special revenue fund. To provide for project costs incurred prior to the actual receipt of the grant, the city might advance $8,000 from the general fund to the special revenue fund. This transaction is recorded in the *general fund* as follows:

Books of General Fund

Due from Special Revenue Fund	8,000	
Cash		8,000
To record advance to special revenue fund.		

A parallel entry is required on the books of the *special revenue fund*:

Books of Special Revenue Fund

Cash	8,000	
Due to General Fund		8,000
To record advance from general fund.		

When the advance is repaid, opposite entries are made by the general and special revenue funds.

Reimbursements occur when Fund A makes a payment on behalf of Fund B, records an expenditure properly chargeable to Fund B, and is subsequently repaid by Fund B. Even though the repayment from B to A is an interfund transaction, the fact that it is a *reimbursement* allows it to be recorded as an expenditure by Fund B and as a reduction of expenditures by Fund A. For example, suppose that the *general fund* paid $4,000 for services used in a special revenue fund project, and recorded the following:

Books of General Fund

Expenditures	4,000	
Cash		4,000
To record purchase of services for special revenue fund project.		

Subsequently, the special revenue fund reimburses the general fund for the services. The entry for the *special revenue fund* to record the expenditure is as follows:

Books of Special Revenue Fund

Expenditures	4,000	
Cash		4,000
To record reimbursement to general fund for services.		

The *general fund* records the reimbursement as a reduction in its previously recorded expenditures:

Books of General Fund

Cash	4,000	
Expenditures		4,000
To record reimbursement from special revenue fund.		

After the reimbursement is made, the expenditure is recorded in the special revenue fund where it is properly chargeable, and there is no net effect on the general fund.

Quasi-external transactions are interfund transactions that would be treated as revenues or expenditures if they involved an organization outside of the governmental unit rather than another fund. Therefore, the two funds involved in quasi-external transactions record them as revenues or expenditures. For example, if the general fund purchases services from an outside vendor, an expenditure is recorded by the general fund. If the same services are purchased from an internal service fund, a quasi-external transaction exists and the accounting is identical: an expenditure is recorded by the general fund and revenue is recorded by the internal service fund. Other examples of quasi-external transactions include the following:

- General fund contributions to a pension trust fund.
- Payments in lieu of property taxes by an enterprise fund to the general fund.
- General fund payments to an enterprise fund for utility services provided to city buildings.

Residual equity transfers occur when resources of a permanent equity nature are transferred from one fund to another. For example, when a city establishes an internal service fund and transfers general fund resources to provide the initial capital of the internal service fund, we have a residual equity transfer. As another example, suppose a construction project funded by a bond issue is completed and the related capital projects fund is closed. Transfer of any cash remaining in the terminated capital projects fund to the debt service fund is accounted for as a residual equity transfer. This type of transfer is accounted for as a direct change in *beginning* fund balances.

Operating transfers involve legally authorized transfers of resources from the fund receiving the revenues (frequently the general fund) to the fund that will make the expenditures. Unlike residual equity transfers, operating transfers are spent by the receiving fund in carrying on its activities rather than serving as permanent equity. Operating transfers are *not* recorded as revenues and expenditures; in the financial statements they are reported as **other financing sources (uses)**. Following are some examples:

- Debt payments (principal and interest) on long-term debt originally issued by the general or capital projects funds are commonly made using general fund resources. Money is transferred from the general fund (*operating transfer out*) to the debt service fund (*operating transfer in*) where the debt-related expenditures are made.
- A business activity of the local government such as the water department is partially subsidized by general fund resources, which are recorded as an *operating transfer out*. Receipt of the resources by the water department enterprise fund is recorded as an *operating transfer in.*
- A construction project is financed in part by a bond issue and in part by general fund resources transferred (*operating transfer out*) to the capital projects fund (*operating transfer in*).

CLOSING ENTRIES

When closing entries are prepared at the end of the reporting period, all nominal accounts, *including the budgetary accounts*, are closed to the Fund Balance. Although a single combined closing entry is possible, use of two closing entries—one for revenues and the other for expenditures—aids in understanding the process.

As noted earlier, the fund balance of a government entity usually consists of an unreserved portion and one or more reserved portions. Closing entries are made to the *unreserved* portion. Both Estimated Revenues (debit balance) and Revenues (credit balance) are closed to Fund Balance—Unreserved. A debit to Fund Balance—Unreserved results when actual revenues are less than budgeted. In contrast, a credit results when actual revenues exceed the amount budgeted.

Similarly, if at the end of the period there are no outstanding purchase orders (that is, encumbrances), we close Expenditures (debit balance) and Appropriations (credit balance) to Fund Balance—Unreserved. When actual expenditures are less than the amount budgeted, the unreserved fund balance is increased; when actual expenditures exceed the budget, the unreserved fund balance is reduced.

To illustrate the closing process, assume that budgeted revenues are $785,000 and budgeted expenditures are $800,000, and that actual revenues amount to $787,000, while actual expenditures amount to $791,000. The following closing entries are made:

Revenues	787,000	
Estimated Revenues		785,000
Fund Balance—Unreserved		2,000
To close revenues and estimated revenues to fund balance.		

Appropriations	800,000	
Expenditures		791,000
Fund Balance—Unreserved		9,000
To close expenditures and appropriations to fund balance.		

As a result of these entries, the unreserved fund balance is increased by $11,000, because actual revenues exceeded the budget by $2,000, and actual expenditures were $9,000 less than planned. Recall that the budget entry at the beginning of the year was as follows:

Estimated Revenues	785,000	
Fund Balance—Unreserved	15,000	
Appropriations		800,000
To record budget for the year and planned decrease in fund balance.		

Whereas the fund balance was originally expected to decrease by $15,000, it actually decreased by only $4,000, as shown in this condensed *budgetary comparison statement*:

	Budget	Actual	Variance— Favorable (Unfavorable)
Revenues	$ 785,000	$ 787,000	$ 2,000
Expenditures	(800,000)	(791,000)	9,000
Change in Fund Balance	$ (15,000)	$ (4,000)	$ 11,000

Note that the $15,000 debit to the fund balance in the budget entry and the $11,000 total credits to the fund balance in the closing entries together account for the actual $4,000 decrease during the year.

OUTSTANDING ENCUMBRANCES AT YEAR-END

When encumbrances are outstanding at the end of the year, it means that a purchase order was issued, but the goods were not received as of year-end. In most jurisdictions, outstanding purchase orders are honored in the next period. As an example, assume that purchase orders amounting to $27,000 are issued late in 20X1, do not lapse, and are still outstanding at year-end. When the orders were issued, the encumbrance entry was as follows:

Encumbrances	27,000	
Fund Balance—Reserved for Encumbrances		27,000
To record purchase orders.		

GAAP Budgetary Basis

Treatment of encumbrances outstanding at year-end depends on the governmental unit's basis of reporting. If appropriations for the year are viewed as **authority to spend**, then outstanding encumbrances are *not* equivalent to expenditures. A budgetary comparison statement shows actual expenditures only, and outstanding encumbrances are removed from the appropriations balance. Next year, expenditures include the actual expenditure associated with last year's encumbrance, and appropriations include the outstanding encumbrance from last year, effectively moving the appropriation and the expenditure to the year when the goods are received and the resources spent. This interpretation is known as the **GAAP budgetary basis**. To illustrate accounting for outstanding encumbrances under the GAAP budgetary basis, we return to the $27,000 of purchase orders outstanding at the end of 20X1. The encumbrances are closed out, while the related Fund Balance—Reserved for Encumbrances remains.

Appropriations	XX	
Fund Balance—Unreserved		XX
Expenditures		XX
Encumbrances		27,000
To close 20X1 appropriations, expenditures, and encumbrances.		

The encumbrances are *not* included in the 20X1 budgetary comparison statement. In 20X2, the $27,000 of encumbrances are restored to the accounts, and the unreserved fund balance is increased, effectively reversing part of the 20X1 closing entry:

Encumbrances	27,000	
Fund Balance—Unreserved		27,000
To restore encumbrances carried over from 20X1.		

The expenditure signifying receipt in 20X2 of the goods and services ordered in 20X1 is recorded in the same manner as all other 20X2 expenditures. The encumbrance is reversed in the amount of $27,000, and the expenditure is recorded at the actual amount owed. Assume the actual expenditure related to the carryover encumbrance is $26,600. In the budgetary comparison statement, total expenditures for 20X2 include the actual $26,600 expenditure related to the carryover encumbrance, and total appropriations include the $27,000 carryover encumbrance.

Legal Budgetary Basis

If appropriations for the year are viewed as **authority to encumber or obligate**, then outstanding encumbrances are equivalent to expenditures, since the obligation arises at the time of the purchase order. A budgetary comparison statement at year-end shows actual expenditures and encumbrances versus appropriations, including the appropriation connected with the outstanding encumbrance. Evidence of the expenditure does not appear on a budgetary comparison statement for the following year. This interpretation is known as the **legal budgetary basis**.

Using the same example as above, when the legal budgetary basis is used, the $27,000 in encumbrances outstanding at the end of 20X1 are included with expenditures in the 20X1 budgetary comparison statement. In the next year, the $26,600 expenditure related to the prior year outstanding encumbrance is recorded separately and closed against the portion of the prior year's fund balance reserved for encumbrances rather than against the budget for 20X2. Entries to record the encumbrance in 20X1 and close the accounts are the same as under the GAAP budgetary basis. At the beginning of 20X2, the reserved fund balance is reclassified, indicating that it is set aside to cover purchase orders issued in 20X1.

Fund Balance—Reserved for Encumbrances	27,000	
Fund Balance—Reserved for Encumbrances (Prior Year) . . .		27,000
To reclassify purchase orders outstanding at beginning of 20X2.		

When the goods and services ordered in 20X1 are received in 20X2 at a cost of $26,600, a separate expenditures account is used to record completion of the transaction initiated in 20X1:

Expenditures—Prior Year Encumbrances	26,600	
Vouchers Payable		26,600
To record invoices for goods and services ordered		
in 20X1.		

Finally, at the end of 20X2 an additional closing entry is required to close the prior year encumbrances and related expenditures to the prior year's unreserved fund balance:

Fund Balance—Reserved for Encumbrances (Prior Year)	27,000	
Expenditures—Prior Year Encumbrances		26,600
Fund Balance—Unreserved		400
To close encumbrances carried over from 20X1 and		
related expenditures.		

The $400 credit to the unreserved fund balance effectively corrects the 20X1 closing entry. Even though that entry charged $27,000 of 20X1 encumbrances against the unreserved fund balance, the actual cost of these goods and services was only $26,600.

Accounting for carryover encumbrances under these two alternative budgetary bases may be summarized as follows. Assume that an encumbrance is outstanding at the end of 20X1. Notice that under both budgetary bases, outstanding encumbrances are closed at year end. Encumbrances are not assets to be reported on a balance sheet.

1. Under the *GAAP budgetary basis*, the encumbered amount is carried into 20X2:
   a. It is temporarily closed to the unreserved fund balance at the end of 20X1, but this entry is reversed in 20X2.
   b. It is not included in comparing budget to actual for 20X1.
   c. When the actual expenditure occurs in 20X2, it is recorded as a regular 20X2 expenditure.
   d. In comparing budget to actual for 20X2, the carryover encumbered appropriation from 20X1 is included in the 20X2 budget.
2. When the *legal budgetary basis* is used, the encumbered amount is treated in the budgetary comparison statement as if it were an expenditure of 20X1:
   a. It is closed to the unreserved fund balance in 20X1.
   b. It is included in comparing budget to actual for 20X1.
   c. When the actual expenditure occurs in 20X2, it is recorded separately from 20X2 expenditures and is closed against the carried-over reserved fund balance; any difference is closed to the unreserved fund balance.
   d. It does not affect the comparison of budget to actual for 20X2.

The governmental unit should report on whatever budgetary basis is prescribed by the applicable laws and regulations in its jurisdiction in order to demonstrate legal compliance with those laws and regulations. If the unit's financial statements are to be certified as being in accordance with GAAP, however, the unit must also provide enough information for a GAAP budgetary basis presentation.[9] Continuing our earlier example, we illustrate one way to accomplish this in the budgetary comparison statement for 20X1. The reconciliation appears in the lower part of the statement. Assume that appropriations for 20X1 are $800,000, the *legal budgetary basis is used* by the governmental unit, expenditures are $791,000, outstanding encumbrances are $27,000, and revenue data are as shown below.

Budgetary Comparison Statement
(Legal Budgetary Basis)

	Budget	Actual	Variance— Favorable (Unfavorable)
Revenues	$ 785,000	$ 787,000	$ 2,000
Expenditures and Encumbrances	(800,000)	(818,000)	(18,000)
Change in Fund Balance (Legal Budgetary Basis)	$ (15,000)	$ (31,000)	$ (16,000)
Adjust for Encumbrances		27,000	
Change in Fund Balance (GAAP Budgetary Basis)		$ (4,000)	

FINANCIAL STATEMENTS FOR THE GENERAL FUND

As discussed above, the required financial statements for the general fund are the **balance sheet**, the **statement of revenues, expenditures, and changes in fund balance**, and the **budgetary comparison statement**.

---

[9] GASB, *Codification*, pars. 2400.104-106.

BALANCE SHEET

Exhibit 12.3 presents a simple balance sheet for the general fund of a city. Notice that the balance sheet is unclassified. Fixed assets and long-term debt are excluded from the general fund balance sheet and are reported in financial statements for their respective account groups. Thus the assets of the general fund are limited to those able to be spent or otherwise consumed during the next fiscal period in carrying on the fund's activities. Similarly, the liabilities of the general fund are limited to claims to be paid during the next fiscal year. The total fund balance includes the portion reserved for encumbrances, which signifies that purchase orders were outstanding at year-end.

City of Norwood
Balance Sheet—General Fund
June 30, 20X1

Assets

Cash	$ 51,000
Short-Term Investments, at Cost	1,850,000
Accounts Receivable (Net of $300 Allowance for Uncollectible Accounts)	1,200
Due from Other Governments	1,040,800
Total Assets	$2,943,000

Liabilities and Fund Balance

Liabilities:	
Vouchers Payable	$ 239,000
Due to Other Funds	170,000
Total Liabilities	$ 409,000
Fund Balance:	
Reserved for Encumbrances	$2,265,000
Unreserved	269,000
Total Fund Balance	$2,534,000
Total Liabilities and Fund Balance	$2,943,000

EXHIBIT 12.3 ILLUSTRATION OF GENERAL FUND BALANCE SHEET

STATEMENT OF REVENUES, EXPENDITURES, AND CHANGES IN FUND BALANCE

The **statement of revenues, expenditures, and changes in fund balance** is the general fund's principal operating statement covering the reporting period. It usually focuses on changes in the *total fund balance*. Exhibit 12.4 presents a simple statement of revenues, expenditures, and changes in fund balance for the general fund of a city.

Revenues are classified by *source*. For the general fund, major sources of revenue include taxes, intergovernmental revenues (that is, revenues from other governmental units), licenses and permits, charges for services, and fines. Various types of expenditure classification also exist. For financial statement purposes, *expenditures* are often classified by character and function. Classification by *character* hinges on the time period (or periods) that the expenditures benefit.

City of Norwood
Statement of Revenues, Expenditures, and Changes
in Fund Balance—General Fund
for the Fiscal Year Ended June 30, 20X1

Revenues

Taxes	$ 6,453,000
Licenses and Permits	800,000
Charges for Services	1,500,000
Miscellaneous Revenues	879,000
Total Revenues	$ 9,632,000

Expenditures

General Government	$ 1,508,000
Public Safety	3,600,000
Health and Welfare	730,000
Education	3,080,000
	$ 8,918,000
Total Expenditures	$ 714,000
Excess of Revenues over (under) Expenditures	

Other Financing Sources (Uses)

Operating Transfers In	$ 670,000
Operating Transfers Out	(850,000)
	$ (180,000)
Total Other Financing Sources (Uses)	$ 534,000
Excess of Revenue and Other Sources over Expenditures and Other Uses	2,000,000
Fund Balance—July 1, 20X0	$ 2,534,000
Fund Balance—June 30, 20X1	

EXHIBIT 12.4 ILLUSTRATION OF GENERAL FUND STATEMENT OF REVENUES, EXPENDITURES, AND CHANGES IN FUND BALANCE

Common character classifications are *current expenditures, capital outlays,* and *debt service.* Classification by *function* identifies groups of related activities designed to accomplish a particular service or regulatory responsibility. Examples of functions are general government, public safety, education, highways, sanitation, health, and recreation. Classification of expenditures by *object classes*—types of goods and services acquired—such as personnel compensation and utilities is also common.

Other financing sources and uses include proceeds of long-term debt issues and operating transfers to or from the general fund. As noted earlier, residual equity transfers are reported as changes to the beginning fund balance.

BUDGETARY COMPARISON STATEMENT

In addition to the statement of revenues, expenditures, and changes in fund balance just discussed, a parallel statement showing the comparison between budget and actual data is presented. The format of the **budgetary comparison statement**, formally called the **statement of revenues, expenditures, and changes in fund balance—budget and actual**, is similar to the format of the statement of revenues, expenditures, and changes in fund balance, except that three columns of numbers are presented: *budget*, *actual*, and *variance*.

In the event that the governmental unit uses a *non-GAAP budgetary basis*, "expenditures" in the budgetary comparison statement could include outstanding encumbrances. Because those amounts would differ from the corresponding amounts in the statement of revenues, expenditures, and changes in fund balance, a reconciliation with GAAP is also required.

An illustration of a budgetary comparison statement on the GAAP budgetary basis appears in Exhibit 12.5. Note that the convention here differs from cost accounting. In cost accounting, favorable variances are commonly enclosed in parentheses, while in governmental accounting, parentheses are used for unfavorable variances.

City of Norwood
Statement of Revenues, Expenditures and Changes
in Fund Balance—Budget and Actual—General Fund
for the Fiscal Year Ended June 30, 20X1

Revenues	Budget	Actual	Variance— Favorable (Unfavorable)
Taxes	$ 6,461,000	$ 6,453,000	$ (8,000)
Licenses and Permits	975,000	800,000	(175,000)
Charges for Services	1,604,000	1,500,000	(104,000)
Miscellaneous Revenues	866,000	879,000	13,000
Total Revenues	$ 9,906,000	$ 9,632,000	$ (274,000)
Expenditures			
General Government	$ 1,764,000	$ 1,508,000	$ 256,000
Public Safety	3,334,000	3,600,000	(266,000)
Health and Welfare	839,000	730,000	109,000
Education	2,886,000	3,080,000	(194,000)
Total Expenditures	$ 8,823,000	$ 8,918,000	$ (95,000)
Excess of Revenues over (under) Expenditures	$ 1,083,000	$ 714,000	$ (369,000)
Other Financing Sources (Uses)			
Operating Transfers In	$ 665,000	$ 670,000	$ 5,000
Operating Transfers Out	(850,000)	(850,000)	—
Total Other Financing Sources (Uses)	$ (185,000)	$ (180,000)	$ 5,000
Excess of Revenues and Other Sources over Expenditures and Other Uses	$ 898,000	$ 534,000	$ (364,000)
Fund Balance—July 1, 20X0	2,000,000	2,000,000	—
Fund Balance—June 30, 20X1	$ 2,898,000	$ 2,534,000	$ (364,000)

EXHIBIT 12.5 ILLUSTRATION OF GENERAL FUND BUDGETARY COMPARISON STATEMENT

ACCOUNTING FOR FIXED ASSETS AND LONG-TERM DEBT

Governmental funds—general fund, special revenue funds, capital projects funds, and debt service funds—use *fund accounting* to report transactions. A major difference between fund accounting and business accounting is the treatment of fixed assets and long-term debt. Recall that the emphasis in fund accounting is on revenues, expenditures, and the availability of current financial resources. Thus the balance sheet of a governmental fund focuses on current financial assets—those yet to be expended—and does not list fixed assets or long-term debt. Fixed assets cannot be expended, and long-term debt does not require the use of current financial resources. Since net increases in fund balance are defined as *inflows of current financial resources*, proceeds from the issuance of long-term debt and sale of fixed assets are shown as "other financing sources" on the statement of revenues, expenditures, and changes in fund balance of a governmental fund. Issuance of long-term debt is a net increase in current financial resources since cash increases and no other current financial resource is affected. Similarly, proceeds from the sale of fixed assets are net increases in current financial resources. Payments on long-term debt and uses of cash to acquire fixed assets are reductions in fund balance, following the same reasoning. As a result, governmental funds do not report long-term debt or fixed assets directly in the fund accounts. Because of this omission, it is necessary to disclose long-term debts and fixed assets of governmental funds in a separate location.

ACCOUNTING FOR FIXED ASSETS

To maintain control and accountability for fixed assets used by governmental funds, an inventory is kept separately, showing the nature and cost of each item of land, buildings, equipment, and improvements owned by the governmental unit. The record of these assets is called the **general fixed assets account group**. It is a set of records listing the fixed assets acquired by a state or local government through its general, special revenue, and capital projects funds. The debt service fund is not expected to acquire fixed assets.

The general fixed assets account group consists of two types of accounts. The first group is comprised of the asset accounts, which show the major classifications of fixed assets owned by a local government. Typical classifications are as follows:

Typical Fixed Asset Classifications

Land
Buildings
Improvements (for example, streets, bridges, sewer systems)
Construction in Progress (costs of uncompleted projects)
Equipment

Whether the governmental unit reports its *infrastructure assets*, such as roads, bridges, and lighting systems (the *improvements* noted above), is optional. It is an accounting policy decision, however, and must be followed consistently.

Purchased and self-constructed assets are recorded at acquisition cost, if known. Otherwise, estimated cost is used, particularly when fixed asset records are being developed long after the items were acquired. Included are assets acquired in substance under noncancellable leases, pursuant to the requirements of *SFAS 13*.[10] Donated assets are recorded at fair market value when received. These book values do not change until disposed. Depreciation is not recorded in the accounts of governmental funds, and recording depreciation in the general fixed assets account group, although permitted,[11] is rare.

The second account type in the general fixed assets account group is a set of accounts showing the specific funds through which the assets were acquired, similar to equity accounts. These fixed asset source accounts are titled as follows:

Typical Fixed Asset Sources

Investment in General Fixed Assets—General Fund
Investment in General Fixed Assets—Special Revenue Fund
Investment in General Fixed Assets—Capital Projects Fund

When fixed assets are acquired by donation, such as for example, roads deeded to a town by a developer or a building turned over to a city by the federal government, an Investment in General Fixed Assets—Donations account is used.

In summary, the sole function of the general fixed assets account group is to provide a record of fixed assets acquired by governmental funds; it has no expendable resources and thus cannot by itself acquire fixed assets. It is not a fund, only a set of accounts showing the amounts and sources of fixed assets.

Accounting for Fixed Asset Transactions

An acquisition of fixed assets by a governmental fund requires two sets of entries. The first is made in the fund itself to record the use of resources to acquire the assets. The second is made in the general fixed assets account group to record the acquisition of the assets and the source of the resources used to acquire them. For example, assume that highway equipment costing $400,000 is purchased by the general fund. The first entry, made in the *general fund*, signifies the expenditure of resources:

Books of General Fund

Expenditures	400,000	
Vouchers Payable		400,000
To record purchase of highway equipment.		

When the expenditure is for an asset "acquired" via a long term noncancellable lease, an account such as Other Financing Sources—Capital Lease is credited instead of Vouchers Payable. Because fixed asset records are not maintained in the general fund, a second entry is also made in the *general fixed assets account group* as follows:

---

[10] Financial Accounting Standards Board, "Accounting for Leases," *Statement of Financial Accounting Standards No. 13* (Stamford, CT: FASB, 1976).
[11] *Codification*, par. 1400.118.

General Fixed Assets Account Group

Equipment	400,000	
Investment in General Fixed Assets—General Fund . .		400,000

To record purchase of highway equipment by
general fund.

As previously mentioned, depreciation of fixed assets is not recorded in governmental funds and is generally not shown in the general fixed asset accounts. This aspect of fund accounting is a long-standing center of controversy. Although some argue that depreciation should be recorded in fund accounting to aid in determining the costs of governmental services, to date this position is not adopted in other than internal managerial accounting contexts.

A sale or other disposition of fixed assets also requires two sets of entries. Assume that old highway equipment, previously acquired with $150,000 of state grant funds accounted for in a special revenue fund, is now sold for $30,000, with the proceeds going to the general fund. The first entry is in the *general fund*:

Books of General Fund

Cash	30,000	
Revenues		30,000

To record proceeds from sale of equipment.

The second entry is a parallel entry in the *general fixed assets account group* that removes the previously recorded cost of the equipment:

General Fixed Assets Account Group

Investment in General Fixed Assets—Special Revenue Fund . . .	150,000	
Equipment		150,000

To record disposition of equipment originally purchased
by special revenue fund.

Note that because the fixed assets sold have no book value in the general fund, no gain or loss is recognized. Instead, the gross proceeds are treated as general fund revenues. If the asset is retired rather than sold, and no proceeds realized, no entry is made in the general fund.

Financial Statements for General Fixed Assets

The principal financial statement for the general fixed assets account group is a balance-sheet-type statement called a **Statement of General Fixed Assets**.

An illustration of this statement appears in Exhibit 12.6. In addition, a statement (or schedule in the notes) detailing the changes in general fixed assets during the year is required, as shown in Exhibit 12.7.

City of Anderson
Statement of General Fixed Assets
General Fixed Assets Account Group
December 31, 20X1

General Fixed Assets

Land	$ 40,000,000
Buildings	196,000,000
Improvements	19,000,000
Equipment	43,000,000
Total	$ 298,000,000

Investment in General Fixed Assets From

General Fund	$ 103,000,000
Special Revenue Funds	50,000,000
Capital Projects Funds	142,000,000
Special Assessments	3,000,000
Total	$ 298,000,000

EXHIBIT 12.6 ILLUSTRATION OF STATEMENT OF GENERAL FIXED ASSETS

City of Anderson
Statement of Changes in General Fixed Assets
General Fixed Assets Account Group
for the Year Ended December 31, 20X1

	Land	Buildings	Improvements	Equipment	Total
General Fixed Assets, January 1, 20X1	$ 39,100,000	$187,150,000	$ 13,370,000	$37,500,000	$ 277,120,000
Additions					
Expenditures from:					
General Fund	$ —	$ 50,000	$ —	$ 4,300,000	$ 4,350,000
Special Revenue Fund . .	600,000	600,000	30,000	700,000	1,930,000
Capital Projects Fund . . .	300,000	8,600,000	5,600,000	500,000	15,000,000
Total Additions	$ 900,000	$ 9,250,000	$ 5,630,000	$ 5,500,000	$ 21,280,000
	$ 40,000,000	$196,400,000	$ 19,000,000	$43,000,000	$ 298,400,000
Dispositions					
Capital Projects Fund	—	400,000	—	—	400,000
General Fixed Assets, December 1, 20X1 . . .	$ 40,000,000	$196,000,000	$ 19,000,000	$43,000,000	$ 298,000,000

EXHIBIT 12.7 ILLUSTRATION OF STATEMENT OF CHANGES IN GENERAL FIXED ASSETS

ACCOUNTING FOR LONG-TERM CAPITAL DEBT

Long-term debt issued by the governmental funds is excluded from the balance sheet and is reported in a separate set of accounts known as the **general long-term debt account group**. Governmental funds' long-term capital debt is often referred to as General Long-Term Obligations. This caption includes such items as bonds of various types, long-term notes payable, unfunded pension costs, and long-term liabilities for compensated absences. It also includes special assessment debt for which the governmental unit is *liable*. As was the case with general fixed assets, the general long-term debt account group is used solely to provide a record of unmatured (outstanding) debt; it does not engage in actual transactions.

The general long-term debt account group is a set of records showing (1) the *principal amounts* and description of general long-term debt, and (2) the extent of resources set aside—usually in the debt service fund—for repayment of the long-term debt *principal*. The statement format for the general long-term debt account group is as follows:

Amount Available for Repayment of Long-Term Debt	XX	Serial Bonds Payable	XX
Amount to be Provided for the		Term Bonds Payable	XX
Repayment of Long-Term Debt	XX		

Note that the general long-term debt account group lists the *principal* of the debt only. Also, the account group contains *no actual resources* accumulated to repay the debt. The actual accumulation of resources for repayment of the debt is typically found in the debt service fund, discussed in Chapter 13.

Accounting for Long-Term Capital Debt Transactions

Incurrence of long-term capital debt by a governmental fund requires two sets of entries. The first is in the fund issuing the debt and spending the proceeds. The second is in the general long-term debt account group. The following example uses long-term bonds to illustrate the accounting; similar procedures are employed for other types of long-term debt.

Assume that $3,000,000 of long-term bonds are issued by the general fund to finance a service project. The first entry records the receipt of proceeds of the bond issue in the *general fund*:

Books of General Fund

Cash	3,000,000	
Bond Proceeds		3,000,000
To record proceeds of bond issue.		

As mentioned previously, bond proceeds are not considered revenue; rather, they are reported as "other financing sources" on the statement of revenues, expenditures, and changes in fund balance.

In addition to the entry in the general fund, a second entry to record the bond liability and the amount of resources required to repay the bond liability is made in the *general long-term debt account group*:

General Long-Term Debt Account Group

Amount to Be Provided for Repayment of Bonds	3,000,000	
Bonds Payable		3,000,000
To record bonds issued by general fund.		

The general long-term debt account group records only the amount of principal of the debt. Interest obligations are not shown, nor is any premium or discount on the original issue.

As resources are set aside in the debt service fund for eventual repayment of the bonds, an entry is needed in the general long-term debt account group to signify that these resources are *available* and no longer need *to be provided* in the future. To illustrate, suppose that in a given year $150,000 was appropriated in the general fund budget for transfer to the debt service fund, where it is held and invested for future debt principal repayments. The entry in the *general fund* is as follows:

Books of General Fund

Operating Transfers Out	150,000	
Cash		150,000
To record transfer to debt service fund.		

The *debt service fund* records receipt of the transfer with the following entry:

Books of Debt Service Fund

Cash	150,000	
Operating Transfers In		150,000
To record transfer from general fund for future		
debt principal payments.		

Finally, the entry in the *general long-term debt account group* is as follows:

General Long-Term Debt Account Group

Amount Available for Repayment of Bonds	150,000	
Amount to Be Provided for Repayment of Bonds . . .		150,000
To record resources set aside in the debt service fund		
for future principal payments.		

Repayment of long-term debt also requires two sets of entries. Assume that $500,000 of long-term bonds mature this year, and that resources are accumulated in the debt service fund to retire these bonds. The following entry is made in the *debt service fund*:

Books of Debt Service Fund

Expenditures	500,000	
Cash		500,000
To record payment of principal of matured bonds.		

The entry in the *general long-term debt account group* is as follows:

General Long-Term Debt Account Group

Bonds Payable	500,000	
Amount Available for Repayment of Bonds		500,000
To record retirement of matured bonds.		

Financial Statements for General Long-Term Debt

A **Statement of General Long-Term Debt** presents balance sheet-type information on long-term debt at year-end. On the credit side, the statement displays General Long-Term Obligations—

unmatured debt such as term and serial bonds payable, capitalized lease obligations, and accrued sick leave. On the debit side, the two accounts—Amount Available for Repayment of Long-Term Debt and Amount to Be Provided for Repayment of Long-Term Debt—are reported and broken down according to the various categories of unmatured general long-term obligations. An example of such a statement is presented in Exhibit 12.8. The GASB *Codification* requires that changes in the various categories of long-term debt be disclosed in a schedule in the notes to the financial statements or in a separate Statement of Changes in General Long-Term Debt. Not illustrated here, this disclosure shows beginning balances, new issues, retirements, other changes, and ending balances in the various categories of long-term debt.

Blackstone County
Statement of General Long-Term Debt
June 30, 20X0

Amount Available for Repayment of Serial Bonds	$ 453,000
Amount to Be Provided for Repayment of Serial Bonds	9,184,000
Total	$ 9,637,000
Serial Bonds Payable	$ 9,637,000

EXHIBIT 12.8 ILLUSTRATION OF STATEMENT OF GENERAL LONG-TERM DEBT

COMPREHENSIVE ILLUSTRATION OF GENERAL FUND ACCOUNTING AND REPORTING

The following illustration incorporates assumed data for Ranford County. Ranford County follows the *GAAP budgetary basis*, uses the *consumption method* for supplies inventory and designates a portion of the fund balance as *Reserved for Supplies Inventory*. Assume that the fiscal year for the Ranford County general fund is the calendar year. On January 1, 20X2, the accounts of the general fund had the following balances:

Ranford County
Trial Balance
January 1, 20X2

Accounts	Debit	Credit
Cash	$ 80,000	
Taxes Receivable—Delinquent	15,000	
Allowance for Uncollectible Taxes—Delinquent		$ 15,000
Due from Special Revenue Fund	10,000	
Supplies Inventory	5,000	
Vouchers Payable		5,000
Fund Balance—Unreserved		83,000
Fund Balance—Reserved for Supplies Inventory		5,000
Fund Balance—Reserved for Encumbrances		2,000
	$ 110,000	$ 110,000

The 20X2 general fund budget included revenues from the following sources:

Property Taxes (95% of Amount Levied)	$ 190,000
State Aid	30,000
Fees and Licenses	8,000
Charges for Services	12,000
Miscellaneous	7,000
Total Estimated Revenues	$ 247,000

Expenditures for 20X2 were estimated to be:

General Services	$ 180,000
Supplies	18,000
Maintenance	14,000
Miscellaneous	6,000
Total Appropriations	$ 218,000

In addition, the county decided to establish an internal service fund to provide supplies used by the general fund and the special revenue fund. A permanent residual equity transfer of $20,000 from the general fund was authorized to enable the internal service fund to purchase the initial supplies inventory. For the first year of operation the general fund plans an $8,000 operating transfer to help defray the operating costs of the internal service fund.

Transactions during the Year

The events and transactions occurring during the year were recorded by Ranford County as follows:

1. The budget was recorded on January 2 as follows:

Estimated Revenues	247,000	
Appropriations		218,000
Estimated Other Financing Uses		8,000
Estimated Residual Equity Transfers Out		20,000
Fund Balance—Unreserved		1,000

   To record 20X2 budget.

2. Taxes were levied:

Taxes Receivable—Current	200,000	
Allowance for Uncollectible Taxes—Current		10,000
Revenues		190,000

   To record property tax levy, estimated to be
   95 percent collectible.

3. The county received $30,000 in state aid:

Cash	30,000	
Revenues		30,000

   To record aid received from state government.

4. Fully reserved delinquent taxes of $4,000 were received; the remainder of 20X1 taxes were reclassified as tax liens:

Cash	4,000	
Allowance for Uncollectible Taxes—Delinquent	4,000	
Taxes Receivable—Delinquent		4,000
Revenues		4,000
To record collection of delinquent taxes.		

Tax Liens Receivable	11,000	
Allowance for Uncollectible Taxes—Delinquent	11,000	
Allowance for Uncollectible Tax Liens		11,000
Taxes Receivable—Delinquent		11,000
To reclassify uncollected delinquent taxes as tax liens and to fully reserve tax liens.		

5. The internal service fund was established, and the $28,000 authorized was transferred from the general fund:

Residual Equity Transfers Out	20,000	
Cash		20,000
To record permanent capital (*residual equity*) transfer to establish the internal service fund.		

Operating Transfers Out	8,000	
Cash		8,000
To record authorized subsidy of internal service fund operating costs.		

6. Ranford County follows the *GAAP budgetary basis* and treats encumbrances outstanding at year-end accordingly. For the miscellaneous amounts encumbered for $2,000 but not received in 20X1, the bill received in 20X2 was $1,800. It was paid in cash.

Encumbrances	2,000	
Fund Balance—Unreserved		2,000
To restore encumbrances carried over from 20X1.		

Fund Balance—Reserved for Encumbrances	2,000	
Encumbrances		2,000
To reverse encumbrances.		

Expenditures	1,800	
Cash		1,800
To record expenditures.		

7. Revenues of $27,600 were received as follows: $8,500 from fees and licenses, $11,800 from charges for services, and $7,300 from miscellaneous sources:

Cash	27,600	
Revenues		27,600
To record revenues.		

8. Supplies of $18,000 were ordered from the internal service fund:

Encumbrances	18,000	
Fund Balance—Reserved for Encumbrances		18,000
To record supplies ordered.		

9. Expenditures of cash were $6,200 for miscellaneous purchases and $40,000 for general services. Orders were issued for maintenance services, $14,000; for general services, $135,000.

Expenditures	46,200	
Cash		46,200
To record cash expenditures.		

Encumbrances	149,000	
Fund Balance—Reserved for Encumbrances		149,000
To record encumbrances for goods and services ordered.		

10. Supplies ordered in 8. were received and the internal service fund was paid cash of $18,000. Ranford County follows the *consumption method* of accounting for inventory expenditures.

Fund Balance—Reserved for Encumbrances	18,000	
Encumbrances		18,000
To reverse encumbrances.		

Supplies Inventory	18,000	
Cash		18,000
To record payment for supplies.		

11. Current taxes of $183,000 were collected:

Cash	183,000	
Taxes Receivable—Current		183,000
To record collection of current taxes.		

12. Invoices for goods and services ordered in 9. and received were maintenance, $14,000, and general services, $137,000. The total vouchers paid in 20X2 amounted to $152,000.

Fund Balance—Reserved for Encumbrances	149,000	
Encumbrances		149,000
To reverse encumbrances.		

Expenditures	151,000	
Vouchers Payable		151,000
To record expenditures.		

Vouchers Payable	152,000	
Cash		152,000
To record payment of vouchers outstanding.		

13. Goods to be used in providing general services were ordered late in December but were not received in 20X2. The anticipated price of the goods was $1,300.

Encumbrances	1,300	
Fund Balance—Reserved for Encumbrances		1,300
To record encumbrances for goods ordered.		

14. Cash of $10,000 was received from the special revenue fund as repayment of a loan made in 20X1:

Cash	10,000	
Due from Special Revenue Fund		10,000
To record repayment of loan.		

15. The year-end count of supplies showed that inventory acquired at a cost of $7,000 was on hand; expenditures for supplies used of $16,000 (= $5,000 + $18,000 − $7,000) are recorded and the reserve maintained by Ranford County is increased to $7,000 from $5,000.

Expenditures	16,000	
Supplies Inventory		16,000
To record cost of supplies used during 20X2.		

Fund Balance—Unreserved	2,000	
Fund Balance—Reserved for Supplies Inventory ...		2,000
To adjust supplies inventory and reserved		
portion of fund balance from $5,000 beginning		
balance to $7,000 ending balance.		

16. Taxes uncollected at year-end were classified delinquent and fully reserved:

Revenues	7,000	
Taxes Receivable—Delinquent	17,000	
Allowance for Uncollectible Taxes—Current	10,000	
Taxes Receivable—Current		17,000
Allowance for Uncollectible Taxes—Delinquent ...		17,000
To reclassify uncollected taxes as delinquent and fully		
reserved, and to reduce revenues by the amount		
uncollected in excess of the estimated uncollectibles.		

The preclosing trial balance for Ranford County at December 31, 20X2, appears as follows:

Ranford County
Preclosing Trial Balance
December 31, 20X2

Account	Debit	Credit
Cash	$ 88,600	
Taxes Receivable—Delinquent	17,000	
Tax Liens Receivable	11,000	
Supplies Inventory	7,000	
Encumbrances	1,300	
Expenditures	215,000	
Operating Transfers Out	8,000	
Estimated Revenues	247,000	
Residual Equity Transfers Out	20,000	
Vouchers Payable		$ 4,000
Revenues		244,600
Appropriations		218,000
Estimated Other Financing Uses		8,000
Estimated Residual Equity Transfers		20,000
Allowance for Uncollectible Taxes—Delinquent		17,000
Allowance for Uncollectible Tax Liens		11,000
Fund Balance—Reserved for Supplies Inventory		7,000
Fund Balance—Reserved for Encumbrances		1,300
Fund Balance—Unreserved		84,000
	$ 614,900	$ 614,900

The county's subsidiary records show the detail of the revenue and expenditure accounts as follows:

Revenues

Property Taxes	$ 187,000
State Aid	30,000
Fees and Licenses	8,500
Charges for Services	11,800
Miscellaneous	7,300
Total Revenues	$ 244,600

Expenditures

General Services	$ 177,000
Maintenance	14,000
Supplies	16,000
Miscellaneous	8,000
Total Expenditures	$ 215,000

Closing Entries

Closing entries at December 31, 20X2, are as follows:

Revenues	244,600	
Fund Balance—Unreserved	2,400	
Estimated Revenues		247,000
To close revenues.		
Appropriations	218,000	
Expenditures		215,000
Encumbrances		1,300
Fund Balance—Unreserved		1,700
To close expenditures and encumbrances.		
Estimated Other Financing Uses	8,000	
Operating Transfers Out		8,000
To close operating transfers.		
Estimated Residual Equity Transfers	20,000	
Residual Equity Transfers Out		20,000
To close residual equity transfers.		

Financial Statements

The financial statements for the general fund of Ranford County can now be prepared. The balance sheet appears in Exhibit 12.9.

Ranford County
Balance Sheet—General Fund
December 31, 20X2

Assets

Cash	$	88,600
Taxes Receivable—Delinquent (net of $17,000 allowance for uncollectible taxes)		—
Taxes Liens Receivable (net of $11,000 allowance for uncollectible tax liens)		—
Supplies Inventory		7,000
Total Assets	$	95,600

Liabilities and Fund Balance

Liabilities:

Vouchers Payable	$	4,000
Total Liabilities	$	4,000

Fund Balance:

Reserved for Supplies Inventory	$	7,000
Reserved for Encumbrances		1,300
Unreserved		83,300
	$	91,600
Total Fund Balance	$	95,600
Total Liabilities and Fund Balance		

EXHIBIT 12.9 BALANCE SHEET OF RANFORD COUNTY

Note that the delinquent taxes receivable and tax liens receivable are both fully reserved, signifying that no revenues are anticipated from these sources.

The statement of revenues, expenditures, and changes in the general fund balance is presented in Exhibit 12.10. The total fund balance—unreserved fund balance plus the reserved portions—appears on this statement. Because the *consumption method* was used for the supplies inventory, only supplies used during the year are included in expenditures. The effect of the increase in the reserve account was to transfer $2,000 to the reserve account from the unreserved fund balance with no change in the total fund balance.

**Ranford County
Statement of Revenues, Expenditures, and
Changes in Fund Balance—General Fund
for the Fiscal Year Ended December 31, 20X2**

Revenues

Property Taxes	$ 187,000
State Aid	30,000
Fees and Licenses	8,500
Charges for Services	11,800
Miscellaneous	7,300
Total Revenues	$ 244,600

Expenditures

General Services	$ 177,000
Maintenance	14,000
Supplies	16,000
Miscellaneous	8,000
	$ 215,000
Total Expenditures	$ 29,600
Excess of Revenues over Expenditures	

Other Financing Sources (Uses)

Operating Transfers Out	$ (8,000)
	$ (8,000)
Total Other Financing Sources (Uses)	$ 21,600
Excess of Revenues and Other Sources over Expenditures and Other Uses	$ 90,000[a]
Fund Balance—January 1	20,000
Less: Residual Equity Transfer	$ 70,000
Adjusted Fund Balance—January 1	$ 91,600
Fund Balance—December 31	

[a] Unreserved Fund Balance	$ 83,000	
Reserved for Supplies Inventory	5,000	
Reserved for Encumbrances	2,000	
	$ 90,000	

EXHIBIT 12.10   STATEMENT OF REVENUES, EXPENDITURES, AND CHANGES IN FUND BALANCE OF RANFORD COUNTY

The budgetary comparison statement for Ranford County appears in Exhibit 12.11. It is prepared on the *GAAP budgetary basis*.

Ranford County
Statement of Revenues, Expenditures and Changes
in Fund Balance—Budget and Actual—General Fund
for the Fiscal Year Ended December 31, 20X2

Revenues	Budget	Actual	Variance—Favorable (Unfavorable)
Property Taxes	$ 190,000	$ 187,000	$ (3,000)
State Aid	30,000	30,000	—
Fees and Licenses	8,000	8,500	500
Charges for Services	12,000	11,800	(200)
Miscellaneous	7,000	7,300	300
Total Revenues	$ 247,000	$ 244,600	$ (2,400)
Expenditures			
General Services	$ 180,000	$ 177,000	$ 3,000
Maintenance	14,000	14,000	—
Supplies	18,000	16,000	2,000
Miscellaneous	6,000	8,000	(2,000)
	$ 218,000	$ 215,000	$ 3,000
Total Expenditures	$ 29,000	$ 29,600	$ 600
Excess of Revenues over (under) Expenditures			
Other Financing Sources (Uses)			
Operating Transfers Out	(8,000)	(8,000)	—
	$ (8,000)	$ (8,000)	$ —
Total Other Financing Sources (Uses) .			
Excess of Revenues and Other Sources	$ 21,000	$ 21,600	$ 600
over Expenditures and Other Uses	$ 90,000	$ 90,000	—
Fund Balance—January 1	20,000	20,000	—
Less: Residual Equity Transfer	$ 70,000	$ 70,000	$ —
Adjusted Fund Balance—January 1	$ 91,000	$ 91,600	$ 600
Fund Balance—December 31			

EXHIBIT 12.11   BUDGETARY COMPARISON STATEMENT FOR RANFORD COUNTY

SUMMARY OF KEY CONCEPTS

State and local governments differ in many ways from for-profit enterprises. Resources are derived from taxes, fees, fines and debt financing. A **legal budget** limits expenditures. The main purpose of the government is to provide services to the citizenry.

External users of governmental financial statements include **credit market representatives**, **elected officials**, and **citizens**. Credit market representatives use the financial statements to judge the governmental unit's ability to generate resources to fund required interest and principal payments. Citizens and legislators are concerned with services provided, and how current activities and plans affect future taxes and ability to provide services.

The **Governmental Accounting Standards Board (GASB)** sets accounting requirements for state and local governmental external reporting. The emphasis in external reporting is on **stewardship**. The governmental unit is made up of several accounting entities known as **funds**, which correspond to the major activities of the unit. Seven standard fund types and two account groups exist, some or all of which may be used by the particular governmental unit. Determination of the appropriate **reporting entity** is based on whether **financial accountability** exists.

The general, special revenue, capital projects, and debt service funds are known as **governmental funds**. These funds focus on sources, uses, and balances of **current financial resources** available to fund current expenditures, and use a method of accounting we call **fund accounting**. Fund accounting is characterized by use of the modified accrual basis for recording revenues and expenditures, and by recognition of **encumbrances** and inclusion of **budgetary accounts**. Required financial statements of governmental funds are the **statement of revenues, expenditures, and changes in fund balance**, the **balance sheet**, and the **budgetary comparison statement**.

The enterprise and internal service funds are known as **proprietary funds** because they are used to conduct business-type activities. Proprietary funds focus on determination of net income, financial position, and cash flows, and follow **accrual accounting** as used in business. Required financial statements of proprietary funds are the **statement of revenues, expenses and changes in retained earnings**, the **balance sheet**, and the **cash flow statement**.

The trust and agency funds are known as **fiduciary funds**. Nonexpendable trust funds generally follow **fiduciary accounting**, since they must separately report principal and income transactions. Expendable trust funds use modified accrual accounting. Agency funds record only assets and liabilities, and do not recognize fund equity.

Under the **modified accrual basis of accounting**, revenues are defined as **inflows of current financial resources**, excluding borrowings and transfers from other funds. Revenues are recognized when they are **measurable** and **available to finance expenditures in the current period**. Expenditures are recognized when they are **measurable** and the **related liability is incurred**, as long as the expenditure is likely to be paid in the current period.

Inventories of supplies can be accounted for by the **consumption method**, which recognizes expenditures when the supplies are used, or by the **purchases method**, which recognizes expenditures when the supplies are purchased.

Alternative treatments also exist for **encumbrances outstanding at year-end**, depending on the **budgetary basis** used by the governmental unit. Under the **GAAP budgetary basis**, expenditures—including those related to carryover encumbrances—are charged against the budget for the year the expenditures are made. Under the **legal budgetary basis**, expenditures are charged against the budget for the year the encumbrances are made. Expenditures related to carryover encumbrances adjust the beginning fund balance.

Fixed assets acquired by the general fund and by other governmental funds are recorded in the **general fixed assets account group**. Depreciation is not recorded in governmental funds; amounts paid to acquire fixed assets are shown as reductions in fund balance. **Long-term liabilities** incurred by the general fund and by other governmental funds are recorded in the **general long-term debt account group**, along with the amount of resources currently available and the amount to be provided in the future to retire the liabilities. Proceeds from issuance of long-term debt are recorded in the governmental funds as additions to fund balance.

QUESTIONS

Q12.1 Identifying the financial reporting entity in state and local government accounting has been the subject of much controversy over the years. Reporting entity possibilities range from individual funds to multiple legal entities. Briefly discuss the issues that arise when evaluating whether a more inclusive reporting entity is appropriate.

Q12.2 Governmental accounting uses both business and fund accounting along with some fiduciary accounting principles in certain situations. The GASB uses the concept of *measurement focus* to guide selection among accounting methods. Define *measurement focus* and briefly explain the measurement focus behind each of the two types of accounting used in local government.

Q12.3 Select the best answer for each of the following questions:

1. Under the modified accrual method of accounting used by a local governmental unit, which of the following is a revenue most susceptible to accrual?
   a. Income taxes.
   b. Business licenses.
   c. Property taxes.
   d. Sales taxes.
2. Within a local governmental unit, two funds that are accounted for in a manner similar to a business entity are
   a. General and debt service.
   b. Enterprise and general.
   c. Enterprise and trust and agency.
   d. Internal service and enterprise.
3. When used in fund accounting, the term *fund* usually refers to
   a. A sum of money designated for a special purpose.
   b. A liability to other governmental units.
   c. The equity of a municipality in its own assets.
   d. A fiscal and accounting entity having a set of self-balancing accounts.
      (*AICPA adapted*)

Q12.4 Identify the major readers of external governmental financial statements. What are the main interests of each group? What types of financial information are useful to each group?

Q12.5 Why are balance sheets of the governmental funds that use fund accounting unclassified as to current and noncurrent items?

Q12.6 Property taxes are the most significant revenue source in local government. If 5% of levied taxes are expected to be uncollectible, calculate the size of the property tax levy needed to produce tax revenue of $1,140,000.

Q12.7 Explain the difference between temporary and permanent interfund transfers and give an example of each type.

Q12.8 What is the effect of each of the following on the fund balance? (Answer "increase," "decrease," or "no effect.")

1. Budgeted expenditures exceed budgeted revenues.
2. Budgeted revenues exceed budgeted expenditures.
3. Actual revenues equal budgeted revenues.
4. Actual expenditures exceed budgeted expenditures.

Q12.9 Select the best answer for each of the following questions:

1. Which of the following accounts is a budgetary account?
   a. Vouchers Payable.
   b. Expenditures.
   c. Encumbrances.
   d. Fund Balance.
2. A town issues purchase orders of $630,000 to vendors and suppliers. Which of the following entries should be made to record this transaction?

		Debit	Credit
a.	Encumbrances	630,000	
	Fund Balance—Reserved for Encumbrances .		630,000
b.	Expenditures	630,000	
	Vouchers Payable		630,000
c.	Expenses	630,000	
	Accounts Payable		630,000
d.	Fund Balance—Reserved for Encumbrances	630,000	
	Encumbrances		630,000

3. If a credit was made to the fund balance in the process of recording a budget for a local governmental unit, it can be assumed that
   a. Budgeted expenditures exceed actual revenues.
   b. Actual expenditures exceed budgeted expenditures.
   c. Budgeted revenues exceed budgeted expenditures.
   d. Budgeted expenditures exceed budgeted revenues.
   (AICPA adapted)

Q12.10 Select the best answer for each of the following multiple choice questions:

1. A city's general fund budget for the forthcoming fiscal year shows estimated revenues in excess of appropriations. The initial effect of recording this results in an increase in
    a. Taxes receivable.
    b. Fund balance—unreserved.
    c. Fund balance—reserved for encumbrances.
    d. Encumbrances.
2. In the current year, what is the effect on the general fund balance of recording a $15,000 purchase for a new fire truck out of general fund resources, for which a $14,600 encumbrance was recorded in the general fund in the previous year, using the legal budgetary basis?
    a. Reduce the general fund balance by $15,000.
    b. Reduce the general fund balance by $14,600.
    c. Reduce the general fund balance by $400.
    d. Have no effect on the general fund balance.
3. In preparing the general fund budget of Brockton City for the forthcoming fiscal year, the city council appropriated a sum greater than expected revenues. This action of the council results in
    a. A cash overdraft during the fiscal year.
    b. An increase in encumbrances by the end of that fiscal year.
    c. A decrease in the fund balance.
    d. An increase in the fund balance.
        (AICPA adapted)

Q12.11 Select the best answer for each of the following multiple choice questions:

1. Which of the following should be accrued as revenues by the general fund of a local government?
    a. Sales taxes held by the state to be remitted to the local government.
    b. Parking meter revenues.
    c. Sales taxes collected by merchants.
    d. Income taxes currently due.
2. Which of the following types of revenue is generally recorded directly in the general fund of a governmental unit?
    a. Receipts from a city-owned parking structure.
    b. Property taxes.
    c. Interest earned on investments held for retirement of employees.
    d. Revenues of internal service funds.
        (AICPA adapted)

Q12.12 Select the best answer for each of the following multiple choice questions:

1. Authority granted by a legislative body to make expenditures and to incur obligations during a fiscal year is the definition of an
    a. Appropriation.
    b. Estimated revenue.
    c. Encumbrance.
    d. Expenditure.

   2. What type of account is used to earmark the fund balance to liquidate the contingent obligations for goods ordered but not yet received?
      a. Appropriations.
      b. Encumbrances.
      c. Expenditures.
      d. Fund balance—reserved for encumbrances.
   3. The Fund Balance—Reserved for Encumbrances (Prior Year) account represents amounts recorded by a government unit for
      a. Anticipated expenditures in the next year.
      b. Anticipated expenditures for which purchase orders were made in the prior year but disbursement will be in the current year.
      c. Excess expenditures in the prior year to be offset against the current year budgeted amounts.
      d. Unanticipated expenditures of the prior year that become evident in the current year.
      (AICPA adapted)

Q12.13 Identify the financial statements required by each of the following fund types:

   1. governmental funds
   2. proprietary funds

   Why are different statements required for each fund type?

Q12.14 For each of the following activities of a governmental unit, identify the fund type typically used to account for the activity.

   1. Expenditures for primary services for which no fee is charged, such as education, public safety, and social services.
   2. Construction of a building.
   3. Accumulation of resources for repayment of general obligation long-term debt.
   4. Services for which a fee, representing the estimated cost of the service, is collected from the public.
   5. Accumulation of federal taxes withheld from the paychecks of county workers.
   6. Collection of property taxes by the county, used to fund primary services.

EXERCISES

E12.1 Identify Fund and Type of Accounting Following are several common activities or financial events in which a local government may participate:

   1. Operations of a public library receiving the majority of its support from property taxes levied for that purpose.
   2. Proceeds of a federal grant made to assist in financing the future construction of an adult training center.
   3. Operations of a municipal swimming pool receiving the majority of its support from charges to users.

4. Monthly remittance to an insurance company of the lump sum of hospital/surgical insurance premiums collected as payroll deductions from employees.

5. Activities of a central motor pool which provides and services vehicles for the use of municipal employees on official business.

6. Activities of a municipal employee retirement plan financed by equal employer and employee contributions.

7. Collections of property taxes for the benefit of local sanitary, park, and school districts. The collections are periodically remitted to these units.

8. Activities of a street improvement project financed by requiring each owner of property facing the street to pay a proportionate share of the total cost.

9. Activities of a central print shop offering printing services at cost to various city departments.

10. Transactions of a municipal police retirement system.

11. Activities of a municipal golf course that receives three-fourths of its total revenue from a special tax levy.

12. Self-supporting activities of government provided on a user-charge basis.

13. Activities of a data-processing center established to service all agencies within a governmental unit.

REQUIRED: For each of the above, indicate the type of fund in which the activity should be recorded by a local government and the type of accounting (business, fiduciary, or fund) that should be followed.
(AICPA adapted)

E12.2 **Identify Fund(s) and Account Group(s)** Each of the following transactions relates to a city government:

1. A sinking fund is set up to accumulate and invest resources for the retirement of a general bond issue which matures in ten years.

2. The city receives a $50,000 grant from the federal government to institute a meal delivery program for senior citizens.

3. New curbing is being installed in a section of the city with resources initially provided by the general fund. No debt is issued. Residents of that section will pay for the cost of the curbing with an additional charge on their property tax bill during each of the next ten years.

4. Same as No. 3, except that initial financing will be provided by issuing bonds for which the city is (a) liable or (b) not liable.

5. To remedy a flooding problem, the city plans a new drainage system in the southern part of the city. It is decided to finance this project by a general bond issue.

6. The city establishes a retirement fund for its fire fighters. Each year, 8 percent of the fire fighters' wages is set aside by the city. The city administers the investment of funds and the payment of benefits.

7. Same as No. 6, except that the city pays a premium to an insurance company, which is fully responsible for investment of funds and benefit payments.

8. The city set up a computer services division to handle payroll and other functions for all city agencies. Each agency is billed by the computer services division for the work done for that agency.

9. Fifteen new police cars are purchased, as provided in the general budget.

10. State aid funds are received. These funds may be used for any of the general operations of the city.
11. The city deducts federal income taxes from its employees' wages and periodically remits them to the federal government.

REQUIRED: Identify the fund(s) and account group(s) affected by each of the above.

E12.3 **Property Tax Rate and Revenues** Local government property taxes are based on the *millage rate* (= tax per $1,000 of assessed valuation) and the assessed valuation of property within the government's jurisdiction. County authorities anticipate appropriations of $600,000 and revenue from the state and other sources to be $80,000. During the last fiscal year, the tax rate was 55 mills applied to property assessed at $8 million. Uncollectible property taxes are negligible.

In the current year, the county's reassessment program caused the aggregate assessed value of property to increase to $8.5 million.

REQUIRED:

1. Compute the property tax revenue raised during the last fiscal year.
2. Compute the millage rate needed to balance the current budget.
3. Assume that the county charter requires a balanced budget and that increasing the millage rate is politically unacceptable. Compute the maximum amount of appropriations that can be funded by property taxes given the increase in assessed valuation.

E12.4 **Computing Available Funds** As the newly-hired assistant controller for the City of Daulton, you are working diligently to unravel the mysteries of governmental accounting. On your desk this morning is a memorandum from the controller asking you to advise her of the amount of available funds. Traditionally, at the end of the fiscal period, every effort is made to spend the full budget in order to avoid a lower budget next year.

After consulting your assistant and the city treasurer, you begin to analyze the following information.

Cash in Bank	$ 38,500
Estimated Revenue	3,100,000
Budgetary Surplus	(100,000)
Revenue	(2,800,000)
Expenditures	2,000,000
Short-term Notes Payable	(280,000)
Fund Balance—Reserved for Encumbrances	(200,000)
Fund Balance—Unreserved	(740,000)

REQUIRED:

1. Calculate the funds available to be encumbered.
2. Suppose only one month remains in the current fiscal period. Operating costs occur evenly throughout the year with no large lumpy items such as an annual maintenance program. Do you expect to see an effort to cut next period's budget? Why?

E12.5 Reconstruct Budget Entry, Compute Fund Balance The following information relates to actual revenues and expenditures for the town of Greenwood:

Revenues	Actual	Over (under) Budget
Property Taxes	$ 3,000,000	$ 150,000
Fines	6,000	6,000
Intergovernmental	12,000	—
Sale of Services	500,000	(75,000)
Miscellaneous	4,000	(1,000)
Expenditures		
Services	2,050,000	55,000
Supplies	500,000	(76,000)
Other	950,000	32,000

REQUIRED:

1. What budget entry was made at the beginning of the year?
2. If the fund balance *before* the budget entry was $2,100,000, what is the fund balance after year-end closing entries?

E12.6 Recording Transactions and Closing Entries The January 1, 20X7, balance sheet for the single fund of the village of Owen is as follows:

Village of Owen
Fund Balance Sheet
January 1, 20X7

Cash	$ 30,000	Vouchers Payable	$ 43,000
Receivables	20,000	Fund Balance	7,000
		Total Liabilities and	
Total Assets	$ 50,000	Fund Balance	$ 50,000

Transactions for the village during 20X7 were as follows:

1. The village council approved a budget estimating revenues of $41,000 in property taxes and $10,000 in user charges. Property taxes are accrued on Owen's books. The budget authorized expenditures of $51,000.
2. Receivables of $18,500 from last year were collected. Of the 20X7 tax levy, $26,500 was collected.
3. Encumbrances of $50,300 were recorded. On December 31, 20X7, purchase orders of $13,000 were outstanding.
4. Bills received exceeded the amounts encumbered by $200.
5. Checks for $44,000 were mailed in payment of vouchers. No payments were made without vouchers.
6. User charges of $11,000 were collected.

REQUIRED:

1. Prepare the journal entries to record the transactions during 20X7.
2. Prepare closing entries at December 31, 20X7.
3. Compute the unreserved fund balance at December 31, 20X7.

E12.7 Property Tax Transactions On July 10, Marchville levied property taxes of $2,500,000. Based on past experience, city management estimated that the city will be unable to collect 4 percent of the taxes. Taxes were due September 30, but $800,000 was received before that date from taxpayers taking advantage of the 1-percent discount for early payment. Marchville treats discounts given as a reduction of revenues.

On January 1, outstanding taxes due of $150,000 were declared delinquent and were fully reserved. By the end of the fiscal year, 40 percent of the delinquent taxes were collected. There were no taxes receivable, either current or delinquent, at the beginning of the fiscal year.

Actual expenditures were $2,000,000, the same amount as appropriations. All expenditures were cash transactions. The budget entry included $2,400,000 of estimated revenues. After the budget entry, the fund balance was $472,000.

REQUIRED:

1. Prepare the journal entries to record the property tax transactions.
2. State the balance sheet accounts and their respective balances relating to the property tax levy and collections as of the end of the fiscal year. Assume that the cash balance at the beginning of the fiscal year was $93,000.

E12.8 Inventory Accounting and Financial Position Starton City reported a physical inventory costing $90,000 at the beginning of the fiscal year. During the year, Starton purchased materials and supplies on account for $165,000; $45,000 remains unpaid at year-end. Materials and supplies costing $105,000 are on hand at the end of the fiscal year. *Excluding the effects of the materials and supplies transactions and related balances*, Starton's ending post-closing trial balance shows the following condensed balances:

Current Assets	$ 550,000
Current Liabilities	300,000
Total Fund Balance	250,000

REQUIRED:

1. Prepare the summary journal entries made this year under the two allowable methods used by governmental funds to account for materials and supplies inventories.
2. Show, with calculations if needed, whether the above balances and Starton's current ratio and total liabilities/total assets ratio are affected differentially by the methods used in 1.

E12.9 **Closing Entries** The Newberry County budget for the 20X7 fiscal year included estimates of revenues of $3,501,000 and appropriations of $3,449,000.

REQUIRED: Prepare the closing entries for 20X7 under each of the following independent assumptions:

1. Actual revenues and expenditures equaled estimates.
2. Actual revenues were as expected, but actual expenditures exceeded estimates by $22,000.
3. Actual revenues of $3,500,000 equaled actual expenditures.
4. The net effect of the closing entries on the fund balance was zero. Actual revenues were $3,576,000.

E12.10 **Carryover Encumbrances** The December 31, 20X0, balance sheet for the special revenue fund of Burnville showed $19,000 reserved for encumbrances. This figure represented $11,000 encumbered for office equipment and $8,000 for supplies. Early in 20X1, the equipment and supplies were delivered and bills received for $11,700 and $7,950, respectively.

REQUIRED: Prepare the journal entries for 20X1 relating to these events, using (1) the legal budgetary basis and (2) the GAAP budgetary basis.

E12.11 **Interfund Transactions** Interfund transfers of the general fund of North Weston City for 20X7 were as follows:

	Inflows	Outflows
1. To the special revenue fund to permit initial expenditures under a project to be fully supported by a federal grant		$ 18,000
2. To a capital projects fund as the city's contribution to a street lighting project		25,000
3. From the capital projects fund, unspent proceeds of a bond issue	$ 7,000	
4. To the enterprise fund as city's cost of services provided		12,000
5. To the internal service fund to finance temporarily a purchase of supplies		35,000
6. From the special revenue fund to repay advance .	18,000	

REQUIRED: What asset and liability accounts appear on the 20X7 general fund balance sheet as a result of these transfers?

E12.12   Adjusting and Closing Entries, Balance Sheet The preclosing trial balance for the general fund of Graystone is given below:

Cash	$ 350,000
Taxes Receivable—Current	80,000
Allowance for Uncollectible Taxes—Current	(45,000)
Estimated Revenues	1,300,000
Expenditures	1,050,000
Expenditures—Prior Year Encumbrances	42,000
Encumbrances	30,000
Due from Other Funds	12,000
	$ 2,819,000

Vouchers Payable	$ 180,000
Due to Other Funds	21,000
Revenues	1,400,000
Appropriations	1,100,000
Fund Balance—Reserved for Encumbrances	30,000
Fund Balance—Reserved for Encumbrances (Prior Year)	45,000
Fund Balance—Unreserved	43,000
	$ 2,819,000

Additional information:

1. At year-end, all uncollected taxes are deemed delinquent. Delinquent taxes are fully reserved.
2. A physical count of inventory revealed $25,000 of supplies on hand. Graystone uses the purchases method and discloses inventory available in the body of its financial statement.

REQUIRED:

1. Prepare all year-end adjusting and closing entries for the general fund of Graystone.
2. Prepare a year-end balance sheet for the general fund of Graystone.

E12.13   Fixed Asset and Long-Term Debt Transactions The city of Margate's accounting system includes all funds and account groups prescribed by GASB standards. During the current year, the following transactions occurred.

1. New fire-fighting equipment was acquired by the general fund at a cost of $225,000.
2. Old fire-fighting equipment acquired ten years ago for $150,000 was sold for $37,000.
3. Cash of $350,000 was transferred from the general fund to the debt service fund.
4. Using the cash transferred in 3. above, the debt service fund immediately paid interest and principal on long-term capital debt of $200,000 and $50,000, respectively; $100,000 is set aside for future repayment of principal.

REQUIRED:

1. Prepare all necessary journal entries made by the city of Margate for the above transactions, identifying each with the fund or account group affected. Explanations are not required.
2. Compute the effect of the foregoing on the general fund unreserved fund balance.

E12.14 Statement of General Fixed Assets The Salinas City Statement of General Fixed Assets as of the beginning of the fiscal year follows:

Salinas City
Statement of General Fixed Assets
July 1, 20X0

General Fixed Assets		**Investment in** **General Fixed Assets**	
Land	$ 150,000	General Fund	$ 1,450,000
Buildings	1,000,000	Capital Projects Fund . .	500,000
Equipment	800,000		
Total	$ 1,950,000	Total	$ 1,950,000

During October 20X0, the city purchases a warehouse for $375,000, of which 40 percent is attributable to the land. The city begins construction of a civic center in 20X0. The entire project is estimated to cost $800,000. By June 30, 20X1, $200,000 is expended on the project, which is estimated to be one-fourth complete.

Old equipment originally costing $20,000 is scrapped, and new equipment is purchased for $35,000 early in 20X1.

REQUIRED: Prepare the General Fixed Assets portion of the June 30, 20X1, statement of general fixed assets for Salinas City.

E12.15 Fixed Asset Transactions The village of Jamesville acquired the following fixed assets during 20X3:

1. Snow removal equipment was purchased by the general fund at a cost of $58,000.
2. A delivery van was purchased by the internal service fund at a cost of $8,300.
3. A building was purchased for $220,000 by the capital projects fund to serve as a youth center. The purchase was financed by a 20-year bond issue.
4. Sewer lines were extended to an undeveloped section of the village at a cost of $700,000. This cost will eventually be paid by the property owners through special tax assessments. To cover the actual construction cost, bonds were issued by the village.

REQUIRED: Prepare the entries needed in the village of Jamesville's general fixed assets account group to reflect the above acquisitions.

E12.16 General Long-Term Debt Transactions The county of Edgewater had the following transactions involving long-term debt during 20X6:

1. A $2,000,000 bond issue by the capital projects fund provided money for construction of new streets and bridges.
2. A $1,500,000 bond issue by the water authority (an enterprise fund) provided money for replacement of water mains.
3. A $3,300,000 bond issue to be repaid by special assessments provided money for improvements to the sewage treatment plant. The county is *not* liable for the debt.
4. $100,000 of principal and $120,000 of interest was paid by the general fund on bonds issued in 20X4 for construction of a fire station.
5. Of the bond proceeds described in No. 1, $80,000 was not spent on the project and was transferred to the debt service fund to be used for principal payments on the bonds in future years.

REQUIRED: Prepare the entries needed in the general long-term debt accounts of the county of Edgewater.

PROBLEMS

P12.1 Determining the Reporting Entity The governmental reporting entity consists of a primary government and may include one or more related governmental enterprises.

REQUIRED: In each of the following independent situations, identify the primary government and explain whether the other governmental enterprise is part of the financial reporting entity centered on the primary government.

1. By a vote of 9-6, the Megalopolis city council voted to establish a Convention Authority (CA). Megalopolis's mayor appoints the CA's governing board with the approval of city council. City council's direct financial commitment to the CA is limited to a $100,000 appropriation of seed money to be repaid from the CA's permanent financing as soon as possible. The CA's initial responsibility is to obtain the funding for a downtown convention center. Funding will likely come from a combination of federal development grant money, tax-exempt bonds issued and backed by the city, and corporate contributions.
2. Consider the same facts as in 1. except that the CA is authorized to issue its own bonds without city backing and may levy a small sales tax to support its activities. The CA's bond issues and sales taxes need not be approved by the city council but, as a matter of courtesy, council is advised of the CA's plans.
3. Many local communities in Gigantic County are served by volunteer fire departments. Each such fire department is a separate not-for-profit corporation governed by a board elected by and from its own membership. The county has a three-year contract with each fire department to pay for the department's fire-fighting services. Also, the county has historically paid for fire trucks and similar equipment used and *owned* by the fire departments.
4. The Winitville Board of Education is elected by the voters. This Board governs the Winitville school district and obtains an annual appropriation from the city to fund

school district activities. The City of Winitville levies whatever taxes and issues whatever bonds it needs to fund its expenditures, including those attributable to the school district, and has no authority over the individual line items in the school district's budget.

5. The State of Michigan, along with seven other states, is participating in a joint venture to examine the water quality of the Great Lakes. Michigan is the largest contributor, and contributions to the Great Lakes Protection Fund (GLPF) are permanently restricted and are not available for disbursement. Each of the participating states is represented by two members on the GLPF's board of directors. The GLPF's financing and budgeting operations are controlled by the directors within requirements established by its own Articles of Incorporation.

6. The Georgia Public Telecommunications Commission is a legally separate entity within the State of Georgia. This commission is a public charitable organization created for the purpose of providing educational, instructional and public broadcasting services to the citizens of Georgia. The budget of the commission must be approved by the State. The Board consists of three State officials designated by statute and six members appointed by the Governor.

P12.2 **Property Tax Levy** In February 20X6, the city of Greenville began planning its budget for the fiscal year beginning July 1, 20X6. The following information was available:

General Fund Balance, January 1, 20X6	$ 352,000
Estimated Receipts from Property Taxes	
(January 1, 20X6—June 30, 20X6)	2,222,000
Estimated Revenue from Investments	
(January 1, 20X6—June 30, 20X7)	442,000
Estimated Proceeds from Sale of General Obligation Bonds in	
August 20X6	3,000,000
	$ 6,016,000
Estimated Expenditures (January 1, 20X6—June 30, 20X6)	$ 1,900,000
Proposed Appropriations (July 1, 20X6—June 30, 20X7)	4,300,000
	$ 6,200,000

Additional information:

1. The general fund balance required by the city council for July 1, 20X7, is $175,000.
2. Property tax collections are due in March and September of each year. During the month of February 20X6, estimated expenditures are expected to exceed available funds by $200,000. Pending collection of property taxes in March 20X6, this deficiency will have to be met by the issuance of 30-day tax anticipation notes of $200,000 at an estimated interest rate of 9 percent per annum.
3. The proposed general obligation bonds will be issued by the city water fund (an enterprise fund) to be used for construction of a new water pumping station.

REQUIRED: Prepare a schedule as of January 1, 20X6, calculating the property tax levy required for the city of Greenville general fund for the fiscal year ending June 30, 20X7. *(AICPA adapted)*

P12.3 **Planning for Tax Anticipation Notes** Stevens County operates on a June 30 fiscal year. Property tax bills are mailed on May 15 of the previous fiscal year. Although taxpayers are offered several payment options, 80% of those that do pay their taxes choose to pay in two equal installments on September 1 and March 1. Remaining taxes are paid in full on September 1. Under the installment plan, the second installment is higher by a 1% penalty for not paying the full amount on September 1. In recent years, 5% of taxes levied were not collected. Revenue sources other than property taxes are insignificant.

Stevens County's operating budget for fiscal 20X8 is $44,000,000, including estimated interest on short-term borrowings. Cash expenditures run about $2,000,000 per month in July and August and $4,000,000 per month thereafter. On July 1, 20X7, the following account balances, unrelated to the 20X8 budget, are projected:

Cash in Bank	$ 100,000
Short-Term Investments	160,000[a]
Taxes Receivable—Delinquent	1,900,000
Allowance for Uncollectible Taxes—Delinquent	(1,900,000)
Vouchers Payable	(210,000)
Fund Balance—Reserved for Encumbrances	(70,000)[b]
Fund Balance—Unreserved	(475,000)

[a] These will be sold to cover any projected shortfall.

[b] These goods and services will be received in July and paid for in August.

REQUIRED:

1. Prepare a schedule indicating Stevens County's needs—amounts and timing—for short-term tax anticipation note financing. It is County policy to maintain a cash balance of at least $30,000.

2. Make a suggestion to enable Stevens County to reduce or eliminate the need for temporary short-term financing.

P12.4 **General Fund—Entries and Financial Statements** The township of Wyatt finances its operations from revenues provided by property taxes, water distribution, fines levied by the municipal court, and interest on savings accounts.

Wyatt maintains only a general fund. The following information is available for the year ended December 31, 20X6:

1. Following are general fund account balances on January 1, 20X6:

Cash in Savings Account	$ 620,000
Cash in Checking Accounts	384,800
Cash on Hand (Undeposited)	1,600
Water Department Supplies	36,400
Accounts Receivable—Water Customers	36,700
Fund Balance—Unreserved	1,079,500

2. The budget for 20X6 adopted by the township commission and the transactions relating to the budget (with all current bills vouchered and paid on December 31, 20X6) for the year were as follows:

	Budget	Actual
Property Taxes	$ 267,500	$ 267,500
Water Department Costs	665,000	643,600[a]
Township Constable and Court Fees Paid by Township	100,000	95,500[a]
Water Revenues	300,000	320,600[b]
Court Fines	125,000	110,250
Commissioners' Salaries and Expenses	60,000	54,700[a]
Interest on Savings Accounts	20,000	22,400
Miscellaneous Expenses	12,000	26,100[a]

[a] Cash Expenditures.
[b] Billings.

3. All property taxes were collected.
4. A count of cash on December 31, 20X6, determined that there was $2,500 on hand that was not deposited until January 2, 20X7.
5. All outstanding water bills on January 1, 20X6, were collected during 20X6. All billings for water during 20X6 were paid with the exception of statements totaling $22,300, which were mailed to customers the last week of December.
6. All water department supplies were consumed during the year on the repair of water mains.

REQUIRED:

1. Prepare 20X6 journal entries and closing entries.
2. Prepare a balance sheet and a statement of revenues, expenditures, and changes in fund balance.
    (AICPA adapted)

P12.5 General Fund—Adjustments and Statements The books for the town of Fountain Inn are maintained by an inexperienced bookkeeper. All transactions were recorded in the town's general fund for the fiscal year ended June 30, 20X6. The bookkeeper prepared the following trial balance:

Town of Fountain Inn
General Fund Trial Balance
June 30, 20X6

Accounts	Debit	Credit
Cash	$ 12,900	
Accounts Receivable	1,200	
Taxes Receivable, Current	8,000	
Tax Anticipation Notes Payable		$ 15,000
Appropriations		350,000
Expenditures	344,000	
Estimated Revenues	290,000	
Revenues		320,000
Town Property	16,100	
Bonds Payable	36,000	
Fund Balance		23,200
Total	$ 708,200	$ 708,200

Additional information:

1. The accounts receivable balance was due from the town's golf course, representing an advance made by the general fund. Accounts for the municipal golf course operated by the town are maintained in a separate enterprise fund.
2. The total tax levy for the year was $280,000, of which $10,000 was abated during the year. The town's tax collection experience in recent years indicates an average loss of 5 percent of the net tax levy for uncollectible taxes. At year-end, all taxes receivable are considered delinquent and are fully reserved.
3. On June 30, 20X6, the town retired at face value 4-percent general obligation serial bonds totaling $30,000. The bonds were issued on July 1, 20X4, in the total amount of $150,000. Interest paid during the year was also recorded in the Bonds Payable account.
4. At the beginning of the year, the town council authorized a supply room with an inventory not to exceed $10,000. During the year, supplies totaling $12,300 were purchased and charged to Expenditures. The physical inventory taken at June 30 disclosed that supplies totaling $8,400 were used. The consumption method is to be used.
5. Expenditures for 20X6 included $2,600 applicable to purchase orders issued in the prior year. Outstanding purchase orders at June 30, 20X6, not recorded in the accounts, amounted to $4,100. The GAAP budgetary basis is used.
6. The amount of $8,200, due from the state for the town's share of state gasoline taxes, was not recorded in the accounts.
7. Equipment costing $7,500 was removed from service and sold for $900 during the year, and new equipment costing $17,000 was purchased. These transactions were recorded in the Town Property account.

REQUIRED:

1. Prepare the adjusting and closing entries for the general fund of Fountain Inn and any corresponding entries to the general fixed assets and general long-term debt account groups. Assume that general fixed assets and general long-term debt accounts were properly maintained in prior years.
2. Prepare a balance sheet and statement of revenues, expenditures and changes in fund balance for Fountain Inn's general fund.
   (AICPA adapted)

P12.6 **Reconstructing Journal Entries** Balance sheets for the city of Golden's general fund appear as follows:

City of Golden
General Fund
Balance Sheets
June 30, 20X1 and 20X0

Assets	20X1	20X0
Cash	$ 39,000	$ 10,000
Investments	140,000	200,000
Due from State Government	50,000	—
Due from Federal Government	—	150,000
	$ 229,000	$ 360,000
Liabilities and Fund Balance		
Vouchers Payable	$ 87,000	$ 180,000
Fund Balance—Reserved for Encumbrances	—	75,000
Fund Balance—Unreserved	142,000	105,000
	$ 229,000	$ 360,000

The following budget entry was made in July 20X0:

Estimated Revenues	50,000	
Fund Balance—Unreserved	13,000	
Appropriations		63,000
To record budget.		

Bills for the June 30, 20X0, encumbrances were $3,000 less than the amount committed. There were no unanticipated revenues. The legal approach is used for outstanding encumbrances.

REQUIRED: Reconstruct the journal entries, including closing entries, for the year ended June 30, 20X1, for Golden's general fund.

P12.7 **Evaluating Municipality Financial Condition** Well-known examples of municipal financial problems, such as New York City in 1975, the San Jose (California) School District in 1983, and Orange County in 1994, seem to have surprised capital market participants and other observers. Perhaps fund accounting and the use of separate account groups for fixed assets and long-term debt complicate analysis of the relationships between a governmental unit's sources and uses of financial resources and changes in its levels of fixed assets and debt. Modestly inappropriate uses of fungible financial resources could mask impending financial difficulties.

Consider the five years of selected data for a hypothetical municipality shown below.

	20X1	20X2	20X3	20X4	20X5
Estimated Revenue—General Fund .	$3,400	$3,650	$3,800	$4,000	$4,100
Actual Revenue—General Fund	3,360	3,570	3,700	3,820	3,900
Short-Term Borrowings	200	250	310	370	500
Change in Long-Term Debt—Capital Projects Funds	440	600	620	550	580
Expenditures—Capital Projects Funds	300	480	510	470	430
Fund Balance—Unreserved (all governmental funds)	810	830	845	815	795

REQUIRED:

1. Explain what is meant by "fungible financial resources."
2. Identify and explain any signals these data provide regarding the evolving financial condition of this municipality.
3. Discuss how the use of fund accounting, rather than business accounting, reduces the ability to evaluate the financial condition of a municipality.

P12.8   **General Fund and Account Groups—Corrections and Adjustments** During the fiscal year ending June 30, 20X7, all transactions of Salleytown were recorded in the general fund due to the inexperience of the town's bookkeeper. The trial balance of Salleytown's general fund is as follows:

Salleytown
General Fund Trial Balance
June 30, 20X7

Accounts	Debit	Credit
Cash	$ 16,800	
Short-Term Investments	40,000	
Accounts Receivable	11,500	
Taxes Receivable—Current	30,000	
Tax Anticipation Notes Payable		$ 50,000
Appropriations		400,000
Expenditures	382,000	
Estimated Revenue	320,000	
Revenues		360,000
General Property	85,400	
Bonds Payable	52,000	
Fund Balance		127,700
	$ 937,700	$ 937,700

The following information is also available:

1. The accounts receivable of $11,500 includes $1,500 due from the town's water utility. Accounts for the municipal water utility operated by the town are maintained in a separate fund.
2. The balance in Taxes Receivable—Current is now considered delinquent, and the town estimates that $24,000 will be uncollectible.
3. On June 30, 20X7, the town retired, at face value, 6-percent general obligation serial bonds totaling $40,000. The bonds were issued on July 1, 20X2, at face value of $200,000. Interest and principal paid during the year ended June 30, 20X7, were charged to Bonds Payable.
4. During the year, supplies totaling $128,000 were purchased and charged to Expenditures. The town conducted a physical inventory of supplies on hand at June 30, 20X7, and this physical count disclosed that supplies exceeding $84,000 were used. The purchases method is used.
5. Expenditures for the year ended June 30, 20X7, included $11,200 applicable to purchase orders issued in the prior year. Outstanding purchase orders at June 30, 20X7, not recorded in the accounts, amounted to $17,500. The legal approach is used.
6. On June 28, 20X7, the state revenue department informed the town that its share of a state-collected, locally shared tax would be $34,000.
7. During the year, equipment with a book value of $7,900 was removed from service and sold for $4,600. In addition, new equipment costing $90,000 was purchased. The transactions were recorded in General Property.
8. During the year, 100 acres of land were donated to the town for use as an industrial park. The land had a value of $125,000. This donation was not recorded.

REQUIRED:

1. Prepare the formal reclassification, adjusting, and closing journal entries for the general fund as of June 30, 20X7.
2. Prepare the formal adjusting journal entries for the general long-term debt account group and the general fixed assets account group as of June 30, 20X7. Assume that proper entries were made in prior years.
(AICPA adapted)

P12.9   **Comprehensive General Fund Review** The Wayne City Council approved and adopted its general fund budget for 20X3. The budget contained the following amounts:

Estimated Revenues	$ 700,000
Appropriations	660,000
Authorized operating transfer to the Library debt service fund	30,000

During 20X3, various transactions and events occurred which affected the general fund. The legal budgetary basis is used.

REQUIRED: For items 1-40, indicate whether the item should be **debited (D), credited (C),** or is **not affected (N)** in the general fund.

a. Items 1-5 involve recording the adopted budget.
    1. Estimated revenues
    2. Fund balance—unreserved
    3. Appropriations
    4. Estimated other financing uses—operating transfers
    5. Expenditures

b. Items 6-10 involve recording the 20X3 property tax levy. It was estimated that $5,000 would be uncollectible.
    6. Property taxes receivable—current
    7. Bad debt expense
    8. Allowance for uncollectibles—current
    9. Revenues
    10. Estimated revenues

c. Items 11-15 involve recording encumbrances at the time purchase orders are issued.
    11. Encumbrances
    12. Fund balance—reserved for encumbrances
    13. Expenditures
    14. Vouchers payable
    15. Purchases

d. Items 16-20 involve recording expenditures which had been previously been encumbered in the current year.
    16. Encumbrances
    17. Fund balance—reserved for encumbrances
    18. Expenditures
    19. Vouchers payable
    20. Purchases

e. Items 21-25 involve recording the operating transfer made to the Library debt service fund. No previous entries were made regarding this transaction.
    21. Residual equity transfers out
    22. Due from Library debt service fund
    23. Cash
    24. Other financing uses—operating transfers out
    25. Encumbrances

f. Items 26-36 involve recording the closing entries (other than encumbrances) for 20X3.
    26. Estimated revenues
    27. Due to special revenue fund
    28. Appropriations
    29. Estimated other financing uses—operating transfers
    30. Expenditures
    31. Revenues
    32. Other financing uses—operating transfers out
    33. Bonds payable
    34. Bad debt expense
    35. Depreciation expense
    36. Residual equity transfers out

g. Items 37-40 involve recording the closing entry related to the $12,000 of outstanding encumbrances at the end of 20X3 and the adjusting entry to signify that these commitments will be honored in 20X4 under the legal budgetary basis.
   37. Encumbrances
   38. Fund balance—reserved for encumbrances
   39. Fund balance—unreserved
   40. Fund balance—reserved for encumbrances (prior year)
   (AICPA adapted)

P12.10 Comprehensive General Fund—Entries and Statements Data relating to the general fund of the Pilotsville School District are as follows:

Pilotsville School District
General Fund Balance Sheet
December 31, 20X6

Assets		Liabilities and Fund Balance	
Cash	$ 36,600	Vouchers Payable	$ 22,000
Taxes Receivable—Current		Due to Enterprise Fund	7,000
(Net of $8,000 Allowance		Fund Balance:	
for Uncollectible Taxes)	42,000	Reserved for Encumbrances . .	4,600
Inventory	17,000	Unreserved	62,000
	$ 95,600		$ 95,600

Additional information:

1. The 20X7 budget included $287,000 in expected revenue, all from property taxes, and a $6,000 planned decrease in the fund balance. The tax levy was for $300,000.
2. Tax collections during 20X7 were as follows:

20X6 Taxes	$ 45,000
20X7 Taxes	238,000
	$ 283,000

   Remaining 20X6 taxes were written off.
3. Taxes due at year-end are not considered delinquent but are 16-percent reserved.
4. Old school desks were sold for $800 in cash. The desks had originally cost $1,200.
5. New desks were purchased for $2,000 in cash.
6. Vandalism to the schools resulted in $3,000 of unexpected repair and cleanup costs.
7. Actual total expenditures by the general fund were $291,000.
8. Supplies on hand at year-end totaled $13,000 per annual physical inventory.
9. Although no vouchers payable were outstanding at the end of 20X7, $7,000 was encumbered for goods ordered but not yet received. The GAAP approach is used.
10. The 20X6 encumbrance for $4,600 was canceled when the goods ordered were found to be defective.
11. Cash of $7,000 was transferred to the enterprise fund.

REQUIRED:

1. Prepare all the 20X7 journal entries and closing entries for the school district's general fund.
2. Prepare a 20X7 balance sheet and a statement of revenues, expenditures, and changes in fund balance for the general fund.

P12.11 **Fixed Asset Transactions and Statements** At January 1, 20X3, the town of Bakersville compiled a current listing of its fixed assets and the means by which they were acquired. The fixed assets are shown below:

Land	**Cost**
Site of Town Hall	$ 17,000
Site of Town Garage and Services Building	48,000
Town Park and Wildlife Preserve	160,000
Buildings	
Town Hall	775,000
Garage	380,000
Services Building	625,000
Park Buildings	63,000
Equipment	
Office Equipment	116,000
Highway Equipment	843,000
Park Equipment	102,000
Other Equipment	477,000
Improvements	
Streets	1,755,000
Sewers and Drainage	2,416,000
Park	288,000

The land and buildings, except for those related to the park, were financed by general obligation bonds through the capital projects fund. The park land was donated by a corporation which has a large plant in Bakersville. The town then applied for and received a state grant of $250,000 to develop the park. The cost of sewers and drainage was financed by assessments to property owners. All other fixed asset costs were paid from general fund appropriations.

During 20X3, the following transactions occurred:

1. Highway equipment purchased ten years ago at a cost of $62,000 was sold for $18,000.
2. New highway equipment costing $77,000 was purchased. An appropriation for this amount was included in the general fund budget.
3. A bond issue of $510,000 was approved to finance the construction of a youth center. Construction will begin in early 20X4.
4. Office equipment costing $2,000 was stolen and has not yet been replaced.
5. The town received a $40,000 federal grant to expand the wildlife preserve. It used the grant plus $5,000 of general fund resources to buy 200 acres of land adjoining the present site.

REQUIRED:

1. Record the transactions in the general fixed assets account group for 20X3.
2. Prepare a statement of general fixed assets as of December 31, 20X3, and a statement of changes in general fixed assets for the year.

P12.12 Capital Lease Transaction On January 1, 20X1, a city leased a new truck for use in general operations. The lease payments are financed by General Fund resources. The following is relevant information concerning this lease:

Fair value of truck on January 1, 20X1	$20,000
Down payment (paid out of general funds)	2,000
Lease interest rate	10%

Lease payments of $4,750 are due at the end of each of the next five years, and will be paid out of general fund resources. The truck has an expected life of five years, with no salvage value.

REQUIRED:

1. Make the necessary journal entries on January 1, 20X1 in the general fund, the general fixed assets account group, and the general long-term debt account group, to record this lease.
2. Make the necessary journal entries on December 31, 20X1 to record the first lease payment. Specify the funds or account groups affected.

P12.13 General Fund Accounting Below is information concerning the State of Michigan's general fund for the fiscal year ended September 30, 1996 (all amounts in thousands):

Revenues and other sources	Actual	Variance Favorable (Unfav)
Taxes	$10,224,470	$36,368
From federal agencies	6,654,865	83,515
From local agencies	134,769	22,679
From services	119,229	2,197
From licenses and permits	189,979	325
Special Medicaid reimbursements	598,654	—
Operating transfers in	839,471	96,016

Expenditures, operating transfers out, and encumbrances		
Legislative	134,300	2,084
Judicial	215,988	11,036
Executive branch	19,203,362	119,695
Intrafund expenditure reimbursements	(770,500)	—

Additional information: Outstanding encumbrances at September 30, 1996 were $99,022. The beginning fund balance for the general fund was $757,523. Residual equity transfers from the general fund to other funds for fiscal year 1996 were $13,704.

REQUIRED:

1. What method does the State of Michigan use to account for encumbrances? How do you know?
2. Reconstruct the budget entry made at October 1, 1995 for the general fund.
3. Prepare a statement of revenues, expenditures, and changes in fund balance—budget and actual—for the general fund for the fiscal year ended September 30, 1996. Include a calculation of the fund balance for the general fund as of September 30, 1996, on the GAAP budgetary basis.

P12.14 **Employee Compensated Absences** Like most employees, governmental employees receive annual compensated sick leave, family leave, and vacation days. Often, employees are compensated for unused accumulated annual leave upon retirement or termination. Per GASB *Statement No. 16*, unpaid leave for employees related to governmental funds is reported in the general long-term debt account group.

Following is information concerning compensated absences in the State of South Carolina for fiscal year 1996 (in thousands):

Unpaid compensated absences as of July 1, 1995 . . . . $154,419
Accumulation of compensated absence pay for fiscal 1996   83,257
Payments to employees for compensated absences in fiscal 1996 . . .   78,569

Payments are made out of general fund resources.

REQUIRED:

1. Present the journal entries necessary to record the above events. Specify the funds and/or account groups affected.
2. Comment on the value of the general fund balance sheet in evaluating South Carolina's future obligation for compensated absences.

CHAPTER 13

ACCOUNTING FOR NONROUTINE ACTIVITIES AND EXTERNAL REPORTING FOR STATE AND LOCAL GOVERNMENT

CHAPTER PREVIEW

In Chapter 12, we studied accounting and reporting for routine activities of governments. These activities are recorded in the general fund. A complex governmental unit, however, engages in a wide range of governmental, proprietary, and fiduciary activities, requiring the use of all seven fund types plus the two account groups. In addition, interactions between funds and account groups must be recorded. The first sections of this chapter discuss accounting and reporting for nonroutine activities of government, and illustrate the use of all fund types and account groups.

The remaining sections of the chapter address the external reporting requirements for state and local governments. The external financial report of a governmental unit is called the Comprehensive Annual Financial Report, or CAFR. This chapter discusses the content and presentation of the CAFR, along with an analysis of the quality of information provided. The Governmental Accounting Standards Board's 1997 *Exposure Draft*, specifying new external reporting requirements for state and local governments, is also examined.

In this chapter, we focus on these topics in financial reporting for state and local governments:

- Accounting for special revenue activities
- Accounting for capital projects
- Accounting for general debt issuance and payment
- Accounting for enterprise and internal service activities
- Accounting for trust and agency activities
- Accounting for investments
- The comprehensive annual financial report
- The GASB's new financial reporting model

Recall from Chapter 12 that a governmental unit typically engages in the following activities, accounted for in separate funds:

Governmental:

- Collection of taxes and revenues from fees and fines, and delivery of primary services such as education, public safety, social and judicial services, and administration; accounted for in the **general fund**.

- Projects or services financed by taxes or other funding sources restricted for specific purposes; accounted for in **special revenue funds**.
- Accumulation of resources for future payment of long-term debt; accounted for in **debt service funds**.
- Acquisition and construction of long-term assets; accounted for in **capital projects funds**.

Proprietary:

- Services for which a cost-based fee is collected from the public; accounted for in **enterprise funds**.
- Services provided to other governmental units in return for a cost-based fee; accounted for in **internal service funds**.

Fiduciary:

- Financial resources held in trust; accounted for in expendable or nonexpendable **trust funds**.
- Financial resources collected for another governmental unit or organization; accounted for in **agency funds**.

The governmental and expendable trust funds use the *modified accrual basis of accounting*, often referred to as *fund accounting*, while proprietary funds use *business accounting*, and nonexpendable trust funds use *fiduciary accounting*. The governmental and expendable trust funds do not recognize long-term debt or fixed assets directly in the funds. Therefore the general long-term debt account group and the general fixed assets account group are used to list the general obligation long-term debt and fixed assets used in activities related to the governmental funds. Agency funds consist of assets and liabilities only, and do not require a particular accounting method.

ACCOUNTING FOR SPECIAL REVENUE ACTIVITIES

Often resources are collected and legally restricted for a particular purpose. Examples are a state gasoline tax raised to fund repairs and improvements in the state transportation system, a property tax levy to fund refuse collection, or federal grants given to states to finance particular social services programs. **Special revenue funds** record inflows of earmarked resources and their expenditure for appropriate activities. Because special revenue funds are *governmental* funds, they follow modified accrual accounting. Because the accounting for special revenue funds is generally the same as for the general fund, an illustration of entries is not necessary.

The number of special revenue funds reported by a governmental unit ranges from zero to ten or more, depending on the number of activities funded by legally restricted revenue sources. See the Authors' Commentary for examples of such funds.

AUTHORS' COMMENTARY

State and local governments report a wide array of special revenue and capital projects funds reflecting their diverse environments and public concerns. The following is a sampling of the funds encountered in state CAFRs.

Special Revenue Funds

The State of Louisiana has a Lottery Proceeds Fund, that collects net lottery proceeds of the Louisiana Lottery Corporation. Use of fund resources is limited by legislative appropriation. The Video Draw Poker Device Fund collects revenue from owner licenses and net device revenue. The fund gives 25% of its revenues to district attorneys and governing authorities in municipalities where these devices are operated, and provides annual appropriations to the Department of Public Safety and Corrections. Any remaining resources revert to the general fund. The Transportation Trust Fund collects money from gasoline and automobile license taxes. This fund is used exclusively for highway construction and maintenance, flood control, ports and airports programs, state police traffic control, and other transportation-related programs.

The State of Massachusetts has an Oil Overcharge Fund that obtains resources from fines and penalties collected under federal regulation from oil companies. The money is used to provide fuel assistance and to fund projects to insulate housing for low income residents of the state.

Capital Projects Funds

The State of Pennsylvania has a Keystone Recreation, Park and Conservation Fund that accounts for bond proceeds used as grants to counties for capital improvements and expansion of parks, recreation facilities, historic sites, zoos, public libraries, natural preserves and wildlife habitats.

The State of South Dakota reports a State Capitol Construction Fund in a recent CAFR. The State of Iowa lists a Recreational Trails Development Fund to account for acquisition and construction of recreational trails in Iowa. The State of Missouri reports a Veterans' Homes Capital Improvement Fund, which accounts for fees from the sale of bingo cards. These fees are then used to construct or renovate veterans' homes and cemeteries in the state.

In the State of Georgia, the Georgia Education Authority (University) accounts for new construction and improvements of facilities under the authority of the Board of Regents of the University System of Georgia. The Georgia Building Authority (Markets) accounts for construction and improvements of farmers markets.

Based on fund descriptions, the choice of fund type is not always clear. For example, Louisiana's Transportation Trust Fund is classified as a special revenue fund, but resources are used for highway construction. Missouri's Veterans' Homes Capital Improvement Fund is a capital projects fund, but might be classified as a special revenue fund.

ACCOUNTING FOR CAPITAL PROJECTS

When a government acquires or constructs long-term assets—land, buildings, equipment, infrastructure such as sidewalks, sewers, street lights—one of three basic approaches are used:

ACQUISITIONS FINANCED THROUGH THE GENERAL FUND OR SPECIAL REVENUE FUND

The budget of the general fund or special revenue fund often includes appropriations for acquisitions of property and equipment, such as land and fire trucks. These acquisitions are illustrated in Chapter 12. Entries for acquisitions of capital assets funded by general fund resources are as follows, for a purchase of equipment costing $5,000:

Books of General Fund

Expenditures	5,000	
Vouchers Payable, Cash		5,000
To record purchase of equipment.		

General Fixed Assets Account Group

Equipment	5,000	
Investment in General Fixed Assets-General Fund		5,000
To record purchase of equipment by the general fund.		

ACQUISITIONS FINANCED THROUGH A PROPRIETARY FUND

Acquisitions by a proprietary fund—enterprise or internal service fund—are recorded using normal business accounting. Entries for the acquisition of $60,000 in new golf carts by a municipal golf course are as follows:

Books of Enterprise Fund

Equipment	60,000	
Vouchers Payable, Cash		60,000
To record purchase of golf carts.		

The golf carts are depreciated over their useful life. Assume the carts are straight-line depreciated over six years. The entry to record yearly depreciation is as follows:

Depreciation Expense	10,000	
Accumulated Depreciation		10,000
To record annual depreciation on golf carts.		

CAPITAL PROJECTS

A governmental unit often engages in large capital projects involving the construction of buildings, equipment, or infrastructure that may extend over more than one year. The projects may be financed by general obligation or revenue bonds issued for the purpose of funding the construction, tax assessments on benefitted property owners, federal or state capital grants, or by transfers from other funds. Unless the project relates to an enterprise or internal service fund, it is accounted for using a **capital projects fund**. The remainder of this section illustrates the accounting for major transactions of a capital projects fund, financed by a general obligation bond issue.

A separate capital projects fund is established for each project. In some cases, the fund is temporary, originating when the project begins, and ending when the fixed asset is completed. More commonly, a capital projects fund is established for ongoing construction and maintenance of particular types of assets such as roads or bridges. See the Authors' Commentary for examples of capital projects found in state CAFRs.

The budget for a capital project typically requires formal approval, and therefore budgetary accounts are often used. If the project is to be financed by general obligation bonds, initial work may be financed by a temporary advance from another fund or by short-term financing known as **bond anticipation notes**—short-term loans from a bank or other financial institution. When the long-term bonds are issued, these temporary loans are repaid from the proceeds. Any bond proceeds not used for the project are used to pay principal and interest on the bonds. Even if the project is financed by property tax assessments, typically bonds are issued to finance the project, in advance of collections from property owners. Then collection of these assessments is used to repay the principal and interest of the bonds.

Capital Projects Fund Cash Flows

Sources of Cash	Uses of Cash
Bond anticipation notes	Construction costs
Bond proceeds	Repayment of advances
Grants	Repayment of bond anticipation notes
Advances or transfers	Investments
from other funds	Transfers to other funds
Investment proceeds	

ACCOUNTING FOR THE CAPITAL PROJECTS FUND

The following example uses a typical construction project to illustrate the accounting procedures for a capital projects fund. Assume that in fiscal 20X1 Lake City decides to construct a new fire station. The total cost is expected to be $1,500,000, funded as follows:

State grant	$1,000,000
General obligation bonds	500,000

Budget Entry

Whether a budget entry is recorded depends on applicable local laws and regulations. If a budget entry is recorded, it appears as follows:

Books of Capital Projects Fund

Bonds Authorized—Unissued	500,000	
Estimated Financing Sources—State Grant	1,000,000	
Appropriations		1,500,000
To record approval of capital project involving		
construction of fire station.		

Note that Bonds Authorized—Unissued and Financing Sources—State Grant are similar to the Estimated Revenues account used in the general fund, signifying the budgeted sources of resources for the project.

Revenue Accrual

Typically grants are accrued as revenue in the capital projects fund, since collection is reasonably assured. The entry to record the accrual is as follows:

Books of Capital Projects Fund

State Grant Receivable	1,000,000	
State Grant Revenue		1,000,000
To record accrual of state grant.		

Temporary Financing

Initial resources for the project might be temporarily advanced from another fund to allow work to begin before the bonds are issued. Suppose that, in this example, $50,000 is advanced from the general fund. It is recorded as follows:

Books of Capital Projects Fund

Cash	50,000	
Due to General Fund		50,000
To record advance from general fund.		

Books of General Fund

Due from Capital Projects Fund	50,000	
Cash		50,000
To record advance to the capital projects fund.		

Note that an **advance** from one fund to another is recorded as a payable of the fund receiving the cash, and a receivable of the fund providing the cash, since the advance is expected to be repaid. In contrast, a **transfer** impacts fund balance as "other financing sources (uses)," since no repayment is expected.

Partial Collection of Grant; Issuance of Bonds

When bonds are issued to finance a construction project, the proceeds must be at least equal to the amount budgeted. Otherwise, additional funding sources must be identified. Therefore, the coupon rate on the bonds is typically set at or above the interest rate demanded by investors to ensure that the bond issue generates sufficient financing for the project. Assume the bonds have a coupon rate of 5% and are issued at 102, and the premium is to be transferred to the debt service fund. Half of the state grant is received. The entries are as follows:

Books of Capital Projects Fund

Cash	510,000	
Bond Proceeds		500,000
Due to Debt Service Fund		10,000
To record issuance of $500,000 face value bonds for $510,000.		

Cash	500,000	
State Grant Receivable		500,000
To record receipt of half of the state grant.		

The account "Bond Proceeds" is similar to a revenue account and appears as "other financing sources" on the capital project fund's Statement of Revenues, Expenditures, and Changes in Fund Balance. The principal of the debt is recorded in the general long-term debt account group as follows:

General Long-Term Debt Account Group

Amount to be Provided for Repayment of Bonds	500,000	
Bonds Payable		500,000
To record the principal of the bonds.		

Legal provisions dictate how the $10,000 premium on the bond issue may be spent. Generally, the premium cannot be spent on construction costs of the project, since the total cost of construction is authorized at $1,500,000. This authorization cannot be increased by issuing bonds at a premium. The premium is typically applied toward repayment of the principal and interest on the bonds. The debt service fund is used to accumulate money toward payment of principal and interest on general obligation debt. The next entries record the transfer of the premium to the debt service fund.

Books of Capital Projects Fund

Due to Debt Service Fund	10,000	
Cash		10,000
To record transfer of premium to the debt service fund.		

Books of Debt Service Fund

Cash	10,000	
Operating Transfers In		10,000
To record receipt of bond premium from capital projects fund.		

The general long-term debt account group lists outstanding general obligation debt principal and the extent to which money has accumulated in the debt service fund to fund future payments of the principal. Assuming the $10,000 will be used toward repayment of the bond **principal**, the following entry is necessary in the general long-term debt account group:

Books of General Long-Term Debt Account Group

Amount Available for Repayment of Bonds	10,000	
Amount to be Provided for Repayment of Bonds		10,000

To record accumulation of $10,000 in debt service fund toward repayment of bond principal.

Repayment of Advance

Repayment of the advance from the general fund is recorded as follows:

Books of Capital Projects Fund

Due to General Fund	50,000	
Cash		50,000

To record repayment of advance from general fund.

Books of General Fund

Cash	50,000	
Due from Capital Projects Fund		50,000

To record repayment of advance to capital projects fund.

Investment of Excess Cash

Governmental units often temporarily invest bond proceeds not yet needed to fund construction. State laws typically restrict investments to U.S. Treasury or state obligations, or similar low-risk investments. Laws also restrict the use of interest earned on such investments. A common restriction is that interest earned on temporary investment of debt proceeds be used to reduce future debt service.

Assume that $200,000 is invested, and that interest earned and received for the year is $6,000. Assume also that by law such interest must be used to reduce future debt service.

Books of Capital Projects Fund

Investments	200,000	
Cash		200,000

To record investment of excess cash.

Cash	6,000	
Interest Income		6,000

To record interest on investments.

Operating Transfers Out	6,000	
Cash		6,000

To record transfer of interest to debt service fund.

Books of Debt Service Fund

Cash	6,000	
Operating Transfers In		6,000

To record transfer from capital projects fund.

If the $6,000 is to be used to finance repayment of bond principal, the following entry is made in the general long-term debt account group:

Books of General Long-Term Debt Account Group

Amount Available for Repayment of Bonds	6,000	
Amount to be Provided for Repayment of Bonds		6,000
To record accumulation of $6,000 in debt service fund		
toward repayment of bond principal.		

Awarding the Contract

Bids are taken for construction of the fire station and a contract for $1,300,000 is awarded to the qualified low bidder. This constitutes an encumbrance, recorded as follows:

Books of Capital Projects Fund

Encumbrances	1,300,000	
Fund Balance—Reserved for Encumbrances		1,300,000
To record award of contract for construction of fire station.		

Expenditure Recognition; Partial Payment

Assume that $400,000 of invoices are received, representing payments due for partial completion of the encumbered construction contract. Encumbrances are reversed and expenditures recorded. Amounts owing are recorded in a short-term liability account.

Books of Capital Projects Fund

Fund Balance—Reserved for Encumbrances	400,000	
Encumbrances		400,000
To reverse encumbrances for amount billed by contractor.		
Expenditures	400,000	
Contracts Payable		400,000
To record billing from contractor.		

As expenditures are recognized on the contract, the fixed asset is recognized as construction in progress in the general fixed assets account group.

Books of General Fixed Assets Account Group

Construction in Progress	400,000	
Investment in General Fixed Assets—Capital Projects . .		400,000
To record fire station construction.		

Contracts of this type often provide for a portion of each billing to be withheld by the governmental unit until the project is completed and passes inspection. Known as **retainage**, this provision helps protect against failure of the contractor to complete the project or against deficiencies that need to be remedied. The retainage account is often a long-term liability for projects of several years. If the Lake City contract provides for a 20% retainage, the following entry records the payment:

Books of Capital Projects Fund

Contracts Payable	400,000	
Cash		320,000
Contracts Payable—Retainage		80,000
To record payment to the contractor and reclassification of retainage.		

End of Year Closing Entries

Assume the fiscal year ends on June 30, 20X1. Year-end closing entries for the capital projects fund are as follows:

Books of Capital Projects Fund

State Grant Revenue	1,000,000	
Bond Proceeds	500,000	
Interest Income	6,000	
Bonds Authorized—Unissued		500,000
Estimated Financing Sources—State Grant		1,000,000
Fund Balance—Unreserved		6,000
To close actual against budgeted revenues and other financing sources.		
Appropriations	1,500,000	
Expenditures		400,000
Encumbrances		900,000
Operating Transfers Out		6,000
Fund Balance—Unreserved		194,000
To close actual expenditures, encumbrances and operating transfers against appropriations.		

The financial statements of the capital projects fund at June 30, 20X1 appear in Exhibit 13.1.

Completion of the Project

Because the budget is usually established at the outset for the entire project, at the beginning of fiscal 20X2, any carryover encumbrances and appropriations are reestablished with the following entries:

Books of Capital Projects Fund

Encumbrances	900,000	
Fund Balance—Unreserved		900,000
To restore encumbrances closed at prior year-end.		
Fund Balance—Unreserved	900,000	
Appropriations		900,000
To establish appropriations for the year.		

Lake City
Capital Projects Fund—Fire Station
Balance Sheet
June 30, 20X1

Assets		Liabilities and Fund Balance	
Cash	$ 480,000	Contracts Payable—Retainage	$ 80,000
Investments	200,000	Fund Balance—Reserved	
State Grant Receivable	500,000	for Encumbrances	900,000
		Fund Balance—Unreserved	200,000
		Total Liabilities	
Total Assets	$1,180,000	and Fund Balance	$1,180,000

Statement of Revenues, Expenditures and Changes in Fund Balance
for the Year Ended June 30, 20X1

Revenues

State Grant Revenue	$1,000,000
Interest Income	6,000
Total Revenues	$1,006,000

Expenditures

Contract Expenditures	400,000
Excess of Revenues over Expenditures	$ 606,000

Other Financing Sources (Uses)

Bond Proceeds	$ 500,000
Operating Transfers Out	(6,000)
Total Other Financing Sources (Uses)	$ 494,000
Excess of Revenues and Other Sources over Expenditures	$1,100,000
Fund Balance, July 1, 20X0	0
Fund Balance, June 30, 20X1	$1,100,000

EXHIBIT 13.1 FINANCIAL STATEMENTS OF LAKE CITY CAPITAL PROJECTS FUND

Assume the fire station is completed and passes inspection in 20X2, and all payments are made as contracted. The remainder of the state grant is received. An additional $150,000 is paid for items not previously encumbered. Investments are liquidated without earning additional interest. Entries to record these events are as follows:

Books of Capital Projects Fund

Cash	500,000	
State Grant Receivable		500,000
To record receipt of remainder of state grant.		
Cash	200,000	
Investments		200,000
To record liquidation of investments.		

Fund Balance—Reserved for Encumbrances	900,000	
Encumbrances		900,000
To record reversal of encumbrances.		
Expenditures	1,050,000	
Contracts Payable—Retainage	80,000	
Cash		1,130,000
To record remaining expenditures and payments under		
contract plus additional expenditures.		

Books of General Fixed Assets Account Group

Construction in Progress	1,050,000	
Investment in General Fixed Assets—Capital Projects . .		1,050,000
To record fire station construction.		

Closing the Capital Projects Fund

Because this capital projects fund was created to account for the construction of the fire station, the fund is closed when the project is complete. The fund shows a cash balance of $50,000, consisting of the unspent bond proceeds and state grant funding ($50,000 = $1,500,000 − $400,000 − $900,000 − $150,000). Assume the remaining $50,000 in the fund represents unspent bond proceeds. Laws or regulations usually specify that unspent bond proceeds be transferred to the debt service fund for payment of principal and interest on the bonds. Because transfer of the $50,000 is the transfer of a residual balance of a terminated fund, it is accounted for as a *residual equity transfer*. We transfer the cash balance and close the capital projects fund in the following entries:

Books of Capital Projects Fund

Residual Equity Transfers Out	50,000	
Cash		50,000
To record transfer of unspent bond proceeds to debt		
service fund.		
Appropriations	900,000	
Fund Balance—Unreserved	150,000	
Expenditures		1,050,000
To close expenditures against appropriations.		
Fund Balance—Unreserved	50,000	
Residual Equity Transfers Out		50,000
To close residual equity transfers out against the		
remaining unreserved fund balance.		

Entries are also made in the general fixed assets account group to reclassify the construction as completed.

Books of General Fixed Assets Account Group
Fire Station   1,450,000
      Construction in Progress   1,450,000
    To record completion of fire station.

The debt service fund records receipt of the residual equity transfer in, as follows:

Books of Debt Service Fund
Cash   50,000
      Operating Transfers In   50,000
    To record receipt of remaining cash transferred when the
capital projects fund is closed out.

If the cash accumulated in the debt service fund is to be used for payment of principal of the bonds, the following entry is also made in the general long-term debt account group:

Books of General Long-Term Debt Account Group
Amount Available for Repayment of Bonds   50,000
      Amount to be Provided for Repayment of Bonds   50,000
    To record resources available in debt service fund for
repayment of principal.

ACCOUNTING FOR GENERAL DEBT ISSUANCE AND PAYMENT

Treatment of long-term debt in governmental accounting depends in part on the source of cash used for repayment, the fund making the payment, and the fund incurring the debt. Debt of proprietary and some fiduciary funds is recorded as a liability of the fund itself. Interest and principal payments are recorded using business accounting procedures. General obligation debt—debt for which the government is liable and which is used to finance general operations or capital projects—is listed in the general long-term debt account group. Accumulation of resources for the payment of principal and interest on general obligation debt is accounted for using a debt service fund.

Special assessment construction activities may be financed by debt for which the affected property owners are liable. Collection of these assessments is recorded as a liability in an agency fund, for future payment to the bondholders. A summary of the treatment of debt in governmental accounting is presented in Exhibit 13.2.

Funding for interest and principal payments on general obligation debt comes primarily from the general fund, although special tax levies for debt payment are also possible. As illustrated earlier in the chapter, some resources for general obligation debt payment may be provided by bond premiums and unspent appropriations on capital projects. The typical components of a debt service fund's cash flow are shown in Exhibit 13.3.

Long-Term Debt Incurred by	Where Liability Is Recorded	Source of Resources to Repay Debt	Payment Made from
General, special revenue, capital projects, expendable trust funds	General long-term debt account group	Provision in general fund budget Special tax levies Bond premium Unspent bond proceeds	Debt service fund
Enterprise, internal service funds	Specific fund (enterprise or internal service)	Revenues from operations	Specific fund
Nonexpendable trust fund	Trust fund	Income of trust fund	Trust fund
Special assessment construction activities	General long-term debt account group when government is liable	Assessments on property owners	Debt service fund
	Not recorded when government is not liable	Assessments on property owners	Agency fund

EXHIBIT 13.2 TREATMENT OF LONG-TERM DEBT IN GOVERNMENTAL ACCOUNTING

Our discussion of debt service funds focuses on servicing conventional bonds. Debt service funds, however, are also used to service capital leases, and for timely and advance debt refundings. Extinguishment of debt via **in-substance defeasance**, whereby risk-free assets sufficient to service the debt are set aside in an irrevocable trust, is permitted in governmental accounting, and debt service funds handle such transactions. Defeasance is a controversial subject in business accounting which was dealt with by the GASB in *SGAS 7*[1] after similar guidance was provided to business firms by the FASB in *SFAS 76.*[2]

As interest rates have declined in recent years, governments find they can reduce interest costs by refunding their outstanding debt. If the debt cannot be immediately called, new debt is issued

---

[1] Governmental Accounting Standards Board, *Statement of Governmental Accounting Standards No. 7*, "Advance Refundings Resulting in Defeasance of Debt" (Stamford, CT: GASB, 1987); also see Sec D20 of the *Codification*.
[2] Financial Accounting Standards Board, *Statement of Financial Accounting Standards No. 76*, "Extinguishment of Debt," (Stamford, CT: FASB, 1983).

Sources of Cash	Uses of Cash
Transfers from general fund (budgetary appropriations for debt service)	Current payments of interest and principal on general obligation debt
Transfers from special revenue fund (proceeds of any special tax levies for debt service)	Investment for future principal and interest payments
Transfers from capital projects fund (bond premium and unspent bond proceeds)	
Special assessments to pay debt for which the government is primarily or residually liable	
Earnings on investments	
Liquidation of investments	

EXHIBIT 13.3 DEBT SERVICE FUND CASH FLOWS

at the lower interest rate and the proceeds invested until the old debt can be called. Under federal law, the interest on investments cannot exceed the interest paid on the new debt. Otherwise, the tax-exempt status of the debt may be revoked. Governments are also restricted in the types of investments they may make. The U.S. Treasury offers investments that meet these restrictions. However, the IRS and SEC have charged investment bankers with using a tactic called **yield burning** to inflate their profits at the expense of the government. Yield burning occurs when investment bankers purchase higher yield investments and resell them to governments at inflated prices, thereby reducing their yield to the level restricted by law. The higher price "burns away" the excess yield the investments normally earn, and the investment banker pockets the difference. At this writing, the IRS and SEC are investigating these activities.

ACCOUNTING FOR THE DEBT SERVICE FUND

Because the debt service fund employs fund accounting techniques, a budget for estimated revenues and appropriations is frequently recorded in the accounts, even though the budget usually results from managerial design rather than from a legal approval process. Moreover, under the modified accrual basis of accounting, *interest on long-term debt is not accrued*. Instead, only interest due is included in appropriations. Resources of a debt service fund come primarily from transfers from other funds and earnings on investments. Special assessments are revenue to the debt service fund when it services special assessment debt for which the governmental unit has some liability. Revenue budget terminology differs depending on whether *serial bonds* or *term bonds* are being serviced.

Serial bonds mature, generally in equal annual installments, over the life of the bond issue so that interest payments, and some principal payments, are made annually according to a predetermined schedule. Budgeted resource inflows are recorded as **Estimated Revenues** or **Estimated Financing Sources**, or both. Because these budgeted resource inflows are normally equal to budgeted resource outflows—appropriations—for interest and principal payments, the annual budget will typically be balanced.

In contrast, **term bonds** mature in total at the end of the bond issue. Although only interest on term bonds is paid currently, sufficient resources must be available in the debt service fund to repay all the bonds on their maturity date. Because the debt service fund generally serves as a *sinking fund* for term bonds, the annual budget calls for the periodic inflows needed to fund current interest payments and future principal retirement. Two estimated revenue accounts are used: **Required Additions** indicates the amount of transfers to be made from the general or special revenue funds (transfers from capital projects funds are difficult to estimate and thus are often not budgeted); **Required Earnings** reflects the estimated income from debt service fund investments.

When the debt service fund is used to accumulate resources for future repayment of term bonds, annual appropriations differ from annual estimated revenues. During years in which resources are accumulated toward future principal payments, appropriations for current interest are less than estimated revenues. For those years in which an accumulation is expended, appropriations for principal retirement exceed estimated revenues.

Illustration of Accounting for Term Bonds

To illustrate the sequence of entries for *term bonds*, suppose that Lake City establishes a debt service fund to make annual interest payments on the 5 percent, $500,000 general obligation bond issue and to accumulate resources for the future retirement of principal. Although the annual amount needed to fund principal retirement is frequently determined actuarially, we assume that an annual general fund operating transfer of $50,000 to the debt service fund, included in the general fund budget, is sufficient. Investment income for the year is estimated to be $2,700. With the only planned expenditure being the $25,000 interest payment on the bonds, the budget entry for the debt service fund is as follows:

Required Additions	50,000	
Required Earnings	2,700	
Appropriations		25,000
Fund Balance—Unreserved		27,700
To record debt service fund budget.		

Assume that early in the year the $50,000 operating transfer is received from the general fund and is immediately invested in interest-bearing securities. The following entries are made:

Cash	50,000	
Operating Transfers In		50,000
To record operating transfer from general fund.		

Investments	50,000	
Cash		50,000
To record acquisition of investments.		

Later in the year, the interest payment on the bonds becomes due. Securities that cost $24,000 are sold for $25,000, and the interest payment is made:

Cash	25,000	
Investments		24,000
Gains on Investments		1,000
To record sale of securities costing $24,000.		
Expenditures	25,000	
Cash		25,000
To record payment of bond interest.		

If, at year-end, interest income accrued on investments is $1,500, and $16,000 is transferred in from the capital projects fund, the following entries are made:

Investments	1,500	
Interest Income		1,500
To record earnings accrued on investments.		
Cash	16,000	
Operating Transfers In		16,000
To record cash transferred from capital projects fund.		

With use of the modified accrual method by all governmental funds, interest on long-term debt is not accrued, and not recorded as an expenditure, by the debt service fund until it becomes legally payable. Thus there is no year-end adjusting entry for the bond interest accrued since the last payment date.

Closing Entries. Closing the nominal accounts in the debt service fund calls for closing budgetary accounts against related actual accounts. Year-end closing entries are as follows:

Operating Transfers In	66,000	
Gains on Investments	1,000	
Interest Income	1,500	
Required Additions		50,000
Required Earnings		2,700
Fund Balance—Unreserved		15,800
To close revenues, transfers in, and budgeted revenues to fund balance.		
Appropriations	25,000	
Expenditures		25,000
To close expenditures and appropriations.		

After the closing entries, the accounts show cash of $16,000, investments of $27,500 (= $50,000 − $24,000 + $1,500), and an unreserved fund balance of $43,500 (= $27,700 + $15,800). The unreserved fund balance is designated for debt service.

Serial Bond Considerations. If *serial bonds* were issued instead of term bonds, the annual budget provides only for interest due and principal amount to be retired this fiscal year. Moreover, unless the bond indenture required that the debt service fund also have a cash reserve to protect the bondholders, the budget is balanced. Account titles such as Required Additions and Required Earnings are not used. No investments are purchased.

Interaction with Other Funds and Account Groups

Several transactions made by debt service funds involve other funds and account groups. The two major interactions are (1) transfers to the debt service fund, which are recorded by the fund making the transfer and (2) accumulation of resources in the debt service fund to be used for repayment of debt principal, which is recognized in the general long-term debt account group.

In the Lake City illustration, there were three transfers to the debt service fund. The operating transfer from the general fund is recorded on the general fund books as follows:

Books of General Fund

Operating Transfers Out	50,000	
Cash		50,000
To record transfer of appropriated operating contribution to debt service fund.		

The other two transfers were from the capital projects fund: (1) transfer of the bond premium and (2) transfer of interest earned on investments.

Books of Capital Projects Fund

Due to Debt Service Fund	10,000	
Cash		10,000
To transfer premium on bonds issued to debt service fund.		
Operating Transfers Out	6,000	
Cash		6,000
To record transfer of interest to debt service fund.		

At year-end, the debt service fund accumulated cash and investments of $43,500. When this amount is to be used for the future repayment of bond principal, it is recorded as resources available for this purpose in the general long-term debt account group:

General Long-Term Debt Account Group

Amount Available for Repayment of Bonds	43,500	
Amount to Be Provided for Repayment of Bonds . . .		43,500
To record resources available in debt service fund.		

Serial Bond Considerations. Again, if we were dealing with *serial bonds*, the above interactions differ. Transfers from the general and capital projects funds still occur. Because no resources need to be accumulated for future principal retirement, however, there is no need for such an entry in the general long-term debt accounts. If an installment of serial bonds is retired, the entry appears as follows:

General Long-Term Debt Account Group

Serial Bonds Payable	XXX	
Amount to Be Provided for Repayment of Bonds . . .		XXX
To record retirement of serial bonds.		

Payments for retirement of bond principal are recorded concurrently in the debt service fund as expenditures when serial and term bonds are retired.

Special Assessment Debt Considerations

When the government is obligated for debt issued to finance a *special assessment project,* special assessments levied on and paid by the property-owners provide the debt service fund with the resources to repay the debt. Par. 115 of *SGAS 6* requires the debt service fund to record Special Assessments Receivable for the total assessments levied, showing the current and deferred (noncurrent) portions. Revenue is recognized for the current portion and deferred revenue for the noncurrent portion. As time passes, each year's currently-due assessment is reclassified from the noncurrent receivables and the corresponding amount of revenue is recognized by reducing deferred revenue.

Resources will accumulate in the debt service fund to repay the debt. In addition to the collected assessments, resources may come from capital projects fund transfers of bond premium and unspent bond proceeds. As these resources accumulate, and special assessment debt is retired, corresponding entries are made in the general long-term debt account group.

FINANCIAL STATEMENTS FOR THE DEBT SERVICE FUND

Financial statements for the debt service fund include a balance sheet, a statement of revenues, expenditures, and changes in fund balance, and a budgetary comparison statement. A separate fund may be used for each bond issue. The balance sheet and statement of revenues, expenditures, and changes in fund balance for the Lake City illustration appear in Exhibit 13.4.

The budgetary comparison statement, not illustrated here, shows an unfavorable variance of $200 (= $2,700 − $2,500) on Earnings on Investments and a $16,000 favorable variance in Other Financing Sources due to the operating transfer from the capital projects fund not budgeted by the debt service fund.

Lake City
Debt Service Fund
Balance Sheet
June 30, 20X1

Cash	$ 16,000	Fund Balance:	
Investments	27,500	Unreserved—Designated	
	$ 43,500	for Debt Service	$ 43,500

Lake City
Debt Service Fund
Statement of Revenues, Expenditures,
and Changes in Fund Balance
for the Year Ended June 30, 20X1

Revenues

Gains on Investments	$ 1,000
Interest Income	1,500
Total Revenues	$ 2,500
Expenditures	
Debt Service—Interest	25,000
Excess of Revenues over (under) Expenditures	$(22,500)
Other Financing Sources (Uses)	
Operating Transfers In	66,000
Excess of Revenues and Other Sources over (under) Expenditures	
and Other Uses	$ 43,500
Fund Balance—July 1	0
Fund Balance—June 30	$ 43,500

EXHIBIT 13.4 FINANCIAL STATEMENTS FOR DEBT SERVICE FUND

ACCOUNTING FOR ENTERPRISE AND INTERNAL SERVICE ACTIVITIES

Enterprise funds are used to account for governmental operations financed and operated in a manner similar to private business enterprise, that is, where the costs of providing goods or services to the general public on a continuing basis are to be recovered primarily through user charges. In addition, an enterprise fund may be used in circumstances where income determination is appropriate for such purposes as capital maintenance, public policy, management control, or accountability.[3] Typical activities for which enterprise funds are used include the following:

- Utilities—municipal water, gas, and electricity.
- Sanitation—sewer systems.

---

[3] *Codification*, Sec. 1100.103b(1).

- Recreational facilities—golf courses, marinas, swimming pools, tennis courts, and stadiums.
- Commercial facilities—airports, ports, and farmers' markets.
- Transportation facilities—buses, rapid transit, and toll bridges.
- Public hospitals and health clinics.
- Public housing projects.

In addition to receiving resources from user charges, these activities are often subsidized by general governmental revenues. The principal source of revenue usually determines whether the activity is accounted for in an enterprise fund or in the general fund. If the majority of the activity's revenue is generated by charges to users, the activity should be accounted for in an enterprise fund; otherwise, it should be accounted for in the general fund. Even when accounted for in the general fund, the activity's revenue is recorded as user fees.

Internal service funds account for goods or services provided by one department or agency of the governmental unit to another, on a cost reimbursement basis.[4] Centralized service functions are the most common examples, including activities such as the following:

- Maintenance and repair services.
- Vehicle pool and transportation services.
- Supply facilities.
- Print shop.
- Computing and information services.

Such activities are centralized so that cost savings may be realized through more efficient use of equipment, volume purchasing, and other economies of scale. The internal service fund pays the cost of operating the central service facility and sets user charges to produce sufficient revenues to recover costs and to perpetuate the facility's activities. See the Authors' Commentary for examples of enterprise and internal service funds from state CAFRs.

ACCOUNTING FOR ENTERPRISE AND INTERNAL SERVICE FUNDS

Because the measurement focus of business accounting is used by enterprise and internal service funds, revenues and expenses (*not* expenditures), including depreciation, are recognized using the accrual basis. Excess of Revenues over Expenses may be used instead of Net Income. Enterprise and internal service funds account for their own fixed assets and long-term debt. Enterprise funds often issue **revenue bonds** secured by the enterprise fund's operating revenues. Fund equity consists of Contributed Capital, such as Contributions from Other Funds and Federal and State Government, and Retained Earnings.

The financial statements of enterprise and internal service funds are patterned after those of a business firm. The balance sheet has the same accounts and structure as a business balance sheet, with the exceptions noted above in the equity section—an enterprise or internal service fund has no capital stock and no stockholders. Thus there are differences in terminology, but not in substance.

---

[4] *Ibid.*

In addition to the balance sheet, a statement of revenues, expenses, and changes in retained earnings and a statement of cash flows are presented. Although the latter two statements are very similar to their business counterparts, the governmental statement of cash flows as required by *SGAS 9* reports cash flows from financing activities in two categories: (1) cash flows from noncapital financing activities and (2) cash flows from capital and related financing activities. Cash flows from *noncapital financing activities* include borrowings and repayment of borrowings (*and interest*) for other than acquisition or improvement of fixed assets. In contrast, cash flows from *capital and related financing activities* refer to borrowings and other receipts related to acquisition of fixed assets, repayment of those borrowings (*and interest*), and payments to acquire fixed assets. Unlike their business counterparts, cash flows from *investing activities* involve purchase, sale, and earnings on equity and debt instruments only, *not* purchase and sale of fixed assets.

Two of the differences between the *SGAS 9* governmental cash flow statement and the *SFAS 95* business cash flow statement are particularly noteworthy. These involve classification of (1) interest payments, and (2) interest and dividend receipts.

	SGAS 9	*SFAS 95*
Interest payments (not capitalized)	Financing outflows	Operating outflows
Interest and dividend receipts	Investing inflows	Operating inflows

Illustrations of financial statements for proprietary funds are found in Exhibits 13.9 and 13.10 later in the chapter.

AUTHORS' COMMENTARY

A sampling of enterprise and internal service funds reported in state CAFRs provides an interesting view of the nature of business-type operations in each state.

Enterprise Funds

The State of Hawaii reports three enterprise funds: the Department of Transportation-Airports Division, the Department of Transportation-Harbors Division, and the State Hospitals Fund. The airports fund accounts for the operation of the state airports as self-sustaining businesses. The harbors fund promotes development of water transportation in Hawaii, finances harbor operations, and promotes preservation of ocean shores and navigational safety. The hospitals fund reports on the operations of all state-owned hospitals, including the Hilo Medical Center, Maui Memorial Hospital, and Kauai Veterans Memorial Hospital.

Colorado reports a Guaranteed Student Loan Fund, reporting the activities of the Colorado Student Loan Division. This division guarantees loans from private lending institutions to college students. The State Lottery Fund is run as an enterprise fund. Net proceeds are used to support conservation and construction in the state. Note from the previous Authors' Commentary that other states report lottery activities in a special revenue fund. Colorado also has enterprise funds for prison canteens and correctional industries, accounting for the production and sale of goods produced by prisoners.

The State of Texas has a Texas Prepaid Higher Education Tuition Board, run as an enterprise fund, which allows Texas families to lock in college costs at today's prices. The Texas Department of Commerce enterprise fund provides funding to Texas cities for loans to local businesses.

Internal Service Funds

The State of Indiana has various internal service funds accounting for services provided to other governmental agencies on a cost-reimbursement basis. Its Communications Revolving Fund accounts for telecommunications services to State agencies. A Printing Revolving Fund and Data Processing Revolving Fund account for printing and data processing services, respectively. The Indiana Political Subdivision Insurance Fund is a risk pool established to provide protection of political subdivisions against liability.

The State of Georgia has an internal service fund to account for a program to remove asbestos and other hazardous materials from state and local facilities. Another fund provides career service to the classified employees of the executive branch of state government. A Tort Claims Fund accounts for funds used to provide liability insurance for losses caused by tort actions of State employees.

ACCOUNTING FOR TRUST AND AGENCY ACTIVITIES

Trust and agency funds, while commonly combined, consist of two distinct elements: *trust funds* and *agency funds*. Although both involve resources collected, held, paid out, and/or managed by the governmental unit acting as a fiduciary, these funds differ in terms of the purpose and duration of the fiduciary responsibility.

ACCOUNTING FOR TRUST FUNDS

Trust funds are used when the governmental unit holds, manages, and spends resources under terms of a trust agreement. Two general types exist. One type, called a **nonexpendable trust fund**, requires that the principal be maintained intact and that the income be spent for a particular purpose. Examples include an endowment fund for the public library or a scholarship fund for students. The other type, called an **expendable trust fund**, does not maintain a distinction between principal and income; all resources of the fund may be spent for the specified purpose. The income portion of a nonexpendable trust is accounted for in an expendable trust fund. In addition, **pension trust funds**, which are expendable, are used to account for Public Employee Retirement Systems. Pension trust funds receive resources from the local government, perhaps from the employees, and from earnings on investments. The resources are then used to pay retirement benefits. Note that, in contrast to most agency funds, discussed below, trust funds normally hold resources for long periods of time.

Nonexpendable trust funds are considered to be *proprietary funds* and follow fiduciary accounting. Because distinction must be maintained between principal and income, the important **fiduciary accounting principle calling for separation of principal and income** (discussed in Module H), must be adhered to. The income portion, which may be spent for the purposes designated by the trust instrument, is transferred to an expendable trust fund.

An *expendable trust fund* is viewed as a *governmental fund* and is accounted for like a special revenue fund. The modified accrual basis and budgetary accounting are used. See the Authors' Commentary for examples of trust funds found in state CAFRS.

Trust Fund Illustration with Nonexpendable and Expendable Components

To illustrate accounting for trust funds, suppose that Lake City receives a $25,000 gift from a wealthy citizen to support the library. The $25,000 is invested, and income generated from the investments will be used to purchase books for the library. The entries are as follows:

Books of Nonexpendable Trust Fund

Cash	25,000	
Fund Balance—Reserved for Endowment		25,000
To record gift of endowment for library.		
Investments	25,000	
Cash		25,000
To record investment of library endowment funds.		

Assume that during the remainder of the year, $1,300 is earned on the investments. There are no expenses or other transactions, and the $1,300 is transferred to an expendable trust (operating) fund for the library.

Books of Nonexpendable Trust Fund

Cash	1,300	
Revenues		1,300
To record earnings on investments.		
Operating Transfers Out	1,300	
Cash		1,300
To record operating transfer out to the library operating fund.		

The expendable trust fund records receipt of the $1,300 and then uses $1,050 to acquire library books. Because the gift and the resultant earnings were unplanned, normal budgetary accounting is not employed.

Books of Expendable Trust Fund

Cash	1,300	
Operating Transfers In		1,300
To record operating transfer in from the library endowment fund.		
Expenditures	1,050	
Cash		1,050
To record purchase of library books.		

Closing entries for both funds are shown next:

Books of Nonexpendable Trust Fund

Revenues	1,300	
Operating Transfers Out		1,300
To close revenues and operating transfers.		

Books of Expendable Trust Fund

Operating Transfers In	1,300	
Expenditures		1,050
Fund Balance—Unreserved		250
To close expenditures and operating transfers.		

A common type of trust fund is the pension fund. Because any meaningful discussion of pension fund accounting—public or private—is beyond the scope of this textbook, no illustrations of *pension trust funds* are provided. Three GASB statements issued in 1994 on this and related subjects should be consulted for additional information.[5]

ACCOUNTING FOR AGENCY FUNDS

When a governmental unit acts as collection agent for another entity, **agency funds** are used. The two most common situations involving agency funds are employee deductions and tax collections. Deductions of various types, such as federal and state taxes, health insurance, retirement contributions, union dues, and payroll savings are taken from the earnings of employees and periodically are remitted on behalf of the employees to appropriate entities. In the case of tax collections, one governmental unit may collect taxes on behalf of another. For example, a state may collect income taxes or sales taxes on behalf of a city or county. A county may collect property taxes on behalf of other legal entities—cities, towns, or special districts—within its jurisdiction. In situations involving employee deductions or tax collection, the resources are likely to be held for only a short time by the agency fund. See the Authors' Commentary for examples of agency funds. As previously mentioned, agency funds are also used to account for the *financing of special assessment activities* when the governmental unit itself has no liability in connection therewith. A capital projects fund is used for the *construction*.

Transactions in most agency funds fall into two categories: *collection* and *payment*. The entries for these two transaction types are straightforward. A **collection transaction** requires a debit to cash and a credit to an appropriate liability account; a **payment transaction** requires a debit to the liability and a credit to cash. Because these transactions involve creation or settlement of a liability, an agency fund has no revenues and expenditures, and consequently has no fund balance. Instead, it has offsetting assets and liabilities. Even fees charged by an agency fund serving as a collector of taxes that are shared by several jurisdictions are not revenue to the

---

[5] Governmental Accounting Standards Board, *Statement of Governmental Accounting Standards No. 25*, "Financial Reporting for Defined Benefit Pension Plans and Note Disclosures for Defined Contribution Plans," *No. 26,* "Financial Reporting for Postemployment Healthcare Plans Administered by Defined Benefit Pension Plans," and *No. 27*, "Accounting for Pensions by State and Local Government Employers" (Norwalk, CT: GASB, all issued in 1994).

agency fund. Instead, the fees are deducted from amounts due to the other jurisdictions and are recorded as liabilities due to the general fund of the governmental unit operating the agency fund.

Illustration of Special Assessment Financing in an Agency Fund

Recall from Chapter 12 that improvements that benefit a limited number of property owners are frequently paid for by special assessments on those property owners. Known as special assessment construction activities, these improvements often require bonds to be issued to provide up-front cash needed for construction. The bonds are then serviced and retired over time with special assessment money collected periodically from the property owners by the governmental unit.

Returning to the Lake City example, assume that the town decides to install new streetlights in a certain area. A ten-year 6 percent serial bond issue totaling $100,000 will provide cash for construction. Residents in the affected area will be assessed $131,800 over ten years to retire the bonds and pay interest on the unmatured bonds. The bondholders agreed to waive Lake City's residual liability if sufficient assessments are not collected, in exchange for liens against the assessed properties. Thus the bonds are secured by commercial and residential buildings where the streetlights are located.

These serial bonds, for which Lake City has *no liability*, mature at the rate of $10,000 per year. Each year the assessments collected will be used to pay the $10,000 principal of the bonds maturing and the current year's interest on all the outstanding bonds. Because Lake City has no liability for the bonds, *SGAS 6* requires that the town use an agency fund to account for transactions related to the financing and the assessments. The general long-term debt account group is not affected. If Lake City has primary or residual liability for the bonds, financing and assessment transactions are accounted for in the debt service fund and the general long-term debt account group.

The first year's assessment is $16,000, which is recorded in the Lake City agency fund:

Assessments Receivable—Current	16,000	
Due to Special Assessment Creditors		16,000
To record levy of special assessments.		

The first installment of the assessments is collected, and the $10,000 of principal and $6,000 (=.06 × $100,000) of interest are paid.

Cash	16,000	
Assessments Receivable—Current		16,000
To record collection of current assessments.		
Due to Special Assessment Creditors	16,000	
Cash		16,000
To record payment of $10,000 of principal and $6,000 of interest.		

At the beginning of the next year, the second year's assessments are recorded. In this year, $15,400 is needed to retire $10,000 in bond principal and to pay interest of $5,400 [= .06($100,000 − $10,000)] on the $90,000 of bonds still outstanding.

Assessments Receivable—Current	15,400	
Due to Special Assessment Creditors		15,400
To record the second year's assessments.		

In each succeeding year, a similar set of entries is made until all assessments are collected and all bondholders are paid. Note that only the current portion of the assessment receivables is recorded in the agency fund each period. This treatment follows from the *SGAS 6* requirement that "Special assessment debt for which the government is not obligated in any manner should not be displayed in the government's financial statements" [par. 17b(2)]. Recording the noncurrent assessments as deferred revenue creates such a liability. Thus the agency fund treatment of the special assessments differs from the debt service fund treatment discussed earlier, because the government has no liability.

FINANCIAL STATEMENTS FOR TRUST AND AGENCY FUNDS

Balance sheets are presented for both trust funds and agency funds. Because agency funds have no revenue and expenditure transactions, and no fund balance, a statement of revenues, expenditures, and changes in fund balance is not used. Rather, a statement of changes in assets and liabilities is used to show the agency fund's activity during the year. This statement is illustrated in Exhibit 13.12 later in the chapter.

Nonexpendable trust funds, like proprietary funds, measure net income and cash flows. Financial statements for nonexpendable trust funds, in addition to the balance sheet, are the statement of revenues expenses and changes in retained earnings and the statement of cash flows.

AUTHORS' COMMENTARY

Following are a few examples of trust and agency funds reported in state CAFRs.

Trust Funds

The State of Georgia reports the following expendable trusts: Housing Trust Fund for the Homeless, providing financial assistance to sponsors of housing programs to aid low income residents in becoming homeowners; Keds Corporation Settlement Fund, providing services to women between the ages of 15 and 44 for job training in non-traditional employment fields; the Sports Hall of Fame Board, which maintains a hall of fame to honor outstanding athletes; a Subsequent Injury Trust Fund, encouraging employers to hire workers with pre-existing impairments.

The State of Florida reports a Ringling Museum Investment Trust Fund, a nonexpendable trust fund accounting for the endowment principal for the John and Mable Ringling Museum of Art. Florida also has an expendable trust fund providing for the prepayment of college expenses by state residents. The Florida Hurricane Catastrophe Fund was created in 1993 to provide reimbursement to insurers for some of their catastrophic hurricane losses. The purpose of the fund is to encourage timely repair and reconstruction of damaged property. It is accounted for as an expendable trust.

From fund descriptions, it is difficult to determine why a government reports an activity using an expendable trust fund or a special revenue fund. In either case, resources are earmarked for a particular purpose and there is no separate accounting for principal versus interest. Trust funds are used when the government holds the resources in a trustee capacity and the government may use these resources for purposes designated in the trust agreement. Special revenue fund resources are legally restricted for specified purposes, but a trust agreement is not involved.

Agency Funds

Wisconsin's agency funds include the following: a Local Government Pooled Investment Fund, accounting for investments of idle cash by local governments; an Inmate and Resident Fund, accounting for the assets of inmates in State institutions; and a Student Activity Fund, accounting for activities of student organizations of the Wisconsin School for the Deaf and the Wisconsin School for the Visually Handicapped.

Pennsylvania has an agency fund to collect and administer funds providing claim payments to owners and operators of underground storage tanks who incur liabilities due to release from such tanks. A Deferred Compensation Fund accounts for money contributed by Commonwealth employees who are deferring a portion of their income to future years for tax purposes. A Fire Insurance Tax Fund collects premiums from out-of-state fire insurance companies that do business in Pennsylvania. This money is then distributed to relief, pension or retirement funds of municipal firefighting organizations.

ACCOUNTING FOR INVESTMENTS

A governmental unit typically invests liquid assets on either a short-term or long-term basis. As seen above, amounts accumulated in the debt service fund for payment of term bond principal may be invested over several years. Nonexpendable trust funds invest the principal of the trust. The governmental unit may invest individually, or may combine resources with other units in the form of an investment pool. In the past, these funds reported investments on a *cost* basis, unless declines in market value below cost were considered permanent. Criteria to distinguish temporary versus permanent declines in value were not always clear. When market value was below cost, the cost basis overstated the value of investments and obscured important information on the financial status of the governmental unit. As a result, the GASB enacted *SGAS 31*, "Accounting and Financial Reporting for Certain Investments and for External Investment Pools." The statement specifies that most investments in debt or equity securities, mutual funds, external investment pools, options, warrants, and stock rights be reported at *fair value*, if the investments have readily determinable fair values. Thus *SGAS 31* parallels the investment accounting now required for not-for-profit organizations under *SFAS 124*, studied in Chapter 14.

Investment income and changes in the fair value of investments are reported as revenue in the operating statement—the Statement of Revenues, Expenditures and Changes in Fund Balance for a governmental or expendable trust fund, or the Statement of Revenues, Expenses, and Changes in Retained Earnings for a proprietary or nonexpendable trust fund.

SGAS 31 allows more accurate reporting of the financial condition of a governmental unit. The financial effects of poor investment decisions will be reported on a more timely basis. Cases of poor investment management by governments have unfortunately been too common in recent years. In the early 1990s, Orange County, California ran a $20 billion investment pool which invested on behalf of 187 California municipalities. The County and its investment pool filed for bankruptcy court protection when the pool lost $1.7 billion due to risky investments. In 1994, the Township of Independence, Michigan was told by the State of Michigan to sell investments believed to be in violation of the State Investment Act. According to the Township's 1994 financial report, these sales were expected to result in losses. Legal counsel was engaged to pursue action against brokers deemed responsible for these investments.

THE COMPREHENSIVE ANNUAL FINANCIAL REPORT

Chapter 12 and prior sections of Chapter 13 study how routine and nonroutine transactions are accounted for in each of the fund types. Now we turn to the *external* presentation of financial information of a governmental unit. The external financial report of a state or local governmental unit is known as the **Comprehensive Annual Financial Report**, or **CAFR**, and is equivalent to the annual report to shareholders for a business. The financial statements are generally presented in either a *combined, individual,* or *combining* format. **Combined statements**, as the name suggests, bring together information on several funds. Their purpose is to provide an overview of the financial affairs of the governmental unit by showing totals of all funds within some or all of the several fund types and account groups that comprise the reporting entity. Memorandum totals across all fund types reported are typically provided. Unlike consolidated statements, however, transactions and financial relationships among the various funds making up the reporting entity are typically *not eliminated* when combined statements are prepared.[6]

Combining statements are presented when the unit has more than one fund of a given type. **Individual statements** are presented for the two account groups and any other fund for which additional disclosure is appropriate. The format of the CAFR, outlined in the GASB *Codification*, is called the "financial reporting pyramid," presented in Figure 13.1.

Major components of the CAFR are described below, and are illustrated using the 1996 CAFR for Erie County, New York.

COMBINED FINANCIAL STATEMENTS

Combined statements show the financial results for several funds and account groups in one statement. They are composed of five **general-purpose financial statements**.

Combined Balance Sheet

The combined balance sheet shows the balance sheets of all governmental funds, proprietary funds, fiduciary funds, and account groups for the primary government, and also any component units. Component units are legally separate organizations for which the elected primary officials of the primary government are financially responsible, or other units which have a relationship with the primary government such that exclusion of financial information on these units is misleading. Assets, liabilities and fund balance/retained earnings are shown by fund type or account group, and memorandum totals for all accounts are also shown.

---

[6] When interfund or similar eliminations *are* reflected in the combined totals, this should be made clear from the statement headings or disclosed in the notes to the financial statements; see pars. 2200.112, 114, and 116 in the *Codification*.

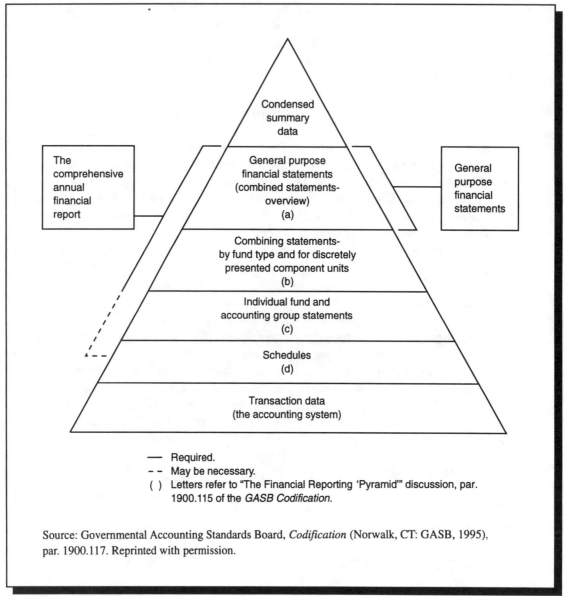

Source: Governmental Accounting Standards Board, *Codification* (Norwalk, CT: GASB, 1995), par. 1900.117. Reprinted with permission.

FIGURE 13.1 THE FINANCIAL REPORTING "PYRAMID"

The combined balance sheet for Erie County, New York appears in Exhibit 13.5. The primary government uses all four governmental fund types: general, special revenue, debt service, and capital projects funds. Erie County does not have any internal service funds and therefore only reports balances for the enterprise fund type, consisting of a medical center and a nursing home. The County also has no trust funds and only reports balances for the agency fund type. Both account groups are used. In addition, the Community College is shown separately, although it is not a separate legal entity, because it has a different fiscal year-end and uses somewhat different accounting procedures. Erie County considers its library as a component unit, since it is a separate legal entity but the County is financially accountable for the library's financial performance.

Some interesting features of the combined balance sheet are:

- The governmental funds do not report inventories, implying that the *purchases* method is used to account for inventories, and that inventories are not significant enough to warrant disclosure of a reserve for inventories.
- The amount shown in the general long-term debt account group as available for retirement of general long-term debt ($20,603,000) equals the fund balance reported by the debt service fund.
- General fund balance is reserved for various purposes in addition to encumbrances. For example, prepaid items of $22,446,000 are shown as both an asset and a reserved fund balance, similar to inventory disclosure using the purchases method. Resources spent for prepaid items are apparently shown as expenditures—reductions in fund balance—but prepaid balances are disclosed as reserved fund balances.
- The "due from" and "due to" accounts do not articulate: the total for "due from other funds" is $71,168, but the "due to other funds" account has a balance of $69,329.
- A significant amount of unreserved fund balances are designated for subsequent year expenditures.

Combined Statement of Revenues, Expenditures, and Changes in Fund Balances

The combined statement of revenues, expenditures, and changes in fund balances is the combined operating statement for governmental funds and component units that use fund accounting. It presents revenues, expenditures, and changes in fund balance for each *governmental* fund type—general fund, special revenue fund, debt service fund, and capital projects fund, for expendable trusts, and for discrete component units using modified accrual accounting. Total balances for all fund types are also presented.

The combined statement of revenues, expenditures, and changes in fund balances for Erie County appears in Exhibit 13.6. The governmental funds are the general, special revenue, debt service, and capital projects funds. The operations of the library, considered a separate governmental-type component unit, are shown in a separate column. Note that revenues are categorized as to where the resources came from. Expenditures are categorized on a **functional** basis, showing expenditures by type of program or service. Other financing sources and uses consist of proceeds of debt financing (all recorded in the capital projects fund), proceeds from sale of property, and operating transfers. The end of year fund balances articulate with the fund balances reported for these funds and component unit in the Combined Balance Sheet.

COUNTY OF ERIE, NEW YORK
Combined Balance Sheet - All Fund Types, Account Groups and Discretely Presented Component Unit
December 31, 1996
(amounts expressed in thousands)

	Governmental Fund Type				Proprietary Fund Type	Fiduciary Fund Type	Account Groups		Community College	Totals (Memorandum Only)	Component Unit	Totals (Memorandum Only)
	General	Special Revenue	Debt Service	Capital Projects	Enterprise	Agency	General Fixed Assets	General Long-Term Debt	August 31, 1996	Primary Government	Library	Reporting Entity
Assets and other debits												
Assets:												
Cash and investments	$ 89,849	$ 21,042	$ 15,693	$ 41,487	$ 2	$ 62,784	$	$	$ 14,644	$ 245,501	$ 2,126	$ 247,627
Patient & residents' trust cash					635					635		635
Receivables (net of allowances)												
Real property taxes, interest, penalties and liens	535,861	89								535,950		535,950
Other	156	13,424	9	255	59,224				1,718	74,786	362	75,148
Due from other funds	37,924	20,782	4,904	7,220	238	100				71,168		71,168
Due from primary government											23,025	23,025
Due from other governments	117,052	19,705	24	843						137,872		137,872
Deferred compensation assets						82,147				82,147		82,147
Bonds and securities held in custody						60				60		60
Inventories					2,763					2,763		2,763
Prepaid items	22,446				1,048				130	23,624		23,624
Advances to Enterprise Funds	5,993									5,993		5,993
Restricted cash and investments					12,053				143	12,196		12,196
Other assets					567					567		567
Fixed assets (net, where applicable, of accumulated depreciation and amortization)					86,541		539,598		15,438	641,577		641,577
Other debits:												
Amount available in debt service fund for retirement of general long-term debt								20,603		20,603		20,603
Amount to be provided in future years budgets for retirement of general long-term debt								256,534		256,534		256,534
Total assets and other debits	$ 809,281	$ 75,042	$ 20,630	$ 49,805	$ 163,071	$ 145,339	$ 539,598	$ 277,137	$ 32,073	$ 2,111,976	$ 25,513	$ 2,137,489

(Continued)

EXHIBIT 13.5 1996 COMBINED BALANCE SHEET—ERIE COUNTY, NY

COUNTY OF ERIE, NEW YORK
Combined Balance Sheet - All Fund Types, Account Groups and Discretely Presented Component Unit
December 31, 1996
(amounts expressed in thousands)

	Governmental Fund Types				Proprietary Fund Type	Fiduciary Fund Type	Account Groups		Community College August 31, 1996	Totals (Memorandum Only) Primary Government	Component Unit Library	Total Reporting Entity (Memorandum Only)
	General	Special Revenue	Debt Service	Capital Projects	Enterprise	Agency	General Fixed Assets	General Long-Term Debt				
Liabilities, equity and other credits												
Liabilities:												
Accounts payable	$ 11,789	$ 3,759	$	$ 4,787	$ 15,284	$	$	$	$ 1,178	$ 36,797	$ 361	$ 37,158
Accrued liabilities	87,264	5,957	27	28	19,186				7,092	119,554	347	119,901
Due to other funds	23,913	13,866		10,214	238	19,719			1,379	69,329		69,329
Due to component unit	23,018			7						23,025		23,025
Due to other governments	239,030				17,275					256,305		256,305
Retained percentages		6		1,691						1,697		1,697
Amounts held in custody for others					635	108,345				108,980		108,980
Deferred revenue	284,808	34,425			520				4,078	323,831	23,406	347,237
Short-term debt	57,060			708	22,940					80,708		80,708
Advances from General Fund					5,993					5,993		5,993
Bonds payable					50,078			223,756		273,834		273,834
Other long-term obligations					22,689			53,381		76,070		76,070
Total Liabilities	726,882	58,013	27	17,435	137,563	145,339		277,137	13,727	1,376,123	24,114	1,400,237
Equity and other credits:												
Investment in fixed assets							539,598		15,438	555,036		555,036
Contributed capital					11,965					11,965		11,965
Retained earnings:												
Reserved for debt service					1,227					1,227		1,227
Unreserved					12,316					12,316		12,316
Fund balances:												
Reserved for encumbrances	13,856	2,435		16,434					1,992	34,717	447	35,164
Reserved for advances to Enterprise Funds	5,993									5,993		5,993
Reserved for debt service			10,299							10,299		10,299
Reserved for prepaid items	22,446									22,446		22,446
Reserved for repairs		1,658								1,658		1,658
Reserved for E-911 system costs		173								173		173
Unreserved												
Designated for subsequent year's expenditures	18,912	4,416	10,304						345	33,977		33,977
Designated for property tax relief	9,400									9,400		9,400
Designated for judgements and claims	5,125									5,125		5,125
Designated for contingencies											254	254
Undesignated	6,667	8,347		15,936					571	31,521	698	32,219
Total equity and other credits	82,399	17,029	20,603	32,370	25,508		539,598		18,346	735,853	1,399	737,252
Total liabilities, equity and other credits	$ 809,281	$ 75,042	$ 20,630	$ 49,805	$ 163,071	$ 145,339	$ 539,598	$ 277,137	$ 32,073	$ 2,111,976	$ 25,513	$ 2,137,489

See accompanying notes to general purpose financial statements

EXHIBIT 13.5 *(Continued)*

COUNTY OF ERIE, NEW YORK
Combined Statement of Revenues, Expenditures and Changes in Fund Balances
All Governmental Fund Types and Discretely Presented Component Unit
For the fiscal year ended December 31, 1996
(amounts expressed in thousands)

	Governmental Fund Types				Totals (Memorandum Only) Primary Government	Component Unit Library	Totals (Memorandum Only) Reporting Entity
	General	Special Revenue	Debt Service	Capital Projects			
Revenues:							
Real property taxes and tax items	$ 203,737	$ 16,652	$	$	$ 220,389	$ 22,029	$ 242,418
Sales and use taxes	207,232	8,825			216,057		216,057
Intergovernmental	223,530	62,483	773	4,830	291,616	2,773	294,389
Interfund revenues	19,559	2,871		1,638	24,068		24,068
Departmental	50,269	15,551		723	66,543	488	67,031
Interest	13,458	894	2,712	32	17,096	19	17,115
Miscellaneous	8,409	222	1,849	78	10,558	181	10,739
Total revenues	726,194	107,498	5,334	7,301	846,327	25,490	871,817
Expenditures:							
Current:							
General government support	65,868	6,098			71,966		71,966
Public safety	62,685	10,564			73,249		73,249
Health	32,543	10,449			42,992		42,992
Transportation	15,861	22,006			37,867		37,867
Economic assistance and opportunity	425,519	49,239			474,758		474,758
Culture and recreation	10,752	1,956			12,708	24,300	37,008
Education	39,053				39,053		39,053
Home and community service	4,028	23,819			27,847		27,847
Capital outlay				35,561	35,561		35,561
Debt service:							
Principal retirement	162		26,768		26,930		26,930
Interest and fiscal charges	3,596		12,691		16,287		16,287
Total expenditures	660,067	124,131	39,459	35,561	859,218	24,300	883,518
Excess (deficiency) of revenues over expenditures	66,127	(16,633)	(34,125)	(28,260)	(12,891)	1,190	(11,701)

(Continued)

EXHIBIT 13.6 1996 COMBINED STATEMENT OF REVENUES, EXPENDITURES, AND CHANGES IN FUND BALANCES—ERIE COUNTY, NY

COUNTY OF ERIE, NEW YORK
Combined Statement of Revenues, Expenditures and Changes in Fund Balances
All Governmental Fund Types and Discretely Presented Component Unit
For the fiscal year ended December 31, 1996
(amounts expressed in thousands)

	Governmental Fund Types				Totals (Memorandum Only) Primary Government	Component Unit Library	Totals (Memorandum Only) Reporting Entity
	General	Special Revenue	Debt Service	Capital Projects			
Other financing sources (uses):							
Proceeds of general obligation debt				34,825	34,825		34,825
Proceeds of contractual debt				1,981	1,981		1,981
Proceeds of installment purchase debt				238	238		238
Sale of property	164	7			171	106	277
Operating transfers in	17,574	25,862	28,685	7,627	79,748		79,748
Operating transfers from component unit			615		615		615
Operating transfers from primary government					0	122	122
Operating transfers out	(77,614)	(5,816)			(83,430)		(83,430)
Operating transfers to primary government					0	(615)	(615)
Operating transfers to component unit	(122)				(122)		(122)
Total other financing sources (uses)	(59,998)	20,053	29,300	44,671	34,026	(387)	33,639
Excess (deficiency) of revenues and other financing sources over expenditures and other financing uses	6,129	3,420	(4,825)	16,411	21,135	803	21,938
Fund balances at beginning of year	76,270	13,609	25,428	15,959	131,266	596	131,862
Fund balances at end of year	$ 82,399	$ 17,029	$ 20,603	$ 32,370	$ 152,401	$ 1,399	$ 153,800

See accompanying notes to general purpose financial statements.

EXHIBIT 13.6 *(Continued)*

Combined Statement of Revenues, Expenditures and Changes in Fund Balances—Budget and Actual

The combined statement of revenues, expenditures and changes in fund balances—budget and actual shows budget versus actual revenues and expenditures for those governmental funds governed by legally adopted annual budgets. The statement addresses accountability of the government by disclosing whether it is in compliance with the legal budget.

The combined statement of revenues, expenditures, and changes in fund balances—budget and actual for Erie County appears in Exhibit 13.7. In Erie County, legally adopted budgets are used for the general fund, the special revenue funds, and the debt service fund. These budgets are submitted to the Erie County Legislature by the County Executive, and the Legislature votes to adopt the budget for the fiscal year beginning January 1, no later than the second Tuesday of the previous December. For the year 1996, the budgeted general fund deficit was $48,158,000 but the actual deficit was $7,727,000, for a favorable variance of $40,431,000, explained as follows: General fund revenues were below budget by $11,178,000, but expenditures were below budget by $33,010,000. Actual other financing net uses were below budget by $18,599,000. The special revenue funds and debt service fund also show lower actual deficits than budgeted.

Combined Statement of Revenues, Expenses and Changes in Retained Earnings

The combined statement of revenues, expenses and changes in retained earnings shows a combined income statement and statement of retained earnings for the proprietary and nonexpendable trust funds, and any component units reported using business accounting. It shows income statements for each fund type, as well as totals for all funds.

Erie County does not report any internal service funds or nonexpendable trusts. Its only proprietary fund type is its enterprise funds. Therefore it does not disclose a separate combined statement for its business-type funds. The enterprise column in the combined balance sheet in Exhibit 13.5 suffices.

Combined Statement of Cash Flows

The combined statement of cash flows shows a combined statement of cash flows for the proprietary funds. The structure of the statement is different from that of a business, however. Cash flows are categorized as:

- **Cash flows from operating activities**, consisting of cash received from customers and users, and cash paid to suppliers and employees; the direct or indirect approach may be used to reconcile operating income to cash from operations
- **Cash flows from noncapital financing activities**, consisting of operating transfers, borrowings and payments on noncapital debt
- **Cash flows from capital and related financing activities**, consisting of borrowings and payments on capital debt and leases, purchase and sale of fixed assets, construction costs
- **Cash flows from investing activities**, consisting of purchase and sale of investments, investment earnings

Erie County again does not report a separate combined statement of cash flows because it only has one proprietary fund type.

COUNTY OF ERIE, NEW YORK
Combined Statement of Revenues, Expenditures and Changes in Fund Balances -
Budget and Actual - Budgetary Basis (Note I(D)) -
General Fund, Special Revenue Funds and Debt Service Fund
For the fiscal year ended December 31, 1996
(amounts expressed in thousands)

	General Fund			Special Revenue Funds			Debt Service Fund		
	Budget	Budgetary Actual	Variance Favorable (Unfavorable)	Budget	Budgetary Actual	Variance Favorable (Unfavorable)	Budget	Budgetary Actual	Variance Favorable (Unfavorable)
Revenues:									
Real property taxes and tax items	$ 204,971	$ 203,737	$ (1,234)	$ 16,607	$ 16,652	$ 45	$	$	$
Sales and use taxes	206,886	207,232	346	7,764	8,825	1,061			
Intergovernmental	236,003	223,530	(12,473)	5,417	55	(5,362)	743	773	30
Interfund revenue	19,464	19,559	95	586	273	(313)			
Departmental	49,086	50,269	1,183	8,474	8,597	123			
Interest	13,148	13,458	310	333	872	539	1,515	2,712	1,197
Miscellaneous	7,814	8,409	595		28	28	3,123	1,849	(1,274)
Total revenues	737,372	726,194	(11,178)	39,181	35,302	(3,879)	5,381	5,334	(47)
Expenditures:									
Current:									
General government support	78,006	71,260	6,746	1,187	1,187		220		220
Public safety	68,421	65,839	2,582	1,888	1,825	63			
Health	45,591	33,856	11,735	30,242	22,863	7,379			
Transportation	15,920	15,920							
Economic assistance and opportunity	447,107	440,033	7,074						
Culture and recreation	11,521	10,899	622						
Education	43,284	39,286	3,998						
Home and community service	4,275	4,075	200	23,444	18,823	4,621			
Debt service:									
Principal retirement	215	162	53				26,768	26,768	0
Interest and fiscal charges	3,596	3,596		232		232	12,691	12,691	0
Total expenditures	717,936	684,926	33,010	56,993	44,698	12,295	39,679	39,459	220
Excess (deficiency) of revenues over expenditures	19,436	41,268	21,832	(17,812)	(9,396)	8,416	(34,298)	(34,125)	173
Other financing sources (uses):									
Sale of property	93	164	71	3	4	1			
Operating transfers in	164	17,574	17,574	15,770	14,859	(911)	18,814	28,685	9,871
Operating transfers from component unit								615	615
Operating transfers out	(67,565)	(66,611)	954	(6,195)	(5,816)	379			
Operating transfers to component unit	(122)	(122)							
Total other financing sources (uses)	(67,594)	(48,995)	18,599	9,578	9,047	(531)	18,814	29,300	10,486
Excess (deficiency) of revenues and other financing sources over expenditures and other financing uses	$ (48,158)	$ (7,727)	$ 40,431	$ (8,234)	$ (349)	$ 7,885	$ (15,484)	$ (4,825)	$ 10,659

See accompanying notes to general purpose financial statements.

EXHIBIT 13.7 1996 BUDGETARY COMPARISON STATEMENT—ERIE COUNTY, NY

COMBINING FINANCIAL STATEMENTS

The combining financial statements follow the same format as the *combined* financial statements, but provide more detailed information on the individual funds. Remember that the combined statements report account balances by *fund type*. *Combining* statements are presented for an individual fund type if there is *more than one fund* of a given fund type. For example, a state typically has several capital projects and special revenue funds—see the Authors' Commentary for examples. A separate debt service fund may be used for each bond issue. A combining Balance Sheet, Statement of Revenues, Expenditures and Changes in Fund Balance, and Budgetary Statement are presented for governmental funds and expendable trust funds. A combining Balance sheet, Statement of Revenues, Expenses and Changes in Retained Earnings and Statement of Cash Flows are presented for enterprise, internal service, and nonexpendable trust funds. When a municipality does not have more than one fund per fund type, a combining statement is not shown for this fund type.

A combining balance sheet is shown in Exhibit 13.8 for Erie County's special revenue funds, consisting of road, sewer, downtown mall, E-911,[7] community development, and grants funds.

Erie County's combining statement of revenues, expenses and changes in retained earnings for its enterprise funds appears in Exhibit 13.9. Its enterprise funds consist of the county medical center, which is a primary health care center, and the county nursing home. The medical center reported a profit of $216,000 for 1996; the nursing home reported a profit of $201,000 for the same period. However, the medical center incurred an operating deficit of $5,113,000, while the nursing home showed an operating income of $11,799,000. The difference between operating income and net income is explained by large transfers—net transfers in for the medical center and net transfers out for the nursing home. Note that no budgetary information is provided for proprietary funds. The combining statement of cash flows for Erie County's two enterprise funds appears in Exhibit 13.10. The *indirect* approach is used to report cash from operations. The total change in cash and cash equivalents for 1996 is $2,432,000, with the majority of the net cash inflow derived from operations.

Individual Financial Statements

Individual statements are presented for the general fixed assets account group and the general long-term debt account group, and for any governmental or proprietary fund when needed for full disclosure or to demonstrate compliance with finance-related legal and contractual provisions. The general fixed assets account group lists fixed assets used in activities accounted for by governmental funds. Usually the assets are carried at historical cost, and no depreciation is recognized. The general long-term debt account group lists the principal portion of general obligation debt. Each statement shows major changes during the year—additions and subtractions of fixed assets, and procurement and payment of the principal portion of debt. The individual statement for the general long-term debt account group is typically found in the notes to the financial statements rather than with the other individual statements, and also includes detailed information on debt maturities and expected interest payments.

---

[7] The E-911 Special Revenue Fund accounts for revenues raised through a telephone access line surcharge, and expenditures of these funds for establishment and maintenance of an Enhanced 911 system.

COUNTY OF ERIE, NEW YORK
Special Revenue Funds
Combining Balance Sheet
December 31, 1996
(amounts expressed in thousands)

	Road	Sewer	Downtown Mall	E-911	Community Development	Grants	Total
Assets							
Cash and investments	$ 5,604	$ 15,337	$ 13	$ 88	$	$	$ 21,042
Receivables (net of allowances)							
Real property taxes, interest, penalties & liens			89				89
Other		2		326	12,977	119	13,424
Due from other funds	2	19,741				1,039	20,782
Due from other governments	2,676	75			1,037	15,917	19,705
Total assets	$ 8,282	$ 35,155	$ 102	$ 414	$ 14,014	$ 17,075	$ 75,042
Liabilities							
Accounts payable	$ 895	$ 670		$ 130	$ 157	$ 1,907	$ 3,759
Accrued liabilities	1,185	3,371	65		473	863	5,957
Due to other funds	2,680	2	8		434	10,742	13,866
Retained percentages		6					6
Deferred revenue	47	19,199			12,950	2,229	34,425
Total liabilities	4,807	23,248	73	130	14,014	15,741	58,013
Fund equity							
Fund balance:							
Reserved for encumbrances	857	1,467		111			2,435
Reserved for repairs	1,658						1,658
Reserved for E-911 system costs				173			173
Unreserved:							
Designated for subsequent year's expenditures		3,082				1,334	4,416
Undesignated	960	7,358	29				8,347
Total fund equity	3,475	11,907	29	284	0	1,334	17,029
Total liabilities and fund equity	$ 8,282	$ 35,155	$ 102	$ 414	$ 14,014	$ 17,075	$ 75,042

EXHIBIT 13.8   1996 COMBINING BALANCE SHEET—SPECIAL REVENUE FUNDS—ERIE COUNTY, NY

COUNTY OF ERIE, NEW YORK
Combining Statement of Revenues, Expenses and Changes in Retained Earnings -
All Enterprise Funds
For the fiscal year ended December 31, 1996
(amounts expressed in thousands)

	Medical Center	Nursing Home	Total
Operating revenues:			
Net patient service revenue	$ 179,419	$ 46,623	$ 226,042
Other operating revenues	11,823	22	11,845
Total operating revenues	191,242	46,645	237,887
Operating expenses:			
Employee wages	81,953	18,477	100,430
Employee benefits	17,624	5,334	22,958
Contractual, professional & temporary services	33,620	4,883	38,503
Supplies	23,808	1,002	24,810
Utilities & telephone	5,780	98	5,878
Provision for depreciation & amortization	10,299	897	11,196
Interest expense	4,379	272	4,651
Provision for bad debts	14,859		14,859
Other operating expense	3,342	306	3,648
Services provided by County of Erie	691	3,577	4,268
Total operating expenses	196,355	34,846	231,201
Operating income (loss)	(5,113)	11,799	6,686
Nonoperating revenues:			
Income from investments	371	153	524
Income (loss) before operating transfers	(4,742)	11,952	7,210
Operating transfers in	8,466	2,315	10,781
Operating transfers out	(3,508)	(14,066)	(17,574)
Net income	216	201	417
Add: Amortization on fixed assets acquired with State capital grants	78		78
Increase in retained earnings	294	201	495
Retained earnings at beginning of year	170	12,878	13,048
Retained earnings at end of year	$ 464	$ 13,079	$ 13,543

See accompanying notes to general purpose financial statements.

EXHIBIT 13.9 1996 COMBINING OPERATING STATEMENT—ENTERPRISE FUNDS— ERIE COUNTY, NY

COUNTY OF ERIE, NEW YORK
Combining Statement of Cash Flows -
All Enterprise Funds
For the fiscal year ended December 31, 1996
(amounts expressed in thousands)

	Medical Center	Nursing Home	Total
Cash flows from operating activities:			
Operating income (loss)	$ (5,113)	$ 11,799	$ 6,686
Adjustments to reconcile operating income (loss) to net cash provided by operating activities:			
Depreciation and amortization	10,299	897	11,196
Change in:			
Accounts receivable	(9,781)	2,900	(6,881)
Due from other funds	1,086	509	1,595
Inventory	405	63	468
Prepaid items	194	2,929	3,123
Other assets	(101)		(101)
Deferred charges	223		223
Accounts payable	2,074	161	2,235
Accrued liabilities (net of interest)	3,163	31	3,194
Due to other funds		(6,109)	(6,109)
Amounts held in custody for others	(19)	19	0
Deferred revenue	(400)		(400)
Other long-term liabilities	48	(155)	(107)
Interest used for noncapital financing activities	1,320	64	1,384
Interest used for capital and related financing activities	3,060	207	3,267
Net cash provided by operating activities	6,458	13,315	19,773
Cash flows from noncapital financing activities:			
Operating transfers in	8,466	2,315	10,781
Operating transfers out	(3,508)	(14,066)	(17,574)
Advances from (to) other funds	93	(312)	(219)
Borrowings under revenue anticipation note arrangement	22,940		22,940
Principal paid on revenue anticipation note arrangement	(18,965)		(18,965)
Interest paid on revenue anticipation note arrangement	(388)		(388)
Net cash provided (used) by noncapital financing activities	8,638	(12,063)	(3,425)

(Continued)

EXHIBIT 13.10   **1996 COMBINING STATEMENT OF CASH FLOWS—ENTERPRISE FUNDS—ERIE COUNTY, NY**

COUNTY OF ERIE, NEW YORK
Combining Statement of Cash Flows -
All Enterprise Funds
For the fiscal year ended December 31, 1996
(amounts expressed in thousands)

	Medical Center	Nursing Home	Total
Cash flows from capital and related financing activities:			
Proceeds from issuance of serial bonds	4,500	414	4,914
Acquisition and construction of capital assets	(5,260)	(1,787)	(7,047)
Principal repayments	(8,483)	(423)	(8,906)
Interest paid	(3,133)	(268)	(3,401)
Net cash used by capital and related financing activities	(12,376)	(2,064)	(14,440)
Cash flows from investing activities:			
Interest earnings	371	153	524
Net increase (decrease) in cash and cash equivalents	3,091	(659)	2,432
Cash and cash equivalents, beginning of year	5,831	4,427	10,258
Cash and cash equivalents, end of year	$ 8,922	$ 3,768	$ 12,690

Noncash investing, capital, and financing activities (000s omitted):
  During the year, equipment with a fair market value of $57
  was donated to the Medical Center Enterprise Fund.

See accompanying notes to general purpose financial statements.

EXHIBIT 13.10   *(Continued)*

The individual statement for the general fixed assets account group of Erie County appears in Exhibit 13.11. It shows each *asset group* separately—land, buildings, improvements, equipment—and by *activity*—general government, public safety, public health, and other activities such as education.

An individual statement for Erie County's agency fund appears in footnote format, in Exhibit 13.12. The majority of the activity in Erie County's agency fund is the collection and disbursement of sales taxes and payroll taxes and withholdings. Collections and payments are generally almost equal, except for deferred compensation plan withholdings from employees, which are held by the County over a period of time before being paid out to the employees.

In summary, the Comprehensive Annual Financial Report of a state or local government consists of the following sets of financial statements:

- Combined financial statements
  - Combined balance sheet—all fund types and account groups and discretely presented component units
  - Combined statement of revenues, expenditures, and changes in fund balances—all governmental fund types and discretely presented component units
  - Combined statement of revenues, expenditures, and changes in fund balances—budget and actual—all governmental funds for which annual budgets are legally adopted
  - Combined statement of revenues, expenses, and changes in retained earnings—all proprietary fund types and discretely presented component units
  - Combined statement of cash flows—all proprietary fund types and discretely presented component units
- Combining statements by fund type—used for any fund type with more than one individual fund
- Individual statements for account groups and funds not shown in the combining statements

ADDITIONAL SCHEDULES AND INFORMATION

Notes to the financial statements and schedules detailing compliance with legal restrictions, and other relevant information aiding readers in assessing the government's activities, are also presented in the CAFR. For example, Erie County's 1996 CAFR shows the following schedules for each of the last ten years:

- General government expenditures by function
- General revenues by source
- Property tax levies and collections
- Assessed value of taxable property
- Property tax rates for Erie County and other local taxing entities
- Ratio of net general bonded debt to assessed value, and net bonded debt per capita
- Ratio of general obligation debt service to total general expenditures

COUNTY OF ERIE, NEW YORK
Schedule of General Fixed Assets
By Function and Activity
December 31, 1996
(amounts expressed in thousands)

	Land	Buildings	Improvements Other than Buildings	Equipment	Total
General government:					
Legislative	$	$	$	$ 150	$ 150
Judicial				694	694
Executive				52	52
Budget, Management and Finance	1,286			112	1,398
Comptroller				130	130
Purchasing				56	56
County clerk				437	437
Law				12	12
Personnel				48	48
Elections				49	49
Public works - administration				6	6
General government buildings	3,138	40,435	4,185	224	47,982
Information and Support				16,126	16,126
Total general government	4,424	40,435	4,185	18,096	67,140
Public safety:					
Administration				13	13
Law enforcement	465	67,180		7,012	74,657
Fire prevention	50	3,765	146	1,767	5,728
Total public safety	515	70,945	146	8,792	80,398
Public health:					
Health				3,040	3,040
Mental health				3,490	3,490
Total public health	0	0	0	6,530	6,530
Economic assistance & opportunity				2,207	2,207
Education	2,841	71,109	58		74,008
Culture and recreation	9,308	111,464	1,053	56,323	178,148
Home & community services				367	367
Sanitation & waste removal	900	93,570	1,365	2,338	98,173
Public welfare	66	2,569		3,188	5,823
Transportation	104	5,864		18,875	24,843
Surplus (warehouse)				1,961	1,961
Total fixed assets	$ 18,158	$ 395,956	$ 6,807	$ 118,677	$ 539,598

EXHIBIT 13.11   1996 INDIVIDUAL STATEMENT—GENERAL FIXED ASSETS ACCOUNT GROUP—ERIE COUNTY, NY

| | | (000s omitted) | | |
	Balance 1-1-96	Additions and Adjustments	Deductions and Adjustments	Balance 12-31-96
ASSETS				
Cash and investments	$ 53,328	$954,150	$944,694	$ 62,784
Due from other funds	48	100	48	100
Due from other governments	0	248		248
Deferred compensation assets	68,821	14,319	993	82,147
Bonds and securities held in custody	5	60	5	60
Total assets	$122,202	$968,877	$945,740	$145,339
LIABILITIES				
Due to other funds	$ 16,228	$ 33,200	$ 25,709	$ 19,719
Due to other governments	12,419	16,310	11,454	17,275
Amounts held in custody for others:				
Sales taxes	0	189,856	189,856	0
Deferred compensation plan obligations to employees	68,894	14,319	1,066	82,147
Court funds	3,346	2,261	2,179	3,428
Mortgage tax	1,684	9,515	9,600	1,599
Social services	2,986	77,471	77,497	2,960
Bail and bid deposits	1,305	366	199	1,472
Payroll taxes and withholdings	6,279	234,555	236,154	4,680
Miscellaneous - Other	9,061	17,576	14,578	12,059
Total amounts held in custody for others	93,555	545,919	531,129	108,345
Total liabilities	$122,202	$595,429	$572,292	$145,339

EXHIBIT 13.12   1996 INDIVIDUAL STATEMENT—AGENCY FUND—ERIE COUNTY, NY

THE GASB'S NEW FINANCIAL REPORTING MODEL

On January 31, 1997, the Governmental Accounting Standards Board (GASB) issued a proposed Statement governing external reporting by state and local governments.[8] The new reporting model proposed in this *Exposure Draft* represents a fundamental change in the way governments report their financial performance. In developing the new reporting model, the GASB took a hard look at the current model and its effectiveness in meeting the needs of interested readers.

[8] Governmental Accounting Standards Board, *Exposure Draft*, "Basic Financial Statements—and Management's Discussion and Analysis—for State and Local Governments" (Norwalk, CT: GASB, 1997).

Remember from Chapter 12 that there are three major users of governmental financial reports: investors and creditors, citizenry, and legislative and oversight bodies. Traditionally, credit market representatives have the greatest interest in the reports. They are concerned with the entity's ability to meet obligations as they come due. Citizens, legislative and oversight bodies are concerned with how much money the government has available to spend, where tax dollars are going, costs of services, sources of funding for various programs, and the implications of the current level of services for future tax obligations. The motivations of financial statement users other than credit market representatives are not always clear, and opinions differ on the value of financial statement information to citizens and oversight groups. The GASB hopes to attract more readers with its new reporting model.

The objective of current reporting requirements is one of **accountability**. Governments are expected to use resources for their intended purpose and comply with legally enacted budgets. Financial information traditionally reports how current activities are financed, how much in current resources is available for future expenditures, budget versus actual revenues and expenditures, and any significant changes in current financial position during the year. The governmental entity is accounted for through separate accounting subentities, each with its own balance sheet and operating statement. The fund basis allows separation of resources dedicated to specific activities, and serves as a control mechanism.

The measurement focus for most activities is the **flow of current financial resources**, defined as cash, cash equivalents and receivables, net of payables and short-term debt. Revenues are inflows of current financial resources, and expenditures are outflows of current financial resources. This focus assures that resources available to finance expenditures of the current period are matched with outflows of resources, and the difference between assets and liabilities, or fund balance, represents financial resources available for future expenditures. It also allows comparison with budgeted inflows and outflows. The full accrual basis of accounting is used only for proprietary funds, where fee-for-service activities make it essential to know the costs of services.

THE PROPOSED FINANCIAL REPORTING MODEL

The GASB believes that its proposed financial accounting model will make the financial reports easier to understand and more informative to users. The focus is not just on current readers of the reports; it is hoped that the new format will draw new readers as well.

Two major changes from current practice are inherent in the proposal:

- *Financial reporting from two perspectives: an entity-wide perspective and a funds perspective*
- *Use of accrual-based accounting for the entity-wide perspective*

The financial report consists of four parts:

- Management's discussion and analysis
- Entity-wide-perspective financial statements
- Fund-perspective financial statements
- Notes and other required supplementary information

Management's Discussion and Analysis

The purpose of the management's decision and analysis (MD & A) section is to provide a readable summary of the year's financial performance, in comparison with last year's performance. Specific requirements include:

- Explanation of the objectives of the two perspectives presented in the financial statements.
- Condensed entity-wide financial statements, comparing the current year to the prior year and analyzing the reasons for significant changes.
- Analysis of significant differences between original and final budget amounts and between budget and actual amounts for the general fund, with emphasis on the effect on future services and liquidity.
- A description of capital asset and long-term debt transactions, including significant commitments for capital expenditures, changes in credit ratings, and the effect of debt limitations on financing of future assets or services.
- Discussion of whether the government's overall financial position, including both governmental and business-type activities, improved or deteriorated, with analysis of significant changes in the financial position of specific funds.
- Explanation of differences between **net assets** of governmental funds using the entity-wide perspective and **fund balances** using the funds perspective.
- Description of currently known circumstances which have or are expected to have an impact on financial performance.

Entity-Wide Financial Statements

There are two required entity-wide statements: a **Statement of Net Assets** and a **Statement of Activities**. These statements show financial performance overall, and are not segregated by fund type or account group. Assets, liabilities and net assets allocated to governmental activities and business-type activities are separately disclosed. Similarly, revenues and expenses are separated into governmental and business-type activities. These statements are prepared using **full accrual accounting**—what the GASB calls the *economic resources measurement focus*.

The **Statement of Net Assets** shows all governmental assets and liabilities, including capital assets and long-term liabilities, in order of liquidity, and classifies *net assets* as follows:

- **Invested in capital assets, net of related debt**. Capital assets net of depreciation, less debt incurred to acquire the capital assets.
- **Restricted net assets**. Contributions, grants and loans subject to an externally imposed constraint on the use of the funds.
- **Unrestricted net assets**. All other net assets.

The **Statement of Activities** shows all changes in net assets during the year. Gross expenses are shown by function or program. The extent to which these expenses are funded by charges for services and/or grants and contributions is shown. This format clearly reveals the extent to which each program uses or contributes to general revenues of the government, such as taxes. The "bottom line" in the statement of activities is the **degree to which current services and activities are financed by current revenues**.

Exhibit 13.13 shows condensed entity-wide statements under the GASB proposal.

Typical County
Statement of Net Assets
December 31, 2000
(amounts in thousands)

	Governmental Activities	Business-type Activities	Total
ASSETS			
Cash and cash equivalents . .	$ 90,000	$ 1,000	$ 91,000
Investments	120,000	3,000	123,000
Receivables (net)	300,000	40,000	340,000
Inventories	50,000	5,000	55,000
Capital assets, net	600,000	100,000	700,000
Total assets	$1,160,000	$149,000	$1,309,000
LIABILITIES			
Accounts payable	$ 15,000	$ 2,000	$ 17,000
Deferred revenue	100,000	10,000	110,000
Long-term liabilities	500,000	50,000	550,000
Total liabilities	$ 615,000	$ 62,000	$ 677,000
NET ASSETS			
Invested in capital assets, net of related debt	$ 350,000	$ 60,000	$ 410,000
Restricted for:			
Capital projects	100,000	—	100,000
Debt service	40,000	10,000	50,000
Development projects	20,000	—	20,000
Unrestricted	35,000	17,000	52,000
Total net assets	$ 545,000	$ 87,000	$ 632,000

EXHIBIT 13.13   ENTITY-WIDE FINANCIAL STATEMENTS

Fund-Perspective Financial Statements

Financial statements are presented for each of the government's fund types—governmental, proprietary, and fiduciary—similar to the combining statements required under current generally accepted accounting principles. The governmental fund financial statements use modified accrual accounting, which emphasizes fiscal accountability for current financial resources. Proprietary fund financial statements use full accrual accounting. Except for elimination of the combined balance sheet, which is replaced by the Statement of Net Assets, the required fund-perspective statements are the same as currently required.

Notes to the Financial Statements

One set of notes is used for both the entity-wide and fund-perspective statements.

Typical County
Statement of Activities
for the year ended December 31, 2000
(amounts in thousands)

Functions/Programs	Expenses	Program Revenues		Net (expense) revenue		
		Charges for Services	Grants & Contracts	Governmental Activities	Business-type Activities	Total
General government . . .	$ 80,000	$ 20,000	$ 2,000	$ (58,000)	—	$ (58,000)
Public safety	70,000	1,000	3,000	(66,000)	—	(66,000)
Health	40,000	25,000	1,000	(14,000)	—	(14,000)
Transportation	20,000	18,000	1,000	(1,000)	—	(1,000)
Economic assistance . . .	400,000	3,000	12,000	(385,000)	—	(385,000)
Culture & recreation . . .	10,000	4,000	3,000	(3,000)	—	(3,000)
Interest on long-term debt	45,000	—	—	(45,000)	—	(45,000)
Medical Center	215,000	190,000	30,000	—	$ 5,000	5,000
Total	$880,000	$261,000	$52,000	$(572,000)	$ 5,000	$(567,000)

General revenues

Property taxes				450,000	—	450,000
Unrestricted grants				100,000	—	100,000
Investment income				5,000	1,000	6,000
Total				$ 555,000	$ 1,000	$ 556,000
Excess (deficiency) of revenues over expenses . . .				(17,000)	6,000	(11,000)
Net assets-beginning				562,000	81,000	643,000
Net assets-ending				$ 545,000	$87,000	$ 632,000

EXHIBIT 13.13   *(Continued)*

DIFFERENCES BETWEEN THE PROPOSAL AND CURRENT PRACTICE

Major changes from current requirements for external reporting are:

- Entity-wide financial statements are required, using **accrual accounting** for all activities. The purpose is to provide readers with longer-term information than is available using the funds structure and modified accrual accounting. Statements reflect the financial performance of the government as one economic entity. *Interfund balances are eliminated*, as they are for consolidated statements of businesses.
- **Capital assets** are reported in the entity-wide financial statements, and **depreciation expense** is shown as a charge to operations. Currently, capital assets of the governmental funds are reported in a separate account group; depreciation is optional and never shown

as a charge to operations. Rather, the expenditure for the capital asset is a charge to operations when it is acquired. The new requirement discloses capital assets more clearly and assigns their cost over time as the assets deteriorate.

■ Long-term debts are reported as **liabilities** on the entity-wide financial statements, rather than being listed in a separate account group, as currently done for the governmental funds. Interest expense is **accrued as incurred**, not necessarily when the interest is due, which is the current timing of recognition.

■ In the Statement of Activities, a "net program cost" format replaces the current operating statement: Combined Statement of Revenues, Expenditures and Changes in Fund Balance for governmental funds; Combined Statement of Revenues, Expenses and Changes in Retained Earnings for proprietary funds. Revenues and expenses are grouped by functional categories—programs and activities rather than by funds. Information is provided in a way that informs readers on how programs and activities are funded.

REASONS WHY A NEW FINANCIAL REPORTING MODEL IS PROPOSED

This new financial reporting model for state and local governments is designed to make the financial statements more readable and informative to users. The major improvements are:

More Accurate Measurement of Long-term Financial Position

Use of full accrual accounting in the entity-wide statements allows a more precise measure of *interperiod equity*—a comparison of financial resources obtained versus financial claims incurred during a period, regardless of whether the claims are due in the current period. The emphasis is on a perceived deficiency in recording financial claims and expenses under the current reporting model.

Under the current model's modified accrual accounting, financial claims incurred in a period but not requiring a disbursement of current financial resources are not recorded in the governmental funds. Examples are **accrued interest on long-term debt** and postemployment benefits such as **unfunded pension liabilities**. On the other hand, outflows of current financial resources for acquisition of capital assets are *expenditures* in the year of acquisition. Under accrual accounting, *expenses* are recorded when a transaction or event results in a claim on a financial resource, regardless of when cash is paid. Therefore interest on long-term debt and an increase in pension liabilities are recorded as expenses in the period when the claim is incurred, not as in current practice, where no recognition takes place until the period when the payment is due. Acquisitions of capital assets are recognized as expenses as the capital assets wear out.

Inflows of current financial resources due to incurrence of long-term debt are viewed as other financing sources—increases in fund balance—under the modified accrual basis, but are increases in liabilities under the full accrual basis.

From a long-term perspective, financing a budget deficit with a bond issue or reducing the funding of pension liabilities does not improve the government's financial position. The full accrual basis reports *no* improvement in financial position for these strategies. However the modified accrual basis reports an *increase in fund balance* for both of these strategies, since revenues and expenditures are measured by the inflow and outflow of current financial resources. In the case of capital assets, the current practice of recording the expenditure in the year of acquisition and ignoring wear and tear on these assets over time tends to obscure declines in the productivity of these assets, possibly encouraging governments to delay necessary upkeep and replacement of capital assets. Use of full accrual accounting allows a better analysis of **whether services provided in the current year will create a burden of payment in future years**—for example, in the form of future tax increases—since costs of current services will be more accurately measured.

Dual Presentation of Short- and Long-Term Financial Position

Providing statements using both the **flow of economic resources** (full accrual accounting) and the **flow of current financial resources** (modified accrual accounting) will meet the needs of a variety of statement users concerning the **focus** of their interests. Readers interested in the current financial status of the government and its ability to meet short-term needs will look at the funds-based statements that focus on short-term financial position, inflows and outflows of current financial resources, amounts available for immediate use and compliance with legal and budgetary restrictions. Readers interested in the longer-term financial position of the government, in terms of ability to provide services and the impact of current performance on future tax levels, will look to the entity-wide, full accrual statements.

Availability of Summary Information

Providing information in the form of MD&A, entity-wide statements, and on a fund-by-fund basis better meets the needs of statement users concerning the **scope** of information desired. A reader may look to the MD&A and entity-wide statements for an overall view of the governmental unit's performance and financial position. If a reader is interested in particular compliance with legal restrictions, or activities connected with a particular fund, the fund-level statements provide this information.

With the new requirements will come a period of transition and learning on the part of both financial statement readers and preparers. The GASB's goal throughout the development of its new reporting model is to make governmental statements more informative to a variety of users. The addition of entity-wide statements on a full accrual basis adds a new dimension of information. A readable summary of financial performance, including condensed financial statements, makes the information more accessible.

SUMMARY OF KEY CONCEPTS

The **nonroutine activities** of a state or local government are reported in five fund types: **capital projects**, **debt service**, **enterprise**, **internal service**, and **trust and agency**.

The capital projects and debt service funds are **governmental funds**. They use the modified accrual basis of accounting and other fund accounting procedures. However, budgetary accounting is less important for these funds than for the general and special revenue funds.

Enterprise and **internal service funds** are **proprietary funds**. Their transactions, accounting, and financial statements closely parallel those for businesses.

Trust and agency funds are **fiduciary funds**. Business-type accounting is used by nonexpendable trust funds, separating principal and income transactions. Expendable trust funds generally use fund accounting. Agency funds have no fund balance and follow no special accounting; cash receipts create liabilities, and cash disbursements liquidate them.

Construction activities are accounted for in the capital projects fund. Typical transactions include temporary financing, collection of debt proceeds, expenditures for construction, temporary investments, and transfers to other funds.

The **debt service fund** accumulates resources and uses them for payment of principal and interest on general obligation debt. The debt service fund for **term bonds** typically also engages in investment activities.

Investments made by governmental units are reported at **fair market value**, with income, realized and unrealized gains and losses reported in the operating statement of the appropriate fund.

The **Comprehensive Annual Financial Report (CAFR)** of a state or local governmental unit presents both **combined statements**, giving an overview of the financial affairs of the entire unit, and **combining** or **individual statements** for each fund type and account group. Notes and statistical information are also provided.

In 1997, the GASB proposed a new **financial reporting model** for state and local governments. This model retains the funds perspective of the current reporting model, but also requires financial reporting on an **entity-wide basis**. The entity-wide statements use the **full accrual basis of accounting**. The entity-wide reports disclose the financial condition of the unit as one economic entity, providing readers with better information with which to assess long term performance.

QUESTIONS

Q13.1 In governmental accounting, the budget for a fund may be entered in the accounting records. Briefly explain the purpose of this entry. For which of the seven fund types is a budget entry usually made?

Q13.2 A governmental unit may have several capital projects underway simultaneously. How must the accounting records and financial statements of the capital projects fund be structured to properly reflect this situation?

Q13.3 Improvement projects undertaken by a governmental unit may be financed by general revenues or by assessments to property owners. What criterion is often used in determining the source of financing for improvements?

Q13.4 The general fund of Taylor City transferred $15,000 to a capital projects fund. Under what assumptions would each of the following entries be made in the general fund?

1.	Due from Capital Projects Fund	15,000	
	Cash		15,000
2.	Operating Transfers Out	15,000	
	Cash		15,000

Q13.5 Where should the liability be recorded for special assessment bonds that carry a secondary pledge of a municipality's general credit?
(AICPA adapted)

Q13.6 Describe the major differences that exist in the purpose of accounting and financial reporting and in the types of financial reports for a large city when compared to those for a large industrial corporation.
(AICPA adapted)

Q13.7 Does accounting for supplies by enterprise and internal service funds differ from the accounting used for similar items by governmental funds? Explain.

Q13.8 Most general municipal debt is repaid by using general fund resources. Why is a debt service fund frequently used, rather than simply recording these payments as expenditures in the general fund?

Q13.9 Distinguish between an expendable and a nonexpendable trust fund. What are the major accounting differences between the two types?

Q13.10 How does interpretation of an interim year unreserved fund balance for a multi-year capital projects fund differ from interpretation of the general fund unreserved fund balance?

Q13.11 Explain why an agency fund normally has no fund balance.

Q13.12 Describe the difference between *Bond Proceeds* and *Bonds Payable*. How are balances in those accounts reported in a municipality's financial statements?

Q13.13 A governmental unit may choose to account for its lottery activities in either a special revenue fund or an enterprise fund. What criteria are used to make this choice?

Q13.14 Outline the major differences between the current external reporting model for state and local governments and the GASB's proposed model. Why is the proposed model viewed as providing a longer-term perspective on performance?

EXERCISES

E13.1 **Capital Project Transactions** On January 14, 20X1, the city of Waterport authorized a $750,000 bond issue for the purchase of a building to be used as a community center. On May 3, the bonds were issued at par, and on June 1, the building was purchased and paid for. On November 1, the general fund paid the semiannual interest of $30,000 on the bonds.

REQUIRED: Record all necessary entries for the above information. Identify the fund or account group for each entry.

E13.2 Capital Project Calculations The town of Kaley recently completed construction of a recreational facility which was accounted for in a capital projects fund. Bonds were issued at the onset of the project to finance construction. Legal constraints prevented use of the $800 premium on the bonds toward construction costs. The premium has not yet been transferred to the debt service fund. Temporary investments of bond proceeds yielded a 3 percent return, or $2,424.

Kaley awarded the construction contract for the facility to the lowest bidder. The contract called for a 15 percent retainage. Kaley's books show $11,550 due the contractor pending final inspection. All other amounts due the contractor have been remitted. Assume interest on temporary investments remain in the capital projects fund.

REQUIRED:

1. What was the face value of the bonds issued?
2. What was the amount of the contract awarded?
3. What was the original authorization for the project?
4. What is the fund balance after closing entries?

E13.3 Adequacy of Capital Project Authorization The Board of Supervisors of Hanover Township authorized construction of a $1,000,000 community center. The township will contribute $100,000 from general fund revenues and bonds will be issued for the rest. Construction activities will last about eighteen months.

The project is reviewed after six months when the construction manager indicates that the project is 41% complete and after the township's $100,000 contribution was made. At that time, the following data from the capital projects fund are presented.

Cash—Construction	$ 150,000
Short-Term Investments	500,000
Cash—Debt Service	15,000
Construction in Progress	450,000
Bonds Payable	900,000
Bond Anticipation Notes Payable	100,000
Encumbrances (balance of construction contract)	650,000

REQUIRED:

1. At what amount were the bonds apparently issued?
2. Calculate the apparent potential cost overrun.
3. Identify the items above that are improperly presented.

E13.4 Debt Service Fund Irregularities A debt service fund's condensed trial balance at December 31, 20X8 shows the following:

Cash	$ 100,000
Due from Water Utility (an enterprise fund)	40,000
Short-Term Investments	900,000
Estimated Revenue	800,000
Expenditures	40,000
Interest Payable	(40,000)
Water Utility Bonds Payable	(800,000)
Appropriations	(40,000)
Fund Balance—Unreserved	(760,000)
Contributions from Property Owners	(240,000)
	$ 0

The water utility bonds were issued on July 1, 20X8 and pay 10% interest annually on June 30. The contributions from property owners represent the proceeds from special assessment debt for which the governmental unit has no liability.

REQUIRED: Identify the apparent irregularities in the above debt service fund trial balance and suggest corrective action for them.

E13.5   Internal Service Fund Balance Sheet At the beginning of fiscal year 20X2, Waller Town established a central supplies storehouse to service its several funds. The general fund contributed $25,000 (nonrefundable) to aid in the establishment of the supplies storehouse. It was agreed that the storehouse would charge other funds for the purchase price of supplies plus 15 percent. During the year, the storehouse purchased $18,000 of supplies, paid operating expenses of $1,500, and billed other funds for $17,250. All accounts are settled except $2,000 remaining to be collected from the general fund for supplies billed.

REQUIRED:

1. Prepare the balance sheet for the central supplies storehouse at the end of fiscal 20X2.
2. State any effects of the transactions on the financial statements of the general fund of Waller Town. Assume the general fund bought supplies for $6,000 and used only $5,500 worth of supplies.

E13.6   Enterprise Fund Profitability Analysis Below are summary data for the first two years of operation of an enterprise fund prepared under *fund accounting* and *business accounting*.

	Fund Accounting		Business Accounting	
	Year 2 '	**Year 1**	**Year 2**	**Year 1**
Revenues	$ 1,100	$ 1,000	$ 1,300	$ 1,150
Expenditures/Expenses . . .	4,000	3,500	1,000	900
Total Assets	320	300	3,550	3,050
Fund Balance/Equity	(3,400)	(500)	2,550	2,250

REQUIRED:

1. Perform a basic profitability analysis for Year 2 using the "DuPont Analysis" shown next.

$$\text{Return on Assets} = \text{Return on Sales} \times \text{Total Assets Turnover}$$

$$\frac{\text{Income}}{\text{Average Total Assets}} = \frac{\text{Income}}{\text{Sales}} \times \frac{\text{Revenue}}{\text{Average Total Assets}}$$

2. Which basis of accounting better reflects the profitability of the enterprise fund during Year 2? To what do you attribute the differences?

E13.7   **Trust Fund Transactions** In March 20X3, a resident of Randall City died, leaving her entire estate to the Randall City School District. The will specified that proceeds from the liquidation of her estate are to be invested, and investment income used to provide scholarships for needy high school students. Three students were to be selected each year by the school superintendent. At the date of the donor's death, the fair market value of the estate was estimated to be $103,000. In December, the estate was liquidated, realizing $105,000. Administrative costs of the estate in 20X3 were $4,000. The net proceeds were then transferred to the school district and were invested in appropriate securities.

In 20X4, income from investments was $7,000. Administrative costs (all related to income) were $250. The first scholarships were awarded in 20X4 for a total of $5,000.

REQUIRED: Record the events described above in an appropriate fund. Include closing entries.

E13.8   **Special Assessment Project** After discussions with property owners in Park City's historic district, City Council authorized installation of a large number of particularly elegant and tasteful street lights in the district. Total cost of the project is $3,300,000. Council will contribute $300,000 and ten-year term bonds will be issued to fund construction of the project. Park City can issue bonds paying 6% annually at par. The principal and interest will be repaid ten equal annual assessments paid by the property owners in the historic district. Because each annual assessment exceeds the interest due on the bonds, the excess is invested at 6% in order to retire the principal.

REQUIRED:

1. Calculate the amount of the total annual assessment needed to pay the annual interest for ten years and retire the bonds.
2. Assume the government is liable for the bonds. Prepare the journal entries and identify the funds/account groups affected when the bonds are issued, the assessments are levied, the first assessment is collected, and the first interest payment is made.
3. Repeat 2. assuming the government has *no* liability for the bonds.

E13.9 Fund/Account Group Interactions Often an entry on the books of one fund triggers corresponding entries in other funds of the governmental unit.

REQUIRED: Record any entries to other funds or account groups that correspond to the entries below. Identify the fund or account group for each entry made.

1. General Fund

Cash	12,000	
Due from Capital Projects Fund		12,000
To record repayment of advance.		

2. Capital Projects Fund

Due to Debt Service Fund	8,000	
Cash		8,000
To transfer bond premium to debt service fund to be used for future repayment of principal.		

3. Internal Service Fund

Cash	40,000	
Bonds Payable		40,000
To record issuance of bonds at par.		

4. Capital Projects Fund

Expenditures	40,000	
Vouchers Payable		40,000
To record final payment for improvements contract totaling $100,000.		

5. Enterprise Fund

Cash	18,000	
Capital Contributed from General Fund		18,000
To record transfer from general fund.		

E13.10 Fund/Account Group Recognition

REQUIRED: List *all* funds or groups of accounts in which each of the following situations requires accounting recognition:

1. Part of the general obligation bond proceeds from a new issue was used to pay for the cost of a new city hall as soon as construction was completed. The remainder of the proceeds was transferred to repay the debt.

2. Equipment in general governmental service that was constructed ten years before by a capital projects fund was sold. The receipts were accounted for as unrestricted revenue.
3. Cash was received from a special tax levy to retire and pay interest on general obligation bonds issued to finance construction of a new city hall.
4. Fixed assets were acquired by a central purchasing and supplies department organized to serve all municipal departments.
5. Several years ago a city established a sinking fund to retire an issue of general obligation bonds. This year, the city made a $50,000 contribution to the sinking fund from general revenues and realized $15,000 in revenue from securities in the sinking fund. The bonds due this year were retired.
6. A municipal electric utility paid $150,000 out of its earnings for new equipment.
7. A municipality issued general obligation serial bonds to finance the construction of a fire station.
8. Expenditures of $200,000 were made during the year on the fire station in No. 7.
9. A municipal electric utility issued bonds to be repaid from its own operations.
   (AICPA adapted)

E13.11 Asset Transactions During 20X1, the city of Reyland acquired a variety of assets.

REQUIRED: For each transaction listed below, identify any asset accounts debited at the time of the transaction. Specify the funds or account groups used.

1. Supplies of $800 were purchased by an internal service fund.
2. Early in the year, a trust fund purchased supplies of $800.
3. Sidewalks were installed at the expense of neighborhood property owners. Cost of installation was $4,000.
4. The city pool facility, which is financed by user charges, bought pool-cleaning equipment for $450.
5. An ambulance garage was constructed by the capital projects fund for $80,000.
6. An ambulance was purchased by the general fund for $35,000.

E13.12 Long-Term Debt Transactions On January 1, a governmental unit issued 7 percent bonds at par for $70,000. On June 30, semiannual interest became due and was paid.

REQUIRED: Make all appropriate entries for January 1 and June 30 given the following independent assumptions. Explanations are not required. Identify each fund or account group affected.

1. The bonds were issued to finance city court expansion. General fund resources were transferred to the debt service fund at the beginning of each year to finance annual interest charges.
2. The bonds were issued to finance city operations. General fund resources are transferred to the debt service fund at the beginning of each year to finance annual interest charges.
3. The bonds were issued by a self-supporting city utility.
4. The bonds were issued by a police retirement fund.

E13.13 **Choice of Fund Type** Following are descriptions of actual funds found in state CAFRs. For each, identify the **type of fund**, and the **method of accounting**.

   a. The Financial Institutions Deposits Fund is used to account for security deposits held by the Michigan State Treasurer on behalf of banks which operate trust departments. Deposits are in the form of securities or other acceptable assets.
   b. The Second Injury Fund insures carriers and self-insured employers against certain workers' compensation losses. The fund is supervised by the administrator who is appointed by the fund's Board of Trustees. Revenue consists of assessments to insurance carriers and self-insured employers. Administrative costs are appropriated in the General Fund with financing provided by operating transfers.
   c. The Iowa Infrastructure Fund is used to account for resources used as directed by the General Assembly for public infrastructure related expenditures.
   d. Iowa's Scholarship and Tuition Grant Reserve Fund receives surplus monies for scholarships and grants at the end of each fiscal year to be used as a reserve for over expenditures in the scholarship and grant accounts.
   e. The Alcoholic Beverage Control Board operates facilities in Alabama for the distribution and sale of alcoholic beverages to the public.
   f. Alabama's Air Transportation Fund provides air transportation for state personnel and maintenance facilities for state aircraft, on a cost-reimbursement basis.

PROBLEMS

P13.1 **Capital Projects Fund** In a special election held on July 1, 20X7, the voters of the city of Nicknar approved a $10,000,000 issue of 6 percent general obligation bonds maturing in 20Z7. The proceeds of this sale will be used to help finance the construction of a new civic center. The total cost of the project was estimated at $15,000,000. The remaining $5,000,000 will be financed by an irrevocable state grant which has been awarded. A capital projects fund was established to account for this project and was designated the "civic center construction fund."

The following transactions occurred during the fiscal year beginning July 1, 20X7, and ending June 30, 20X8:

1. On August 1, the general fund loaned $500,000 to the civic center construction fund for defraying engineering and other expenses.
2. Preliminary engineering and planning costs of $320,000 were paid to Akron Engineering Company. There had been no encumbrance for this cost.
3. On December 1, the bonds were sold at 101. The premium on bonds was transferred to the debt service fund to be used for future payment of bond principal.
4. On March 15, a contract for $12,000,000 was entered into with Candu Construction Company for the major part of the project.
5. Orders were placed on March 23 for materials estimated to cost $55,000.
6. On April 1, a partial payment of $2,500,000 was received from the state.
7. The materials previously ordered were received on June 7 at a cost of $51,000, were used in construction, and payment was made.

8. On June 15, a progress billing of $2,000,000 was received from Candu Construction for work done on the project. According to the terms of the contract, the city will withhold 6 percent of any billing until the project is completed.
9. The general fund was repaid the $500,000 previously loaned.

REQUIRED: Based on the transactions presented above, prepare the following:

1. Journal entries to record the transactions in the civic center construction fund for the period July 1, 20X7, through June 30, 20X8, and the appropriate closing entries at June 30, 20X8.
2. A balance sheet for the civic center construction fund as of June 30, 20X8.
   (AICPA adapted)

P13.2 Capital Projects Fund During the fiscal year ended June 30, 20X2, the city of Westgate authorized construction of a new library and sale of general obligation term bonds to finance construction of the library. The authorization imposed the following restrictions: (1) construction cost was not to exceed $5,000,000, and (2) the annual interest rate was not to exceed 8½ percent. The city does not record project authorizations, but other budgetary accounts are maintained. The following transactions relating to financing and constructing the library occurred during the fiscal year ended June 30, 20X3:

1. On July 1, 20X2, Westgate issued $5,000,000 of 30-year, 8 percent general obligation bonds for $5,100,000. The semiannual interest payment dates are December 31 and June 30. The premium of $100,000 was transferred to the library debt service fund.
2. On July 3, 20X2, the library capital projects fund invested $4,900,000 in short-term commercial paper. These purchases were at face value with no accrued interest. Interest on cash invested by the library capital projects fund must be transferred to the library debt service fund. During the fiscal year ending June 30, 20X3, estimated interest to be earned is $140,000.
3. On July 5, 20X2, Westgate signed a contract with F&A Construction Company to build the library for $4,980,000.
4. On January 15, 20X3, the library capital projects fund received $3,040,000 from the maturity of short-term notes purchased on July 3. The cost of these notes was $3,000,000. The interest of $40,000 was transferred to the library debt service fund.
5. On January 20, 20X3, F&A Construction Company properly billed the city $3,000,000 for work performed on the new library. The contract calls for 10 percent retention until final inspection and acceptance of the building. The library capital projects fund paid F&A $2,700,000.
6. On June 30, 20X3, the library capital projects fund made the proper adjusting entries, including accrued interest receivable of $103,000, and closing entries.

REQUIRED:

1. Prepare journal entries to record the six preceding sets of facts in the library capital projects fund. Do not record journal entries in any other fund or group of accounts.
2. Prepare in good form a balance sheet for the City of Westgate—Library Capital Projects Fund as of June 30, 20X3.
   (AICPA adapted)

P13.3 Capital Projects and Debt Service Funds The information below relates to the construction of a new recreation building in the city of Lander.

20X0 Transactions

1. A bond issue in the amount of $1,000,000 was authorized by vote on March 1, 20X0, to provide funds for the construction. The bonds are to be repaid, in 20 annual installments, from a debt service fund, with the first installment due on March 1, 20X1.
2. An advance of $80,000 was received from the general fund to make a deposit on the land contract of $120,000. The deposit was made.
3. Bonds having a face value of $900,000 were sold for cash at 102. Since the cost of the land was much less than anticipated, the city decided to postpone the sale of the remaining bonds.
4. Contracts amounting to $780,000 were awarded to the lowest bidder for the construction of the recreation center.
5. The temporary advance from the general fund was repaid, and the balance on the land contract was paid.
6. The architect certified that work in the amount of $640,000 had been completed, and bills for that amount were received.
7. Vouchers paid by the treasurer relative to the completed work amounted to $620,000.
8. The bond premium was transferred to the debt service fund.

20X1 Transactions

9. Due to engineering modifications in the construction plans, the contract was revised to $880,000. The remaining bonds were sold at 101.
10. The recreation center was completed and billed at a further cost of $230,000. The building passed final inspection.
11. The treasurer paid all bills.
12. The cash balance remaining was transferred to the debt service fund.

Interest on the bond issue is paid directly from the general fund. Transfers from the general fund to the debt service fund were $25,000 in 20X0 and $30,000 in 20X1. All cash was invested in certificates of deposit which yielded interest income of $1,000 in 20X0 and $800 in 20X1. Expected investment income was $1,000 in each year. The first installment on the bonds ($45,000) was paid when due.

REQUIRED:

1. Prepare the journal entries for the recreation center fund for 20X0 and 20X1.
2. Prepare the balance sheet for the recreation center fund on December 31, 20X0.
3. Prepare the journal entries for the debt service fund and the general long-term debt account group for 20X0 and 20X1.

P13.4 Evaluating Status of Capital Project As a newly elected member of the Wannabe Area School Board, you are exhausted after listening to two hours of discussion on an obscure and inconsequential administrative issue. Now, at 11PM, as part of the Business Manager's monthly report, a post-closing trial balance at the end of the first year of a two-year school construction project is circulated to update the Board. All financing authorized for the project has been recorded. Amounts are in thousands.

Because of your technical accounting background, you look sharply at the trial balance displayed below. While doing so, you recall that the Board just passed its largest budget ever, requiring a tax increase opposed by several citizens taxpayer groups.

Wannabe Area School District
E-4 School Capital Projects Fund
Trial Balance at June 30, 20X5

	Dr.(Cr.)
Cash in Bank	$ 1,400
Supplies	750
Interest Receivable	200
Temporary Investments	9,700
Due from General Fund	1,000
Vouchers Payable	(960)
Contracts Payable	(1,340)
Fund Balance—Reserved for Encumbrances	(12,600)
Fund Balance—Unreserved	1,850
	$ 0

REQUIRED:

1. Another member of the School Board wants to move on to the next item of business. You object. Why?
2. Prepare an analysis designed to get the attention of your colleagues, citing specific items in the trial balance. Be sure to discuss the status of the project in relation to its budget.

P13.5   Special Assessment Activity Early in 20X1, the town of Jacobs authorized widening of streets and installation of curbs in a residential area known as Woodside. The project was expected to cost $400,000 and to be financed by $50,000 from the 20X1 general fund budget and $350,000 from Woodside residents. Residents were assessed for equal principal payments over ten years plus interest on bonds as due. Ten-year, 6 percent general obligation bonds with a face value of $350,000 were issued at par on July 1, 20X1. Interest is due on December 31 and June 30. Proceeds from the bonds not currently needed to finance construction and proceeds of the assessments after payment of interest were invested in appropriate securities. Assessments to residents for interest are to be reduced by the prior year's earnings on investments.

Regarding the street improvement project, the following occurred:

1. Investments yielded $8,000 in 20X1 (collected in 20X2) and $18,000 in 20X2 (collected in 20X3). The balance in the capital projects fund cash account was $40,000 on December 31, 20X1.
2. Project costs of $400,000 were encumbered at the start of the project.
3. Construction costs billed in 20X1 were $150,000, of which $20,000 was not paid at year-end.

4. The improvement project was completed in 20X2 at a total cost of $400,000. All amounts due the contractor were paid.
5. Of the 20X1 assessment, $15,000 was not collected until 20X2. All 20X2 assessments were collected when due.

REQUIRED:

1. Prepare a schedule showing amounts to be assessed in 20X1 and 20X2.
2. Prepare a balance sheet for the capital projects fund at December 31, 20X1, and for the debt service fund at December 31, 20X1 and December 31, 20X2.
3. What other funds or account groups are affected by the street improvement project? Explain.

P13.6 Internal Service Fund The city of Merlot operates a central garage through an internal service fund to provide garage space and repairs for all city-owned and operated vehicles. The central garage fund was established by a contribution of $200,000 from the general fund on July 1, 20X1, at which time the building was acquired. The post-closing trial balance at June 30, 20X3, was as follows:

	Debit	Credit
Cash	$ 150,000	
Due from General Fund	20,000	
Inventory of Materials and Supplies	80,000	
Land	60,000	
Building	200,000	
Allowance for Depreciation—Building		$ 10,000
Machinery and Equipment	56,000	
Allowance for Depreciation—Machinery and Equipment		12,000
Vouchers Payable		38,000
Contribution from General Fund		200,000
Retained Earnings		306,000
	$ 566,000	$ 566,000

The following information applies to the fiscal year ended June 30, 20X4:

1. Materials and supplies were purchased on account for $74,000.
2. The inventory of materials and supplies at June 30, 20X4, was $58,000, which agreed with the physical count taken.
3. Salaries and wages paid to employees totaled $230,000, including related fringe benefit costs.
4. A billing was received from the enterprise fund for utility charges totaling $30,000, and was paid.
5. Depreciation of the building was recorded in the amount of $5,000. Depreciation of the machinery and equipment amounted to $8,000.
6. Billings to other departments for services rendered to them were as follows:

General Fund	$ 262,000
Water and Sewer Fund	84,000
Special Revenue Fund	32,000

7. Unpaid interfund receivable balances at June 30, 20X4, were as follows:

General Fund .... $ 6,000
Special Revenue Fund 16,000

8. Vouchers payable at June 30, 20X4, were $14,000.

REQUIRED:

1. For the period July 1, 20X3, through June 30, 20X4, prepare journal entries to record all of the transactions in the central garage fund accounts.
2. Prepare closing entries for the central garage fund at June 30, 20X4.
   (AICPA adapted)

P13.7 **Critique Enterprise Fund Accounting** Two years ago, Mightyfine Township took over the swimming pool of a defunct private swim club and converted it into a community pool financed by user charges. Most user charges are in the form of low-cost family season passes sold to Township residents; the fee charged to nonresidents is five times the fee charged to residents.

The township manager boasts about how he can provide such fine swimming facilities at a low cost (to residents). He dismisses last year's dismal financial results—the first year the Township ran the pool—as an aberration. During that year, a diving board and baby pool were added to the facilities. In his report to the Board of Supervisors, the manager presents the following schedule, taken from a subsidiary ledger in the township's general fund without adjustment.

Mightyfine Township Community Swimming Pool
Operating Statement

Season Passes—Residents.............................. $ 22,400
Season Passes—Nonresidents 5,000
Daily Admission Fees 1,300
Concessions, Net.................................... 3,700
     Total Revenues .... $ 32,400
Salaries—Pool Manager and Lifeguards .... $ 22,800
Maintenance and Repairs 6,700
     Total Expenditures .... $ 29,500
Excess of Revenues over Expenditures .... $ 2,900

Notes:
1. Fair value of original pool (20-year life) .... $ 300,000
2. Cost of baby pool addition (25-year life) 50,000
3. Cost of diving board (10-year life) 15,000
4. Cost of rider to Township's liability insurance
    (paid by Township) 4,200

REQUIRED:

1. Discuss the basis of accounting used in the above report.
2. What deficiencies in the report cause it to depart from GAAP as defined by the GASB?
3. Evaluate whether the township manager is justified in boasting. Support your evaluation with a numerical analysis.
4. A township resident who teaches accounting at Superfine U., states that the pool is never crowded and that more revenue could be generated by reducing the cost of nonresident season passes from $200 per family to $120 per family. She estimates that the price elasticity of demand $[= -(\Delta q/q)/(\Delta p/p)]$ for a nonresident season pass is 2.5. Using the professor's numbers, calculate the additional revenue generated from nonresident season passes.

P13.8 Agency Fund In compliance with a newly enacted state law, Dial County assumed the responsibility of collecting all property taxes levied within its boundaries as of July 1, 20X5. A composite property tax rate per $1,000 of net assessed valuation was developed for the fiscal year ending June 30, 20X6, and is presented below:

Dial County General Fund . . . . $ 60
Eton City General Fund   30
Bart Township General Fund   10
Composite Tax Rate . . . . $ 100

All property taxes are due in quarterly installments, and when collected they are distributed to the governmental units represented in the composite rate. In order to administer collection and distribution of such taxes, the county has established a tax agency fund.

Additional information:

1. In order to reimburse the county for estimated administrative expenses of operating the tax agency fund, the tax agency fund is to deduct 2 percent from the tax collections each quarter for Eton City and Bart Township. The total amount deducted is to be remitted to the Dial County general fund.
2. Current year tax levies to be collected by the tax agency fund are as follows:

	Gross Levy	Estimated Amount to Be Collected
Dial County	$ 3,600,000	$ 3,500,000
Eton City	1,800,000	1,740,000
Bart Township	600,000	560,000
	$ 6,000,000	$ 5,800,000

3. As of September 30, 20X5, the tax agency fund had received $1,440,000 in first-quarter payments. On October 1, this fund made a distribution to the three governmental units.

REQUIRED: For the period July 1, 20X5, through October 1, 20X5, prepare journal entries to record the transactions described above for the following funds:

- Dial County tax agency fund.
- Dial County general fund.
- Eton City general fund.
- Bart Township general fund.

Your solution should be organized as follows:

	Dial County Tax Agency Fund		Dial County General Fund		Eton City General Fund		Bart Township General Fund	
Accounts	Debit	Credit	Debit	Credit	Debit	Credit	Debit	Credit

(AICPA adapted)

P13.9 Expendable and Nonexpendable Trust Funds On July 1, 20X7, the city of Warwick received a bequest from the estate of a wealthy citizen. The terms of the bequest call for the property bequeathed to the city, including a performing arts center, to be maintained in perpetuity and the earnings therefrom to be transferred semiannually and used to subsidize the operating expenses of the arts center. The fair values of the specific items of property bequeathed are:

Cash	$ 200,000
$3,000,000 par value bonds of Nurnberg Corp. (10% annual coupons, paid semiannually, due June 30, 20Y7; 12% yield to maturity; effective interest amortization method required) . . .	2,655,903
Building (20-year life, $100,000 residual value)	4,900,000
Fixtures (10-year life, no residual value)	800,000
	$ 8,555,903

The cash is immediately invested in money market mutual funds yielding 5% and, once a budget is determined, the arts center will begin scheduling exhibits and performances during the remainder of 20X7. Moreover, the city council authorizes an operating transfer of $200,000 to support the arts center during its first fiscal year ending June 30, 20X8 and estimates revenue of $60,000 from ticket sales and $20,000 from concessions for the first six months.

REQUIRED:

1. Assuming there are no further resources placed in the nonexpendable trust fund, and that earnings are transferred to the expendable trust fund semiannually, prepare an interim operating statement and balance sheet for the nonexpendable portion of the trust as of December 31, 20X7, after the semiannual transfer of earnings.
2. Taking the above facts into account, prepare the budget entry made by the expendable trust fund covering the six-month period ending December 31, 20X7. Assume that half of the $200,000 operating transfer will be received during this six-month period.

A balanced budget is contemplated and planned expenditures fully utilize available resources. Show supporting calculations.

3. If you had reviewed the above facts *before* the city accepted the bequest, what would you have advised the city council?

P13.10 Budgeting for Various Funds The Laurens city council passed a resolution requiring a yearly cash budget by fund for the city beginning with its fiscal year ending September 30, 20X3. The city's financial director prepared a list of expected cash receipts and disbursements, but he is having difficulty subdividing them by fund. The list is given in Exhibit 13.14.

The financial director provides you with the following additional information:

1. A bond issue was authorized in 20X2 for the construction of a civic center. Future civic center revenues are to account for 20 percent of the repayment of debt. The remainder is to come from general property taxes.
2. A bond issue was authorized in 20X2 for additions to the library. The debt is to be paid from general property taxes.
3. General obligation bonds are paid from general property taxes collected by the general fund.
4. Ten percent of the total annual school taxes represents an individually voted tax for payment of bonds, the proceeds of which were used for school construction. School operations are accounted for in the general fund.
5. In 20X0, a wealthy citizen donated rental property to the city. Net income from the property is to be used to assist in operating the library. The net cash increase attributable to the property is transferred to the library on September 30 of each year.
6. All sales taxes are collected by the city; the state receives 85 percent of these taxes. The state's portion is remitted at the end of each month.
7. Payment of the street construction bonds, for which the city has no liability, is to be made from assessments previously collected from the respective property owners. The proceeds from the assessments were invested and the principal of $312,000 will earn $15,000 interest during the coming year.
8. In 20X2, a special assessment in the amount of $203,000 was made on certain property owners for sewer construction. During fiscal 20X3, $50,000 of this assessment is expected to be collected. The remainder of the sewer cost is to be paid from a $153,000 bond issue to be sold in fiscal 20X3. Future special assessment collections will be used to pay principal and interest on the bonds, for which the city has residual liability.
9. All sewer and sanitation services are provided by a separate enterprise fund.
10. The federal grant is for fiscal 20X3 school operations.
11. The proceeds remaining at the end of the year from the sale of civic center and library bonds are to be invested.

Cash Receipts			**Cash Disbursements**		
Taxes:			General Government	$	671,000
General Property		685,000	Public Safety		516,000
School		421,000	Schools		458,000
Franchise		223,000	Sanitation		131,000
		$1,329,000	Library		28,000
			Rental Property		17,500
Licenses and Permits:			Parks		17,000
Business Licenses	$	41,000			$1,838,500
Automobile Inspection Permits . . .		24,000			
Building Permits		18,000	Debt Service:		
	$	83,000	General Obligation Bonds	$	618,000
			Street Construction Bonds		327,000
Intergovernmental Revenue:			School Bonds		119,000
Sales Tax	$	1,012,000	Sewage Disposal Plant Bonds . .		37,200
Federal Grants		128,000			$1,101,200
State Motor Vehicle Tax		83,500	Investments	$	358,000
State Gasoline Tax		52,000	State Portion of Sales Tax	$	860,200
State Alcoholic Beverage Licenses . .		16,000	Capital Expenditures:		
		$1,291,500	Sewer Construction (Assessed		
Charges for Services:			Area)	$	114,100
Sanitation Fees	$	121,000	Civic Center Construction		73,000
Sewer Connection Fees		71,000	Library Construction		36,000
Library Revenues		13,000		$	223,100
Park Revenues		2,500	Total Disbursements		$4,381,000
	$	207,500			
Bond Issues:					
Civic Center	$	347,000			
General Obligation		200,000			
Sewer		153,000			
Library		120,000			
	$	820,000			
Other:					
Proceeds from Sale of					
Investments	$	312,000			
Sewer Assessments		50,000			
Rental Revenue		48,000			
Interest Revenue		15,000			
	$	425,000			
Total Receipts		$4,156,000			

EXHIBIT 13.14   CASH RECEIPTS AND DISBURSEMENTS, TO BE USED IN P13.10

REQUIRED: Prepare a budget of cash receipts and disbursements by fund for the year ending September 30, 20X3. Include all interfund transfers involving cash. Your solution should be organized as follows, with appropriate subtotals and totals:

Description	General Fund	Capital Projects Fund	Debt Service Fund	Trust Fund	Agency Fund	Enterprise Fund
Cash Receipts						
:						
Cash Disbursements						
:						
Interfund Transfers						
:						

(AICPA adapted)

P13.11 Comprehensive Fund Accounting—Worksheet The balance sheet presented below was prepared by the city of Bayside's bookkeeper:

City of Bayside
Balance Sheet
June 30, 20X6

Assets

Cash	$ 160,000
Taxes Receivable—Current	32,000
Supplies on Hand	8,000
Marketable Securities	250,000
Land	1,000,000
Buildings	7,000,000
Total Assets	$ 8,450,000

Liabilities and Fund Balance

Vouchers Payable	$ 42,000
Bonds Payable	3,000,000
Fund Balance—Reserved for Supplies Inventory	8,000
Fund Balance—Unreserved	5,400,000
Total Liabilities and Fund Balance	$ 8,450,000

Additional information:

1. An analysis of the fund balance account disclosed the following:

Fund Balance, June 30, 20X5		$ 2,100,000
Add:		
Donated Land	$ 800,000	
Federal Grant-in-Aid	2,200,000	
Creation of Endowment Fund	250,000	
Excess of Actual Tax Revenue over Estimated Revenue	24,000	
Excess of Appropriations over Actual Expenditures and Encumbrances	20,000	
Net Income from Endowment Funds	10,000	3,304,000
		$ 5,404,000
Deduct:		
Excess of Cultural Center Operating Expenses over Income		4,000
Fund Balance, June 30, 20X6		$ 5,400,000

2. In July 20X5, land appraised at a fair market value of $800,000 was donated to the city for a cultural center that opened on April 15, 20X6. Building construction expenditures for the project were financed from a federal grant-in-aid of $2,200,000 and from an authorized ten-year, $3,000,000 issue of 7 percent general obligation bonds sold at par on July 1, 20X5. Interest is payable on December 31 and June 30. The fair market value of the land and the cost of the building are included in the Land and Buildings accounts, respectively.

3. The cultural center receives no direct state or city subsidy for current operating expenses. A cultural center endowment fund was established by a gift of marketable securities having a fair market value of $250,000 at date of receipt. The endowment principal is to be kept intact. Income is to be applied to any operating deficit of the center.

4. It is anticipated that $7,000 of the 20X5-X6 tax is uncollectible.

5. The physical inventory of supplies on hand at June 30, 20X6, amounted to $12,500. No minimum amount of supplies must be maintained.

6. Unfilled purchase orders for the general fund at June 30, 20X6, totaled $5,000.

7. On July 1, 20X5, an all-purpose building was purchased for $2,000,000. Of the purchase price, $200,000 was assigned to the land. The purchase was authorized under the budget for the year ended June 30, 20X6.

REQUIRED: Prepare a working paper showing adjustments and distributions to the proper funds and account groups. The working paper should have the following column headings:

1. Balance per Books
2. Adjustments—Debit
3. Adjustments—Credit
4. General Fund
5. City Cultural Center Endowment Fund:
      Principal
      Income
6. General Fixed Assets Account Group
7. General Long-Term Debt Account Group

Number all adjusting entries. Formal journal entries are not required. Supporting computations should be in good form.
(AICPA adapted)

P13.12 Comprehensive Fund Accounting—Entries The village of Dexter was recently incorporated and began financial operations on July 1, 20X8, the beginning of its fiscal year.

The following transactions occurred during this first fiscal year, July 1, 20X8, to June 30, 20X9:

1. The village council adopted a budget for general operations during the fiscal year ending June 30, 20X9. Revenues were estimated at $400,000. Legal authorizations for budgeted expenditures were $394,000.

2. Property taxes were levied in the amount of $390,000; it was estimated that 2 percent of this amount would prove to be uncollectible. These taxes are available as of the date of levy to finance current expenditures.

3. During the year a resident of the village donated marketable securities valued at $50,000 to the village under the terms of a trust agreement. The terms of the trust agreement stipulated that the principal amount is to be kept intact; use of revenue generated by the securities is restricted to financing college scholarships for needy students. Revenue earned and received on these marketable securities amounted to $5,500 through June 30, 20X9.

4. A general fund transfer of $5,000 was made to establish an internal service fund to provide for a permanent investment in inventory.

5. The village decided to install lighting in the village park, and a special assessment project was authorized to install the lighting at a cost of $75,000. The appropriation was formally recorded.

6. The assessments were levied for $72,000, with the village contributing $3,000 out of the general fund. All assessments were collected during the year, including the village's contribution.

7. A contract for $75,000 was let for installation of the lighting. At June 30, 20X9, the contract was completed but not approved. The contractor was paid all but 5 percent, which was retained to ensure compliance with the terms of the contract. Encumbrances and other budgetary accounts are maintained.

8. During the year the internal service fund purchased various supplies at a cost of $1,900.

9. Cash collections recorded by the general fund during the year were as follows: property taxes, $386,000; licenses and permits, $7,000.

10. The village council decided to build a village hall at an estimated cost of $500,000 to replace space occupied in rented facilities. The village does not record such project authorizations. It was decided that general obligation bonds bearing interest at 6 percent would be issued. On June 30, 20X9, the bonds were issued at their face value of $500,000, payable in 20 years. No contracts have been signed for this project and no expenditures have been made.

11. A fire truck was purchased for $15,000 and the voucher approved and paid by the general fund. This expenditure was previously encumbered for $15,000.

REQUIRED: Prepare journal entries to record each of the above transactions in the appropriate fund(s) or account groups of the village of Dexter for the fiscal year ended June 30, 20X9. Use the following funds and account groups:

- General Fund.
- Capital Projects Fund.
- Internal Service Fund.
- Trust Fund.
- General Long-Term Debt Account Group.
- General Fixed Assets Account Group.

Closing entries are not required.
(AICPA adapted)

P13.13 **Special Revenue Fund** In 20X4, Grand City established a special revenue fund to account for acquisitions of wildlife by the city zoo. Acquisitions were scheduled to begin in January 20X5. Appropriations were not recorded until 20X5. Financing for the project was to be provided as follows:

From Federal Grant to Be Received in March 20X5	$ 90,000
From 20X4 General Fund Revenue	45,000
From 20X5 General Fund Revenue	45,000
	$ 180,000

The special revenue fund balance sheet for December 31, 20X4, follows:

Grand City Special Revenue Fund
Balance Sheet
December 31, 20X4

Assets		Liabilities and Fund Balance	
Cash	$ 13,000	Deferred Revenue	$ 90,000
Investments	32,000	Fund Balance	45,000
Accounts Receivable			
(Federal Grant)	90,000		
	$ 135,000		$ 135,000

During 20X5, the following occurred:

1. An appropriation of $180,000 was made for the project.
2. Contracts for $175,000 for the acquisition of wildlife were signed. Animals, reptiles, and birds were delivered, and Grand City was billed for $175,000.
3. Cash from the general fund and federal grant was received as scheduled.
4. Investments yielded $1,800 in revenues, $200 less than anticipated.
5. Vouchers remaining to be paid at year-end totaled $8,000.
6. Any remaining resources were reclassified for transfer to the general fund.

REQUIRED:

1. What was the 20X4 budget entry?
2. Prepare all 20X5 journal entries and closing entries for the special revenue fund.
3. Prepare the balance sheet for the special revenue fund as of December 31, 20X5.

CHAPTER 14

ACCOUNTING AND REPORTING BY NOT-FOR-PROFIT ORGANIZATIONS

CHAPTER PREVIEW

Business firms and governmental units are two of the three major types of economic entities in our society. The third type of economic entity is the **not-for-profit (NFP) organization**. Accounting and reporting by NFPs is problematic because the NFP organization has the characteristics of both a business entity and a governmental unit. NFPs are similar to governmental units in the sense that contributors of resources generally do not expect to receive services in proportion to their contributions. The NFP's goal is not to generate profits, but to provide services to society. However, NFPs also have characteristics of a business entity. Unlike a governmental unit, NFPs do not have automatic sources of funding, but must generate resources from donations, grants, debt, and user charges. Donors and creditors generally want to assess the NFP organization's financial health and management decisions before making contributions or granting loans.

If a significant amount of an NFP organization's assets are restricted to particular uses, either by private donors or by funding organizations, an NFP may organize its internal accounting structure on a fund basis, similar to a governmental entity. However, the requirements of *SFAS 117*, "Financial Statements of Not-For-Profit Organizations," do not allow external reporting on a fund basis, but require reporting for the NFP entity as a whole. This chapter emphasizes the *external reporting requirements* for not-for-profit organizations. A commonly-encountered NFP internal fund structure, and the process by which internal fund information can be used to create external reports, are discussed in Appendix 2. In this chapter we examine the following major topics:

- Characteristics of not-for-profit organizations
- Reporting concepts for not-for-profit organizations
- The financial reporting display model
- Accounting for contributions received
- Accounting for investments
- Comprehensive illustration of NFP accounting: Northeastern Heart Society
- Effects of FASB requirements on financial analysis of NFPs
- Application: New York State Society of Certified Public Accountants (Appendix 1)
- Internal fund structure and preparation of external reports (Appendix 2)

CHARACTERISTICS OF NOT-FOR-PROFIT ORGANIZATIONS

NFP organizations typically share the following characteristics:

- Significant amounts of the organization's resources are received from providers who expect to receive neither payment nor economic benefits proportionate to the resources provided.
- The primary mission of the organization is to provide services to some segment of society; the mission does *not* involve generating a profit. An excess of revenues over expenses is expected to be used to provide future services.
- There are no ownership interests that can be sold, transferred, or redeemed, or that convey entitlement to a share of resources in the event the organization is liquidated.[1] The NFP is owned by its members or by the public, and is run by a board of directors or trustees.
- Assets are often restricted either to a particular use or for use during a certain period of time, either by the donor or by an institution which provides resources through grants.

NFP organizations can be categorized as follows:

Voluntary health and welfare organizations. These organizations derive support from voluntary contributions rather than user charges, and offer their services to the public in general. Services may be in the form of social welfare, health, or community services. Examples include the American Heart Association, the Salvation Army, the YMCA, and Habitat for Humanity.

Colleges and universities. This category includes all two- and four-year colleges and universities, but does not include for-profit schools, which are typically technical schools. Support is derived from user charges, alumni contributions, and some state and federal funding.

Hospitals and other medical organizations. These organizations include not-for-profit hospitals, nursing homes, health maintenance organizations, medical groups, ambulatory care facilities, and clinics. Major support comes from user charges, including third party payments, contributions, and grants.

This chapter deals with the reporting requirements for *private NFP organizations*. Private NFPs are those controlled by a governing board. Private NFPs may receive a significant amount of public funding, but they are run by a nongovernmental group. These organizations fall within the jurisdiction of the FASB. Public NFPs must follow the accounting requirements of the GASB, as covered in Chapters 12 and 13. Therefore, when deciding whether the FASB requirements for NFP reporting apply to a particular organization, one must consider two important issues: Is the organization under the jurisdiction of a private or public group? If private, is it a not-for-profit or a for-profit organization? The latter question cannot be answered merely by identifying the nature of the services rendered. For-profit forms of voluntary health and welfare organizations, colleges and universities, and health care organizations have proliferated in recent years. In addition, an organization which has traditionally been an NFP may reorganize on a for-profit basis.

---

[1] Financial Accounting Standards Board, *Statement of Financial Accounting Concepts No. 4*, "Objectives of Financial Reporting by Nonbusiness Organizations," (Stamford, CT:FASB, 1980), para. 6.

SOURCES OF ACCOUNTING PRINCIPLES

The FASB provides generally accepted accounting principles for private NFPs, while public NFPs are under the jurisdiction of the GASB. Reporting requirements of the GASB can differ significantly from the FASB. For example, in current practice, *SFAS 93* requires private NFPs to recognize depreciation on long-lived assets.[2] The GASB, in *SGAS 8*, denied *SFAS 93's* applicability to public colleges and universities, although the proposed reporting model for public colleges and universities requires recognition of depreciation.[3] Differences in reporting requirements thus depend on whether the organization is a for-profit or not-for-profit organization, even though the mission and method of operations may be similar.

Prior to 1980, the FASB devoted little effort to NFP accounting, and accounting principles developed informally through practice and professional organizations such as the American Hospital Association, the National Health Council, and the National Association of College and University Business Officers. Since 1980, the FASB has actively developed uniform accounting principles for NFPs.

Important FASB pronouncements for NFPs are as follows:

- *SFAS 117* (1993), "Financial Statements of Not-for-Profit Organizations"
- *SFAS 116* (1993), "Accounting for Contributions Received and Contributions Made"
- *SFAS 124* (1995), "Accounting for Certain Investments Held by Not-for-Profit Organizations"
- FASB *Statement of Financial Accounting Concepts No. 4* (1980), "Objectives of Financial Reporting by Nonbusiness Organizations," and sections of FASB *Statement of Financial Accounting Concepts No. 6* (1985), "Elements of Financial Statements"

Remember that the accounting principles identified above are for *external reporting* purposes. For internal reporting, NFPs may use a fund structure similar to that of governmental accounting. However, this chapter looks exclusively at external reporting requirements, where funds are *not* used. The internal fund structure of an NFP organization and its reconfiguration into external reports are covered in Appendix 2.

THE DEMAND FOR EXTERNAL FINANCIAL INFORMATION

In the past, NFPs prepared financial statements using fund accounting, focusing on the stewardship of resources. The financial data provided by fund group allowed readers to track resources received and expended for particular functions and activities. However, the financial climate and the information demands on NFPs changed over the last two decades. NFPs increasingly look to external financial markets to finance escalating costs, and solicit contributions from corporations and foundations, as well as individuals. As the number of NFPs grew, there is greater competition

---

[2] Financial Accounting Standards Board, *Statement of Financial Accounting Standards No. 93*, "Recognition of Depreciation by Not-for-Profit Organizations," (Stamford, CT: FASB, 1987).

[3] Governmental Accounting Standards Board, *Statement of Governmental Accounting Standards No. 8*, "Applicability of *FASB Statement No. 93*, Recognition of Depreciation by Not-for-Profit Organizations, to Certain State and Local Governmental Entities," (Norwalk, CT: GASB, 1988), and Governmental Accounting Standards Board, *Exposure Draft*, "Basic Financial Statements—and Management's Discussion and Analysis—for Public Colleges and Universities," (Norwalk, CT: GASB, 1997).

for limited resources. In turn, donors increasingly demand information to support their resource allocation decisions. This demand for financial accountability put pressure on the FASB to develop accounting and reporting requirements that provide external readers with useful and readable financial statements for the NFP organization as a complete entity. As a result, although NFPs may maintain internal records using the fund structure, the external reporting model has changed to report on the organization as a whole, and to provide more understandable and user-friendly information.

Goals of Financial Reporting by NFPs

Unlike for-profit businesses, NFPs are not expected to generate net income from their activities. However, they are expected to use contributions for their intended purposes, choose activities which effectively further the organization's goals, and operate efficiently. Readers of an NFP's financial statements should be able to find evidence on these dimensions of performance. Readers may be contributors, lenders, organization members, watchdog groups, managers, or the general public.

Contributors and watchdog groups are interested in what part of each dollar contributed is spent on administration and fund raising, and how much is spent on services for members or the community. Most charity watchdog groups expect an organization to spend at least 60 cents of every dollar collected on programs, and evaluate organizations on various dimensions of financial performance.

Lenders are concerned with the organization's ability to meet obligations as they come due. Bond ratings are affected by management, governance, debt structure, and debt history, as well as the revenue and expenditure base and financial reserves. To assess credit-worthiness, lenders need information on what portion of unrestricted net assets is available to meet debt payments and planned and unplanned expenditures. The stability and expected future level of revenue sources are also assessed.

All external readers are likely to be interested in whether the activities of the organization are above-board and within the organization's mission, whether the organization is fiscally responsible, and whether it is able to continue to provide services and pay its bills in the future. These concepts form the basis for current GAAP for NFPs.

AUTHORS' COMMENTARY

A look at the standards set by two watchdog groups—the National Charities Information Bureau, and the Better Business Bureau—provides insight into the financial information now demanded by external readers.

The National Charities Information Bureau—http://www.give.org—lists nine areas of evaluation for charitable organizations, such as governance of the Board and availability of financial information. The area "use of funds" lists four standards:

- spend at least 60% of annual expenses for program activities
- ensure that fund-raising expenses are reasonable over time in relation to fund-raising results
- net assets available for the following year are usually not more than twice the current year's expenses or next year's budget, whichever is higher
- no persistent or increasing deficit in unrestricted net assets

An organization is expected to supply on request audited financial statements prepared in accordance with GAAP. Expenses should be presented functionally by program and activity. The budget should show detail by major classification.

The Council of the Better Business Bureau (CBBB)—http://www.bbb.org—has similar standards. For example, the standards under "use of funds" are:

- at least 50% of total income from all sources be spent on programs and activities directly related to the organization's purposes
- at least 50% of public contributions be spent on programs and activities described in solicitations
- fund-raising costs not exceed 35% of related contributions
- total fund-raising and administrative costs not exceed 50% of total income

The CBBB also requires organizations to provide "adequate" financial information, described as:

- significant categories of contributions and other income
- expenses by major programs and activities
- detailed schedules of expenses by natural classification, such as salaries and postage, for each program or activity
- accurate presentation of all fund-raising and administrative costs
- if a significant activity combines fund-raising with other purposes, such as a direct mail campaign combining fund-raising and public education, the financial statements should specify the total cost of the activity and the basis for allocating its costs

REPORTING CONCEPTS FOR NOT-FOR-PROFIT ORGANIZATIONS

FASB *Concepts Statement No. 4* presents the basic principles and objectives of NFP reporting. The three broad objectives are:

- Financial information should be useful to contributors, lenders, suppliers, organization members, oversight bodies, and managers in making resource allocation decisions—either how much to give to the organization, or how much to allocate within the organization to alternative activities.
- Financial information should be useful in evaluating the services provided by the organization and in determining its ability to continue to provide these services.
- Financial information should be useful in assessing the performance of management.

FASB *Concepts Statement No. 6* concluded that the net assets ("equity") section of an NFP's balance sheet be partitioned into three classes:

- **Permanently restricted net assets**. Contributions or other net inflows where donor-imposed restrictions limit use indefinitely.
- **Temporarily restricted net assets**. Contributions or other net inflows subject to donor-imposed restrictions that will expire either through the passage of time or by actions of the organization.
- **Unrestricted net assets**. All other net assets.

These principles and objectives were later implemented in the contributions and financial statement requirements of *SFAS 116* and *SFAS 117*. *SFAS 117* explicitly defines the purpose of NFP financial statements as follows:

> The primary purpose of financial statements is to provide relevant information to meet the common interests of donors, members, creditors, and others who provide resources to not-for-profit organizations. Those external users of financial statements have common interests in assessing (a) the services an organization provides and its ability to continue to provide those services and (b) how managers discharge their stewardship responsibilities and other aspects of their performance.[4]

SFAS 117 goes on to specify that the financial statements include information on the organization's assets, liabilities, and net assets, transactions affecting net assets, how the organization obtains and uses cash, and its service efforts.

THE FINANCIAL REPORTING DISPLAY MODEL

SFAS 117 calls for a common structure in financial reporting by NFPs, and also calls for reporting financial results for the entity as a whole. *SFAS 117* requires that an NFP organization present the following statements: a **Statement of Financial Position**, a **Statement of Activities**, and a **Statement of Cash Flows**. The general format of these statements is illustrated in Exhibits 14.1, 14.2, and 14.3.

The **Statement of Financial Position** presents assets, liabilities, and net assets of the organization. Important features are as follows:

- Net assets must be presented in the three net asset categories discussed above.
- Assets and liabilities are classified according to liquidity.
- Basic concepts of business accounting are followed in valuing assets and liabilities, except for investments in debt and equity securities, where *SFAS 124* requires that fair values be used for all investments in debt securities and investments in equity securities with determinable fair values.
- Cash or other assets donor-restricted in a way that limits their use over the long-term, such as for acquisition or construction of long-term assets, should be separated in a different category from unrestricted cash and other assets that are available for current use.

The **Statement of Activities** shows changes in each of the net asset categories during the year. Important features are as follows:

- Inflows—from contributions, sales, and so forth—are reported as increases in the appropriate net asset category. For example, unrestricted donations are reported as increases in unrestricted net assets; contributions restricted by the donor for use in a particular time period or for a particular purpose are reported as increases in temporarily restricted net assets; contributions where the donor stipulates that the principal is to be kept intact and only the income earned on the contribution is to be used, are reported as increases in permanently restricted net assets.

---

[4] Financial Accounting Standards Board, *Statement of Financial Accounting Standards No. 117*, "Financial Statements of Not-for-Profit Organizations," para. 17.

Sample NFP Organization
Statement of Financial Position
December 31, 20X1

Assets
Current Assets

Cash and Cash Equivalents	$ 50,000
Accounts and Interest Receivable	400,000
Inventories and Prepaid Expenses	150,000
Contributions Receivable	75,000
Short-term Investments	40,000
	$ 715,000

Noncurrent Assets

Assets Restricted to Investment in Land, Buildings, and Equipment	$ 200,000
Land, Buildings, and Equipment (net)	800,000
Long-term Investments	300,000
	$ 1,300,000
Total Assets	$ 2,015,000

Liabilities and Net Assets

Liabilities
Current Liabilities

Accounts Payable	$ 150,000
Refundable Contributions	20,000
Grants Payable	600,000
	$ 770,000

Noncurrent Liabilities

Notes Payable	$ 100,000
Annuity Obligations	350,000
Long-term Debt	150,000
	$ 600,000
Total Liabilities	$ 1,370,000

Net Assets

Unrestricted	$ 250,000
Temporarily Restricted	270,000
Permanently Restricted	125,000
Total Net Assets	$ 645,000
Total Liabilities and Net Assets	$ 2,015,000

EXHIBIT 14.1 STATEMENT OF FINANCIAL POSITION

■ As donor-imposed temporary restrictions are met, either because time passed or the contributions were used for the intended purpose, temporarily restricted net assets are reduced and unrestricted net assets are increased. These items are shown separately on the Statement of Activities as *net assets released from restrictions* with equal amounts shown as reductions in temporarily restricted net assets and increases in unrestricted net assets. By definition, there can be no release of permanently restricted net assets.

Sample NFP Organization
Statement of Activities
For the Year Ended December 31, 20X1

	Unrestricted	Temporarily Restricted	Permanently Restricted	Total
Revenues, Gains, and Other Support:				
Contributions	$ 750,000	$ 120,000	$ 40,000	$ 910,000
Fees	130,000			130,000
Investment Income	35,000	5,000		40,000
Net Realized and Unrealized Gains				
on Long-term Investments	100,000	35,000	15,000	150,000
Net Assets released from restrictions:				
Satisfaction of program restrictions .	50,000	(50,000)		
Expiration of time restrictions	24,000	(24,000)		
Total Revenues, Gains				
and Other Support	$1,089,000	$ 86,000	$ 55,000	$1,230,000
Expenses and Losses:				
Childcare Programs	$ 400,000			$ 400,000
Family Support Programs	145,000			145,000
Community Education Programs	250,000			250,000
Administrative	135,000			135,000
Fund-raising	150,000			150,000
Total Expenses	$1,080,000			$1,080,000
Change in Net Assets	$ 9,000	$ 86,000	$ 55,000	$ 150,000
Net Assets, beginning of year	241,000	184,000	70,000	495,000
Net Assets, end of year	$ 250,000	$ 270,000	$ 125,000	$ 645,000

EXHIBIT 14.2   STATEMENT OF ACTIVITIES

- *Expenses are reported as reductions in the unrestricted net assets category only*. When restricted resources are used, they must be reported as released from restrictions—moved from the temporarily restricted category to the unrestricted category—and the expense is shown as a reduction in unrestricted net assets.
- Expenses are classified **functionally**, separating out expenses of each major program service, and showing support costs—*administrative, membership development, and fundraising*—separately.
  - **Administrative** costs are those not specifically related to a particular program, fundraising activity, or membership development activity, but are required for the organization's continued operations. Administrative costs include accounting, financing, and business management costs.
  - **Membership development** costs include costs of soliciting prospective members, collection of dues, and membership relations.

- **Fund-raising** costs are incurred to influence potential donors to make contributions and mount fund-raising campaigns, including the cost of preparing and distributing printed material. It is important to provide readers with an accurate breakdown of fund-raising costs, since donors have an avid interest in the proportion of their contributions spent on programs versus fund-raising. This breakdown becomes complicated when an organization uses an activity for both educational and fund-raising purposes. Organizations incurring such joint costs must disclose the fact that costs have been allocated between functional categories, and the amounts allocated to each classification.

- For voluntary health and welfare organizations, a **natural or object** classification of expenses—for example, salaries, rent, depreciation—is required in addition to the functional classification. These organizations must show expenses by functional and natural classification, using a matrix format, in a separate financial statement. Other organizations are *encouraged* but not required to show a natural classification of expenses. Expense classifications may appear in the Statement of Activities or in the notes to the financial statements.

- *SFAS 124* requires that investments in debt and equity securities be valued at fair market value. Therefore changes in investment values are shown in the Statement of Activities. Unless these value changes are donor-restricted, they are shown as changes in unrestricted net assets. Similarly, investment income is unrestricted unless the donor specifically says otherwise.

- The general format of the Statement of Activities shows changes in each of the three classifications of net assets, with the change in net assets as the "bottom line." However, NFPs are encouraged to include additional classifications within the Statement, which provide better disclosure of the organization's performance. For example, changes in net assets may be classified as operating and nonoperating, recurring and nonrecurring, or realized and unrealized.

The **Statement of Cash Flows** follows the format of *SFAS 95*, which shows cash flows from operations, investing, and financing, except that contributions and income which are donor-restricted for long-term purposes, such as plant assets and endowment, are reported as **financing** cash flows, not as operating cash flows. Also, the reconciliation of income to operating cash flow appears as a reconciliation of the **change in net assets**—the bottom line of the Statement of Activities—to cash from operations. Either the direct or indirect method of reporting cash from operating activities is allowed. While the direct method is illustrated in this chapter, the required reconciliation of the change in assets to cash from operations illustrates the reporting of operating cash flows under the indirect method.

A detailed analysis of procedures to develop the required statements using the Northeastern Heart Society illustration appears in a separate section below. Analysis of published financial statements appears in Appendix 1, using New York State Society of Certified Public Accountants financial statements.

Sample NFP Organization
Statement of Cash Flows
For the Year Ended December 31, 20X1

Cash Flows from Operating Activities

Cash received from service recipients	$ 102,000
Cash received from contributors	700,000
Investment income received	40,000
Cash paid to suppliers and employees	(1,000,000)
Cash paid for grants	(100,000)
Net cash used for operating activities	$ (258,000)

Cash Flows from Investing Activities

Purchase of equipment	$ (35,000)
Purchase of long-term investments	(28,000)
Proceeds from sale of investments	350,000
Net cash from investing activities	$ 287,000

Cash Flows from Financing Activities

Contributions restricted to investment in endowment	$ 40,000
Payments on long-term debt	(32,000)
Payments on notes payable	(15,000)
Payments of annuity obligations	(60,000)
Proceeds of notes	75,000
Net cash from financing activities	$ 8,000

Net increase in cash and cash equivalents	$ 37,000
Cash and cash equivalents at beginning of year	13,000
Cash and cash equivalents at end of year	$ 50,000

Reconciliation of change in net assets to net cash from operating activities:

Change in net assets	$ 150,000
Depreciation	30,000
Increase in accounts and interest receivable	(95,000)
Decrease in inventories and prepaid expenses	5,000
Increase in contributions receivable	(100,000)
Decrease in accounts payable	(58,000)
Decrease in refundable contributions	(25,000)
Decrease in grants payable	(15,000)
Net realized and unrealized gains on long-term investments	(150,000)
Net cash from operating activities	$ (258,000)

EXHIBIT 14.3   STATEMENT OF CASH FLOWS

ACCOUNTING FOR CONTRIBUTIONS RECEIVED

Accounting requirements for recognition of contributions appear in *SFAS 116*, "Accounting for Contributions Received and Contributions Made." Contributions are measured at *fair value*. As contributions are recognized, they are categorized as increases in **unrestricted, temporarily restricted**, or **permanently restricted net assets**, as described above.

Contributions received may be in the form of cash, other assets, or forgiveness of liabilities. Contributions may also take the form of volunteer services. According to *SFAS 116*, "[a] contribution is an unconditional transfer of cash or other assets to an entity or a settlement or cancellation of its liabilities in a voluntary **nonreciprocal transfer** by another entity acting other than as an owner."[5] In this context, **unconditional** implies that there are no circumstances under which the contribution would be returned. An example of a **conditional** contribution occurs when a donor agrees to make a $100,000 contribution when the total level of contributions from other sources reaches $100,000. Until other contributions reach $100,000, the donor's contribution is conditional. In a **nonreciprocal transfer**, the donor does not receive something of significant value in return. Therefore if a donor receives goods or services, other than a minor thank-you item, it is not a contribution but is instead *payment for goods or services*, and normal business accounting is appropriate.

UNCONDITIONAL AND UNRESTRICTED CONTRIBUTIONS OF CASH

Unconditional and unrestricted cash contributions are those having no donor-imposed conditions or restrictions. An example is the cash deposited in the Salvation Army kettles at the holiday season. Notice that determination of the existence of conditions or restrictions depends on the existence of *donor-imposed* conditions or restrictions *only*. If the Board of the NFP organization decides to set aside certain contributions for a designated purpose, such as funding a particular program or building a sinking fund for repayment of debt, the contributions are still unrestricted. Unconditional contributions of cash not subject to donors' restrictions are recorded as increases in *unrestricted net assets* on the Statement of Activities. The journal entry to record unconditional contributions of cash is of the following form:

Cash	1,000	
Contribution Revenue—Unrestricted		1,000
To record unconditional cash contributions of $1,000.		

UNCONDITIONAL AND UNRESTRICTED CONTRIBUTIONS OF GOODS AND SERVICES

Unconditional contributions of goods not subject to donors' restrictions are shown as increases in *unrestricted net assets*. Such contributions are valued at the fair market value of the goods, at the date they are contributed. The book value or basis in the goods to the contributor is irrelevant. An NFP organization is required to make a good faith estimate of the goods received. This may require appraisal information.

---

[5] Financial Accounting Standards Board, *Statement of Financial Accounting Standards No. 116*, "Accounting for Contributions Received and Contributions Made," para. 5.

The requirement that contributions of goods be recorded at the date received is a significant departure from pre-*SFAS 116* practice, when such contributions were typically recorded as the goods were liquidated. For example, organizations such as the Salvation Army and Goodwill Industries receive a significant amount of contributions in the form of used clothing, furniture and appliances. These contributions are sold either in thrift stores or to brokers. Before *SFAS 116*, such contributions were not recognized until the goods were turned into cash. This simplified the process of estimating their value. With the advent of *SFAS 116*, these organizations must estimate the value of the contributions before they are liquidated. Of course, this does not imply that the value of all contributions must be estimated when contributions are received. Most contributions are received and liquidated in the same accounting period. Only those contributions received in one period and sold in another period must be appraised. If it is determined that the estimate was in error, normal business accounting for a change in estimate applies.

Revenue from contributed goods not subject to donors' restrictions appears as an addition to unrestricted net assets on the Statement of Activities. The entry to record unconditional contributions of goods takes the following form:

Merchandise	8,000	
Revenue from Contributed Goods—Unrestricted		8,000
To record an unconditional contribution of		
merchandise with a fair market value of $8,000.		

Unconditional contributions of services are recorded as increases in *unrestricted net assets* if the services

(a) create or enhance nonfinancial assets or (b) require specialized skills, are provided by individuals possessing those skills, and are typically purchased if not provided by donation. Services requiring specialized skills are provided by accountants, architects, carpenters, doctors, electricians, lawyers, nurses, plumbers, teachers, and other professionals and craftsmen. Contributed services and promises to give services that do not meet the above criteria shall not be recognized.[6]

Specialized services that do not create or enhance nonfinancial assets, such as services donated by a lawyer in handling a lawsuit against an organization, are valued at the *fair value of the services rendered*. Services that create or enhance nonfinancial assets, such as services donated by a contractor to build an addition to the organization's community center, are valued at the *fair value of the asset created*.

Note that the entry to record unconditional contributions of services typically involves both an increase *and* a decrease in unrestricted net assets. Unless the service creates or enhances nonfinancial assets, an entry such as the following is made:

General Expenses	10,000	
Revenue from Contributed Services—Unrestricted		10,000
To record the donation of accounting		
services valued at $10,000.		

---

[6] *SFAS 116*, para. 9.

General Expenses are shown as a reduction in unrestricted net assets, while Contributed Services are shown as an increase in unrestricted net assets on the Statement of Activities.

Services that create or enhance nonfinancial assets, such as the efforts of a contractor in building a facility to house abused families, are recorded as follows:

Building	75,000	
Revenue from Contributed Services—Unrestricted		75,000
To record services donated to construct a new		
family facility. The services are estimated to		
add $75,000 to the fair value of the facility.		

DONOR-IMPOSED TEMPORARY RESTRICTIONS

There are two types of temporary restrictions which donors may impose on their contributions: **time restrictions** and **use restrictions**. With time-restricted contributions, the donor specifies that the contribution be used in a future time period. For example, a donor may make a contribution with the stipulation that it be spent in the following year. With a use-restricted contribution, the donor specifies that the contribution must be used for a particular purpose. This restriction may be explicitly stated by the donor, or may be inferred because of the way the contribution was solicited. For example, a donor may make a donation to a university, with the explicit stipulation that the donation be used to finance scholarships for accounting students. Alternatively, the accounting department may solicit contributions in the form of a scholarship fund drive. Although the donor may not specifically state the restriction, donations to the fund drive are implicitly restricted to scholarship use.

Both time and use restrictions are **temporary restrictions** since the restrictions will disappear either with the passage of time or by using the contributions for the intended purpose. Temporarily restricted contributions are initially recorded as an increase in temporarily restricted net assets. When the restriction is met, net assets are released from temporarily restricted to unrestricted net assets. For example, assume a donor contributes $5,000 to a local food bank to be used to purchase a used car to deliver food to the homeless. Entries are as follows:

Cash	5,000	
Contribution Revenue—Temporarily Restricted		5,000
To record the cash contribution.		
Net Assets Released from Restrictions—Temporarily Restricted ..	5,000	
Net Assets Released from Restrictions—Unrestricted		5,000
To record the release of net assets.		
Automobiles and Equipment	5,000	
Cash		5,000
To record the acquisition of the car.		

Contribution Revenue is added to temporarily restricted net assets on the Statement of Activities. The "net assets released" accounts are shown as a reduction in temporarily restricted net assets and an increase in unrestricted net assets, respectively. As a practical matter, if donations restricted to a particular use are used for this purpose in the same accounting period, it is not necessary to first classify the donations as temporarily restricted and then release them from restriction when the expenditures are made. Although this practice does not report restricted contributions as accurately, such donations may be included with unrestricted net assets in the period received.

Unconditional Promises

According to *SFAS 116*, **unconditional promises** to give in the future, where the promises have verifiable documentation, are reported in the period the promise is given, as an increase in unrestricted, temporarily restricted, or permanently restricted net assets. This requires that a receivable be recognized. These promises are valued at *net realizable value, net of estimated uncollectibles*. If the contributions are expected to be collected over more than one year, they should be measured at the present value of the future cash flows.

Most promises to contribute, where the donor will make payments over more than one year, are recorded as *time-restricted contributions*. Because the organization will not receive the payments immediately, their use is automatically restricted to the period(s) in which payment is received. Thus if the promise has the documentation which allows it to be recorded in the period the promise is made, the contribution revenue is considered to be temporarily restricted.

As an example of an unconditional promise that qualifies for recognition in the year the promise is made, assume a donor agrees in writing to contribute $5,000 per year for the next five years. At the time the agreement is signed, the following entry is made:

Contributions Receivable	18,954	
Contribution Revenue—Temporarily Restricted		18,954
To record the present value of the written agreement, using a discount rate of 10%—$18,954 is the present value of an annuity of $5,000 per year for five years. The promise is assumed to be 100% collectible.		

Each year, interest is recognized on the receivable and the $5,000 cash donation is recorded. The interest is included in *contribution revenue*, not interest income, and accumulates in temporarily restricted net assets until the donation is available for use (*SFAS 116*, paragraph 20). Entries for the first year are as follows:

Contributions Receivable	1,895	
Contribution Revenue—Temporarily Restricted		1,895
To record interest earned on outstanding contributions receivable; $1,895 = 10% × $18,954.		

Cash	5,000	
Contributions Receivable		5,000
To record the donor's cash contribution for the year.		

Net Assets Released from Restrictions—Temporarily Restricted . .	5,000	
Net Assets Released from Restrictions—Unrestricted		5,000
To show satisfaction of the time restriction.		

The requirement that promises be recorded as revenue in the period the promise is made is a significant deviation from pre-*SFAS 116* practice, where contributions were reported in the period when the cash was received. This requirement has been a major source of criticism for *SFAS 116*. In order to comply with the new requirements, NFP organizations must keep careful records of promises and payments, and make judgments as to their collectibility and whether the promise is backed by verifiable documentation. Clearly a donor's written agreement to contribute $5,000 per year for the next five years is recognized as revenue in the year the agreement is signed. Just as clearly, a phone pledge during a telethon, where the potential donor asks if he can "think it over" before making the donation, is not recognized until the cash is received. However, other situations may not be as clear. Sufficient verifiable documentation supporting recognition of contribution revenue includes written agreements, pledge cards, or follow-up written confirmations of oral agreements. It is important to distinguish an *intention* from a *promise*. For example, an individual may indicate that he or she has included the organization as a beneficiary in his or her will. Since the will may be legally modified before death, this is an intention to give which is not recognized as revenue by the organization. However, if the individual dies without modifying the will, the organization recognizes the contribution as revenue at the date of death.

DONOR-IMPOSED CONDITIONS

A donor-imposed **condition** refers to an uncertain future event that could void the contribution. Conditional promises to give are recognized *in the period the condition is met*. If the uncertain event needed to remove the condition occurs, the revenue is recognized. If a donor makes the contribution before the condition is met, a liability is recognized. For example, a donor promises to contribute $1,000,000 if contributions by others total a certain amount. When that condition is met, the $1,000,000 promise is recorded as revenue. If the donor pays $1,000,000 to the organization *before* the condition is met, entries are as follows:

Cash	1,000,000	
Refundable Contributions		1,000,000
To record the receipt of a conditional contribution,		
where the required condition has not yet been met.		
Refundable Contributions	1,000,000	
Contribution Revenue—Unrestricted		1,000,000
To record contribution revenue when the condition is		
met, assuming the contribution does not involve any		
donor-imposed restrictions.		

If the donation is made *after* the condition is met, it is immediately recognized as contribution revenue. If the donation is a *promise* to contribute supported by verifiable documentation, the contribution is recognized as revenue and a receivable is recorded when the condition is met, as discussed above.

DONOR-IMPOSED PERMANENT RESTRICTIONS

Donors of permanently restricted contributions generally stipulate that the principal of the donation be maintained, while any income earned on investment of the principal may be unrestricted, or may be limited to a particular purpose. The principal of the donation is a **permanent endowment** and is added to permanently restricted net assets. Income on the endowment is either unrestricted or temporarily restricted, depending on the donor's wishes.

Assume a donor gives $1,000,000 to a hospital in 20X0. The principal is to be left intact, and income earned on the principal is to be used to support AIDS research. The $1,000,000 is invested in securities that generate income of $50,000 in 20X1. This $50,000 is used in AIDS research in 20X2. Entries are as follows:

20X0	Cash	1,000,000	
	Contribution Revenue—Permanently Restricted		1,000,000
	To record receipt of the permanent endowment.		
20X1	Cash	50,000	
	Investment Income—Temporarily Restricted		50,000
	To record receipt of the investment income.		
20X2	Net Assets Released from Restrictions—Temporarily Restricted	50,000	
	Net Assets Released from Restrictions—Unrestricted		50,000
	To record release of funds from temporary restrictions.		
	AIDS Research Expenses	50,000	
	Cash		50,000
	To record use of the funds for AIDS research.		

The expenses are shown as a reduction in unrestricted net assets on the Statement of Activities.

CONTRIBUTIONS OF FIXED ASSETS

Donations of long-lived assets, valued at fair market value at the date of donation, may be reported as increases in unrestricted net assets or temporarily restricted net assets when the use of assets is donor-restricted in some way, the donation is an increase in temporarily restricted net assets. When the organization intends to liquidate the assets, the donation is probably an increase in unrestricted net assets. When the asset is restricted to a particular use or sale is precluded for a specified period of time, the donation increases temporarily restricted net assets. The organization must have a consistent policy with respect to such donations. Assume a local mission receives a donation of office equipment, and the donor specifies that the equipment be used in the regular operations of the mission. If the equipment is used for this purpose irrespective of donor stipulations, it is not clear that the restriction is real. The organization must make a judgment on whether to record the contribution as an increase in unrestricted or temporarily restricted net assets. In making this decision, the organization must decide whether the donor intended to prevent immediate liquidation of the equipment. If the organization recognizes such contributions as **time restricted**, it must use the same reporting policy for long-lived assets acquired with cash donations restricted for this use.

If the organization elects to record a donation of a depreciable asset as temporarily restricted, the restriction expires as the asset wears out. Depreciation on the asset is shown as a release from temporarily restricted to unrestricted net assets, and the depreciation expense is then shown as a reduction in unrestricted net assets. For example, assume that the local mission receives a building with a fair market value of $150,000. The donor stipulates that the building must be retained for five years. Depreciation will be recorded on a straight-line basis over the building's estimated 15-year life, with no salvage value. Entries are as follows:

Building	150,000	
Contribution Revenue—Temporarily Restricted		150,000
To record receipt of the building.		

Each year, for the first five years, depreciation on the building is recorded as follows:

Net Assets Released from Restrictions—Temporarily Restricted	10,000	
Net Assets Released from Restrictions—		
Unrestricted		10,000
To record release of restrictions as the building		
wears out.		

Depreciation Expense	10,000	
Accumulated Depreciation—Building		10,000
To record depreciation expense.		

At the end of five years, the organization is free to retain or sell the building.

Net Assets Released from Restrictions—Temporarily		
Restricted	100,000	
Net Assets Released from Restrictions—		
Unrestricted		100,000
To record the lifting of restrictions on the building's		
use; $100,000 = $150,000 − ($10,000 × 5)$.		

An NFP may also receive donations of nondepreciable assets, such as land or artworks. Contributions of land are recorded as increases in permanently restricted, temporarily restricted or unrestricted net assets, depending on donor stipulations. Organizations are *not* required to report as revenue donations of collections of works of art or items of historical value, if the items meet all of the following conditions:

- Are held for public exhibition, education, or research in furtherance of public service rather than financial gain
- Are protected, kept unencumbered, cared for, and preserved
- Are subject to an organizational policy that requires the proceeds from sales of collection items to be used to acquire other items for collections.[7]

---

[7] *SFAS 116*, para. 11.

ANNUITY AND LIFE INCOME CONTRIBUTIONS

One means of fund-raising by NFPs is the *annuity* or *life income agreement*. A donor contributes a sum of money or other resources that is recorded at fair market value. In exchange, the organization agrees to make periodic payments, either to the donor or to other specified individuals, for a period of time. When the periodic payment is a fixed amount, the agreement is called an **annuity agreement**; when the payment is defined as the amount of income earned on the contributed assets, it is a **life income agreement**.

In the case of an *annuity agreement*, the present value of the annuity payments is calculated and recorded as a liability. The difference is the value of the agreement to the organization, and is an increase in net assets. If this amount becomes part of a permanent endowment when the agreement terminates, the increase is to permanently restricted net assets. If it is available for restricted purposes, or available for unrestricted use when the agreement terminates, the increase is to temporarily restricted net assets. In the case of a *life income agreement*, because future payments to beneficiaries are equal to future income, the present value of the liability is zero, and the entire contribution increases net assets, classified according to donor intent.

Annuity Agreement Illustration

Suppose that an elderly alumnus, who has a life expectancy of nine years, donates $50,000 to McKinley College under an *annuity agreement* whereby he is to receive $7,000 annually for life. It is determined that a 10 percent discount rate is appropriate. The present value of the liability is calculated as $7,000 × present value of an ordinary annuity of nine years at 10% = $7,000 × 5.759 = $40,313. The college has unrestricted access to the value of the annuity in excess of the present value of the related obligation, at the termination of the agreement. The contribution is recorded as follows:

Cash	50,000	
Annuity Payable		40,313
Contribution Revenue—Temporarily Restricted		9,687
To record the contribution and		
corresponding annuity agreement.		

Suppose further that $40,000 was invested at 12 percent, and that $10,000 was invested at 6 percent. Entries for the first year are as follows:

Investments	50,000	
Cash		50,000
To record investment of the $50,000.		

Cash	5,400	
Investment Income—Temporarily Restricted		5,400
To record income for the year from investments		
[$5,400 = ($40,000 × 12%) + ($10,000 × 6%)].		

Interest expense for the year of $4,031 (= $40,313 × 10%) is recognized on the Annuity Payable. Since expenses cannot be reductions in temporarily restricted net assets, an entry is made to release the restricted net assets before the expense can be recognized.

Net Assets Released from Restrictions—Temporarily Restricted	4,031	
Net Assets Released from Restrictions—Unrestricted		4,031
To record release of net assets.		

Interest Expense	4,031	
Annuity Payable	2,969	
Cash		7,000
To record interest expense on the annuity obligation and reduction of the annuity liability.		

Life Income Agreement Illustration

When the same contribution is made under *a life income agreement*, no initial liability is recorded. The donor is entitled to receive whatever income is generated each year. Assuming the same facts as above, the entries for a life income agreement are as follows:

Cash	50,000	
Contribution Revenue—Temporarily Restricted		50,000
To record contribution under a life income agreement.		

Investments	50,000	
Cash		50,000
To record investment.		

Cash	5,400	
Life Income Payable		5,400
To record income for year from investments, and corresponding obligation to donor.		

Life Income Payable	5,400	
Cash		5,400
To record payment of current income to donor per agreement.		

ACCOUNTING FOR INVESTMENTS

NFP organizations frequently invest endowment and other restricted resources on a long-term basis and invest unrestricted resources on a temporary basis. *Purchased investments* are recorded at *cost* and *donated investments* at *fair value when received. SFAS 124* specifies the accounting for investments held by NFP organizations, subsequent to acquisition.

SFAS 124 requires that investments in *equity securities with determinable fair values* and *all debt securities* be carried at **fair (market) value**. Unrealized value changes are reported in the Statement of Activities. Note that no distinction is made between securities held for trading, available-for-sale, and held-to-maturity, as specified for investments held by business entities under *SFAS 115*—see Authors' Commentary for further discussion. *SFAS 124* is a significant departure from previous practice, where organizations typically used the lower-of-cost-or-market method, which does not recognize appreciation in the value of investments.

Realized and unrealized gains and losses on investments are categorized as changes in unrestricted, temporarily restricted, or permanently restricted net assets, depending on the existence of donor restrictions or applicable laws. In many cases, a donor specifies a restriction on investment *gains* but not investment *losses*. If no donor-specified restrictions exist, all value changes are changes in unrestricted net assets, even if the NFP Board's policy is to restrict such value changes to a particular use.

When the donation is a specific investment, such as 5,000 shares of AT&T common stock, and the donor specifies that the shares be held as a permanent endowment, any change in their value is a change in permanent net assets. However, if the donation is $40,000 in cash, donor-restricted as a permanent endowment, and the organization invests the cash in equity securities, classification of value changes is more complicated. Assume the donor restricts income and gains to a particular use, such as specified program activities. Unrealized losses are reductions in temporarily restricted net assets, unless the value of the investment goes below $40,000, when the losses become reductions in unrestricted net assets. Unrealized gains which bring the investment value back up to $40,000 are increases in unrestricted net assets, whereas unrealized gains above this point are increases in temporarily restricted net assets.

AUTHORS' COMMENTARY

Those familiar with *SFAS 115*, "Accounting for Certain Investments in Debt and Equity Securities" (1992), will recall that statement's three-portfolio approach: such investments are assigned to the *trading, available-for-sale* or *held-to-maturity* portfolios based on management's intent. The *trading* and *available-for-sale* portfolios are carried at *market* with value changes recognized in earnings or carried directly to stockholders' equity, respectively. In contrast, the *held-to-maturity* portfolio, reserved for investments in debt securities that management intends and has the ability to hold to maturity, is carried at *amortized cost*. This controversial provision of SFAS 115 was strongly favored by financial institutions.

In its "Basis for Conclusions" in *SFAS 124*, the board decided that not-for-profits do not need a "held-to-maturity" portfolio in the same way as financial institutions subject to *SFAS 115*. Financial institutions

> . . . manage their interest rate risk by coordinating the maturity and repricing characteristics of their investments and their liabilities. Reporting unrealized holding gains and losses on only the investments, and not the related liabilities, could cause volatility in earnings that is not representative of how financial institutions are affected by economic events (par. 43).

Not-for-profits do not generally use investments as hedges against interest rate risk on their liabilities. Thus recognizing value changes on investments in debt instruments by a not-for-profit does not possess the same potential for distortion such recognition would create for financial institutions.

COMPREHENSIVE ILLUSTRATION OF NFP ACCOUNTING: NORTHEASTERN HEART SOCIETY

This section illustrates the accounting and reporting requirements for NFP organizations. The Northeastern Heart Society supports research, education, and public awareness programs on the prevention of heart disease. The Society's resources are generated from contributions, bequests, and grants. A trial balance at December 31, 20X1 appears below.

Cash	$ 117,000
Pledges Receivable (net)	64,000
Investments	720,000
Land	20,000
Equipment (net)	24,000
Vouchers Payable	(33,000)
Net Assets—Unrestricted	(192,000)
Net Assets—Permanently Restricted	(720,000)
	$ -0-

The following events occurring during 20X2, and the entries to record these events, are as follows:

1. Contributions pledged by the public during 20X2 amounted to $1,300,000, of which $1,150,000 was collected during the year. In addition, $67,000 of the $80,000 in gross pledges outstanding at January 1 were collected; the balance was written off. The beginning balance in the allowance account was $16,000. The society records pledges at gross and provides an allowance for uncollectibles equal to 20 percent of pledges outstanding at year-end. Revenue of $46,000 was earned from programs which the society conducted for employee groups of various corporations.

Cash	1,150,000	
Pledges Receivable	150,000	
Public Contributions—Unrestricted		1,300,000
To record contributions and cash collections for 20X2.		

Cash	67,000	
Pledges Receivable		67,000
To record collection of receivables outstanding on January 1, 20X2.		

Allowance for Uncollectible Pledges	13,000	
Pledges Receivable		13,000
To write off the remaining January 1, 20X2 receivables balance.		

Public Contributions—Unrestricted	27,000	
Allowance for Uncollectible Pledges		27,000
To adjust the Allowance for Uncollectibles account to its correct ending balance of $30,000 (= 20% × $150,000); prior to adjustment, the allowance stood at $3,000 (= $16,000 beginning balance − $13,000 writeoffs).		

Cash	46,000	
Educational Program Revenue—Unrestricted		46,000
To record revenue from educational programs.		

2. Cash disbursements amounted to $1,155,000 in 20X2, as follows:

Research	$ 400,000
Public Awareness Programs	350,000
Corporate Programs	35,000
General Administration	195,000
Fund-Raising	175,000
Total	$ 1,155,000

Vouchers payable increased from $33,000 to $48,000; all unpaid vouchers at beginning and end of year relate to general administration costs.

Expenses—Research	400,000	
Expenses—Public Awareness Programs	350,000	
Expenses—Corporate Programs	35,000	
Expenses—General Administration	210,000	
Expenses—Fund-Raising	175,000	
Cash		1,155,000
Vouchers Payable		15,000
To record expenses for 20X2.		

3. During 20X2 the Society received a federal grant of $200,000 to expand its public awareness programs into smaller communities where it had not been active. The grant period expires on March 31, 20X3. By the end of 20X2, $143,000 was spent on the project under the terms of the grant; the balance of $57,000 is designated by the grantor for expenditure in 20X3 and remains temporarily restricted.

Cash	200,000	
Federal Grant Support—Temporarily Restricted		200,000
To record receipt of the federal grant.		

Net Assets Released from Restrictions—Temporarily Restricted	143,000	
Net Assets Released from Restrictions— Unrestricted		143,000
To record release of assets from temporary restrictions.		

Expenses—Public Awareness Programs	143,000	
Cash		143,000
To record expenditures for designated programs.		

4. The Society has a permanent endowment containing donor-restricted money to be used for research scholarships. Several years ago, the Society received a $500,000 bequest to establish this fund. The donor stipulated that the principal be maintained intact, with income used for research scholarships. Subsequent bequests and contributions increased the principal of the fund to $720,000 at the beginning of 20X2. During 20X2, contributions of $3,500 and a bequest of $10,000 were received as additions to principal. Investment income of $80,000 was earned. At year-end, all but $5,000 of principal was invested.

Cash	13,500	
Public Contributions—Permanently Restricted		13,500
To record support designated for endowment.		

Investments	8,500	
Cash		8,500
To record purchase of investments;		
$8,500 = $3,500 + $10,000 − $5,000.		

Cash	80,000	
Investment Income—Temporarily Restricted		80,000
To record income from investments.		

5. In 20X2, $75,000 was spent for research scholarships, pursuant to the fund restrictions.

Net assets Released from Restrictions—Temporarily Restricted	75,000	
Net Assets Released from Restrictions— Unrestricted		75,000
To record release of purpose restriction.		

Expenses—Research Scholarships	75,000	
Cash		75,000
To record disbursement of scholarship funds.		

6. During 20X2, construction began on an office building estimated to cost the Society $400,000. The Society borrowed $300,000 from the bank on a short-term building loan. During 20X2, construction costs were $240,000, and $28,000 in interest was paid on the loan. Investment of excess cash balances in time deposits yielded $7,700 in interest revenue; the Society's board of directors authorized the use of this money for unanticipated construction costs. Office equipment depreciation of $3,000 was charged to general administration.

Cash	300,000	
Loan Payable		300,000
To record financing for the building.		

Construction in Progress	240,000	
Cash		240,000
To record construction activity during 20X2.		

Interest Expense	28,000	
Cash		28,000
To record interest expense on the loan.		

Cash	7,700	
Investment Income—Unrestricted		7,700
To record interest revenue on investments of excess cash.		

Expenses—General Administration	3,000	
Accumulated Depreciation		3,000
To record depreciation on the office equipment.		

The Statement of Financial Position for Northeastern Heart Society at December 31, 20X2, and the Statement of Activities and Statement of Cash Flows for the year ended December 31, 20X2, appear in Exhibits 14.4, 14.5, and 14.6 below. An analysis of expenses, by natural and functional classification, appears in Exhibit 14.7.

Northeastern Heart Society
Comparative Statements of Financial Position
at December 31, 20X2 and 20X1

	December 31	January 1
Assets		
Cash	$ 331,700	$ 117,000
Pledges Receivable (net)	120,000	64,000
Investments	728,500	720,000
Land	20,000	20,000
Equipment (net)	21,000	24,000
Construction in Progress	240,000	—
Total Assets	$ 1,461,200	$ 945,000
Liabilities and Net Assets		
Liabilities		
Vouchers Payable	$ 48,000	$ 33,000
Loan Payable	300,000	—
Total Liabilities	$ 348,000	$ 33,000
Net Assets		
Unrestricted	$ 317,700	$ 192,000
Temporarily Restricted	62,000	—
Permanently Restricted	733,500	720,000
Total Net Assets	$ 1,113,200	$ 912,000
Total Liabilities and Net Assets	$ 1,461,200	$ 945,000

EXHIBIT 14.4   NORTHEASTERN HEART SOCIETY STATEMENTS OF FINANCIAL POSITION

REPORTING ISSUES FOR SPECIFIC TYPES OF NOT-FOR-PROFIT ORGANIZATIONS

In this section, reporting issues specific to each of the three types of NFP organizations are discussed.

VOLUNTARY HEALTH AND WELFARE ORGANIZATIONS

VHWOs generate most of their resources from **public support**—contributions, bequests, and grants—and **revenues**—provision of goods and services. In accounting for expenses, donors to VHWOs take a strong interest in the distinction between program service expenses and administrative and fund-raising expenses. The discussion earlier in the chapter on the functional classification of expenses and treatment of joint educational and fund-raising costs is particularly applicable to VHWOs.

Northeastern Heart Society
Statement of Activities
For the Year Ended December 31, 20X2

Changes in Unrestricted Net Assets:

Revenues and Gains:

Public Contributions (net)	$1,273,000
Educational Programs	46,000
Investment Income	7,700
Net assets Released from Program Restrictions	218,000
Total Unrestricted Revenues, Gains,	
Other Support	$1,544,700

Expenses and Losses:

Research Programs	$ 400,000
Public Awareness Programs	493,000
Corporate Programs	35,000
Research Scholarships	75,000
General Administration	213,000
Interest	28,000
Fund-Raising	175,000
Total Expenses and Losses	$1,419,000
Increase in Unrestricted Net Assets	$ 125,700

Changes in Temporarily Restricted Net Assets:

Grants	$ 200,000
Investment Income	80,000
Net Assets Released from Program Restrictions	(218,000)
Increase in Temporarily Restricted Net Assets	$ 62,000

Changes in permanently Restricted Net Assets:

Contributions	$ 13,500
Increase in Net Assets	$ 201,200
Net Assets at Beginning of Year	912,000
Net Assets at End of Year	$1,113,200

EXHIBIT 14.5 NORTHEASTERN HEART SOCIETY STATEMENT OF ACTIVITIES

Accounting for revenues and expenses related to providing goods and services should be carefully separated from activities related to contributions. Revenue recognition principles from regular business accounting are followed in accounting for the sale of goods or services by a not-for-profit organization. For example, the YWCA provides childcare services to the public. Goodwill Industries does contract work for local businesses. Revenue on such services and contracts is recognized when earned, and expenses are matched against revenue using business accounting principles. All such activities are included as changes in unrestricted net assets.

Specific guidelines for financial reporting by VHWOs can be found in the *AICPA Audit Guide*, "Not-for-Profit Organizations."[8]

---

[8] *AICPA Audit Guide: Not-for-Profit Organizations* (New York: AICPA, 1997).

Northeastern Heart Society
Statement of Cash Flows
For the Year Ended December 31, 20X2

Cash Flows from Operating Activities:

Public Contributions	$ 1,217,000
Investment Income	80,000
Program Revenue	46,000
Grant Support	200,000
Interest	7,700
Program Expenditures	(1,401,000)
Net Cash from Operating Activities	$ 149,700

Cash Flows from Investing Activities:

Investments	$ (8,500)
Construction	(240,000)
Net Cash Used for Investing Activities	$ (248,500)

Cash Flows from Financing Activities:

Loan	$ 300,000
Restricted Contributions	13,500
Net Cash from Financing Activities	$ 313,500

Net Increase in Cash	$ 214,700
Beginning Cash Balance	117,000
Ending Cash Balance	$ 331,700

Reconciliation of change in net assets
to net cash provided by operating activities

Change in Net Assets	$ 201,200
Adjustments:	
Depreciation Expense	3,000
Restricted Contributions	(13,500)
Change in Pledges Receivable	(56,000)
Change in Vouchers Payable	15,000
Net Cash Provided by Operations	$ 149,700

EXHIBIT 14.6   NORTHEASTERN HEART SOCIETY STATEMENT OF CASH FLOWS

Northeastern Heart Society
Statement of Functional Expenses
for the Year Ended December 31, 20X2

	Program Services			Supporting Services		
	Research	Public Programs	Corporate Programs	General Administration	Fund-Raising	Total Expenses
Salaries	$ 65,000	$ 160,000	$ 22,000	$ 110,000	$ 20,000	$ 377,000
Employee Benefits	15,000	30,000	4,000	20,000	5,000	74,000
Payroll Taxes	7,000	15,000	2,000	10,000	2,000	36,000
Total Personnel Costs . . .	$ 87,000	$ 205,000	$ 28,000	$ 140,000	$ 27,000	$ 487,000
Professional Fees	—	—	—	—	70,000	70,000
Supplies	45,000	23,000	—	10,000	10,000	88,000
Telephone	10,000	50,000	—	10,000	25,000	95,000
Postage	10,000	30,000	—	5,000	5,000	50,000
Occupancy Costs	15,000	15,000	5,000	20,000	5,000	60,000
Equipment Rental and Maintenance	35,000	20,000	—	15,000	—	70,000
Printing and Publications	20,000	90,000	—	—	30,000	140,000
Travel	40,000	40,000	2,000	—	3,000	85,000
Conferences and Meetings . . .	35,000	20,000	—	10,000	—	65,000
Research Grants	103,000	—	—	—	—	103,000
Scholarship Awards	75,000	—	—	—	—	75,000
Interest	—	—	—	28,000	—	28,000
Total before Depreciation	$ 475,000	$ 493,000	$ 35,000	$ 238,000	$ 175,000	$ 1,416,000
Depreciation	—	—	—	3,000	—	3,000
Total Expenses	$ 475,000	$ 493,000	$ 35,000	$ 241,000	$ 175,000	$ 1,419,000

EXHIBIT 14.7 NORTHEASTERN HEART SOCIETY STATEMENT OF FUNCTIONAL EXPENSES

COLLEGES AND UNIVERSITIES

Private colleges and universities derive much of their resources from student tuition and fees, contributions, contracts, and grants. FASB pronouncements apply only to those institutions that are privately controlled. Oversight in these institutions is through a Board of Trustees. Tuition revenue is typically shown gross, with adjustments such as scholarships and waivers shown as either a revenue deduction or as expenses. If the tuition adjustments are in return for services provided, such as tuition waivers for graduate teaching assistantships, the adjustments are shown as expenses. If the tuition adjustments do not involve any services, as is the case with scholarships, the adjustments are shown as revenue deductions. Functional classification of expenses includes the following: **education** costs, such as faculty salaries, supplies, and classroom facility costs, **support** costs, such as student services and maintenance, and **self-supporting** services, such as dormitories, food service, and health service.

Authoritative guidance on reporting for colleges and universities include the AICPA's *Audit Guide*, referenced above, and the National Association of College and University Business Officers, which issues information on accounting and reporting practices.

Colleges and universities must be especially diligent in tracking donations restricted to particular uses. They usually have a **permanent endowment** consisting of funds that are donor-restricted indefinitely, with the income either unrestricted or donor-restricted for particular purposes. For example, a business school may have an endowment where the income from the endowment is restricted to expenditures for upgrading the accounting curriculum. Donors often establish an **annuity** fund, where the university must pay a specified amount each year to the donor, with any excess remaining when the agreement terminates going to the university. A **life income** fund pays the donor the income on fund investments for life, with the remainder going to the university upon the donor's death. Each of these funds is accounted for separately for internal reporting purposes.

HEALTH CARE ORGANIZATIONS

The business environment for health care organizations has changed substantially in recent years, causing changes in the information required to make decisions. These organizations face increased costs and increased competition. Most hospital bills are paid by third parties such as Medicare, Medicaid, and insurance carriers. Third-party payers reimburse many services based on the patient's diagnosis, *not* the actual treatment cost incurred. Third-party payers require a detailed analysis of costs incurred to establish reimbursement rates by diagnosis. Such information is also used to rank health care providers. These rankings help determine whether a particular health care facility qualifies for reimbursement, and can strongly influence its ability to attract patients.

Operating revenues of health care organizations consist of **patient service revenue**, generated from patient charges, and **other revenue**, from research grants, gift shops, etc. Amounts realizable from third-party payers are typically less than recognized gross revenues. On the Statement of Activities, gross patient service revenue is shown, with provisions for contractual and other adjustments deducted from gross revenue to determine net service revenue. Charity care must be distinguished from bad debt expense. Charity care represents services performed with no expectation that payment will be received, and is **not** recorded as revenue. Services provided to patients, with the expectation that payment will be received, **are** recorded as patient service revenue. Uncollectible portions of this patient service revenue are typically shown as bad debt expense and not netted against revenue. Health care expenses fall into the following major classifications: nursing services, other professional services, general services, administrative services, uncollectible accounts, and depreciation.

Professional associations providing assistance to health care organizations in developing financial information include the American Hospital Association and the Healthcare Financial Management Association. An AICPA *audit guide* for health care organizations is also updated annually.[9]

EFFECTS OF FASB REQUIREMENTS ON FINANCIAL ANALYSIS OF NFPs

The FASB requirements for NFPs are supported by some and criticized by others. In this section, the major issues on both sides are discussed, in terms of the impact of the requirements on the external reader's ability to evaluate the financial performance of NFPs.

---

[9] *AICPA Audit Guide: Health Care Organizations* (New York: AICPA, 1997).

STRENGTHS OF FASB REQUIREMENTS

Strengths of FASB requirements include:

■ The requirements provide a more standardized presentation of financial performance and condition by all NFP organizations. Prior to these standards, each type of NFP organization had its own presentation methodology. In addition, certain disclosures were often omitted, such as the Statement of Cash Flows and a functional classification of expenses.

■ Presentation and disclosure requirements must be followed by all NFPs. However, this does not preclude an NFP from tailoring its financial statements to meet readers' needs. For example, although the "bottom line" on the Statement of Activities is the change in net assets, the NFP may include a measure of operating performance that it feels best reflects its activities.

■ The presentation requirements focus on the entity as a whole. Prior presentation typically followed the governmental model, showing results of activity by fund. Creditors, donors, members, and other interested readers can now evaluate the performance of the entire organization.

CRITICISMS OF FASB REQUIREMENTS

Criticisms of FASB requirements include:

■ Investments in debt and equity securities are reported at fair value rather than at cost. Critics fear that the unrealized value changes, which generally appear as changes in unrestricted net assets, will be misinterpreted as funds available for the organization's activities. The FASB, on the other hand, believes that fair value more accurately measures resources available to provide services. Critics also object to treating investment income and unrealized value changes on temporarily or permanently restricted contributions as unrestricted unless the donor specifically restricts such income. Some believe that income and value changes on restricted assets are implicitly restricted as well, and the required accounting treatment overstates unrestricted net assets.

■ Contributions are recognized as revenue in the period they are promised, rather than waiting until the contributions are received. Critics contend that promises are not resources available for use and that financial statements are misleading to the extent that promised contributions are shown as increases in net assets.

■ Recognition of contributions in the period received has special complications for those organizations receiving large amounts of contributions in the form of goods, such as used clothing. Prior to *SFAS 116*, these contributions were not recognized until the contributions were liquidated by sale through thrift centers or clothing brokers. *SFAS 116* requires that these organizations estimate the market value of contributions when received, which may be subject to a high degree of error.

■ Restricted contributions are recognized as increases in net assets in the period received. Critics say that these contributions are not revenues until the period the restrictions are met. For example, amounts received that are donor-restricted to be used in some future year are not available to meet the organization's current obligations. Showing them as increases in net assets could be misleading, even though they are segregated under temporarily restricted net assets.

- Donations of long-lived assets are recognized as increases in net assets in the period received. The full fair value of the asset is shown as revenue in the period received, but the asset will benefit many periods in the future. Even though the organization may elect to treat such donations as temporarily restricted, critics feel that this causes a mismatching of revenues with expenses, and overstates the resources available to the organization to fund program services.

- Net assets are classified according to donor restrictions, not internal Board restrictions. Critics feel that classification by management intention provides a more meaningful presentation of resources available for future use. For example, in practice, income on restricted funds is used for the same purpose as the original restricted funds. However, unless the income is donor-restricted, it appears as an increase in unrestricted assets.

- Assets are not classified according to intended use. Critics feel that assets to be used as a part of operations should be clearly separated from those assets which are held as part of a restricted endowment.

- Organizations find it difficult to distinguish between **restrictions** and **conditions**. Restricted contributions are shown as increases in net assets, while conditional contributions are shown as increases in liabilities. A contribution to a building fund may be considered *restricted*, in the sense that the donor intends that it be used to finance building construction. On the other hand, the contribution is *conditional* in the sense that if total contributions are too low, plans to build may be scrapped and the money returned.

Criticism of the FASB requirements generally follows one major theme—that the required reporting of changes in net assets may cause readers of the financial statements to believe resources that are unrestricted and available for organization activities are greater than they really are. Although it is true that GAAP requires that the Statement of Activities present the change in each of the categories of net assets, and the overall change in total net assets, organizations are encouraged to show other measures of performance. Therefore if an organization feels that the change in net assets is not an accurate reflection of the change in resources available for future activities, it may show a separate item in the Statement of Activities, such as "increase in net assets from operations," or provide a more detailed presentation of changes in unrestricted net assets.

CONCLUDING REMARKS

The requirements of *SFAS 116, SFAS 117,* and *SFAS 124* dramatically changed the way NFPs report their financial performance for external readers, and illustrate a continuing trend to apply a similar reporting model to all types of organizations, whether they be governmental, not-for-profit, or for-profit organizations. NFP organizations may maintain their internal records on a fund basis, to segregate resources by their intended purpose. However, there is no explicit requirement that NFPs use fund accounting internally, and fund accounting is explicitly prohibited for external reporting. It seems likely that NFPs will increasingly change their internal accounting systems to meet the information requirements for external reporting. A brief overview of internal fund accounting for NFPs and procedures to recast the fund information to meet external reporting requirements appears in Appendix 2.

SUMMARY OF KEY CONCEPTS

Not-for-profit organizations have an objective other than providing goods and services at a profit. Contributors generally do not expect direct benefits. There are no ownership interests to be sold or transferred. Most not-for-profit organizations are **voluntary health and welfare organizations, colleges and universities,** or **hospitals and other health care organizations**.

Demands for more understandable and user-friendly information by **donors, lenders, organization members, and watchdog groups** led to major changes in reporting by NFP organizations in recent years.

Accounting principles for external reporting by **private NFPs** are prescribed in *SFAS 116, SFAS 117,* and *SFAS 124*. Three financial statements are required: a **statement of financial position**, a **statement of activities**, and a **statement of cash flows**.

The **statement of financial position** reports the organization's net assets classified as **unrestricted, temporarily restricted,** or **permanently restricted**. The **statement of activities** reports changes in each of the three net asset categories. **Expenses** are reported only in the **unrestricted net asset** category, whereas **revenues** can appear in each category.

The **statement of cash flows** reconciles the change in total net assets to cash flow from **operating activities**. Cash flows from **investing** and **financing activities** complete the analysis of the change in **cash and cash equivalents** during the period.

Contributions increase unrestricted net assets unless donor-restricted. **Temporary restrictions** take the form of **time** or **use restrictions**. When donor restrictions on contributions expire, net assets are **released** by reducing temporarily restricted net assets and increasing unrestricted net assets. If the donor stipulates that the principal of the donation be maintained, it is added to **permanently restricted net assets**. **Promises to contribute** are recognized when they are supported by verifiable documentation. **Contributions of services** are recognized when they meet conditions prescribed in *SFAS 116*.

Investments held by NFP organizations are reported at **fair market value** under *SFAS 124*. **Value changes** and **investment income** are reported in the statement of activities as changes in unrestricted net assets unless subject to donor restrictions.

APPLICATION: FINANCIAL STATEMENTS OF THE NEW YORK STATE SOCIETY OF CERTIFIED PUBLIC ACCOUNTANTS

This appendix examines the 1997 financial statements of the New York State Society of Certified Public Accountants (Society), and consolidated entities. This NFP was chosen as one which is representative of the type of professional association with which many accounting students are familiar.

The Society financial statements include two related but separate entities, the Foundation for Accounting Education, Inc. (Foundation) and the New York State Society of Certified Public Accountants Benevolent Fund, Inc. (Benevolent Fund). All are not-for-profit entities which share facilities and personnel. The Society provides member services such as conferences, publications, and a web site. It also represents the interests of the profession in legislative and regulatory arenas, and subsidizes the operations of its regional chapters. The Foundation sponsors educational and research activities in accounting-related fields, such as continuing education courses, promotion of accounting careers, and undergraduate scholarships. The Benevolent Fund provides financial and counseling assistance to members and their families. The financial statements represent a consolidation of the three entities. Consolidation policies are the same as those used by for-profit organizations, studied in Chapters 3-7 in this text. **Consolidated** statements show the financial statements of the organization as a whole, with inter-entity transactions eliminated. **Consolidating** statements show the financial balances of the individual entities that comprise the consolidated entity. The comparative 1996 statements are "restated" because the Society discovered an omission of pension liability for years prior to 1996. As a result, a prior period adjustment was made to beginning net assets for 1996.

Consolidating Statement of Financial Position (Exhibit 14.8). The largest asset held by the Society is cash and cash equivalents, which includes bank deposits and short-term investments. Foundation assets are mostly temporarily restricted, and consist of long-term investments. Note 4 shows the composition of long-term investments. The Benevolent Fund accumulates cash from unrestricted sources and pays it out as needed. Note 7 discloses the nature of the $46,900 in permanently restricted net assets. Income from investment of these assets is restricted to lecture series and scholarships. The income from these investments is included in the $155,254 in investment income earned in 1997, shown on the Statement of Activities.

Consolidating Statement of Activities (Exhibit 14.9). Membership dues and registration fees constitute the major sources of net assets, and all are unrestricted. Revenues received which pertain to future events, such as dues, *CPA Journal* subscriptions and conference registration fees are deferred until the related service is performed—see the "Deferred revenues" account on the Statement of Financial Position. Most contributions are donor-restricted to undergraduate scholarships and to the Career Opportunities in the Accounting Profession (COAP) program, which is aimed at attracting minority candidates to the accounting profession. Note 7 shows that $36,190 in temporarily restricted net assets were used to fund COAP activities in 1997, and $120,785 in undergraduate scholarships were granted. Note that the Society subsidizes the Foundation's decrease in unrestricted net assets—see the transfer of $554,040 shown toward the bottom of the Statement of Activities. Following consolidation principles, all such transfers are eliminated in the consolidated balances.

Consolidated Statement of Cash Flows (Exhibit 14.10). The main source of operating cash inflows is fees for member services, such as dues, subscriptions, and conferences. Cash paid to suppliers and employees comprises the major operating use of cash. Investing activities consist of purchases of fixed assets, including furniture and equipment, data processing, and leasehold improvements, and acquisition of long-term investments. Contributions to permanently restricted net assets are normally included as sources of cash from financing activities. Since no financing activities are disclosed, it appears that the $600 in contributions were deemed immaterial and included elsewhere in the Statement of Cash Flows.

Consolidating Statement of Functional Expenses (Exhibit 14.11). This statement shows expenses by functional and natural classification, and also by entity. As expected, the Society's expenses are mostly for membership and professional development activities, although a significant amount is spent for publications and general management costs. The Foundation, whose activities center on education and research, categorizes most of its expenses as educational. The Benevolent Fund's expenses all relate to membership activities.

Notes to Consolidated Financial Statements (Exhibit 14.12). The Society's report presents 11 notes to the financial statements. To conserve space, only Note 4 (long-term investments) and Note 7 (restricted net assets) are reproduced here.

NEW YORK STATE SOCIETY OF CERTIFIED PUBLIC ACCOUNTANTS AND CONSOLIDATED ENTITIES

CONSOLIDATING STATEMENT OF FINANCIAL POSITION

MAY 31, 1997

	Consolidated Total	New York State Society of Certified Public Accountants	Foundation for Accounting Education, Inc.	New York State Society of Certified Public Accountants Benevolent Fund, Inc.
ASSETS				
Cash and cash equivalents	$3,624,261	$2,846,256	$ 420,104	$357,901
Accounts receivable - net of allowance for doubtful accounts of $438,871	519,789	300,995	218,794	
Inventory	19,595		19,595	
Prepaid expenses	894,514	740,851	153,663	
Long-term investments	1,854,590	508,515	1,346,075	
Fixed assets - net	1,459,842	1,459,842		
Total assets	$8,372,591	$5,856,459	$2,158,231	$357,901
LIABILITIES AND NET ASSETS				
Liabilities				
Accounts payable and accrued expenses	1,334,116	938,786	393,930	1,400
Deferred revenues	4,205,307	3,896,653	308,654	
Other liabilities	2,037,930	2,037,930		
Due to (from) related entities		(122,192)	125,285	(3,093)
Total liabilities	7,577,353	6,751,177	827,869	(1,693)
Net assets				
Unrestricted	(576,881)	(894,718)	(41,757)	359,594
Temporarily restricted	1,325,219		1,325,219	
Permanently restricted	46,900		46,900	
Total net assets	795,238	(894,718)	1,330,362	359,594
Total liabilities and net assets	$8,372,591	$5,856,459	$2,158,231	$357,901

EXHIBIT 14.8 CONSOLIDATING STATEMENT OF FINANCIAL POSITION FOR NEW YORK STATE SOCIETY OF CERTIFIED PUBLIC ACCOUNTANTS

NEW YORK STATE SOCIETY OF CERTIFIED PUBLIC ACCOUNTANTS AND CONSOLIDATED ENTITIES

CONSOLIDATING STATEMENT OF ACTIVITIES

YEAR ENDED MAY 31, 1997

	Consolidated Total	New York State Society of Certified Public Accountants Unrestricted	Foundation for Accounting Education, Inc. Unrestricted	Temporarily Restricted	Permanently Restricted	New York State Society of Certified Public Accountants Benevolent Fund, Inc. Unrestricted
Revenues and Other Support						
Contributions	$ 121,530	$	$	$ 119,595	$ 600	$ 1,335
Membership dues	6,087,509	6,087,509				
Registration fees	4,031,488	120,118	3,911,370			
The CPA Journal	894,183	894,183				
Self-study and in-firm training	149,385		149,385			
Shows and exhibits	502,873		502,873			
Meetings and conferences	450,358	450,358				
Member services	603,245	603,245				
Public relations	75,449	75,449				
Investment income	353,022	162,448	19,271	155,254		16,049
Unrealized/realized gains	4,263	4,263				
Other revenues	130,282	46,651	83,631			
Net assets released from restrictions			156,975	(156,975)		
Total revenues and other support	13,403,587	8,444,224	4,823,505	117,874	600	17,384
Expenses						
Membership activities	2,543,496	2,534,996				8,500
Professional development	2,827,169	2,322,083	505,086			
Career development	157,594	619	156,975			
Educational activities	3,885,719		3,885,719			
Publications	1,794,759	1,794,759				
Management and general	2,626,373	1,796,608	829,765			
Total expenses	13,835,110	8,449,065	5,377,545			8,500
(Decrease) increase in net assets before transfers (to) from related entities	(431,523)	(4,841)	(554,040)	117,874	600	8,884
Transfers (to) from related entities		(554,040)	554,040			
Change in net assets	(431,523)	(558,881)		117,874	600	8,884
Net assets, beginning of year	1,226,761	(335,837)	(41,757)	1,207,345	46,300	350,710
Net assets, end of year	$ 795,238	$ (894,718)	$ (41,757)	$1,325,219	$ 46,900	$359,594

EXHIBIT 14.9 CONSOLIDATING STATEMENT OF ACTIVITIES FOR NEW YORK STATE SOCIETY OF CERTIFIED PUBLIC ACCOUNTANTS

NEW YORK STATE SOCIETY OF CERTIFIED PUBLIC ACCOUNTANTS AND CONSOLIDATED ENTITIES

CONSOLIDATED STATEMENTS OF CASH FLOWS
YEARS ENDED MAY 31, 1997 AND 1996

	1997	1996 (Restated)
Cash flows from operating activities		
Cash received from service recipients	$ 13,029,843	$ 12,705,501
Cash received from contributors	121,530	173,820
Investment income received	353,022	297,366
Cash paid to suppliers and employees	(13,560,005)	(13,540,138)
Awards and grants paid	(120,784)	(79,688)
Net cash used by operating activities	(176,394)	(443,139)
Cash flows from investing activities		
Purchase of fixed assets	(99,398)	(229,389)
Purchase of long-term investments	(74,496)	(1,211,581)
Proceeds from maturity of long-term investments		500,000
Net cash used by investing activities	(173,894)	(940,970)
Net decrease in cash and cash equivalents	(350,288)	(1,384,109)
Cash and cash equivalents, beginning of year	3,974,549	5,358,658
Cash and cash equivalents, end of year	$ 3,624,261	$ 3,974,549

See accompanying notes to consolidated financial statements.

EXHIBIT 14.10   CONSOLIDATED STATEMENT OF CASH FLOWS FOR NEW YORK STATE SOCIETY OF CERTIFIED PUBLIC ACCOUNTANTS

NEW YORK STATE SOCIETY OF CERTIFIED PUBLIC ACCOUNTANTS AND CONSOLIDATED ENTITIES

CONSOLIDATED STATEMENTS OF CASH FLOWS
(Continued)

YEARS ENDED MAY 31, 1997 AND 1996

	1997	1996 (Restated)
Reconciliation of change in net assets to net cash used by operating activities		
Change in net assets	$(431,523)	$ 38,656
Adjustments to reconcile change in net assets to net cash used by operating activities:		
Depreciation and amortization	478,504	475,121
Amortization of deferred rent expense	(47,566)	(47,566)
Amortization of lease incentive	(135,920)	(135,920)
Unrealized/realized loss (gains) on investments	(4,263)	14,704
Increase (decrease) in allowance for doubtful accounts	(31,501)	28,026
Decrease (increase) in:		
Accounts receivable	(13,586)	(204,197)
Inventory	30,023	(14,583)
Prepaid expenses	103,371	(94,972)
Increase (decrease) in:		
Accounts payable and accrued expenses	75,337	(118,890)
Deferred revenues	225,158	36,844
Other liabilities	(424,428)	(420,362)
Net cash used by operating activities	$(176,394)	$(443,139)

See accompanying notes to consolidated financial statements.

EXHIBIT 14.10   *(Continued)*

NEW YORK STATE SOCIETY OF CERTIFIED PUBLIC ACCOUNTANTS AND CONSOLIDATED ENTITIES

CONSOLIDATING STATEMENT OF FUNCTIONAL EXPENSES

YEAR ENDED MAY 31, 1997
(With comparative totals for 1996)

	Membership Activities	Professional Development	Career Development	Educational Activities	Publications	Management and General	Total 1997	Total 1996 (Restated)
New York State Society of Certified Public Accountants								
Salaries, wages, and benefits	$ 507,980	$ 1,845,618	$	$	$ 859,659	$ 742,434	$ 3,955,691	$ 3,772,257
Awards and grants	7,488	2,151					9,639	78,318
Printing and distribution	518,660	42,838	619		665,010	147,769	1,374,896	1,416,589
Supplies and travel	852,755	69,926			25,873	275,533	1,224,087	1,002,951
Services and professional fees	434,619	38,887			89,899	398,936	962,341	607,414
Office and occupancy	57,708	204,197			97,660	84,342	443,907	398,461
Depreciation and amortization	155,786	118,466			56,658	147,594	478,504	475,121
	2,534,996	2,322,083	619		1,794,759	1,796,608	8,449,065	7,751,111
Foundation for Accounting Education, Inc.								
Salaries, wages, and benefits		174,417		1,046,504		523,253	1,744,174	1,687,755
Awards and grants			120,784				120,784	79,688
Printing and distribution		93,498	9,351	1,399,378		13,396	1,515,623	1,785,495
Supplies and travel		42,253	24,218	1,014,335		53,647	1,134,453	1,048,206
Services and professional fees		171,769	2,622	205,234		170,022	549,647	559,195
Office and occupancy		23,149		220,268		69,447	312,864	345,014
		505,086	156,975	3,885,719		829,765	5,377,545	5,505,353
New York State Society of Certified Public Accountants Benevolent Fund, Inc.								
Services and professional fees	8,500						8,500	6,190
Totals	$2,543,496	$2,827,169	$ 157,594	$3,885,719	$1,794,759	$2,626,373	$13,835,110	$13,262,654
Consolidated								
Salaries, wages and benefits	$ 507,980	$2,020,035	$	$1,046,504	$ 859,659	$1,265,687	$ 5,699,865	$ 5,460,012
Awards and grants	7,488	2,151	120,784				130,423	158,006
Printing and distribution	518,660	136,336	9,970	1,399,378	665,010	161,165	2,890,519	3,202,084
Supplies and travel	852,755	112,179	24,218	1,014,335	25,873	329,180	2,358,540	2,051,157
Services and professional fees	443,119	210,656	2,622	205,234	89,899	568,958	1,520,488	1,172,799
Office and occupancy	57,708	227,346		220,268	97,660	153,789	756,771	743,475
Depreciation and amortization	155,786	118,466			56,658	147,594	478,504	475,121
Consolidated totals	$2,543,496	$2,827,169	$ 157,594	$3,885,719	$1,794,759	$2,626,373	$13,835,110	$13,262,654

EXHIBIT 14.11   CONSOLIDATING STATEMENT OF FUNCTIONAL EXPENSES FOR NEW YORK STATE SOCIETY OF CERTIFIED PUBLIC ACCOUNTANTS

NOTES TO CONSOLIDATED FINANCIAL STATEMENTS

4. Long-term Investments

Long-term investments are comprised of the following:

	1997	1996
Market value		
Equity securities	$ 579,103	$ 658,813
U.S. Government obligations	1,038,955	514,295
Money Market accounts held for investments	232,605	603,059
Estimated value		
Other	3,927	3,927
Total	$1,854,590	$1,780,094

7. Restricted Net Assets

Temporarily restricted net assets at May 31, 1997 and 1996 are available for the following career development activities:

	1997	1996
Career Opportunities in the Accounting Profession	$ 61,104	$ 53,765
Undergraduate scholarships	1,264,115	1,153,580
	$1,325,219	$1,207,345

Net assets released from restrictions consist of the following for the years ended May 31, 1997 and 1996:

	1997	1996
Career Opportunities in the Accounting Profession	$ 36,190	$ 34,303
Undergraduate scholarships	120,785	79,772
	$156,975	$114,075

Permanently restricted net assets at May 31, 1997 and 1996 are restricted to investment in perpetuity, the income from which is expendable to support the following career development activities:

	1997	1996
Lecture series	$15,000	$15,000
Scholarships	31,900	31,300
	$46,900	$46,300

EXHIBIT 14.12   NOTES TO CONSOLIDATED FINANCIAL STATEMENTS FOR NEW YORK STATE SOCIETY OF CERTIFIED PUBLIC ACCOUNTANTS

INTERNAL FUND ACCOUNTING FOR NOT-FOR-PROFIT ORGANIZATIONS

This appendix introduces the internal fund structure of not-for-profit organizations, and the process by which internal fund data are recast to meet the external reporting requirements of *SFAS 117*. Because many different types of organizations fall into the broad category of not-for-profit organizations, considerable variation in the specific titles of funds exists. We can, however, identify the **types of funds** commonly used. It is important to note that NFPs generally follow *full accrual accounting* in the internal accounts, including providing for depreciation.

INTERNAL FUND STRUCTURE FOR NFPs

The internal fund structure for NFPs generally takes the following form.

UNRESTRICTED CURRENT FUNDS

The **unrestricted current fund**, also commonly called an **unrestricted operating fund** or **general fund**, is analogous to the general fund of a local governmental unit. This fund accounts for the organization's day-to-day operating activities funded by resources having no *operating* restriction on their use. These resources are unrestricted as to *how* they can be used in operations but may be restricted as to *when* they can be used. Thus resources contributed for general operations but restricted by donors for use in future periods were traditionally treated as unrestricted current fund resources. In external financial reports, however, unrestricted operating resources subject to donors' "time restrictions" are reported as temporarily restricted net assets.

For most not-for-profits, unrestricted investments in plant assets are not included here. In other words, unrestricted fund assets may be spent, at the discretion of management, for any activity of the organization. Such resources come from sources such as voluntary contributions, user charges, and unrestricted grants for operating purposes. Expenditures are made from the unrestricted current fund to cover the costs of providing the primary services or activities of the organization.

RESTRICTED CURRENT FUNDS

The **restricted current fund**, also called a **restricted operating fund** or **specific purpose fund**, is analogous to the special revenue fund of a local government. Expenditures from this fund are also made for the day-to-day operating activities or services of the organization. In this case, however, use of the fund's resources is restricted by their providers to certain operating activities. Such resources typically come from grants or contributions. For example, a hospital may receive a grant for a research program, or a church may receive a contribution for its missionary work.

Traditionally, internal fund accounting treated *restricted current fund revenue* as unearned until the related expenditures are made. Restricted operating grants were often recorded as deferred revenue or liabilities until the terms of the grants were satisfied, signifying that the grant "revenue" may need to be returned to the grantor if the specified expenditures do not comply with the terms of the grant. Under *SFAS 116,* though, restricted operating grants not subject to donors' *conditions* are reported as revenue in temporarily restricted net assets. When the grant's terms are satisfied, the applicable amount of temporarily restricted net assets is reclassified as unrestricted net assets and the related expenses are recorded in the unrestricted category.

PLANT FUNDS

The **plant fund** of a not-for-profit organization, also called a **land, building, and equipment fund**, accounts for various aspects of the investment in land, buildings, and equipment (hereafter called **plant assets**). Hospitals, however, account for their plant assets in current (general) funds. A plant fund is often a complex entity consisting of several self-balancing subfunds, containing some or all of the following:

- *Unexpended resources* to be used for the *acquisition* of plant assets. This component is analogous to the capital projects fund of a local government.
- *Resources set aside* for the *renewal or replacement* of plant assets. When expended, the costs may be capitalized as additional plant assets or may be expensed. The resources of this component are usually transfers from operating funds set aside by management for future needs. There is currently no counterpart to this component in local governmental accounting.
- *Resources set aside* for the *payment of interest and principal* on indebtedness related to past acquisitions of plant assets. This component is analogous to the debt service fund of a local government.
- *Information relating* to amounts *already invested* in plant assets and the *unpaid balance* of related indebtedness. This component is analogous to both the general fixed assets and general long-term debt account groups of a local government.

Even though an organization may use the plant fund with its various subfunds internally, most plant fund transactions are reported externally as transactions affecting unrestricted net assets, unless there are specific donor restrictions on plant fund resources.

ENDOWMENT FUNDS

The **endowment fund** accounts for resources that the organization holds for the generation of income and is analogous to a nonexpendable trust fund of a local government. A **permanent endowment** consists of *permanently restricted resources* provided by outside donors or agencies that stipulated that the principal is to be maintained indefinitely and invested to produce income which often must be spent in a specified way. A **term endowment** consists of *temporarily restricted resources* and is similar to a permanent endowment, except that at some point the principal may be spent. A **quasi-endowment**, also called *funds functioning as endowment*, consists of resources that management of the organization set aside to be retained and invested for certain purposes. In this case, any restrictions are imposed by management rather than by an outside donor and thus can be easily modified in the future. Under *SFAS 117,* the organization's external financial statements could report endowment fund resources in all three net asset categories—*unrestricted* (quasi-endowment), *temporarily restricted* (term endowment) and *permanently restricted* (permanent endowment).

AGENCY FUNDS

The **agency fund** of a not-for-profit organization, also called a **custodian fund**, is analogous to the agency fund of a local government. It accounts for resources held by the organization as a custodian or fiscal agent. For example, if a college holds the resources of student clubs and organizations, these resources are recorded in an agency fund.

LOAN FUNDS

The **loan fund**, found primarily in educational organizations, accounts for loans outstanding and resources available for lending to students and employees. A loan fund is usually said to be *revolving*; that is, the interest and principal payments on current loans provide the resources for future loans. The initial capital needed to establish the fund is typically provided either by outside gifts or by allocation of internal resources. As a revolving, self-sustaining fund which mainly serves individuals within the organization, a loan fund is somewhat similar to an internal service fund of a local government. Loan fund resources, unless subject to donors' restrictions, are reported in the unrestricted net asset category.

ANNUITY FUNDS

The **annuity fund** accounts for resources acquired by a not-for-profit organization in exchange for a promise to make specified payments to the donor or other designated individuals for a given period of time. Depending upon the donor's stipulations, these resources are permanently or temporarily restricted and will be reported as such in the organization's external financial statements. Many types of not-for-profit organizations, especially colleges and universities and religious organizations, offer annuities as a means of deferred fund-raising. For example, assume an individual contributes $50,000 to a religious organization. In return, the organization agrees to pay the individual $4,000 annually for life. The organization invests the $50,000 and uses the income (and, if necessary, some of the principal) to make the annual payments. Upon the donor's death, the remaining funds become available to the organization for other uses. Annuity terms may vary from those in the above example; payments may be made to an individual other than the donor, or the payments may be for a specified number of years rather than for life.

These *annuity agreements* are attractive to both donors and organizations. Donors assure themselves, or others, of a specified income, while also assuring that the remaining funds eventually go to the charity of their choice. In addition, there may be tax advantages to transferring assets to a charity while living rather than after death via bequest. From the organization's point of view, annuity agreements enable them to attract sizable contributions, even though it may be several years until the resources become unrestricted and available for the organization's programs.

A variation of an annuity agreement is a *life income agreement*. Such an agreement provides that all income earned on the contributed resources be paid annually to the donor or to his or her designates for life. Under a life income agreement, therefore, the annual payment may vary, whereas under an annuity agreement the annual payment is fixed. Resources received pursuant to life income agreements are recorded in the annuity fund or in a separate **life income fund.**

Annuity funds and life income funds have no direct counterparts in local governmental accounting. Until the resources become unrestricted, though, these funds are similar to governmental nonexpendable trust funds.

RECASTING INTERNAL FUND DATA TO MEET EXTERNAL REPORTING REQUIREMENTS

When internal accounting records are maintained in a fund accounting system, two major steps must be taken to recast these data for external reporting purposes:

- Fund balances must be recast into the three classes of net assets—*unrestricted, temporarily restricted*, and *permanently restricted*.
- Interfund transfer accounts must be eliminated.

RECASTING OF FUND BALANCES INTO NET ASSET BALANCES

The following shows the fund balances which typically comprise each category of net assets. Categorization is highly situation-specific, and depends on the existence of donor-imposed restrictions.

Unrestricted Net Assets

- *Unrestricted current fund* net assets *reduced* by any net assets restricted to future years but unrestricted as to use, such as the noncurrent portion of multi-year pledges receivable.
- *Plant fund* net assets not subject to donor restrictions, including resources set aside by management or debt covenants for (1) *renewal or replacement* of plant assets or (2) *payment of interest and principal* on debt related to past plant asset acquisitions.
- *Loan fund* net assets not subject to donor restrictions.

Temporarily Restricted Net Assets

- *Unrestricted current fund* net assets restricted to future years.
- *Restricted current fund* net assets (normally the total restricted current fund net assets are restricted by donors for use in specific programs).
- *Plant fund* net assets subject to donors' temporary restrictions, such as donated assets or assets purchased with donations, and contributed resources temporarily restricted for replacement and renewal of plant assets.
- *Endowment fund* net assets that are *term endowments*.
- *Annuity and life income fund* net assets that become available for temporarily restricted or unrestricted use upon the donor's death.

Permanently Restricted Net Assets

- *Endowment fund* net assets that are *permanent endowments*.
- *Plant fund* net assets restricted by donors to permanent use as plant assets, including use of sale proceeds, and contributions of resources permanently restricted by donors for replacement and renewal of plant assets.
- *Annuity and life income fund* net assets that become permanent endowments upon the donor's death.

ELIMINATION OF INTERFUND TRANSFER ACCOUNTS

Within the internal fund system, transactions between funds are recorded as if the transaction were with an external party. For example, unrestricted current fund assets may be transferred to the plant fund to finance acquisitions of long-term assets. That transfer is recorded as a transfer out of the unrestricted current fund and a transfer in to the plant fund. Both accounts must be eliminated for external reporting.

ILLUSTRATION

The Northeastern Heart Society illustration presented in the chapter is used to demonstrate the recasting of internal fund data to meet the external reporting requirements of *SFAS 117*.

The Northeastern Heart Society uses the following internal funds: unrestricted current fund, restricted current fund, endowment fund, and plant fund. Balances at December 31, 20X1 are shown in Exhibit 14.13. Compare these internal fund balances with the December 31, 20X1 Statement of Financial Position appearing previously in Exhibit 14.4. The fund balances of the unrestricted current fund and plant fund become the balance in unrestricted net assets. The fund balance in the endowment fund becomes the balance in permanently restricted net assets. Events occurring in 20X2 are recorded in the various funds as follows:

Books of Unrestricted Current Fund

Cash	1,150,000	
Pledges Receivable	150,000	
Public Contributions		1,300,000
To record contributions and cash collections during 20X2.		
Cash	67,000	
Pledges Receivable		67,000
To record collections of prior year pledges.		
Allowance for Uncollectible Pledges	13,000	
Pledges Receivable		13,000
To write off uncollected pledges from 20X1.		
Public Contributions	27,000	
Allowance for Uncollectible Pledges		27,000
To adjust allowance to 20 percent of year-end balance.		
Cash	46,000	
Program Revenue		46,000
To record revenue from educational programs.		
Expenses—Research	400,000	
Expenses—Public Awareness Programs	350,000	
Expenses—Corporate Programs	35,000	
Expenses—General Administration	210,000	
Expenses—Fund Raising	175,000	
Cash		1,155,000
Vouchers Payable		15,000
To record expenses for 20X2.		

Transfer to Plant Fund	100,000	
Cash		100,000

To record transfer to plant fund, to cover construction
costs and interest on short-term financing of building
construction.

Books of Restricted Current Fund

Cash	200,000	
Federal Grant Support		200,000

To record federal grant received.

Expenses—Public Awareness Programs	143,000	
Cash		143,000

To record cost of public awareness programs incurred
in 20X2.

Cash	80,000	
Transfer from Endowment Fund		80,000

To record money received from endowment fund
to be used for research scholarships.

Expenses—Research Scholarships	75,000	
Cash		75,000

To record payment of scholarships.

Books of Endowment Fund

Cash	13,500	
Public Contributions		13,500

To record support designated for endowment.

Investments	8,500	
Cash		8,500

To record purchase of investments.

Cash	80,000	
Investment Income		80,000

To record income from investments.

Transfer to Restricted Current Fund	80,000	
Cash		80,000

To record transfer of money to be used for
research scholarships.

Books of Plant Fund

Cash   100,000

        Transfer from Unrestricted Current Fund   100,000

    To record transfer from unrestricted current fund.

Cash   300,000

        Loan Payable   300,000

    To record building loan.

Construction in Progress   240,000

        Cash   240,000

    To record building construction costs.

Interest Expense   28,000

        Cash   28,000

    To record interest paid on loan.

Cash   7,700

        Interest Revenue   7,700

    To record interest earned on time deposits.

Expenses—General Administration   3,000

        Accumulated Depreciation—Equipment   3,000

    To record depreciation on office equipment.

Balances in the various fund accounts at December 31, 20X2 appear in Exhibit 14.13. Compare these balances with the December 31, 20X2 Statement of Financial Position in Exhibit 14.4. Again, the fund balances of the unrestricted current fund and the plant fund become the balance in unrestricted net assets. The fund balance in the restricted current fund becomes the balance in temporarily restricted net assets. The fund balance for the endowment fund becomes the balance in permanently restricted net assets.

Northeastern Heart Society
Fund Balance Sheets
at December 31, 20X2 and 20X1

Unrestricted Current Fund

	12/31/X2	12/31/X1		12/31/X2	12/31/X1
Cash	$ 125,000	$ 117,000	Vouchers Payable . .	$ 48,000	$ 33,000
Pledges Receivable . . .	120,000	64,000	Fund Balance	197,000 (1)	148,000 (4)
Total	$ 245,000	$ 181,000	Total	$ 245,000	$ 181,000

Restricted Current Fund

	12/31/X2	12/31/X1		12/31/X2	12/31/X1
Cash	$ 62,000	$ —	Fund Balance	$ 62,000 (2)	$ —

Endowment Fund

	12/31/X2	12/31/X1		12/31/X2	12/31/X1
Cash	$ 5,000	$ —	Fund Balance	$ 733,500 (3)	$ 720,000 (5)
Investments	728,500	720,000			
Total	$ 733,500	$ 720,000	Total	$ 733,500	$ 720,000

Plant Fund

	12/31/X2	12/31/X1		12/31/X2	12/31/X1
Cash	$ 139,700	—	Loan Payable	$ 300,000	$ —
Land	20,000	20,000	Fund Balance	120,700 (1)	44,000 (4)
Equipment (net)	21,000	24,000			
Construction in Progress	240,000	—			
Total	$ 420,700	$ 44,000	Total	$ 420,700	$ 44,000

(1) $197,000 + $120,700 = $317,700, unrestricted net assets at 12/31/X2, per Exhibit 14.4.

(2) $62,000 is temporarily restricted net assets at 12/31/X2, per Exhibit 14.4.

(3) $733,500 is permanently restricted net assets at 12/31/X2, per Exhibit 14.4.

(4) $148,000 + $44,000 = $192,000, unrestricted net assets at 12/31/X1, per Exhibit 14.4.

(5) $720,000 is permanently restricted net assets at 12/31/X1, per Exhibit 14.4.

EXHIBIT 14.13   INTERNAL FUND BALANCES FOR NORTHEASTERN HEART SOCIETY

QUESTIONS

Q14.1 Contributions subject to donors' *restrictions* are reported as increases in net assets whereas contributions subject to donors' *conditions* are not. Explain the rationale behind this distinction.

Q14.2 Identify the major readers of the external financial statements of an NFP organization, and the types of information important to each.

Q14.3 A donor contributes $1,000,000 to an organization, with the stipulation that it be used to fund scholarships. Another $1,000,000 is set aside by the Board of the organization to fund payments on debt. Are each of these events accounted for in the same way? Explain.

Q14.4 Money contributed in a previous year, and donor-restricted for a particular medical research project, was spent on the research project in the current year. Explain how these events are disclosed on the statement of activities.

Q14.5 Hospital volunteers visit patients daily, selling items such as newspapers and magazines. Proceeds from the sales go to the hospital. How should the volunteers' services be recorded?

Q14.6 *SFAS 124* prescribes the accounting for investments by NFP organizations. How are these investments valued on the statement of financial position? How is investment income reported in the statement of activities? How are gains and losses measured and reported?

Q14.7 Many not-for-profit organizations prepare a *statement of functional expenses* in addition to the *statement of activities*. How does the information provided in the two statements differ?

Q14.8 A not-for-profit organization received an unconditional promise from a donor in 20X1, specifying that the amount promised be used in 20X3. The promise is supported by verifiable documentation. How should the organization account for this promise in 20X1 and receipt and use in 20X3?

Q14.9 Identify the major categories of expenses that must be shown on the statement of activities.

Q14.10 The statement of cash flows groups cash flows by operating, investing, and financing activities. Explain how contributions and income which are donor-restricted for long-term purposes, such as plant assets and endowment, are reported on the statement of cash flows.

Q14.11 Contributions of services must meet certain requirements to be shown on the statement of activities. Explain these requirements, and the accounting for contributions of services.

Q14.12 Critics of the FASB reporting requirements generally believe that the organization's resources available to support operations are overstated. Identify two specific requirements that can cause overstatement of resources currently available.

EXERCISES

E14.1 **Recognition of donations** A voluntary health and welfare organization receives the following donations:

1. A donor contributes cash, with no restrictions or conditions.
2. An accountant provides services in maintaining organization records.

3. Volunteers provide services in staffing the local soup kitchen.
4. A donor signs an agreement promising to contribute cash next year.
5. A donor contributes land.
6. A donor contributes cash, specifying that it be used to fund a specific research project.

REQUIRED: For each of the above events, identify the effect on net assets. Use the following alternatives:

UR	affects unrestricted net assets
TR	affects temporarily restricted net assets
PR	affects permanently restricted net assets
N	does not affect net assets

E14.2   **Recognition of Donations** Donations are received by NFP organizations as indicated below:

1. A donor contributes $50,000, with the stipulation that it be used to fund a building project. The organization doesn't know whether it can accumulate enough money to go ahead with the project.
2. A donor contributes $100,000 to a college, with the stipulation that the principal remain intact and any investment income be used to buy library books. The college invests the $100,000 in securities, which earn income of $5,000. The $5,000 is spent on library books.
3. A citizen notifies a university that he has specified in his will that $2,000,000 of his estate be paid to the university.
4. A donor promises to contribute $100,000 if the organization can raise $100,000 from other sources. The organization raises the $100,000 and the donor contributes the additional $100,000.
5. A citizen donates a car valued at $20,000, specifying that the car be used to deliver food to the homeless and not be sold by the organization.
6. The car in item 5. depreciates by $5,000.
7. Cash contributions for the year total $400,000. The organization's Board sets aside $20,000 for repairs to its administrative building.

REQUIRED: For each of the above events, make the appropriate journal entry or entries. If the event affects net assets, specify which category of net assets is affected.

E14.3   **Donated Building** On January 1, 20X0, the City Mission receives a building with a fair market value of $50,000. The donor specifies that the building is not to be sold, but is to be used to house homeless families. City Mission estimates that the building has a remaining useful life of 10 years, and uses straight-line depreciation.

REQUIRED: Make the journal entries necessary in 20X0 and 20X1 to account for this donation and subsequent depreciation. If the entry affects net assets, indicate which category of net assets is affected.

E14.4 **Accounting for Investments** A private not-for-profit health care facility receives donated debt securities with a fair market value and par value of $200,000 in 20X0. The donor specifies that the debt securities be held as a permanent endowment, and investment income earned on these securities may be used for any purpose. The securities have a fair market value of $180,000 at the end of 20X0, and $230,000 at the end of 20X1. Investment income earned on the securities is $15,000 in each of the two years.

REQUIRED:

1. Make the journal entries necessary to record the above events in 20X0 and 20X1, for external reporting purposes. Indicate the balance in each account and its placement in the external financial statements.
2. Assume the same facts as above, except the donation was $200,000 in cash, and the organization invested the $200,000 in debt securities. How do the entries in 1. change?

E14.5 **Donors' Restrictions/Conditions on Contributions** Consider the following potential contributions to a not-for-profit organization.

1. Pledge cards signed by church members pledge $200,000 to a facilities improvement campaign. Church officials expect 90% will be collected.
2. A university phone-a-thon produces $75,000 of "intentions to give;" respondents asked for time to think it over.
3. A prominent alumnus pledges $5,000,000 to support the MBA program in the business school of a state university. She will pay the $5,000,000 within 48 hours of the school's being cited in the annual *Business Week* survey of MBA programs.
4. Contributors sign pledge cards for $150,000 to support ongoing programs at a local teaching hospital. Past experience indicates that 75% will be collected.
5. A college receives cash gifts of $250,000 restricted by donors to a new program the college is promoting. College officials believe $1,000,000 is needed before the new program can start.

REQUIRED: State whether each of the above items is recognized as a contribution. If recognized, give the amount of revenue and whether it is unrestricted or temporarily restricted. If it is not recognized, explain why.

E14.6 **Recognition of Various Donations** Hopeville Retreat is a not-for-profit organization that counsels former drug addicts in readjusting to productive community life. Donations provide the major support for Hopeville Retreat. During 20X2, the following gifts were received by the organization:

1. Cash from fund-raising campaign, $25,000.
2. Cash from rehabilitated clients of the organization, $10,000.
3. Clothing donated by a local department store. Cost to the store was $2,800; market value was $3,600.
4. A television set, valued at $300, donated by a private citizen.
5. Medicine used for drug withdrawal symptoms, donated by a pharmaceutical company. Cost of drugs was $3,000; market value was $5,000.

6. Secretarial and bookkeeping services for necessary paperwork and record-keeping performed by volunteers, valued at $7,000.
7. Door-to-door fund solicitation time donated by local high school students. The organization estimates this service to be worth $2,800 when valued using minimum wage rates.
8. Free radio announcements of the fund-raising campaign given by a local radio station. The normal charge for advertisements of comparable length is $400.

REQUIRED: For each gift, indicate at what amount the donation is recorded on the books of Hopeville Retreat, and where it would appear in the statement of activities.

E14.7 **Effect of Transactions on Net Assets** The following items relate to a voluntary health and welfare organization:

1. A gift of cash is received with no stipulations as to use.
2. The organization borrows money to finance construction of a new office building.
3. Money is collected and held for distribution to an unaffiliated organization.
4. Money is collected and held for distribution to the beneficiaries of one of the organization's programs.
5. An automobile is donated for use in transporting officials on organization business.
6. Depreciation is computed on the automobile in No. 5.
7. General revenues are set aside to repay the loan in No. 2.
8. Used toys are collected for holiday distribution to needy children.

REQUIRED: For each item, identify the category of net assets affected, if any.

E14.8 **Promises of Future Gifts** On July 1, 20X1, John Smith, a wealthy college alumnus, promises in writing to contribute $100,000 at the beginning of each of the next ten fiscal years to help offset the expenses of operating the Greek Affairs Office in those years. The first two $100,000 payments are received on July 1, 20X2 and July 1, 20X3, and the college's fiscal year runs from July 1 through June 30.

REQUIRED: Discuss, using calculations as needed and assuming a 10% discount rate, how this gift affects (a) the organization's accounts on July 1, 20X1 and (b) the organization's financial statements at June 30, 20X2, June 30, 20X3 and June 30, 20X4.

E14.9 **Reporting Temporary Investments** A not-for-profit organization maintains a portfolio of temporary debt and equity investments. At December 31, 20X3, the following securities are owned:

Security	Cost	Fair Value
8% Short-term notes (face value ($20,000)	$ 20,000	$ 21,000
10% Long-term bonds (par value $300,000)	300,000	298,000
Common stock (1,000 shares)	42,000	49,000

Interest on the notes and bonds is paid annually; the premium on the Long-Term bonds is amortized by the straight-line method over 10 years. Quarterly dividends of $.50/share were paid on the common stock.

At December 31, 20X4, fair values of the above securities are as follows. No securities were bought or sold during 20X4.

Security	Fair Value
8% Short-term notes (face value $20,000)	$ 19,700
10% Long-term bonds (par value $300,000)	304,000
Common stock (1,000 shares)	46,800

REQUIRED: Prepare a schedule showing the investment income recognized on the organization's 20X4 statement of activities, including unrealized gains/losses, according to *SFAS 124*.

E14.10   College Transactions The following items relate to a not-for-profit college:

1. An alumna donates cash for purchase of library books.
2. An alumna donates cash, stipulating that income generated by investment of the cash be paid to the donor during the donor's lifetime. At the donor's death, the gift and all future income belong to the college.
3. An alumna donates cash, stipulating that income generated by investment of the cash be used for student scholarships. The principal is to remain intact.
4. A gymnasium is constructed.
5. Salaries to faculty are paid.
6. Loans are made to faculty members.
7. Student activity fees for student organizations are collected with tuition payments.
8. Depreciation on the gymnasium is computed.

REQUIRED: For each item, identify the accounts affected and their placement on the college's external statements.

E14.11   Journal Entries—College

1. The school's general fund-raising campaign generates pledges of $80,000. Past history shows pledges to be 90 percent collectible.
2. A previously recorded pledge for scholarship money is received ($7,000).
3. An employee borrows $1,000 from the school and signs a note for repayment within one year.
4. Previously collected student activity fees of $6,000 are transferred to student organizations.
5. Salaries of $20,000 are paid to employees. An accrual had not been recorded.
6. A loan of $11,000 is taken to buy audiovisual equipment.
7. An $800 scholarship is awarded.

REQUIRED: For each of the above transactions of Canton College, record the journal entry. Explanations may be omitted.

E14.12 **Annuity/Life Income Transactions** On January 1, 20X0, Patricia Dahlene gave Stokely College $100,000 in cash with the provision that the cash be invested in income-producing securities. Actuarial estimates set Dahlene's life expectancy at 15 years from the date of the gift. The annual discount rate associated with the arrangements outlined below is 8 percent.

REQUIRED: Record Patricia Dahlene's gift on the college's books under each of the following *independent* arrangements:

1. The college is to pay Patricia Dahlene $7,500 every December 31 of her remaining life. If earnings of the principal are insufficient to meet the payments, then the principal is to be depleted. Any earnings exceeding the required payment can be spent by the college without restriction. Gains and losses on principal assets must be added to (deducted from) principal. Upon Dahlene's death, remaining resources become available to the college with no restrictions as to use.
2. The college is to pay Patricia Dahlene all earnings of the principal for life. Any gains and losses pertaining to principal assets are treated as income and therefore affect payments to the donor. Upon Dahlene's death, remaining resources become available to the college with no restrictions as to use.

E14.13 *SFAS 117* **Balance Sheet** *(Appendix)* The Seaside Safety Society, a not-for-profit organization, maintains three funds for its internal accounting. The December 31, 20X8 fund balance sheets appear below.

	Unrestricted Current Fund	Restricted Current Fund	Plant Fund
Assets			
Cash	$ 55,000	$ 15,000	$ 10,000
Pledges Receivable, Net	50,000	25,000	80,000
Investments	68,000	—	150,000
Plant Assets, Net	—	—	200,000
	$ 173,000	$ 40,000	$ 440,000
Liabilities and Fund Balance			
Trade Accounts Payable	$ 75,000	$ —	$ —
Bank Loans Payable	—	—	190,000
Fund Balance	98,000	40,000	250,000
	$ 173,000	$ 40,000	$ 440,000

Restricted current fund assets are restricted by donors for use in certain current year operating programs. Unrestricted current fund assets include $15,000 restricted by donors for expenditure on general operations in the next fiscal year. Of the plant fund assets, the pledges receivable are restricted by donors for plant maintenance in subsequent years. No other plant fund assets are subject to donor restrictions.

REQUIRED: Recast the above December 31, 20X8, fund balance sheets into the format required by *SFAS 117*.

E14.14 Financial Statement Effects of Plant Fund Transactions *(Appendix)* Davis College's plant fund had the following balance sheet at June 30, 20X7:

Davis College
Plant Fund
Balance Sheet
June 30, 20X7

Cash	$ 70,000	Mortgage Payable	$ 4,600,000
Land	400,000	Fund Balance	2,020,000
Buildings	3,700,000		
Equipment	2,450,000		
	$ 6,620,000		$ 6,620,000

During the year ended June 30, 20X8, the following transactions occurred:

1. Resources in the amount of $500,000 were transferred from the unrestricted current fund.
2. Resources in the amount of $80,000 were transferred from the restricted current fund and spent on the purchase of audiovisual equipment.
3. Interest of $330,000 and principal of $200,000 were paid on the mortgage.

REQUIRED: Indicate how, and in what amounts, the foregoing plant fund transactions and ending balances are reported in Davis College's Statement of Activities and Statement of Financial Position for the year ended June 30, 20X8. Classify the amounts reported as relating to unrestricted net assets or temporarily restricted net assets. Ignore depreciation.

PROBLEMS

P14.1 Journal Entries and Financial Statements The Southside Counseling Center was established on January 10, 20X1, to provide a variety of counseling services to community residents, including marital and family counseling and treatment for alcoholism and drug abuse. The center's initial resources were provided by the county government in the form of a $100,000 capital grant. Of this sum, $50,000 was designated for building and equipment, and $25,000 was designated for the establishment of a special program for counseling parolees; the remaining funds were unrestricted. The following transactions occurred during 20X1:

1. Contributions of $80,000 were received through the local United Way campaign, and an additional $13,000 was received in direct contributions. Of the direct contributions, $1,000 was for the parolees' program and $3,000 was for the building fund; the remaining $9,000, of which $4,000 was in the form of pledges, expected to be 75 percent collectible, was unrestricted.
2. Operating expenses for the year were $93,000, of which $85,000 had been paid by year-end.

3. The special parolees' program had not yet begun as of December 31, 20X1. All resources dedicated to this program were invested in short-term securities. Investment income for the year, which was reinvested, was $2,000.

4. The center purchased a building for $220,000 ($180,000 is owed on the mortgage at year-end) and equipment for $24,000, of which $14,000 is owed on a three-year note.

REQUIRED:

1. Prepare journal entries to record the transactions for 20X1.
2. Prepare a statement of activities and a statement of financial position at December 31, 20X1.

P14.2 **Recognition of Contributions** The following events relate to not-for-profit organizations. Assume the discount rate, if required, is 10% per annum.

1. In a telephone solicitation, A promises to contribute $1,000 in 30 days.
2. In a telephone solicitation, B requests a that pledge card be mailed, suggesting that a $500 contribution may be forthcoming.
3. C promised to contribute $50,000 when the organization has raised $50,000 in matching funds; $20,000 in matching funds have been raised to date.
4. Same as 3. except that D agrees to contribute up to $50,000 by giving $1 for each $1 of matching funds raised.
5. A local church group volunteers to serve meals at a homeless shelter; the time of those serving is valued at $250.
6. E signs an agreement to contribute $1,000 now and $1,000 at the beginning of each of the next four years to help defray annual operating expenses.
7. F contributes $10,000, stating that half is to be used to fund "Meals on Wheels" this year and half is to be used for the same purpose next year.
8. On January 2, G contributes a building worth $300,000 and requires that it be used to house the organization's administrative offices over the building's 20-year estimated useful life.
9. H, a registered plumber, performs plumbing repairs worth $350 for the local church at no charge to the church.
10. I contributes $1,000,000 par value of 12% bonds to her alma mater's endowment fund. Income generated from the bonds is to be used for scholarships. Donated between interest payment dates, the bonds' $1,200,000 value includes accrued interest of $80,000.

REQUIRED: In each case, identify (a) whether the item should be recorded as a contribution and (b) if recorded, the dollar amount of the item to be considered unrestricted, temporarily restricted or permanently restricted.

P14.3 **Journal Entries and Statements** Several years ago, a group of civic-minded merchants in the city of Albury organized the "Committee of 100" for the purpose of establishing a community sports club, a not-for-profit sports organization for local youth. Each of the committee's 100 members contributed $1,000 towards the club's capital, and in turn received a participation certificate. In addition, each participant agreed to pay dues of $200 a year for the club's operations. All dues are collected in full by the end of each fiscal year ending March 31. Members who discontinued their participation were replaced by an equal number of new members through transfer of the participation certificates from the former members to the new ones. Following is the club's trial balance at April 1, 20X2:

	Debit	Credit
Cash	$ 9,000	
Investments (at market, equal to cost)	58,000	
Inventories	5,000	
Land	10,000	
Building	164,000	
Accumulated Depreciation—Building		$ 130,000
Furniture and Equipment	54,000	
Accumulated Depreciation—Furniture and Equipment		46,000
Accounts Payable		12,000
Participation Certificates (100 at $1,000 each)		100,000
Cumulative Excess of Revenue over Expenses		12,000
	$ 300,000	$ 300,000

Transactions for the year ended March 31, 20X3, were as follows:

1. Collections from participants for dues .... $ 20,000
2. Snack bar and soda fountain sales 28,000
3. Interest and dividends received 6,000
4. Additions to voucher register:
    House expenses 17,000
    Snack bar and soda fountain expenses 26,000
    General and administrative expenses 11,000
5. Vouchers paid 55,000
6. Assessments for future capital improvements (assessed on
    March 20, 20X3; none collected by March 31, 20X3; deemed
    100% collectible during year ending March 31, 20X4) 10,000
7. Unrestricted bequest received 5,000

Additional information:

1. Investments are valued at market, which amounted to $65,000 at March 31, 20X3. There were no investment transactions during the year.
2. Depreciation for the year: building—$4,000, furniture and equipment—$8,000.
3. Allocation of depreciation: house expenses—$9,000, snack bar and soda fountain—$2,000, general and administrative—$1,000.
4. Actual physical inventory at March 31, 20X3, was $1,000, and pertains to the snack bar and soda fountain.

REQUIRED:

1. Record the transactions and adjustments in journal entry form for the year ended March 31, 20X3. Omit explanations.
2. Prepare a statement of activities for the year ended March 31, 20X3.
   (AICPA adapted)

P14.4 **Budgeting for a College** Crosby College, a not-for-profit school, is developing its budget for the upcoming 20X1-X2 academic year. The following data relate to the current academic year (20X0-X1):

	Lower Division (Freshman/Sophomore)	Upper Division (Junior/Senior)
Average Number of Students per Class	25	20
Average Salary of Faculty Members	$ 48,000	$ 48,000
Average Number of Credit Hours Carried Each Year per Student	33	30
Enrollment, Including Scholarship Students	2,000	1,360
Average Faculty Teaching Load in Credit Hours per Year (8 Classes of 3 Credit Hours)	24	24

Additional information:

1. For 20X1-X2, lower division enrollment is expected to increase by 10 percent, while the upper division's enrollment is expected to remain stable. Faculty salaries will be increased by a standard 8 percent, and additional merit increases to be awarded to individual faculty members will be $300,000 for the lower division and $270,000 for the upper division.
2. The current budget is $768,000 for operation and maintenance of plant and equipment; this includes $360,000 for salaries and wages. Experience of the past three months suggests that the current budget is realistic but that expected increases for 20X1-X2 are 8 percent in salaries and wages and $36,000 in other expenditures for operation and maintenance of plant and equipment.
3. The budget for the remaining expenditures for 20X1-X2 is as follows:

Administrative and General	$ 560,000
Library	440,000
Health and Recreation	300,000
Athletics	480,000
Insurance and Retirement	660,000
Interest	192,000

4. The college expects to award 15 free-tuition scholarships to lower division students and 10 to upper division students. Tuition is $88 per credit hour, and no other fees are charged.

5. Budgeted revenues for 20X1-X2 are as follows:

Endowments . . . . $ 684,000
Net Income from Auxiliary Services   1,000,000
Athletics   920,000

The college's remaining source of revenue is an annual support campaign held during the spring.

REQUIRED:

1. Compute by division (a) the expected enrollment, (b) the total credit hours to be carried, and (c) the number of faculty members needed for 20X1-X2.
2. Compute the budget for 20X1-X2 faculty salaries by division.
3. Compute the 20X1-X2 tuition revenue budget by division.
4. Compute the amount that must be raised during the annual support campaign in order to cover the 20X1-X2 expenditures budget.

P14.5 *SFAS 117* **Statement of Financial Position** The bookkeeper for the Jacob Vocational School resigned on March 1, 20X8, after preparing the general ledger trial balance and analysis of cash as of February 28, 20X8. These schedules appear in Exhibits 14.14 and 14.15.

At the end of the fiscal year, August 31, 20X8, an examination of the records showed the following:

1. D. E. Marcy donated 100 shares of Trans, Inc., stock in September 20X7 with a market value of $110 per share at the date of donation. The terms of the gift provide that the stock and any income thereon are to be retained intact. At any date designated by the board of directors, the assets are to be liquidated and the proceeds used to assist the school's director in acquiring a personal residence. The school will not retain any financial interest in the residence.
2. E. T. Pearce donated 6 percent bonds in September 20X7 with par and market values of $150,000 at the date of donation. Annual payments of $3,500 are to be made to the donor during his lifetime, although in no case is the annual payment to exceed interest earned on the bonds. Earnings in excess of these payments are to be used for current operations in the following fiscal year. Upon the donor's death, the fund is to be used to construct a school cafeteria.

Jacob Vocational School
General Ledger Trial Balance
February 28, 20X8

Debits

Cash for Current Operations	$ 258,000
Cash for Restricted Current Uses	30,900
Stock Donated by D. E. Marcy	11,000
Bonds Donated by E. T. Pearce	150,000
Building	33,000
Land	22,000
General Current Operating Expenses	38,000
Faculty Recruitment Expenses	4,100
Total	$ 547,000

Credits

Mortgage Payable on Fixed Assets	$ 30,000
Income from Gifts for General Operations	210,000
Income from Gifts for Restricted Uses	196,000
Student Fees	31,000
Net Assets	80,000
Total	$ 547,000

EXHIBIT 14.14   TRIAL BALANCE FOR THE JACOB VOCATIONAL SCHOOL, TO BE USED IN P14.5

3. No transactions were recorded on the school's books since February 28, 20X8. An employee of the school prepared the following analysis of the checking account for the period from March 1 through August 31, 20X8:

Balance, March 1, 20X8			$ 288,900
Deduct:			
Unrestricted Current Operating Expenses	$ 14,000		
Purchase of Equipment	47,000	$ 61,000	
Less: Student Fees		8,000	
Net Expenses		$ 53,000	
Payment for Director's Residence	$ 11,200		
Less: Sale of 100 Shares of Trans, Inc., Stock	10,600	600	53,600
Total			$ 235,300
Add: Interest on 6% Bonds		$ 9,000	
Less: Payments to E. T. Pearce		3,500	5,500
Balance, August 31, 20X8			$ 240,800

Jacob Vocational School
Analysis of Cash
For the Six Months Ended February 28, 20X8

Unrestricted Cash for Current Operations:			
Balance, September 1, 20X7		$ 80,000	
Add: Student Fees	$ 31,000		
Gift of W. L. Jacob	210,000	241,000	
		$ 321,000	
Deduct: General Current Operating Expenses . .	$ 38,000		
Payment on Land and Building	25,000	63,000	$ 258,000
Cash for Restricted Uses:			
Gift of W. L. Jacob for Faculty Recruitment . . .		$ 35,000	
Less: Faculty Recruitment Expenses		4,100	30,900
Checking Account Balance, February 28, 20X8 . . .			$ 288,900

EXHIBIT 14.15   ANALYSIS OF CASH FOR THE JACOB VOCATIONAL SCHOOL, TO BE USED IN P14.5

REQUIRED: Prepare a statement of financial position as of August 31, 20X8 in accordance with SFAS 117.
(AICPA adapted)

P14.6   Hospital Journal Entries The following information was taken from the books of Garden Court Hospital for the year ended December 31, 20X5:

1. The hospital received $6,000,000 in cash from patients it cared for during the year. Another $3,000,000 is due from patients, and $1,500,000 is due from various insurance companies, all at standard charge rates. Revenues from other nursing services amounted to $250,000 and revenues from other professional services were $600,000. Only $400,000 of those revenues were collected in cash during the year; half of these cash collections related to nursing services. Other revenue, mostly from cafeteria sales, amounted to $200,000. Except for cafeteria sales, all revenues flowed through accounts receivable.

2. Garden Court has certain agreements with various insurance companies under which standard rates were adjusted downward by $210,000. Furthermore, Garden Court is involved in a community assistance program; the hospital provided $160,000 of charity and other free services. An allowance for uncollectible accounts was established based on 1 percent of accounts receivable that arose in 20X5. Receivables written off in 20X5 were $80,000.

3. The annual budget indicated that supplies estimated to cost $510,000 will be needed in 20X5. These materials have been ordered and received; however, only half have been paid for as of the end of 20X5. Mr. G. Khurabi donated medicine that would normally be purchased in the market for $200,000. In addition, Ms. A. Jansen unexpectedly donated a large refrigeration unit; its book value to her was $400,000 and its fair market value was $600,000.

4. Garden Court's principal expense categories (object classes) are salaries and wages, supplies and other materials, and other operating expenses. An allocation of these expenses among the principal service categories (functional classes) shows the following:

| | Object Classes | | |
Functional Classes	Wages and Salaries	Supplies	Other Expenses
Nursing Services	$ 200,000	$ 180,000	$ 170,000
General Services	190,000	160,000	130,000
Fiscal Services	140,000	120,000	150,000
Professional Services	240,000	80,000	110,000
	$ 770,000	$ 540,000	$ 560,000

Of these expenses, $100,000 of wages and $120,000 of other operating expenses remain unpaid at year-end.

5. Early in 20X5, Garden Court received a gift to be used for conducting research on a deadly and intractable disease. Of the $400,000 received, $180,000 was expended on the research. Another $200,000 was invested in high yield bonds and earned interest of $30,000. The donor specified that investment income is restricted for the designated research purposes.

6. Maureen MacInnis donated marketable securities worth $2,000,000. These securities cost her $1,500,000 in 20X1. The principal is to be maintained and 75 percent of the income is restricted for research on brain tissue; the balance is transferred currently for normal operating expenses. During 20X5, $160,000 in dividends were received and $100,000 was expended on the designated research.

7. The hospital is replacing its scanning equipment. Volunteers conducted a fund-raising campaign to finance the new equipment and have raised $1,600,000. Of these contributions, all but $100,000 were collected as of the end of 20X5. In order to cover the $4,000,000 cost of the equipment, a $2,500,000 loan was obtained. The new equipment was purchased in late November. Proceeds of $250,000 were received from sale of the old equipment (book value, $200,000).

REQUIRED: Prepare journal entries for the transactions of Garden Court Hospital for 20X5, per *SFAS 116* and *117*. Explanations may be omitted.

P14.7 Hospital Statement of Activities The following information pertains to the activities of Montclair Hospital for the year ended December 31, 20X1.

1. Gross patient service revenue .... $ 8,000,000
    Charity allowances   1,500,000
    Contractual discounts to third-party payers   500,000
    Provision for uncollectibles: to be calculated based on 5%
      of net patient service revenue ....   ?
2. Fair market value of noncash donations:
    Volunteer workers in public-relations campaign   20,000
    Medical supplies given by pharmaceutical firm   80,000

3. Operating expenses, of which $300,000 are unpaid at year end:

Professional care of patients	3,300,000
General services	950,000
Nursing services	1,000,000
Administrative services	350,000

4. The hospital conducts various educational programs for which it received fees of $50,000 during 20X1.
5. The cafeteria and gift shop reported profit of $12,000 on sales of $132,000; operating costs are classified as administrative services.
6. Oscar Moritani, a retired doctor, provided $100,000 to be used in validating the accuracy of a new cholesterol testing procedure. The funds were spent this year and were recorded as general services expenses.
7. In July, Mr. and Mrs. Mallett established a trust in the amount of $600,000. Income from the trust is to be paid to the hospital until the death of Mr. Mallett. At that time, the principal is to be given to a local university. The Second National Bank is appointed as trustee. Income received by the trust, and due to be distributed in 20X1, amounted to $10,000. As of December 31, the bank had remitted only $6,000 to the hospital.
8. The will of Gladys Chickering provided for a bequest to the hospital of common stock of a company listed with the New York Stock Exchange. Ms. Chickering had inherited the stock four years ago, when it was worth $100,000, from a decedent who purchased it for $50,000. When Ms. Chickering died on March 15, the stock was worth $150,000; at year-end it is worth $127,000.
9. A new X-ray machine was purchased for $400,000, using unrestricted cash.

REQUIRED: Prepare a statement of activities for the year ended December 31, 20X1. Ignore beginning and ending net asset balances.

P14.8   Hospital Accounting—Insurance Reimbursements Grady Hospital completed its first year of operation as a qualified institutional provider under the health insurance (HI) program for the aged and wishes to receive maximum reimbursement for its allowable costs from the government. The following financial, statistical, and other information is available:

1. The hospital's charges and allowable costs for departmental inpatient services were as follows:

Departments	Charges for HI Program Beneficiaries	Total Charges	Total Allowable Charges
Inpatient Routine Services			
(Room, Board, Nursing)	$ 425,000	$ 1,275,000	$ 1,350,000
Inpatient Ancillary Service			
Departments:			
X-ray	$ 56,000	$ 200,000	$ 150,000
Operating Room	57,000	190,000	220,000
Laboratory	59,000	236,000	96,000
Pharmacy	98,000	294,000	207,000
Other	10,000	80,000	88,000
Total Ancillary Services ..	$ 280,000	$ 1,000,000	$ 761,000
Totals	$ 705,000	$ 2,275,000	$ 2,111,000

2. For the first year, the reimbursement of settlement for inpatient services may be calculated at the option of the provider under either of the following apportionment methods:
    a. *The departmental RCC (ratio of cost centers) method* provides for listing on a departmental basis the ratios of beneficiary inpatient charges to total inpatient charges, with each departmental beneficiary inpatient charge ratio applied to the allowable total cost of the respective department.
    b. *The combination method (with cost finding)* provides that the cost of routine services be apportioned on the basis of the average allowable cost per day for all inpatients applied to the total inpatient days of beneficiaries. The residual part of the provider's total allowable cost attributable to ancillary (nonroutine) services is to be apportioned in the ratio of the beneficiaries' share of charges for ancillary services to the total charges to all patients for such services.
3. Statistical and other information is as follows:
    a. Total inpatient days for all patients: 20,000.
    b. Total inpatient days applicable to HI beneficiaries (600 aged patients whose average length of stay was 12.5 days): 7,500.
    c. A fiscal intermediary acting on behalf of the government's Medicare program negotiated a fixed allowance rate of $90 per inpatient day subject to retroactive adjustment as a reasonable cost basis for reimbursement of covered services to the hospital under the HI program. Interim payments based on an estimated 500 inpatient days per month were received during the 12-month period subject to an adjustment for the provider's actual cost experience.

REQUIRED:

1. Prepare schedules computing the total allowance cost of inpatient services for which the provider should receive payment under the HI program and the remaining balance due for reimbursement under each of the following methods:
    a. Departmental RCC method.
    b. Combination method (with cost finding).
2. Under which method should Grady Hospital elect to be reimbursed for its first year under the HI program, assuming the election can be changed for the following year with the approval of the fiscal intermediary? Why?
3. Grady Hospital wishes to compare its charges to HI program beneficiaries with published information on national averages for charges for hospital services. Compute the following (show your computations):
    a. The average total hospital charge for an HI inpatient.
    b. The average charge per inpatient day for HI inpatients.
    (AICPA adapted)

P14.9 Transactions and Financial Statements Irvine Services is a private not-for-profit organization that provides community services for the prevention of substance abuse. The following events occur in 20X0:

1. Contributions of $600,000 are received. Of this amount, $400,000 is donor-designated for educational program activities. The rest is unrestricted.

2. Contributions of $250,000 are promised to the organization during the year. Irvine has signed agreements from the donors that payment will be received in 20X1. It is estimated that 70% of these promises are collectible.
3. A donor contributes marketable securities valued at $150,000, with the stipulation that the securities be held intact. The income is unrestricted. The value of the securities at year-end is $180,000. Income earned on the securities during 20X0 is $10,000.
4. Expenses for the year are as follows:

General services	$ 20,000
Program services	500,000
Fund-raising	60,000

Included in the program services expenses above are $300,000 from contributions made last year which were donor-designated for educational program activities, and $100,000 from contributions made this year (see 1. above) which were donor-designated for educational program activities.

5. Volunteers contributed services as follows:

   a. Accounting and payroll services valued at $15,000 were provided by a local CPA.
   b. A contractor donated his services to finish the upper floor in the organization's main building. It is estimated that $25,000 was added to the value of the building.

REQUIRED: Prepare a Statement of Activities for Irvine Services for the year 20X0, using the format required by *SFAS 117*. A supplemental schedule of expenses by natural classification is *not* required.

P14.10 Accounting for Investments American Hereditary Disease Association, a private not-for-profit organization supporting research and education related to hereditary diseases, has long-term investments at December 31, 20X1 as follows:

	December 31, 20X1 Market Value
Investment in Bonds	$ 100,000
Investment in Debentures	40,000
Investment in Equity Securities	600,000

All investments were purchased at par value.

Notes:
1. The bonds were donated several years ago; the donor stipulated that the securities be held as a permanent endowment, and income on the securities be used for research projects relating to sickle cell disease. The market value of these securities was $60,000 when donated.
2. The debentures are a recent investment of permanently restricted cash contributions of $40,000.

3. The equity securities are investments of permanently restricted cash contributions of $700,000. The donor specified that income and gains be restricted to community educational programs on Crabbe's Disease. The decline in value to $600,000 was properly recorded.

Income on investments during 20X2 was as follows:

Bonds	$ 10,000
Debentures	2,000
Equity securities	40,000

Market values at December 31, 20X2 are as follows:

Bonds	$ 106,000
Debentures	45,000
Equity securities	625,000

REQUIRED: Show how the events of 20X2 are disclosed in the Statement of Activities, per *SFAS 124*. Be careful to identify the effect on each category of net assets.

P14.11 Financial Statement Effects of University Transactions *(Appendix)* Baxter University is a private not-for-profit institution. In addition to various routine transactions in its restricted and unrestricted current funds, Baxter had the following activity during the year ended June 30, 20X4:

1. A loan fund was established by transferring $75,000 from the unrestricted current fund and $20,000 from endowment fund income. During the year, $32,000 was loaned to students; there were no principal repayments during the year. Five percent of the loans are expected to be uncollectible. Interest earned on the loans was $2,000, of which $1,300 was received in cash. In addition, interest of $5,200 was earned on the unexpended cash, which is maintained in interest-bearing bank accounts.

2. At July 1, 20X3, the plant fund showed:

Land	$ 100,000
Buildings	12,200,000
Equipment	6,600,000
Mortgage Payable	(3,000,000)
Cash for Replacements	30,000

During the year, $78,000 was transferred from the unrestricted current fund for equipment replacement. In addition, $100,000 in principal and $210,000 in interest on the mortgage was paid by the unrestricted current fund. Plant fund resources of $83,000 were spent for new equipment; old equipment which cost $46,000 was retired, with no proceeds. Although plant assets are not subject to any restrictions, "cash for replacements" is restricted by donors for that purpose.

3. An annuity fund was established in July 20X3, as two alumni made substantial contributions to the university in exchange for guaranteed annual payments. One, who has a life expectancy of 10 years, contributed $40,000 and is to receive $4,800

annually. The other, who has a life expectancy of 12 years, contributed $75,000 and is to receive $8,400 annually (first payment for each annuity is June 30, 20X4). Baxter uses an 8 percent rate to account for the annuities. Interest earned on invested funds during the year was $13,000. Upon death of the donors, remaining resources may be used for general operations.

4. At July 1, 20X3, Baxter's endowment fund had cash of $10,000 and investments of $284,000. The fund balance—principal was $250,000. During the year, securities which cost $61,000 were sold for $78,000, and all proceeds were reinvested. Baxter attributes all gains and losses to principal. Interest and dividends of $22,000 were received, along with $15,000 in new principal contributions. In addition to the transfer to the loan fund, $25,000 of income was spent for faculty research grants, pursuant to donors' stipulations.

REQUIRED:

1. Prepare journal entries internally by fund to record the transactions for the year.
2. Indicate how, and in what amounts, the foregoing transactions and ending balances will be reported in Baxter University's Statement of Activities and Statement of Financial Position for the year ended June 30, 20X4. Classify the amounts reported as relating to unrestricted, temporarily restricted or permanently restricted net assets.

P14.12 **University Accounting** *(Appendix)* Presented in Exhibit 14.16 is the current funds balance sheet of Mayville University as of the end of its fiscal year ended June 30, 20X7.

The following transactions occurred during the fiscal year ended June 30, 20X8:

1. On July 7, 20X7, a gift of $100,000 was received from an alumnus. The alumnus requested that one-half of the gift be used to purchase books for the university library and the remainder be used to establish a scholarship fund. The alumnus further requested that the income generated by the scholarship fund be used annually to award a scholarship to a qualified disadvantaged student. On July 20, 20X7, the board of trustees resolved that the resources of the newly established scholarship fund would be invested in savings certificates. On July 21, 20X7, the savings certificates were purchased.
2. Revenue from student tuition and fees applicable to the year ended June 30, 20X8, amounted to $1,900,000. Of this amount, $66,000 was collected in the prior year, and $1,686,000 was collected during the year ended June 30, 20X8. In addition, at June 30, 20X8, the university had received cash of $158,000, representing fees for the session beginning July 1, 20X8.
3. During the year ended June 30, 20X8, the university collected $349,000 of the outstanding accounts receivable at the beginning of the year. The balance was determined to be uncollectible and was written off against the allowance amount. At June 30, 20X8, the allowance account was increased to $11,000.
4. Interest charges of $6,000 were earned and collected on late payments of student fees.
5. The state appropriation was received. An additional unrestricted appropriation of $50,000 was made by the state but was not paid to the university as of June 30, 20X8.

Mayville University
Current Funds Balance Sheet
June 30, 20X7

Assets		Liabilities and Fund Balances	
Current Funds—Unrestricted:		Current Funds—Unrestricted:	
Cash	$ 210,000	Accounts Payable	$ 45,000
Accounts Receivable—		Deferred Revenues	66,000
Student Tuition and		Fund Balance	515,000
Fees, less Allowance			$ 626,000
for Doubtful Accounts			
of $9,000	341,000		
State Appropriations			
Receivable	75,000		
	$ 626,000		
Current Funds—Restricted:		Current Funds—Restricted:	
Cash	$ 7,000	Fund Balances	$ 67,000
Investments	60,000		
	$ 67,000		
Total Current Funds . . .	$ 693,000	Total Current Funds . . .	$ 693,000

EXHIBIT 14.16   CURRENT FUNDS BALANCE SHEET, TO BE USED IN P14.12

6. An unrestricted gift of $25,000 cash was received from alumni of the university.
7. During the year, pre-20X7 investments of $21,000 were sold for $26,000. Investment income amounting to $1,900 was also received. Gains and losses on the sale of investments by the restricted current fund are considered to be restricted.
8. During the year, unrestricted operating expenses of $1,777,000 were recorded. At June 30, 20X8, $59,000 of these expenses remained unpaid.
9. Restricted cash of $13,000 was spent for authorized purposes during the year.
10. The accounts payable at June 30, 20X7, were paid during the year.
11. During the year, $7,000 interest was earned and received on the savings certificates purchased in accordance with the board of trustees' resolution discussed in No. 1.

REQUIRED:

1. Prepare journal entries to record in summary the above transactions for the year ended June 30, 20X8. Each journal entry should be numbered to correspond with the transaction described above. Organize your answer sheet as follows:

	Current Funds				Endowment	
	Unrestricted		Restricted		Fund	
Accounts	Debit	Credit	Debit	Credit	Debit	Credit

2. Prepare a statement of activities for the year ended June 30, 20X8 in accordance with *SFAS 117*.
    (AICPA adapted)

CHAPTER 15

PARTNERSHIPS: FORMATION, OPERATION, AND EXPANSION

CHAPTER PREVIEW

Despite the popularity of the corporate form of business organization, most businesses in the United States are organized as sole proprietorships or partnerships rather than as corporations. This chapter introduces the partnership form of business organization, along with some accounting procedures peculiar to it. These procedures appear to stem from a consideration of the nature of the partnership entity and its relationship with the individual partners. An appendix that examines certain issues related to tax considerations in partnerships is also provided. The chapter covers the following major topics:

- Characteristics of a partnership
- Important accounting issues
- Formation of the partnership
- Allocation of net income to partners
- Admission of a new partner
- Tax aspects of partnerships (Appendix)

Readers will note that the nature of partnership formation and the events that occur when there are changes in partnership personnel result in *goodwill* being recorded under a wider variety of circumstances than in corporate accounting. This development raises questions about the propriety of recording goodwill so frequently in partnership accounting, especially in light of corporate accounting principles applicable in similar circumstances.

Partnerships provide us with some interesting accounting applications, ranging from income-related issues to dramatically different accounting procedures for recording the admission of new partners. Moreover, the extensive use of cash-basis accounting among smaller partnerships often requires adjustments to produce accrual-basis accounting records. Unlike personal financial statements prepared for individuals, however, financial reporting by partnerships does *not* incorporate current value accounting.

CHARACTERISTICS OF A PARTNERSHIP

The organizational and operational rules for partnerships derive from two sources: *law*—the Uniform Partnership Act, and *contract*—the partnership agreement.

LEGAL PROVISIONS

Partnerships are subject to the laws of the particular state in which they are organized. Many states have adopted the provisions of the Uniform Partnership Act (the Act). The Act has sections dealing with

- The nature of a partnership.
- Relations of partners to others.
- Relations among partners.
- Partners' property rights.
- Termination and dissolution of the partnership.

The Nature of a Partnership

The Uniform Partnership Act defines a **partnership** as "an association of two or more persons to carry on as co-owners a business for profit." Thus, the actions of individuals as they jointly conduct a business activity and share profits and losses legally create a partnership even if no formal agreement among the individuals exists. The term *persons* in this definition is not limited to individuals. Corporations or other legal entities may be partners. An association of two or more corporations is often called a *joint venture*; this topic is discussed in Chapter 16.

Relations of Partners to Others

Each partner is considered an agent of the partnership. That is, for most transactions, any one partner can act for the entire partnership and can legally enter into binding contracts, representing other partners as well. Only a few transactions, such as disposing of the goodwill of the business or confessing a judgment in court, require authorization of all the partners. This characteristic, known as **mutual agency**, is of great convenience to partners in transacting business. One partner may act for the entire partnership, and outsiders know that any partner they deal with legally represents the entire partnership.

There is another significant aspect to this section of the Act: although any one partner may enter into transactions on behalf of the partnership, all partners are liable for the partnership's obligations. The partners are said to be *liable jointly and severally*. This means that as a group they are liable for the obligations of the partnership, and also that each partner has personal liability which could extend to the entire partnership obligation. In other words, creditors of the partnership can seek to collect the full amount of the partnership debt from a single partner. Because partners' obligations are not limited to their investments in the partnership—personal assets are also at risk—partners are said to assume **unlimited liability**. This matter will be considered more fully in the next chapter, in the context of partnership liquidations.

Relations among Partners

In dealing with the rights and duties of partners, the Act sets forth the following:[1]

---

[1] Uniform Partnership Act, Part IV, Section 18.

The rights and duties of the partners in relation to the partnership shall be determined, subject to any agreement between them, by the following rules:

a. Each partner shall be repaid all contributions, whether by way of capital or advances to the partnership property, and share equally in the profits and surplus remaining after all liabilities, including those to partners, are satisfied; and must contribute toward the losses, whether of capital or otherwise, sustained by the partnership according to each partner's share in the profits.

b. The partnership must indemnify every partner in respect of payments made and personal liabilities reasonably incurred by a partner in the ordinary and proper conduct of its business, or for the preservation of its business or property.

c. A partner, who in aid of the partnership makes any payment or advance beyond the amount of capital which the partner agreed to contribute, shall be paid interest from the date of payment or advance.

d. A partner shall receive interest on the capital contributed only from the date when repayment should be made.

e. All partners have equal rights in the management and conduct of the partnership business.

f. No partner is entitled to remuneration for acting in the partnership business, except that a surviving partner is entitled to reasonable compensation for services in winding up the partnership affairs.

g. No person can become a member of a partnership without the consent of all the partners.

h. Any difference arising as to ordinary matters connected with the partnership business may be decided by a majority of the partners; but no act in contravention of any agreement between the partners may be done rightfully without the consent of all the partners.

Note that any of the above rules may be modified by the partnership agreement. For example, the partners may agree to a division of profits and losses in unequal shares. When no specific agreement exists, however, the provision of the Act regarding equal sharing applies.

Partners' Property Rights

The Act defines three specific property rights which a partner possesses:

1. The partner is a co-owner of all property held by the partnership and has no claim on specific assets.
2. The partner possesses a **partnership interest**—a right to a share of the capital and profits.
3. The partner has a right to participate in the management of the partnership.

Termination and Dissolution of the Partnership

The Act deals extensively with the dissolution of partnerships, covering ways in which dissolution occurs, the impact of dissolution on the rights of various parties, and the rules for distribution of partnership assets. These issues are discussed in Chapter 16.

CONTRACTUAL PROVISIONS

The **partnership agreement**, sometimes referred to as the **articles of partnership**, is a contract among the partners. On certain matters, such as the allocation of income among partners, the contractual agreement takes precedence over the provisions of the Uniform Partnership Act. On other matters, such as the rights of outside parties, the contract cannot be at variance with the law. In general, the partnership agreement deals with the following matters:

- Characteristics of the partnership, such as its name, nature, location of business activity, duration, and fiscal year.
- Methods of allocating partnership income to the partners.
- Procedures for admitting new partners and for settling a partner's interest upon withdrawal or death, including life insurance to be carried on partners and buy-sell agreements.

Thus the partnership agreement specifies the various aspects of the relationship among the partners. It has little if anything to say about the relationship of the partnership to outside parties.

LIMITED PARTNERSHIPS

The discussion thus far has focused on **general partnerships** in which all partners can participate in the management of the firm and all are liable for the partnership's obligations. Another type of partnership, the **limited partnership**, has both general partners and limited partners. The *general partners*, of whom there must be at least one, manage the firm and have all the rights and obligations previously discussed. The *limited partners* invest capital and have the right to a specified share of income or loss but have no right to participate in management. Moreover, their liability for the partnership's obligations is limited to their investment in the partnership. Therefore, limited partners have *no personal liability* for partnership obligations, as general partners do.

Limited partnerships are often used when large amounts of investment capital are needed and tax treatment as a partnership is desired. A general partner initiates the project, such as real estate development or natural resource exploration, and finance it by selling limited partnership interests to a number of investors. The general partner acquires the needed capital without relinquishing management control, and investors acquire a right to share in income without bearing any personal responsibility for partnership liabilities. Limited partnerships are discussed further in Chapter 16.

LIMITED LIABILITY COMPANIES AND PARTNERSHIPS

A relatively new form of organization is the **limited liability company (LLC)**, which combines many of the organizational and tax treatments of a noncorporate entity—a partnership or proprietorship—with the limited liability protection of a corporation. This form of organization was first enacted in Wyoming in 1977. In 1988, the Internal Revenue Service ruled that such entities would be taxed as partnerships rather than as corporations. This ruling created a great interest in the LLC form of organization, and all states have now adopted LLC statutes.

An alternative to the LLC is the **limited liability partnership (LLP)**, which has an underlying partnership structure. By contrast, an LLC has an underlying structure that is more similar to a corporation, including articles of organization (similar to a corporate charter) and, in many states, a governing board. The LLP form was first adopted by Texas in 1991, and has since been enacted in nearly all states. The LLP form is now widely used by professional firms, which have a long history of organizing as partnerships. The LLC and LLP are typically considered to be superior forms of organization to the general partnership, because they retain most of the desirable characteristics of a general partnership, but largely eliminate the unlimited liability that individual partners face for actions of the partnership. Most LLC/LLP laws limit liability to a partner's investment; personal liability exists only for personal involvement in, or supervision of, the specific wrongful act. For example, if a CPA firm is organized as a limited liability partnership, an individual partner who was involved in a negligent audit would be personally liable, but a partner who was not involved in the engagement in any way, including a supervisory role, would not be personally liable.

In recent years, most general partnerships converted their legal status to an LLC or LLP. Once the LLC/LLP form of organization was adopted by most states, virtually all the large CPA firms, as well as entities in other professions registered as LLPs, thus changing their legal form of ownership from a general partnership to a limited liability partnership. However, the general characteristics of partnership operation and the accounting procedures for an LLP remain the same as they were for the general partnership.

AUTHORS' COMMENTARY

Many partnerships are small local businesses with few partners. In such cases, *mutual agency* and *joint and several liability* may be manageable characteristics; each partner is likely to be aware of the actions of the other partners.

Some partnerships, however, are large national or international enterprises with hundreds or thousands of partners. The international CPA firms are prime examples of large partnerships. Here, mutual agency and joint and several liability may cause major problems. For example, suppose a partner in the Los Angeles office of a CPA firm presides over an audit failure which leads to a large liability judgment against the firm. Under general partnership law, every partner in the firm, whether in New York or Grand Rapids, has potential personal liability for the judgment, even though he or she had absolutely no involvement with the failed audit.

Historically, professionals such as CPAs, attorneys and physicians were not allowed to limit personal liability by organizing their affairs as corporations. **Professional corporations,** allowed in many jurisdictions, provide corporate income tax treatment, but do not offer limited liability. Creation of the LLC and LLP forms of organization has largely remedied the problem of joint and several liability for professionals. Under these new organizational arrangements, partners involved in a particular engagement are personally liable for damages arising out of that engagement but their liability does not extend to their partners who are *not* involved in the engagement.

OTHER ORGANIZATIONAL FORMS

Many other types of entities exist that have characteristics similar to partnerships. In a **joint venture**, two or more entities which themselves may be large corporations form a new entity, usually to carry out a particular transaction or activity rather than to engage in an ongoing business. The accounting implications of joint ventures are discussed in Chapter 16.

In a **syndicate**, a group, usually composed of individuals, is formed to pool resources for a particular transaction, such as a real estate deal or the acquisition of a professional sports franchise. A **cooperative** is an entity formed by various parties to provide a service to its members, typically without profit. For example, a group of merchants forms a cooperative to buy certain goods and services in larger quantities, so as to qualify for lower prices. Or a neighborhood group forms a cooperative to buy organic food products and resell them to members.

These, and other similar organizational forms, all would use partnership-type accounting. Thus, *partnership accounting* has applicability beyond firms that are specifically called *partnerships*.

COMPARISON OF PARTNERSHIP AND CORPORATE FORMS OF BUSINESS ORGANIZATION

Each form of partnership organization possesses advantages and disadvantages, as does the corporate form, depending on the situation. In addition to the above characteristics, a **general partnership** ceases to exist legally when a new partner enters or an existing partner retires or dies. The partnership agreement can provide for continued business operations seemingly unaffected by changes in partnership personnel. All partners must consent to transfers of ownership interests.

In a **limited partnership,** the entity ceases to exist when at least one general partner is no longer present. Interests of the limited partners are freely transferable whereas changes in the general partner's interest are subject to consent of all other partners. From an income tax perspective, *all qualified partnerships* are **conduits.** Transactions with tax effects are passed through to the partners; no income tax is levied on the partnership itself.

A **corporation** is formed under a charter granted by a governmental entity. Shareholders have no right to participate in management, although they do elect the governing board of directors, and have no personal liability for the corporation's debts. Life of a corporation is generally unlimited and shares are freely transferable. Corporations are *taxable entities*, as are those partnerships that possess corporate characteristics. Income taxes are levied on the corporation and on certain distributions to shareholders, thereby creating "double taxation."

IMPORTANT ACCOUNTING ISSUES

Because a partnership is a business entity, it uses many of the same accounting principles used by corporations. For example, general topics such as revenue and expense recognition and asset valuation are given the same treatment. There are, however, a few important areas where partnership accounting differs from corporate accounting. Most of these differences are due to the particular nature of the partnership entity.

Like a corporation, a partnership is an entity distinct from the individual partners. However, the partners typically are actively involved in the firm; they are not absentee owners. This fact influences the concept of net income for a partnership as well as the treatment of owners' equity. Corporate owners' equity is reflected in several accounts—Common Stock, Additional Paid-In Capital, and Retained Earnings—but no attempt is made to maintain equity accounts for each stockholder. Partnership equity, on the other hand, is recorded in **capital accounts**, which reflect the partners' shares of invested capital and accumulated earnings. A separate capital account is maintained for each partner. These accounting considerations also apply to sole proprietorships, although only a single capital account is needed for the sole proprietor.

INCOME ALLOCATIONS VERSUS PAYMENTS TO PARTNERS

When discussing the distribution of partnership income to the individual partners, two separate events must be distinguished. *First* are the **allocations to partners**, which are *credits* to the partners' capital accounts for their respective shares of partnership income (or debits for their shares of partnership loss). Much of the following discussion is devoted to these allocations. *Second* are the **payments to partners**, which are *debits* to their capital accounts reflecting the transfer of resources from the partnership to the partners. Also called **drawings**, these payments create no special accounting problems, except in cases where the partnership is being liquidated, as will be discussed in Chapter 16.

INCOME DETERMINATION

Although partnerships employ the standard revenue and expense recognition criteria, *net income* has a special meaning within the context of the partnership. In corporate accounting, net income signifies the return to the corporation; the return to the owners/shareholders is in the form of dividends and capital gains. In partnership accounting, however, net income signifies the return to the owners/partners. In most cases partners are actually involved in the operation of the firm. In addition to being investors, partners may also render personal services in the day-to-day conduct of business and may loan money to the partnership. Stockholders of a corporation may also be employees of, or lenders to, that corporation, but salaries and interest paid to them are subtracted from revenue in computing corporate net income.

Accounting and tax requirements necessitate a careful distinction between the corporate entity and the individual, along with a distinction among the individual's possible roles as stockholder, employee, and lender. These distinctions are not particularly useful in the case of a partnership because a partnership does not have the formal legal status of a corporation, nor is it a taxable entity. As a result, when partners have multiple involvement in the financial affairs of the partnership—as investors, employees, and lenders—it is difficult to distinguish among: (1) compensation for services performed, (2) interest on loans, and (3) return on capital invested. Certain income allocations may be called *salaries*, other allocations *interest*, and still others *shares of profit*. The lack of arm's-length transactions in establishing the amounts of these allocations causes the various role distinctions to be disregarded and *all allocations to partners are considered to be divisions of partnership net income*. In other words, *net income of a partnership is determined before any allocations are made to partners*; salaries to partners and interest to partners are *not* treated as expenses. Similarly, net income of a sole proprietorship is the return to the proprietor; no compensation to the proprietor is subtracted.

A second area of difference between corporation and partnership net income is the treatment of income taxes. As noted earlier, a corporation is a taxable entity, but a partnership is not. A partnership is considered a **conduit** through which income flows to the individual partners. Thus *no federal income tax is imposed directly on the partnership*; rather, the individual partners include their share of partnership income—their *allocations*—on their personal income tax returns. The income statement of the partnership does not provide for income tax expense. The appendix to this chapter provides a brief discussion of other tax issues related to partnerships.

Cash to Accrual Conversions

In very small businesses, including many partnerships, records are often maintained on a cash basis. This system may be adequate for the partners' information needs and for tax reporting. Moreover, there may be no need to prepare formal financial statements for external parties on a regular basis. When cash basis records are maintained and business financial statements suitable for external use are prepared, perhaps when applying for a bank loan, a conversion from cash basis to accrual basis is needed. Because converting from cash basis to accrual basis is typically studied in introductory or intermediate accounting courses, it is only reviewed here. The basic approach is to adjust the cash basis data for the accruals, deferrals, and prepayments present under accrual basis accounting. Conversion changes the *timing* of revenue and expense recognition, not the ultimate amount.

For example, consider the conversion *from cash basis sales* (collections from customers) *to accrual sales* (total billings during the period). If accounts receivable—uncollected billings not formally recorded in cash basis accounting—*increased* during the period, then total billings exceed collections from customers and the increase is *added* to cash basis sales. Conversely, if accounts receivable *decreased*, then collections from customers exceed total billings and the decrease is *subtracted* from cash basis sales. In this latter case, the decrease in accounts receivable represents collection of prior period billings. These relationships are summarized as follows:

Accrual sales   =   Cash sales plus ending accounts receivable minus beginning accounts receivable,

or alternatively:

Accrual sales   =   Cash sales plus increase (or minus decrease) in accounts receivable.

Other revenue accounts, such as interest, are converted in the same way.

Similarly, conversion of an *expense account* from cash basis to accrual basis is expressed as follows:

Accrual expense   =   Cash expense plus increase (or minus decrease) in related accounts payable and/or accrued liability account(s).

When accounts payable or accrued liabilities related to a given expense item *increased* during the period, total accrual basis expense exceeds cash basis expense—the amount *paid* to vendors—and the increase is *added* to cash basis expense. A *decrease* in accounts payable and accrued expenses indicates that amounts paid to vendors are greater than accrual expense incurred this period. Thus some prior period expenses are paid in the current period and the decrease is *subtracted* from cash basis expense.

When *inventories* are significant to the business operation, the accrual method is generally used for sales and cost of goods sold, since it is required for tax purposes. Should a conversion from *cash purchases to accrual cost of goods sold* be required, however, the relationship is as follows:

Accrual cost of goods sold   =   Cash purchases plus increase (or minus decrease) in related accounts payable plus decrease (or minus increase) in inventories.

An *increase* in accounts payable for merchandise—signifying that more merchandise was purchased this period than was paid for—is *added* to cash purchases. An *increase* in inventories—indicating that not all merchandise purchases were sold—is *subtracted* from cash purchases.

The approach just shown for cost of goods sold also applies to other expenses that involve *prepayments*. For example, accrual basis insurance expense consists of insurance payments paid plus (minus) the decrease (increase) in prepaid insurance.

As a final illustration of converting from the cash basis to the accrual basis, consider the establishment of an *allowance for doubtful accounts*. After other needed conversions are made, bad debt expense under the allowance method is subtracted to obtain accrual basis income. If the allowance should have been established in a prior period, the *pro forma* allowance account must be reconstructed and analyzed to determine the effect on prior period income. This relationship is as follows:

> Income after allowance = Income before allowance plus decrease (or minus increase) in the *pro forma* allowance for doubtful accounts.

When the *pro forma* allowance *increased* in a given year, bad debt expense exceeded net accounts written off and a *subtraction* results. When the *pro forma* allowance *decreased*, net accounts written off exceeded bad debt expense and an *addition* to cash basis income is needed.

As an example, suppose that accrual income is $75,000 after all conversions *except* for bad debt expense. Uncollectible accounts receivable that were written off, or were never recorded under cash basis accounting, amount to $8,000. Accrual bad debt expense is estimated at $12,000. Because the $8,000 in bad receivables is *not included as income* in the $75,000, only the additional $4,000 (= $12,000 − $8,000)—the *increase* in the *pro forma* allowance—is considered. Accrual basis income is therefore $71,000 (= $75,000 − $4,000).

PARTNERSHIP INCOME ALLOCATIONS

Once the partnership's net income is determined, perhaps after converting cash basis accounts to the accrual basis, it must be allocated among the individual partners. As discussed, all allocations to partners are viewed as divisions of net income. It is not surprising, therefore, that in providing for the division of net income, partnership agreements frequently consider the various roles—investor, employee, lender—that partners hold.

The partnership agreement should specify the rules for the allocation of income. These rules may be simple or complex, sometimes calling for salary, interest, and bonus allocations. If the partnership agreement is silent as to the allocation of income, then it is assumed that income is to be divided equally among all partners as required by law. Various approaches to allocation are discussed and illustrated in a subsequent section.

CAPITAL CHANGES

Another important issue in accounting for partnerships involves changes in the capital structure of the partnership. Such changes occur for many reasons other than investments and withdrawals by the partners. This chapter and the next consider initial formation of partnerships, subsequent entry and exit of individual partners, and eventual liquidation of partnerships.

These various capital changes are frequently summarized in a **schedule of changes in capital accounts**. Similar to the corporate statement of changes in stockholders' equity, the schedule of changes in capital accounts often becomes a formal partnership financial statement.

SUMMARY OF ACCOUNTING FOR PARTNERSHIP OPERATIONS

Rules covered in introductory and intermediate accounting courses regarding corporate revenue and expense recognition and asset and liability valuation apply in general to partnerships. As a result, accounting matters specific to partnerships tend to focus on events affecting the capital accounts representing the owners' equity.

The capital accounts for the partners serve as the set of owners' equity accounts. These accounts combine invested capital and undistributed income. Three events have an impact on capital account balances:

1. **Investment of capital.** An individual partner's capital account is affected not only by the partner's own investment, as illustrated in discussing partnership formation, but also by the investments of new partners and retirements of existing partners. Admission of new partners is discussed later in this chapter; retirements are addressed in Chapter 16.

2. **Allocation of net income.** Although no new issues arise in measuring partnership revenues and expenses, *partnership net income*—the return to the partners—is determined before subtracting any compensation to the partners. Once the partnership's net income is determined, it is allocated to the partners in accordance with the partnership agreement, or in equal shares if the partners have not agreed otherwise. Each partner's *income share* is *credited* to each partner's capital account. When a loss occurs, the partners' *loss shares* are *debited* to their capital accounts.

3. **Withdrawal of capital.** Amounts withdrawn by partners, whether from invested capital or from accumulated income allocations, are debited to each partner's capital account. Often, withdrawals are made in anticipation of income allocations and are debited to a separate **drawing account** for each partner. Drawing accounts are closed at year-end to the capital accounts. For example, if partner Burns draws $500 per month to help with living expenses, the following entry is made monthly:

Drawing—Burns	500	
Cash		500
To record monthly drawing.		

At year-end, the balance in the drawing account is closed, as follows:

Capital—Burns	6,000	
Drawing—Burns		6,000
To close drawing account to capital.		

Use of drawing accounts is optional; instead, drawings may be directly debited to the capital accounts.

FORMATION OF THE PARTNERSHIP

Accounting for the formation of a partnership requires determining values of assets contributed by the partners and establishing the initial balances in the partners' capital accounts. Following Generally Accepted Accounting Principles (GAAP), assets contributed to a partnership in exchange for a capital interest are valued at fair market value.[2] This use of fair market values often causes the accounting basis and the tax basis of some contributed assets to diverge. The principal concern of this chapter is the accounting basis. Issues related to the tax basis are briefly examined in the appendix to this chapter.

BONUS AND GOODWILL APPROACHES

Establishing the opening balance in each partner's capital account can be complicated even though fair market values of the contributed assets are known. One straightforward approach is to set each partner's capital account equal to the fair market value of net assets invested. For example, assume that Prince and Quinn form a partnership. Prince invests $30,000 cash, and Quinn invests land and a building having a combined fair market value of $75,000, subject to a mortgage of $35,000, which the partnership assumes. Thus Quinn invested net assets with fair market value of $40,000 (= $75,000 − $35,000). If each partner's capital account is set equal to net assets invested at fair market value, the following entry is used to record the partnership's formation:

Cash	30,000	
Land and Building	75,000	
Mortgage Payable		35,000
Capital—Prince		30,000
Capital—Quinn		40,000

    To record formation of partnership.

Alternatively, the partners could specify a **capital percentage** for each partner, indicating that each partner will have an agreed-upon percentage interest in *initial total partnership capital*. Such an approach could generate several different entries for recording the partnership's formation, depending on the details of the agreement between Prince and Quinn. One possibility is to assign the total capital according to the agreed-upon *capital percentages* of the respective partners. For example, suppose that Prince and Quinn decide that each will have a 50 percent interest in the partnership's initial capital. We may argue, for example, that the reason the partners agreed on equal capital balances while making unequal tangible investments is that one partner, Prince in this case, brings certain talents, contacts, or other intangible benefits to the partnership.

Because Prince invested $30,000 and Quinn invested $40,000, they must decide how to apply their capital percentages to determine their opening capital balances. Two approaches are possible: *One approach* calls for dividing the total capital of $70,000 in proportion to the capital percentages, in this case equally, and credit each partner with $35,000. In this situation there is an implied transfer of $5,000 of capital from Quinn to Prince. The following entry is therefore used to record formation of the partnership:

---

[2] Accounting Principles Board, *Opinion No. 29*, "Accounting for Nonmonetary Transactions" (New York: AICPA, 1973).

Cash	30,000	
Land and Building	75,000	
Mortgage Payable		35,000
Capital—Prince		35,000
Capital—Quinn		35,000
To record formation of partnership.		

This is called the **bonus approach to partnership formation**. Quinn is assumed to be paying Prince a bonus of $5,000.

A *second approach* involves assuming that enough unrecorded *intangible assets* have been contributed to bring the investments, and the capital balances, into the desired relationship. We may record this intangible asset, called **goodwill**, in an amount sufficient to achieve the desired relationship among the capital accounts. In the current example, we need to record $10,000 (= $40,000 − $30,000) of goodwill in order to make Prince's investment equal to Quinn's. Our entry to record formation of the partnership is as follows:

Cash	30,000	
Land and Building	75,000	
Goodwill	10,000	
Mortgage Payable		35,000
Capital—Prince		40,000
Capital—Quinn		40,000
To record formation of partnership.		

This approach is called the **goodwill approach to partnership formation**. When forming a partnership, the partners must specify which accounting approach is to be used. The bonus and goodwill methods are examined more thoroughly later in the chapter when we consider how to record the admission of a new partner.

INVESTMENT OF AN EXISTING BUSINESS

Rather than investing individual assets, a partner may have an existing business entity, currently operated as a proprietorship, which becomes that partner's investment in the partnership. No new accounting problems arise here. Revaluation of proprietorship assets may be necessary to reflect the fair market value of assets being transferred to the partnership, and intangible assets may need to be recognized. After these matters are settled, the investments by the partners are recorded in an entry signifying formation of the partnership.

ALLOCATION OF NET INCOME TO PARTNERS

As previously discussed, partners' salaries or interest are not considered expenses in determining the partnership's net income. Rather, all such provisions are considered in dividing or allocating partnership net income among the individual partners. Thus, a multifactor allocation procedure may be used. Although partners may agree to use any factors they wish, three common ones are as follows:

1. A **salary factor**, representing compensation for the personal services a partner provides to the operations of the partnership.
2. An **interest factor**, representing a return on the capital each partner has invested.
3. A **percentage factor**, reflecting an agreed **income-sharing ratio** to be used to allocate income or loss remaining after providing for any salaries and interest.

SALARIES TO PARTNERS

Allocations of net income to partners in the form of salary allowances are typically established by formal agreement among the partners. This agreement usually specifies (1) the amount each partner is to receive or (2) a formula, such as a bonus formula, for calculating the amount. Specified amounts can be based on the time, effort, or experience that each partner contributes to the business. For example, the DEF partnership might agree that D is to receive an annual salary of $20,000, E is to receive an annual salary of $6,000, F is to receive no salary, and any remaining income or loss is to be divided equally among the partners. If partnership net income for the year is $38,000, the allocation first provides for the $26,000 in salaries and then divide the remaining $12,000 according to the income-sharing ratio. This yields the following allocation of partnership net income:

	D	E	F	Total
Salaries	$ 20,000	$ 6,000	$ 0	$ 26,000
Balance	4,000	4,000	4,000	12,000
Net Allocation	$ 24,000	$ 10,000	$ 4,000	$ 38,000

The partnership agreement should specify whether salary and other allocations are to be **fully implemented**, even if they exceed the partnership net income. *We assume full implementation unless otherwise stated.* In the DEF example, assume that net income is $17,000 and that salaries are to be fully implemented. The salary allocation of $26,000 exceeds net income by $9,000. This $9,000 "loss" is then allocated by the income-sharing ratio, producing the following allocations:

	D	E	F	Total
Salaries	$ 20,000	$ 6,000	$ 0	$ 26,000
Balance	(3,000)	(3,000)	(3,000)	(9,000)
Net Allocation	$ 17,000	$ 3,000	$ (3,000)	$ 17,000

When partners' salaries or other income allocation devices are *not* to be fully implemented, the partnership agreement must specify the order in which the devices are to be used. Thus the partners could agree that salaries are implemented first, followed by interest on capital balances, and so forth. Moreover, the partners must agree on a procedure for partial implementation of any income-sharing device. In the above example, there is not enough income to implement even the salaries, let alone any other income allocation device. Two of the many possible approaches are (1) allocating D's salary first or (2) allocating the $20,000 salary of D and the $6,000 salary of E in the proportion that the salary of each bears to total salaries of $26,000. If the proportional basis in (2) is selected, the $17,000 of income is allocated as follows:

	D	E	F	Total
Net Allocation	$ 13,077*	$ 3,923**	$ 0	$ 17,000

*$13,077 = ($20,000/$26,000) $17,000
**$3,923 = ($6,000/$26,000) $17,000

BONUS TO PARTNERS

Allocation of net income to partners for services rendered might also be based on a bonus related to profit, perhaps in addition to a fixed salary. In discussing various bonus relationships, we use the following symbols:

$$X = \text{Net income before bonus}$$
$$B = \text{Amount of bonus}$$
$$Y = \text{Net income after bonus } (Y = X - B)$$
$$R = \text{Percentage rate of bonus}$$

When the bonus is defined as a percentage of net income *before* the bonus, its calculation is simply

$$B = RX$$

Sometimes the bonus is defined as a percentage of the net income that remains *after* the bonus. This involves a somewhat more complex formula:

$$B = RY$$
$$B = R(X - B)$$
$$B = RX/(1 + R)$$

For example, assume net income before the bonus, X, is $30,000, and the bonus rate, R, is 25 percent of net income after the bonus, Y, a figure that is presently unknown. Using the above formula, we calculate the bonus as follows:

$$B = RX/(1 + R)$$
$$B = .25(30,000)/1.25$$
$$B = 7,500/1.25$$
$$B = 6,000$$

We can then easily verify that the $6,000 bonus is indeed 25 percent of the net income after the bonus, Y, of $24,000 ($Y = \$30,000 - \$6,000$).

Many other bonus possibilities exist. There could be different percentages based on different levels of income. Or the bonus could be determined after an income-sharing device, such as salaries, is implemented, but before another, such as interest on capital accounts, is implemented.

INTEREST ON PARTNERS' CAPITAL ACCOUNTS

Allocations of net income may also be made on the basis of interest allowances on partners' capital accounts. An interest rate is specified, which usually applies to weighted average capital balances.[3] We calculate the **weighted average capital balance** by multiplying each different amount of a partner's capital balance by the fraction of the year during which that amount existed.

---

[3] The partnership agreement should specify the base for the calculation of interest. For example, beginning-of-year capital balance or a simple average of beginning and ending balances could be used.

For example, suppose a partner's capital account has a balance of $6,000 on January 1. On March 1, additional capital of $20,000 is invested, and on September 1, $2,000 is withdrawn. The weighted average capital balance for the year is calculated as follows:

Period	Capital Balance	Fraction of Year	Weighted Average
1/1-2/28	$ 6,000	2/12	$ 1,000
3/1-8/31	26,000	6/12	13,000
9/1-12/31	24,000	4/12	8,000
			$ 22,000

If an interest rate of 8 percent is specified, $1,760 (= .08 × $22,000) of the partnership net income is allocated to this partner for interest on the average capital balance.

As is the case with salary allocations to partners, any allocation of net income in the form of interest may be made fully, even if it exceeds total net income. Again, any remaining income, or loss created by previous allocations, is divided according to the percentages in the income-sharing ratio.

PERCENTAGE ALLOCATION BY INCOME-SHARING RATIO

A percentage allocation formula, or **income-sharing ratio**, *always* exists for a partnership. The entire net income of the partnership may be allocated by this percentage formula or, alternatively, some income may be allocated by salaries, by interest, or both. In the latter case, the amount of partnership net income remaining *after* salaries and interest are fully implemented, whether positive or negative, is allocated by the income-sharing ratio.

The partnership agreement sets forth the income-sharing ratio. Normally a single set of percentages is applied to all forms of income. The partners may, however, agree that different types of income, or expense, will be divided in different ways. When the partnership agreement *fails to specify* an income-sharing ratio, it is assumed, by law, that all partners share *equally*.

ILLUSTRATION OF ALLOCATION OF PARTNERSHIP NET INCOME

Thomas, Underwood, and Vickers are partners in a printing firm. Their partnership agreement contains the following provisions regarding income allocation:

- Thomas is to devote two days per week to partnership business and receives an annual salary of $15,000. Underwood and Vickers are to work full time and receive annual salaries of $35,000 and $30,000, respectively.
- Vickers, who is responsible for sales, is to receive a bonus equal to 10 percent of any net income, before allocations, in excess of $100,000.
- The partners are to receive 10 percent interest on their weighted average capital balances. Allocations of salaries and bonus are ignored for purposes of this calculation.
- After these three allocations are implemented, any remaining income or loss is to be allocated 50 percent to Thomas, 30 percent to Underwood, and 20 percent to Vickers.

Suppose that partnership net income for 19X6 was $150,000. The partners' capital balances at the beginning of the year were as follows: Thomas, $69,000; Underwood, $40,000; and

Vickers, $40,000. Underwood invested an additional $10,000 on March 31, 19X6. At the end of each quarter, the partners withdrew a total of $6,000, divided according to the income-sharing percentages in the last provision above; that is, Thomas withdrew $3,000, Underwood $1,800, and Vickers $1,200. Thomas withdrew an additional $18,000 on October 31, 19X6. The allocation of income for 19X6 is shown in Exhibit 15.1.

	Thomas	Underwood	Vickers	Total
Salaries	$ 15,000	$ 35,000	$ 30,000	$ 80,000
Bonus[a]	—	—	5,000	5,000
Interest[b]	6,150	4,480	3,820	14,450
				$ 99,450
Balance[c]	25,275	15,165	10,110	50,550
	$ 46,425	$ 54,645	$ 48,930	$ 150,000

[a] Bonus is 10 percent of $50,000 (= $150,000 − $100,000).
[b] Weighted average capital is calculated as follows:

	Thomas			Underwood			Vickers		
1/1–3/31	$ 69,000 × 3/12 =	$ 17,250		$ 40,000 × 3/12 =	$ 10,000		$ 40,000 × 3/12 =	$ 10,000
4/1–6/30	66,000 × 3/12 =	16,500		48,200 × 3/12 =	12,050		38,800 × 3/12 =	9,700
7/1–9/30	63,000 × 3/12 =	15,750		46,400 × 3/12 =	11,600		37,600 × 3/12 =	9,400
10/1–10/31	60,000 × 1/12 =	5,000						
11/1–12/31	42,000 × 2/12 =	7,000	{	44,600 × 3/12 =	11,150	{	36,400 × 3/12 =	9,100
Weighted average		$ 61,500			$ 44,800			$ 38,200

Ten percent of the weighted average capital is the amount of interest.

[c] The balance of $50,550 is allocated 50 percent to Thomas, 30 percent to Underwood, and 20 percent to Vickers.

EXHIBIT 15.1 ILLUSTRATION OF INCOME ALLOCATION

SCHEDULE OF CHANGES IN CAPITAL ACCOUNTS

Partnerships frequently summarize all the events affecting the partners' capital accounts during an accounting period in a **schedule of changes in capital accounts**. This schedule is illustrated in Exhibit 15.2 using the information for the year ended December 31, 19X6 just presented for the partnership for Thomas, Underwood, and Vickers.

The schedule of changes in capital accounts is often included with the formal financial statements prepared by a partnership. When this is done, items such as Drawings are summarized in total on a single line.

| Event | Capital Accounts | | | |
	Thomas	Underwood	Vickers	Total
Beginning Balance				
(Jan. 1)	$ 69,000	$ 40,000	$ 40,000	$ 149,000
Investment (Mar. 31)	10,000	—	—	10,000
Drawings (Mar. 31)	(3,000)	(1,800)	(1,200)	(6,000)
Drawings (June 30)	(3,000)	(1,800)	(1,200)	(6,000)
Drawings (Sept. 30)	(3,000)	(1,800)	(1,200)	(6,000)
Withdrawal (Oct. 31)	—	(18,000)	—	(18,000)
Income Allocation*				
(Dec. 31)	46,425	54,645	48,930	150,000
Drawings (Dec. 31)	(3,000)	(1,800)	(1,200)	(6,000)
Ending Balance				
(Dec. 31)	$ 113,425	$ 69,445	$ 84,130	$ 267,000

*From Exhibit 15.1.

EXHIBIT 15.2 ILLUSTRATION OF SCHEDULE OF CHANGES IN CAPITAL ACCOUNTS

ADMISSION OF A NEW PARTNER

Admission of a new partner gives rise to another important accounting problem for partnerships. Technically, there is no such thing as "admission of a new partner." When a new partner is admitted, the old partnership legally ends, and a new partnership is created. For practical purposes, however, business operations are likely to continue without interruption. As is often the case in accounting, the *economic substance*—the continuing business activity—takes precedence over the *legal form*—termination of the old partnership and the creation of a new one. It is in this economic sense, therefore, that we speak of admission of a new partner.

In the illustrations that follow, assume the partnership of Arthur Associates has a balance sheet at June 30, 19X2, as follows:

Arthur Associates
Balance Sheet
June 30, 19X2

Various Assets	$ 140,000	Liabilities		$ 50,000
		Capital:		
		Arthur . . .	$ 31,000	
		Bradley . .	26,000	
		Crowe . . .	33,000	90,000
	$ 140,000			$ 140,000

Assume further that the partners' *income-sharing ratio* is as follows: Arthur, 50 percent; Bradley, 20 percent; and Crowe, 30 percent.

ADMISSION BY PURCHASE OF AN EXISTING PARTNERSHIP INTEREST

One way in which a new partner may enter an existing partnership is by purchasing the interest of one or more existing partners. Such a transaction occurs between the old and new partners as individuals and usually has no direct effect on the partnership accounts. This is parallel to the case in which one individual sells shares of stock in a corporation to another individual. Only those two are involved in the transaction; the corporation makes no entry other than to update its stockholder records. In a similar manner, when one individual buys an existing partnership interest, the only partnership entry usually needed is a transfer of the capital account from the old partner to the new.

Transfer of Capital Interests

The usual method of accounting for a purchase of a partnership interest is to transfer the capital balance of the selling partner to a new capital account established for the entering partner. The amount of the entry is the existing capital balance of the selling partner, which may be different from the selling price.

Purchase from One Partner. In the case of Arthur Associates, suppose that on July 1, 19X2, Findley purchases Crowe's entire partnership interest for $45,000. The partnership records the following entry to show transfer of Crowe's capital balance to Findley:

Capital—Crowe	33,000	
Capital—Findley		33,000
To record transfer of partnership interest from Crowe to Findley.		

Note that the purchase price of $45,000 has no bearing on the partnership entry. The $45,000 was received by Crowe directly, not by the partnership. Crowe realized a gain of $12,000 on the sale of the partnership interest, assuming Crowe's basis is the book figure of $33,000. The cost (and tax basis) of Findley's partnership interest is $45,000, despite the fact that the partnership books show the capital account as $33,000. Findley's cost of $45,000 has no effect on any capital-based distributions the partnership makes. In contrast, the $45,000 cost affects the amount of taxable gain or loss recognized by Findley when that partnership interest is sold.

Purchase from Several Partners. A new partner may purchase a portion of the interest of several partners. For example, suppose that Grogan buys a 25 percent interest in Arthur Associates by purchasing 25 percent of each partner's interest for a total of $28,000. Following the procedure illustrated in the preceding section, we could simply record the transfer of capital interests. By this method, 25 percent of each partner's capital at the date of entry is transferred to the new partner, Grogan. The following entry is:

Capital—Arthur	7,750	
Capital—Bradley	6,500	
Capital—Crowe	8,250	
Capital—Grogan		22,500
To record transfer of 25 percent interest to Grogan.		

The debits to the capital accounts of the three existing partners represent 25 percent of their respective capital balances, and Grogan's capital of $22,500 is 25 percent of the total capital of $90,000. Note that, as before, the $28,000 purchase price has no bearing on the entry. The three existing partners recognize gains or losses as individuals on the sale of part of their partnership interests.

A *new income-sharing ratio* must be established for the four partners. For convenience, we typically assume that the contract for the new partnership specifies that (1) the new partner's percentages of income and of the initial capital balance are equal and (2) the old partners maintain their income-sharing relationship. After Grogan joins the firm, therefore, the partners share income as follows: Arthur, 37.5 percent; Bradley, 15 percent; Crowe, 22.5 percent; and Grogan, 25 percent. These percentages are based on the fact that the old partners now own 75 percent of the partnership: Arthur has 50 percent of 75 percent, or 37.5 percent; Bradley has 20 percent of 75 percent; and Crowe has 30 percent of 75 percent.

Recognition of Implied Goodwill

Admission of a new partner by purchase of an existing partnership interest is usually recorded by transferring capital accounts as described above. Another possible method involves the recognition of **implied goodwill**. Under this approach, the purchase price is used to infer the value of the entire partnership. To illustrate, again consider the case where Grogan buys 25 percent of each partner's interest for a total of $28,000.

If Grogan is willing to pay $28,000 to buy a 25 percent interest in the partnership, the entire partnership capital must be worth $112,000 (= $28,000/.25). But the partnership books show only $90,000, the total capital of Arthur, Bradley, and Crowe. This implies that $22,000 (= $112,000 implied total value − $90,000 recorded capital) of unrecorded assets exist. For convenience, we call these unrecorded assets **goodwill**. We first record the goodwill, apportioning a share to each existing partner according to the established income-sharing ratio of 50 percent for Arthur, 20 percent for Bradley, and 30 percent for Crowe. The entry to record the implied goodwill is as follows:

Goodwill	22,000	
Capital—Arthur		11,000
Capital—Bradley		4,400
Capital—Crowe		6,600
To record implied goodwill.		

We now make an entry to transfer 25 percent of each partner's capital to Grogan:

Capital—Arthur (25% × 42,000)	10,500	
Capital—Bradley (25% × 30,400)	7,600	
Capital—Crowe (25% × 39,600)	9,900	
Capital—Grogan		28,000
To record transfer of 25 percent interest to Grogan.		

Note that when this approach is used, the credit to the new partner's capital account equals the amount paid to acquire the interest. This is so even though Grogan's payments were made to Arthur, Bradley, and Crowe as individuals.

Unless the agreement covering the purchase of partners' interests specifically provides for the recognition of implied goodwill on the partnership books, the transfer of capital accounts method should be used. Moreover, suppose the implied value of the partnership, calculated by capitalizing the purchase price, is *less* than total capital. If specific assets are deemed to be overvalued, they should be written down. After this write-down, if the implied value is still less than total capital, the transfer of capital accounts method should be used to eliminate the difference. *Negative goodwill should not be recorded.* Alternatively, an argument may be made in some cases that goodwill should be attributed to the new partner. If so, the capital credit to the new partner is increased, and additional intangible assets recorded, so that the implied value of the partnership equals total capital.

ADMISSION BY INVESTMENT OF NEW CAPITAL

The second way in which a new partner may enter an existing partnership is by investing directly in the partnership. In this case, the new partner contributes an agreed-upon amount of assets, which may be cash or property, or services, to the partnership. The new partner receives an agreed-upon share of capital at the date of entry and a specified share of subsequent income and loss. This agreed-upon *capital percentage* is used to establish the new partner's *initial capital balance*. Thereafter, the income percentage is of primary importance, because it guides the division of subsequent profits and losses among the partners. In many cases, the capital percentage and income percentage are equal. When they are not equal, their use is guided by the following rule:

Capital percentage (capital-sharing ratio) is used to establish the value of the firm and hence the total amount of goodwill.

Income percentage (income-sharing ratio) is used to allocate goodwill or bonus to partners as well as to allocate income.

The partnership records the investment of assets by the new partner, the capital account of the new partner, and, perhaps, some adjustments to reconcile the two. When the investment by the new partner equals the new partner's capital percentage times the new capital—old capital plus assets invested—no accounting problem exists. For example, suppose that on July 1, 19X2, Edwards invests $10,000 in Arthur Associates in exchange for a 10 percent interest in capital and income (hereafter referred to simply as a 10 percent interest). We have the following:

1. Investment by Edwards = $10,000.
2. Edwards's share of new capital = 10% × ($90,000 old capital + $10,000 invested by Edwards) = 10% × $100,000 = $10,000.

Since Items 1 and 2 are equal, we simply make the following entry:

Assets   10,000
      Capital—Edwards   10,000
      To record investment by Edwards.

Suppose, however, that Edwards invested $9,000 for the 10 percent interest. We then have the following:

Case A
1. Investment by Edwards = $9,000.
2. Edwards's share of new capital = 10% × ($90,000 + $9,000) = $9,900.

Alternatively, suppose Delano invests $12,000 for a 10 percent interest:

Case B
1. Investment by Delano = $12,000.
2. Delano's share of new capital = 10% × ($90,000 + $12,000) = $10,200.

In each of the two preceding cases, the investment differs from the computed share of capital. When this situation occurs, the disparity must be reconciled before the entry recording the investment can be made. Reconciliation can be achieved in one of two ways:

1. Consider the share of capital amount (item 2 in Cases A and B) to be the correct amount credited to the new partner's capital account. The difference between this amount and the amount invested is treated as an adjustment of the existing partners' capital accounts. This is known as the **bonus method of admission**.
2. Bring the investment (item 1 in Cases A and B) and the share of capital (item 2) amounts into agreement by inferring the existence of intangible assets and adding these either to the capital of the new partner or to the capital of the existing partners. This is known as the **goodwill method of admission**.

The partnership agreement should specify which of these methods is to be used when a new partner is admitted to the partnership. In the following sections, both methods are discussed and illustrated.

Bonus Method of Admission

The bonus method of admission avoids both revaluing assets and recognizing goodwill when a new partner enters.

> Under the **bonus method of admission**, the total capital of the new partnership after admission of the new partner equals the capital before admission plus the investment of the new partner. The new partner's capital account is credited with the appropriate share of the total capital.

Suppose that the new partner's investment is *less* than the computed share of capital, as in Case A above, where Edwards invests $9,000 but receives a $9,900 share in capital. In such a situation, the existing partners have some reason for admitting Edwards at this less-than-fair-share price. Perhaps Edwards brings some important talents or resources to the firm, and to obtain these the existing partners are willing to subsidize Edwards' admission by giving a $9,900 share for only $9,000.[4] The $900 difference is charged against the existing partners' capital accounts in their income-sharing percentages. In effect, each existing partner is transferring a portion of capital to Edwards. The entry to record Edwards' admission for a 10 percent interest with an investment of $9,000 is as follows:

Cash	9,000	
Capital—Arthur	450	
Capital—Bradley	180	
Capital—Crowe	270	
Capital—Edwards		9,900

To record Edwards' admission under the bonus method.

This situation, in which the new partner's investment is *less* than the computed capital balance, results in a **bonus to the new partner**.

The second possibility is that the new partner's investment is *more* than the computed share of capital, as in Case B above, where Delano invests $12,000 but has a $10,200 share in total capital. We assume that the existing partners are able to command a premium when admitting a new partner. Perhaps the assets of the partnership are worth more than their book value. Perhaps the partnership has above-average earning potential. Or perhaps the existing partners wish to be compensated for the risk and effort they incurred in establishing the firm. In any event, to gain admittance Delano must contribute not only a fair share of assets, $10,200, but also an additional $1,800, which is credited to the capital accounts of the existing partners in their income-sharing percentages. The entry to record Delano's admission, reflecting an investment of $12,000 in exchange for a 10 percent interest, is as follows:

Cash	12,000	
Capital—Arthur		900
Capital—Bradley		360
Capital—Crowe		540
Capital—Delano		10,200

To record Delano's admission under the bonus method.

This situation, in which the new partner's investment is *more* than the computed capital balance, results in a **bonus to the existing partners**.

Formulas for the Bonus Method of Admission. The bonus method may be summarized in formula terms. We calculate the amount to be credited to the new partner's capital account (NC) as follows:

$$NC = S(OC + I) \text{ where}$$
$$OC = \text{Total capital of the old partners}$$
$$I = \text{Amount invested by the new partner}$$
$$S = \text{New partner's percentage share in the partnership capital}$$

[4] Another possible reason for the low price is that the partnership's assets are overvalued. However, we generally ignore this possibility in this textbook. If generally accepted accounting principles have been followed, write-downs to market for current assets such as marketable securities and inventories should have been made as losses occurred. Fixed assets are generally not written down, unless there is evidence that an impairment has occurred as provided in *SFAS 121*, "Accounting for the Impairment of Long-Lived Assets and for Long-Lived Assets to Be Disposed Of" (1995).

For example, when two existing partners each have capital balances of $43,000, and a new partner invests $50,000 for a 25 percent interest in the partnership, the balance of the new partner's capital account is calculated as follows:

$$NC = S(OC + I)$$
$$= 25\% \times (86,000 + 50,000)$$
$$= 25\% \times 136,000$$
$$= 34,000$$

The difference between the credit to the new partner's capital account and the amount invested ($NC - I$) is divided among the existing partners in accordance with their income-sharing percentages and is debited or credited to their capital accounts, depending on whether the new investment was less than or greater than the balance in the new partner's capital account.

Goodwill Method of Admission

The goodwill method of admission specifically provides for asset revaluation and goodwill recognition supported by the amount of the new partner's investment.

> Under the **goodwill method of admission**, the discrepancy between the amount invested by the new partner and the share of capital initially calculated is attributed to the presence of unrecorded intangible assets or to undervalued other assets. To reconcile the discrepancy, amounts signifying these unrecorded or undervalued assets must be recorded.

For example, suppose the new partner's investment of tangible assets is *less* than the initially computed share of capital, as in Case A above, where Edwards invests $9,000 cash but has a $9,900 share in net assets. To explain this imbalance, we infer that Edwards must be bringing something more to the firm than $9,000 cash—perhaps some special skills or talents—such that the existing partners are willing to admit Edwards as a 10 percent partner. Thus we conclude that Edwards is also investing some intangible assets or *goodwill* in the partnership. We determine this amount so that the investment (cash plus goodwill) and the share of capital are brought into balance. Note that as we add assets in the form of goodwill, Edwards' share of capital increases. *Calculation of the goodwill* proceeds as follows:

1. Determine the total value of the new firm implied by the capital of the existing partners. In the current example, existing capital amounts to $90,000, and the existing partners will have a 90 percent interest in the new partnership. This implies a total value of the new partnership of $100,000 (= $90,000/.9).
2. Calculate the new partner's share of this total value. In the current example, Edwards' share is $10,000 (10 percent of $100,000).
3. The goodwill invested by the new partner is the difference between the calculated share of the value of the firm and the amount of tangible assets invested. In this example, Edwards is assumed to invest $1,000 of goodwill (= $10,000 share of firm's value − $9,000 cash invested).

The entry to record Edwards' admission follows:

Cash	9,000	
Goodwill	1,000	
Capital—Edwards		10,000

To record Edwards' admission under the goodwill method.

This situation, in which the new partner's investment of tangible assets is *less* than the initially computed share of capital, is referred to as **goodwill to the new partner**.

The second possibility is that the new partner's investment of tangible assets is *more* than the initially computed share of capital, as in Case B above, where Delano invests $12,000 cash for only a $10,200 share in net assets. To explain this imbalance, the net assets of the existing partnership are assumed to be understated. Perhaps some of the firm's tangible assets have market values in excess of their book values. Or perhaps the firm has unrecorded goodwill in the form of established customers, product recognition, and skillful management. The fact that a new partner is willing to pay more than book value for a partnership interest gives credence to the idea that undervalued or unrecorded assets exist. To bring the new partner's investment into balance with the share of net assets, we must acknowledge these unrecorded asset amounts. We now proceed to *calculate the goodwill*:

1. Determine the total value of the new firm as implied by the investment of the new partner. In the current example, Delano invests $12,000 for a 10 percent interest. This relationship implies a total value of the new partnership of $120,000 (= $12,000/.10).
2. Calculate the amount by which assets are understated. In this example, present net assets are recorded at $90,000. Delano will invest an additional $12,000, bringing the total to $102,000. Because we calculated the value of the new firm to be $120,000, assets are understated by $18,000 (= $120,000 − $102,000).
3. Correct the understatement of assets by recognizing the presence of an intangible asset, goodwill, with offsetting credits to the capital accounts of the existing partners in their income-sharing percentages. This procedure recognizes the fact that the unrecorded increase in net assets occurred in the past and is attributable to the existing partners. Revaluation of tangible assets to remove the understatement is generally not proper unless objective evidence, such as a quoted market value of securities, substantiates the revaluation.

The following entry is used to record Delano's admission:

Cash	12,000	
Goodwill	18,000	
Capital—Arthur		9,000
Capital—Bradley		3,600
Capital—Crowe		5,400
Capital—Delano		12,000

To record Delano's admission under the goodwill method.

A situation in which the new partner's investment of tangible assets is *more* than the initially computed share of capital is referred to as **goodwill to the existing partners**. Any goodwill recorded in admitting a new partner should be amortized over its estimated life. According to *APBO 17*, this life should not exceed 40 years.[5]

Comparison of Bonus and Goodwill Methods

The mechanics of the bonus and goodwill methods can be expressed in formulas using the following notation:

$$I = \text{Amount invested by new partner}$$
$$S = \text{New partner's percentage share in the partnership capital}$$
$$(1 - S) = \text{Percentage share in the partnership capital which will be held by the existing partners}$$
$$OC = \text{Total capital of the existing partners (\textit{old capital})}$$
$$TV = \text{Calculated total value of the partnership}$$
$$G = \text{Goodwill to be recorded}$$
$$B = \text{Bonus to be recorded}$$

In comparing the two methods, we must first determine whether bonus or goodwill will apply to the new partner or to the existing partners. We may identify two general cases, which correspond to the Edwards (Case A) and Delano (Case B) illustrations.

Case A: $I < S(OC + I)$. When the investment by the new partner, I, is *less* than that partner's share in the firm's total capital, $S(OC + I)$, the difference is accounted for by recording either a bonus or goodwill to the *new partner*. Under the *bonus method*, the bonus to the new partner is the difference between the new partner's capital share and investment:

$$B = S(OC + I) - I$$

Under the *goodwill method*, we first calculate the implied total value of the firm:

$$TV = OC/(1 - S)$$

The total amount of goodwill to be associated with the new partner is the difference between the calculated total value, TV, and the old capital plus the new partner's tangible investment:

$$G = TV - (OC + I)$$

The relationship between the amount of goodwill and the amount of bonus can be seen by expanding and rearranging the above goodwill formula:

$$G = TV - (OC + I)$$
$$G = OC/(1 - S) - (OC + I)$$

---

[5] Accounting Principles Board, *Opinion No. 17*, "Intangible Assets" (New York: AICPA, 1970), par. 29.

This simplifies to

$$(1 - S)G = S(OC + I) - I$$

Recall that the bonus formula is

$$B = S(OC + I) - I$$

Thus we see that

$$B = (1 - S)G$$

Case B: $I > S(OC + I)$. When the investment by the new partner, I, *exceeds* that partner's share in the firm's total capital, $S(OC + I)$, we record either a bonus or goodwill to the *existing* partners. Under the *bonus method*, the total bonus to the existing partners is the difference between the new partner's investment and capital share:

$$B = I - S(OC + I)$$

Under the *goodwill method*, we first calculate the implied total value of the firm:

$$TV = I/S$$

The total amount of goodwill to be allocated to the existing partners is the difference between the calculated total value and the new capital:

$$G = TV - (OC + I)$$

Again, the relationship between the amount of goodwill and the amount of bonus can be seen by expanding and rearranging the above goodwill formula:

$$G = TV - (OC + I)$$
$$G = I/S - (OC + I)$$
$$SG = I - S(OC + I)$$

Recall that the bonus formula is

$$B = I - S(OC + I)$$

and thus

$$B = SG$$

These results are summarized in Exhibit 15.3. Formulas relating bonus and goodwill may be useful in problem solving. If the bonus was already calculated for a given situation, the goodwill can be readily determined by use of a formula, and vice versa.

	Relation of New Partner's Investment to Capital Share	
	$I < S\,(OC + I)$	$I > S\,(OC + I)$
Bonus Method	$B = S\,(OC + I) - I$	$B = I - S\,(OC + I)$
	(Bonus to new partner)	(Bonus to existing partners)
Goodwill Method	$G = \dfrac{OC}{(1 - S)} - (OC + I)$	$G = \dfrac{I}{S} - (OC + I)$
	(Goodwill to new partner)	(Goodwill to existing partners)
Relationship of Bonus to Goodwill	$B = (1 - S)\,G$	$B = SG$

EXHIBIT 15.3 SUMMARY OF BONUS AND GOODWILL FORMULAS

Effects of Bonus and Goodwill Methods on Partners' Capital

In general, the bonus and goodwill methods do *not* yield the same capital balances for the individual partners or the same total capital for the partnership.

Total Partnership Capital after Admission of New Partner

Bonus Method	**Goodwill Method**
Total capital before admission + Amount invested by new partner	Total capital before admission + Amount invested by new partner + Goodwill recorded

Compare the bonus and goodwill results obtained in the illustrations for Arthur Associates. The total capital before admission was $90,000. Edwards invested $9,000 and was admitted as a partner. Under the goodwill method, $1,000 of goodwill was attributed to Edwards. The capital balances after admission are as follows:

	Bonus Method	Goodwill Method
Arthur	$ 30,550	$ 31,000
Bradley	25,820	26,000
Crowe	32,730	33,000
Edwards	9,900	10,000
Total	$ 99,000	$ 100,000

In the other illustration, Delano invested $12,000 and was admitted as a partner. Under the goodwill method, $18,000 of goodwill was attributed to the existing partners. The capital balances after admission are as follows:

	Bonus Method	Goodwill Method
Arthur	$ 31,900	$ 40,000
Bradley	26,360	29,600
Crowe	33,540	38,400
Delano	10,200	12,000
Total	$ 102,000	$ 120,000

In *only one case* do the bonus and goodwill approaches lead to the same initial result. This happens when the amount invested *equals* the new partner's capital share; when $I = S(OC + I)$. In this case, the amount of bonus is zero, the amount of goodwill is zero, and the capital balances are the same, both individually and in total, under both the bonus and goodwill methods.

Although the bonus and goodwill methods lead to the same *initial* result only in the limited case where goodwill and bonus are zero, they lead to the same *ultimate* result in a broader set of cases. Consider the situation where goodwill is initially recorded and is subsequently written off through amortization. After write-off, the goodwill method yields the same capital balances as the bonus method in cases when *two conditions are met*:

1. The new partner's initial capital percentage and income percentage are equal, and
2. The existing partners retain their relative income percentages, thereby keeping their income-sharing ratio intact.

Observe that these two conditions are met in both the bonus and goodwill illustrations given above. Edwards' capital percentage and income percentage are both 10 percent in the first example. The same holds for Delano in the second example. Arthur, Bradley, and Crowe retain their 5:2:3 income-sharing ratio. Originally, their income percentages were 50, 20, and 30 percent, respectively; after admitting a new partner with a 10 percent share, their income percentages become 45, 18, and 27 percent.

The ultimate equivalence of the two methods is demonstrated below for the Edwards example. The far right column reflects the initial capital balances following Edwards' admission under the bonus method.

	Goodwill Method before Write-Off	Write-Off of Goodwill	Goodwill Method after Write-Off	Bonus Method
Arthur	$ 31,000	$ 450 (= $1,000 × 45%)	$ 30,550	$ 30,550
Bradley	26,000	180 (= $1,000 × 18%)	25,820	25,820
Crowe	33,000	270 (= $1,000 × 27%)	32,730	32,730
Edwards	10,000	100 (= $1,000 × 10%)	9,900	9,900
	$ 100,000	$1,000	$ 99,000	$ 99,000

Similar results are obtained in the Delano example.

Evaluation of Bonus and Goodwill Methods

In comparing the bonus and goodwill methods, we find the rationales for the discrepancy between investment and share of net assets to be similar, but the accounting conclusions are quite different. An investment that is less than the computed share of net assets—Case A in the preceding illustrations—is explained in terms of the intangible benefits the new partner brings to the firm. The goodwill method records these intangibles as an asset, whereas the bonus method leaves them unrecorded. Rather, the bonus method represents side payments by the existing partners, in the form of capital transfers to the new partner, made to obtain these intangible benefits for the firm.

An investment that is more than the computed share of net assets—Case B in the preceding illustrations—is explained in terms of understated or unrecorded asset values presently existing in the partnership. The goodwill method records these increases in asset values and the bonus method leaves them unrecorded. Now the bonus method represents side payments by the new partner, in the form of capital transfers to the existing partners, in order to obtain an interest in these assets.

In sum, both the bonus and goodwill methods deal with the presence of unrecorded assets signalled by the amount invested by an incoming partner. The bonus method suppresses the unrecorded assets. Instead, it assigns additional capital to either the new or the old partners, as indicated by comparison of the new partner's investment with the share of capital acquired. The bonus method is conservative in that it avoids recording intangible assets whose presence and value are difficult to verify and which are likely to have little, if any, realizable value upon liquidation.

In contrast, we believe that the goodwill approach has a better theoretical foundation. Because admission of a new partner creates a new legal entity, and probably a new economic entity, a new basis of asset accountability is appropriate. The transaction that occurs—investment by the new partner—forms the basis for revaluing the assets. The goodwill approach is consistent with the general principles set forth in *APBO 29* dealing with nonmonetary transactions. Although this opinion does not specifically deal with partnerships, in paragraph 18 it sets forth the general principle that "accounting for nonmonetary transactions should be based on the fair values of the assets involved." It would be logical to extend this principle to investment of the existing interests of the old partners.

AUTHORS' COMMENTARY

To conclude this discussion, we compare the bonus/goodwill approaches to recording a new partner's investment in a partnership with *corporate accounting practices*. Admission to a partnership is conceptually similar to the acquisition of one corporation by another in a business combination. Thus we consider the bonus and goodwill approaches used in partnership accounting in light of the purchase and pooling approaches used in corporate accounting discussed in detail earlier in this book.

The *bonus approach* to admission of new partners is roughly comparable to *pooling of interests* accounting for corporate business combinations. The assets of the combining entities—the acquiring and acquired corporations or the existing partnership and new partner—are simply added together. No revaluation of assets occurs in a pooling; under the bonus method, no goodwill is recognized. The equity accounts are then adjusted to reflect the new ownership relationships. Under pooling, transfers occur among the Common Stock, Additional Paid-In Capital, and Retained Earnings accounts. Under the bonus method, transfers occur among the capital accounts of the old and new partners.

The *goodwill approach* to admission of new partners shares some similarities with *purchase accounting* for corporate business combinations. Under both methods, the amount of investment may cause assets to be revalued. The purchase-goodwill analogy is not perfect, however. When the purchase method is used in corporate acquisitions, goodwill is recorded only with respect to the *acquired firm's* assets—comparable to *goodwill to the new partner*. This principle recognizes that the value of the investment or consideration given exceeds the value of tangible assets acquired; goodwill is recorded to make up the difference. In corporate accounting, goodwill is *not* recognized with respect to the assets of the *acquiring* (existing) firm. Yet in partnership accounting, goodwill may be recognized on the existing firm's assets, a method referred to earlier as *goodwill to the existing partners*. We should, however, note an important difference in circumstances. In the corporate case, the acquiring corporation continues to exist, while in the partnership case, the acquiring (old) partnership is terminated and a new one created. Therefore, the corporate and partnership approaches share the following results:

■ Goodwill may be recognized with respect to an addition to the firm—an acquired corporation or a new partner.
■ A new basis of accountability may be established when a new entity is created—the new partnership is a new entity; the acquiring corporation is not.

SUMMARY OF KEY CONCEPTS

Partnership law specifies the general conditions under which partnerships operate. Many specific details are subject to the contractual terms established by the partners in the **partnership agreement**.

Because **net income** of a partnership represents **return to the partners**, it does not include deductions for salaries to partners or interest to partners. Salaries, bonus, interest, and percentage formulas all may be used to **allocate** net income to partners. **Full implementation** of such allocations is common.

In the **formation of a partnership**, assets are recorded at **fair market value**. Initial capital balances may be based on amounts actually invested or on a preestablished capital ratio. In the latter case, either the **bonus** or **goodwill** approach is applied to reconcile any difference between the amount invested and the calculated share of capital.

Admission of a new partner may occur by **purchase of existing interest** or **direct investment in the partnership**. In the case of a purchase, transfer of capital accounts is the usual accounting method. In the case of investment, either the bonus or goodwill approach is used to account for any difference between the new partner's investment and the share of capital acquired.

The **bonus and goodwill approaches** are based on different conceptual views of the nature of admission of a new partner. The two approaches may be related by formula. The **bonus method** recognizes transfers of capital among partners, similar to **pooling of interests accounting** in corporate business combinations. In contrast, the **goodwill method** calls for asset revaluations, often in the form of intangibles, and is similar to **purchase accounting** in corporate business combinations.

TAX ASPECTS OF PARTNERSHIPS

Not a taxable entity, a partnership is a **conduit** through which taxable income, gains, and losses flow to individual partners. A partnership files an information return, Form 1065, with the IRS but pays no tax. Nevertheless, certain tax issues arise because of the way partnership accounting is carried on, and deserve an introductory discussion here. This appendix focuses primarily on implications of differences between accounting and tax amounts with respect to the basis of partnership assets and the basis of partners' capital accounts.

TAX BASIS OF PARTNERSHIP ASSETS

When an individual transfers assets to a partnership in exchange for an interest in that partnership, no gain or loss is recognized on the transfer for tax purposes. The tax basis of the asset carries over from the individual to the partnership. Recall, however, that for book purposes the asset would be recorded at its fair market value. As an example, assume that a machine having a tax basis to Partner A of $6,000 has a fair market value of $15,000 when it is transferred to the AB Partnership. For book purposes, the machine is recorded at $15,000, and depreciation on the income statement is based on this amount. The asset retains its tax basis of $6,000, however, and for purposes of calculating taxable income, depreciation is based on the $6,000 amount. Similarly, if the machine is subsequently sold after providing for depreciation, the book gain or loss differs from the tax gain or loss because the net book value differs from the adjusted tax basis.

When differences between accounting basis and tax basis exist, dual records must be kept with respect to basis, depreciation, and income. This in turn creates the need to examine how the deviation between book income and taxable income should affect the partners. Assume, for simplicity of discussion, that the machine in the current example has a useful life of three years with no salvage value; that A and B share income equally; and that partnership book and taxable income, before depreciation on the machine, is $20,000. After deducting straight-line depreciation, *book income* is as follows:

Book Income before Depreciation	$ 20,000
Depreciation (Book)	(5,000)
Net Income per Books	$ 15,000

With equal income sharing, $7,500 is allocated to each partner for accounting purposes. For tax purposes, though, the partnership reports the following *taxable income*:

Taxable Income before Depreciation	$ 20,000
Depreciation (Tax)	(2,000)
Taxable Income	$ 18,000

How much income should each partner report for tax purposes? One possibility is $9,000 each, reflecting equal division. If taxable income is divided equally, though, Partner B will be taxed on A's previously unrecognized and untaxed gain. This potentially inequitable situation must be remedied as follows.

> Depreciation or amortization on the **difference between the tax bases and fair values of partners' contributed assets** is assigned to those partners when their shares of *taxable income* are calculated.

To illustrate this procedure, recall that A had an *economic gain* of $9,000 (= $15,000 fair market value − $6,000 tax basis) when the machine was transferred to the partnership and that the gain was not taxed. To avoid having B pay part of the tax attributable to A's gain, tax law requires that *taxable income* be allocated as follows:

	A	B	Total
Book Income Divided Equally	$ 7,500	$ 7,500	$ 15,000
Adjustment Resulting from Lower Tax Basis of Machine—Allocated to Partner A	3,000	—	3,000
Taxable Income	$ 10,500	$ 7,500	$ 18,000

In this way, the tax effect of the $9,000 gain that went untaxed when A transferred the machine to the partnership is attributed solely to A. By including the $3,000 annual difference between book and tax depreciation in A's share of partnership taxable income, B is relieved of the tax on this amount.

TAX BASIS OF PARTNERSHIP INTEREST

The **tax basis of each partner's interest** begins with the tax basis of property contributed to the partnership. This amount is increased by the partner's share of taxable income, and is decreased by the partner's share of losses and by amounts withdrawn from the partnership. In addition, *each partner's share of partnership liabilities[6] is considered part of the tax basis of the partner's interest*. The logic of this provision is that, under the unlimited liability provision of general partnership law, a partner's capital plus his/her share of the partnership liabilities indicates the total amount the partner has at risk. This definition of the tax basis of a partner's interest is clearly different from the accounting definition of partner's capital.

Tax law permits partners to deduct their share of partnership losses up to the tax basis of their partnership interest. Suppose that Keller and Lehman are equal partners whose partnership interests, excluding liabilities, have tax bases of $4,000 and $2,800, respectively. Suppose that the partnership has liabilities of $6,000, and that there is a net tax loss for the year of $15,000. Although each partner's share of the loss is $7,500, the loss deductible on their individual income tax returns is limited to $7,000 for Keller (= $4,000 capital + $3,000 liabilities) and $5,800 for Lehman (= $2,800 + $3,000).

---

[6] We assume for this discussion that all liabilities of the partnership are such that creditors may proceed against the individual partners when collection cannot be made from the partnership. Such liabilities are termed **liabilities with recourse**. On the other hand, **nonrecourse liabilities** are those where the creditor typically has a security interest in some asset of the partnership, but no ability to collect from the individuals. The effect of nonrecourse liabilities on partnership taxation is beyond the scope of this appendix.

In an illustration presented earlier in the chapter, Prince and Quinn formed a partnership. Prince contributed $30,000 in cash, while Quinn contributed land and a building having a fair market value of $75,000, subject to a mortgage of $35,000 which the partnership assumed. Recall the three ways of determining the partners' initial capital for accounting purposes:

Capital Accounts Based on:	Prince	Quinn
Net Assets Invested	$ 30,000	$ 40,000
Equal Interests, Bonus Method	35,000	35,000
Equal Interests, Goodwill Method	40,000	40,000

Regardless of the method used for accounting purposes, the *initial tax basis of each partnership interest* is calculated as follows:

> Individual's tax basis in assets transferred
> + Share of liabilities assumed *from* others
> − Share of liabilities assumed *by* others
> = **Initial tax basis of partnership interest**.

If the tax basis of the land and building is equal to the fair market value of $75,000, we get the following result:

	Prince	Quinn
Individual's Basis in Assets Transferred	$ 30,000	$ 75,000
Liabilities Assumed from (by) Others	17,500	(17,500)
Tax Basis of Partnership Interest	$ 47,500	$ 57,500

These amounts result because, by having the partnership assume the $35,000 mortgage, Prince in effect assumes half of Quinn's previous obligation. We may view these same amounts in another manner, which may more clearly indicate the fact that the tax basis of a partnership interest includes the partner's share of partnership liabilities:

	Prince	Quinn
Basis in Net Assets Transferred	$ 30,000	$ 40,000
Share of Partnership Liabilities	17,500	17,500
Tax Basis of Partnership Interest	$ 47,500	$ 57,500

If the tax basis of the land and building had not been $75,000, the basis of Quinn's interest, but not Prince's, would be affected accordingly. Suppose Quinn's tax basis in the land and building was $52,000. The tax basis of each partner's interest is as follows:

	Prince	Quinn
Individual's Basis in Assets Transferred	$ 30,000	$ 52,000
Liabilities Assumed from (by) Others	17,500	(17,500)
Tax Basis of Partnership Interest	$ 47,500	$ 34,500

As the partnership pays off the $35,000 mortgage, the tax bases of the partners' interests are correspondingly reduced. Similarly, as the partnership incurs new liabilities, the tax bases are increased. In effect, incurring liabilities is treated as an investment by the partners, and repaying liabilities is treated as a distribution to partners. Partnership liabilities can logically be viewed as individual partners' liabilities, since the partners are legally liable for them.

The tax basis of the partner's interest is particularly important when there is a loss. As mentioned, tax law permits a partner to deduct a loss only to the extent of the tax basis; that is, the tax basis cannot become negative. Note, however, that even if the partner's *capital account* for accounting purposes is *negative*, the partner's *tax basis*—capital account for tax purposes plus the partner's share of partnership liabilities—may be *positive*.

QUESTIONS

Q15.1 Define *partnership* and identify the information that a partnership agreement contains.

Q15.2 When a partnership is formed it is governed by the Uniform Partnership Act. Among other things, the Act calls for equal sharing of profits and losses by the partners. How can partners who seek *unequal* sharing of profits and losses override the Act? If partners wish to limit their personal liability, how can they do so?

Q15.3 Many professional service firms are organized as partnerships. What advantages are associated with options available to those groups of professionals who prefer *not* to be treated as general or limited partnerships?

Q15.4 Describe briefly the power of a partner to bind fellow partners in business contracts. What is meant by saying that all partners are liable jointly and severally?

Q15.5 Three individuals come to you for advice on starting a new business. They wish to avoid as much paperwork and legal fees as possible. What pitfalls might they face?

Q15.6 1. X and Y are forming a partnership. X invests assets worth $100,000, and Y invests assets worth $120,000. Prepare the journal entry to record the formation.
　　　2. If X and Y agree that each is to have a 50 percent interest in partnership capital, discuss two ways to record the investments described in No. 1.

Q15.7 Suppose you are charged with analyzing the financial statements of a small partnership applying for a loan. What peculiar features of partnership accounting should you be familiar with?

Q15.8 Explain the difference between the terms *partners' salaries* and *partners' drawings*.

Q15.9 Select the best answer for each of the following multiple choice questions:

　　　1. Partners Cox and Kaler share profits and losses equally after each has been credited in all circumstances with annual salary allowances of $15,000 and $12,000, respectively. Under this arrangement, Cox will benefit by $3,000 more than Kaler in which of the following circumstances?

   a. Only if the partnership has earnings of $27,000 or more for the year.
   b. Only if the partnership does not incur a loss for the year.
   c. In all earnings or loss situations.
   d. Only if the partnership has earnings of at least $3,000 for the year.
2. Partners Hutton and Elbert share profits in a 2:1 ratio, respectively. Each partner receives an annual salary allowance of $6,000. If the salaries are recorded in the accounts of the partnership as an expense rather than treated as a division of net income, the total amount allocated to each partner for salaries and net income would be
   a. less for both Hutton and Elbert.
   b. unchanged for both Hutton and Elbert.
   c. more for Hutton and less for Elbert.
   d. more for Elbert and less for Hutton.
3. If A is the total capital of a partnership before the admission of a new partner, B is the total capital of the partnership after the admission of a new partner, C is the amount of the new partner's investment, and D is the amount of capital credited to the new partner, then there is
   a. a bonus to the new partner if $B = A + C$ and $D < C$.
   b. goodwill to the old partners if $B > (A + C)$ and $D = C$.
   c. neither bonus nor goodwill if $B = A - C$ and $D > C$.
   d. goodwill to the new partner if $B > (A + C)$ and $D < C$.
4. If E is the total capital of a partnership before the admission of a new partner, F is the total capital of the partnership after the admission of the new partner, G is the amount of the new partner's investment, and H is the amount of capital credited to the new partner, then there is
   a. goodwill to the new partner if $F > (E + G)$ and $H < G$.
   b. goodwill to the old partners if $F = E + G$ and $H > G$.
   c. a bonus to the new partner if $F = E + G$ and $H > G$.
   d. neither bonus nor goodwill if $F > (E + G)$ and $H > G$.
   (AICPA adapted)

Q15.10 Identify and briefly discuss two ways a new partner can enter an existing partnership.

Q15.11 Alice, Thelma, and Dee are partners with capital balances of $50,000, $30,000, and $20,000, respectively. The partners share profits and losses equally. For an investment of $50,000 cash, Mary is to be admitted as a partner with a one-fourth interest in capital and profits. Based on this information, the amount of Mary's investment can best be justified by which of the following?

   1. Mary will receive a bonus from the other partners upon her admission to the partnership.
   2. Assets of the partnership were overvalued immediately prior to Mary's investment.
   3. The book value of the partnership's net assets was less than their fair market value immediately prior to Mary's investment.
   4. Mary is apparently bringing goodwill into the partnership, and her capital account will be credited for the appropriate amount.

If Mary invested $20,000 (rather than $50,000) for a one-fourth interest in capital and profits, how could you justify the amount of her investment using (1) the bonus method and (2) the goodwill method?

• **Q15.12** *(Appendix)* Eisenman is investing securities worth $15,000 in a new partnership. She purchased these securities several years ago for $6,000, which became her tax basis. Corman, the other (equal) partner, does not suggest any change in the terms of the proposed partnership agreement which provide that the partnership's allocation of taxable income shall be identical to its allocation of accounting income. Assuming Corman is subject to a 40 percent tax rate, what is the impact of this decision on Corman?

EXERCISES

E15.1 **Accrual Basis Trial Balance** The Ellis Housecleaning Service keeps its books on the cash basis. Partners Bob and Ray agreed that they will share profits and losses via salaries of $35,000 and $25,000, respectively; remaining profits and losses will be shared equally. They prepare the following trial balance at December 31, 19X5, the end of their first year of operations.

Cash	$ 18,000
Temporary Investments	25,000
Equipment (4-year life, salvage value: $2,000)	40,000
Note Payable, 12%	(10,000)
Capital—Bob	(32,000)
Capital—Ray	(7,000)
Sales	(68,000)
Interest Income	(1,000)
Wages Expense	22,000
Supplies Expense	12,700
Interest Expense	300
	$ 0

Additional information:

1. Wages earned by employees but unpaid amount to $3,500.
2. Supplies that cost $3,700 are on hand.
3. Services billed but not collected are $15,000.
4. Temporary investments yield 8% and pay interest on the first day of each quarter.
5. Interest on the note payable is due on the first day of each month.

REQUIRED: Prepare a trial balance for the Ellis Housecleaning Service on the accrual basis of accounting.

E15.2 **Cash to Accrual Conversions** Moretti Auto Repair maintains its books on a cash basis. Selected account balances for 19X2 show the following:

Sales Revenue	$ 71,600
Wages Paid to Employees	11,000
Parts and Supplies Purchased	21,300
Insurance Expense	1,500

At the end of the year, the Moretti brothers make a note of (but do not record) various information:

	12/31/X2	12/31/X1
Owed to Suppliers	$ 2,200	$ 1,800
Owed to Employees	600	800
Owed by Customers	3,700	1,400
Unexpired Insurance	200	100
Parts and Supplies on Hand	900	1,200

REQUIRED: Calculate sales revenue, wages expense, parts and supplies expense, and insurance expense, using an accrual basis.

E15.3 Partnership Formation On March 1, 19X7, Rowen and Evans formed a partnership with each contributing assets having the following fair market values:

	Rowen	Evans
Cash	$ 70,000	$ 70,000
Machinery and Equipment	25,000	75,000
Building	—	225,000
Furniture and Fixtures	10,000	—

The building is subject to a mortgage loan of $180,000, which is to be assumed by the partnership. The partnership agreement provides that Rowen and Evans share profits and losses 30 percent and 70 percent, respectively.

REQUIRED:

1. Compute the balance in each partner's capital account on March 1, 19X7, if the partners do not specify any capital relationship.
2. Compute the balance in each partner's capital account if the partners agree that each is to have a 50 percent interest in partnership capital, and they specify the bonus approach to recording the formation.
3. Compute the balances as in No. 2, except the partners specify the goodwill approach. *(AICPA adapted)*

E15.4 Partnership Formation Max, Nat and Roberta formed a partnership to operate a dry-cleaning business. They agreed to share initial capital and subsequent income in a 3:2:1 ratio. Each partner's contributions to the new venture are listed next.

Max: $20,000 cash, dry-cleaning equipment worth $150,000 and the ability to keep the equipment in good operating condition.

Nat: $40,000 cash and extensive experience in the dry-cleaning business.

Roberta: $15,000 cash and a 2-year $60,000 note, payable to the firm, with 12% interest on the unpaid balance.

REQUIRED:

1. Record the formation using the goodwill approach.
2. Record the formation using the bonus approach.

E15.5 **Compute Partnership Net Income** Ralph Greene, a partner in the Brite Partnership, has a 30 percent participation in partnership profits and losses. Greene's capital account had a net decrease of $60,000 during the calendar year 19X4. During 19X4, Greene withdrew $130,000 (charged against his capital account) and contributed property valued at $25,000 to the partnership.

REQUIRED: Compute the net income of the Brite Partnership for 19X4.
(AICPA adapted)

E15.6 **Partnership Income Allocation** On January 1, 19X7, Melvin and Lacey formed a partnership with each contributing $75,000 cash. The partnership agreement provided that Melvin would receive a guaranteed salary of $20,000 and that partnership profits and losses (computed after deducting Melvin's salary) would be shared equally for the year ended December 31, 19X7. The partnership's operations resulted in a net income of $2,000; Melvin's entire salary was paid in cash during 19X7.

REQUIRED:

1. Compute the balance in Melvin's partnership capital account as of December 31, 19X7.
2. Compute the balance in Melvin's partnership capital account as of December 31, 19X7, assuming net income of $42,000.
    (AICPA adapted)

E15.7 **Partnership Income Allocation—Various Options** The January 1, 19X0, balance sheet of the partnership of Linda Kingston and Jeannette Allen is shown below. The partnership reported revenues of $80,000 and expenses of $55,000 for 19X0. Neither partner withdrew funds from the partnership during the year. Kingston invested $8,000 in the firm on June 28, 19X0.

Assets		**Liabilities and Capital**	
Cash	$ 20,000	Liabilities	$ 60,000
Other Assets	180,000	Capital—Kingston	56,000
		Capital—Allen	84,000
	$ 200,000		$ 200,000

REQUIRED: Compute the December 31, 19X0, capital balance for each partner under each of the following assumptions:

1. The partnership agreement does not specify how income is to be divided.
2. The partnership agreement specifies that Kingston receives 65 percent of income and Allen 35 percent.
3. The partnership agreement specifies that income is divided equally after paying each partner 10 percent interest on her weighted average capital balance.
4. The partnership agreement specifies that Kingston and Allen receive salaries of $12,000 and $8,000, respectively, and that each partner receives 5 percent interest on her capital balance at the beginning of the year. Salary and interest allocations are to be fully implemented if they exceed total income. Any remaining income is to be divided equally.

E15.8 **Multiple Income Allocation Provisions** Partners Judi, Ken and Lee agreed to the following provisions for sharing profit or loss from their partnership:

1. Judi, Ken and Lee receive salaries of $22,000, $18,000 and $30,000, respectively.
2. Interest on average capital investment is credited at the rate of 12% per annum.
3. Residual profit or loss is shared in the ratio 4:5:1.
4. All provisions are to be fully implemented.

The average capital investments for the year are:

Judi	$ 200,000
Ken	300,000
Lee	100,000

REQUIRED:

1. Prepare a schedule to allocate partnership income of $180,000.
2. Repeat 1. for income of $116,000.
3. Refer to 1. Suppose Judi, as managing partner, is entitled to a bonus of 10% of profit after the bonus but before other allocation provisions. Without re-doing the complete schedule, calculate the effect of the bonus on the net allocation to Judi and the other partners.

E15.9 **Admission of New Partner** Lancer and Day are partners with capital balances of $80,000 and $40,000, respectively. The partners share profits and losses in the ratio of 6:4, respectively. The partners agree to admit Corey, upon his investment of $30,000, as a partner with a one-third interest in capital and profits and losses.

REQUIRED: Compute the balances in the capital accounts of Lancer, Day, and Corey after Corey's admission, assuming that the parties agree that the admission is to be recorded without recognizing goodwill.
(AICPA adapted)

E15.10 **Compute Amount of Investment** The following balance sheet is for the Amos, Grant, and Derrick partnership. The partners share profits and losses in the ratio of 5:3:2, respectively.

Cash	$ 30,000	Liabilities	$ 70,000
Other Assets	270,000	Capital—Amos	140,000
		Capital—Grant	80,000
		Capital—Derrick	10,000
	$ 300,000		$ 300,000

The partnership wishes to admit Martin as a new partner with a one-fifth interest.

REQUIRED: Compute the amount of cash or other assets Martin should contribute if the partners agree that the admission is to be recorded without recognizing goodwill or bonus.
(AICPA adapted)

E15.11   Admission of New Partner Felix and Hubert are partners who share profits and losses equally in a highly successful partnership. The capital accounts of Felix and Hubert are currently $90,000 and $60,000, respectively. Taylor wishes to join the firm and offers to invest $70,000 for a one-fourth interest in the capital and profits and losses of the firm.

REQUIRED: Compute the balances in the capital accounts of Felix, Hubert, and Taylor after Taylor's admission, assuming

1. the parties agree that the admission is to be recorded by recognizing goodwill.
2. the parties agree that the admission is to be recorded without recognition of goodwill. *(AICPA adapted)*

E15.12   Admission of New Partner Partners Ivan and Juan share income in a 3:2 ratio and have capital balances of $70,000 and $32,000, respectively. Knute proposes to invest $50,000 in the firm for a 25% interest in capital and income.

REQUIRED:

1. Record Knute's admission using the bonus method.
2. Record Knute's admission using the goodwill method.
3. Suppose instead that Knute purchases 25% of each partner's interest by paying them a total of $40,000 directly. Record Knute's admission using the implied goodwill method.

E15.13   Bonus and Goodwill Formulas Each of the following independent situations shows either a bonus or goodwill recognized upon admission of a new partner to an existing partnership.

REQUIRED: In each case, calculate the amount of bonus or goodwill that would have been recognized if the alternative accounting treatment had been followed. That is, if the bonus method was used, calculate the goodwill to be recognized under the goodwill method and vice versa.

1. D and E admit F as an equal partner. A bonus to F of $3,000 is recorded.
2. O, P, and Q admit R as a new partner. R is to have a one-third interest in the new partnership. Goodwill of $6,000 is attributed to R.
3. H purchases a one-fifth interest in the partnership of I, J, and K. Goodwill of $6,000 to the existing partners is recorded.
4. L and M admit N as an equal partner for $10,000. No goodwill is recognized under the goodwill method.

E15.14   Admission of New Partner Presented below is the condensed balance sheet of the partnership of Kane, Clark, and Lane, who share profits or losses in the ratio of 6:3:1, respectively:

Cash	$ 85,000	Liabilities	$ 80,000
Other Assets	415,000	Capital—Kane	252,000
		Capital—Clark	126,000
		Capital—Lane	42,000
	$ 500,000		$ 500,000

REQUIRED:

1. The assets and liabilities on the above balance sheet are fairly valued, and the partnership wishes to admit Bayer with a 25 percent interest in the capital and profits and losses without recording goodwill or bonus. How much should Bayer contribute in cash or other assets?
2. Assume that the partners agree instead to sell Bayer 20 percent of their respective capital and profit and loss interests for a total payment of $90,000. The payment by Bayer is to be made directly to the individual partners. The partners agree that implied goodwill is to be recorded prior to the acquisition by Bayer. What are the capital balances of Kane, Clark, and Lane, respectively, after the acquisition by Bayer?

(AICPA adapted)

E15.15 Tax Aspects of Partnerships *(Appendix)* Burriss, Culpepper, and Downstreet formed a partnership with each individual contributing assets as shown here:

	Cost	Fair Value
Burriss—Cash	$ 15,000	$ 15,000
Culpepper—Equipment	13,000	15,000
Accumulated Depreciation	(3,000)	—
Downstreet—Land	30,000	30,000

The equipment had an original life of 13 years, has no salvage value, and has been depreciated on a straight-line basis for 3 years. The land has an outstanding mortgage of $15,000, which the partnership assumes.

The partners agreed to share profits and losses equally. Profit for the first year was $6,000 before depreciation.

REQUIRED:

1. Compute the tax basis of each partner's interest in the partnership at the date of formation.
2. Compute the taxable income of each partner, assuming Culpepper is to bear any tax related to the equipment appreciation.

PROBLEMS

P15.1 Worksheet—Cash to Accrual Conversions Jacob Petersen owns a warehouse which he operates as a sole proprietorship. He has applied for a bank loan to expand the facilities. Jacob maintains his accounting records on a cash basis. The lending institution has requested a balance sheet and income statement for the proprietorship prepared on the accrual basis. Below is the trial balance of accounts in the general ledger as of December 31, 19X5.

General Ledger Trial Balance
December 31, 19X5

	Debit	Credit
Cash	$ 170,000	
Investments	425,000	
Property, Plant, and Equipment	1,200,000	
Accumulated Depreciation		$ 350,000
Payroll Taxes Withheld		12,000
Capital, Jacob Peterson		1,318,000
Rental and Service Income		400,000
Operating Expenses	220,000	
Insurance Expense	30,000	
Administrative Expenses	70,000	
Investment Income		35,000
Total	$ 2,115,000	$ 2,115,000

Details of unrecorded accruals and other information follow:

	December 31	
	19X4	**19X5**
Accounts Receivable—Rents and Services (includes doubtful accounts totaling $700 at December 31, 19X5; all doubtful accounts were for 19X5 services)	$ 27,000	$ 37,000
Rental Deposits from Lessees ($7,500 of 19X5 amount was received in 19X5 and recorded in Rental and Service Income; $600 of the 19X4 amount was applied to final month's rentals in 19X5)	2,100	9,000
Interest Income Receivable from Investments	1,000	2,600
Market Value of Investments (all investments are corporate bonds)	460,000	475,000
Accounts Payable (Operating Expenses)	8,000	9,700

The amount in the Insurance Expense account is a February 1 payment for insurance premiums: $6,000 for a one-year liability insurance policy and $24,000 for a three-year fire insurance policy. The coverage under both policies commenced on January 1.

Payroll Taxes Withheld includes employees' FICA taxes of $800. Administrative Expenses includes a payment of $300 for 19X4 employer FICA taxes.

REQUIRED: Prepare a worksheet for the preparation of financial statements on the accrual basis. The worksheet should have debit and credit columns for each of the following: (1) trial balance (cash basis); (2) adjustments; (3) income statement (accrual basis); (4) balance sheet (accrual basis).
(AICPA adapted)

P15.2 Partnership Formation: Working Backward Brian and two other friends from college decide to form a CPA firm specializing in forensic accounting. The three had worked for different Big Six firms for several years and accumulated a wealth of experience as well as a variety of other assets the new firm could use. After agreeing on a 2:3:1 capital and income ratio, the three listed what they intend to contribute to the new firm:

Brian: Cash ($12,000), office and computer equiprment ($18,000), knowledge of potential client base

Jennifer: Cash ($15,000), tax library ($11,000), specialized tax skills

Eric: Note, payable to the firm ($10,000), extensive computer audit experience

Pro-forma capital balances under three formation scenarios appear below.

	Scenario #1	Scenario #2	Scenario #3
Capital—Brian	$ 30,000	$ 22,000	$ 36,000
Capital—Jennifer	45,000	33,000	54,000
Capital—Eric	15,000	11,000	18,000

REQUIRED:

1. In each scenario, identify the flow of bonuses or the amount and beneficiaries of goodwill recorded.
2. Discuss the relative advisability of the three scenarios, paying particular attention to their effects on the new firm's future profitability and leverage (or credit-worthiness).

P15.3 Formation of Partnership Augustus Berrini, the sole proprietor of the Berrini Company, is planning to expand the company and establish a partnership with Fiedler and Wade. The partners plan to share profits and losses as follows: Berrini, 50 percent; Fiedler, 25 percent; Wade 25 percent. They also agree that the beginning capital balances of the partnership will reflect this same relationship.

Berrini asked Fiedler to join the partnership because his many business contacts are expected to be valuable during the expansion. Fiedler is also contributing $28,000. Wade is contributing $11,000 and a block of marketable securities which the partnership expects to liquidate as needed during the expansion. The securities, which cost Wade $42,000, are currently worth $57,500.

Berrini's investment in the partnership is the Berrini Company. He plans to pay off the notes with his personal assets. The other partners have agreed that the partnership will assume the accounts payable and the mortgage. The balance sheet for the Berrini Company follows. The three partners agree that the inventory is worth $85,000; the equipment is worth half its original cost; the building and land are worth $65,000 and $25,000, respectively; and the allowance established for doubtful accounts is correct.

Berrini Company
Balance Sheet
Date of Partnership Formation

Assets			Liabilities		
Cash	$	7,000	Accounts Payable	$	53,000
Accounts Receivable (Net) . . .		48,000	Notes Payable		7,000
Inventory		72,000	Mortgage Payable		55,000
Equipment (Net of $12,000					$ 115,000
Accumulated Depreciation) .		18,000			
Building (Net of $20,000					
Accumulated Depreciation) .		40,000	**Owner's Equity**		
Land		15,000	Capital, Berrini		85,000
			Total Liabilities and		
Total Assets	$	200,000	Owner's Equity . . .	$	200,000

REQUIRED: Prepare the balance sheet of the partnership on the date of formation under each of the following independent assumptions:

1. The partners agree to follow the bonus method to record the formation.
2. The partners agree to follow the goodwill approach to record the formation.

P15.4 Partners' Disputes Over Income Allocation Bill, Al and Hillie generally get along well as business associates in their consulting firm. Recently, however, the income-sharing provisions of their partnership agreement have become contentious. With these provisions, partnership net income is shared as follows:

	Salary	Interest on Capital	% of Remainder
Bill	$ 80,000	4%	20%
Al	50,000	4%	40%
Hillie	0	20%	40%

Note: Salary and interest provisions are to be implemented in that order only to the extent of the available income.

Hillie was originally to have been a silent partner, an investor without active participation in the business. Al, on the other hand, was to have had a large voice in business decisions as well as a modest capital investment. As it turns out, Al has been shunted to the side whereas Hillie appears to be running the business much of the time. Bill spends a lot of time on practice development and generates few chargeable hours.

In the last three years, partnership income and partners' average capital balances were:

Partnership Net Income			Average Capital Balances		
19X3	**19X2**	**19X1**	**Bill**	**Al**	**Hillie**
$ 125,000	$ 160,000	$ 185,000	$ 30,000	$ 50,000	$ 134,000

REQUIRED:

1. Explain why the income-sharing provisions have become contentious.
2. Would a provision allowing Hillie a 25% bonus of net income before any allocations satisfy her? What would Al's reaction be?
3. Suppose the partners adopt the provision in 2. for 19X4 except that the bonus is based on 25% of net income before allocations but after the bonus. Net income in 19X4 amounts to $175,000 and average capital balances are unchanged. Compare the 19X4 income allocations with and without the bonus. Comment on the income redistribution you observe.

P15.5 Income Allocation; Schedule of Changes in Capital Accounts A December 31, 19X5, balance sheet for the Silverstone Partnership is shown below:

Silverstone Partnership
Balance Sheet
December 31, 19X5

Assets		Liabilities and Capital	
Cash	$ 10,000	Accounts Payable	$ 60,000
Accounts Receivable .	50,000	Long-Term Liabilities .	100,000
Equipment	85,000	Capital—Lamke	55,000
Buildings	125,000	Capital—Perez	80,000
Land	30,000	Capital—Sills	5,000
		Total Liabilities and	
Total Assets	$ 300,000	Capital	$ 300,000

Additional information:

1. The partners agreed that each will be paid 5 percent interest on his or her capital balance as of the beginning of the year.
2. Salaries are as follows: Lamke, $15,000; Perez, $20,000; and Sills, $10,000.
3. Sills is to receive a bonus of 10 percent of income before salaries, bonus, and interest to partners.
4. Any income remaining after salaries, bonus, and interest to partners is to be allocated equally.
5. During 19X5, Lamke withdrew $3,300 from the firm. All other allocations to Lamke for salary, interest, and profit were retained in the business.
6. Perez withdrew all but $10,000 of 19X5 allocations.
7. In 19X5 Sills withdrew $15,000 and all salary, bonus, interest, and profit allocations.
8. Total capital investment at the beginning of the year was $120,000.
9. Income for 19X5 after deducting interest to partners but before deductions for salaries and bonus was $90,000.

REQUIRED: Prepare a schedule of changes in capital accounts for the partners in the Silverstone Partnership. The schedule should begin with capital balances as of January 1, 19X5.

P15.6 Financial Statement Effects of Partnership Expansion Graham and Hyde currently share profits and losses in a 3:1 ratio and are considering admitting Ingalls as a new partner with a 20% interest in capital as well as in profits and losses. The different approaches to accounting for partnership expansion affect the financial statements of the new partnership. Condensed balance sheets for the Graham/Hyde partnership and the Graham/Hyde/Ingalls partnership under alternative admission approaches appear below.

	G/H	G/H/I #1	G/H/I #2	G/H/I #3	G/H/I #4
Cash and Receivables .	$ 37,000	$ 37,000	$ 77,000	$ 77,000	$ 49,000
Other Assets	142,000	142,000	142,000	222,000	150,000
	$ 179,000	$ 179,000	$ 219,000	$ 299,000	$ 199,000
Accounts Payable . . .	$ 48,000	$ 48,000	$ 48,000	$ 48,000	$ 48,000
Long-Term Debt	51,000	51,000	51,000	51,000	51,000
Capital—Graham . . .	50,000	40,000	62,000	110,000	50,000
Capital—Hyde	30,000	24,000	34,000	50,000	30,000
Capital—Ingalls	—	16,000	24,000	40,000	20,000
	$ 179,000	$ 179,000	$ 219,000	$ 299,000	$ 199,000

REQUIRED:

1. As a user of financial statements in credit-granting or investment decisions, which of the above balance sheets look strongest? Why? Discuss any red flags that whet your appetite for additional information.
2. Explain whether Ingalls will likely prefer a particular alternative. Which one?
3. Reconstruct the journal entries recording the four alternatives.

P15.7 Income Restatements; Admission Under Goodwill Approach Wright and Koehler formed a partnership on January 1, 19X6. They agreed to admit Robertson as a partner on January 1, 19X9. The books for the year ending December 31, 19X8, are closed. The following additional information is available:

1. Wright and Koehler shared profits equally until January 1, 19X8, when they agreed to share profits 40 percent and 60 percent, respectively. The profit-sharing ratio after Robertson is admitted will be 32 percent to Wright, 48 percent to Koehler, and 20 percent to Robertson.
2. Robertson will invest $25,000 cash for a one-fifth interest in the capital of the partnership.
3. The partnership reported earnings of $22,000 in 19X6, $35,000 in 19X7, and $32,000 in 19X8.
4. The partnership of Wright and Koehler did not use accrual accounting for some items. It was agreed that before Robertson's admission is recorded, adjustments should be made in the accounts retroactively to report properly on the accrual basis of accounting.
5. Use of a modified cash basis of accounting led to overstatements of net income of $7,000 in 19X6 and $6,000 in 19X7 and an understatement of net income of $1,000 in 19X8.

REQUIRED:

1. Prepare a schedule presenting computation of the adjustments necessary to report Wright's and Koehler's correct capital account balances at December 31, 19X6, 19X7, and 19X8.
2. Assume the capital balances as originally reported on December 31, 19X8, were Wright, $66,100 and Koehler, $81,900. Adjust these capital balances to reflect accrual accounting and determine (a) Robertson's capital balance if admission is recorded under the goodwill approach and (b) the amount of goodwill to be recognized. *(AICPA adapted)*

P15.8   Admission—Various Cases Given below are account balances for the partnership of Simpson and Scott before the admission of a new partner, Lansing. Each case presents account balances of the partnership immediately after the admission of Lansing. The cases are independent of each other.

Balance Sheet Accounts	Balances before Lansing's Admission	Balances after Lansing's Admission				
		Case 1	Case 2	Case 3	Case 4	Case 5
Cash	$ 10,000	$ 10,000	$ 10,000	$ 20,000	$ 10,000	$ 30,000
Other Assets	80,000	130,000	80,000	80,000	170,000	80,000
Goodwill	10,000	10,000	10,000	10,000	30,000	20,000
Liabilities	(30,000)	(30,000)	(30,000)	(30,000)	(80,000)	(30,000)
Capital—Simpson . .	(35,000)	(42,500)	(35,000)	(30,000)	(35,000)	(40,000)
Capital—Scott	(35,000)	(42,500)	—	(30,000)	(35,000)	(40,000)
Capital—Lansing . .	—	(35,000)	(35,000)	(20,000)	(60,000)	(20,000)

REQUIRED: For each independent case, answer the following questions. Show supporting computations.

1. What method of accounting was used to record the admission (bonus, goodwill, neither)?
2. How much did Lansing invest in the partnership?
3. What percentage of ownership does Lansing have in the new partnership?

P15.9   Cash to Accrual Basis—Admission of Partner The partnership of Kraft, Mills, and Farmer engaged you to adjust its accounting records and convert them uniformly to the accrual basis in anticipation of admitting Ward as a new partner. Some accounts are on the accrual basis and others are on the cash basis. The partnership's books were closed at December 31, 19X6, by the bookkeeper, who prepared the general ledger trial balance that appears below.

Kraft, Mills, and Farmer
General Ledger Trial Balance
December 31, 19X6

	Debit	Credit
Cash	$ 10,000	
Accounts Receivable	40,000	
Inventory	26,000	
Land	9,000	
Buildings	50,000	
Accumulated Depreciation—Buildings		$ 2,000
Equipment	56,000	
Accumulated Depreciation—Equipment		6,000
Goodwill	5,000	
Accounts Payable		55,000
Allowance for Future Inventory Losses		3,000
Capital—Kraft		40,000
Capital—Mills		60,000
Capital—Farmer		30,000
Total	$ 196,000	$ 196,000

Your inquiries disclosed the following:

1. The partnership was organized on January 1, 19X5, with no provision in the partnership agreement for the distribution of partnership profits and losses. During 19X5, profits were distributed equally among the partners. The partnership agreement was amended effective January 1, 19X6, to provide for the following profit-and-loss-sharing ratio: Kraft, 50 percent; Mills, 30 percent; and Farmer, 20 percent. The amended partnership agreement also stated that the accounting records were to be maintained on the accrual basis and that any adjustments necessary for 19X5 should be allocated according to the 19X5 distribution of profits.

2. The following balances were not recorded as prepayments or accruals:

	December 31	
	19X6	19X5
Prepaid Insurance	$ 700	$ 650
Advances from Customers	200	1,100
Accrued Interest Payable	—	450

The advances from customers were recorded as sales in the year the cash was received.

3. In 19X6 the partnership recorded a provision of $3,000 for anticipated declines in inventory prices. You convinced the partners that the provision was inappropriate and the provision and related allowance should be removed from the books.

4. The partnership charged equipment purchased for $4,400 on January 3, 19X6, to expense. The equipment has an estimated life of ten years and an estimated salvage value of $400. The partnership depreciates its capitalized equipment under the double-declining-balance method.

5. The partners agreed to establish an allowance for doubtful accounts at 2 percent of current accounts receivable and 5 percent of past due accounts. At December 31, 19X5, the partnership had $54,000 of accounts receivable, of which only $4,000 was past due. At December 31, 19X6, 15 percent of accounts receivable was past due, of which $4,000 represented sales made in 19X5, and was generally considered collectible. The partnership had written off uncollectible accounts in the year the accounts became worthless as follows:

	Accounts Written Off	
	19X6	19X5
19X6 Accounts	$ 800	—
19X5 Accounts	1,000	$ 250

6. Goodwill was recorded on the books in 19X6 and credited to the partners' capital accounts in the profit-and-loss-sharing ratio in recognition of an increase in the value of the business resulting from improved sales volume. No amortization of goodwill was recorded. The partners agreed to write off the goodwill before admitting the new partner.

REQUIRED:

1. Prepare the journal entries to convert the accounting records to the accrual basis and to correct the books before admitting the new partner.
2. Without prejudice to your solution to No. 1 above, assume that the assets were properly valued and that the adjusted total of the partners' capital account balances at December 31, 19X6, was $140,000. On that date, Ward invested $55,000 in the partnership. Record the admission of Ward using the goodwill method. Ward is to be granted a one-fourth interest in the partnership. The other partners will retain their 50:30:20 income-sharing ratio for the remaining three-fourths interest.
   (AICPA adapted)

P15.10 Partnership Income Statement and Cash Flow Analysis The following trial balance has been prepared from the books of the Aston Refinishing Company at December 31, 19X1, the end of its first year of operations:

Cash	$ 9,000
Equipment (at cost; 5-year life, no salvage value)	12,000
Supplies Inventory	4,000
Prepaid Rent	3,000
Accounts Payable	(4,460)
Notes Payable	(10,000)
Partners' Capital	(6,160)
Revenues	(59,840)
Supplies Expense	9,500
Labor Expense	8,000
Salary Expense (Aston)	34,000
Interest Expense	960
	$ 0

Additional information:

1. Wages owed on December 31, 19X1 are $600.
2. Daniel Aston, the principal partner, earned a salary of $35,000 in 19X1. Of this amount, $1,000 is unpaid at December 31, 19X1.
3. Prepaid rent at December 31, 19X1 should be $1,000.
4. Semiannual interest of $720 on the note is due on February 28, 19X2. The note was taken out on January 2, 19X1. Two months' interest were paid on February 28, 19X1 and the first semiannual interest payment was made on August 31, 19X1.
5. Unrecorded billings to customers at December 31, 19X1 amount to $11,000. These are expected to be collected in full.

REQUIRED:

1. Prepare an income statement for the Aston Refinishing Company on the accrual basis of accounting after making adjustments suggested by the data.
2. Calculate the company's cash flow from operations.
3. As a potential new partner examining Aston's income and operating cash flow data, comment on the company's profitability and apparent quality of earnings.

P15.11 Partnership Accounting—Comprehensive You have been engaged to prepare financial statements for the partnership of Allison, Reed, and Werner as of June 30, 19X2. You obtained the following information from the partnership agreement as amended and from the accounting records:

1. The partnership was formed originally by Allison and Bailey on July 1, 19X1. At that date, the situation was as follows:
    a. Bailey contributed $400,000 cash.
    b. Allison contributed land, building, and equipment with fair market values of $110,000, $520,000, and $185,000, respectively. The land and building were subject to a mortgage securing an 8 percent per annum note (interest rate of similar notes at July 1, 19X1, was 8 percent). Quarterly payments of $5,000 plus interest are due on the note on January 1, April 1, July 1, and October 1 of each year. Allison made the July 1, 19X1, principal and interest payment personally. The partnership then assumed the obligation for the remaining $300,000 balance.
    c. The agreement further provided that Allison had contributed a certain intangible benefit to the partnership due to his many years of business activity in the area to be serviced by the new partnership. The assigned value of this intangible asset plus the net tangible assets he contributed gave Allison a 60 percent initial capital interest in the partnership. The intangible asset is amortized over ten years.
    d. Allison was designated the only active partner at an annual salary of $24,000 plus an annual bonus of 4 percent of net income after deducting his salary but before deducting the bonus and interest on partners' capital investments.
    e. Each partner is to receive a 6 percent return on his average capital investment. The average is based on the capital balances at the beginning of each month.
    f. All remaining profits or losses are to be shared equally.

2. On October 1, 19X1, Bailey sold his partnership interest and rights as of July 1, 19X1, to Werner for $370,000. Allison agreed to accept Werner as a partner if he would contribute sufficient cash to meet the October 1, 19X1, principal and interest payment on the mortgage note. Werner made the payment from personal funds.

3. On January 1, 19X2, Allison and Werner admitted a new partner, Reed. Reed invested $150,000 cash and received a 10 percent capital interest based on the July 1, 19X1, original investments of Allison and Bailey. The January 1, 19X2, capital balances of Allison and Werner were ignored for this calculation. At January 1, 19X2, the book values of the partnership's assets and liabilities approximated their fair market values. Reed contributed no intangible benefit to the partnership.

   Similar to the other partners, Reed is to receive a 6 percent return on his average capital investment. His investment also entitles him to 20 percent of the partnership's profits or losses as defined above. However, for the year ended June 30, 19X2, Reed will receive one-half of his pro rata share of the profits or losses.

4. The accounting records show that on February 1, 19X2, Miscellaneous Expenses had been charged $3,600 for payment of hospital expenses incurred by Allison's eight-year-old daughter.

5. Allison's salary was paid in one lump sum on June 29, 19X2, and charged to his drawing account. On June 1, 19X2, Werner made a $33,000 withdrawal. These are the only transactions recorded in the partners' drawing accounts.

6. Presented below is a trial balance summarizing the partnership's general ledger balances at June 30, 19X2. The general ledger has not been closed.

	Debit	Credit
Current Assets	$ 307,100	
Fixed Assets, Net	1,285,800	
Current Liabilities		$ 157,000
8% Mortgage Note Payable		290,000
Capital—Allison		515,000
Capital—Reed		150,000
Capital—Werner		400,000
Drawing—Allison	24,000	
Drawing—Reed	0	
Drawing—Werner	33,000	
Sales		872,600
Cost of Sales	695,000	
Administrative Expenses	16,900	
Miscellaneous Expenses	11,100	
Interest Expense	11,700	
	$ 2,384,600	$ 2,384,600

REQUIRED: Prepare a schedule of changes in the partners' capital accounts. Show supporting calculations.

(AICPA adapted)

P15.12 **Partners' Tax Bases and Taxable Income** *(Appendix)* Refer to the data in P15.3 concerning the formation of a partnership by Berrini, Fiedler, and Wade.

The equipment had an original life of five years with no salvage value. The building had an original life of thirty years, also with no salvage value. The straight-line method of depreciation is used.

Accounting net income for the first year of operations is $30,000. All of the inventory transferred from the Berrini Company was charged to cost of goods sold under the FIFO method. The marketable securities contributed by Wade were sold during the year for $65,000 (the $7,500 accounting gain is included in the net income figure cited above).

The partners agreed that accounting income will be divided according to the 50:25:25 percentage ratio. As the partnership realizes the gains or losses that were unrecognized at the time of the original transfer of assets, these will be included in the taxable income of the partner(s) who invested the assets.

REQUIRED:

1. Compute the tax basis of each partner's interest in the partnership at the date of formation.
2. Compute the taxable income to be reported by each partner.

CHAPTER 16

PARTNERSHIPS: CONTRACTION, TERMINATION, AND LIQUIDATION

CHAPTER PREVIEW

This chapter completes our discussion of accounting for partnerships. The following major topics are studied in this chapter:

- Retirement of a partner
- Introduction to partnership liquidations
- Simple liquidations
- Installment liquidations
- Other uses of the partnership form of business organization

The possibility of recognizing *goodwill* is encountered again in the partnership context when a partner retires, and is suspect because all parties to the retirement transaction are insiders. Accounting for partnership liquidations involves no new accounting principles. Rather, the emphasis is on determining the proper sequence of distributions to the partners when the liquidation extends over a period of time. Such a procedure is necessary to preserve equity among the partners, particularly when the liquidation fails to provide enough cash for each partner's capital investment to be recovered. Lastly, some variations in use of the partnership form of business organization are introduced.

A partnership terminates legally whenever the composition of the partnership changes, as in the admission of a new partner or the retirement or death of an existing partner. Accounting, however, is concerned with the economic entity rather than the legal entity. This chapter addresses one legal situation—legal dissolution of a partnership—with two economic interpretations: the partnership may continue as an economic entity or it may cease to exist.

When a partnership terminates legally but the business activities are maintained by a successor partnership, the economic entity is intact. This occurs when a partner leaves the business due to retirement, resignation, or death.

On the other hand, when the assets of a partnership are liquidated and distributed, the partnership ceases to exist as an economic entity. There are several possible reasons for this type of termination. Bankruptcy of the partnership leads to termination. Or the partners may have initially specified that the partnership would exist for only a limited time or until a certain purpose was accomplished. For example, a partnership is created to buy a tract of land and to develop and sell subdivision lots. When all lots are sold and paid for, the partnership is dissolved. In other cases, partners mutually agree to terminate a partnership because it is unsuccessful or because they wish to pursue other activities. In yet other cases, a partnership is converted to a sole proprietorship by the remaining partner or the partners decide to reorganize their business as a corporation.

RETIREMENT OF A PARTNER

Ownership composition of a partnership changes when a partner withdraws. Accounting for such changes varies, depending on whether the interest of the withdrawing partner is purchased by one or more remaining partners with their personal assets or by the partnership with partnership assets. Because the accounting treatment is similar regardless of the reason for withdrawal—resignation, retirement, or death—we discuss only the case of retirement.

PURCHASE WITH PERSONAL ASSETS

First consider the situation in which the remaining partners, as individuals, purchase the interest of the retiring partner with their personal assets. Because this transaction, which is between the retiring partner and the remaining partners, occurs outside the partnership, the only entry made on the partnership books is to transfer the capital balances. Suppose, for example, that the partners in KLM Associates have capital balances and income-sharing percentages as follows:

Partner	Capital Balance	Income Share
Keenan	$ 75,000	45%
Ludlow	60,000	30%
Morris	30,000	25%
Total	$ 165,000	100%

If Keenan and Ludlow buy Morris' interest for $60,000, Morris' $30,000 capital balance must be transferred to Keenan and Ludlow. If the purchasers retain their relative income-sharing ratio (45:30, or 3:2), $18,000 is credited to Keenan and $12,000 to Ludlow. The transfer of capital is recorded as follows:

Capital—Morris	30,000	
Capital—Keenan		18,000
Capital—Ludlow		12,000
To record Morris' retirement and purchase of her interest by Keenan and Ludlow.		

This treatment is similar to procedures discussed in Chapter 19 for admitting a new partner by purchase of an existing interest. In that case, however, the purchase transaction with an outside party could lead to recognition of implied goodwill on the partnership books. No outside party is involved in this retirement case; all participants are partners. Without the presence of an arm's-length transaction, the argument that market value has been determined and goodwill can be recognized is weak.

PURCHASE WITH PARTNERSHIP ASSETS

We now examine the situation in which the retiring partner receives assets directly from the partnership in settlement of that individual's capital interest. In effect, the partnership buys out the retiring partner. The remainder of this section explains procedures for dealing with this retirement scenario.

Determination of Payment to Retiring Partner

Settlement with a retiring partner should be based on the *fair value* of the partner's interest. There is no reason to expect that this value will equal the balance in the partner's capital account at time of retirement. Some equitable manner of determining the value of the retiring partner's interest, and hence the payment to the retiring partner, is needed. In general, we expect the partnership agreement to answer this question. When forming the partnership, the partners should consider and agree upon a method of valuing a partner's interest in the event of resignation, retirement, or death. They might decide that a formula, such as "5 times the partner's average share of income over the preceding 3 years, plus the balance in the capital account" is equitable. Or they might agree to base the value on an outside appraisal of the partnership's assets, both tangible and intangible. Whatever the partnership agreement specifies is used to determine the value of the retiring partner's interest. When the agreement is silent on the question of retirement, the parties must agree on valuation procedures at the time of retirement.

Accounting for Retirement

As stated above, payment of partnership assets to a retiring partner is not necessarily based on the balance in the retiring partner's capital account. Upon retirement, however, the capital account must be eliminated from the partnership books, and any differences between the payment and the capital balance accounted for.

The illustrations that follow assume that the retiring partner is paid with partnership cash. When part or all of the payment is made with other partnership assets, the assets are adjusted on the books to fair market value before their distribution to the retiring partner is recorded. Any difference between fair market value and book value is entered in the partners' capital accounts according to their income-sharing percentages.

Accounting for the retirement of a partner via distribution of partnership assets is similar to accounting for the admission of a new partner via direct investment in the partnership. In the simplest case, where payment to the retiring partner *does* equal that partner's capital balance, the retirement is recorded as follows:

> Capital—Retiring Partner   XXX
>   Cash (or Other Assets)   XXX
>   To record retirement of partner.

When the payment does *not* equal the capital balance, however, we must account for the difference by either the bonus or goodwill method. In discussing application of these methods, we return to the capital account and income-sharing data for KLM Associates:

Partner	Capital Balance	Income Share
Keenan	$ 75,000	45%
Ludlow	60,000	30%
Morris	30,000	25%
Total	$ 165,000	100%

Bonus Method. To illustrate the **bonus method of recording a partner's retirement**, assume that the partners determine that Morris, the retiring partner, is to receive $55,000, *more* than the capital balance. Under the bonus method, the $25,000 difference between the payment, $55,000, and the balance in Morris' capital account, $30,000, is treated as a bonus from Keenan and Ludlow to Morris. We use two entries to show this; the first records the bonus.

Capital—Keenan	15,000	
Capital—Ludlow	10,000	
Capital—Morris		25,000
To record retirement bonus to Morris.		

Note that the bonus is charged against Keenan and Ludlow in their respective income shares (45:30, or 3:2). The second entry records the payment to Morris with concurrent removal of Morris' capital account.

Capital—Morris	55,000	
Cash		55,000
To record retirement payment to Morris.		

If, instead, Morris is to receive *less* than the $30,000 capital balance, the difference is treated as a bonus from Morris to Keenan and Ludlow. For example, if Morris is paid $22,000, we can make the following single entry:

Capital—Morris	30,000	
Capital—Keenan		4,800
Capital—Ludlow		3,200
Cash		22,000
To record Morris' retirement under the bonus method.		

Now the bonus of $8,000 (= $30,000 − $22,000) is credited to the remaining partners according to their income-sharing ratio of 3:2, with $4,800 going to Keenan and $3,200 to Ludlow.

Thus the assumption underlying the bonus method of recording a partner's retirement is that a bonus is being paid either by or to the retiring partner. The bonus accounts for the difference between the settlement amount and the retiring partner's capital balance.

Goodwill Method. In contrast to the bonus method, use of the **goodwill method of recording a partner's retirement** calls for asset revaluations when there is a positive or negative difference between the settlement amount and the retiring partner's capital balance. When the difference is positive, existing assets may be written up, or intangible assets—goodwill—may be recorded, or both. Alternatively, when the payment is less than the capital balance, existing assets are written down. When existing assets are written up, retirement can be recorded under the goodwill method without making an entry to an account entitled Goodwill.

Two interpretations of the goodwill method exist: the *partial goodwill approach* and the *total goodwill approach*. Either can be applied to upward or downward asset revaluations. As noted earlier, use of the retirement payment to justify asset revaluations is less supportable in the retirement case than in the admission case. In the retirement case, the transaction is with one of the partners and cannot be viewed as arm's-length. Moreover, the retirement payment could represent an inducement to buy out an unproductive or dissident partner, and thus not be evidence of undervalued assets or goodwill at all.

Under the **partial goodwill approach**, revaluations of assets triggered by a partner's retirement are limited to the difference between the settlement price and the retiring partner's capital account. When the payment is greater than the capital balance, undervaluation of existing assets is corrected, with any remaining difference being attributed to goodwill. When the payment is less than the capital balance, assets are written down only to the extent of the difference, even though evidence may imply a need for further write-downs. With the partial goodwill approach, asset revaluations are charged or credited only to the capital account of the retiring partner; the capital accounts of other partners are unaffected. In contrast, the **total goodwill approach** calls for *all* asset revaluations apparent at the time of retirement to be recorded. These revaluations are charged or credited to the capital accounts of all partners according to their income-sharing ratio.

Illustration of Goodwill Approaches. An illustration will clarify the differences between these two approaches. Returning to the example of Morris' retirement from KLM Associates, assume that Morris receives $55,000, that Morris' capital account balance is $30,000, and that the partners determine that existing assets are appropriately valued. The *partial goodwill approach* calls for recognition of $25,000 of goodwill—the difference between the settlement price and the capital balance. The *total goodwill approach* follows the logic that if $25,000 of goodwill is attributable to Morris' 25 percent interest, then total goodwill of the firm is $100,000 (= $25,000/.25) This entire amount should be recognized and allocated to the partners according to their income-sharing percentages. Note that the income percentage, rather than the capital percentage, is used here to calculate the total goodwill. Capital percentages are useful for recording partnership formation but are generally meaningless thereafter, since different patterns of additions to and withdrawals from capital disturb any constant relationship among capital accounts.

The total goodwill approach yields total partnership capital, before Morris' retirement, of $265,000, the original $165,000 capital plus $100,000 of goodwill. In general, this result *cannot* be obtained by capitalizing the total payment to Morris. Capitalizing the total payment yields total partnership capital of $220,000 (= $55,000/.25); the results derived from capitalizing the excess paid to the retiring partner are the same *only* when the dollar balance in the retiring partner's capital account is exactly equal to that partner's income-sharing percentage times total capital.[1]

---

[1] To see this point, suppose that A, B and C have capital balances of $40,000, $40,000 and $20,000, respectively, and share income in the ratio 5:3:2. C is retiring and will receive a $30,000 payment from the partnership. Note that C's capital account balance of $20,000 equals C's 20 percent income share times total capital of $100,000 (= $40,000 + $40,000 + $20,000). *Partial goodwill* is $10,000 (= $30,000 − $20,000), and *total goodwill* is $50,000 (= $10,000/.2); total capital amounts to $150,000. Capitalizing the $30,000 payment to C also produces total capital of $150,000 (= $30,000/.2).

Calculation of total goodwill when partners retire does *not* parallel the Chapter 15 calculation of goodwill when new partners are admitted. In the retirement case, payment to a retiring partner includes the retiree's existing capital balance—not a fractional share of total capital—as well as any goodwill. If that payment is capitalized, and goodwill is determined by subtracting existing capital from the capitalized payment, the goodwill depends directly on the retiree's capital balance. Thus, the retiree could influence the amount of goodwill simply by making investments to, or withdrawals from, the capital account. In order to avoid this type of manipulation, total goodwill is determined in retirement situations from the goodwill attributable to the retiring partner rather than from the payment made to the retiring partner.

Exhibit 16.1 illustrates application of these two variations of the goodwill method under three independent assumptions regarding Morris' retirement from KLM Associates.

Assumption	Partial Goodwill Approach			Total Goodwill Approach		
Morris' capital balance	Goodwill	25,000		Goodwill	100,000	
= $30,000.	Capital—Morris		25,000	Capital—Keenan		45,000
Payment upon retirement				Capital—Ludlow		30,000
= $55,000.	Capital—Morris	55,000		Capital—Morris		25,000
Excess payment	Cash		55,000			
is attributable				Capital—Morris	55,000	
to goodwill.				Cash		55,000
Morris' capital balance	Assets	15,000		Assets	15,000	
= $30,000.	Capital—Morris		15,000	Capital—Keenan		6,750
Payment upon retirement				Capital—Ludlow		4,500
= $55,000.	Goodwill	10,000		Capital—Morris		3,750
Excess payment	Capital—Morris		10,000			
is attributable to				Goodwill	85,000	
undervalued existing	Capital—Morris	55,000		Capital—Keenan		38,250
assets ($15,000) and	Cash		55,000	Capital—Ludlow		25,500
to goodwill.				Capital—Morris		21,250
				Capital—Morris	55,000	
				Cash		55,000
Morris' capital balance	Capital—Morris	8,000		Capital—Keenan	14,400	
= $30,000.	Assets		8,000	Capital—Ludlow	9,600	
Payment upon retirement				Capital—Morris	8,000	
= $22,000.	Capital—Morris	22,000		Assets		32,000
Difference is	Cash		22,000			
attributable to				Capital—Morris	22,000	
overvalued assets.				Cash		22,000

EXHIBIT 16.1 COMPARISON OF THE PARTIAL AND TOTAL GOODWILL APPROACHES: KLM ASSOCIATES

AUTHORS' COMMENTARY

Arguments similar to those encountered in the controversy between the parent theory and the entity theory in consolidations exist with respect to the choice between the two goodwill variations in partnership accounting. Proponents of the partial goodwill approach argue that the partnership should record goodwill only to the extent that it is purchased or paid for, consistent with the parent theory of consolidations. Total goodwill advocates argue that the transaction provides evidence for inferring the total fair value of the partnership. Under the total goodwill approach, therefore, the accounts of the new entity (the successor partnership) should reflect this total fair value, consistent with the entity theory of consolidations. The argument essentially comes down to an entity question. If one views the successor partnership as a continuation of the old entity, then partial goodwill is reasonable. In contrast, if the successor partnership is viewed as a new entity, then total goodwill should be used. Following the concept of economic entity advocated in this text, we believe the partial goodwill approach is superior.

Accountants should evaluate the propriety of recognizing goodwill upon retirement on a case-by-case basis. The lack of an arm's-length transaction and the presence of motives for "excess" payments which do not signify the presence of goodwill must be kept in mind. Accountants should insist that other evidence supporting the existence of goodwill in the amount specified be provided to substantiate recording the goodwill.

INTRODUCTION TO PARTNERSHIP LIQUIDATIONS

Our discussion thus far has addressed situations in which a partnership continued as an economic entity despite legal dissolution through retirement of a partner. Now we turn to cases where a partnership terminates economically as well as legally. The business ceases operation, liquidates its assets, and makes distributions to creditors and, when possible, to the partners.

PRIORITIES FOR PAYMENTS

One issue central to the study of partnership liquidations is the sequence in which the proceeds derived from liquidating partnership assets are distributed. Outside creditors have claims against partnership assets. Partners have claims on partnership assets resulting from loans of personal assets to the partnership, investments in the partnership, and the right to share in undistributed income of the partnership.

Simply stated, *liquidation distributions go first to outside creditors and then to partners.* Technically, the sequence of liquidation distributions can be much more complicated.[2] With respect to partners' claims, the law identifies three subcategories: partners' loans, partners' invested capital, and partners' undistributed income. As a practical matter, though, there is little

---

[2] The first priority of distribution to outside creditors is subdivided among fully secured, partially secured, and unsecured creditors. Such distinctions are discussed in the section on bankruptcy accounting in Chapter 8. For purposes of illustrating partnership liquidation, this chapter treats all outside creditors as a single category.

difference between partners' invested capital and undistributed income, which is closed annually to the capital accounts. Drawings by partners are typically not differentiated as to withdrawals of capital or income. Similarly, there is little practical difference between partners' loans or partners' invested capital, even though *loans* to the partnership are to be paid off before *invested capital*.

To see this equivalence, note that because liquidation often produces losses when assets are sold, the balance of a partner's capital account could become negative when the losses are allocated. Partnership law requires partners to contribute sufficient capital to cover a **capital deficiency**—a debit balance in the capital account. If a partner with a capital deficiency has made loans from personal assets to the partnership, then the **right of offset** provides for the loan balance to be applied to the deficiency. Thus if the partner has insufficient invested capital, the loan payable *to* the partner, which otherwise would be paid off first, is treated as another component of invested capital and added to the capital balance. Similarly, a loan receivable *from* a partner is subtracted from the capital balance.

For example, suppose Partner A has a capital deficiency—an amount due to the partnership—of $8,000 and has made a loan to the partnership—an amount due to Partner A—of $10,000. The net effect of the *right of offset* enables Partner A to receive $2,000 of the liquidation proceeds. Similarly, if the partnership has a loan receivable from a partner—an amount due to the partnership—the right of offset calls for the loan to be deducted from the capital balance.

Although more complexity may exist in particular cases, we use the following **two-step priority sequence for distribution of cash in a partnership liquidation**:

1. Outside creditors
2. Partners' combined loans and capital

In partnership liquidations, therefore, the first concern is to meet obligations to outside creditors. After providing for payment of outside creditors, we focus on the proper sequence for distributing, to the partners, any remaining cash arising during the liquidation process.

RIGHTS OF CREDITORS

Both the creditors of the partnership and the creditors of individual partners have legal rights to available resources during a partnership liquidation. These rights influence the accounting procedures. *Creditors of the partnership* must first seek payment of their claims from partnership assets. If the partnership is insolvent, the partnership creditors may then seek payment from any partner. Thus a partner can be individually liable for any and all claims against the partnership. When an individual partner uses personal assets to pay partnership creditors, this payment is recorded as an investment of capital in the partnership.

Creditors of an individual partner must first seek payment of their claims from the individual. If the individual is insolvent, the creditors then have a claim against partnership assets remaining after satisfaction of partnership creditors. Any claim of a partner's personal creditors against partnership assets is limited to that partner's equity in the partnership.

The above provisions conform to the *Uniform Partnership Act* and may be restated from an asset viewpoint. In this form, they are often referred to as the *marshaling of assets rule*, and lead to the following payment priorities.

Under the **marshaling of assets rule**, assets of the *partnership* are applied in the following order:

1. Partnership creditors
2. Creditors of individual partners, but only to the extent of each partner's capital balance

Assets of the *individual partner* are applied in the following order:

1. Creditors of the individual partner
2. Partnership creditors
3. Other partners (to remedy a capital deficiency)

Under *common law and federal bankruptcy law*, however, a partner's fellow partners have the same standing as that partner's personal creditors. In states that have not adopted the Uniform Partnership Act, liquidated assets of the individual partner are applied in the following order:

1. The partner's creditors, including other partners
2. Partnership creditors

Following the *right of offset*, mentioned earlier, loans payable to a partner are offset against a capital deficiency. This effectively gives the other partners first claim on this asset (loan receivable *from* the partnership) of the deficient partner.[3] As seen above, under either the marshaling of assets rule or federal bankruptcy law, other creditors may rank ahead of the other partners. In cases where the deficient partner is personally insolvent and higher-ranking creditors exist, the above rights of creditors supersede the other partners' right of offset. Court cases on this matter have not clearly settled the question of the relative standing of creditors. For purposes of our subsequent illustrations and problems, we assume that the right of offset is operable.

SIMPLE VERSUS INSTALLMENT LIQUIDATIONS

Liquidation of a partnership may be carried out in several ways. One possibility is for all assets to be sold in a single transaction, at a going-business price, to a competitor or to others wishing to continue the business. Another is for the assets to be sold in a single transaction at distress prices, perhaps at a bankruptcy auction. Or some assets might be sold individually over a period of time, as buyers for specific items are found, while other assets, such as receivables and prepayments, are liquidated by means other than sale. In this last case, the partners often seek payment of cash as it becomes available, rather than wait for all assets to be liquidated before any cash is distributed.

The timing of cash distributions to partners influences the accounting procedures. In a **simple liquidation**, sometimes called a **lump-sum liquidation**, all assets are sold before any cash is distributed to partners. When cash is distributed to partners before the sale of assets is complete, an **installment liquidation** occurs. Some assets are sold and some cash is distributed, then

---

[3] See Stephen A. Zeff, "Right of Offset vs. Partnership Act in Winding-Up Process," *The Accounting Review* (January, 1957) 68-70.

additional assets are sold and more cash is distributed, and so on, producing a series of payments to the partners.

SIMPLE LIQUIDATIONS

Determining the proper distribution of cash to partners of a liquidating partnership can be a straightforward task or a complex one. Even in the simple liquidation situation, settlement becomes more complex when any partners have initial capital deficiencies or develop them while the partnership is being liquidated.

SUCCESSFUL LIQUIDATING PARTNERSHIPS

One views a liquidating partnership as *successful* if, in the process of liquidation, all partners receive a return of capital. This means that the sale of partnership assets results in either a net gain, or in a net loss small enough that no capital deficiencies result. When a successful liquidating partnership exists, proper distribution of cash to outside creditors and to partners is easily accomplished.

As an illustration, suppose that the JKL partnership has the following balance sheet immediately prior to liquidation.

JKL Partnership
Balance Sheet
(Prior to Liquidation)

Cash	$ 12,000	Liabilities	$ 17,000
Other Assets	48,000	Capital—J	21,000
		Capital—K	6,000
		Capital—L	16,000
	$ 60,000		$ 60,000

The three partners share income in a 2:1:1 ratio so that J has a 50 percent share and K and L each have 25 percent. If the Other Assets are sold for $64,000 and the resulting $16,000 gain is allocated to the partners, the accounts show the following:

Cash	$ 76,000	Liabilities	$ 17,000
		Capital—J	29,000
		Capital—K	10,000
		Capital—L	20,000
	$ 76,000		$ 76,000

Because there is sufficient cash to pay off the outside creditors, and no partner has a capital deficiency, the $76,000 can be distributed in amounts equal to the liability and capital balances: $17,000 to the outside creditors, $29,000 to J, $10,000 to K, and $20,000 to L.

UNSUCCESSFUL LIQUIDATING PARTNERSHIPS

A liquidating partnership is viewed as *unsuccessful* if losses from the sale of assets result in one or more capital deficiencies. When a partner still has a capital deficiency after offsetting any loans payable to that partner against the debit balance in the capital account, two possibilities exist. One possibility is that the partner is able to invest resources sufficient to remedy the deficiency. Enough assets are then available to pay the creditors and the other partners. The other possibility is that the deficient partner is unable to invest any resources or cannot invest enough to eliminate the deficiency. In this case, the deficiency is allocated to the other partners before assets are distributed.

To illustrate the unsuccessful case, suppose that the balance sheet of the XYZ partnership appears as follows:

XYZ Partnership
Balance Sheet
(Prior to Liquidation)

Cash	$ 10,000	Liabilities	$ 20,000
Loan Receivable—Z	8,000	Loan Payable—X	6,000
Other Assets	100,000	Loan Payable—Y	4,000
		Capital—X	41,000
		Capital—Y	10,000
		Capital—Z	37,000
	$ 118,000		$ 118,000

The partners share income and loss in a 5:3:2 ratio, respectively. Suppose now that the Other Assets are sold for $30,000. The $70,000 (= $100,000 − $30,000) loss on the sale is allocated to the capital accounts as follows:

	Capital Accounts before Loss	Loss Allocation		Capital Accounts after Loss
Partner X	$ 41,000	− (.5 × 70,000)	=	$ 6,000
Partner Y	10,000	− (.3 × 70,000)	=	(11,000)
Partner Z	37,000	− (.2 × 70,000)	=	23,000
	$ 88,000			$ 18,000

Thus Y has a capital deficiency of $11,000, before considering the loan payable to Y of $4,000.

Suppose now that Y invests additional resources. Since the partnership owes $4,000 to Y, Y's net deficiency is $7,000. If Y invests $7,000, and we offset Y's loan against the capital account, the accounts appear as follows. Note that the cash balance of $47,000 includes the original $10,000, the $30,000 sale proceeds, and Y's investment of $7,000.

Cash	$ 47,000	Liabilities	$ 20,000
Loan Receivable—Z	8,000	Loan Payable—X	6,000
		Capital—X	6,000
		Capital—Y	0
		Capital—Z	23,000
	$ 55,000		$ 55,000

After the loan receivable from Z is offset against Z's capital account, the cash is distributed as follows:

Outside Creditors	$ 20,000
Partner X	12,000
Partner Y	0
Partner Z	15,000
Total Cash Distributed	$ 47,000

In contrast, suppose that Y is personally insolvent. Recall that the capital accounts after allocation of the $70,000 loss are as follows: X, $6,000; Y, ($11,000); and Z, $23,000. Being insolvent, Y is unable to invest any resources to remedy the deficiency. After the $4,000 owed to Y by the partnership is offset against Y's capital account—reducing the deficiency to $7,000—the accounts show the following:

Cash	$ 40,000	Liabilities	$ 20,000
Loan Receivable—Z	8,000	Loan Payable—X	6,000
		Capital—X	6,000
		Capital—Y	(7,000)
		Capital—Z	23,000
	$ 48,000		$ 48,000

Because Y is unable to invest further, X and Z must absorb Y's deficiency. We allocate Y's $7,000 deficiency to X and Z according to their income-sharing ratio (5:2). Thus X is charged with $5,000 of the loss, Z is charged with $2,000, and the new account balances are as follows:

Cash	$ 40,000	Liabilities	$ 20,000
Loan Receivable—Z	8,000	Loan Payable—X	6,000
		Capital—X	1,000
		Capital—Y	0
		Capital—Z	21,000
	$ 48,000		$ 48,000

Again, after offsetting the Loan Receivable from Z against Z's capital account, the $40,000 cash is distributed as follows:

Outside Creditors	$ 20,000
Partner X	7,000
Partner Y	0
Partner Z	13,000
Total Cash Distributed	$ 40,000

A summary of the accounting procedures employed in simple partnership liquidations appears next:

In summary, to account for **simple partnership liquidations**, we use the following sequence of accounting procedures:

1. Determine the gain or loss on the sale of assets.
2. Allocate the gain or loss to the partners' capital accounts according to the income-sharing ratio.
3. Subtract loans receivable from capital accounts.
4. When a debit balance exists in a capital account (capital deficiency), offset loans payable against the deficiency.
5. Record any investments by partners in response to capital deficiencies.
6. Allocate any remaining deficiencies to partners with positive capital account balances. If this step produces new capital deficiencies, repeat Steps 4 through 6.
7. Distribute the cash.

INSTALLMENT LIQUIDATIONS

The preceding sections focused on simple liquidations characterized by the complete sale of all assets before any cash is distributed to the partners. Such cases enable all gains and losses to be determined and allocated to the partners' capital accounts prior to determining how the cash will be distributed.

Suppose, however, that the partners request cash distributions before all assets are sold. Because the amount of net gain or loss on future asset sales is unknown, how to distribute cash to the partners as it becomes available is not immediately evident. Clearly, outside creditors have the first claim; they must be paid before any cash is distributed to the partners. Once the creditors are paid, a method for determining an equitable distribution of available cash to the partners is needed. Two general approaches are available: determination of *safe payments* and preparation of a *cash distribution plan*. Both approaches yield the same ultimate results.

SAFE PAYMENT APPROACH

The **safe payment approach** is a way of determining how the cash available in a single installment is to be distributed. The calculation, which is repeated prior to distribution of each installment, is based on two simple assumptions:

1. *All remaining assets will be a total loss*; that is, no more cash will be realized.
2. *Deficient partners will not invest any additional resources*; that is, other partners will be charged with those deficiencies.

Together, these two assumptions constitute the *worst possible outcome*. Thus at each installment cash is distributed first to those partners having the greatest ability to absorb future losses.

To illustrate the safe payment approach, assume that the ABC partnership decided to terminate business and liquidate its assets. Assets will be sold or otherwise converted into cash over a period of time, and the partners intend to distribute cash as it becomes available. The partners share income and loss in a 4:4:2 ratio and the balance sheet presently appears as follows:

ABC Partnership
Balance Sheet
(Prior to Liquidation)

Cash	$ 3,000	Liabilities	$ 30,000
Receivables	30,000	Loan Payable—A	20,000
Inventory	47,000	Capital—A	86,000
Land	25,000	Capital—B	140,000
Building, Net	72,000	Capital—C	41,000
Equipment, Net	140,000		
	$ 317,000		$ 317,000

Suppose that half of the receivables are collected and that the entire inventory is sold for $35,000. After distributing the realized loss of $12,000 (= $47,000 − $35,000) on the inventory to the capital accounts ($4,800 to A, $4,800 to B, and $2,400 to C), the accounts show the following:

Cash	$ 53,000	Liabilities	$ 30,000
Receivables	15,000	Loan Payable—A	20,000
Land	25,000	Capital—A	81,200
Building, Net	72,000	Capital—B	135,200
Equipment, Net	140,000	Capital—C	38,600
	$ 305,000		$ 305,000

If the partners wish to distribute the $53,000, then $30,000 goes first to the outside creditors, and $23,000 is available for the partners. How is this $23,000 to be distributed?

First, we combine the partners' loans with the partners' capital accounts. In this example, the $20,000 loan payable to A is combined with A's capital balance of $81,200. For convenience, we refer to the total of $101,200 as *capital*. *Second*, we assume that all remaining noncash assets will result in a total loss, which is allocated by the income-sharing ratio. When additional expenses are anticipated as part of the liquidation process, these should also be included in the loss allocation. Book values of these remaining assets—receivables, land, building, and equipment—total $252,000. If these do produce a total loss, the partners' capital accounts are affected as follows:

	Capital Accounts before Loss	Loss Allocation		Capital Accounts after Loss
Partner A (Includes $20,000 Loan) . . .	$ 101,200	− (.4 × 252,000)	=	$ 400
Partner B	135,200	− (.4 × 252,000)	=	34,400
Partner C	38,600	− (.2 × 252,000)	=	(11,800)
	$ 275,000			$ 23,000

Third, we make the assumption that Partner C is unable to invest additional capital. We continue by allocating C's $11,800 deficiency equally to A and B since they have equal (4:4) income shares, leading to the following:

	Capital Accounts before Loss	Loss Allocation		Capital Accounts after Loss
Partner A	$ 400	$- (.5 \times 11{,}800)$	=	$ (5,500)
Partner B	34,400	$- (.5 \times 11{,}800)$	=	28,500
Partner C	(11,800)			0
	$ 23,000			$ 23,000

Fourth, we assume that A is also unable to invest additional capital, and we allocate A's entire $5,500 deficiency to B, resulting in the following capital balances:

Partner A	$ 0
Partner B	23,000
Partner C	0
	$ 23,000

The $23,000 is therefore distributed entirely to Partner B. This is called a **safe payment** because it is based on the worst possible circumstances; namely, that no more cash will be generated by the sale of assets and that deficient partners are unable to invest additional capital. Following distribution of $30,000 to the creditors and $23,000 to Partner B, the accounts show the following:

Receivables	$ 15,000	Loan Payable—A	$ 20,000
Land	25,000	Capital—A	81,200
Building, Net	72,000	Capital—B	112,200
Equipment, Net	140,000	Capital—C	38,600
	$ 252,000		$ 252,000

When the next stage in the liquidation is complete, and more cash becomes available for distribution, the next safe payment is computed. Suppose that $6,000 of receivables are collected, the remaining receivables are deemed uncollectible, and the equipment is sold for $90,000. After these transactions are recorded, including allocation of the $9,000 loss from uncollectible receivables and the $50,000 loss on sale of equipment to the partners in the 4:4:2 ratio, we have the following:

Cash	$ 96,000	Loan Payable—A	$ 20,000
Land	25,000	Capital—A	57,600
Building	72,000	Capital—B	88,600
		Capital—C	26,800
	$ 193,000		$ 193,000

As before, assume no recovery of the remaining assets having total book value of $97,000 (= $25,000 + $72,000) and allocate this potential loss to the partners as shown below:

	Capital Accounts before Loss	Loss Allocation		Capital Accounts after Loss
Partner A (Includes $20,000 Loan) . . .	$ 77,600	$- (.4 \times 97{,}000)$	=	$ 38,800
Partner B	88,600	$- (.4 \times 97{,}000)$	=	49,800
Partner C	26,800	$- (.2 \times 97{,}000)$	=	7,400
	$ 193,000			$ 96,000

Because this loss creates no capital deficiencies, the $96,000 is distributed thus: $38,800 to A, $49,800 to B, and $7,400 to C. After this cash distribution is made, an updated balance sheet is prepared, the next batch of assets is sold, and so forth. This process continues until the liquidation is complete. The safe payment approach to cash distribution in installments is a fairly easy procedure. Its principal disadvantages are that (1) new calculations must be made for each installment distribution and (2) no information on future installment distributions is provided. The cash distribution plan, discussed next, remedies these disadvantages.

CASH DISTRIBUTION PLAN

As an alternative to calculating the proper cash distribution as each cash installment becomes available, we can develop a comprehensive *cash distribution plan*. By focusing on the ability of the partners to absorb future losses, at the beginning of the liquidation process, the **cash distribution plan** provides a sequence of cash distributions satisfying safe payment criteria. Once the plan is prepared, we refer to it to determine how available cash is to be distributed.

The balances of the partners' capital accounts continue to be critical for determining cash distributions according to this plan. Throughout partnership accounting, we noted that partners' shares of capital and profits are not necessarily the same. Conceptually, the cash distribution plan is based on integrating the partners' income shares and capital balances to develop standard measures of ability to absorb future losses.

This concept can be understood with a simple example. Suppose Black and Jones share profits and losses equally, but Black's capital account has a balance of $45,000, while Jones' has a balance of $30,000. Despite the fact that they are equal partners for income-sharing purposes, Black has more capital, due to Black's having either invested more or withdrawn less than Jones. Fairness suggests that when the partnership is liquidated, Black should receive $15,000 before Jones receives anything so as to equalize their capital positions. Once Black's capital is reduced to $30,000, they should share any remaining cash equally, in accordance with their equal income-sharing ratio. Thus the following cash distribution plan applies in this simple situation:

Jones and Black's Cash Distribution Plan

1. All liabilities are paid.
2. Black receives the next $15,000.
3. Any further distributions are divided equally between Black and Jones.

When several partners with different income-sharing percentages are liquidating their partnership in installments, derivation of the cash distribution plan requires a more formal approach. This approach is explained in the following box. The logic is the same as in the simple example above: cash distributions should follow a sequence designed to bring the capital accounts of the partners into proper alignment with respect to each other. This means that the partner having the *largest capital balance relative to his or her income percentage* will be the first to receive cash. In the preceding example, Black, with more capital and a 50 percent income percentage, received the first distribution. After all the imbalances in relative capital strength are remedied, subsequent distributions are made to all partners in proportion to their income percentages.

> The **cash distribution plan** is prepared *prior* to the liquidation of a partnership and incorporates the follow steps:
>
> 1. *Standardize* the capital relationship among the partners by dividing each capital balance by that partner's income-sharing percentage. The results provide a **measure of each partner's ability to absorb losses** that may occur during liquidation. The larger a partner's standardized capital balance, the greater is that partner's ability to absorb losses before his or her capital balance is eliminated.
> 2. *Equalize* the standardized capital balances in steps. Begin with the largest balance, and determine the adjustment (subtraction) needed to equalize it with the next largest. Continue this process until all standardized capital amounts are equal. These equalization adjustments signify the **incremental amounts of loss** which can be absorbed by partners with larger standardized capital balances over and above what can be absorbed by partners with smaller standardized balances.
> 3. *Convert* the equalization adjustments back into terms of the respective partners' capital accounts by multiplying each adjustment, in the order made, by that partner's income-sharing percentage. This gives the amounts and priorities of cash distributions to the partners.
> 4. *Organize* the results of Step 3 into a formal cash distribution plan. Remember to provide first for the payment of amounts due to all outside creditors.

Cash Distribution Plan Illustration

To illustrate preparation of a more complex cash distribution plan, consider again the ABC partnership discussed in the previous section. At the beginning of the liquidation process, the right-hand side of the balance sheet appeared as follows:

ABC Partnership
Liabilities and Capital
(Prior to Liquidation)

Liabilities	$ 30,000
Loan Payable—A	20,000
Capital—A	86,000
Capital—B	140,000
Capital—C	41,000
	$ 317,000

The partners share income in a 4:4:2 ratio. As before, A's capital of $86,000 and loan of $20,000 will be combined prior to proceeding, so that Partner A has total capital of $106,000.

First, standardize the capital accounts to find each partner's loss-absorption ability by dividing each partner's actual capital by the income-sharing percentage:

	Actual Capital	Income Percentage	Standardized Capital
Partner A	$ 106,000	.4	$ 265,000
Partner B	140,000	.4	350,000
Partner C	41,000	.2	205,000

This calculation tells us that when we standardize for the different income shares, Partner B has the greatest amount of relative capital, and Partner C has the least. In other words, Partner B can absorb the greatest amount of loss, and Partner C the least amount. If the partnership incurs a $205,000 loss, Partner C's share of $41,000 (= .2 × $205,000) eliminates C's capital balance. Partners A and B have shares of $82,000 (= .4 × $205,000), which leaves them with positive capital balances. It is reasonable to expect that B will receive money first, then A, then finally C.

Second, equalize the standardized capital balances, starting with the largest:

	Partner A	Partner B	Partner C
Standardized Capital	$ 265,000	$ 350,000	$ 205,000
a. Equalize A with B	—	(85,000)	—
	$ 265,000	$ 265,000	$ 205,000
b. Equalize A and B with C	(60,000)	(60,000)	—
	$ 205,000	$ 205,000	$ 205,000

This process is repeated in iterations, noted *a* and *b* above, until the standardized capital balances of all partners are equalized. Each adjustment represents incremental loss-absorption ability. Thus B can absorb a partnership loss on liquidation of $85,000 more than A, and $145,000 (= $85,000 + $60,000) more than C. When the equalization process is complete, all partners have the same loss-absorption ability remaining. The number of iterations is, at most, one fewer than the number of partners.

Third, convert these adjustments back into the equivalents of actual capital balances as follows:

	Partner A	Partner B	Partner C
a.	—	$85,000 × .4 = $34,000	—
b.	$60,000 × .4 = $24,000	$60,000 × .4 = $24,000	—

This calculation indicates that after the $30,000 of liabilities are paid, Partner B should receive $34,000, and then Partners A and B should each receive $24,000. Because B's loss-absorption ability exceeds that of A by $85,000, B will still have capital of $34,000 (= .4 × $85,000) after elimination of A (and C). Once these distributions are made, the standardized capital balances of each partner are equal, and their actual capital balances are in the 4:4:2 income-sharing ratio. Any further distributions of cash should be made according to this income-sharing ratio.

A worksheet combining the second and third steps is shown in Exhibit 16.2. The left side of the worksheet shows the equalization of standardized capital to determine the partners' incremental loss-absorption abilities. The right side shows the conversion back to the partners' actual capital account balances. The amounts on the left side are multiplied by the respective income percentages to get the figures on the right side. Note that the adjustments that equalize the standardized capital represent the predetermined sequence of cash distributions that bring the partners' capital accounts into line with the income-sharing ratio.

Fourth, organize the results into a formal cash distribution plan, such as that shown below. This plan shows how to distribute any amount of cash that becomes available. Remember that distributions are *cumulative*; that is, each distribution starts where the previous one ended.

ABC Partnership's Cash Distribution Plan

Distribution	Amount	Payment Made to
1	First $30,000	Creditors
2	Next $34,000	Partner B
3	Next $48,000	Partners A and B in equal amounts up to $24,000 each
4	Any further amount	Partners A, B and C in 4:4:2 ratio

	Equalization of Standardized Capital				Actual Capital Accounts and Cash Distributions		
	Partner A	**Partner B**	**Partner C**		**Partner A (40%)**	**Partner B (40%)**	**Partner C (20%)**
Standardized Capital	$ 265,000	$ 350,000	$ 205,000	Actual Capital	$ 106,000	$ 140,000	$ 41,000
a. Equalize A with B .	—	(85,000)	—		—	(34,000)	—
	$ 265,000	$ 265,000	$ 205,000		$ 106,000	$ 106,000	$ 41,000
b. Equalize A and B with C . . .	(60,000)	(60,000)	—		(24,000)	(24,000)	—
	$ 205,000	$ 205,000	$ 205,000		$ 82,000	$ 82,000	$ 41,000
				Capital Share	40%	40%	20%

EXHIBIT 16.2 WORKSHEET FOR CASH DISTRIBUTION PLAN

Equivalence of the Cash Distribution Plan and Safe Payments

To illustrate the equivalence of the cash distribution plan and safe payments, recall that we previously calculated the proper safe payment distribution of the first two installments in the liquidation of the ABC partnership—$53,000 ($30,000 to the creditors and $23,000 to B) and $96,000 ($38,800 to A, $49,800 to B and $7,400 to C). We now use the cash distribution plan to verify the safe payment amounts.

First, the $53,000 is considered. The cash distribution plan states that the first $30,000 is paid to creditors and the next $34,000 is paid to Partner B. Available cash of $53,000 permits us to complete the first distribution—to pay the creditors $30,000—and to partially complete the second distribution—to pay Partner B $23,000 of the required $34,000. Thus the $53,000 is paid as follows:

Creditors	$ 30,000
Partner B	23,000
	$ 53,000

Second, we have $96,000 to distribute. We must complete the second distribution called for by the plan—to pay Partner B an additional $11,000 (for a total of $34,000)—before moving to the third distribution. According to the cash distribution plan, we perform the following steps:

1. Pay $11,000 to Partner B to complete the second distribution, leaving $85,000 (= $96,000 − $11,000) available to pay out.
2. Divide the next $48,000 equally between A and B, thus completing the third distribution indicated by the plan. Cash of $37,000 (= $85,000 − $48,000) remains to be paid.
3. Divide the $37,000 among A, B, and C in the 4:4:2 income-sharing ratio, as specified by the fourth and final distribution in the plan.

Proper payment of the entire $96,000 is summarized here:

		Payment Made To		
Distribution	**Amount**	**Partner A**	**Partner B**	**Partner C**
2	$ 11,000	$ 0	$ 11,000	$ 0
3	48,000	24,000	24,000	0
4	37,000	14,800	14,800	7,400
	$ 96,000	$ 38,800	$ 49,800	$ 7,400

Observe that this result is identical to that achieved by the safe payment approach.

Deviations from the Plan and Distributions in Kind

Not all available cash need be paid to the partners immediately. Cash may be retained for anticipated liquidation expenses or other purposes. Both the safe payment approach and the cash distribution plan—which is actually a *schedule of safe payments*—are specifically aimed at the distribution of *cash* in a partnership liquidation. Occasionally, though, temporary deviations from the safe payments determined by either approach do occur. For example, when a specific asset is distributed to a partner in lieu of cash, and the value of the asset exceeds the amount to which that partner is entitled. Subsequent payments must be adjusted in favor of other partners until the excess is absorbed. We illustrate how distribution of a noncash asset in liquidation can temporarily disrupt scheduled safe payments by using the following hypothetical cash distribution plan.

Distribution	**Amount**	**Payment Made to**
1	First $10,000	Creditors
2	Next $16,000	Partner D
3	Next $30,000	Partners D and E in 6:3 ratio
4	Any further amount	Partners D, E and F in 6:3:1 ratio

Suppose that when considering the third distribution, in lieu of the $10,000 cash, E receives a truck worth $14,200. In effect, E received an advance on the fourth distribution, and appropriate payments to D and F in a 6:1 ratio must be made before making the fourth distribution in the 6:3:1 ratio. The excess payment of $4,200 to E (= $14,200 − $10,000 = 3 × $1,400) is remedied in the fourth distribution by paying $8,400 to D (= 6 × $1,400) and $1,400 to F (= 1 × $1,400) before E receives any further payment. In other words, of the next $14,000 considered in the fourth distribution, E's share of $4,200 (= .3 × $14,000) was *prepaid* as part of the truck value. D and F are paid the remaining $9,800 (= $14,000 − $4,200) in their 6:1 ratio. When more than $9,800 in cash is available in the fourth distribution, the excess is paid in the 6:3:1 ratio.

Suppose, instead, that we are working with individually calculated safe payments. In this case, distributing the truck to E could serve to prepay some of the next safe payment to which E is otherwise entitled. If so, calculation of that next safe payment is modified to incorporate the effect just illustrated on the cash distribution plan.

When dealing with partnership liquidations occurring over an extended period of time, the accountant must ensure an equitable distribution of partnership assets. Consideration must be given to actual and prospective losses on sales of assets and to the potential inability of partners to remedy capital deficiencies. These factors are considered, either directly or indirectly, in the two procedures discussed for installment liquidations—the safe payment approach and the cash distribution plan.

OTHER USES OF THE PARTNERSHIP FORM OF BUSINESS ORGANIZATION

The partnership form of business organization is often associated only with small business. It is common to think of a partnership as an association of a very small number of individuals, perhaps only two or three, operating a relatively small firm. In some professions, though—especially accounting and law—we find large firms with hundreds or thousands of partners organized as partnerships, largely because of historical impediments to organizing these activities as corporations. For example, the largest international accounting firms, organized as partnerships, have thousands of partners, tens of thousands of employees and billions of dollars of annual revenue. In other areas of business, such as manufacturing or retailing, the need for massive amounts of equity capital to finance fixed assets makes it uncommon to find a large enterprise organized as a partnership.

Although the image of the partnership as being almost exclusively related to small business activities is generally correct, recent years have seen the partnership form of business organization increasingly used in other entrepreneurial contexts. Two common examples of this phenomenon are *joint ventures* and *limited partnerships*.

JOINT VENTURES

A **joint venture** is an entity formed by a small group of individuals or firms that contribute resources and *jointly share* in managing and controlling the venture. Joint ventures are traditionally established to carry out a single business transaction or activity, often over a limited period of time. Frequently, the owners of a joint venture are themselves large firms, either partnerships or corporations. A **corporate joint venture** exists when the venture is organized as a corporation.

Participants form joint ventures for activities where it is mutually desirable to combine expertise, special technology, capital, or access to certain markets. Examples include research projects or development of new products, in which two areas of technology must be joined, and large-scale construction projects, in which the capital and facilities of two or more contractors are needed. Corporate joint ventures are frequently found in the automobile industry; NUMMI—General Motors' joint venture with Toyota—produces vehicles sold under the Toyota and Chevrolet nameplates. Thus, although joint ventures are frequently short-lived, they can last several years and their initial projects may lead to ongoing business activities.

Joint ventures also may enable their owners to obtain **off-balance-sheet financing**. When a venture is established, perhaps to perform a particular production process, research activity or financing function—such as carrying receivables—debt incurred by the venture is not reported on the owners' balance sheets. Measures of the extent of owners' financial leverage may therefore be understated and solvency or available debt capacity overstated. Applying **proportionate consolidation**—discussed in Module A—to joint ventures could remedy this deficiency in their owners' financial reporting.

Numerous issues related to (1) accounting for investments in joint ventures and (2) accounting by joint venture entities were addressed in a 1979 AICPA *Issues Paper*.[4] More recently, the 1991 FASB *Discussion Memorandum*, "New Basis Accounting,"[5] considers whether a *new basis* should be assigned to property contributed when forming a joint venture and whether sale of a joint venture interest should trigger a *new basis* for the venture's property.

Accounting for Investments in Joint Ventures

When a joint venture is formed, the agreement between the parties should clearly specify how joint control is to be achieved, how costs or profits are to be shared, and how any remaining assets are to be distributed when the venture is terminated. Each owner establishes an Investment in Joint Venture account. The initial carrying value reflects either the transferor's cost of the property transferred or the property's fair value. Until the FASB resolves the "new basis" issue, use of fair value seems appropriate only when a clear measure of the fair value exists and the transfer signifies completion of an earnings process.[6]

After the joint venture is formed, its owners usually account for their investments by the *equity method*, as explained in Chapter 4 of this text. In most cases the number of owners is small, often two or three, and the 20 percent ownership threshold for use of the equity method is easily met. *APBO 18* specifies use of the equity method for investments in joint ventures organized as corporations;[7] it is commonly also used for investments in joint ventures organized as partnerships. Because no single investor controls the venture, the *equity method income accrual* should be decreased (increased) by the investor's *proportionate* share of any unconfirmed profit (loss) on investor/venture transactions.

Recall that under the equity method, neither the assets nor the liabilities of the venture (investee) appear on the balance sheet of the investor, thereby facilitating off-balance-sheet financing. Although *proportionate consolidation* effectively discloses such financing commitments, and is found in some industries where venture investors have undivided interests in venture assets and are proportionately liable for venture liabilities, it is *not* required. A technique known as the **expanded equity method**, also *not* required, replaces the equity method's one-line consolidation concept with separate disclosure of the investor's proportionate share of venture assets and liabilities.[8]

Illustration of Reporting Joint Venture Investments. Suppose L Company contributes $2,400,000 for a 40% interest in the LMN joint venture. At the end of the venture's first year of operation, condensed balance sheets (in thousands) for LMN and L, under alternative reporting formats, appear in Exhibit 16.3. L Company's data appear in the second ("equity") column. L's Investment in LMN and L's Retained Earnings both include the $2,000,000 that is L's 40% share of LMN's retained earnings.

---

[4] Accounting Standards Executive Committee, *Issues Paper*, "Joint Venture Accounting" (New York: AICPA, 1979).

[5] Financial Accounting Standards Board, *Discussion Memorandum*, "New Basis Accounting," (Norwalk, CT: FASB, 1991)

[6] Price Waterhouse, "Accounting for Joint Ventures" (New York: Price Waterhouse, 1992), pp. 2-3.

[7] Accounting Principles Board, *Opinion No. 18*, "The Equity Method of Accounting for Investments in Common Stock" (New York: AICPA, 1971), par. 16.

[8] Dieter, Richard, and Arthur R. Wyatt, "The Expanded Equity Method—An Alternative in Accounting for Investments in Joint Ventures," *The Journal of Accountancy* (June, 1978); pp. 89-94.

	LMN Joint Venture	L Company		
		Equity: 40%	Proportionate Consolidation	Expanded Equity: 40%
Current Assets	$ 9,000	$ 15,000	$ 18,600	$ 15,000
Plant Assets	18,000	22,000	29,200	22,000
Share of LMN Joint Venture:				
Current Assets	—	—	—	3,600
Plant Assets	—	—	—	7,200
Investment in LMN	—	4,400*	—	—
	$ 27,000	$ 41,400	$ 47,800	$ 47,800
Liabilities	$ 16,000	$ 21,400	$ 27,800	$ 21,400
Share of LMN Joint Venture:				
Liabilities	—	—	—	6,400
Contributed Capital	6,000	5,000	5,000	5,000
Retained Earnings	5,000	15,000*	15,000*	15,000*
	$ 27,000	$ 41,400	$ 47,800	$ 47,800

* Includes 40% of LMN's retained earnings.

EXHIBIT 16.3 ALTERNATIVE APPROACHES TO REPORTING A JOINT VENTURE INVESTMENT

To see how the *off-balance-sheet financing* works, note that the equity method suppresses L's interest in LMN's assets and liabilities. L's leverage (measured by Total Liabilities/Total Assets; TL/TA) is *.517* (= $21,400/$41,400) in the second column. Including L's share of LMN's assets and liabilities raises L's measured leverage to *.582* (= $27,800/$47,800) in the optional third and fourth columns! We prefer the expanded equity presentation as it enables the reader to distinguish L's separable assets and liabilities from L's share of LMN's amounts. Proportionate consolidation commingles the assets and liabilities of L and LMN.

Accounting by Joint Venture Entities

In a sense, accounting for the joint venture activity itself poses few special accounting problems. Contributed property is generally recorded by the venture at fair value unless no clear measure of fair value exists or recovery of the fair value is in doubt. Because the amount of initial investment is usually recorded by the venturer at venturer's cost, this amount differs from the fair value amounts at which the venture usually records contributed property. Partnership accounting principles apply when a joint venture has the legal form of a partnership; corporate accounting principles apply for corporate joint ventures. Whether corporate joint ventures should record contributed goodwill is an issue being addressed by the FASB's "New Basis" project.

LIMITED PARTNERSHIPS

A **limited partnership** consists of at least one *general partner* who has all the usual characteristics of a partner, and one or more *limited partners* who are essentially investors only. The limited partners have no role in management, and their liability is limited to their capital balances. Limited partnership interests are typically freely transferable in the same manner as shares of stock, as long as a market exists for them. In recent years, limited partnerships have also been used for investment programs, especially those characterized as tax shelters. **Tax shelter investments** generally possess one or more of the following characteristics:

- Creation of tax-deductible losses by various tax-accounting rules, such as fast depreciation write-offs, immediate deductibility of costs having long-term benefit (research and development, intangible drilling costs for oil and gas), and tax credits on certain capital, rehabilitation and low income housing expenditures.
- Concentration of tax losses in the early years of the investment.
- Aggregate tax losses possibly exceeding the amount invested. Recall, from the Appendix to Chapter 19, that a partner's tax basis in his or her partnership interest is the capital account balance plus the partner's share of partnership liabilities. A partner's ability to deduct tax losses, however, has been restricted in recent years. These restrictions refer to the extent to which the partner is economically *at risk*, which excludes some liabilities otherwise included in the tax basis of the partnership interest, and to limits placed on deductibility of losses from passive activities.
- Eventual profit from sale of the investment qualifying for favorable tax treatment as a long-term capital gain.[9]

To illustrate, suppose that a real estate investment is structured as a limited partnership. A **promoter**, who typically also serves as the general partner, enters into a contract to purchase, develop, and perhaps manage, a shopping center. As with most real estate acquisitions, much of the purchase price is to be financed with mortgage debt. For the equity portion, the promoter sells a number of limited partnership interests. Money received from the investors is used for the down payment, closing costs on the property (such as legal fees and commissions), working capital to meet initial operating costs, and compensation of the promoter. The limited partnership agreement typically provides (1) that virtually all of the annual profits or losses are allocated to the limited partners, and (2) that the eventual gain on the sale of the property is shared by the general partner and the limited partners.

The limited partnership form has several attractions as a vehicle for investment programs. The investor's risk is limited, and the partnership form allows the pass-through of tax losses to the individual partners to be offset against other sources of taxable income, subject to the at-risk and passive activity restrictions mentioned earlier. Because limited partnerships generally seek noncash losses in the early years of the project, the first provision above enables the limited partners to convert those *noncash losses* into *cash inflows* produced by income tax savings. Also, many limited partnerships fall under the *small offering* provisions of the SEC, exempting them from the

---

[9] Preferential tax treatment of long-term capital gains has consistently been a feature of U.S. tax law. The Tax Reform Act of 1986 eliminated the capital gain rate preference but left the structure for determining long-term and short-term capital gains intact. Although a small capital gain preference became available in 1991, larger cuts in effective tax rates on long-term capital gains were enacted by Congress in 1997.

full SEC registration process. Limited partnerships are traditionally used for investments in real estate, oil and gas exploration, farming, and cattle breeding. In recent years, new areas such as research and development have emerged as limited partnership investments.

No new accounting problems are introduced by limited partnerships. Note that there are two classes of partners: *general* and *limited*. Formation of the partnership is typically recorded on the basis of amounts invested. Because limited partners generally invest cash in equal amounts, no valuation or bonus/goodwill adjustments are needed. The general partner often makes little or no tangible investment; goodwill may be recorded to reflect the general partner's intangible services in organizing the venture. Income allocation is governed by the partnership agreement, which may provide any one of a variety of possibilities of how income is to be divided between the general partner and the limited partners. The agreement further governs how liquidation proceeds are to be allocated between the general partner and the limited partners.

SUMMARY OF KEY CONCEPTS

The interest of a **retiring partner** may be purchased with the **personal assets of one or more of the remaining partners** or with **partnership assets**. In the latter case, the **bonus** and **goodwill** approaches are used to account for any difference between the payment to the retiring partner and the amount of the retiring partner's capital account.

When the **partial goodwill** approach is used, asset revaluations are recognized only in connection with the **retiring partner's interest**. In contrast, use of the **total goodwill** approach infers asset revaluations pertaining to **all of the partners**, based on capitalizing the excess of the payment to the retiring partner over the retiree's capital balance.

If the partnership is to be **liquidated**, the **rights of creditors** are usually based on the **marshaling of assets rule**. Loans payable to partners are combined with those partners' capital balances under the **right of offset**. When a partner has a **capital deficiency**, that partner is obligated to invest additional assets in the partnership to remedy the deficiency; if this is impossible, the deficiency is allocated to the other partners in their income-sharing ratio.

A **simple** or **lump-sum liquidation** is characterized by the complete sale of all assets before any cash is distributed to the partners. In an **installment liquidation**, cash payments are made to the partners before the sale of assets is complete.

Under an **installment liquidation**, equitable division of each cash distribution among the partners is derived from either the **safe payment approach** or the **cash distribution plan**. Both methods address the partners' relative abilities to absorb a **total loss** on all remaining assets and produce the same sequence of cash payments.

Both large and small enterprises may be organized as partnerships. **Joint ventures**—frequently of short duration—often use partnership accounting principles as do limited partnerships which feature limited-liability investors. **Corporate joint ventures** follow corporate accounting principles and are subject to unresolved **new basis issues.**

Reporting **joint venture investments** via the **equity method** facilitates **off-balance-sheet financing.** Optional techniques—**proportionate consolidation** and the **expanded equity method**—provide improved disclosure of joint venture investments.

QUESTIONS

Q16.1 How do the concepts of *legal* and *economic entity* relate to a partnership that continues after the retirement of one partner?

Q16.2 Recognition of *implied goodwill* is possible when a new partner enters by purchasing an interest directly from existing partners. Discuss the propriety of recognizing implied goodwill when the remaining partners use their personal funds to purchase a retiree's interest.

Q16.3 To calculate *total goodwill* in a retirement situation, the excess of the retirement payment over the retiree's capital balance (i.e., the *partial goodwill*) is capitalized—divided by the retiree's income-sharing percentage. Explain why capitalizing the entire payment to the retiree is inappropriate.

Q16.4 Upon what assumption is the goodwill method of accounting for partnership retirements based? How does this reasoning apply to the partial and total goodwill approaches?

Q16.5 How is the sequence of payments in a cash distribution plan affected if the partners decide to hold back cash pending resolution of contingencies?

Q16.6 Assume that a partnership is being liquidated and that the obligations to creditors exceed the assets of the partnership. What, if any, rights do the creditors have in attempting to collect the full amount owed them?

Q16.7 Suppose that A receives a noncash asset worth $5,000 instead of $3,000 cash to which she was entitled at a particular stage of an installment liquidation. How does this affect subsequent distributions?

Q16.8 Discuss the procedure followed in accounting for simple partnership liquidations.

Q16.9 What advantage does the cash distribution plan have over the safe payment approach in determining cash payments to partners during liquidation? How do the results of the two approaches differ?

Q16.10 What purpose do the safe payment approach and the cash distribution plan serve during partnership liquidation? Why is this important?

Q16.11 A large company is developing a new product involving an area of technology in which it has little experience. Why might this company consider forming a joint venture with another (noncompeting) company having expertise in that technology?

Q16.12 Why is the limited partnership form, rather than the regular partnership form or the corporate form, often used for real estate investments?

EXERCISES

E16.1 **Post-Retirement Capital Balances** On June 30, 19X8, the balance sheet for the partnership of Winston, Barker, and Langley, together with the partners' respective income-sharing ratios, was as follows:

Assets, at Cost	$ 300,000
Loan—Winston	$ 15,000
Capital—Winston (20%)	70,000
Capital—Barker (20%)	65,000
Capital—Langley (60%)	150,000
	$ 300,000

Winston has decided to retire from the partnership, and by mutual agreement the assets are to be adjusted to their fair value of $360,000 at June 30, 19X8. It was agreed that the partnership would pay Winston $102,000 cash for his partnership interest exclusive of his loan, which is to be repaid in full. No goodwill is to be recorded in this transaction.

REQUIRED: After Winston's retirement, what are the capital account balances of Barker and Langley, respectively?
(AICPA adapted)

E16.2 **Retirement: Bonus and Goodwill Calculations** Ellery Stevens, senior partner in a rapidly growing local CPA firm, has decided to retire. His share in the firm's profits and losses is 30% and his capital account, before considering drawings of $50,000, has a balance of $240,000. Total capital of the firm is $780,000, before considering total drawings of $180,000. Under the partnership agreement, Stevens will receive $250,000.

REQUIRED:

1. Calculate the bonus to Stevens and the total capital of the firm after Stevens' retirement.
2. What balance sheet accounts will change after Stevens' retirement, and by what amounts, if the partial goodwill approach is used?
3. If the total goodwill method is used, calculate the amount of goodwill recognized and the total capital of the firm after Stevens' retirement.

E16.3 **Retirement Journal Entries: Various Assumptions** Baxter is planning to retire from the partnership of Baxter, Helman, and Caines. The partners' income-sharing ratio is 2:1:1. Helman and Caines will continue as a partnership, sharing profits and losses equally. The partners are considering various ways to pay Baxter $90,000, which is the fair market value of her interest in the business. Prior to retirement, Baxter's capital account balance is $70,000.

REQUIRED: Prepare the journal entry to record Baxter's retirement on the partnership books under each of the following assumptions:

1. Helman and Caines each pay Baxter $45,000 from personal funds.
2. Partnership cash is used to pay Baxter. The bonus method is followed.
3. Partnership cash is used to pay Baxter. The total goodwill approach is followed.
4. Partnership cash is used to pay Baxter. The partial goodwill approach is followed.
5. Helman and Caines each pay Baxter $10,000 from personal funds; the rest is paid with partnership cash.

E16.4 **Reconstructing Retirement Entries** Schmidt, Hayes and Hollins are partners who share income in a 5:3:2 ratio. Hayes is forced to retire by the other partners and is paid $82,000 for his partnership interest.

REQUIRED:

1. Assuming the bonus method is not used, identify the approach used and prepare the journal entries made to record Hayes' retirement if total capital of the remaining partners *increases* by $98,000 after Hayes' retirement.
2. Identify the approach used and prepare the journal entries assuming total capital of the remaining partners *decreases* by $42,000 after Hayes' retirement. All assets are fairly valued.
3. Using the pre-retirement balance in Hayes' capital account implied by *1.* and *2.*, determine the change in total assets after Hayes' retirement, assuming no change in the remaining partners' capital. Identify the approach that produces this result.

E16.5 **Lump-Sum Liquidation** The following balance sheet is for the LMN partnership. The partners share profits and losses in the ratio of 5:3:2, respectively.

Cash	$ 30,000	Liabilities	$ 70,000
Other Assets	270,000	Capital—L	140,000
		Capital—M	80,000
		Capital—N	10,000
	$ 300,000		$ 300,000

Assume that L, M, and N agreed to liquidate the partnership by selling the other assets.

REQUIRED: What should each partner receive if the other assets are sold for $200,000? *(AICPA adapted)*

E16.6 **Admission, Liquidation Calculations** The following condensed balance sheet is presented for the partnership of Bond, Whit, and Tell, who share profits and losses in the ratio of 5:3:2, respectively:

Cash	$ 120,000	Liabilities	$ 240,000
Other Assets	600,000	Capital—Bond	300,000
		Capital—Whit	160,000
		Capital—Tell	20,000
	$ 720,000		$ 720,000

REQUIRED:

1. Assume that the assets and liabilities are fairly valued on the balance sheet, and that the partnership decided to admit Eller as a new partner with a one-fifth interest. No goodwill or bonus is to be recorded. How much should Eller contribute?
2. Assume that instead of admitting a new partner, the partners decided to liquidate the partnership. If the other assets are sold for $460,000, how much of the available cash should be distributed to Bond?
    (AICPA adapted)

E16.7 Admission, Liquidation Calculations The following condensed balance sheet is presented for the partnership of Cooke, Dorry, and Evans, who share profits and losses in the ratio of 4:3:3, respectively:

Cash	$ 90,000	Accounts Payable	$ 210,000
Other Assets	820,000	Loan—Evans	40,000
Loan—Cooke	30,000	Capital—Cooke	300,000
		Capital—Dorry	200,000
		Capital—Evans	190,000
	$ 940,000		$ 940,000

REQUIRED:

1. Assume that the assets and liabilities are fairly valued on the balance sheet and the partnership decides to admit Fisher as a new partner with a one-fourth interest. No goodwill or bonus is to be recorded. How much should Fisher contribute in cash or other assets?
2. Assume that instead of admitting a new partner, the partners decide to liquidate the partnership. If the other assets are sold for $600,000, how much of the available cash should be distributed to Cooke?
    (AICPA adapted)

E16.8 Marshaling of Assets The following are data for the AB Partnership and for A and B as individuals. Assume that A and B are equal partners.

AB Partnership	Case 1	Case 2
Assets	$ 48,000	$ 31,000
Liabilities	42,000	51,000
Capital—A	3,000	(8,000)
Capital—B	3,000	(12,000)
Partner A		
Assets	10,000	30,000
Liabilities	17,000	17,000

Partner B	Case 1	Case 2
Assets	50,000	15,000
Liabilities	9,000	16,000

REQUIRED: For each case, following the marshaling of assets rule, indicate how the assets of the partnership and the assets of each partner are applied if creditor claims are satisfied as fully as possible.

E16.9 **Safe Payment Calculation** Partners James, Storm, and Hadley share profits and losses in the ratio of 5:3:2, respectively. The partners vote to dissolve the partnership when its assets, liabilities, and capital are as follows:

Cash	$ 40,000	Liabilities	$ 60,000
Other Assets	210,000	Capital—James	48,000
		Capital—Storm	72,000
		Capital—Hadley	70,000
	$ 250,000		$ 250,000

The partnership will be liquidated over a prolonged period of time. As cash becomes available, it will be distributed to the partners. The first sale of noncash assets having a book value of $120,000 realizes $90,000.

REQUIRED: How much cash should be distributed to each partner after this sale? *(AICPA adapted)*

E16.10 **Lump-Sum Liquidation** Conley and Lewis, who share income in a 3:2 ratio, decide to liquidate their partnership. A condensed balance sheet prior to liquidation appears below.

Cash	$ 70,000	Liabilities	$ 190,000
Receivables	130,000	Loan Payable—Lewis . .	80,000
Inventory	100,000	Capital—Conley	140,000
Other Assets	200,000	Capital—Lewis	90,000
	$ 500,000		$ 500,000

REQUIRED: Assuming noncash assets are sold for $450,000, prepare a schedule showing how available cash should be distributed.

E16.11 **Simple Cash Distribution Plan** At the time they decided to liquidate their partnership, Whitehead, Ellis and Riley had capital balances of $75,000, $60,000 and $100,000, respectively. Liabilities were $48,000 and the balance sheet showed a note receivable from Riley in the amount of $40,000. The partners share income in a 5:3:2 ratio.

REQUIRED: Prepare a schedule showing how cash is to be distributed as it becomes available during the liquidation process.

E16.12 Limited Partnership Balance Sheet A firm called 1368 Main Associates is formed as a limited partnership to acquire and operate an apartment building. A promoter/general partner, who makes a $2,000 investment, sells 15 limited partnership interests for $10,000 each. The building costs $850,000; a down payment of $100,000 is made, with the remaining $750,000 financed via a 20-year mortgage. The general partner is paid $40,000 for services; this amount is to be expensed. Net loss for the first year, exclusive of the payment to the general partner, is $14,000; all items except depreciation of $37,500 are assumed to be cash transactions. Also, a payment of $20,000 is made on the principal of the mortgage. The partnership agreement provides that income is to be allocated 10 percent to the general partner and 90 percent to the limited partners.

REQUIRED: Prepare a balance sheet for the partnership at the end of its first year of operation.

PROBLEMS

P16.1 Retirement of Partner Horton, Fischer, and Walker are partners in a trucking firm. They share income in a 3:4:2 ratio, respectively. On March 8, the date Fischer retires from the partnership, the balances of the partners' capital accounts are Horton, $35,000; Fischer, $15,000; and Walker, $21,000. Fischer agreed to surrender his interest to Horton and Walker (who plan to continue the business) for $18,000 and a pick-up truck owned by the partnership. The cash payment is to be made from partnership funds. The truck cost $8,000 and has accumulated depreciation of $5,000. Fair value of the used truck is $3,900.

REQUIRED: Make the entries to record Fischer's retirement and compute the capital balances for Horton and Walker after the retirement (1) under the bonus approach and (2) under the partial goodwill approach.

P16.2 Retirement of Two Partners Thirty years ago, five mechanics formed a partnership and established an automobile repair shop. Two of the partners, Dewitt and Galax, are now retiring. The other three partners, Farber, Wayne, and Lane, are continuing the partnership. The original agreement called for an equal division of income. The remaining partners plan to continue this arrangement.

The following balance sheet is prepared for the partnership as of the retirement date:

Cash	$ 65,000	Accounts Payable	$ 90,000
Accounts Receivable .	80,000	Loan Payable	40,000
Inventory of Parts . . .	40,000	Capital—Dewitt	50,000
Equipment, Net	90,000	Capital—Galax	40,000
Building, Net	30,000	Capital—Farber	70,000
Land	25,000	Capital—Wayne	7,500
		Capital—Lane	32,500
	$ 330,000		$ 330,000

All partners agreed that Dewitt should receive $62,500 for his interest in the business and Galax should receive $50,000. Farber proposed the bonus method for recording the retirements. Wayne objects to this method and suggests the partial goodwill approach.

REQUIRED:

1. Prepare the journal entry to record the retirements under the bonus method.
2. Prepare the journal entry to record the retirements under the partial goodwill approach.
3. Why is Wayne objecting to the bonus method of accounting?
4. Regardless of the accounting method employed, what immediate problem for the business can you identify at the time of retirement? Propose a solution to this problem.

P16.3 Retirement—Various Cases Given below are account balances for the partnership of Flint, Yancy, and Goldsmith before the retirement of Goldsmith. Each case presents account balances of the Flint and Yancy partnership immediately after Goldsmith's retirement. The cases are independent of each other. In Case 4, no bonus was recorded.

Balance Sheet Accounts	Balances before Goldsmith's Retirement	Balances after Goldsmith's Retirement				
		Case 1	Case 2	Case 3	Case 4	Case 5
Cash	$ 50,000	$ 20,000	$ 0	$ 50,000	$ 50,000	$ 0
Other Assets	130,000	130,000	130,000	130,000	100,000	130,000
Goodwill	10,000	10,000	20,000	10,000	10,000	40,000
Liabilities	(70,000)	(70,000)	(70,000)	(70,000)	(70,000)	(70,000)
Capital—Flint	(40,000)	(45,000)	(40,000)	(80,000)	(45,000)	(50,000)
Capital—Yancy	(40,000)	(45,000)	(40,000)	(40,000)	(45,000)	(50,000)
Capital—Goldsmith . .	(40,000)	0	0	0	0	0

REQUIRED: For each independent case, answer the following questions. Show supporting calculations.

1. What method of accounting was used to record the retirement (bonus, goodwill, neither)?
2. How much did Goldsmith receive upon retirement?

P16.4 Financial Statement Effects of Retirement/Admission Moore, Mills, Sinclair & Co. (MMS) is a rapidly-growing regional CPA firm. It actively recruits new staff accountants at major colleges and universities and aggressively pursues exceptional partners and near-partners at other CPA firms. Concurrently, MMS's founders have been retiring. Moore left last year and Mills and Sinclair are contemplating retiring soon.

Prior to retirement of Mills and Sinclair, who each have a 20% share in profits and losses, the firm's condensed balance sheet appears as follows:

Moore, Mills, Sinclair & Co.
Balance Sheet
December 31, 19X3

Cash and Cash Equivalents	$ 178,000
Accounts Receivable—Clients	430,000
Notes Receivable—Sinclair	100,000
Prepayments	60,000
Fixed Assets, Net	500,000
Goodwill, Net	800,000
	$ 2,068,000
Trade Payables	$ 47,000
Accrued Liabilities	209,000
Notes Payable—1st National Bank	600,000
Notes Payable—Moore	200,000
Capital—Mills	270,000
Capital—Sinclair	195,000
Capital—Other Partners	547,000
	$ 2,068,000

After some discussion, the firm agrees to pay Mills $350,000 upon retirement, intending to borrow the cash to do so from 1st National Bank. Shortly thereafter, Luh, a highly competent and entrepreneurial information systems specialist, is offered a 10% interest in capital and profits for a $50,000 cash investment.

REQUIRED:

1. Discuss the ways in which the methods of accounting for the retirement could weaken the above balance sheet and illustrate with calculations.
2. Suppose Mills' retirement is accounted for by the total goodwill method. After Mills' retirement is recorded by the total goodwill approach, prepare pro-forma balance sheets for MMS that reflect Luh's admission under the two alternative admission methods described in Chapter 15.
3. Briefly describe the principal differences between the two balance sheets in 2. above. Which seems to portray the healthier firm? Why?

P16.5 Partnership Admission and Liquidation The following balance sheet is for the partnership of Alex, Stanley, and George (figures shown parenthetically reflect agreed income-sharing ratio):

Cash	$ 20,000		Liabilities	$ 50,000
Other Assets	180,000		Capital—Alex (40%) . . .	37,000
			Capital—Stanley (40%) . .	65,000
			Capital—George (20%) . .	48,000
	$ 200,000			$ 200,000

REQUIRED:

1. If the assets are fairly valued on the balance sheet and the partnership wishes to admit Day as a new partner having a one-sixth interest without recording goodwill or bonus, how much cash or other assets should Day contribute?
2. If assets on the initial balance sheet are fairly valued, Alex and Stanley consent, and Day pays George $51,000 for his interest, what would the revised capital balances of the partners be?
3. Assume that the firm, as shown on the original balance sheet, is dissolved and liquidated by selling assets in installments. The first sale of noncash assets, having a book value of $90,000, realized $50,000, and all cash available after settlement with creditors is distributed. How much cash would the respective partners receive (to the nearest dollar)?
4. If the facts are as in No. 3 above, except that $3,000 cash is to be withheld for expenses of liquidation, the respective partners would then receive how much cash (to the nearest dollar)?
5. Assume that each partner properly received some cash in the distribution after the second sale, the cash to be distributed amounts to $12,000 from the third sale, and unsold assets with an $8,000 book value remain. Ignoring Nos. 3 and 4 above, which of the following would the respective partners receive?
   a. Alex, $4,800; Stanley, $4,800; George, $2,400.
   b. Alex, $4,000; Stanley, $4,000; George, $4,000.
   c. Alex, 37/150 of $12,000; Stanley, 65/150 of $12,000; George, 48/150 of $12,000.
   d. Alex, $0; Stanley, $8,000; George, $4,000.
   (AICPA adapted)

P16.6 **Partnership Liquidation—Safe Payments** Several years ago, Judith Able, Leslie Bowen, Janice Cratz, and Donna Ogleby formed a partnership to operate the Abco Delicatessen. Rerouting of bus lines caused declines in patronage to the extent that the partners have agreed to dissolve the partnership and liquidate the assets.

The November 2, 19X0, balance sheet of the Abco Delicatessen and other data are given below. The partnership agreement did not specify how profits and losses were to be shared.

Abco Delicatessen
Balance Sheet
November 2, 19X0

Cash	$ 30,000		Liabilities	$ 40,000
Supplies	14,000		Loan—Ogleby	13,000
Equipment	35,000		Capital—Able	16,000
Fixtures	15,000		Capital—Bowen	7,000
			Capital—Cratz	3,000
			Capital—Ogleby	15,000
	$ 94,000			$ 94,000

Additional information:

1. During November, half of the fixtures were sold for $4,000. Equipment with a book value of $9,000 was sold for $4,000.
2. During December, all outside creditors were paid. A neighboring restaurant bought Abco Delicatessen's supplies at 85 percent of cost. The remaining fixtures were sold for $3,100.
3. During January, equipment with a book value of $6,000 was sold for $4,500.

REQUIRED: Following the safe payment approach, specify how cash is to be distributed at the end of November, December, and January.

P16.7　Partnership Liquidation—Cash Distribution Plan Assume the same data as in P16.6.

REQUIRED: Develop a cash distribution plan for the liquidation of Abco Delicatessen. Show each step in the development of the plan.

P16.8　Partnership Liquidation—Safe Payments On January 1, 19X2, partners Allen, Brown, and Cox, who share income in the ratio of 5:3:2, respectively, decide to liquidate their partnership. The partnership trial balance at this date is as follows:

	Debit	Credit
Cash	$ 18,000	
Accounts Receivable	66,000	
Inventory	52,000	
Machinery and Equipment (Net)	189,000	
Loan—Allen	30,000	
Accounts Payable		$ 53,000
Loan—Brown		20,000
Capital—Allen		118,000
Capital—Brown		90,000
Capital—Cox		74,000
	$ 355,000	$ 355,000

The partners plan a program of piecemeal conversion of assets in order to minimize liquidation losses. All available cash, less an amount retained to provide for future expenses, is to be distributed to the partners at the end of each month. A summary of the liquidation transactions is as follows:

January 19X2
1. $51,000 was collected on accounts receivable; the balance is uncollectible.
2. $38,000 was received for the entire inventory.
3. $2,000 liquidation expenses were paid.
4. $50,000 was paid to outside creditors, after offset of a $3,000 credit memorandum received on January 11, 19X2.
5. $10,000 cash was retained in the business at the end of the month for potential unrecorded liabilities and anticipated expenses.

February 19X2

6. $4,000 liquidation expenses were paid.
7. $6,000 cash was retained in the business at the end of the month for potential unrecorded liabilities and anticipated expenses.

March 19X2

8. $146,000 was received on sale of all items of machinery and equipment.
9. $5,000 liquidation expenses were paid.
10. No cash was retained in the business.

REQUIRED: Prepare a schedule to compute safe installment payments to the partners at the end of January, February, and March.
(AICPA adapted)

P16.9   Close Books and Prepare Cash Distribution Plan A, B and C agree to liquidate their partnership as soon as possible. The partnership agreement calls for salaries of $20,000 and $30,000 for A and B, respectively; any remaining profit or loss is divided in a 2:3:5 ratio. The preclosing trial balance for the partnership at July 31, 19X4, the end of the firm's fiscal year, is:

Account	Dr.	Cr.
Cash	$ 55,000	
Other Assets	210,000	
Liabilities		$ 69,000
Loan Payable—C		20,000
Capital—A		80,000
Capital—B		51,000
Capital—C		30,000
Sales		310,000
Operating Expenses	240,000	
Drawings—A	30,000	
Drawings—B	15,000	
Drawings—C	10,000	
	$ 560,000	$ 560,000

REQUIRED:

1. Prepare a schedule showing the closing of the books prior to liquidation.
2. Prepare a cash distribution plan for the liquidation.
3. Compute the amount that must be realized from the Other Assets to liquidate the Liabilities and drive all capital accounts to zero.

P16.10   Analysis of Liquidation Scenario Partners Green and Blue have operated a coin laundry business in a strip shopping center for several years. Their income-sharing ratio is 3:2. The business was generating decent operating cash flow but in the last 18 months, cash flow declined precipitously. On alternate days each partner empties the coins from the laundromat's machines and deposits them in the bank.

Green is experiencing personal financial problems relating to a messy divorce and investments that went "in the tank." She is urging Blue to sell out and liquidate their partnership. The following trial balance is prepared by the partners' accountant.

Cash	$ 2,300
Supplies and Prepayments	900
Equipment	42,000
Accumulated Depreciation	(17,000)
Accounts Payable	(1,350)
Loan Payable—Blue	(11,000)
Sales	(25,000)
Operating Expenses	13,000
Depreciation Expense	6,000
Capital—Green	(5,000)
Capital—Blue	(4,850)
	$ 0

In addition, the partnership has a noncancellable lease (remaining term: 2 years) on the building where the laundromat is located, classified as an operating lease under *SFAS 13*. The monthly payments of $500 are based on an implicit annual interest rate of 9% and are consistently made on time. Although the lessor would like to rent the space to a pizza shop which would bring more traffic to the strip shopping center, he stands behind the lease agreement that requires a $10,000 payment to release the lessees.

REQUIRED:

1. Identify the weakness in the partnership's internal control which could produce the pattern of declining cash flow.
2. If the partners decide to liquidate, explain whether they should pay the $10,000 or the present value of the remaining lease payments.
3. Using cash distribution plan methodology, explain whether it is in Green's interest to liquidate at this time.

P16.11 **Joint Venture Investments; Off-Balance-Sheet Financing** For years the Klingon Corporation has sought ways to accelerate collection of accounts receivable without alienating its customers. It sold receivables to factors in the past before the cost of doing so became prohibitive. At a recent industry convention in Atlantic City, New Jersey, the CFOs of Klingon and three other companies discussed the problem while enjoying submarine sandwiches at the renowned White House Sub Shop.

The four CFOs decided to form a "captive" finance company to purchase, service and collect their companies' customer receivables. A joint venture, the new Save-It Finance Company issues short-term securities backed by the companies' customer receivables for the cash needed to purchase the receivables from Klingon and friends. In this way, Klingon gets cash out of its receivables well in advance of the usual collection period.

After its first year of operation, Save-It Finance Company reported the following condensed balance sheet.

Save-It Finance Company
Balance Sheet
December 31, 19X1

Accounts Receivable	$ 200,000,000
Other Current Assets	10,000,000
	$ 210,000,000
Notes Payable	$ 208,000,000
Capital	2,000,000
	$ 210,000,000

On the same date, Klingon's condensed balance sheet showed:

Klingon Corporation
Balance Sheet
December 31, 19X1

Current Assets	$ 150,000,000
Plant Assets, Net	599,500,000
Investment in Save-It (25%)	500,000
	$ 750,000,000
Current Liabilities	$ 100,000,000
Noncurrent Liabilities	200,000,000
Stockholders' Equity	450,000,000
	$ 750,000,000

REQUIRED:

1. Prepare Klingon's balance sheet using (1) proportionate consolidation and (2) the expanded equity method to report the investment in Save-It.
2. Considering Klingon's financial leverage (TL/TA) under these alternatives, what other reason might Klingon have for forming Save-It?

P16.12 **Limited Partnership Distributions, Rate of Return** Judith Jamison formed Suburban Properties IX as a limited partnership to acquire a shopping center. Jamison, who serves as general partner, made a $5,000 investment. Nineteen limited partnership interests were sold at $25,000 each.

The shopping center was purchased for $3,600,000. A down payment of $250,000 was made, with the balance financed by a mortgage. In addition, $200,000 was paid to Jamison as a commission on the transaction; this amount is to be capitalized as part of the cost of the shopping center. The center is to be depreciated straight-line over 20 years, with zero salvage value.

The limited partnership agreement contains the following terms:

1. Operating profit or loss is to be allocated 95 percent to the limited partners and 5 percent to the general partner.

2. If cash flow from operations in any year exceeds $10,000, a distribution of $10,000 is to be made, 95 percent to the limited partners and 5 percent to the general partner. If cash flow in a given year does not exceed $10,000, no distribution is to be made that year. For this purpose, principal payments on the mortgage count as operating disbursements.

3. Upon sale of the property, sale proceeds net of mortgage repayment are to be distributed as follows:
   a. One hundred percent to limited partners until they have received their original investment net of any distributions received to date.
   b. Thereafter, 57 percent to the limited partners and 43 percent to the general partner.

4. Any remaining operating cash shall be distributed 95 percent to the limited partners and 5 percent to the general partner.

Operating results were as follows:

	Year 1	Year 2	Year 3	Year 4
Revenues (Cash)	$ 700,000	$ 720,000	$ 735,000	$ 740,000
Cash Expenses (Including Interest)	610,000	610,000	600,000	605,000
Principal Payments	100,000	110,000	120,000	130,000

The shopping center was sold at the end of Year 4 for $4,500,000, and the partnership was terminated in accordance with the limited partnership agreement.

REQUIRED:

1. Determine, by year, the cash distributions to
   a. the limited partners.
   b. the general partner.
2. Calculate the internal rate of return earned by a limited partner on this investment.

P16.13 Analyze Limited Partnership Viability The Wildcat Natural Resources Exploration Partnership (WINREP) was formed on January 2, 19X6 and began generating cash flow later in 19X6. The essentials of the partnership agreement were:

- Fifty limited partnership shares were authorized, and sold, for $100,000 each. The resulting proceeds were used to acquire drilling equipment, well casing and other tangible assets.
- Each limited partner is to receive 1.8% of the net cash flow from each economically viable project, including any liquidation proceeds.
- The general partner contributes expertise and access to leases on various properties in exchange for 10% of the net cash flow from each economically viable project.
- Cash distributions occur at year-end.
- The general partner decides when a project is economically viable, based on geological data and cash flow forecasts.
- All partners are charged with cash outflows on unsuccessful projects in the proportions indicated above.

During the life of WINREP, the general partner demonstrated an extraordinary drilling record, only selecting projects that ultimately were economically viable. Net cash flows occur at year end and were as follows:

	19X9	19X8	19X7	19X6
Net Cash Flow	$ 250,000	$ 300,000	$ 240,000	$ 90,000

In response to inquiries by several limited partners, the general partner estimated that likely annual cash flows will approximate $280,000 in the future.

REQUIRED:

1. Given the above information, from the limited partners' perspective does WINREP appear to have been a good investment as of January 2, 19X6? Do a present value analysis assuming an annual discount rate of 10%. Ignore income tax factors.
2. Some limited partners have threatened to sue the general partner. What is the likely nature of their complaint?
3. How would you revise the partnership agreement to better protect the rights of the limited partners?

THE SEC AND ITS ROLE IN FINANCIAL REPORTING

MODULE PREVIEW

Accounting students who are relatively familiar with the Financial Accounting Standards Board (FASB), and its predecessor standard-setting organizations from the private sector, sense that the federal government also plays a role through the Securities and Exchange Commission (SEC). The work of the SEC is alluded to in previous accounting courses but is not examined in depth. Because the SEC has the statutory authority (1) to set accounting principles (this authority is delegated to the FASB) and (2) to regulate the securities markets, the SEC deserves more detailed consideration in an advanced financial accounting course.

Accordingly, the purpose of this module is to discuss the rationale for and nature of securities regulation, the SEC, its role in financial reporting, and some of the regulations it has created and enforced. Of special interest is the relationship between the SEC and the FASB; this relationship is discussed at the end of the module. Important areas to be studied are

- The setting for the establishment of the SEC
- Securities legislation and the SEC
- Organization and structure of the SEC
- Registration of new securities
- Periodic reporting requirements
- Corporate accountability and governance
- The SEC and accounting standards

Complying with SEC regulations in professional practice often requires highly specialized expertise, and many professional accountants dedicate themselves to becoming experts in this field. It represents another important way in which the professional can contribute to sound financial reporting and efficient securities markets.

Previous chapters addressed selected accounting and reporting issues encountered when dealing with large, complex corporate entities. Financial reporting for such large publicly held companies encompasses more than periodic reports to shareholders prepared in accordance with generally accepted accounting principles. Additional rules and regulations, with which the company's accountants and independent auditors must be familiar, apply. While some state regulations may apply, by far the most significant and extensive requirements have been established by the U.S. **Securities and Exchange Commission (SEC).**

THE SETTING FOR THE ESTABLISHMENT OF THE SEC

The stock market crash of 1929 started a financial panic unparalleled in American history.[1] Market averages lost about *50 percent* of their value during the autumn of 1929. The averages hit bottom in the summer of 1932, having plummeted to about *20 percent* of their precrash levels. At the same time, the value of extensive holdings of foreign bonds by U.S. citizens had collapsed. According to one estimate, by 1932 the bonds of 16 European nations had lost about 43 percent of par; similar losses for bonds of Latin American nations amounted to 74 percent of par, including a drop of 93 percent in Peruvian bonds.[2] Considerable discussion ensued as to the role the federal government might play in regulating the issuance and trading of securities. Several years of debate led to the passage of the Securities Act of 1933 and the Securities Exchange Act of 1934. The latter act established the Securities and Exchange Commission (SEC). Despite the Great Crash, though, the 1933 and 1934 acts were part of a more comprehensive tapestry depicting disaster and response.

> Securities legislation was conceived during the worst financial and social crisis in our history. It was part of a much broader program of social reform that promised to give a New Deal to Mr. Everyman at a time when the economy was prostrate. Twenty-five percent of the labor force was unemployed in 1933. Four thousand banks failed that year, and 252,400 nonfarm properties were foreclosed. The GNP in 1933 declined to 53 percent of its 1929 level.[3]

The enactment of this legislation, however, did not end the debate over the federal government's role in regulating the securities markets. That discussion still continues, as evidenced by several well-known congressional hearings in recent years. Moreover, a number of studies of security price behavior during periods before and after the SEC was formed fail to establish a strong empirical case for SEC regulation of financial disclosures.[4]

SECURITIES LEGISLATION AND THE SEC

The mission of the SEC is to administer federal legislation that promotes efficient capital allocation by ensuring that securities markets function fairly and honestly. Embedded in the SEC's mission are protection of investors by requiring full disclosure of material information by issuers of securities, and prevention of fraudulent activities in securities trading and markets. The SEC is charged with administering the following federal securities laws:

- Securities Act of 1933
- Securities Exchange Act of 1934

---

[1] For a highly readable account of the Great Crash and its immediate aftermath, see John K. Galbraith, *The Great Crash*: 1929, 2d ed. (Boston: Houghton Mifflin Company, 1961).

[2] Joel Seligman, "The SEC and Accounting: A Historical Perspective." In *The SEC and Accounting: The First 50 Years—1984 Proceedings of the Arthur Young Professors' Roundtable*, edited by Robert H. Mundheim and Noyes E. Leech, (New York: North-Holland, 1986), 5.

[3] John W. Buckley, Marlene H. Buckley, and Tom M. Plank, *SEC Accounting*, (New York: John Wiley & Sons, 1980), 1.

[4] For a readable account of issues surrounding the need for and desirability of SEC regulation, see E. Richard Brownlee II and S. David Young, "The SEC and Mandated Disclosure: At the Crossroads," *Accounting Horizons* (Sept., 1987), 17-24.

- Public Utility Holding Company Act of 1935
- Trust Indenture Act of 1939
- Investment Company Act of 1940
- Investment Advisers Act of 1940

The **Securities Act of 1933** deals primarily with the issuance of new securities. It regulates the public offering of securities, prohibiting (subject to certain exemptions) the offering and sale of securities unless they are registered with the government. It also prohibits fraudulent or deceptive practices in the offering or sale of securities.

The **Securities Exchange Act of 1934** established the **Securities and Exchange Commission** and granted it jurisdiction over the securities markets. The 1934 act deals with trading in securities once they have been issued and are outstanding. This act authorizes the government, *through the SEC*, to establish accounting, reporting, and disclosure requirements for publicly owned corporations, and it prohibits deceptive and manipulative practices in the purchase or sale of securities.

Although the 1933 and 1934 acts are the primary focus of our discussion, several other laws also relate to the securities markets and contribute to the work of the SEC. To prevent abuse of the holding company device in controlling and manipulating public utility operating companies, the **Public Utility Holding Company Act of 1935** was enacted. This act requires public utility holding companies to register with the SEC, provides for SEC-influenced reorganization of such holding companies when dictated by the public interest, and calls for equitable distribution of voting power among security holders in a public utility system.

The **Trust Indenture Act of 1939** deals with the issuance of bonds. It requires a formal trust agreement, or *indenture*, specifying the rights of the bondholders, and provides for the appointment, by the issuing company, of an independent trustee to represent the bondholders. The **Investment Company Act of 1940** regulates investment companies, such as *open-end mutual funds* and *closed-end investment companies*. When such companies register with the SEC, they fulfill certain disclosure requirements involving their investment policies, management fees, etc., and solicit shareholder participation in company policy. The **Investment Advisers Act of 1940** requires that those who provide paid advice to the public concerning securities must register with the SEC. Activities of such advisers are also regulated; for example, they may not receive a share of the gains in their clients' portfolios.

More recently, the **Securities Investor Protection Act of 1970** created the Securities Investor Protection Corp. (SIPC), which insures customer accounts held by brokers. The SIPC must file annual reports and financial statements with the SEC, and all of its activities are subject to inspection by the SEC. The **Foreign Corrupt Practices Act (FCPA) of 1977**, enacted to stop U.S. companies from making illegal payments to foreign entities, requires companies to maintain accurate accounting records and to maintain a system of effective internal accounting controls. These provisions of the FCPA, which are administered by the SEC, apply to all companies that register with or report to the commission. Another key law, the **Insider Trading Sanctions Act of 1984**, drastically increased penalties assessed for violating the insider trading rules. Under this legislation, "the SEC can seek fines of up to the greater of $1 million or three times the profits gained or losses avoided by those insiders who inappropriately use material nonpublic information."[5]

The **Private Securities Litigation Reform Act of 1995** also involves the SEC. This act provides the long-sought tort liability reform limiting the liability of public accountants to their

---

[5] K. Fred Skousen, *An Introduction to the SEC*, 5th ed. (Cincinnati: South-Western Pub. Co., 1991), 39.

"fair share" in certain securities suits. It also creates new safe harbors—protection against lawsuits—that apply to certain forward-looking financial information reported by registrants to the SEC and illegal acts reported by auditors to the SEC.

DEFINITION OF SECURITY

The Securities Act of 1933 established a broad definition of the meaning of a **security**, as follows:

> Any note, stock, treasury stock, bond, debenture, evidence of indebtedness, certificate of interest or participation in any profit-sharing agreement, collateral trust certificate, preorganization certificate or subscription, transferable share, investment contract, voting trust certificate, certificate of deposit for a security, fractional undivided interest in oil, gas, or other mineral rights, or, in general, any interest or instrument commonly known as a "security," or any certificate of interest or participation in, temporary or interim certificate for, receipt of, guarantee of, or warrant or right to subscribe to or to purchase, any of the foregoing.[6]

The law provided several categories of securities that are exempt from the SEC's registration and reporting rules, although other provisions, such as the antifraud rules, generally apply to these securities. The following are among the *exempt securities*:

- Securities issued or guaranteed by federal, state, or local government.
- Securities issued or guaranteed by a bank or savings and loan association. These securities, however, are subject to the provisions of the 1934 act.
- Commercial paper, that is, short-term notes (original maturity not exceeding nine months) issued for working capital purposes.
- Securities issued by not-for-profit organizations. These also are subject to the provisions of the 1934 act.

Subsequent legislation and litigation clarified the securities status of other financial instruments. The basic question to be addressed in deciding whether a financial instrument is a *security* is whether "the person invests his money in a common enterprise and is led to expect profits solely from the efforts of the promoter or a third party."[7] Thus interests in real estate condominiums, interests in oil drilling programs, variable annuities (where the return depends on the performance of a portfolio of securities), and commodity option contracts have all been held to be securities. On the other hand, bank certificates of deposit, savings and loan "shares," life insurance policies, and notes representing ordinary bank loans are *not* securities. Because the definition of a security is so broad, many financial transactions fall under the jurisdiction of the securities laws.

ORGANIZATION AND STRUCTURE OF THE SEC

As previously mentioned, the SEC administers and enforces the federal securities laws. The SEC consists of five commissioners, collectively known as the *commission*. The president appoints one commissioner each year for a staggered five-year term. No more than three of the five commissioners can be from the president's political party. As an independent, nonpartisan agency,

---

[6] Securities Act of 1933, Sec. 2(1).
[7] *SEC v. W.J. Howey Co.*, 328 U.S. 293(1946).

the SEC is not part of the legislative or executive branches of government. It is funded by a combination of user charges and congressional appropriations. The commission has a support staff of about 2,000 employees; the staff position best known to accountants is that of *Chief Accountant of the SEC*.

The SEC is organized into several divisions. The division most frequently encountered by accountants is the **Division of Corporate Finance**. It processes documents known as *filings*, that are filed with the SEC, such as registration statements and periodic reports, and closely examines a sample of perhaps 20 percent of these filings, including all first-time registration statements. This division primarily administers the disclosure requirements of the securities laws, but it is also involved in matters concerning proxy statements, insider trading, and tender offers.

The **Division of Enforcement** is charged with enforcing the securities laws except for the Public Utility Holding Company Act. It investigates possible violations by market participants, such as corporate officers, brokers, financial analysts, and accountants, who are suspected of violating laws and regulations. The division then makes recommendations to the Justice Department concerning administrative proceedings (consent decrees and settlements), injunctions, and criminal prosecution.

The **Division of Market Regulation** oversees the operations of the secondary securities markets and the trading of already-outstanding securities, including the monitoring of trading activities and stock market operations. It also administers the provisions of the Investment Advisers Act.

Finally, the **Division of Investment Management** has oversight and investigative responsibilities for the Investment Company Act of 1940, the Investment Advisors Act of 1940, and the Public Utility Holding Company Act of 1935. These duties include monitoring sales practices, advertising, and new products of mutual funds; processing investment company filings; and analyzing the legal and financial structure of public utility holding companies.

Several staff offices serve as technical advisors to the commission. They cooperate extensively with the SEC divisions in fulfilling the SEC's mission. Current staff offices include

- Office of the General Counsel
- Directorate of Economic and Policy Analysis
- Office of the Chief Economist
- Office of Administrative Law Judges
- Office of the Chief Accountant

The **Chief Accountant of the SEC** is the SEC's expert on accounting principles, auditing standards, and financial disclosures. The Chief Accountant advises the commission on these topics, supervises the preparation of SEC accounting and auditing pronouncements, and reviews investigations of questionable accounting and auditing practices made by the Division of Enforcement. Assisted by about 15 technical experts, the Chief Accountant also serves as the link between the SEC and the accounting profession, and has *oversight powers over the FASB and the AICPA*. The Chief Accountant expresses the SEC's views in speeches, papers, and appearances before standard-setting groups.

SEC PRONOUNCEMENTS ON ACCOUNTING AND AUDITING

Recall that the goal of the SEC is to promote efficient allocation of capital by helping to maintain honest and fair securities markets. One important means for accomplishing this goal is to communicate relevant information about securities to market participants. This in turn should lead to improved methods of security analysis and increased public confidence in the securities markets. Indeed, the Securities Acts are largely disclosure acts. Although the SEC delegates its authority to set accounting principles—recognition and measurement issues—to the private sector, it occasionally requires additional disclosures of its registrants and frequently comments on accounting and auditing matters. The SEC communicates its views on accounting and auditing-related matters in formal published pronouncements and through less formal methods, as follows.

- *Financial Reporting Releases (FRR or FR)*, which are formal pronouncements analogous to statements of the FASB. By law, the SEC has the power to establish accounting and reporting standards for companies whose securities are under its jurisdiction. The *FRR*s therefore are viewed as the highest-ranking authoritative source of accounting principles for publicly held companies.

     Early in 1982, the *FRR*s replaced a similar series of pronouncements known as *Accounting Series Releases (ASR)*, which were issued since 1937 on both accounting principle issues and SEC enforcement proceedings. In 1982 the SEC organized relevant portions of the current *ASR*s to form a coherent reference document known as the *Codification of Financial Reporting Policies*.[8] This *Codification* is updated when affected by newly issued *FRR*s, of which there are now more than 40.

- *Staff Accounting Bulletins (SAB)*, which are similar, but not identical, to FASB *Technical Bulletins*. *SAB*s are issued by the SEC staff, including the Chief Accountant, without due process, and without a vote by the commission. They represent the staff's current position on the proper reporting of controversial accounting issues in documents submitted to the SEC. Three *SAB*s studied in this text are *SAB 54* and *SAB 73* on "push-down" accounting, and *SAB 51* and *SAB 84* on reporting gains from subsidiary stock issuances.

- *Emerging Issues Task Force (EITF)* Established by the FASB in 1984, the EITF addresses certain narrow, technical accounting issues requiring quick resolution. A key participant in EITF deliberations is the Chief Accountant of the SEC. In this role, the Chief Accountant has the authority to not permit an EITF consensus to apply to public companies and may make statements at EITF meetings that have the force of *Staff Accounting Bulletins*.

- *Accounting and Auditing Enforcement Releases (AAER)*, which report disciplinary or other enforcement actions against accountants. These matters previously were reported in *Accounting Series Releases*. Thus, the topics covered in the *ASR*s prior to early 1982 are now covered in two series: accounting pronouncements in the *FRR*s and enforcement matters in the *AAER*s. Unlike the *SAB*s, all such releases require an affirmative vote by the SEC commissioners.

- Forms, or lists of items to be reported (unlike preprinted IRS forms which taxpayers fill in), plus instructions for the nature and detail of disclosures, as presented in Regulation S-K, Regulation S-X, and the General Rules.

- Private rulings to companies concerning particular transactions. Referred to as *no-action and interpretation letters*, these rulings indicate that the SEC will not object if a transaction is handled in the proposed manner. Such rulings frequently relate to the accounting treatment of a merger or acquisition.

---

[8] This *Codification* is included in the *SEC Accounting Guide* published and updated periodically by Commerce Clearing House, Chicago, IL.

■ Informal statements by commissioners or top staff, such as the Chief Accountant. These statements, often in the form of speeches or written releases, convey informally the views of key individuals on certain matters. This format is frequently used to express views on matters being considered by the FASB or by the accounting profession.

■ The SEC's annual reports.

REGISTRATION OF NEW SECURITIES

The key feature of the Securities Act of 1933 is registration of new security issues. This requirement is a direct response to the deceptive and manipulative environment frequently encountered by investors in the 1920s and early 1930s. Because the SEC acts as a conduit for information provided by issuers of securities to other market participants, its **full disclosure** requirement that new security issues of public companies be registered

> is intended to provide adequate and accurate disclosure of material facts concerning the company and the securities it proposes to sell. Thus, investors may make a realistic appraisal of the merits of the securities and then exercise informed judgment in determining whether or not to purchase them.[9]

The 1933 act provides that, with a few exemptions, no security may be offered or sold to the public unless it is registered with the SEC. Most corporate equity and publicly held debt securities are registered. Achieving registration does not mean that the SEC passes judgment on the merits of the security; rather, it means only that certain disclosure requirements have been satisfied. In other words, the SEC performs *compliance reviews*, not *merit reviews*. The 1933 act also sets forth the registration procedure and establishes liabilities for misstatements or omissions.

A prospective issuer becomes an SEC **registrant** and must file a **registration statement**—the set of documents needed to register securities—with the SEC. The registration statement consists of two parts: (1) information generally included in a *prospectus*, which must also be furnished to each purchaser of the security, and (2) other information and exhibits, which must be publicly available but need not be supplied to each investor. The **prospectus** is a small booklet describing the issuing company, its business operations, its financial statements, historical financial information, the securities to be sold, and the expected uses of the proceeds.[10] Typically a **registration team**, consisting of the issuer's chief financial officer, legal counsel and independent public accountant, and the underwriter (investment banker) and underwriter's counsel, is assembled to prepare the registration statement.

A registration statement could become effective as early as 20 days after it is filed. The SEC's Division of Corporation Finance has 20 days to review the statement to see if it meets disclosure requirements. Reviews may be complete or partial, and a **letter of comment** stating any suggestions or criticisms is sent to the issuing company. Responses to SEC comments and amendments to the registration statement frequently create additional 20-day waiting periods, thereby delaying the effective date. Even a cursory SEC review, however, does not relieve the registrant of the obligation to provide complete and accurate disclosures. Once the registration statement becomes effective, the issuer may sell the securities to the public.

---

[9] U.S. Securities and Exchange Commission, *The Work of the SEC* (Washington, DC: SEC, 1986), 5.

[10] To help promote their securities before the registration process becomes effective, companies distribute *preliminary prospectuses*, with those words stamped in red on the cover, to a small group of potential investors. Because changes were often made to these red-stamped preliminary prospectuses after SEC review, they became known as **red herrings**.

Form S-1 is the basic form for the registration of new issues. Other commonly used forms (again, lists of required disclosures) are short forms **S-2** and **S-3** used by issuers meeting specified criteria, **Form S-4** for securities issued in business combinations, and **Form S-18** for smaller security offerings by smaller companies. Companies may be able to file the simpler Form S-2 or S-3 if they have already filed an annual Form 10-K within the SEC's Integrated Disclosure System (discussed later in this module). The logic here is that, since information about such companies is already available to the market, less additional information is needed from them than from the company going public for the first time.

Financial data presented in a registration statement include a balance sheet dated within 90 days of filing, income statements and statements of cash flows for the past three years, summaries of operations for the past five years, and various other schedules and disclosures. Such data must be accompanied by an auditor's report covering at least through the end of the last fiscal year. The period from the last audited statement to the date of the registration statement, known as the **stub period**, is generally covered by an accountant's review report. Accountants also commonly write **comfort letters** to the underwriter providing negative assurance on non-financial statement information contained in the registration statement.

There are two major exemptions to the registration requirements. One is for small offerings; there are various rules as to the maximum dollar size and number of investors that are allowed under this provision. The second exemption is for **private placements**; that is, securities issued to a single investor or small group of investors who have access to the kind of information otherwise disclosed during registration. Institutional investors such as insurance companies and pension funds frequently absorb private placements.

The flow of the securities in a typical issuance is

$$\text{Issuer} \rightarrow \text{Underwriter} \rightarrow \text{Dealer} \rightarrow \text{Public,}$$

where the underwriter advises the company about the terms and structure of the issue and markets the securities to the public. An underwriter agrees to handle a security issue under one of three types of arrangements.

- A **firm commitment** underwriting means that the underwriter buys the entire issue at a fixed price, and it is responsible for selling the issue to dealers, who will in turn sell it to the public. The underwriter bears the risk that the issue will not find market acceptance at the asking price.

- A **best efforts** underwriting means that the underwriter sells as many shares as possible, receiving a commission based on sales. The issuing company bears the risk of nonacceptance in the market.

- An **all or none** underwriting means that if the underwriter is unable to sell all, or a predetermined portion, of the issue, then the issue may be cancelled and the "sold" shares redeemed. This arrangement relieves the issuing company of the risk that not enough capital will be raised to sustain the project or projects for which the securities are being sold.

After a new security issue is registered and sold, it normally is traded in a secondary market. Depending upon the size and nature of the issue, it may be traded *over-the-counter* by dealers or listed and traded on one of the organized securities exchanges. The issuing company now has a continuing obligation to the SEC, and to the public, to provide full and complete disclosure of relevant information, and must satisfy the SEC's periodic reporting requirements.

PERIODIC REPORTING REQUIREMENTS

The Securities Exchange Act of 1934 subjects currently traded securities to the same "full disclosure" philosophy that the 1933 act applies to newly offered securities in order to promote efficient allocation of the country's capital resources. Thus issuers of currently traded securities also are SEC registrants and file periodic reports with the SEC so that important information about issuers' affairs becomes public and improves the efficiency of the securities markets. The **periodic reporting requirements** of the SEC cover all companies that have securities listed on a national securities exchange, along with all companies that have more than 500 stockholders and more than $3,000,000 in assets. About 3,000 listed companies, and several thousand unlisted, over-the-counter companies, are subject to the SEC's reporting and disclosure rules.

Prior to 1982, separate disclosure systems existed under the two major securities acts. The disclosure system under the 1933 act was oriented toward companies making public offerings of their securities, whereas disclosure under the 1934 act emphasized timely disclosure of current information about companies whose securities were already publicly traded. Each system had its own set of requirements and reports. Moreover, a company's annual report to shareholders represented a third similar, but far from identical, financial reporting system.

Addressing this problem, the SEC implemented changes beginning with *ASR 279* in 1979 and ending with *ASR 306* in 1982, when the final components of an **Integrated Disclosure System** were put in place.[11] To reduce the burden of complying with SEC requirements, major efforts were made to standardize the disclosures required by the 1933 and 1934 acts, and to bring financial statement data published in annual reports to shareholders into conformity with reports required by the SEC, along with other changes and simplifications.

Under the current system, the principal reports made by issuers to the SEC are the annual report (Form 10-K), quarterly reports (Form 10-Q), and special reports (Form 8-K) that are filed for any month in which certain specified events occur. Contents of these reports are largely governed by two sets of regulations: *Regulation S-X* addresses accounting and financial statement requirements for both annual and quarterly reports, and *Regulation S-K* covers all other disclosures. *Regulation S-B* integrates and simplifies the registration and periodic reporting requirements for small businesses.

THE ANNUAL REPORT: FORM 10-K

The **annual report** to the SEC, which follows the requirements specified in **Form 10-K**, is an extensive document presenting both financial statements and a variety of disclosures and descriptive information. Exhibit E.1 outlines the structure of the annual report required by Form 10-K. Note that financial statements comprise only one of the fourteen categories of information; financial disclosures and a variety of nonfinancial information account for the remainder.

In the interest of standardizing reporting and disclosure, the Integrated Disclosure System requires that a company's annual financial report to its stockholders must conform to SEC financial statement requirements set forth in Regulation S-X. Moreover, the SEC encourages

---

[11] Discussion of the Integrated Disclosure System is found in Sec. 102 of the SEC's *Codification of Financial Reporting Policies.*

Item	Description
	Part I
1	Description of the business
2	Description of properties
3	Legal proceedings involving the company
4	Submission of matters to a vote of stockholders
	Part II
5	Market price of common stock, dividends, and related stockholder matters
6	Selected financial data
7	Management's discussion and analysis of financial condition and results of operations
8	Financial statements and supplementary financial information
9	Disagreements with accountants on accounting and financial disclosure
	Part III
10	Directors and executive officers
11	Executive compensation and transactions with executives
12	Security ownership by certain beneficial owners and by management
13	Certain relationships and related-party transactions
	Part IV
14	Exhibits
	Signatures

EXHIBIT E.1   STRUCTURE AND CONTENTS OF FORM 10-K

inclusion of other SEC-required disclosures in the annual report to stockholders. Such information can be incorporated into the 10-K report by reference to the annual report to shareholders. **Incorporation by reference** means that the data already appear, in the required form, in the annual report to shareholders. When presenting a particular item in the 10-K, or in another report to the SEC, specific reference is made to the location of the information in the annual report. For example, the following disclosure appeared in a recent 10-K filed by Union Pacific Corporation.

Item 8. Financial Statements and Supplementary Data

The consolidated financial statements and related notes of Union Pacific are presented on pages 31 through 40 of the Annual Report. Selected quarterly financial data are set forth under Selected Quarterly Data, appearing on page 41 of the Annual Report. Information about oil and gas producing activities is set forth under Supplementary Information, appearing on pages 41 though 44 of the Annual Report. All of this information is incorporated herein by reference.

A company's 10-K report must be filed with the SEC within 90 days of the end of the registrant's fiscal year. It is also filed with the exchange on which the stock is traded. In addition, copies must be made available by the registrant to company stockholders and others upon request. Although the SEC does not provide copies of 10-Ks, the public may photocopy 10-Ks and other SEC filings in the SEC's public reference room.

The 10-K is signed by the company, its principal executive officer, its principal financial officer, its principal accounting officer (usually the controller), and a majority of the board of directors. This requirement signifies the broad responsibility of officers and directors for proper reporting and disclosure.

Electronic Data Gathering, Analysis, and Retrieval System (EDGAR)

In addition to benefits of the Integrated Disclosure System on registrants, discussed above, the SEC has further expedited the filing process with modern computer technology. Known as **EDGAR**, and governed by *Regulation S-T,* the new **Electronic Data Gathering, Analysis, and Retrieval System** reduces the amount of paperwork processed and stored by the SEC and reflects the following policy objectives:[12]

- To provide investors, securities analysts, and the public with instant access to filers' disclosure documents.
- To allow companies to make required filings electronically by using their existing equipment.
- To allow the commission and its staff to process and analyze filings more efficiently.

After a document to be filed is prepared and converted into a format acceptable to EDGAR, it is filed by direct transmission using a modem or by physically delivering a diskette or magnetic tape to the SEC. Hardcopy documents such as the annual report to shareholders are sometimes not available in a word processing format compatible with EDGAR. When such documents are *incorporated by reference* into an SEC filing, they are filed separately in hardcopy form using Form SE. The ability to submit SEC filings using EDGAR can also enable companies to communicate electronically with analysts, underwriters, and counsel involved with security issuances.[13] Registrants were phased into EDGAR over three years; by 1996 all domestic registrants were required to file registration statements and periodic reports electronically.

REGULATION S-K

The accounting, reporting, and disclosure requirements for preparing the 10-K are set forth in Regulations S-X and S-K. In Exhibit E.1, Item 8—financial statements and supplementary financial information—is governed by Regulation S-X; the other 13 items are governed by **Regulation S-K**. Following is a brief discussion of the content of many of these 13 items. This discussion indicates the broad range of information required by the SEC, extending far beyond what is commonly found in the annual financial report to stockholders.

---

[12] These objectives originated in an SEC document as reported in Jerry L. Arnold and Michael A. Diamond, *EDGAR: The SEC's Pilot Program and Its Impact* (Morristown, NJ: Financial Executives Research Foundation, 1986), 2.

[13] Robert C. Folbigg, "Behind the Scenes with EDGAR: It Works!" *Financial Executive* (March/ April, 1988), 43-45.

Item 1: Description of Business

Item 1 provides a narrative overview of the registrant's business operations, including principal products or services, major markets served, and primary methods of distribution. Any significant organizational developments since the beginning of the year are reported, such as mergers or acquisitions, or bankruptcy proceedings. In addition, financial information about industry segments, foreign and domestic operations, and export sales is presented. Accounting standards governing these disclosures are discussed in Module D. Item 1 disclosures explain the scope and diversity of company business operations, and allow assessment of the company's potential susceptibility to industry changes and regional, national, and international economic trends.

Item 2: Description of Properties

Item 2 contains descriptions of the location and general character of the company's principal plants; oil, gas, or other mineral deposits; and other physical properties. Users of the report need these physical descriptions to appreciate what lies behind the dollar amounts of plant assets reported in the corporate balance sheet. Property descriptions may be extremely brief or very detailed.

Item 3: Legal Proceedings

Item 3 describes, in some detail, significant legal proceedings involving the company. Because this disclosure is usually more detailed than that presented in the annual report to stockholders, interested readers become better informed about the company's potential legal exposure and may be able to sense the adverse effects of significant liabilities lying beneath the surface.

Item 5: Stock Prices and Dividends

Data in Item 5 indicate the approximate number of stockholders of the company and the principal markets in which the stock is traded. The high and low stock price for each quarter of the past two years is presented, along with the amount and frequency of dividends during the past two years. Companies are encouraged to make a statement of expectation that dividends will or will not be paid in the near future. This convenient item indicates in one place how widely-held the stock is, a rough picture of the stock's recent price volatility, and the recent dividend payment record.

Item 6: Selected Financial Data

Item 6 presents summaries of financial data to highlight trends in the company's financial condition and operating results, and to provide a basis for evaluating the company's performance and financial position in the current year. These summaries include, for each of the past five years, at least the following:

- Net sales or operating revenues.
- Income or loss from continuing operations.
- Income or loss per share from continuing operations.
- Total assets.
- Long-term obligations and redeemable preferred stock.
- Cash dividends declared per common share.

Companies may disclose additional items that they believe are informative with respect to trends in their financial condition and operating results. Current value and/or constant dollar financial results, which are no longer mandatory, represent an additional item that could be disclosed.

Item 7: Management's Discussion and Analysis

A major disclosure is Item 7, **management's discussion and analysis (MD&A)** of the company's financial condition and operating results, with particular emphasis on the company's liquidity and capital resources. The principal objective of MD&A is to allow the reader to examine the company through the eyes of management. It represents management's opportunity, indeed obligation, to provide analytical commentary on the current state of the company's business operations and likely significant future developments. The key areas to be discussed are *liquidity, capital resources*, and *operations*.

Liquidity is the ability of the company to generate adequate amounts of cash to meet its needs. Any known commitments or events that will significantly affect liquidity, or any major uncertainties that, if realized, will have a material effect on liquidity, should be identified. If major liquidity problems exist, management should discuss actions it is taking or plans to remedy the problems.

Capital resources involve both sources of long-term funding and expenditures on long-term assets. Major commitments or plans for capital expenditures, such as plant expansions, acquisition of pollution control equipment, or energy-saving investments, should be described. Trends or anticipated changes in the sources of long-term capital—debt, equity, and off-balance-sheet forms of financing—should also be discussed.

With respect to **operations**, any unusual or infrequent events or transactions that materially affected income should be disclosed. Trends or uncertainties that may significantly affect revenues—whether favorably or unfavorably—should be discussed, along with events that are expected to change the relationship between costs and revenues. Significant year-to-year changes in line items on the financial statements should be explained.

As a sign of the importance of MD&A, the SEC performed a multiphase review of companies' filings. In 1989, the SEC issued *FRR 36* in response to a review of 10-K filings made by more than 350 companies in which major shortcomings in MD&A were identified. Following that review, comment letters were sent to *over 96 percent* of the companies whose filings were reviewed.

A principal thrust of *FRR 36* involves improved disclosure of **prospective information**. In particular, the SEC now requires disclosure of management's expectations regarding the future consequences of currently known trends, events, and uncertainties unless (1) such consequences are not reasonably likely to occur or (2) such consequences are not likely to have a material effect on the company's financial conditions or operations. Although technically required, such disclosures become voluntary in that evaluating the significance and likelihood of future consequences of current events and trends becomes a judgment call on the part of the company.

FRR 36 also calls for registrants to provide *MD&A on a line-of-business basis* when one or more business segments affect revenues, profits, or cash flow disproportionately. Moreover, companies that invest in *junk bonds* or other noninvestment-grade, high-yield financial instruments should include discussion of the attendant unusual risks and returns in the MD&A.

Item 9: Disagreements with Accountants

One area of concern in recent years is the extent to which firms replace their outside auditors because of disagreements over accounting or financial disclosure matters. A change of accountants is a special event that calls for filing a special report in accordance with the rules for Form 8-K (discussed later in this chapter). The report must indicate whether the registrant and the former auditors disagreed on an issue concerning auditing procedures, accounting principles, or financial statement disclosures. When such an 8-K was filed within the past 24 months, Item 9 of the annual 10-K must disclose, for the transactions or events under dispute, the difference between the company's reporting method and that proposed by the former auditors.

As part of the SEC's response to recommendations of the **National Commission on Fraudulent Financial Reporting (Treadway Commission)**, the SEC issued *FRR 31* in July 1988 to strengthen the 8-K reporting requirements after a change in independent auditors. Of particular concern is the phenomenon of **opinion shopping**, alleged to occur when a company seeks a new auditor willing to support a proposed accounting treatment that might be inconsistent with reliable financial reporting. Although opinion shopping can be viewed benignly—companies are entitled to a second opinion just as medical patients are—unless done very professionally it impairs the credibility of the auditing profession and the financial reporting process. Registrants replacing auditors must now also disclose (1) unresolved concerns expressed by the former auditors, (2) the substance of consultations with new auditors prior to their appointment and (3) whether the former auditors resigned or were discharged.

AUTHORS' COMMENTARY

As pointed out, the SEC seeks to promote financial information disclosure via a truthful and reliable financial reporting system to enhance capital market efficiency and equity among market participants. This commentary focuses on the mission, findings and recommendations of the *National Commission on Fraudulent Financial Reporting*. Known as the *Treadway Commission* in recognition of its chairman, former SEC Commissioner James C. Treadway, Jr., this independent private-sector group was established in 1985 to address concerns shared by the SEC and others over the quality of financial reporting.

Nature of Fraudulent Financial Reporting. In its 1987 report, the Treadway Commission defined *fraudulent financial reporting* as "intentional or reckless conduct, whether act or omission, that results in materially misleading financial statements."* Events that can produce fraudulent financial reporting include

- deliberate distortion of company records, such as misstatement of inventory, which can manipulate reported income and financial position.
- fictitious transactions designed to increase reported income and financial position; for example, recording bogus sales and receivables.
- accounting principles applied improperly in the circumstances; for example, taking advantage of full absorption costing by raising production in order to bolster income by capitalizing excessive amounts of fixed manufacturing overhead.
- improperly timing the recognition of accounting events by, for example, recording next year's January sales at the end of December this year.

For two years ending in September 1987, the Treadway Commission conducted interviews and commissioned research studies to assess the extent of fraudulent financial reporting, to pinpoint the factors that produce it, and to recommend actions to minimize it. The Treadway Commission concluded that fraudulent financial reporting is a serious problem and found that the potential for its occurrence relates to the interplay of incentives provided by such factors as a company's operating environment, external business conditions (including the credit markets), internal controls, top management attitude, and ineffective external audits.

Recommendations Addressed to the SEC. Recommendations were grouped according to the constituency addressed: public companies, including those that register with the SEC; independent public accountants; the SEC and other regulatory bodies; and providers of education and professional certifying examinations. The principal recommendations addressed to the SEC are that it

- obtain authority to assess monetary penalties in administrative proceedings, issue cease and desist orders, and suspend corporate officers and directors from future service in those capacities in public companies.
- increase criminal prosecution in cases of fraudulent financial reporting.
- mandate and monitor quality assurance programs for public accounting firms that audit public companies.
- secure the increase in resources needed to review a larger portion of SEC filings and implement the above recommendations.

In sum, the Treadway Commission shares the SEC's objectives with respect to the proper functioning of the financial reporting disclosure system. Although it supports the SEC's financial fraud enforcement program, the Treadway Commission recommends that SEC sanctions be broadened and strengthened.

---

* National Commission on Fraudulent Financial Reporting, *Report of the National Commission on Fraudulent Financial Reporting*, October, 1987, 2.

Item 10: Directors and Executive Officers

The company's directors, executive officers, and certain other key employees are identified, and their business experience is described in Item 10. In addition, any family relationships among directors and executive officers is disclosed, along with any involvement of directors or executive officers in certain legal proceedings.

Item 11: Executive Compensation and Transactions

Item 11 describes various aspects of the compensation of officers and directors. The total compensation of all officers and directors as a group is disclosed, along with the number of such individuals. In addition, the names and amount of compensation (if over $60,000) of the five highest-paid officers and directors are disclosed. Narrative descriptions of deferred compensation plans, pension and profit-sharing plans, stock option plans, and the like are presented, as well as any proposed changes in the compensation of officers and directors. Finally, management indebtedness to the company and other transactions with management (if over $60,000) are disclosed.

Item 12: Security Ownership

Item 12 discloses the security holdings of major stockholders and management of the company.

REGULATION S-X

Regulation S-X governs the form and content of financial reporting to the SEC and related matters.[14] This regulation is actually a collection of rules derived from original SEC pronouncements such as the *Financial Reporting Releases* (*FRRs*; formerly *ASRs*). It is, together with *FASB Statements* and *Interpretations*, the body of accounting and reporting principles to be followed for SEC reports.

Regulation S-X is organized into the several articles outlined in Exhibit E.2. Of major concern are Articles 4 and 5, which present accounting and reporting rules broadly applicable to most companies; Article 10, which deals with interim reports; and Article 12, which deals with the disclosure of detailed information in the form of schedules to be included in the 10-K report. Many of the other sections address accounting and reporting issues appropriate to particular industry types.

Article	Contents
1	Application of Regulations S-X
2	Qualifications and reports of accountants
3	General instructions as to financial statements
3A	Consolidated and combined financial statements
4	Rules of general application
5	Commercial and industrial companies
5A	Companies in the development stage
6	Registered investment companies
6A	Employee stock purchase, savings, and similar plans
7	Insurance companies other than life insurance
8	Committees issuing certificates of deposit
9	Bank holding companies
10	Interim financial statements
11	*Pro forma* financial statements
12	Form and content of schedules

EXHIBIT E.2   CONTENTS OF REGULATION S-X

In most cases, the SEC accounting rules are the same as Generally Accepted Accounting Principles (GAAP) as issued by the FASB and its predecessors. Section 101 in the SEC's

---

[14] For example, Article 2 of Regulation S-X is concerned with the *qualifications and actions of accountants*. Disciplinary actions sanctioning the improper or unprofessional work of accountants are generally brought under *Rule 2(e)* of this article.

Codification of Financial Reporting Policies endorses the work of the FASB. Pronouncements of the FASB and its predecessors are automatically accepted by the SEC, unless the SEC issues its own pronouncement on the particular subject. Historically, most accounting standard-setting has been done directly by the private sector with SEC oversight rather than by the SEC itself, even though the SEC has the statutory authority to set accounting principles. The SEC accepts and encourages this procedure, except in a few cases where the SEC acted first to spur the private standard-setting body into action on some pressing matter.

General Accounting and Reporting Rules

Article 4 of Regulation S-X deals with selected accounting and reporting matters applicable to companies in general, independent of their industry. It provides for the usual form, order, and terminology. Some examples of its treatment of various items are presented in the following paragraphs.

Article 4 defines current assets and current liabilities in terms of the usual one-year criterion. If the normal operating cycle is longer than one year, companies may follow normal industry practice with respect to including items of longer duration. When such longer-term items are included, an explanation should be provided, along with an estimate of the amount not realizable or payable within one year. If such items extend over several years, there should be disclosure of the amounts maturing each year and the related interest rates.

With respect to the presentation of *income tax expense*, SEC rules go beyond the tax allocation requirements of GAAP. Temporary differences whose effect exceeds 5 percent of the total tax expense are to be separately identified. In addition, a reconciliation is to be provided between the amount actually reported as income tax expense and the amount computed by multiplying the income before tax by the statutory federal tax rate. This reconciliation aids in determining the difference between the *statutory tax rate* and the company's *effective tax rate*.

Significant transactions involving the registrant and **related parties**, such as management, principal owners and affiliated companies, must be disclosed. The disclosure should provide the following information:

■ The nature of the relationship.
■ A description of the transactions.
■ The dollar volume of the transactions.
■ Amounts due to or from related parties, and terms of settlement.
■ Amount of investment in related parties.

These rules encompass the disclosures set forth in *SFAS 57*, "Related Party Disclosures," and *SAS 6*, "Related Party Transactions."[15] When separate financial statements are prepared for the registrant or certain investees and subsidiaries, those statements must disclose amounts eliminated and not eliminated in the related consolidated statements. Similarly, the effect of intercompany profits/losses not eliminated in the separate statements shall be disclosed. Material related party items, such as receivables, payables, revenue, expense, gain or loss, or cash flows, must appear on the face of the respective financial statement, not merely in the notes.

---

[15] Auditing Standards Executive Committee, *Statement on Auditing Standards No. 6*, "Related Party Transactions" (New York: AICPA, 1975).

Schedules of Information

The schedule requirements of Regulation S-X provide for considerable detail on a number of items. Their purpose is to enhance understanding of the financial statements through disclosure of details behind, and analysis of changes in, certain account balances. In general, schedules are required on the following items:

1. Condensed financial information of the registrant
2. Valuation and qualifying accounts, such as allowance for bad debts and valuation allowance for deferred tax assets.
3. Real estate and accumulated depreciation.
4. Mortgage loans on real estate.
5. Supplemental information on property-casualty insurance companies.

THE QUARTERLY REPORT: FORM 10-Q

Firms that are required to file an annual report with the SEC also must file **quarterly reports**, as prescribed in **Form 10-Q**. Such quarterly reporting is intended to provide investors and others with an *update of the most recently filed 10-K report*. Quarterly reports are therefore not stand-alone documents and are not designed to forecast the next 10-K. Rather, they foster timely disclosure of important developments affecting the registrant; one result is that the annual report should contain few big surprises. The 10-Q report must be filed within 45 days after the end of each of the first three quarters of the company's fiscal year; no fourth quarter report is required.

APBO 28,[16] *SFAS 3,*[17] and *IFAS 18*[18] are the primary sources of accounting principles for interim reports. The SEC requires that quarterly data be presented in the annual reports of all registrants whose equity securities are "actively traded" and that meet certain size requirements. Although these data need not be audited, they must at least be reviewed by the independent accountants.

Quarterly reports are typically much shorter than the annual report. Form 10-Q contains quarterly and year-to-date financial statements—balance sheet, income statement and statement of cash flows—for the current quarter and the corresponding quarter of the previous year. The statements themselves may have fewer categories as compared to the annual statements. On the balance sheet, for example, a major caption, such as Receivables, is needed only if the item exceeds 10 percent of total assets or if the item has changed by more than 25 percent from the latest year-end balance. If these tests are not met, the caption may be combined with others so long as the general format of the statements is maintained; for example, current items are not combined with noncurrent items.

Selected other disclosures are also included in the 10-Q. One major disclosure is management's discussion and analysis (MD&A). Other disclosures include any legal proceedings during the quarter, changes in the company's securities, defaults on senior securities, and matters

---

[16] Accounting Principles Board, *Opinion No. 28*, "Interim Reporting" (New York: AICPA, 1973).

[17] Financial Accounting Standards Board, *Statement of Financial Accounting Standards No. 3*, "Reporting Accounting Changes in Interim Financial Statements" (Stamford, CT: FASB, 1974).

[18] Financial Accounting Standards Board, *Interpretation of Financial Accounting Standards No. 18*, "Accounting for Income Taxes in Interim Periods," (Stamford, CT: FASB, 1977).

reported via Form 8-K during the quarter. The extensive financial disclosures found in the annual report are not required on a quarterly basis.

SPECIAL REPORTS: FORM 8-K

Firms make regular reports to the SEC annually via Form 10-K and quarterly via Form 10-Q. In addition, a **special report** or **current report** known as **Form 8-K** is required when certain significant events occur. These events include the following:

- Change in control of the registrant
- A major acquisition or disposition
- Initiation or settlement of major legal matters
- Default by the company on a debt obligation
- Change of auditors (see related discussion under Item 9 of Regulation S-K)

In addition, voluntary disclosure of other events of significance to investors is encouraged. Because Form 8-K must be filed within 15 days of any of these occurrences, without waiting for the next 10-Q or 10-K report, timely disclosure of these important events is assured. Financial statements normally do not accompany Form 8-K. When a major acquisition is being reported, however, the financial statements of the acquired company are included with the 8-K filing. If they are not available by the 15-day deadline when the 8-K is filed, the financial statements are to follow as soon as possible.

CORPORATE ACCOUNTABILITY AND GOVERNANCE

In addition to concerns over corporate *accounting*, there is considerable interest in recent years in the broader notion of corporate *accountability*. Compliance with a requirement for corporate accounting is one example of how the corporation fulfills its obligation to be accountable for its actions. The ways in which a corporation conducts its affairs and relates to its security holders, employees, and the public are major aspects of **corporate accountability**. The SEC plays an important role, both directly and indirectly, in setting guidelines for corporate accountability and governance.

One of its indirect influences was on the *Foreign Corrupt Practices Act (FCPA)* of 1978. The FCPA prohibits certain activities in the conduct of international transactions. Moreover, this act requires management to maintain accurate books and records, so that any illegal transactions are not hidden, and to maintain an adequate system of internal control to reduce the occurrence of such transactions. These two provisions were originally proposed by the SEC in 1977 as amendments to Regulation S-X.

AUDIT COMMITTEES

The board of directors plays an important role in the governance of the corporation. In representing the stockholders, the board oversees the activities of management. To strengthen the independence of the board, the SEC requires that the identity of each director, or nominee for director, be disclosed, along with any relationship the individual has with the company, such as whether the director is also a member of management or is the corporation's banker or attorney. Companies are encouraged to have a number of "outside" or "independent" directors, although this is not a requirement. In addition, companies are encouraged to have committees on the board of directors, such as an *audit committee* and a *compensation committee*.

The **audit committee** is responsible for seeing that management fulfills its responsibilities with respect to accounting, reporting, and controlling the operations and safeguarding the assets of the corporation. It monitors the financial accounting and reporting system as well as the external and internal audit functions. The exact role of the committee varies among companies. In some companies, the audit committee is responsible for hiring the independent auditor, and the auditor reports to it. The internal audit department is responsible to either the audit committee or management. At a minimum, the internal audit department needs direct access to the audit committee for special problems, and the audit committee should be able to use the internal audit department for special investigations. The audit committee also interacts with top management on financial accounting, reporting, and control issues. Although the SEC does not require audit committees, it can require that a registrant disclose whether it has an audit committee and who the members are. The New York Stock Exchange, however, does require all domestic companies listed on the Exchange to have an audit committee composed solely of "outside directors" who are independent of management. One of the Treadway Commission's recommendations is that the SEC require all public companies to have an audit committee.

The board may also form other committees. For example, a **compensation committee** is responsible for making recommendations regarding salaries and benefits for top management. The SEC cannot prescribe management compensation, but it does require that compensation of top executives be disclosed.

ANTIFRAUD PROVISIONS AND INSIDER TRADING

A broad set of rules known as the **antifraud provisions**, found in both the 1933 and 1934 acts, promotes fair capital markets that allocate resources efficiently. These rules seek a "level playing field" for all capital market participants by prohibiting fraud, deceit, and manipulative practices connected with the issuance or trading of securities. Efficient allocation of resources is enhanced when the public has confidence in the integrity of the capital markets. Under these provisions, a corporation cannot issue false or misleading statements about the company or its stock. Underwriters of a stock issue cannot artificially stimulate demand or hold back stock in order to profit from a price rise. Various kinds of corporate mismanagement are also prohibited, such as issuing corporate stock for less than adequate compensation. These antifraud provisions are also used to attack mergers or acquisitions that are not in the interest of minority shareholders.

A special example of fraud is **insider trading**, which refers to the purchase or sale of a company's stock by individuals who have access to information not yet available either to those with whom they are dealing or to the market in general. An *insider* may be a company officer, director, major stockholder, or anyone else who utilizes confidential nonpublic information for the purpose of trading in securities. The exact definitions of *insider* and *inside information*, however, are still unsettled and are the subjects of many legal proceedings.

A major objective of the securities laws is to promote full disclosure of material information to all participants in the market. Trading by insiders having access to special knowledge is at variance with this objective. Although it is impossible to completely prevent use of inside knowledge, certain rules help to constrain it. One rule under the 1934 act requires that officers, directors, and stockholders who own more than 10 percent of a class of equity securities, whether directly or indirectly—*beneficial owners*—report their holdings and their transactions in these securities to the SEC. This report is a public record, and hence serves to disclose any insider transaction that does occur. A second rule permits the company, or a stockholder acting on behalf of the company, to sue to recover *short-swing profit* earned by an insider from in-and-out trading—either purchase-sale or sale-purchase—within a six-month period.

The *Insider Trading Sanctions Act of 1984* dramatically increased the penalties imposed on those who participate in insider trading, market manipulations, and other prohibited activities. It also expanded the potential scope of *inside information* and *insiders* to include situations not yet fully understood.

PROXY STATEMENTS

Proxy statements are communications to shareholders of matters for stockholder action, such as the election of directors, the appointment of an auditor, a change in the corporate charter or bylaws, the issuance of new securities, or the approval of a business combination. The proxy statement discloses these matters to the stockholder and advises the stockholder of the procedure for voting. When security issuances and business combinations are being considered, accountants become involved because the proxy statement must include the most recent annual report with financial statements presented in accordance with Regulation S-X.

In many cases, voting occurs at the annual meeting of stockholders. Since many stockholders are unable to attend this meeting, their voting right, or *proxy*, is often solicited by management. "The proxy statement is intended to provide shareholders with the information needed to determine how to assign their proxies."[19] SEC regulation of proxy statements follows from its emphasis on full disclosure and the belief that the capital markets work better when registrants' managers are kept accountable to the stockholders. Typically, the stockholder may mark the proxy as to how he or she wishes to vote on the major items.

The proxy statement also provides a mechanism for action on stockholder proposals that are not supported by management. Notice of such a proposal must be given to the company at least 90 days prior to the mailing of the proxy statement. The proposal must be personally presented at the annual meeting by a stockholder. Virtually any proposal can be offered, although resubmitted proposals must satisfy tests as to timing and votes previously received, except one that was rejected by the stockholders within the past five years.

In addition, the proxy statement often contains a variety of detailed information on nonvoting matters, such as committees of the board, litigation, management compensation plans (including the amount of compensation paid to top management), and related-party transactions.

THE SEC AND ACCOUNTING STANDARDS

As previously mentioned, although the Securities Exchange Act of 1934 gave the SEC the statutory authority to set accounting standards for companies under its jurisdiction, the SEC historically left the bulk of this task to private-sector standard-setting bodies—the FASB and its predecessors. In 1938, *ASR 4* indicated that "substantial authoritative support" is required when accounting principles used in financial statements submitted to the SEC are not addressed in SEC pronouncements. Until 1973, when the FASB began work, the SEC generally looked to the AICPA's Committee on Accounting Procedure (1938-1959) and Accounting Principles Board (1959-1973) for substantial authoritative support on accounting matters. Then, in *ASR 150* (1973),

---

[19] Larry Gene Pointer and Richard G. Schroeder, *An Introduction to the Securities and Exchange Commission* (Plano, TX: Business Publications, Inc., 1986), 83.

the SEC formally recognized the FASB as being principally responsible for establishing accounting standards; *ASR 280* (1980) reaffirmed the SEC's support of the FASB.

Nevertheless, the SEC actively oversees the standard-setting process and continually reviews registrants' filings. It promotes a balance-sheet emphasis, favoring inclusion of "hard" assets and liabilities and readily challenges cost deferrals and potentially premature revenue recognition practices. The SEC staff is always on the lookout for improper application of the pooling-of-interests method of accounting for business combinations.

The working relationship between the government's SEC and the private-sector's FASB is described by former FASB member Robert Sprouse as "mutually advantageous, eminently effective, and surprisingly sensible" due to the spirit of cooperation among members of both bodies.[20] Sprouse identifies three ways that the SEC, primarily through its ongoing review of financial statements filed by registrants, contributes to the standard-setting process.

1. Observing lack of comparability among registrants' accounting treatments of apparently similar events, which can signify weaknesses or ambiguities in existing standards.
2. Detecting increasing use of questionable accounting methods which, although generally accepted, are not covered by existing pronouncements.
3. Noting the presence of new or unusual transactions which appear questionable and for which the accounting is evolving.

As an example of item 2 in the above list, capitalization of interest during construction became a controversial issue during the era of rising interest rates in the early 1970s because it allowed deferral of an otherwise immediately expensed interest cost. Detecting use of this income-increasing treatment by growing numbers of registrants, the SEC issued *ASR 163*[21] in 1974, placing a moratorium on the adoption of this accounting practice until the FASB took a position on it. Finally, in 1979, *SFAS 34*[22] was issued, whereupon *ASR 163* was withdrawn.

Although many of the accounting-related *ASR*s issued over the years dealt with disclosure requirements for public companies rather than accounting measurement issues, the SEC began playing a more active role in standard-setting in the early 1970s. To illustrate a disclosure matter that was not adequately addressed by private standard-setting bodies, consider **inflation accounting**. In the mid-1970s, there was much discussion about the need for disclosure of the impact of inflation on financial statements. The APB issued nonbinding guidance on this subject in 1969.[23] The FASB then debated this matter for some time, and finally seemed to be moving toward a pronouncement requiring supplemental disclosure of historical cost/constant dollar data. In 1976, the SEC intervened and issued *ASR 190*,[24] requiring disclosure of current replacement cost data, not historical cost/constant dollar data. By this action, the SEC clearly indicated its opposition to the FASB's proposal. The FASB proposal

---

[20] Robert T. Sprouse, "Commentary on the SEC-FASB Partnership," *Accounting Horizons* (Dec. 1987), 92-95.

[21] Securities and Exchange Commission, *Accounting Series Release 163*, "Capitalization of Interest by Companies Other than Public Utilities" (1974).

[22] Financial Accounting Standards Board, *Statement of Financial Accounting Standards No. 34*, "Capitalization of Interest Cost," (Stamford, CT: FASB, 1979).

[23] Accounting Principles Board, *Statement No. 3*, "Financial Statements Restated for General Price-Level Changes" (New York: AICPA, 1969).

[24] Securities and Exchange Commission, *Accounting Series Release 190*, "Notice of Adoption of Amendments to Regulation S-X Requiring Disclosure of Certain Replacement Cost Data" (1976).

was withdrawn; finally in 1979 *SFAS 33*[25] was issued, calling for disclosure of historical cost/constant dollar *and* current cost data. Following issuance of *SFAS 33*, the SEC rescinded *ASR 190*.

Some noteworthy conflicts between the SEC and the private sector include the SEC's overruling of the APB in the early 1960s on the proper accounting treatment of the investment tax credit and the flap over oil and gas accounting in 1977 and 1978. In the latter case, the FASB issued *SFAS 19* calling for immediate expensing of "dry-hole costs" incurred in drilling unsuccessful wells, a method called *successful efforts accounting*. Complaints by many companies that capitalized such costs under *full cost accounting* led the SEC to override the FASB in *ASRs 253, 257* and *258* and to seek a new method called *reserve-recognition accounting (RRA)* in *ASR 269*. Subsequently, *SFAS 25* amended *SFAS 19* to allow both full cost and successful efforts accounting. Reserve-recognition accounting was withdrawn by the SEC early in 1981 when *ASR 289*, "Financial Reporting by Oil and Gas Producers," was issued. The kinds of disclosures sought by the SEC when RRA was proposed, however, surfaced late in 1982 when the FASB adopted *SFAS 69*, "Disclosures about Oil and Gas Producing Activities."

In recent years, the SEC, primarily through the chief accountant, has become a much stronger force in accounting standard-setting. In some cases, an SEC pronouncement is issued or threatened; in other cases, the position of the commission is conveyed through public speeches, papers, the EITF and comments by SEC observers at FASB proceedings. Clearly, the SEC's statutory authority requires it to remain an active participant in the accounting standard-setting process.

SUMMARY OF KEY CONCEPTS

The **Securities Act of 1933** regulates the issuance of new securities. The **Securities Exchange Act of 1934** regulates the trading of securities and also established the **Securities and Exchange Commission (SEC)**. The SEC is responsible for the administration and enforcement of the federal securities laws.

The SEC has authority to establish accounting and reporting principles for publicly held companies. Although it relies heavily on the private sector (the FASB) for standard-setting, the SEC does issue its own pronouncements—**Financial Reporting Releases (FRR), Accounting and Auditing Enforcement Releases (AAER)** and **Staff Accounting Bulletins (SAB).**

Companies under SEC jurisdiction file annual reports **(Form 10-K)** and quarterly reports **(Form 10-Q)**. They also file special reports **(Form 8-K)** when certain events occur. The contents of these reports are largely governed by **Regulation S-X,** which covers accounting and financial statement requirements, and **Regulation S-K**, which covers all other disclosures.

Besides its role in accounting and reporting, the SEC has also played an important role in **corporate governance**. It provides **proxy statement** requirements, encourages **audit committees**, and regulates **insider trading**.

---

[25] Financial Accounting Standards Board, *Statement of Financial Accounting Standards No. 33*, "Financial Reporting and Changing Prices" (Stamford, CT: FASB, 1979). Disclosures required in *SFAS 33* were made optional in *SFAS 89*, "Financial Reporting and Changing Prices" (1986).

Although the SEC has **statutory authority** over establishment of accounting principles, it has largely delegated this authority to private-sector bodies such as the FASB. The SEC monitors the work of the FASB, contributes to it on a continuing basis, and occasionally overrules it.

QUESTIONS

QE.1 Distinguish the major purpose of the Securities Act of 1933 from the major purpose of the Securities Exchange Act of 1934.

QE.2 What companies must file reports with the SEC?

QE.3 How does Form 10-K relate to the annual report to stockholders?

QE.4 Distinguish between Regulation S-K and Regulation S-X.

QE.5 What are the broad topics covered by "management's discussion and analysis"?

QE.6 What has been the impact of the Integrated Disclosure System on the filing of reports with the SEC?

QE.7 What is a *proxy statement*?

QE.8 What is the function of an underwriter?

EXERCISES

EE.1 Multiple Choice—Securities Laws and SEC Functions Each of the following multiple choice questions deals with the federal securities laws and the organization, structure, and authority of the SEC.

REQUIRED:

1. Assuming that all other criteria regarding the issuing organization and its "security" are met, which one of the following is *not* a "security" under the jurisdiction of the SEC?
    a. A trust certificate.
    b. A municipal bond.
    c. An oil drilling venture participation unit.
    d. A limited partnership share.
    e. A subordinated debenture.
2. Which of the following is the act that gives the SEC the ultimate power to suspend trading of a security, delist a security, and prevent brokers and dealers from working in the securities market?
    a. Securities Investors Protection Act of 1970.
    b. Securities Act of 1933.
    c. Securities Exchange Act of 1934.
    d. Investment Company Act of 1940.
    e. Investment Advisers Act of 1940.

3. The SEC is organized into several divisions and principal offices. Which of the following is the organizational unit that reviews registration statements, annual reports, and proxy statements that are filed with the commission?
   a. Office of the Chief Accountant.
   b. Division of Corporation Finance.
   c. Division of Enforcement.
   d. Division of Market Regulation.
   e. Office of the Comptroller.

4. The SEC was established in 1934 to help regulate the United States securities market. Which of the following statements is true concerning the SEC?
   a. The SEC prohibits the sale of speculative securities.
   b. The SEC regulates only securities offered for public sale.
   c. Registration with the SEC guarantees the accuracy of the registrant's prospectus.
   d. The SEC's initial influence and authority has diminished in recent years as the stock exchanges have become more organized and better able to police themselves.
   e. The SEC's powers are broad with respect to enforcement of its reporting requirements as established in the 1933 and 1934 acts but narrow with respect to new reporting requirements because these require confirmation by the Congress. *(CMA adapted)*

EE.2 Multiple Choice—Securities Laws and SEC Functions Each of the following multiple choice questions deals with the federal securities laws and the organization, structure, and authority of the SEC.

REQUIRED:

1. Which of the following are *not* requirements imposed by the Securities Exchange Act of 1934 and its amendments?
   a. Proxy solicitation requirements.
   b. Prospectus requirements.
   c. Insider trading requirements.
   d. Tender offer requirements.
   e. Accounting, recordkeeping, and internal control requirements.

2. The Securities Exchange Act of 1934 specifies the types of companies that must report periodically to the SEC. Which of the following types of companies is *not* required to report to the SEC under this act?
   a. Banks and carriers subject to the Interstate Commerce Act.
   b. Companies whose securities are listed on the National Securities Exchanges.
   c. Companies whose securities are traded over the counter, if those companies have total assets in excess of $3 million and 500 or more stockholders.
   d. Companies whose securities are traded over the counter that voluntarily elect to comply with the reporting requirements even though they have total assets less than $3 million and less than 500 stockholders.
   e. Companies with over 300 stockholders of a class of securities that are registered under the Securities Act of 1933.

3. Which of the following is *not* a purpose of the Securities Exchange Act of 1934?
    a. To establish federal regulation over securities exchanges and markets.
    b. To prevent unfair practices on securities exchanges and markets.
    c. To discourage and prevent the use of credit in financing excessive speculation in securities.
    d. To approve the securities of corporations that are to be traded publicly.
    e. To control unfair use of information by corporate insiders.
4. Which of the following is a category *not* registered by the SEC?
    a. Securities brokers who deal in over-the-counter markets.
    b. Securities brokers who deal only in interstate markets.
    c. Public accounting firms.
    d. Securities exchanges.
    e. Securities of publicly traded companies.
    (*CMA adapted*)

EE.3   Multiple Choice—SEC Reporting Requirements Each of the following multiple choice questions deals with the reporting requirements of the SEC.

REQUIRED:

1. Nonfinancial statement disclosures are specified in which of the following?
    a. Regulation S-K
    b. *Financial Reporting Releases.*
    c. *Staff Accounting Bulletins.*
    d. *Accounting and Auditing Enforcement Releases.*
    e. Regulation S-X.
2. Which of the following items is *not* required by the SEC in either the Securities Act of 1933 or the Securities Exchange Act of 1934?
    a. Identification of directors and executive officers with the principal occupation and employer of each.
    b. Line-of-business or product-line reports for the last five fiscal years.
    c. Identification of the principal markets in which the securities of the firm are traded.
    d. Range of market prices and dividends for each quarter of the two most recent fiscal years.
    e. Comfort letter to the underwriter and legal counsel from the company's independent accountant.
3. SEC regulations provide for a procedure known as *incorporation by reference.* Which of the following best illustrates the concept of *incorporation by reference*?
    a. A partnership is incorporated by reference to the U.S. Tax Code.
    b. The incorporation of a proprietorship or partnership.
    c. Inclusion of information on officers' renumeration in Form 10-K by reference to the same information in the proxy statement to shareholders.
    d. Footnote reference to market data per share since incorporation.
    e. Footnote disclosure that financial statements are incorporated into the annual report by reference from Form 10-K.
4. The SEC requires Form 8-K to be filed with the commission within 15 days after the end of the month in which a significant event transpired. However, financial

statements accompany Form 8-K only under certain conditions. Which of the following events require financial statements to accompany Form 8-K?
a. A material default on a senior security.
b. A write-down, write-off, or abandonment of assets, where such assets represent more than 15 percent of total assets.
c. An acquisition in which the acquired company represents more than 15 percent of total assets or revenues of the registering company.
d. An increase or decrease of more than 5 percent in any class of outstanding security.
e. A change in the registrant's certifying accountants.
    (CMA adapted)

EE.4 Multiple Choice—SEC Reporting Requirements Each of the following multiple choice questions deals with the reporting requirements of the SEC.

REQUIRED:

1. A significant event affecting a company registered under the Securities and Exchange Act of 1934 should be reported on which of the following?
    a. Form 10-K.
    b. Form 10-Q.
    c. Form S-1.
    d. Form 8-K.
    e. Form 11-K.
2. The primary intent of the Integrated Disclosure Rules issued by the SEC is which of the following?
    a. To reduce the influence of SEC regulations in public financial reporting.
    b. To replace generally accepting accounting principles with Regulation S-X.
    c. To replace Regulation S-X with generally accepted accounting principles.
    d. To minimize the differences between published financial reports and financial reports filed on Form 10-K.
    e. To integrate the materiality criteria of Regulation S-X with generally accepted accounting principles.
3. The Management Discussion and Analysis section of Form 10-K has been revised by the SEC's Integrated Disclosure System. The revised Management Discussion and Analysis section does not require a description of which of the following?
    a. Factors affecting financial condition as well as the results of operations.
    b. Factors affecting international markets and currency exchange.
    c. Factors that are likely to increase or decrease liquidity materially.
    d. Material commitments for capital expenditures, including the purpose of and source of financing for such commitments.
    e. The impact of inflation and changing prices on net sales and revenues and on income from continuing operations.
4. The Securities and Exchange Commission substantially increased the disclosure requirements on Form 10-Q quarterly reports to the point where all but one of the following items must be disclosed. Select the item that does *not* need to be filed with the quarterly 10-Q.
    a. Signature of either the chief financial officer or chief accounting officer.

    b. Management analysis of reasons for material changes in the amount of revenue and expense items from one quarter to the next.

    c. In case of a change in accounting principle, a letter indicating that the public accountant believes the new principle is preferable for measuring business operations.

    d. Income statements for the most recent quarter and for the equivalent quarter from the preceding year, and year-to-date data for both years.

    e. A statement by the public accountant that he or she has reviewed the financial data in Form 10-Q and that all necessary adjustments are reflected in the statements.

    (CMA adapted)

EE.5 Multiple Choice—SEC Reporting Requirements Each of the following multiple choice questions deals with the reporting requirements of the SEC.

REQUIRED:

1. Which of the following describes Regulation S-X?
    a. Specifies the information that can be incorporated by reference from the annual report into the registration statement filed with the SEC.
    b. Specifies the regulations and reporting requirements of proxy solicitations.
    c. Provides the basis for generally accepted accounting principles.
    d. Specifies the general form and content requirements of financial statements filed with the SEC.
    e. Provides explanations and clarifications of changes in accounting or auditing procedures used in reports filed with the SEC.

2. The SEC integrated disclosure of financial information sets forth criteria for conditions for "Management Discussion and Analysis of Financial Conditions and Results of Operations." Which of the following is one of these criteria?
    a. Forward-looking information is encouraged but not required to be disclosed.
    b. A discussion of financial conditions for the most recent seven fiscal years is to be included.
    c. Information on the effects of inflation is to be provided only when the registrant is already subject to the reporting requirements of *SFAS 33*, "Financial Reporting and Changing Prices."
    d. An analysis of income from foreign operations is to be included even if such operations are not material to the results of the firm.
    e. Identification of all equity security investments in defense contractors and oil and gas subsidiaries is to be included whether or not such investments are material to the overall financial statements and operations.

3. Within 15 days after the occurrence of any event of material importance to the stockholders, a company must file a Form 8-K Information Report with the SEC to disclose the event. Which of the following is an example of the type of event required to be disclosed?
    a. Salary increases to the officers.
    b. A contract to continue to employ the same certified public accounting firm as in the prior year.
    c. A change in projected earnings per share from $12 to $12.11 per share.

　　d.　The purchase of bank certificates of deposit.

　　e.　The acquisition of a large subsidiary other than in the ordinary course of business.

4.　Which of the following items is not required to be included in a company's periodic 8-K report filed with the SEC when significant events occur?

　　a.　Acquisition or disposition of a significant amount of assets.

　　b.　Instigation or termination of material legal proceedings other than routine litigation incidental to the business.

　　c.　Change in certifying public accountants.

　　d.　Election of new vice-president of finance to replace the retiring incumbent.

　　e.　Default in the payment of principal, interest, or sinking fund installment.
　　(CMA adapted)

EE.6 Multiple Choice—Corporate Governance Each of the following multiple choice questions deals with matters of corporate governance.

REQUIRED:

1.　Formation and meaningful utilization of an audit committee of the board of directors is required of publicly traded companies that are subject to the rules of which of the following?

　　a.　Securities and Exchange Commission.

　　b.　Financial Accounting Standards Board.

　　c.　New York Stock Exchange.

　　d.　National Association of Securities Dealers.

　　e.　SEC Practice Section of the American Institute of Certified Public Accountants' Division of Firms.

2.　The SEC's antifraud rules prohibit trading on the basis of inside information of a business corporation's stock by which of the following?

　　a.　Officers.

　　b.　Officers and directors.

　　c.　All officers, directors, and stockholders.

　　d.　Officers, directors, and beneficial holders of 10 percent of the corporation's stock.

　　e.　Anyone who bases his or her trading activities on inside information.

3.　An audit committee of the board of directors consisting of outside directors should be objective in arbitrating disputes between a company's top management and the external auditor because audit committee members

　　a.　have only limited contacts with the external auditor.

　　b.　have no direct responsibility for the results of a company's operations.

　　c.　usually have no influence on the hiring of the external auditor.

　　d.　rely on opinions of senior management in resolving disputes with the external auditor.

　　e.　are required by the Securities Exchange Act of 1934 to oversee the progress of the annual external audit.

4.　Shareholders may ask or allow others to enter their vote at a shareholders meeting that they are unable to attend. The document furnished to shareholders to provide background information for their vote is a

　　a.　registration statement.

　　b.　proxy statement.

    c.   10-K report.

    d.   prospectus.

    e.   proxy.

       (CMA adapted)

EE.7 **Multiple Choice—SEC and Accounting Standards** Each of the following multiple choice questions deals with the role of the SEC in establishing accounting and reporting standards.

REQUIRED:

1. The role of the SEC regarding financial accounting for public companies is that the SEC does which of the following?

    a.   Promulgates generally accepted accounting principles.

    b.   Adopts pronouncements of the Financial Accounting Standards Board in every case.

    c.   Regularly adopts requirements that conflict with the pronouncements of the Financial Accounting Standards Board.

    d.   Makes regulations and rules pertaining to filings with the SEC but not to annual or quarterly reports to shareholders.

    e.   Makes regulations and rules pertaining more to disclosure outside the financial statements than to the setting of accounting measurement principles.

2. *Financial Reporting Releases (FRRs)* and *Staff Accounting Bulletins (SABs)* are two pronouncements issued by the SEC. How do *FRR*s and *SAB*s differ?

    a.   *FRR*s are part of the 1934 Securities Exchange Act while *SAB*s are not.

    b.   *SAB*s represent official rules of the SEC while *FRR*s do not.

    c.   *SAB*s pertain to the 1933 Securities Act while *FRR*s pertain to the 1934 Securities Exchange Act.

    d.   *SAB*s represent amendments to Regulation S-X while *FRR*s do not.

    e.   *FRR*s represent requirements applicable to the form and content of financial statements filed with the SEC while *SAB*s represent accounting interpretations followed by the SEC.

3. Two interesting and important topics concerning the SEC are the role the commission plays in the development of accounting principles and the impact the SEC has had and will continue to have on the accounting profession and business in general. Which of the following statements concerning the SEC's authority relative to accounting practice is *false*?

    a.   The SEC has the statutory authority to regulate and to prescribe the form and content of financial statements and other reports it receives.

    b.   Regulation S-X of the SEC is the principal source relating to the form and content of financial statements to be included in registration statements and financial reports filed with the SEC.

    c.   The SEC has little, if any, authority over disclosures in corporate annual reports mailed to shareholders with proxy solicitations. Here, the type of information disclosed and the format to be used are left to the discretion of management.

    d.   If the SEC disagrees with some presentation in the registrant's financial statements but the principles used by the registrant have substantial authoritative support, the SEC often will accept footnotes to the statements in lieu of correcting the statements to the SEC view, provided the SEC has not previously expressed its opinion on the matter in published material.

    e. The SEC has reserved the right to rule against a registrant even if the registrant follows principles having substantial authoritative support, as well as to determine which accounting principles have substantive authoritative support.

4. While the SEC has generally allowed the private sector to establish accounting principles, the commission has often exerted pressure to force the private sector into action. In some cases, the SEC may establish a moratorium on certain practices or require that a particular principle be used. In oil and gas accounting, the SEC requires the use of

    a. full cost accounting.

    b. flow through accounting.

    c. successful efforts accounting.

    d. either full cost or successful efforts accounting.

    e. either full cost or flow through accounting.

    (CMA adapted)

EE.8 Multiple Choice—Registration of Securities Each of the following multiple choice questions deals with the registration of new security issues with the SEC.

REQUIRED:

1. In the registration and sale of new securities issues, the SEC

    a. endorses the investment merit of a security by allowing its registration to "go effective."

    b. provides a rating of the investment quality of the security.

    c. may not allow the registration to "go effective" if it judges the security's investment risk to be too great.

    d. allows all registrations to "go effective' if the issuing company's external accountant is satisfied that disclosures and representations are not misleading.

    e. does not make any guarantees regarding the material accuracy of the registration statement.

2. In cases of false or misleading disclosure in a registration statement that the SEC has allowed to become effective in conjunction with the public sale of securities, investors have the potential for legal recourse (for example, damage suits) against all of the following *except*

    a. the Securities and Exchange Commission.

    b. the issuing entity.

    c. the underwriter (managing broker) of the sale.

    d. the issuing entity's legal counsel.

    e. the issuing entity's external accountant.

3. Which of the following is *not* required for the registration statements filed under the Securities Act of 1933?

    a. Nature and history of the issuer's business.

    b. Description of the securities being registered.

    c. Estimate of the net proceeds and the uses to which such proceeds will be put.

    d. Financial forecasts for the next two fiscal years.

    e. Salaries and security holdings of officers and directors.

4. The 1933 Securities Act provides for a 20-day waiting period between the filing and the effective date of the registration. During this waiting period the registrant is prohibited from engaging in which of the following activities?
   a. Preparing any amendments to the registration statement.
   b. Announcing the prospective issue of the securities being registered.
   c. Accepting offers to purchase the securities being registered from potential investors.
   d. Placing an advertisement indicating by whom orders for the securities being registered will be accepted.
   e. Issuing a prospectus in preliminary form.

PROBLEMS

PE.1 **Origins and Objectives of Securities Legislation** During the late 1920s, approximately 55 percent of all personal savings in the United States were used to purchase securities. Public confidence in the business community was extremely high as stock values doubled and tripled in short periods of time. The road to wealth was believed to be through the stock market, and everyone who was able participated. Thus, the public was severely affected when the Dow Jones Industrial Average fell 89 percent between 1929 and 1933. The public outcry arising from this decline in stock prices motivated the passage of major federal laws regulating the securities industry.

REQUIRED:

1. Describe the investment practices of the 1920s that contributed to the erosion of the stock market.
2. Explain the basic objectives of each of the following:
   a. Securities Act of 1933.
   b. Securities Exchange Act of 1934.
3. More recent legislation has resulted from abuses in the securities industry. Explain the provisions of each of the following:
   a. Foreign Corrupt Practices Act of 1977.
   b. Insider Trading Sanctions Act of 1984.
   (CMA adapted)

PE.2 **Annual Reports to Stockholders and Form 10-K** The Jerford Company is a well-known manufacturing company with several wholly owned subsidiaries. The company's stock is traded on the New York Stock Exchange, and the company files all appropriate reports with the Securities and Exchange Commission. Jerford's financial statements are audited by a public accounting firm.

Jerford's Annual Report to Stockholders for the year ended December 31, 1974, contained the following phrase in boldface type: **The Company's 10-K is available upon written request**.

REQUIRED:

1. What is Form 10-K, and who requires that the form be completed? Why is the phrase "The Company's 10-K is available upon written request" shown in the annual report?

2. What information not normally included in the company's annual report could be ascertained from the 10-K?
3. Indicate three items of financial information that are often included in annual reports that are not required for the 10-K.
   (CMA adapted)

PE.3 **Quarterly Reports to the SEC** In order to aid in integrating quarterly reports to shareholders with Form 10-Q, the SEC issued *Accounting Series Release (ASR) 286* in February 1981. The *ASR* modifies and expands the financial information content of the previous Form 10-Q disclosures. Specific guidelines are set forth in the *ASR* as to what information must be included on Form 10-Q.

REQUIRED:

1. Corporations are required by the SEC to file a Form 10-Q.
   a. What is Form 10-Q, and how often is it filed with the SEC?
   b. Explain why the SEC requires corporations to file Form 10-Q.
2. Discuss the disclosure requirements now pertaining to Form 10-Q with specific regard to the following:
   a. Condensed balance sheet.
   b. Condensed income statement.
   c. Condensed statements of cash flows.
   d. Management's discussion and analysis of the interim period(s).
   e. Footnote disclosures.
   (CMA adapted)

PE.4 **Special Reports to the SEC** The purpose of the Securities Act of 1933 is to regulate the initial offering of a firm's securities by ensuring that investors are given full and fair disclosure of all pertinent information about the firm. The Securities Exchange Act of 1934 was passed to regulate the trading of securities on secondary markets and to eliminate abuses in the trading of securities after their initial distribution. To accomplish these objectives, the 1934 act created the Securities and Exchange Commission (SEC). Under the auspices of the SEC, public companies must not only register their securities but must also periodically prepare and file Forms 8-K, 10-K, and 10-Q.

REQUIRED:

1. With regard to Form 8-K, discuss
   a. the purpose of the report.
   b. the timing of the report.
   c. the format of the report.
   d. the role of financial statements in the filing of the report.
2. Identify five circumstances under which the SEC requires the filing of Form 8-K.
3. Discuss how the filing of Form 8-K fosters the purpose of the SEC.
4. Does the SEC pass judgment on securities based on information contained in periodic reports? Explain your answer.
   (CMA adapted)

PE.5 Audit Committees An early event leading to the establishment of audit committees as regular subcommittees of boards of directors occurred in 1940 as part of the consent decree relative to the McKesson-Robbins scandal. An audit committee composed of outside directors was required as part of the consent decree.

Another major development affecting audit committees occurred in June 1978 when the New York Stock Exchange required all domestic listed members to establish and maintain an audit committee composed solely of directors independent of management. By June 1979 the Securities and Exchange Commission had issued an interpretive release, *ASR 264*, which dealt with the scope of services by independent accountants. Although the *ASR* is now rescinded because the SEC believes the *ASR* is no longer necessary, the release had advised audit committees, boards of directors, and managements about factors that should be considered in determining whether to engage their independent accountants to perform nonaudit services.

Despite the increasing interest in audit committees and the official actions taken as described above, no specific role, duties, or liabilities have been established for them by the SEC, the NYSE, or any of the accounting organizations. Nevertheless, a commonly accepted set of duties and expectations has developed for the conduct and performance of audit committees.

REQUIRED:

1. Explain the role the audit committee generally assumes with respect to the annual audit conducted by the company's external auditors.
2. Identify duties other than those associated with the annual audit that might be assigned to the audit committee by the board of directors.
3. Discuss the relationship that should exist between the audit committee and a company's internal audit staff.
4. Explain why board members appointed to serve on the audit committee should be outside (independent of management) board members.
   (CMA adapted)

PE.6 Proxy Statements The SEC has the authority to regulate proxy solicitation. This authority is derived from the Securities and Exchange Act of 1934 and is closely tied to the disclosure objective of this act. Regulations established by the SEC require that a proxy statement be mailed by a corporation's management to each shareholder shortly before the annual shareholders meeting.

REQUIRED:

1. Explain the purpose of proxy statements.
2. Identify four types of events or actions for which proxy statements normally are solicited.
3. Identify the conditions that must be met in order to have a dissident shareholder proposal included in a proxy statement.
   (CMA adapted)

PE.7 **Registration of New Securities** Bandex Inc. has been in business for 15 years. The company has compiled a record of steady, but not spectacular, growth. Bandex's engineers have recently perfected a product that has an application in the small computer market. Initial orders have exceeded the company's capacity and the decision has been made to expand.

Bandex has financed past growth from internally generated funds and, since the initial stock offering in 1970, no further shares have been sold. Bandex's Finance Committee has been discussing methods of financing the proposed expansion. Both short-term and long-term notes were ruled out because of high interest rates. Mel Greene, the chief financial officer, said, "It boils down to either bonds, preferred stock, or additional common stock." Alice Dexter, a consultant employed to help in the financing decision, stated, "Regardless of your choice, you will have to file a Registration Statement with the SEC."

Bob Schultz, Bandex's chief accountant for the past five years, stated, "I've coordinated the filing of all the periodic reports required by the SEC—10-Ks, 10-Qs, and 8-Ks. I see no reason why I can't prepare a Registration Statement also."

REQUIRED:

1. Identify the circumstances under which a firm must file a Registration Statement with the SEC.
2. Explain the objectives of the registration process required by the Securities Act of 1933.
3. Identify and explain the SEC publications Bob Schultz would use for guidance in preparing the Registration Statement.
   (CMA adapted)

PE.8 **Role of the SEC in Standard Setting** The development of accounting theory and practice is influenced directly and indirectly by many organizations and institutions. Two of the most important institutions have been the Financial Accounting Standards Board (FASB) and the Securities and Exchange Commission (SEC).

The FASB is a relatively new, independent body that was established in 1972 as a result of the recommendation of the Study Group on Establishment of Accounting Principles (commonly referred to as the Wheat Committee). The FASB is composed of seven persons who represent the field of public accounting and fields other than public accounting.

The SEC is a governmental regulatory agency that was created in 1934 to administer the Securities Act of 1933 and the Securities Exchange Act of 1934. These acts and the creation of the SEC resulted from the widespread collapse of business and the securities markets in the early 1930s.

REQUIRED:

1. What official role does the SEC have in the development of financial accounting theory and practice?
2. What is the interrelationship between the FASB and SEC with respect to the development and establishment of financial accounting theory and practices?
   (CMA adapted)

ENVIRONMENTAL LIABILITIES

MODULE PREVIEW

Accounting for environmental costs and environmental liabilities emerged as an increasingly important topic in recent years. Because of its growing importance and its limited treatment in intermediate accounting texts, we present extended coverage of environmental liabilities in this text.

During the past 25 years, a large number of environmental laws were passed, both at the federal and state levels. Once a law is passed, it typically takes some years until the operational meaning of the law is developed, through regulations and court cases. Hence the implications of environmental laws for financial reporting continue to unfold.

In this module, we introduce this emerging area in financial reporting by examining the following:

- Types of environmental laws
- Accounting issues raised by these laws
- Current financial reporting of environmental matters

Thus this module summarizes major environmental laws, and addresses the issues of contingent liability recognition and cost capitalization in the context of these laws.[1]

Environmental laws fall into two broad categories. One category is **pollution control and prevention laws**, which deal with issues such as recycling, handling of hazardous wastes, and emission or discharge of pollutants. A second category is **environmental remediation liability laws**, which seek to alleviate the effects of environmental damage arising from past actions.

Environmental laws and concerns raise several accounting issues. One important issue is to determine when, under environmental laws, a company has a **recognizable contingent liability**. A second important issue is to determine the conditions under which environmental costs are properly **capitalized**.

POLLUTION CONTROL AND PREVENTION LAWS

Pollution control and prevention laws relate to *current actions* designed to prevent environmental problems from occurring, and to minimize the effects in cases where some degree of pollution

---

[1] This module draws heavily from *Statement of Position 96-1*: "Environmental Remediation Liabilities," (New York: AICPA, 1996).

cannot be avoided. The costs involved are costs of current compliance and costs of investments in facilities needed to provide future control. Accordingly, the major accounting policy decision is typically whether particular costs should be capitalized or expensed.

REGULATION OF HAZARDOUS WASTES

The Resource Conservation and Recovery Act of 1976 (RCRA) regulates various aspects of *hazardous wastes*, including generation, transport, treatment, storage, and disposal. A **hazardous waste** is any solid, liquid, or gas that, either singly or in combination with other matter, is specified by regulation as being hazardous, or that possesses in sufficient quantity and concentration at least one of four characteristics:

- toxicity (the substance is poisonous)
- corrosivity (it consumes or deteriorates other substances)
- reactivity (it interacts with other substances to cause chemical changes)
- ignitability (it can be set on fire)

Matter with these characteristics may be hazardous to human health or to the environment. Proper handling, treatment, storage, transport, and disposal are required to mitigate these hazards.

As suggested by the breadth of the above description, there is a wide range of potentially hazardous wastes. Hazardous wastes are not limited to the industrial and medical arenas; even such common office products as correction fluid ("white-out") and laser printer toner are likely to be deemed hazardous wastes.

A company that generates hazardous wastes incurs a variety of costs under RCRA. It must determine whether specific items are hazardous, provide appropriate packaging and labeling, maintain records, and file reports with the **Environmental Protection Agency** (EPA). When a company accumulates hazardous wastes for more than 90 days, or treats the waste in some way, it is considered to be operating a **treatment, storage, or disposal facility** (TSDF). Such a situation imposes additional costs on the company, including the cost of a TSDF permit, monitoring costs to ensure that hazardous wastes are not released into the environment, costs of storage containers and facilities, and costs of appropriate treatment processes.

Underground storage tanks are one mechanism for storage. Such tanks and the associated piping must meet established standards with respect to structural integrity, corrosion protection, control of spillage, detection of leaks, and ongoing maintenance.[2] When old tanks do not meet current standards, they must be upgraded and brought into compliance by December 22, 1998, or else be closed. Closure also involves costs, as the tanks must be emptied, cleaned, and either removed or filled with inert solid material.

Other storage mechanisms include above-ground containers, open surface storage (waste piles), and landfills. Each is subject to a variety of regulations that cause compliance costs to be incurred.

THE CLEAN WATER ACT

The **Clean Water Act** (1977) regulates the discharge of pollutants into U.S. waterways. Different standards apply to different types of materials discharged. The EPA issues permits that limit the quantity and character of pollutants that a company may discharge.

---

[2] These provisions apply to underground tank systems used for petroleum products as well as those used for hazardous wastes.

Costs imposed on companies under this act include the cost of installing appropriate pollution control technology, costs of treatment prior to discharge, costs of pre-treatment prior to discharge into a publicly-owned treatment works—the local sanitary sewer system—and costs of analyzing and evaluating proposed discharges. In addition, cleanup costs are incurred when oil spills and similar mishaps occur.

THE CLEAN AIR ACT

The **Clean Air Act** (1970) regulates the discharge of pollutants into the atmosphere. The air quality in a given locality affects the requirements under this law. If a company is located in an area where desired air quality standards are not currently attained, a new or significantly modified production facility must use the *most effective pollution control technology available, without regard to cost*. On the other hand, a company located in an area where the desired air quality levels are currently achieved need only use the *best available* control technology. What constitutes the *best available* is determined on a case-by-case basis, giving consideration to cost, energy use, and environmental factors.

Many amendments to the Clean Air Act occurred over the years, covering a variety of topics such as acid rain and use of chemicals that affect the earth's ozone layer. The 1990 Amendments, for example, affect the emission of sulfur dioxide and nitrogen oxides by public utility generating plants.

ACCOUNTING ISSUES AND STANDARDS: POLLUTION CONTROL

The major accounting issue for control and prevention costs is whether to capitalize or to expense these costs. Capitalization vs. expensing is, of course, a broad issue in accounting that extends to many other types of costs as well. Such specific accounting guidance as exists on this topic is found in the pronouncements of the **Emerging Issues Task Force (EITF)**. An arm of the FASB, the EITF considers accounting topics that are too narrow or specialized to qualify for the FASB's agenda, but where timely guidance is needed. When the EITF achieves **consensus** on an issue—defined as agreement by 13 of its 15 members—the finding has status as GAAP.

One of the first issues considered in this area was the treatment of the costs of asbestos removal. In *EITF Issue No. 89-13*, the following conclusions were reached:

■ When a building is acquired having a known asbestos problem, and the problem is treated within a reasonable time after acquisition, the costs should be **capitalized**. However, an *impairment test* is then required, to ascertain that the total capitalized cost for the property does not exceed its future recoverable amount.

■ When an existing property is treated for an asbestos problem, the costs may be **capitalized** as constituting a *betterment* of the asset, again subject to an impairment test.

■ When asbestos removal costs are incurred to prepare a property for sale, the costs are **deferred** until the period of sale, provided that the costs can be recovered from the estimated sales price.

The broader issue of environmental contamination treatment costs in general was discussed in *EITF Issue No. 90-8*. The costs in question are those incurred to remove, contain, neutralize, or prevent existing or future environmental contamination. There are many such types of costs. Costs may be incurred to *remove existing contamination*, such as that caused by an oil spill. Costs may be incurred to *acquire equipment or technology* needed, for example, to control emissions. Costs may be incurred for *indirect actions*, such as environmental engineering studies or the fines assessed under the environmental laws. Which of these costs should be capitalized, and which should be expensed?

The consensus in *EITF Issue No. 90-8* was that, in general, environmental contamination treatment costs should be **expensed**. These costs may be **capitalized** if they are expected to be recoverable in the future *and at least one of the following criteria are met*:

■ The costs extend the life, increase the capacity, or improve the safety or efficiency of the company's property, relative to its condition when acquired.

■ The costs mitigate or prevent environmental contamination that *has not yet occurred* and that otherwise could result from future operations or activities. In addition, the costs must improve the property relative to its condition when acquired.

■ The costs are incurred in preparing for sale a property currently being held for sale.

The conclusions of *EITF Issue No. 89-13* with respect to asbestos removal costs were not changed by the above general standards, as they are deemed to meet the first criterion above.

As one example of the application of *EITF Issue No. 90-8*, consider the case of an oil spill from a tanker operating on the waterways. Costs to clean up the effects of the spill on the waterway and the adjoining land are expensed. The first and third criteria above are not applicable, because it is not the *Tanker Company's property* that is affected. The second criterion is not met either, as the cleanup does nothing to mitigate or prevent *future* oil spills. Costs to reinforce the hulls of the company's tanker fleet, in order to reduce the probability of future spills, however, could be capitalized under either the first or second criterion.

CURRENT PRACTICES IN REPORTING: POLLUTION CONTROL

Disclosures of specific capitalize/expense decisions are not usually found in annual reports, and the environmental cost area is no exception. Thus, it is difficult to assess current practice from an examination of annual reports, although some companies disclose relevant information.

Bethlehem Steel Corporation's 1997 annual report describes the company's accounting policy for environmental expenditures as follows:

[E]nvironmental expenditures that increase the life or efficiency or property, plant and equipment, or that reduce or prevent environmental contamination are capitalized. Expenditures that relate to existing conditions caused by past operations and which have no significant future economic benefit are expensed.

In its 1997 annual report, Eastman Kodak Company discloses that its environmental expenditures for the year amounted to $115 million. It provides the following analysis of this amount:

Recurring costs for managing hazardous substances and pollution prevention	*$ 88 million*
Capital expenditures to limit or monitor hazardous substances and pollutants	*25*
Site remediation costs	*2*
Total	*$115 million*

In the context of the above discussion, Kodak expensed $88 million and capitalized $25 million. The remaining $2 million appears to be a payment of site remediation liabilities accrued and expensed in an earlier period. These are discussed in a subsequent section.

ENVIRONMENTAL REMEDIATION LAWS

Environmental remediation laws relate to *past actions* that resulted in currently-identified environmental problems. As environmental standards and technical knowledge grow over time, there may be a determination that past actions, especially with respect to disposal of materials, created a current problem. The legal issue becomes one of identifying responsible parties and seeking to have them bear some or all of the cost of correcting the problem. Because this is often a lengthy procedure, the principal accounting problem is deciding *when* a liability for these remediation costs is properly recognizable. A measurement problem also results, from the need to *estimate* these costs.

SUPERFUND

Most of the environmental remediation provisions are contained in a collection of laws commonly referred to as **Superfund** laws. The major statutes are the Comprehensive Environmental Response, Compensation, and Liability Act of 1980 (CERCLA) and the Superfund Amendments and Reauthorization Act of 1986 (SARA).

CERCLA was originally adopted to focus on the remediation of abandoned waste sites. The EPA was to:

- identify sites containing hazardous substances that have been, or might in the future be, released into the environment.
- see that the sites are remediated, either by responsible parties or by the government.
- compensate federal, state, and local governments for damages to natural resources.
- establish a procedure whereby parties that remediated waste sites or restored natural resources could file claims against those responsible for the problem.

CERCLA also provided a trust fund of $1.6 billion to cover remediation costs. Some of these costs might later be recovered from parties responsible for the problem, though there may be some sites for which no responsible party can be identified. These are known as **orphan sites**.

Potentially Responsible Parties

Identification of those parties responsible for environmental problems is an important element in the recognition of environmental liabilities. The Superfund Law identifies four classes of responsible parties:

- The *current owner or operator* of a site where hazardous substances were disposed or abandoned. Note that the current owner need not have any connection to the problem; the mere fact that one owns, or operates, the property currently is sufficient to establish responsibility. Companies must therefore make careful examination of a property's history before buying real estate, lest they inherit a previous owner's problems. Even financial institutions must be very careful in lending for real estate acquisitions, lest they someday become the owners by foreclosure.

- *Previous owners or operators* of the site at the time of disposal of the hazardous substances.
- Parties that *arranged for the disposal* of the hazardous substances found at the sites. This often means the company that produced the wastes in question.
- Parties that *transported* hazardous substances to the site, having selected that site as the place to treat or dispose of the materials.

Companies, individuals, or other kinds of organizations identified by the EPA as *possibly* falling into one of the above categories are known as **potentially responsible parties (PRP**s).

Liability Standards

Liability under the Superfund Laws is known as **strict liability**. That is, if a company falls into one of the categories of responsibility, it does not matter whether they acted negligently with respect to the hazardous materials. Liability is also **retroactive**; it does not matter that the site was in compliance with the environmental laws and regulations that existed at the time the disposals occurred. Nor does it matter whether the company participated in the disposals, or benefited in any way from the disposals. If there has been—or could be—a release of hazardous substances into the environment from that site, any PRP may be liable for the remediation costs. Further, liability is **joint and several**, meaning that any *one* PRP could be held responsible for the *entire* cost of remediation.

Note that the term *hazardous substance* used in environmental remediation laws is a broader term than *hazardous waste* described earlier in the section on pollution control and prevention laws. A **hazardous substance** is any substance identified as hazardous by the EPA, under a variety of federal laws. There are more than one thousand chemicals and chemical compounds on the EPA's list of hazardous substances. Moreover, these substances are often components of products that do not by themselves constitute hazardous wastes. For example, suppose a company disposed of a piece of equipment that was painted with lead-based paint. Because lead is a hazardous substance, if this piece of equipment is found at a Superfund site, the company that disposed of the equipment could be identified as a PRP and held responsible for cleanup costs. There is no minimum threshold quantity under the law; *any amount of a hazardous substance, in any form,* is sufficient to establish potential liability.

There are few defenses against liability under CERCLA. An *act of God* and an *act of war* are mentioned, but the operational meaning of these is unclear. There is also the *innocent landowner defense,* applicable when property is acquired after the hazardous substances were disposed on the property and the new owner did not know or have reason to know about this condition. To use this defense, one must show that "all appropriate inquiry into the previous ownership and uses of the property consistent with good commercial or customary practice" was made. Whether sufficient inquiry was made is often the subject of litigation.

The provisions of strict, retroactive, and joint and several liability are quite harsh. The law does permit PRPs to sue other PRPs to force them to contribute to remediation costs or to recover amounts previously spent. Nonetheless, significant liability exposure may exist for any company identified as a PRP.

The Remediation Process

Since 1981, the EPA identified more than 30,000 sites that may contain hazardous substances. After preliminary assessment, some sites are dropped, and others are investigated further by a site visit and some sampling of contents. A scoring system is used to establish the severity of the problems at the site; those with sufficiently high scores are proposed in this **identification** stage for addition to the **National Priorities List** for remedial action. Remediation is typically a long-term activity seeking permanent solutions to the greatest possible extent.

Unless emergency removal action is deemed necessary, the process next moves to the **remedial investigation** stage. Conducted by environmental engineers, this investigation assesses the nature and extent of substances present, the potential risks, and extensive sampling of soil and ground water in the area of the site. The next stage is a **feasibility study** to identify potential remedial actions, their costs, and their technical requirements. The combined remedial investigation and feasibility study (RI/FS) can require two years or more to complete and cost in excess of $1 million. At the conclusion of the RI/FS, a **remedial action plan** is proposed by the EPA and, after appropriate public comment, is formalized by the issuance of a **record of decision** (ROD).

Once the ROD is in place, actual work begins. A detailed remedial design is developed, followed by its actual implementation. Even after the remediation is completed, monitoring and maintenance activities may continue for as many as 30 years or more.

Impact on PRPs

At any stage in the process—though usually at an early stage—the EPA may notify a company that it has been identified as a potentially responsible party. Often, multiple PRPs are identified and notified. Once notified, the PRPs seek to organize themselves so as to negotiate with the government from a united position. Sometimes, the PRP group assumes responsibility for the remediation; in other cases, the government handles it and then assesses the costs. The PRPs also negotiate among themselves as to cost-sharing. The EPA may assist this process by issuing a nonbinding allocation of responsibility that suggests each PRP's share. Parties with very minor involvement (less than one-percent responsibility) may negotiate a cash settlement with the EPA and be excused from further involvement.

The remaining PRPs typically establish and contribute to a trust fund that pays the remediation contractors; PRPs rarely perform the remediation work themselves. PRPs typically sue any nonparticipating PRPs to force them to contribute their fair share of the costs. Because long time periods often elapse between the creation of the problem and its remediation, some PRPs may not be located, or may no longer be solvent.

To date, most costs imposed on companies have been remediation costs. But CERCLA also allows the government to recover for damage to, or loss or, natural resources. These resources include land, fish and wildlife, other biological life, air, and water. Damage claims may include restoration costs, loss of use, and loss of non-use values such as beauty and enjoyment.

ACCOUNTING ISSUES AND STANDARDS: REMEDIATION COSTS

The primary accounting issue relating to environmental remediation cases is the determination of whether a **contingent liability** should be recognized and accrued. As described above, the legal process under CERCLA is lengthy; many years may elapse from the time when a company first has an indication of possible responsibility to the time when actual remediation costs are incurred. The issues involve both *timing—when* should the company record the cost—and *measurement— how much* should be recorded? The complexity of the process and the long time periods involved complicate the accounting.

Accounting for contingencies is guided by FASB *Statement No. 5*, issued in 1975. Although the standard addresses both gain contingencies and loss contingencies, only the latter is relevant here.

> A **[loss] contingency** is defined as an existing condition, situation, or set of circumstances involving uncertainty as to possible ...loss ...to an enterprise that will ultimately be resolved when one or more future events occur or fail to occur. Resolution of the uncertainty may confirm the ... loss or impairment of an asset or the incurrence of a liability.[3]

The issues addressed by *SFAS 5* include conditions under which a loss should be accrued, and conditions under which disclosure without accrual is appropriate. The standard provides that a loss contingency shall be accrued and charged against income if *both* of the following conditions are met:

> 1. Information available prior to issuance of the financial statements indicates that it is **probable** that an asset had been impaired or a liability had been incurred at the date of the financial statements. It is implicit in this condition that it must be probable that one or more future events will occur confirming the fact of the loss.
> 2. The amount of the loss can be **reasonably estimated**.[4]

The loss must meet the fairly strong requirement of being **probable**, and must be capable of reasonable estimation as to its amount. Both factors require management judgment. If estimation is deemed impossible, no accrual is made but disclosure of the situation occurs. Similarly, if the loss is deemed only **reasonably possible**, the test of *probable* is not met but disclosure still occurs.

A subsequent *Interpretation* of *SFAS 5* emphasized that a single estimate of the amount is essential. A range of estimates may exist. If some amount in that range is more likely than other amounts, that figure should be used for the accrual; otherwise, the *minimum of the range* should be accrued and the potential additional exposure disclosed.[5]

APPLICATION TO ENVIRONMENTAL LIABILITIES

Two issues must be addressed in applying *SFAS 5* to environmental matters, *timing* and *measurement*.

---

[3] Financial Accounting Standards Board, *Statement of Financial Accounting Standards No. 5*, "Accounting for Contingencies," (Stamford, CT: FASB, 1975), par. 1.

[4] *Ibid*, par. 8.

[5] Financial Accounting Standards Board, *Interpretation No. 14*, "Reasonable Estimation of the Amount of a Loss: An Interpretation of FASB Statement No. 5," (Stamford, CT: FASB, 1976), par. 3.

With respect to **timing**, it is probable that an environmental liability has been incurred when:

- It has been asserted by a governmental agency—or it is probable that it will be asserted—that the company is responsible for participating in an environmental remediation because of a past connection with a given site, and
- It is probable that the outcome of this assertion will be unfavorable.

Unlike most legal processes, where good defenses against an assertion of wrongdoing may exist, there are almost no defenses to an assertion of an environmental claim, other than a clear lack of connection to the site. Thus, if a company determines that it is associated with a site in any of the ways discussed earlier, the company should assume an unfavorable outcome. Once there is an assertion of responsibility—usually at the stage where the EPA notifies a company that it is believed to be a PRP—and the company concludes that it is in fact associated with the site, it is probable that an environmental remediation liability exists.

The issue of **measurement** is considerably more difficult to resolve. Especially at early stages of the process, costs are difficult to estimate, as they depend on such factors as:

- Types and quantities of hazardous substances present at the site
- Available technologies for remediation
- Determination of what constitutes acceptable remediation
- The number of other PRPs
- Financial condition of other PRPs
- Percent of the total cost that the company is likely to have to bear

These uncertainties often produce a range of estimates for the amount of the liability that is quite broad, especially early in the process. The minimum of the range is initially likely to be low, based on favorable outcomes to the above uncertainties, and thus a modest accrual may initially be made. As the process unfolds, the range of estimates is clarified by new information. As a result, accruals are frequently adjusted on an annual basis. Such adjustments constitute a *change of estimate* and therefore are expensed in the adjustment year.

Measurement of the future costs of remediation includes both *incremental direct* costs and an allocation of the compensation and benefit costs of company employees who will devote time directly to the remediation effort. **Incremental direct costs** of remediation include:

- Fees paid to outside law firms for related legal work
- Costs of completing the RI/FS
- Fees paid to outside engineering and consulting firms for site investigation and development of remedial action responses
- Costs of contractors for actual remedial work
- Reimbursement of costs incurred by the government
- Costs related to coordinating or participating in a PRP group
- Costs of operating, maintaining, and monitoring the site

The long time period involved in remediation claims and the resultant cleanup create a further complication. Over that time, laws and regulations change, as does technology available to accomplish the cleanup. Costs are also affected by inflationary factors. *Current laws* and *current technology* should be assumed in making the cost estimates, though a company may disclose the uncertainties that exist. Inflation can be considered, and future costs can be discounted to a present value. Usually, companies neither discount nor consider inflation; these two factors may be deemed to offset each other, so that ignoring both does not create a significant distortion.

The possible recovery of remediation costs from other parties also must be considered. Although a given company could bear full responsibility under the *joint and several liability* provisions of the environmental laws, in most cases multiple PRPs exist and are expected to share the cost. In addition, claims may exist for coverage under insurance contracts. When cost-sharing and/or insurance recoveries are *probable*, the company's liability is reduced accordingly.

CURRENT PRACTICES IN REPORTING: REMEDIATION COSTS

Because of the many uncertainties involved, environmental remediation liabilities are a difficult accounting and reporting problem. A high degree of management judgment is involved. Accordingly, a wide range of outcomes is found in practice. This section presents a sampling of disclosures from corporate annual reports.

Inability to Estimate

Some companies focus on the difficulty of making a *reasonable estimate* of environmental remediation liabilities, and conclude that such an estimate cannot be made. For example, Triton Energy Ltd., an international oil and gas exploration and production company, presents the following disclosure in its 1997 annual report:

> *The Company is subject to extensive environmental laws and regulations. These laws regulate the discharge of oil, gas, or other materials into the environment and may require the Company to remove or mitigate the environmental effects of the disposal or release of such materials at various sites. . . . The Company believes that the level of future expenditures for environmental matters, including clean-up obligations, is impractical to determine with a precise and reliable degree of accuracy. . . .*

Though engaged in an industry that often incurs significant environmental costs, this company appears to indicate that no accrual is made because the amounts cannot be reasonably estimated.

Accrual and Detailed Disclosure of Uncertainties

Most companies with potential environmental obligations disclose an estimate and some discussion of the uncertainties surrounding that estimate. One example is the disclosure by Reynolds Metal Company in its 1997 annual report:

> *The Company is involved in various worldwide environmental improvement activities resulting from past operations, including designation as a potentially responsible party (PRP), with others, at various Environmental Protection Agency-designated Superfund sites. Amounts have been recorded (on an undiscounted basis) which, in management's best estimate, will be sufficient to satisfy anticipated costs of known remediation requirements. At December 31, 1997, the accrual for environmental remediation costs was $171 million. . . . This amount is expected to be spent over the next 15 to 20 years with the majority to be spent by the year 2002.*

Estimated environmental remediation costs are developed after considering, among other things, the following:

- *currently available technological solutions*
- *alternative cleanup methods*
- *risk-based assessments of the contamination*
- *estimated proportionate share of remediation costs (if applicable)*

The Company may also use external consultants, and consider, when available, estimates by other PRPs and governmental agencies and information regarding the financial viability of other PRPs. Based on information currently available, the Company believes it is unlikely that it will incur substantial additional costs as a result of failure by other PRPs to satisfy their responsibilities for remediation costs.

Estimated costs for future environmental compliance and remediation are necessarily imprecise because of factors such as:

- *continuing evolution of environmental laws and regulatory requirements*
- *availability and application of technology*
- *identification of presently unknown remediation requirements*
- *costs allocations among PRPs*

Further, it is not possible to predict the amount or timing of future costs of environmental remediation that may subsequently be determined. Based on information presently available, such future costs are not expected to have a material adverse effect on the Company's competitive or financial position or its ongoing results of operations. However, such costs could be material to results of operations in a future interim or annual reporting period.

This disclosure is one of the more detailed ones that exist. Although it describes various uncertainties that are present, the Company settled on an accrual of $171 million. Note the long time frame (15-20 years) over which the actual expenditures are expected and that discounting is *not* employed.

Range of Estimates

Many companies disclose a range of estimates for their environmental obligations. Although the minimum of the range is typically used as the accrual, some other amount, presumably the most likely amount within the range, is sometimes used. Following are some examples.

In some cases, the range is quite narrow. National Fuel Gas Company, in its 1997 annual report, states:

[The] Corporation has estimated that clean-up costs related to the above-noted sites are in the range of $9.3 million to $9.9 million. At September 30, 1997, [the] Corporation has recorded the minimum liability of $9.3 million.

A much broader range is illustrated in the 1997 annual report of MCN Energy Group, Inc., a company also in the natural gas exploration and distribution business:

The findings of these investigations indicate that the estimated total expenditures for investigation and remediation at all 17 former MGP [manufactured gas plant] sites will be between $30,000,000 and $170,000,000 based on undiscounted 1995 costs. As a result of these studies, MCN accrued an additional liability . . . . of $35,000,000.

Observe here that the accrual was slightly above the minimum of the range.

A different approach to the presentation of a range, coupled with a best estimate of the liability, is found in the 1997 annual report of Newmont Mining Corporation, which is primarily engaged in gold mining.

Based upon the Corporation's best estimate of its liability for these matters, $52.2 million . . . . [was] accrued for such obligations at December 31, 1997. . . . Depending upon the ultimate resolution of these matters, the Corporation believes that it is reasonably possible that the liability for these matters could be as much as 70% greater or 15% lower than the amount accrued at December 31, 1997.

Future Recovery of Costs

A company may have claims against others for recovery of some of its environmental remediation costs. Claims are made against other PRPs, especially those unwilling to agree to cost sharing, and against insurers. The outcome of such claims is often quite uncertain. As a result, receivables for these claims are usually not recorded unless their collection is deemed *probable*. Bethlehem Steel's disclosure on this matter is typical.

Bethlehem's policy is to not discount any recorded obligations for future remediation expenditures to their present value nor to record recoveries of environmental remediation costs from insurance carriers and other third parties, if any, as assets until their receipt is deemed probable.

Another form of recovery, peculiar to the public utility industry, is the ability to incorporate remediation costs in the base for ratemaking purposes. When these costs are allowed, the company eventually recovers them by future charges to utility users. Future recovery of these costs justifies their treatment as assets. This is illustrated in the 1997 annual report of New York State Electric and Gas:

The company's estimate for all costs related to investigation and remediation of the 38 sites is a range of $81 million to $182 million at December 31, 1997. That estimate is based on both known and potential site conditions and multiple remediation alternatives for each of the sites. The estimate has not been discounted and is based on costs in 1996 dollars that the company expects to incur through the year 2017. The estimate could change materially, based on facts and circumstances derived from site investigations, changes in required remedial action, changes in technology relating to remedial alternatives and changes to current laws and regulations.

The liability . . . is reflected in the company's consolidated balance sheet at December 31, 1997 . . . in the amount of $81 million. . . . The company has recorded a corresponding regulatory asset, since it expects to recover such expenditures in rates. The company has notified and entered into negotiations with its former and current insurance carriers so that *it may recover from them certain of the cleanup costs. The company is unable to predict the amount of insurance recoveries, if any, that it may obtain.*

Anticipating Future Costs

In industries such as mining, it is known that reclamation and restoration costs will be incurred when the operating life of the property ends. These costs are often accrued as an operating cost during the active life of the mine. As example of such treatment is found in the following disclosure by Newmont Mining Corporation:

> *Estimated future reclamation and remediation costs are based principally on legal and regulatory requirements. Such costs related to active mines are accrued and charged over the expected operating lives of the mines using a unit-of-production method. Future reclamation and remediation costs for inactive mines are accrued based on management's best estimate at the end of each period of the undiscounted costs expected to be incurred at a site. Such cost estimates include where applicable, ongoing care, maintenance and monitoring costs. Changes in estimates are reflected in earnings in the period an estimate is revised.*

SUMMARY OF KEY CONCEPTS

Environmental laws deal with two broad topics: the **control and prevention** of future environmental problems, and the **remediation** of the effects of past actions. AICPA *Statement of Position 96-1* provides background and guidance on these topics.

The primary accounting issue under pollution control and prevention laws is whether the costs incurred should be **capitalized** or **expensed**. Guidance on this issue is found in pronouncements of the **Emerging Issues Task Force**, primarily *EITF Issue No. 90-8*.

Environmental remediation laws contain very strong liability provisions. A company's liability is typically **strict**, **retroactive**, and **joint and several**.

The primary accounting issue under environmental remediation laws is the recognition of a **contingent liability** for future environmental costs. This issue is guided primarily by *SFAS No. 5*, which requires that the obligation be both **probable** and **capable of reasonable estimation**. Because of the liability standards contained in the laws, the *probable* criterion is usually satisfied; the estimation criterion may be more difficult.

While examples of pollution control and prevention are difficult to find in company **annual reports**, examples of environmental remediation liabilities are numerous.

QUESTIONS

QF.1　Distinguish between the main purpose of pollution control and prevention laws compared to environmental remediation laws.

QF.2   If a company incurs costs for pollution control and prevention, under what conditions are such costs capitalized?

QF.3   Describe the liability provisions of the Superfund laws.

QF.4   What is the accounting significance of a company being notified by the Environmental Protection Agency that it is a Potentially Responsible Party with respect to a contaminated site?

QF.5   In assessing its future liability for environmental remediation costs, a company is able to develop a range of estimates, but not a single best estimate. Assuming the conditions of *SFAS No. 5* are otherwise met, how should the company determine the amount to accrue?

QF.6   A company that has recordable contingent liabilities for environmental remediation costs also has insurance coverage that it believes covers the actions that led to the obligations. Should the claim for insurance recovery be offset against the contingent liability?

EXERCISES

EF.1   **Accounting for Environmental Costs** In its 1997 annual report, Motorola, Inc. made the following disclosure:

The Company accrues costs associated with environmental matters when they become probable and reasonably estimable, and these totaled $87 million at both December 31, 1997 and 1996, respectively. The amount of such charges to earnings was $36 million, $29 million and $24 million in 1997, 1996 and 1995, respectively.

REQUIRED: Present the likely entries that Motorola made in 1997.

EF.2   **Contingent Environmental Liability** Goodlife Products has not incurred any significant environmental costs to date. However, a recent environmental assessment against a competitor caused the company to examine its current exposure. A consultant concluded that Goodlife's waste disposals are similar in nature to that of its competitor, and that Goodlife is likely to be required to undertake remediation. The consultant estimates that the cost will be in the range of $800,000 to $4 million. The consultant is also aware of new technology currently being tested; if successful, this technology will reduce remediation costs by about 40 percent. The consultant, whose firm is involved in evaluating the new technology, personally feels that success is almost certain.

REQUIRED: How should Goodlife report the above information?

EF.3   **Pollution Control Costs** In its 1997 annual report, Inland Steel Industries, Inc. reported the following:

It is anticipated that the company will make capital expenditures of $2 million to $5 million annually in each of the next five years for the construction, and have ongoing annual expenditures of $40 million to $50 million for the operation, of air and water *pollution control facilities to comply with current federal, state and local laws and regulations.*

REQUIRED: How is Inland likely to treat each of the items mentioned?

EF.4   **Capitalization of Pollution Control Costs** Damon Company uses several hazardous chemicals in its manufacturing process. Its inventories of such chemicals are stored in above-ground tanks located in a secure outdoor area. Due to age, some of the tanks are showing signs of rust, which could eventually lead to leakage. Damon is considering several actions with respect to the tanks:

1. Regularly maintain to remove rust and paint the tanks with a rust-resistant paint.
2. Line the inside of the existing tanks with a rust-resistant material.
3. Build a spill-collection system under the tanks so that any leakage would not enter the ground or water.
4. Replace all metal tanks with ones made of new nonmetallic materials.

REQUIRED: For each of the above four alternatives, should the company capitalize or expense the cost?

PROBLEMS

PF.1   **Pollution Control Costs** In its 1997 annual report, Eastman Kodak Company reported the following:

In October 1994, the Company, the Environmental Protection Agency (EPA), and the U.S. Department of Justice announced the settlement of a civil complaint alleging noncompliance by the Company with federal environmental regulations at the Company's Kodak Park manufacturing site in Rochester, New York. The Company paid a penalty of $5 million. A Consent Decree was signed under which the Company is subject to a Compliance Schedule by which the Company improved its waste characterization procedures, upgraded one of its incinerators, and is evaluating and upgrading its industrial sewer system. The total expenditures required to complete this program are currently estimated to be approximately $55 million over the next eight years.

REQUIRED: Discuss the proper accounting for the $5 million and $55 million amounts.

PF.2   **Understanding Environmental Disclosures** Dominion Resources, Inc., an electric power utility with primary operations in the state of Virginia (a subsidiary operating under the name of Virginia Power), presented the following environmental disclosure in its 1997 annual report:

Environmental costs have been historically recovered through the ratemaking process; however, should material costs be incurred and not recovered through rates, Virginia Power's results of operations and financial condition could be adversely impacted.

The EPA has identified Virginia Power and several other entities as Potentially Responsible Parties (PRPs) at two Superfund sites located in Kentucky and Pennsylvania. The estimated future remediation costs for the sites are in the range of $61.5 million to

$72.5 million. Virginia Power's proportionate share of the costs is expected to be in the range of $1.7 million to $2.5 million, based upon allocation formulas and the volume of waste shipped to the sites. As of December 31, 1997, Virginia Power had accrued a reserve of $1.7 million to meet its obligations at these two sites. Based on a financial assessment of the PRPs involved at these sites, Virginia Power has determined that it is probable that the PRPs will fully pay the costs apportioned to them.

Virginia Power generally seeks to recover its costs associated with environmental remediation from third-party insurers. At December 31, 1997 pending claims were not recognized as an asset or offset against recorded obligations.

REQUIRED:

1. It appears that Dominion/Virginia Power has not yet incurred any costs with respect to the two Superfund sites. Why should a liability be recorded?
2. Given that remediation costs for the two Superfund sites are estimated to be in the range of $60 to $70 million, why did Dominion record only $1.7 million?
3. What debit was likely made when the $1.7 million liability was recorded?
4. The company appears to have insurance coverage. Why does it not record a receivable for claims made?

PF.3 **Environmental Remediation Costs** Following are four excepts from the 1997 annual report of Potomac Electric Power Company, an electric utility, relating to potential environmental remediation obligations of the company.

1. *On October 6, 1997, the Company received notice from the U.S. Environmental Protection Agency (EPA) that it, along with 68 other parties, may be a Potentially Responsible Party (PRP) under the Comprehensive Environmental Response Compensation and Liability Act (CERCLA or Superfund) at the Butler Mine Tunnel Superfund site in Pittstown Township, Luzerne County, Pennsylvania. The site is a mine drainage tunnel with an outfall on the Susquehanna River where waste oil was disposed via a borehole in the tunnel. The letter notifying the Company of its potential liability also contained a request for a reimbursement of approximately $.8 million for response costs incurred by EPA at the site. The letter requested that the Company submit a good faith proposal to conduct or finance the remedial action contained in a July 1996 Record of Decision (ROD). The EPA estimates the present cost of the remedial action to be $3.7 million.*
2. *In December 1995, the Company received notice from the EPA that it is a PRP with respect to the release or threatened release of radioactive and mixed radioactive and hazardous wastes at a site in Denver, Colorado, operated by RAMP Industries, Inc. Evidence indicates that the Company's connection to the site arises from an agreement with a vendor to package, transport and dispose of two laboratory instruments containing small amounts of radioactive material at a Nevada facility.*
3. *In October 1995, the Company received notice from the EPA that it, along with several hundred other companies, may be a PRP in connection with the Spectron Superfund Site located in Elkton, Maryland. The site was operated as a hazardous waste disposal, recycling, and processing facility from 1961 to 1988. A group of PRPs allege, based on records they have collected, that the Company's share of*

liability at this site is .0042%. The EPA has also indicated that a de minimis settlement is likely to be appropriate for this site.

4. *In October 1994, a Remedial Investigation/Feasibility Study (RI/FS) report was submitted to the EPA with respect to a site in Philadelphia, Pennsylvania. Pursuant to an agreement among the PRPs, the Company is responsible for 12% of the costs of the RI/FS. Total costs of the RI/FS and associated activities prior to the issuance of a ROD by the EPA, including legal fees, are currently estimated to be $7.5 million. The Company has paid $.9 million as of December 31, 1997. The report included a number of possible remedies, the estimated costs of which range from $2 million to $90 million. In July 1995, the EPA announced its proposed remedial action plan for the site and indicated it will accept comments on the plan from any interested parties. The EPA's estimate of the costs associated with implementation of the plan is approximately $17 million. The Company cannot predict whether the EPA will include the plan in its ROD as proposed or make changes as a result of comments received.*

Potomac Electric Power's 1997 financial statements showed revenues of $1.8 billion, net income of $181 million, total assets of $6.7 billion, and stockholders' equity of $4.0 billion.

REQUIRED: Discuss the accounting treatment you recommend for each of the above four situations.

PERSONAL FINANCIAL STATEMENTS

MODULE PREVIEW

This module examines individuals as accounting and reporting entities. Personal financial statements require a current value presentation and encompass some unique issues in accounting for income taxes. Principal topics studied are as follows:

- Introduction to personal financial statements
- Valuation of assets and liabilities
- Preparation of personal financial statements

Accounting principles stressed in this module frequently diverge from conventional corporate accounting principles. Nevertheless, they are designed to respond to the needs of users of financial information provided by individuals. In an era where greater use of current values is often suggested for corporate reporting, personal financial statements offer an opportunity to study an entire reporting system built on current values.

Although the individual might be considered to be the basic accounting entity, relatively little attention is devoted to it other than in a business context. This module discusses problems peculiar to an individual-oriented accounting entity. Some of these problems appear more complex than the nature of the entity itself suggests they should be.

INTRODUCTION TO PERSONAL FINANCIAL STATEMENTS

Frequently it becomes necessary to prepare financial statements covering all the financial affairs of an individual or group of individuals, including business interests as well as nonbusiness items. Such statements are called **personal financial statements**. The need for personal financial statements may arise on an *ad hoc* basis—for example, in connection with an application for a bank loan; a major investment in a business activity, such as formation of a partnership; or election or appointment to public office.

Personal financial statements may also be required on a more regular basis as part of an individual's *personal financial planning*, a subject briefly introduced in the next section. Whatever the case, though, personal financial statements constitute financial reporting for the most basic accounting entity—the individual.

PERSONAL FINANCIAL PLANNING

Personal financial planning is an activity receiving increased attention in recent years, and for which a group of specialized professionals has emerged, combining skills in accounting, taxation, investments, and insurance. **Personal financial planning** is a process that begins with an assessment of an individual's resources, income, financial requirements, and goals, and then develops strategies to meet these requirements and goals.

Personal financial statements are useful in evaluating one's resources and income because they provide a framework for collection, valuation, and presentation of this information. Financial goals and requirements are then considered: wealth accumulation for education, investment, or retirement; general financial security; and eventual wealth transfer to others.[1] A sound financial plan integrates investment strategies, insurance policies, interim wealth transfers such as creation of trusts, and use of tax-saving devices such as tax shelters. The plan should be monitored on a regular basis—again, personal financial statements are useful here—and revised as appropriate.

Because of the growing importance of personal financial planning, familiarity with personal financial statements is desirable. In addition, study of this subject offers exposure to complete use of a *current value*, rather than historical cost, accounting and reporting system.

SOURCE OF ACCOUNTING PRINCIPLES

Accounting principles for personal financial statements were initially established in *Audits of Personal Financial Statements*, an audit guide issued by the AICPA in 1968.[2] This guide recommended a dual presentation of assets and liabilities, along with the change in net assets, on both a historical cost and current value basis. In 1982, the guide was amended by *Statement of Position 82-1*,[3] which specified *current value* as the *sole basis* for reporting an individual's assets and liabilities. This conclusion was based on the belief that the uses of personal financial statements, such as loan applications, financial planning, and information about candidates for public office, were better served by current value data than by historical cost data. *SOP 82-1* is still current as the source of GAAP for personal financial statements.

Although generally-accepted accounting principles require current value presentation for personal financial statements, a non-GAAP basis may be deemed appropriate for a particular reporting purpose. Such reporting is referred to as a *comprehensive basis of accounting other than generally accepted accounting principles*, or, for short, an *other comprehensive basis of accounting* or *OCBOA*. Common OCBOAs used for non-GAAP personal financial statements include cash basis, historical cost basis, and income tax basis.

THE REPORTING ENTITY IN PERSONAL FINANCIAL STATEMENTS

Normally, personal financial statements are prepared for an individual or for a husband and wife jointly. Occasionally, it is appropriate for a larger family group to constitute the reporting entity. The purposes for which the statements will be used and the ownership status of major assets are important considerations in defining the reporting entity. *Multiple ownership of assets* may complicate the definition of the reporting entity. Several forms of **multiple ownership** exist:

---

[1] See the section on estate planning and taxation in Module H for a brief discussion of this aspect of financial planning.

[2] American Institute of Certified Public Accountants, *Audits of Personal Financial Statements* (New York: AICPA, 1968).

[3] American Institute of Certified Public Accountants, *Statement of Position 82-1: Accounting and Financial Reporting for Personal Financial Statements* (New York: AICPA, 1982). Further details on the compilation, review, and audit of personal financial statements are provided in the Accounting Standards Division's *Personal Financial Statements Guide* (New York: AICPA, 1997).

- **Tenancy in common** means that two or more persons own undivided interests in an asset. These interests need not be equal and may be transferred to others.
- **Joint tenancy** means that two or more persons own equal interests in an asset with **rights of survivorship**; at death, the interest of the decedent passes to the other owners. A joint tenant may transfer the interest to a third party, in which case the joint tenancy ceases and a tenancy in common is created.
- **Tenancy by the entireties** is a joint tenancy involving a husband and wife, in which neither party can eliminate the right of survivorship by transferring the interest to a third party.
- **Community property laws**, which exist in some states, provide for joint ownership in any asset acquired by either spouse during a marriage, even if title is in one spouse's name, unless the asset was acquired with resources possessed by that spouse prior to the marriage.

State laws generally define the rights of multiple owners; not all of the forms just listed exist in all states. Where the reporting entity does not correspond to the ownership of assets or liabilities, the *appropriate proportionate share* should be reported in the financial statements, with full disclosure of the details of ownership in the notes. For example, if statements are being prepared for an individual who holds a one-third interest in a parcel of land as a tenant in common, one-third of the value of the land is presented with a footnote explaining the ownership.

TYPES OF PERSONAL FINANCIAL STATEMENTS

A **statement of financial condition**, the principal financial statement for individuals, *must* be prepared. *Assets* are presented at estimated current values, in order of liquidity. *Liabilities* are presented at estimated current amounts, in order of maturity. Receivables and payables, which may not appear in an individual's cash basis records, must be recognized. Current/noncurrent classifications are not used, though, since the concept of working capital is not particularly meaningful in the individual, nonbusiness context. Comparative statements are presented when desired. Exhibit G.1 presents an illustration of comparative statements of financial condition. Several items in this statement are discussed in more detail in subsequent sections.

In addition to the required statement of financial condition, a **statement of changes in net worth** (or **net assets**) is *optional* and may be prepared. This statement is generally omitted when a beginning-of-year balance sheet is not available, or when detailed records of transactions were not maintained. As illustrated in Exhibit G.2, this statement presents major *components of increase and decrease in net worth*: income; expenses; changes in current values of assets, distinguished as to *realized* versus *unrealized*; and changes in liabilities. The statement of changes in net worth is similar to the old business statement of changes in financial position, now replaced by the statement of cash flows, except that it deals with changes in *net assets* rather than a short-term definition of funds, such as cash or working capital.

James and Jane Person
Statements of Financial Condition
December 31, 19X3 and 19X2

	December 31	
Assets	**19X3**	**19X2**
Cash	$ 3,700	$ 15,600
Bonus Receivable	20,000	10,000
Investments		
Marketable Securities (Note 2)	160,500	140,700
Stock Options (Note 3)	28,000	24,000
Kenbruce Associates (Note 4)	48,000	42,000
Davekar Company, Inc. (Note 5)	550,000	475,000
Vested Interest in Deferred Profit-Sharing Plan	111,400	98,900
Remainder Interest in Testamentary Trust (Note 6)	171,900	128,800
Cash Value of Life Insurance ($43,600 and $42,900),		
Less Loans Payable to Insurance Companies ($38,100		
and $37,700) (Note 7)	5,500	5,200
Residence (Note 8)	190,000	180,000
Personal Effects (Note 9)		
Jewelry	40,000	36,500
Other Personal Effects	55,000	50,000
	$ 1,384,000	$ 1,206,700
Liabilities		
Income Taxes—Current Year Balance	$ 24,600	$ 400
Demand 10.5% Note Payable to Bank	25,000	26,000
Mortgage Payable (Note 10)	98,200	99,000
Contingent Liabilities (Note 11)	—	—
	$ 147,800	$ 125,400
Estimated Income Taxes on the Differences between the		
Estimated Current Values of Assets and the Estimated		
Current Amounts of Liabilities and Their Tax Bases		
(Note 12)	217,500	187,800
Net Worth	1,018,700	893,500
	$ 1,384,000	$ 1,206,700

The notes to financial statements are an integral part of these statements.

Source: The illustrative statements and notes in Exhibits G.1, G.2, and G.3 are based on those in *Statement of Position 82-1: Accounting and Financial Reporting for Personal Financial Statements* (New York: AICPA, 1982), Appendix A, and reflect certain modifications made by Professor Jerry D. Hansen of Eastern Montana College. Copyright © 1982 by the American Institute of Certified Public Accountants, Inc.; reprinted with permission.

EXHIBIT G.1   ILLUSTRATIVE STATEMENT OF FINANCIAL CONDITION

James and Jane Person
Statements of Changes in Net Worth
for the Years Ended December 31, 19X3 and 19X2

	December 31	
	19X3	**19X2**
Realized Increases in Net Worth		
Salary and Bonus	$ 95,000	$ 85,000
Dividend and Interest Income	2,300	1,800
Income Distribution from Limited Partnership	5,000	4,000
Gains on Sales of Marketable Securities	79,100	500
	$ 181,400	$ 91,300
Realized Decreases in Net Worth		
Income Taxes	41,800	22,000
Interest Expense	13,000	14,000
Real Estate Taxes	4,000	3,000
Personal Expenditures	36,700	32,500
	$ 95,500	$ 71,500
Net Realized Increase in Net Worth	$ 85,900	$ 19,800
Unrealized Increases (Decreases) in Net Worth		
Marketable Securities (Note 2)	$ (75,100)	$ 500
Stock Options	4,000	500
Davekar Company, Inc.	75,000	25,000
Kenbruce Associates	6,000	—
Deferred Profit Sharing Plan	12,500	9,500
Remainder Interest in Testamentary Trust	43,100	25,000
Jewelry	3,500	—
Change in Estimated Income Taxes on the Differences between the Estimated Current Values of Assets and the Estimated Current Amounts of Liabilities and Their Tax Bases	(29,700)	(49,800)
Net Unrealized Increase in Net Worth	$ 39,300	$ 10,700
Net Increase in Net Worth	$ 125,200	$ 30,500
Net Worth at Beginning of Year	893,500	863,000
Net Worth at End of Year	$1,018,700	$ 893,500

The notes to financial statements are an integral part of these statements.

EXHIBIT G.2 ILLUSTRATIVE STATEMENT OF CHANGES IN NET WORTH

Disclosures in personal financial statements, typically found in the **notes to financial statements**, include information on valuation methods, ownership of major assets, descriptive details concerning assets and liabilities, and tax information. Exhibit G.3 presents an illustration of such notes.

James and Jane Person
Notes to Financial Statements

NOTE 1. The accompanying financial statements include the assets and liabilities of James and Jane Person. Assets are stated at their estimated current value, and liabilities at their estimated current amounts.

NOTE 2. The estimated current values of marketable securities are either (a) their quoted closing prices or (b) for securities not traded on the financial statement date, amounts that fall within the range of quoted bid and asked prices.

Marketable securities consisted of the following:

	December 31, 19X3		December 31, 19X2	
	Number of Shares or Bonds	Estimated Current Values	Number of Shares or Bonds	Estimated Current Values
Stocks				
Jaiven Jewels, Inc.	1,500	$ 98,813		
McRae Motors, Ltd.	800	11,000	600	$ 4,750
Parker Sisters, Inc.	400	13,875	200	5,200
Rosenfield Rug Co.	—		1,200	96,000
Rubin Paint Company	300	9,750	100	2,875
Weiss Potato Chips, Inc.	200	20,337	300	25,075
		$ 153,775		$ 133,900
Bonds				
Jackson Van Lines, Ltd. (12% due 7/1/X9)	5	$ 5,225	5	$ 5,100
United Garvey, Inc. (7% due 11/15/X6)	2	1,500	2	1,700
		$ 6,725		$ 6,800
Total Marketable Securities		$ 160,500		$ 140,700

Substantially all of the realized gains on sales of marketable securities reported in 19X3 accrued in previous years. The effect of realizing these gains was to report an unrealized decrease in current value of marketable securities during 19X3.

NOTE 3. Jane Person owns options to acquire 4,000 shares of stock of Winner Corp. at an option price of $5 per share. The options expire on June 30, 19X5. The quoted market price per share for Winner Corp. was $12 on December 31, 19X3.

NOTE 4. The investment in Kenbruce Associates is an 8-percent interest in a real estate limited partnership. The estimated current value is determined by the projected annual cash receipts and payments capitalized at a 12-percent rate.

EXHIBIT G.3   ILLUSTRATIVE NOTES TO PERSONAL FINANCIAL STATEMENTS

NOTE 5. James Person owns 50 percent of the common stock of Davekar Company, Inc., a retail mail order business. When estimating the current value of the investment, consideration was given to the trend in earnings of the business, the current market value of the net assets, and a provision of a shareholders' agreement which restricts the sale of the stock and, under certain conditions, requires the company to repurchase the stock based on a price equal to the book value of the net assets plus an agreed amount for goodwill. James Person's share of the agreed amount of goodwill was $112,500 on December 31, 19X3, and $100,000 on December 31, 19X2.

A condensed balance sheet of Davekar Company, Inc., prepared in conformity with generally accepted accounting principles, follows:

	December 31	
	19X3	**19X2**
Current Assets	$ 3,147,000	$ 2,975,000
Plant, Property, and Equipment—Net	165,000	145,000
Other Assets	120,000	110,000
Total Assets	$ 3,432,000	$ 3,230,000
Current Liabilities	$ 2,157,000	$ 2,030,000
Long-Term Liabilities	400,000	450,000
Total Liabilities	$ 2,557,000	$ 2,480,000
Stockholders' Equity	875,000	750,000
Total Liabilities and Stockholders' Equity	$ 3,432,000	$ 3,230,000

The sales and net income for 19X3 were $10,500,000 and $125,000, respectively, and for 19X2 were $9,700,000 and $80,000.

NOTE 6. Jane Person is the beneficiary of a remainder interest in a testamentary trust under the will of the late Joseph Jones. The amount included in the accompanying statements is her remainder interest in the estimated current value of the trust assets, discounted at 10 percent.

NOTE 7. At December 31, 19X3, and December 31, 19X2, James Person owned a $300,000 whole life insurance policy. The cash value of the policy was $43,600 on December 31, 19X3, and $42,900 on December 31, 19X2. Policy loans payable to the insurance company amounted to $38,100 on December 31, 19X3, and $37,700 on December 31, 19X2.

NOTE 8. The estimated current value of the residence is its purchase price plus the cost of improvements. The residence was purchased in December 19X1, and improvements were made in 19X2 and 19X3.

NOTE 9. The estimated current value of jewelry and other personal effects are the appraised values of those assets, determined by an independent appraiser for insurance purposes.

NOTE 10. The mortgage (collateralized by the residence) is payable in monthly installments of $815 each, including interest at 10 percent a year through 20Y8.

NOTE 11. James Person has guaranteed the payment of loans of Davekar Company, Inc., under a $500,000 line of credit. The loan balance was $300,000 at December 31, 19X3, and $400,000 at December 31, 19X2.

EXHIBIT G.3   *(Continued)*

NOTE 12. The estimated current amount of liabilities at December 31, 19X3, and December 31, 19X2, equaled their tax bases. Estimated income taxes have been provided on the excess of the estimated current values of assets over their tax bases as if the estimated current values of the assets had been realized on the statement date, using applicable tax laws and regulations. These provisions will probably differ from the amounts of income taxes that eventually might be paid because those amounts are determined by the timing and the method of disposal or realization and the tax laws and regulations in effect at the time of disposal or realization. The estimated current value of assets exceeded their tax bases by $790,800 at December 31, 19X3, and $711,800 at December 31, 19X2. The excess of estimated current values of major assets over their tax bases are as follows:

	December 31	
	19X3	**19X2**
Investment in Davekar Company, Inc.	$ 430,500	$ 355,500
Vested Interest in Deferred Profit-Sharing Plan	111,400	98,900
Investment in Marketable Securities	24,900	100,000
Remainder Interest in Testamentary Trust	97,000	53,900

EXHIBIT G.3   *(Continued)*

VALUATION OF ASSETS AND LIABILITIES

As mentioned earlier, assets are to be reported at their *estimated current values* and liabilities at their *estimated current amounts*.

> **Current value of an asset** follows from the *standard definition of fair market value*: the price at which an item could be exchanged between a buyer and a seller, each of whom is well informed and neither of whom is compelled to buy or sell.

Applying this definition in practice, however, often poses difficulties. It is recognized that the resulting current amounts are *estimates* with varying reliability. Several techniques for estimating current values exist; it is the accountant's task to select the most appropriate in each particular case. These techniques include

- inference of value from recent transactions involving similar assets.
- appraisal by experts.
- calculation by present value of future cash flows, using an appropriate discount rate.
- use of an earnings-capitalization formula.
- historical cost adjusted by an appropriate price index.

Liabilities are to be reported at the *estimated current amount*, which means the present value of the cash to be paid. Hence, an appropriate discount rate must be selected. If the debt can be discharged currently at an amount lower than the calculated present value, the lower amount is presented.

RECEIVABLES AND PAYABLES

Personal financial statements must reflect the accrual basis of accounting. Hence, receivables and payables are to be recognized. Short-term items, such as balances due on charge accounts, are reported at face value. Longer-term items include any definite obligations, such as alimony, which are noncancelable and have known amounts and durations. Such long-term items are typically stated at the discounted present value of their future cash flows.

INVESTMENTS

Investments of various types constitute a significant portion of assets for many individuals. Estimates of the current value of investments range from very precise to very imprecise. Investments in *publicly held companies* have market quotations which serve as current values. When an individual holds a large block of a given stock, however, one may question whether current market quotations are the best estimate of the stock's current value. On the one hand, a large block may be difficult to sell. When the market for the stock is thin, a large block might be salable only at lower prices. On the other hand, a large block might be worth more than current prices to a buyer interested in achieving control. Thus, some judgment is required to estimate current value.

Some individuals have investments in *closely held nonpublic companies*, including proprietorships, general and limited partnerships, and corporations. In such situations, lack of market quotations makes estimation of current value difficult. **Earnings-capitalization formulas** are often used; these range from simple formulas, such as "four times average earnings for the last three years," to more complex relationships like "excess earnings over the average industry rate of return, discounted at 20 percent." Other possible approaches include appraisals by business brokers or business valuation experts, estimates of reproduction cost of assets, or inflation-adjusted book value. The nature of the business activity and the character of its assets may, in part, determine the method to be used. For example, a law practice might be valued at a multiple of earnings, while an appraised value of land, buildings, and equipment could be used for a farm. *On the statement of financial condition, investment in a business is reported as a single net item; the business's individual assets and liabilities are not shown separately.* In other words, investment in a business is presented in the same way as an equity investment or unconsolidated subsidiary on a corporate balance sheet.

Life insurance is also viewed as an investment. Its current value is reported as the *cash surrender value* of the policy, not the face value, *less* any outstanding loans against the policy. This is a departure from the usual rule against offsetting of assets and liabilities.

REAL ESTATE

Valuation of real estate may also prove difficult. Among the factors considered are recent sales of similar property and appraisals by real estate brokers. When assessed values for property tax purposes are considered, one must take into account the relationship between assessed value and market value. Often a clear and consistent relationship between assessed value and market value does not in fact exist, making assessed value a weak indicator of current value. In the case of rental property, a discounted cash flow approach might also be considered to estimate the present value of expected cash flows from the property. When presenting real estate on the statement of financial condition, any related mortgage liabilities are shown in the liability section, not netted against the asset.

FUTURE INTERESTS

An individual may have several assets in the form of nonforfeitable rights to receive known amounts of future cash payments, or **future interests**. Examples include deferred compensation, guaranteed or vested benefits in pension or profit-sharing plans, individual retirement accounts (IRAs), annuities, alimony, or interests in trust funds. These assets should be presented at their current values, which may be known directly, such as the current balance in profit-sharing plan or IRA accounts, or may be calculated by discounting expected future cash flows.

INCOME TAXES

Two income tax liabilities are presented on the statement of financial condition. The first such liability, **Income Taxes Payable**, includes estimated income taxes for the current year, net of any payments, as well as any unpaid balances for prior years.

The second liability account is formally called *Estimated Income Taxes on the Differences Between the Estimated Current Values of Assets and the Estimated Current Values of Liabilities and Their Tax Bases*. Although this title is very descriptive, it is also very long. This textbook uses a shortened version of this title: **Estimated Income Taxes on Unrealized Asset Appreciation**. This *asset appreciation* allows for increases and decreases in asset and liability values. Because assets and liabilities are presented at current values on the statement of financial condition, this estimated tax liability is needed to demonstrate that the full current value may be offset in part by a contingent tax liability. Taxes may be incurred when the current value is realized. Thus the true net worth of the individual is current value of net assets minus estimated taxes on the unrealized appreciation in net assets.

Calculation of estimated income taxes on unrealized appreciation requires knowledge of applicable tax laws and data on the tax basis of each asset and liability. The difference between current value and tax basis of each asset and liability, which may be positive or negative, must be evaluated along the following lines:

- Is the gain taxable, or the loss deductible? For example, losses on the actual or potential sale or exchange of assets held for personal use are not deductible.
- Are there any special tax provisions? An example is the $500,000 exclusion of gain on sale of personal residence.
- Are there any provisions that tax different sources of income differently? For example, long-term capital gains are currently taxed at a lower effective tax rate than ordinary income. Depending upon current law, whether the gain or loss constitutes ordinary income or capital gain may affect the tax rate.

In answering questions such as these, current income tax rules should be followed. To illustrate the calculation of estimated income taxes on unrealized appreciation, assume an individual has the following assets:

- Investments in securities having current value of $200,000 and tax basis of $70,000, all long-term.
- Residence with current value of $210,000 and tax basis of $50,000; individual qualifies for the special exclusion.

- Pension plan rights having a current value of $150,000 and zero tax basis which were fully funded by the employer.
- Household furnishings with current value of $8,000 and tax basis of $15,000.
- Investment in rental property (long-term) with current value of $80,000 and tax basis of $90,000. Assume no depreciation recapture is called for.

Suppose further that the individual is subject to a 40-percent marginal tax rate on ordinary income. For illustrative purposes, *assume* that ordinary income is taxed at a higher rate (40 percent) than net long-term capital gains (16 percent). The estimated income tax on unrealized appreciation is calculated as follows:

**Calculation of Estimated Income Taxes
on Unrealized Asset Appreciation**

Description	Current Value	Tax Basis	Unrealized Appreciation	Taxable Amount	Effective Tax Rate	Estimated Income Tax
Securities	$ 200,000	$ 70,000	$ 130,000	$ 130,000	16%	$ 20,800
Residence	210,000	50,000	160,000	0		0
Pension	150,000	0	150,000	150,000	40	60,000
Furnishings	8,000	15,000	(7,000)	0		0
Rental Property .	80,000	90,000	(10,000)	(10,000)	16	(1,600)
	$ 648,000	$ 225,000	$ 423,000	$ 270,000		$ 79,200

The appreciation on the residence is not taxable because the $500,000 exclusion applies and the unrealized loss on the household furnishings—personal use items—would not be deductible if realized. The pension will be taxed as ordinary income and is subject to the full 40-percent rate. Appreciation on the securities and the rental property constitute long-term capital gains or losses.

The above calculation provides the estimated tax liability on the statement of financial condition. On the *statement of changes in net worth*, the *change in estimated income taxes on unrealized asset appreciation* is shown as an *unrealized decrease in net worth*, assuming estimated income taxes *increased* during the year. For convenience, the change may be calculated as ending balance minus beginning balance; there is no need to trace the effect of each asset value change.

PREPARATION OF PERSONAL FINANCIAL STATEMENTS

In practice, preparation of personal financial statements can be somewhat difficult. Most individuals do not maintain a comprehensive set of accounting records. When preparing personal financial statements, the individual's assets and liabilities must first be identified. Data sources include income tax returns, checkbooks, statements from security brokers, property tax bills, loan statements, and similar items. Once the assets and liabilities are identified, the second step is to estimate their current values, as discussed in the preceding sections. Finally, all the information must be presented in the proper format. Textbook problems emphasize the last, and easiest, step—preparing statements from given information; they cannot adequately convey the difficulty of the two preceding steps—identification and valuation of assets and liabilities.

Once assets and liabilities are identified and valued, the required statement of financial condition is easily prepared. Calculation of the estimated income taxes on unrealized asset appreciation may be difficult; it was illustrated in the last section. The $217,500 shown at December 31, 19X3, in Exhibit G.1 for James and Jane Person is based on the $790,800 excess mentioned in Note 12 of Exhibit G.3—current value of $1,384,000 less assumed tax bases of $593,200—multiplied by a composite tax rate of approximately 27.5 percent. This rate reflected a weighted average of ordinary and capital gains rates in effect when that example was prepared.

STATEMENT OF CHANGES IN NET WORTH

Preparation of the optional statement of changes in net worth, however, is more complicated than preparation of the statement of financial condition. **Realized increases and decreases in net worth** are the changes in net worth caused by *transactions* which also affect assets or liabilities. These transactions could result in changes to cash or changes in other assets or liabilities. For example, the $95,000 Salary and Bonus shown in the *Realized Increases* section on the statement of changes in net worth in Exhibit G.2 was produced by an $85,000 increase in cash for salary received *plus* the increase in Bonus Receivable of $10,000 (= $20,000 − $10,000) shown on the statement of financial condition in Exhibit G.1. The $41,800 of Income Taxes in the *Realized Decreases* section on the statement of changes in net worth represents a $17,600 cash payment *plus* the increase of $24,200 (= $24,600 − $400) in the liability for Income Taxes—Current Year Balance from the statement of financial condition.

    Unrealized increases and decreases in net worth are the *changes in current values of assets and liabilities* during the year; there are no explicit transactions. For example, the $6,000 increase in Kenbruce Associates, shown in the *Unrealized Increases (Decreases)* section, represents the change in the current value of that investment during the year.

    Preparation of a statement of changes in net worth requires analysis of all changes in assets and liabilities on comparative statements of financial condition. For each change the following questions must be asked:

- Does the change in the asset/liability constitute a *change in net worth*? Some asset/liability changes are offset by other asset/liability changes, with no net impact on net worth. Collection of a receivable (increase cash, decrease receivable), payment of a liability (decrease cash, decrease liability), and purchase of an investment (increase investment, decrease cash or increase liability) are examples of transactions that do *not* appear on the statement of changes in net worth.
- Given that the change in the asset/liability *does* constitute a change in net worth, was the change caused by a *transaction*—realized increase or decrease—or by a *change in value*—unrealized increase or decrease?

Additional examples of the determination of realized and unrealized changes in net worth from the Persons' illustration follow.

    The $36,700 shown as Personal Expenditures in the *Realized Decreases* section is a *plug*—the amount needed to arrive at the ending cash balance after considering the beginning cash balance plus all cash receipts minus all cash payments for items such as investments, taxes, and interest. If James and Jane Person also had charge accounts, such as Mastercard or Visa, and the unpaid amount *decreased* by $1,500 during 19X3, then their personal expenditures would be $35,200 (= $36,700 from Exhibit G.2 *minus* $1,500 paid to reduce liabilities).

    A current year transaction that realizes a gain that was unrealized at the beginning of the year represents a *realized increase* in net worth offset by an *unrealized decrease* in net worth. In the case of the Persons, the realized gains on marketable securities of $79,100 during 19X3 are shown in the *Realized Increases* section. Note 2 in Exhibit G.3 explains that these gains were unrealized at the beginning of 19X3. Marketable securities held at year-end increased in value by $4,000 during the year. Overall, the current value of the Persons' marketable securities fell by the $75,100 shown in the *Unrealized Increases (Decreases)* section.

Another example is the stock options owned by Jane Person, described in Note 3 in Exhibit G.3. At December 31, 19X3, Jane has an unrealized gain of $7 per option, equal to the excess of the stock's $12 current market price over the $5 exercise price. The current value of $28,000 for the 4,000 options owned is shown on the Persons' statement of financial condition; $4,000, the increase in current value from $24,000 at the beginning of 19X3 to $28,000 at the end of 19X3, is shown in the *Unrealized Increases (Decreases)* section on the statement of changes in net worth.

The final example involves the $29,700 change in the estimated income taxes on unrealized asset appreciation shown in the *Unrealized Increases (Decreases)* section. This is the amount by which the contingent tax liability increased—from $187,800 to $217,500—on the statement of financial condition. It is an *unrealized decrease* in net worth.

AUTHORS' COMMENTARY

Current value accounting has been officially used as a valuation basis in personal financial statements since 1968. Most observers understand that *value*, not acquisition cost, measures a person's wealth. Yet the use of current values in the corporate context has been spotty—only a few public companies issue financial statements on a current value or similar basis. Even during the period from 1979 to 1985 when the requirements of *SFAS 33* were in effect, disclosures were made as supplementary information,* not as part of the basic financial statements. Current valuation methods are attractive in theory but suffer in practice because it is difficult to obtain reliable value estimates that can be audited.

Reporting Value Changes. Students attempting to prepare an individual's *statement of changes in net worth* on a current value basis are sometimes confused over realized and unrealized gain and loss concepts that were well-understood in more familiar corporate settings. Current value accounting seeks to include in income or in the change in net worth *only* those value changes that occurred during the *current period*. All such changes are referred to as **realizable gains and losses**. Because some realiz*able* gains are realiz*ed*, and some remain *un*realized, at first glance we have the following:

Realiz*able* Gains = Realiz*ed* Gains + *Un*realized Gains

In any given year, though, realiz*ed* gains include some gains that were realiz*able* in previous years and were included in *un*realized gains at the beginning of the current year. Therefore, realiz*able* gains are best viewed in the following way:

Realiz*able* Gains = Realiz*ed* Gains + *Change* in *Un*realized Gains

To illustrate, suppose Tracy purchases 1,000 shares of Tasty Baking Corp. common stock at $12 per share for $12,000 on March 15, 19X1. The stock is worth $14 per share or $14,000 at December 31, 19X1. Tracy's 19X1 statement of changes in net worth reports an *unrealized increase in net worth* of $2,000 (= $14,000 − $12,000). Then on April 15,

19X2, Tracy sells 200 shares for $15 per share, a total of $3,000. If at December 31, 19X2, the remaining 800 shares are worth $12,400, or $15.50 per share, Tracy's 19X2 statement of changes in net worth reports the following:

Realized increase in net worth [$3,000 − (200 × $12)] . . . . $ 600
Unrealized increase in net worth
    [800 × ($15.50 − $14) − 200 × ($14 − $12)   800
                                        $ 1,400

Of the $600 total gain realized when Tracy sold the shares in 19X2, only $200 [= 200 × ($15 − $14)] was realizable in 19X2. The other $400 was realizable and unrealized in 19X1 and is realized but not realizable in 19X2. To avoid counting the $400 as an increase in net worth twice—in 19X1 and in 19X2—it is deducted from the 19X2 realizable and unrealized increase of $1,200 [= 800 × ($15.50 − $14)] on the other 800 shares still owned.

In conclusion, the current value accounting approach to personal financial statements shares an important attribute of current value accounting in general: value changes are recognized in income or net worth during the year in which they occurred and only in that year. This is in sharp contrast to conventional acquisition cost accounting which generally recognizes value changes only when realized, regardless of when the changes occurred.

---

* Financial Accounting Standards Board, *Statement of Financial Accounting Standards No 33*, "Financial Reporting and Changing Prices" (Stamford, CT: FASB, 1979). The provisions of *SFAS 33* were made optional when it was superseded in 1986 by another standard bearing the same title—*SFAS 89*.

SUMMARY OF KEY CONCEPTS

Personal financial statements consist of a **statement of financial condition,** an optional **statement of changes in net worth,** and **notes to financial statements**. Information presented reflects **accrual accounting** on a **current value basis**.

Information presented on personal financial statements is based on **accrual accounting**. Assets and liabilities are reported on a **current value basis**.

Income taxes are calculated and accrued on any **unrealized asset appreciation** (positive or negative) that will be subject to taxation when realized.

The **statement of changes** in net worth presents both **realized** and **unrealized** changes in asset and liability values.

QUESTIONS

QG.1 Briefly describe *personal financial planning* and indicate how an individual's personal financial statements can aid in the planning process.

QG.2 Assets and liabilities in a personal statement of financial condition are to be reported at current value. At the same time, accrual accounting applies so that certain aspects of an individual's cash basis records must be converted to the accrual basis. Give an example of such a conversion that is needed if historical cost valuation is being used.

QG.3 The statement of changes in net worth distinguishes between *realized* and *unrealized* changes in net worth. Kyle Jones owns securities worth $25,000 (cost: $10,000) at the beginning of the year. Early in the year, Kyle sells one-half of those securities for $13,500. The remaining securities are worth $14,000 at year-end. What amount of *realized* increase or decrease in net worth is to be reported? What amount of *unrealized* increase or decrease is to be reported?

QG.4 The statement of financial condition is always prepared when presenting financial statements for an individual or group. The statement of changes in net worth, however, is optional. Under what circumstances might a statement of changes in net worth *not* be presented?

QG.5 What are future interests, and how are they presented on personal financial statements?

QG.6 Current values of material items are presented on personal financial statements. How could the current value of the following assets be determined?

1. Postage stamp collection.
2. Vacant lot in a housing development.
3. Antique furniture.
4. Life insurance policy.
5. Household appliances.
6. Inventory of a proprietorship.
7. Jewelry.
8. Minority interest in a closely held corporation.

EXERCISES

EG.1 **Income Tax on Unrealized Appreciation** James Cromwell, age 45, is employed as an engineer. He participates in his employer's pension plan, which requires that he contribute 4 percent of his annual salary to the plan. To date, he has contributed $8,947 to the plan. His benefits, which are vested, will be based on his past and future salary levels. Given reasonable assumptions about his future salary growth, he anticipates benefits of approximately $10,500 per year upon retirement at age 65, at which time his life expectancy will be 12 years.

REQUIRED: Assuming that a 10-percent discount rate and a 40-percent tax rate are appropriate, indicate the amounts that would be presented for pension rights and for estimated income tax on unrealized appreciation on Cromwell's personal statement of financial condition.

EG.2 Current Value of Residence James and Elaine Vincent are preparing a personal statement of financial condition. They are attempting to estimate a current value for their personal residence. The residence was acquired 15 years ago at a cost of $40,000. At the time, it was assessed for local property tax purposes at $13,000 (the locality assesses at about 30 percent of market value). Eight years ago, the house was reassessed at $16,000; there has been no further change in the assessed value.

Over the years, the Vincents have made improvements to the house, beyond routine painting, redecorating, etc., costing about $8,000. Fire insurance carried on the house (exclusive of contents) is currently $75,000 (this amount was revised 3 years ago to reflect then-current replacement cost).

Within the last year, two homes in the neighborhood were sold at prices of $86,000 and $91,000. All houses in the neighborhood are of approximately the same age and size, but they vary as to design, condition, and amenities. A friend who is a real estate agent estimated that the Vincent house would have an asking price of $90,000 to $95,000, and that houses sell for about 93 percent of the asking price.

REQUIRED: On the basis of the above information, recommend a single figure which the Vincents should present as the current value of their residence. Justify your selection.

EG.3 Income Tax on Unrealized Appreciation Ann Laurence is preparing a personal statement of financial condition as of December 31, 19X3, which will include the following assets:

1. A bonus of $9,000 receivable from her employer for services performed in 19X3; the bonus will be paid in March 19X4.
2. Investment in stocks and bonds having a current value of $38,000. Cost (tax basis) is $27,500, and all have been held for the long-term holding period.
3. An IRA account having a current balance (including accumulated interest) of $7,300. In each of the last three years, $2,000 has been deposited in this account.
4. A recreational vehicle purchased two years ago for $18,000, with a current value of $14,000.

Laurence's marginal tax rate is 40 percent on ordinary income and 16 percent on long-term capital gains.

REQUIRED: Calculate the estimated income tax on unrealized appreciation which should be included in the statement of financial condition.

EG.4 Statement of Financial Condition Prepare a statement of financial condition for Michael Fenway as of December 31, 19X3, given the following information:

1. Fenway's unincorporated business yielded a profit of $42,000 on the cash basis and $50,000 on the accrual basis.

2. The book value of Fenway's equity in the business is $30,000 at year-end. However, the market value of the business is estimated to be $100,000. The books are kept on the accrual basis.
3. Fenway, a cash basis taxpayer, is subject to a tax rate of 40 percent on all income. During the year, estimated tax payments of $12,000 were made.
4. Fenway's only income is derived from the business. His only other asset is cash of $15,000.

EG.5 Current Value of Investment Arthur Randolf owns 75 percent of the Granitville Services Company. The book value of the firm's total assets is $700,000; liabilities are $300,000. The normal rate of return on total assets for similar firms in the same industry is 15 percent. Because of its long-standing reputation for quality service, Granitville has repeatedly enjoyed excess earnings. Net income before extraordinary items for the last 6 years is shown below:

19X4	$ 140,000	19X7	$ 132,500
19X5	$ 130,000	19X8	$ 120,000
19X6	$ 127,500	19X9	$ 130,000

A capitalization rate of 10 percent for excess earnings is considered appropriate.

REQUIRED: Calculate the values of the investment to be shown on Randolf's personal statement of financial condition under each of the following assumptions:

1. Excess earnings will continue indefinitely.
2. Excess earnings will continue for 15 years.

EG.6 Statement of Changes in Net Worth Comparative statements of financial condition are given below for Jonathan Flanders, along with additional information.

Jonathan Flanders
Comparative Statements of Financial Condition

| | 12/31/X4 | | 12/31/X5 | |
| | | Current | | Current |
Assets	Cost	Value	Cost	Value
Cash	$ 4,000	$ 4,000	$ 3,500	$ 3,500
Marketable Securities (Note 1)	10,000	12,000	8,500	13,600
Total Assets	$ 14,000	$ 16,000	$ 12,000	$ 17,100
Liabilities				
Accrued Income Taxes	$ 600	$ 600	$ 450	$ 450
Estimated Income Taxes on Unrealized				
Asset Appreciation (Note 2)	—	300	—	765
Total Liabilities	$ 600	$ 900	$ 450	$ 1,215
Excess of Assets Over Liabilities	$ 13,400	$ 15,100	$ 11,550	$ 15,885

Note 1: Marketable securities are 100 shares in Weber Company at 12/31/X4.
Note 2: Taxes on unrealized appreciation are accrued at a rate of 15 percent.

Additional information:

1. During 19X5, Flanders sold 15 shares of Weber Company for $195 each. He paid $125 in taxes on the sale. No other sale or purchase of marketable securities occurred in 19X5.
2. Dividends of $238 on Weber stock were received during 19X5.
3. Flanders' salary during 19X5 was $14,000. He paid income taxes totaling $3,700 (not including taxes on sale of stock).

REQUIRED: Prepare a statement of changes in net worth for Jonathan Flanders for 19X5.

PROBLEMS

PG.1 **Preparation of Statement of Financial Condition** Marilyn Gray is sole owner and operator of Gray's Art Shop. The balance sheet and income statement for the current year are presented below:

Gray's Art Shop
Balance Sheet
December 31, 19X9

Assets		Liabilities and Capital	
Cash	$ 10,000	Accounts Payable	$ 5,000
Accounts Receivable	20,000	Short-Term Loan	30,000
Inventory	130,000	Loan on Automobile	800
Automobile (Net)	1,800		$ 35,800
Equipment, Fixtures (Net)	20,000	Capital—Marilyn Gray	150,200
Prepaid Expenses	4,200	Total Liabilities and	
Total Assets	$ 186,000	Capital	$ 186,000

Gray's Art Shop
Income Statement
for the Year Ended December 31, 19X9

Sales	$ 250,000
Cost of Goods Sold	150,000
Gross Profit	$ 100,000
Other Expenses:	
Rent	$ 24,000
Car Expense	3,800
Insurance and Security	10,000
Interest	3,500
Depreciation	5,000
Miscellaneous	2,300
Total Expenses	$ 48,600
Net Income	$ 51,400

Gray has been renting space in a building since she began business. The owner has offered to sell her the building if she can raise the necessary money. As her accountant, you instructed Marilyn to assemble both personal and business financial information so that you can prepare a personal financial statement to be included with her loan application. The information received is as follows:

1. The mortgage on her house, which she owns jointly with her husband Neil, has a current balance of $17,500. The Grays purchased the house ten years ago for $50,000. A real estate broker estimates current market value to be $70,000.
2. Their joint checking account shows a balance of $2,000 on the last statement date. Since then, the Grays have written checks totaling $1,400 and deposited $230 up to December 31.
3. A joint savings account shows a balance of $25,000, including interest, at December 31.
4. Outstanding charge accounts (joint) total $5,000 from the purchase of personal items.
5. Marilyn estimates that household effects purchased at various times at a cost of $30,000 now have a resale value of $10,000 (jointly owned).
6. Data on securities held in Marilyn's name are as follows:

Security	Purchase Date	Shares	Cost	Market Value
A	2/1/X6	300	$ 3.83	$ 5.60
B	4/1/X8	250	15.80	35.20
C	10/1/X8	1,500	.35	.50
D	5/1/X9	150	2.34	2.00

7. The automobile Marilyn uses only for business purposes is in her name. It cost $5,400 and has a market value of $1,000. Balance due on the loan for the car is $800. The Grays use Neil's car for personal purposes. He owes $4,000 on the principal of the car loan. Neil paid $5,900 for the car. He estimates it to be worth $3,500 now.
8. Recently a local art gallery offered to purchase Gray's Art Shop for $200,000.
9. Income taxes owed on December 31, 19X9, that are attributable to Marilyn's income are $1,200. The effective tax rate on unrealized appreciation of assets is 20 percent.

REQUIRED: Prepare a personal statement of financial position for Marilyn Gray, with accompanying notes.

PG.2 Statement of Financial Condition—Comprehensive James Bolan, M.D., and Louis Scott, M.D., are applying for a $115,000 loan to purchase additional equipment for their medical practice. The bank has requested a personal statement of financial condition as of June 30, 19X3, from James Bolan and his wife, Frances. Pertinent facts about the Bolans follow. Unless stated otherwise, all facts are presented as of June 30, 19X3.

1. The Bolans have $8,000 in a checking account and $30,000 in a savings account, including interest through June 30, 19X3.
2. The Bolans paid $7,500 in 19X1 for a 15-percent interest in Crown Corporation, which has 100,000 shares outstanding. The stock is traded on a Midwestern exchange. In recent months, the stock has traded in blocks of 100 shares or less at $1.50 per share. Dr. Bolan was recently offered $1.10 per share for all his shares. The offer is still outstanding.

3. Dr. Bolan and Dr. Scott each own a 50-percent interest in the Suburban Medical Group, a partnership. The balance sheet of the Suburban Medical Group, prepared on a cash basis, is presented below.

Suburban Medical Group
Balance Sheet

Assets		Liabilities	
Cash (in Non-Interest-Bearing		6% Notes Payable (Principal	
Account)	$ 10,400	and Interest Payable	
30-day Treasury Bills		Monthly until 19Y0 ...	$ 39,000
(Maturing July 30, 19X3)	11,000	Capital	120,300
Drugs and Supplies Inventory ...	6,100		
Equipment and Office Furniture			
(Net of $14,000 Accumulated			
Depreciation)	66,000		
Automobiles (Net of $1,150			
Accumulated Depreciation) ...	10,800		
Building (Purchased June 28,			
19X3)	55,000		
Total	$159,300	Total	$ 159,300

4. As of June 30, 19X3, the Suburban Medical Group had unrecorded accounts receivable of $12,451 and unrecorded accounts payable of $1,327. Payments on the notes are current. The partnership prepares its tax returns on the accrual basis.

5. Dr. Bolan and Dr. Scott were offered $260,000 for their practice by the Rural Medical Center. The offer is still outstanding. Counsel has advised that if the offer is accepted, any difference between the proceeds and the partners' tax bases in the partnership will be taxed as ordinary income.

6. The Bolans purchased their residence in 19X0 for $85,000. The balance of the thirty-year, 10-percent mortgage is $64,498. The current rate charged on similar mortgages is 10 percent. Payments on the mortgage are current. Similar homes in the area have increased in value approximately 30 percent since 19X0. The assessed real estate value was determined in March 19X3 to be $108,500 based on fair value.

7. Frances Bolan owns a 19X0 automobile which cost $7,100. Current newspaper advertisements indicate that her car could be sold for $4,800.

8. Fifteen years ago the Bolans bought a painting by an artist who has since become internationally famous. The Bolans paid $6,000 for the painting. In June 19X3, the painting was appraised at $16,000.

9. The Bolans have maintained cost records on their major household effects. The costs aggregate $27,500. A local business which specializes in auctioning this type of merchandise estimated in July 19X3 that the household effects have a net realizable value of $12,000. Other household effects are of nominal value.

10. Dr. Bolan has a vested interest of $14,175 in a group-participating pension plan. The present value of the vested benefits is $6,818. Dr. Bolan's contributions to the plan (tax basis) have been $5,432.

11. On July 1, 19X0, Dr. Bolan paid $9,000 for 25 percent of the capital stock of Medical Instruments, Inc., a closely held business which designs medical instruments. A summary of financial data of the corporation follows:

	Balance Sheet at June 30, 19X2	Earnings Summary for the Years Ended June 30		Dividends Paid	
Assets	$ 112,800				
Liabilities . . .	$ 46,650	19X1	$ 12,050		
Equity	66,150	19X2	18,100		
	$ 112,800	19X3	28,050	$ 6,200	June 10

Similar businesses in the area have been sold recently for ten times the average of the last three years' earnings.

12. The Bolans owed $810 on charge accounts and $220 on a national credit card account at June 30, 19X3.

13. In early July 19X3, the Bolans estimated their federal income tax for their 19X3 return to be $26,000. Estimated tax payments of $8,000 had been made as of June 30, 19X3. A tax rate of 40 percent is assumed for all tax considerations, with capital gains taxed at a 16-percent rate.

REQUIRED:

1. Prepare for James and Frances Bolan a statement of financial condition in good form as of June 30, 19X3. Do not prepare accompanying notes.

2. Identify the items of the statement of financial condition that require explanatory and disclosure notes. Do not prepare the notes.
   (AICPA adapted)

PG.3 **Statement of Changes in Net Worth** Janice Tucker graduated in May 19X1 from Great Lakes University and accepted a position as a staff accountant at a CPA firm. At the end of 19X1, she summarized her personal transactions for the year as follows:

Cash Receipts		Cash Disbursements	
Student Loan	$ 2,000	Living Expenses	$ 10,200
Salary—CPA Firm	9,800	Tuition	3,000
Salary—Part-Time Job While		Payment on Student Loan	300
Student	1,750	Purchase of Furniture	2,100
Gifts	800	Down Payment on New Car . . .	1,000
Proceeds from Sale of Old Car . . .	950	Income Taxes Paid	1,200
	$ 15,300		$ 17,800

Additional information:

1. Tucker's bank account balance declined from $4,100 to $1,600 during the year.

2. Following graduation, Tucker bought furniture for her apartment at a cost of $3,000; she still owes the store $900 (no interest is accrued). Current value of the furniture is estimated to be 80 percent of its cost.

3. In December, Tucker sold her old car, which had a current value of $1,300 at the beginning of 19X1. She bought a newer car for $8,800, making a $1,000 down payment and financing the balance. She estimates the current value of the new car at December 31 to be $8,000.

4. A preliminary calculation of her 19X1 income tax indicates an expected refund of $250. Tucker is subject to a marginal rate of 20 percent on any unrealized appreciation.
5. The student loan had a balance of $6,200 at the beginning of the year. Interest at 7 percent begins to accrue on January 1, 19X2.

REQUIRED: Prepare a statement of changes in net worth for 19X1.

PG.4 Statement of Changes in Net Worth Allen and Jean Goldman had the following assets and liabilities (current values) at the beginning and end of 19X7:

	1/1/X7	12/31/X7
Cash	$ 5,000	$ 7,000
Marketable Securities	28,000	20,000
Residence	75,000	78,000
Household Furnishings	8,000	9,000
Automobile	6,000	10,000
Vacation Home	0	26,000
Pension Plan	19,000	24,000
Charge Accounts	(700)	(1,100)
Auto Loan	0	(5,000)
Mortgage—Residence	(29,000)	(27,000)
Mortgage—Vacation Home	0	(15,000)
Accrued Income Taxes	(500)	(500)
Estimated Income Tax on Unrealized Appreciation	(14,100)	(15,600)

Additional information:

1. Securities were sold in January for $11,000 (which was their value at January 1, 19X7). No securities were purchased during the year.
2. The Goldmans earned salaries of $46,000 and interest and dividend income of $5,400 during 19X7.
3. The Goldmans sold their automobile for $4,200 and purchased a new one at a cost of $10,000 (half of which was financed by a loan).
4. A summary of the Goldmans' checkbook produced the following expenditures for the year:

Personal Living Expenditures	$ 35,600
Income Taxes Paid	10,000
New Auto (Net of Loan)	5,000
Vacation Home (Net of Loan)	11,000
Mortgage Payments—Residence	2,000
Purchase of Furniture	1,000

REQUIRED: Prepare a statement of changes in net worth for the Goldmans for 19X7.

PG.5 Personal Financial Statements Howard Schulman is retired. At the end of 19X3, his personal statement of financial condition was as follows:

Howard Schulman
Statement of Financial Condition
December 31, 19X3

Cash	$ 73,000	Accounts Payable	$	1,500
Pension Receivable (Present		Mortgage Payable		38,000
Value)	81,400	Estimated Income Tax on		
Marketable Securities—Stocks ...	157,500	Unrealized Appreciation ...		58,200
Marketable Securities—Bonds ...	120,000	Net Worth		500,200
Investment in Real Estate	143,000			
Automobile	8,000			
Household and Personal Items ...	15,000			
		Total Liabilities and Net		
Total Assets	$ 597,900	Worth		$ 597,900

During 19X4, the following transactions occurred:

1. Schulman received the following in cash: $18,000 from his employer-funded pension late in 19X4 (the present value of the undistributed portion grows at 10 percent each year); $5,000 from Social Security; $10,000 in dividends; $12,500 in bond interest; and $8,300 net rental income from his real estate investments.
2. Schulman's cash disbursements included $25,700 for living expenses (his accounts payable increased to $1,800), $16,000 for income taxes (this should cover his 19X4 tax liability), and $7,000 for gifts to his grandchildren.
3. Stocks with a current value of $32,000 at January 1 were sold for $35,500. New stocks were purchased at a cost of $40,000. His total stock portfolio had a value of $191,000 at December 31, 19X4.
4. There were no transactions involving the bonds other than the receipt of interest noted above. However, due to increasing interest rates in the economy, the value of his bond holdings dropped to $105,000.
5. Real estate owned at January 1 was estimated to have increased in value by 10 percent during 19X4. The mortgage principal was reduced by $6,000 due to payments (interest payments are reflected in the net income from rental). In October, Schulman bought an additional property for $70,000, financing $55,000 via a new mortgage. By year-end, $700 of principal had been paid, and there was no change in the value of the property.
6. The values of the automobile and the household and personal items are estimated to have decreased by 10 percent during 19X4. Their tax bases exceed their current values.
7. Schulman is subject to an average tax rate of 30 percent on asset appreciation.

REQUIRED: Prepare a statement of changes in net worth for 19X4, and a statement of financial condition as of December 31, 19X4.

PG.6 Personal Financial Statements Z. D. Sanberry, who practices dentistry as a sole proprietor, recently filed as a candidate for mayor of his city. He has requested your assistance in preparing combined personal financial statements for himself and his wife, June. Your firm rendered an unqualified opinion on similar statements last year in connection with an examination conducted to support Sanberry's application for a bank loan. Last year's statement of financial condition (based on current values) is as follows:

Z. D. and June Sanberry
Statement of Financial Condition
April 30, 19X0

Cash	$ 6,120	Accounts Payable	$	2,850
Marketable Securities	21,400	Income Taxes—Current		1,900
Cash Value of Life Insurance	3,900	Mortgage Payable		35,300
Dental Practice	27,000		$	40,050
Interest in Dental Supply, Inc.	8,600	Estimated Income Tax on		
Residence	94,000	Unrealized Appreciation		10,970
Automobile	5,800	Net Worth		136,300
Paintings	12,700			
Household Furnishings	7,800			
		Total Liabilities and Net		
Total assets	$ 187,320	Worth		$ 187,320

Sanberry's bookkeeper has provided you with a trial balance listing the Sanberrys' assets and liabilities on the *cost basis* at April 30, 19X1, as follows:

Cash	$ 3,300	Accounts Payable	$	3,100
Marketable Securities	23,000	Income Taxes Payable—		
Cash Value of Life Insurance	4,250	Current		2,225
Net Assets of Dental Practice	19,500	Mortgage Payable		34,000
Interest in Dental Supply, Inc.	6,100	Net Worth		118,225
Residence	65,000			
Automobile	11,300			
Paintings	11,000			
Household Furnishings	14,100			
		Total Liabilities and Net		
Total assets	$ 157,550	Worth		$ 157,550

Additional information:

1. A summary of cash receipts and disbursements for the year ended April 30, 19X1, follows:

   Disbursements

Personal Expenditures, Including Personal Life		
Insurance Premium	$ 16,000	
Purchase of Kindred Company 6% Bonds at Par	8,000	
Income Taxes	4,100	
Interest on Mortgage	1,400	
Mortgage Principal Amortization	1,300	
Real Estate Taxes	900	$ 31,700

Receipts

Withdrawals from Sanberry's Dental Practice	$ 21,000	
Sale of Inco Stock (Purchased 6/1/W8 for $3,200;		
Market Value on 4/30/X0, $4,500)	6,100	
Dividends on Stock	1,540	
Interest on Bonds	240	28,880
Decrease in Cash		$ 2,820

2. The bonds were purchased on July 31, 19X0. Interest is payable semiannually on January 31 and July 31.

3. In 19W4, Sanberry invested $10,000 to begin his dentistry practice and since has made additional investments. On April 2, 19X1, Sanberry was offered $31,000 for the net assets of his dental practice.

4. Sanberry owns 25 percent of the outstanding stock of the closely held corporation, Dental Supply, Inc.

5. The April 30, 19X1, statements of net assets of Sanberry's dental practice and Dental Supply, Inc., both accompanied by unqualified opinions rendered by a CPA, were composed of the following assets and liabilities:

	Sanberry's Dental Practice	Dental Supply, Inc.
Current Assets	$ 6,000	$ 30,000
Noncurrent Assets	36,000	70,000
Current Liabilities	3,650	17,000
Long-Term Liabilities	16,350	35,000
Deferred Credits	2,500	4,000

6. Investments in marketable securities on April 30, 19X1, were composed of the following:

	April 30, 19X1 Bid	Latest Price Asked
Stocks		
Steele, Inc.	$ 15,100	$ 15,500
Gilliam Corp.	4,000	4,200
Bonds		
Kindred Company 6% Bonds	7,800	7,900
	$ 26,900	$ 27,600

7. The valuation (at 100 percent of fair market value) of other property owned by the Sanberrys on April 30, 19X1, was as follows:

Residence	$ 100,000
Automobile	4,300
Paintings	14,500
Household Furnishings	7,600

8. The accounts payable as of April 30, 19X0, and April 30, 19X1, represent liabilities for personal living costs.

9. The Sanberrys would have to pay a capital gains tax at an effective rate of 25 percent if the assets were sold.

10. Accrued income taxes payable of $2,225 as of April 30, 19X1, represent the Sanberry's appropriate tax liability for the current year to date.

REQUIRED: Prepare a statement of financial condition and a statement of changes in net worth for Z. D. and June Sanberry at April 30, 19X1.

ACCOUNTING AND REPORTING FOR ESTATES AND TRUSTS

MODULE PREVIEW

This module examines accounting and reporting by the estates of deceased individuals and includes a brief introduction to personal trusts. Accounting in this area stresses the stewardship and accountability of the fiduciary appointed to manage the assets of the estate or trust. A section on estate planning and taxation completes the module. Principal topics studied are as follows:

- Introduction to estates and trusts
- Estates of individuals
- Personal trusts
- Estate planning and taxation

INTRODUCTION TO ESTATES AND TRUSTS

Estates and trusts are characterized by the involvement of three parties:

- The **creator** of the estate or trust, namely the person or persons who transfers assets for the benefit of others. This transfer may occur during one's lifetime, in the case of certain forms of trusts, or at death, in the case of estates and other forms of trusts.
- **Beneficiaries** of the transfer, namely those individuals who will receive income from the assets, or the assets themselves, or both.
- A **manager** of the assets, who is typically someone other than the creator or a beneficiary. In accordance with the instructions of the creator and any relevant provisions of law, this individual manages the assets on behalf of the beneficiaries.

The **stewardship function of accounting** is relevant to estates and trusts. The responsibility of the accountant is to report on management of the assets to the concerned parties.

One important aspect that distinguishes an estate or trust from a corporation is the responsibility of management. Corporate management has a considerable amount of discretion in managing the assets of the firm, and the focus is on management's performance measured by income or other statistics. The manager of a trust or estate has much less flexibility, being subject to legal restrictions such as wills, bankruptcy laws, and trust agreements that constrain the management and disposition of assets. Since assets are managed on behalf of beneficiaries, the focus is on the manager's **fiduciary responsibility**—the custodial or stewardship responsibility for property belonging to others. Thus the executor of an estate, the receiver of a firm in bankruptcy, or the trustee of a trust is commonly called a **fiduciary**.

Adherence to laws affecting estates and trusts is essential in accounting for these entities. Laws exist both to protect those incapable of self-protection and to safeguard the interests of beneficiaries while their assets are managed by others. Thus the accountant must be aware of the legal framework within which estates and trusts operate. A basic legal principle concerns classification of assets of estates and trusts into one of two categories:

- **Principal** (also called **corpus**) consists of the property and rights to property existing at the date the entity is created. Examples are buildings, marketable securities, and interest receivable.
- **Income** consists of the additional assets generated from the investment or use of principal assets. Examples are rental revenue from buildings and interest or dividends from securities.

Because laws often dictate that this division be maintained, and because the beneficiaries of principal and income assets may be different, accounting for estates and trusts, known as **fiduciary accounting**, recognizes this distinction. Accounts for these entities are classified as either principal or income. Financial statements of estates and trusts report on the two elements separately.

ESTATES OF INDIVIDUALS

An **estate** is an entity created at death to hold, manage, and account for the real and personal property of a deceased person, the **decedent**, until the property can be properly distributed to the appropriate beneficiaries. These beneficiaries and their rights to property are specified in the decedent's **will** or in the law if the individual died *intestate*—without a valid will. An estate is managed by a **personal representative**: a representative named by the will is an **executor** or **executrix**; a court-appointed representative is called an **administrator**. The personal representative of an estate is a fiduciary with numerous duties and responsibilities and may become personally liable if lax in performing these functions. Therefore, most states require an accounting by the representative in order to monitor performance of these duties. Interim accountings enable the court to oversee and review the representative's performance, while the final accounting provides beneficiaries with the opportunity to object to the representative's actions. After the final accounting is approved by all interested parties, the representative is released from further liability relating to discharge of his or her fiduciary responsibilities.

The estate may exist as an entity for a few months or several years. Note that the going-concern assumption underlying most business entities is absent. An estate is created with the assumption of a limited life; it ends when the assets are distributed. In this respect, it resembles a limited-life partnership created to accomplish a specific purpose.

LEGAL ASPECTS OF ESTATES

Because accounting for estates is influenced by law, understanding the legal proceedings surrounding the creation and operation of an estate is essential for the accountant. First, it must be determined if the decedent had a will. Once the will is validated by a process called *probate*, it governs the distribution of the decedent's property. **Probate** involves court hearings at which parties may question the validity of the will. Early in the probate proceedings, the personal representative takes possession and control of the decedent's assets to manage them until final distribution to the beneficiaries. Even if there is no will and the laws of intestacy govern the ultimate property distribution, there is a lapse of time between death and distribution during which the property must be managed. In either case, the time period is at least six months. A longer period is not unusual, since it may be neither practical nor desirable to distribute the assets quickly.

Once the claims are settled and the beneficiaries are determined through probate, the personal representative can distribute the assets and close the estate. Beneficiaries of real property are called **devisees**; of personal property, **legatees**. A gift of property, either a **devise** or a **legacy**, can be *specific* (an identified object), *general* (an indicated quantity of something, such as cash), or *residuary* (property remaining after specific and general gifts are met). The legal classification of the beneficiaries as well as the legal classification of assets is important for proper distribution of estate assets. Following are some *legal responsibilities of the personal representative*:

- *Notify the decedent's heirs* of the appointment as personal representative.
- *Establish a family allowance* for the decedent's surviving spouse and dependent children. The Uniform Probate Code specifies the amount and timing of payment. This allowance is exempt from claims against the estate.
- *Prepare an inventory of the assets* based on the fair value of property or rights owned at date of death.
- *List any liens* against the property.
- *Publish a notice requesting creditors to present claims* against the estate of the decedent. The law dictates the appropriate vehicle and timing for such publication. Creditors have four months to present claims.
- *Manage the decedent's business and investments*. When the decedent was a sole proprietor, the personal representative has the right to manage the business for four months after being appointed.
- *Establish an accounting system* which classifies the property as to principal or income assets. *All assets existing at the date of death are principal.* As income assets are generated, the personal representative must maintain records to retain the distinction between principal and income.
- *Pay claims* against the estate.
- *Distribute the assets* to the beneficiaries.

Preparing the Inventory

The fiduciary should prepare a complete inventory of the assets of the estate as soon as possible after the decedent's death. The Uniform Probate Code stipulates that within three months after appointment, the personal representative must prepare an inventory of property owned by the decedent at the time of death together with a listing of any liens against the property. When the representative anticipates a delay in appointment, perhaps because the will is contested, he or she may have an objective party, such as an attorney, prepare the inventory. A prompt inventory of assets should be made in order to prevent any losses or misunderstandings regarding the existence, valuation, and location of the decedent's assets.

A properly prepared inventory includes the following information:

- Type of asset
- How the asset was held by the decedent (for example, outright or in trust)

- Location of the asset
- Fair value of the asset at date of death
- Income tax basis of the asset to the decedent
- Date the asset was brought under the control of the fiduciary
- Any other distinguishing features such as description of jewelry and antiques

Services of a professional appraiser may be required to estimate the value of assets for which markets are not readily available.

Along with the inventory of assets, the representative should obtain any pertinent documents such as stock certificates, bank statements, deeds, life insurance policies, and income tax returns. Once the inventory is completed, it is filed with the probate court and copies may be provided to interested parties. If the representative subsequently discovers other assets, they should be listed on a separate schedule to be filed with the court and are considered part of principal.

Claims against the Estate

Although the personal representative has the duty of satisfying all claims against the estate, he or she also has the authority to allow or disallow a claim. Holders of disallowed claims can bring action to establish the validity of their claims, but the burden of proof lies with holders of the claims. The representative can also negotiate compromise settlements of claims.

As a general rule, the personal representative should publish notice to creditors in a newspaper with general circulation. The Uniform Probate Code requires that a notice be published at least once a week for three consecutive weeks. Creditors must then respond within four months from the date of first publication, or forever be barred from asserting their claims.

When the estate's assets are sufficient to cover all claims, the order of debt payment is irrelevant. If assets are insufficient to pay all claims in full, however, the following is a *generally accepted order for payment of claims*, closely following that prescribed by the Uniform Probate Code:

1. Debts secured by liens on assets, such as the mortgage on the decedent's residence
2. Expenses of administering the estate
3. Funeral expenses and expenses of last illness
4. Debts given preference under federal or state law
5. Taxes assessed on decedent's property prior to death
6. Bonds and notes issued by the decedent
7. All other claims

When the will is silent as to which assets are to be used for debt payment, *estate assets should be used in the following order to satisfy creditors' claims*:

1. Personal property not bequeathed
2. Personal property bequeathed generally
3. Personal property bequeathed specifically
4. Real property not devised
5. Real property devised generally
6. Real property devised specifically

Distributions to Beneficiaries

Another duty of the personal representative is to distribute the estate assets to the beneficiaries named in the will. The representative should, if possible and if so specified in the will, distribute assets in kind rather than converting them into cash before distribution.

When the estate assets are insufficient to cover both creditors' claims and devises or legacies, then the devises (or legacies) are reduced (or *abated*) according to the sequence provided for in the will. The Uniform Probate Code provides an *order of abatement* to be used when the will does not specify an order. This order is the same as that just listed for the use of assets to pay debts.

Accounting and Reporting

The personal representative must maintain proper accounting records for the estate. It is usually desirable for the representative to open a checking account in the name of the estate so that the estate's cash transactions are kept separate from the representative's personal transactions. The primary financial statement presented for estates is the **charge and discharge statement**. This statement, illustrated in Exhibit H.1, identifies what assets were placed under the control of the personal representative and any distributions made of such property. The financial report for the estate is subject to court review in the interest of the beneficiaries. Note that the legal division of principal and income is carried into the accounting report. The accounting system for an estate must maintain this distinction to ensure legal compliance and facilitate statement preparation.

Identification of Estate		
Identification of Executor		
Charge and Discharge Statement		
for the Period _____		
First, As To Principal		
I charge myself as follows:		
Inventory of Assets	$ XX	
Assets Subsequently Discovered	XX	
Gain on Disposal of Principal Assets	XX	$ XXX
I credit myself as follows:		
Debt of Decedent Paid	$ XX	
Administrative Expenses Paid	XX	
Loss on Disposal of Principal Assets	XX	
Distributions to Beneficiaries	XX	XXX
Balance, End of Period		$ XX
Second, As To Income		
I charge myself as follows:		
Revenues		$ XX
I credit myself as follows:		
Expenses	$ XX	
Distributions to Beneficiaries	XX	XX
Balance, End of Period		$ XX

EXHIBIT H.1 FORMAT OF CHARGE AND DISCHARGE STATEMENT

The charge and discharge statement is usually accompanied by *supporting schedules* that provide details of various items on the statement. For example, the assets comprising the initial inventory, the gains and losses on disposal of principal assets, and the distributions made to beneficiaries are each detailed on supporting schedules. These schedules are illustrated in a subsequent section.

The financial report for a small estate may be prepared only once, at the time of final distribution of estate assets. For a more complex estate, several interim reports may be made. Since an estate is a limited-life entity, reports are usually cumulative, covering the estate from the date of death to the date of the report.

Closing the Estate

Under the Uniform Probate Code, the personal representative must file a **petition** with the probate court to close the estate. This may be done no earlier than six months after appointment and not until the time for presenting claims against the estate has expired. *In the petition*, the representative must state that he or she has

- published notice to creditors at least four months prior to the date of the petition.
- fully administered the decedent's estate—paid all claims, administration expenses, and taxes, and perhaps distributed certain assets to beneficiaries.
- distributed a copy of the petition to all beneficiaries, creditors, and unpaid or barred claimants.

A charge and discharge statement must accompany the petition. Having collected all the decedent's assets, paid the debts, and carried out the appropriate tax duties and responsibilities, the personal representative is ready to prepare the final estate accounting and make the final distribution of the decedent's assets.

ACCOUNTING FOR PRINCIPAL AND INCOME

Because the personal representative is charged with the responsibility of managing the estate's assets, the accounting system must stress accountability for these assets. As mentioned before, a significant aspect of estate accounting is the distinction between *principal and income*. This distinction, and the need for separate records to account for principal and income transactions, was encountered previously in the study of *nonexpendable trust funds* in local government accounting.

The Revised Uniform Principal and Income Act, drafted in 1962 and since adopted by most states, defines *principal* as the property that has been set aside by the owner or the person legally empowered to be held in trust until eventually delivered to a beneficiary. As a general rule, principal includes any property or rights the decedent had at date of death. For example, wages earned prior to death, interest receivable at date of death, and dividends receivable declared prior to death are all included in principal, even though payment is not received until later.

The act defines *income* as "the return in money or property derived from the use of principal." Thus any earnings on principal assets that arise after the date of death are income. Each transaction of the estate must be analyzed to determine if it affects principal or income. Exhibit H.2 shows the treatment of various common transactions. Certain administrative costs, such as the executor's fee, attorney and accountant fees, and income taxes, must be allocated between principal and income.

Increases in Principal

Subsequent discovery of assets existing at date of death (not included in original inventory)

Gain resulting from disposition of principal assets.

Charges against Principal

Cost of investing and reinvesting principal

Expenditures incurred in preparing principal property for sale or rent

Costs of administering and preserving the non-income-producing property of the estate (for example, property taxes, repairs, and maintenance)

Extraordinary repairs or permanent improvements

Income taxes on profit, gains, or other receipts allocable to principal (for example, capital gains tax)

Decedent's debts, expenses of last illness, funeral expenses

Fees of executor, estate attorney, accountant, and other administrative costs

Federal estate tax and state inheritance tax

Payment of devises and other distributions of principal

Loss resulting from any change in the form of principal (for example, sale or destruction)

Increases in Income

Rent on real or personal property

Interest (but premium or discount on debt securities is generally not amortized)

Cash dividends

Business profits

Annuities

Other income earned during administration of decedent's estate

Charges against Income

Expenses of administering and preserving the income-producing property of the estate (for example, property taxes, utilities, wages, office expenses, repairs, and maintenance)

Depreciation on assets subject to depreciation under GAAP

Interest on mortgage and other indebtedness

Income taxes on profit, gains, or other receipts allocable to income

Fees of executor, estate attorney, accountant, and other administrative costs

Distributions of income

EXHIBIT H.2   TREATMENT OF SOME COMMON ESTATE TRANSACTIONS AS THEY AFFECT PRINCIPAL OR INCOME

Note that designation of assets as principal has long-term implications. *Principal* is viewed, according to the Revised Uniform Principal and Income Act, "not as a certain amount of monetary value, but ... as a certain group of assets which must be capable of isolation from the assets which compose the undistributed net income." Once an item is classified as a principal asset, its character is unaffected by subsequent transactions involving the item. For example, if a principal asset is sold, all proceeds are considered to be part of principal. In other words, gains and losses on sales of principal assets are recorded as principal, *not* as income.

A special aspect of estate accounting is that *liabilities are generally not recorded in the accounts*. In practice, this rule may be followed literally—record no liabilities at all—or an exception may be made to record those liabilities that constitute a lien on specific property, such as a mortgage and accrued interest thereon. The illustrations in this chapter follow the second practice.

Estate accounting follows an unusual pattern with respect to the use of *cash versus accrual accounting*. Assets are *accrued at date of death* so that the estate principal is correctly established. *Accruals are also recognized at final settlement of the estate* so that the rights of income beneficiaries are not affected by timing of receipts and payments. *During the life of the estate, however, accruals are not recorded*; interim charge and discharge statements are presented on a *cash basis*. Other than these special accounting characteristics, estate accounting follows generally accepted accounting principles common to other entities.

ILLUSTRATION OF ESTATE ACCOUNTING

Helen Corbett, a widow with two children—Janice Nelson and William Corbett—died on June 28, 19X1. Helen was 75 at the time of her death. In her will, Helen named her daughter as executrix and specified that she receive 2 percent of the gross estate at time of death as compensation for administering the estate. This compensation was to be in addition to the following specifications in the will:

- Janice is to receive the residence. The estate is to pay off the mortgage.
- The Society for the Prevention of Cruelty to Animals is to receive $5,000 and all income of the estate earned between the date of death and settlement of the estate.
- William is to receive all other assets remaining after payment of administrative expenses, claims against the estate, mortgage, and the bequest to charity.

The will entered probate proceedings. Janice notified her brother and the Society for the Prevention of Cruelty to Animals of her appointment as executrix. Soon after Helen Corbett's death, Janice took an inventory of her mother's assets. She valued marketable securities at their quoted prices. The residence and her mother's art collection were appraised to establish value at the date of death. Current values of other items were estimated by Janice. The entry that follows shows the recording of the inventory. Note that (1) the only liabilities recorded are those with liens against estate property and (2) the cash account is specifically labeled *Principal Cash*.

Principal Cash	25,700	
Marketable Securities	22,000	
Interest Receivable	250	
Residence	84,000	
Automobile	2,800	
Furniture	3,200	
Personal Effects	3,500	
Art Collection	12,000	
Mortgage Payable (Secured)		23,000
Interest Payable on Mortgage		140
Estate Principal Balance		130,310

To record inventory of principal assets for Estate of Helen Corbett.

The *Estate Principal Balance* account reflects the excess of assets over liens against them. At the time of inventory, all assets are classified as principal assets. The *gross estate*—total assets—is $153,450.

As required by law, Janice published a notice requesting that claims against her mother's estate be filed. She received the following bills: funeral expenses, $2,000; utility bills, $91; charges at a local clothing store, $150; charges at a book store, $30. No entry was made to the accounts of the estate upon receipt of the bills. Two months after taking the inventory, Janice discovered a cache of commemorative coins worth $6,000 at her mother's home. The discovery increased the gross estate to $159,450, and was recorded as follows:

Coin Collection	6,000	
Assets Subsequently Discovered		6,000
To record discovered assets.		

It is important to note that post-inventory discoveries of assets do not affect the Estate Principal Balance. The balance in that account remains intact until closing entries are made after court acceptance of the charge and discharge statement. This treatment enhances the accountability function of the records.

During the period of administration, $320 of dividends and $850 in interest, of which $250 was accrued and included in the gross estate, were received by the estate and recorded as follows:

Principal Cash	250	
Interest Receivable		250
To record receipt of accrued interest.		

Income Cash	920	
Dividend Revenue		320
Interest Revenue		600
To record receipt of interest and dividends earned after Helen Corbett's death.		

Janice then paid off the mortgage as indicated in the following entry:

Mortgage Payable	23,000	
Interest Payable on Mortgage	140	
Principal Cash		23,140
To record settlement of mortgage.		

To generate cash needed to meet the remaining claims against the estate and to pay the general devise to the SPCA, marketable securities with a recorded value of $7,000 and the car were sold. Despite its estimated value of $2,800, the car sold for only $2,500. The marketable securities yielded $7,150.

Principal Cash	2,500	
Loss on Disposal of Principal Assets	300	
Automobile		2,800
To record sale of automobile.		

Principal Cash	7,150	
Marketable Securities		7,000
Gain on Disposal of Principal Assets		150
To record sale of securities.		

Note that any gains or losses on disposals of assets are identified as to the type of asset—*principal* versus *income*—involved. Claims against the estate, including Janice's fee for administering the estate, were then paid. Because the coin collection was part of the estate at date of death, its value was included in the calculation of the administrative fee.

Administrative Expenses	3,189	
Debts of Decedent Paid	2,271	
Principal Cash		5,460

To record payment of:

Administrative expenses (2% of $159,450)	$ 3,189	
Funeral expenses	2,000	
Various charge accounts	180	
Utility bills	91	

After all claims were paid, Janice distributed the assets to the beneficiaries. The following entries record those distributions:

Distributions to Principal Beneficiaries	5,000	
Principal Cash		5,000
To record distribution of principal cash to the SPCA according to the specifications of the will.		

Distributions to Income Beneficiaries	920	
Income Cash		920
To record distribution of income cash to the SPCA according to the specifications of the will.		

Distributions to Principal Beneficiaries	84,000	
Residence		84,000
To record distribution of residence to Janice Nelson according to the specifications of the will.		

Distributions to Principal Beneficiaries	41,700	
Principal Cash		2,000
Marketable Securities		15,000
Furniture		3,200
Personal Effects		3,500
Art Collection		12,000
Coin Collection		6,000
To record distribution of residuary principal assets to William Corbett according to the specifications of the will.		

The books of the estate were closed on December 28, 19X1, as follows:

Estate Principal Balance	130,310	
Assets Subsequently Discovered	6,000	
Gain on Disposal of Principal Assets	150	
Dividend Revenue	320	
Interest Revenue	600	
Loss on Disposal of Principal Assets		300
Debts of Decedent Paid		2,271
Administrative Expenses		3,189
Distributions to Principal Beneficiaries		130,700
Distributions to Income Beneficiaries		920
To close estate of Helen Corbett.		

The charge and discharge statement for Janice Nelson, Executrix, appears in Exhibit H.3; the supporting schedules are shown in Exhibit H.4.

Estate of Helen Corbett
Janice Nelson, Executrix
Charge and Discharge Statement
for the Period June 28 through December 28, 19X1

First, As To Principal
I charge myself as follows:

Inventory (Schedule 1)	$ 130,310	
Assets Subsequently Discovered (Schedule 2)	6,000	
Gain on Disposal of Principal Assets (Schedule 3)	150	$ 136,460

I credit myself as follows:

Debt of Decedent Paid (Schedule 4)	$ 2,271	
Administrative Expenses	3,189	
Loss on Disposal of Principal Assets (Schedule 5)	300	
Distributions to Beneficiaries (Schedule 6)	130,700	136,460
Balance, December 28, 19X1		$ 0

Second, As To Income
I charge myself as follows:

Dividend Revenues	$ 320	
Interest Revenues	600	$ 920

I credit myself as follows:

Distributions to Beneficiaries (Schedule 6)		920
Balance, December 28, 19X1		$ 0

EXHIBIT H.3　CHARGE AND DISCHARGE STATEMENT

Schedule 1: Inventory of Assets

Cash	$ 25,700	
Marketable Securities	22,000	
Accrued Interest Receivable	250	
Residence	84,000	
Automobile	2,800	
Furniture	3,200	
Personal Effects	3,500	
Art Collection	12,000	$ 153,450
Less:		
Mortgage Payable	$ 23,000	
Accrued Interest Payable	140	23,140
Total Net Assets		$ 130,310

Schedule 2: Assets Subsequently Discovered

Coin Collection	$ 6,000

Schedule 3: Gain on Disposal of Principal Assets

Marketable Securities:

Proceeds of Sale	$ 7,150
Value per Inventory	7,000
Gain on Disposal	$ 150

Schedule 4: Debts of Decedent Paid

Funeral Expenses	$ 2,000
Charge Accounts	180
Utility Bills	91
Total Debts Paid	$ 2,271

Schedule 5: Loss on Disposal of Principal Assets

Automobile:

Proceeds of Sale	$ 2,500
Value per Inventory	2,800
Loss on Disposal	$ 300

Schedule 6: Distributions to Beneficiaries

Principal:

Janice Nelson	$ 84,000
William Corbett	41,700
SPCA	5,000
Total Principal Distributed	$ 130,700

Income:

SPCA	$ 920

EXHIBIT H.4   SCHEDULES FOR CHARGE AND DISCHARGE STATEMENT

PERSONAL TRUSTS

A **trust** is an entity established by a legal process to hold and manage assets on behalf of beneficiaries. Trusts are widely used for a variety of purposes. All have certain common characteristics:

- A *donor or grantor* transfers assets to the trust.
- A *trust agreement* sets forth the purposes of the trust, the duration of the trust, identification of the beneficiaries, identification of the trustee or the process for appointing the trustee, and other relevant matters.
- A *trustee* is appointed to take possession of the assets, to manage the assets, and to make distributions to the beneficiaries.
- One or more *beneficiaries*, who are entitled to receive the income and the principal of the trust, are identified.

Despite the variety of origins and purposes for trusts, three major types of trusts can be identified: *personal trusts*, *public trusts*, and *group trusts*. Although each type has some special accounting characteristics, only personal trusts are examined here.[1]

Individuals create **personal trusts** for the benefit of other individuals. For example, an individual's will may provide for the establishment of a trust for the spouse, children, or others. Such a trust, created by will to be effective at the grantor's death, is known as a **testamentary trust**. Another example is a **living trust**, also called an ***inter vivos* trust**, which takes effect while the grantor is living. In both cases, the trust usually has a limited life, perhaps extending for a spouse's lifetime or until a child reaches age 21. An individual who will periodically receive the trust's income is known as an **income beneficiary** or **life tenant**. A person who will receive the trust's principal, typically at the end of the trust's life, is known as a **principal beneficiary** or **remainderman**. In some cases, the income beneficiary and principal beneficiary are different individuals. For example, a husband may create a testamentary trust providing for his widow to be the income beneficiary and receive the income of the trust during her lifetime, and for the principal to be distributed to their children as principal beneficiaries upon the widow's death.

Personal trusts follow principles of **fiduciary accounting** similar to those discussed earlier for estates of individuals. The distinction between **principal** and **income** is important, since different beneficiaries may exist and their respective shares of the property are affected by whether transactions are considered principal or income. Financial reporting by the trustee may take the form of a **charge and discharge statement**, as was illustrated earlier. Alternatively, principal and income transactions may be reported separately in a **statement of trust principal** and a **statement of trust income**. The formats of these latter two statements are shown in Exhibits H.5 and H.6 respectively.

---

[1] **Public trusts**, often known as *charitable trusts* or *foundations*, generally benefit an activity or a cause and tend to have an indefinite life. Examples include a trust established to fund medical research and a foundation that supports educational initiatives. **Group trusts** are formed to benefit members of a designated group and also have an indefinite life. Examples include a company's pension trust established to accumulate and pay retirement funds and an investment trust that manages specific investment assets on behalf of investors.

Identification of Trust
Name of Trustee
Statement of Trust Principal
for the Period January 1, 19X1, to December 31, 19X1

Trust Principal, January 1, 19X1 (Detailed list) . . . . $ XX
Increases (Detailed list)   XX
                                                                                                           $ XXX
Decreases (Detailed list)   XX
Trust Principal, December 31, 19X1 . . . . $ XX

(A schedule showing the assets that make up the ending balance would be attached.)

EXHIBIT H.5   FORMAT OF STATEMENT OF TRUST PRINCIPAL

Identification of Trust
Name of Trustee
Statement of Trust Income
for the Period January 1, 19X1, to December 31, 19X1

Undistributed Trust Income, January 1, 19X1 . . . . $ X
Revenues (Detailed list)   X
                                                                                                           $ XX
Expenses and Distribution (Detailed list)   X
Undistributed Trust Income, December 31, 19X1 . . . . $ X

(A schedule showing the assets that make up the ending balance would be attached.)

EXHIBIT H.6   FORMAT OF STATEMENT OF TRUST INCOME

Personal trusts are also commonly used in *gift and estate tax planning*, as seen in the following section.

ESTATE PLANNING AND TAXATION

In addition to accounting and reporting for estates, accountants also participate in estate planning and determination of estate taxes. Both are complex topics requiring considerable study; this section introduces a few important aspects of these subjects.

Estate planning may be described as a process by which an individual (1) provides for the transfer of assets to desired beneficiaries and (2) attempts to reduce taxes on the transfers. The first of these objectives can be accomplished in several ways:

- A *will* should be prepared to specify disposition of the individual's property at death. If no will exists, state intestacy laws govern the distribution of property.
- *Gifts* may be made during the individual's lifetime.

■ *Personal trusts* may be established, either during the individual's lifetime or at death, to hold and manage assets on behalf of beneficiaries.

The second objective of estate planning is to minimize the tax cost of these asset transfers. Gift taxes apply to transfers of property during the individual's lifetime, and estate taxes apply to transfers at death. Minimizing gift and estate taxes involves planning the *timing* and *form* of these asset transfers.

FEDERAL ESTATE AND GIFT TAXATION

The U.S. estate tax and gift tax are both levied on the transfer of property from one individual to another. These taxes are imposed on the *transferor*, not on the *recipient*, of the property. Thus the giver is responsible for paying the gift tax, and the estate of a decedent is responsible for paying the estate tax. In contrast, some states impose inheritance taxes on the recipient.

Under the **unified gift and estate tax**, the same progressive rate schedule applies to both types of transfers. Current marginal tax rates range from 18 percent on the first $10,000 of taxable transfers to 55 percent on taxable transfers over $3,000,000, as shown in Exhibit H.7. The *tax base is cumulative* in that the tax is based on the aggregate amount of taxable transfers to date.

Amount Subject To Tax		Amount of Tax	
At Least	**But Less than**		
$ 0	$ 10,000	18% of taxable amount	
10,000	20,000	1,800 + 20% of excess over $	10,000
20,000	40,000	3,800 + 22% of excess over	20,000
40,000	60,000	8,200 + 24% of excess over	40,000
60,000	80,000	13,000 + 26% of excess over	60,000
80,000	100,000	18,200 + 28% of excess over	80,000
100,000	150,000	23,800 + 30% of excess over	100,000
150,000	250,000	38,800 + 32% of excess over	150,000
250,000	500,000	70,800 + 34% of excess over	250,000
500,000	750,000	155,800 + 37% of excess over	500,000
750,000	1,000,000	248,300 + 39% of excess over	750,000
1,000,000	1,250,000	345,800 + 41% of excess over	1,000,000
1,250,000	1,500,000	448,300 + 43% of excess over	1,250,000
1,500,000	2,000,000	555,800 + 45% of excess over	1,500,000
2,000,000	2,500,000	780,800 + 49% of excess over	2,000,000
2,500,000	3,000,000	1,025,800 + 53% of excess over	2,500,000
3,000,000		1,290,800 + 55% of excess over	3,000,000

Source: Internal Revenue Code, Section 2001 (c).

EXHIBIT H.7   FEDERAL ESTATE AND GIFT TAX RATES

Transfers Subject to Tax

Estate and gift taxes are generally based on the fair market value of the property at time of transfer. All transfers of property by gift are generally subject to the gift tax, with the following major *exclusions*:

- Gifts to *qualified charitable* and *political organizations*.
- Gifts to a spouse, due to an *unlimited marital deduction*.
- *Annual gifts* to other donees *up to $10,000* per donee, made to as many donees as the donor wishes. By "splitting" their gifts, married couples obtain an annual exclusion of $20,000 per donee.[2]

Determining the amount of an estate subject to tax can be considerably more complex than determining whether gifts are subject to gift taxes. The **gross estate** consists of the value of all property which the decedent owned or possessed an interest in at time of death. *Jointly-owned property*, such as real estate, is generally included to the extent of the decedent's interest; for example, one-half of the value of the property is included if there are two equal co-owners. In addition to cash, securities, real estate, and automobiles, other property is also part of the decedent's gross estate, including the following:

- Life insurance, even though payable directly to a beneficiary, if the decedent possessed *incidents (rights) of ownership* in the policy, such as the right to cancel the policy or to change beneficiaries.
- Value of decedent's pension and annuity benefits to be paid to a beneficiary.
- *Gift taxes* paid on gifts made within three years of death.[3]

To determine the **taxable estate**, the gross estate is reduced by the following *deductions*:

- Funeral expenses.
- Administrative expenses of the estate.
- Debts of the decedent.
- Losses of estate property due to casualty or theft during the period of administration.
- An unlimited marital deduction for property that passes to the surviving spouse.
- Transfers or bequests to qualified charitable organizations.

Calculation of Tax

The amount of taxable gifts or taxable estate is taxed according to the rate schedule shown in Exhibit H.7. As mentioned earlier, *the tax base is the cumulative amount of taxable transfers*. To determine the tax on a current gift, the tax on all gifts to date is calculated, and the tax applicable to previous gifts is then deducted. For example, assume an individual who has previously made taxable gifts of $470,000 now makes a taxable gift of $80,000 *more* than the $10,000 annual exclusion. The **gift tax** on the current gift is calculated as follows, using the rates in Exhibit H.7:

Tax on Cumulative Gifts of $550,000 [$155,800 + (37% × $50,000)] ..	$ 174,300
Less Tax on Prior Gifts of $470,000 [$70,800 + (34% × $220,000)] ...	(145,600)
Tax on Current Gift of $80,000	$ 28,700

---

[2] Under provisions of the *Taxpayer Relief Act of 1997*, the $10,000 and $20,000 amounts will be adjusted annually for inflation, beginning in 1999.

[3] Taxable gifts made within three years of death are considered to have been made "in contemplation of death." Including the related gift tax in the estate tax base prevents taxpayers from making "deathbed gifts" solely to reduce their taxable estate by the amount of the gift tax.

A **lifetime tax credit of $202,050** is available (in 1998) and is applied against gift and estate taxes until consumed. This credit is sometimes called the **unified credit**, because it applies to *both* gift taxes and estate taxes, which are *unified* into a single rate structure. The effect of the credit is to exempt from taxation a portion of the taxable gifts or taxable estate. The 1998 credit of $202,050 has the effect of offsetting the tax on the first $625,000 of taxable transfers, as seen below:

Tax on $625,000 from Exhibit H.7:	
Tax on first $500,000	$ 155,800
Tax on excess over $500,000, at	
rate of 37% (= $125,000 × .37)	46,250
	$ 202,050

The *Taxpayer Relief Act of 1997* provides for regular increases in this credit through the year 2006. Future credits, and the equivalent exemption from the estate and gift tax, are scheduled as follows:

Year	Amount of Credit	Equivalent Exemption
1999	$211,300	$ 650,000
2000-01	220,550	675,000
2002-03	229,800	700,000
2004	287,300	850,000
2005	326,300	950,000
2006	345,800	1,000,000

The process for calculating the **estate tax** is similar to the gift tax calculation above. In schedule form, the calculation is as follows:

Format of Estate Tax Computation

Gross estate
Less: Deductions for expenses, losses, and debts
Equals: Adjusted gross estate
Less: Marital and charitable contribution deductions
Equals: Taxable estate
Plus: Previous taxable transfers (gifts)
Equals: Tax base (cumulative taxable transfers)
Times: Appropriate rates from Exhibit H.7
Equals: Tentative tax
Less: Tax on prior transfers
Less: Portion of lifetime credit remaining
Equals: Estate tax due

Illustration

George Johnson died on July 17, 19X5, leaving half of his adjusted gross estate to his wife. The gross estate amounted to $1,730,000. The personal representative paid funeral expenses, administrative costs, and debts of the decedent from principal in the amount of $253,000. George made taxable gifts of $75,000 five years ago but, by applying a portion of his lifetime credit, paid no gift tax. Calculation of the *estate tax* follows:

Gross Estate	$ 1,730,000
Less Expenses and Debts	(253,000)
Adjusted Gross Estate	$ 1,477,000
Less Marital Deduction	(738,500)
Taxable Estate	$ 738,500
Previous Taxable Transfers	75,000
Cumulative Taxable Transfers	$ 813,500
Tentative Tax on Cumulative Transfers of $813,500 [$248,300 +	
(39% × $63,500)]	$ 273,065
Less Tax on Prior Transfers of $75,000 [$13,000 + (26% × $15,000)] .	(16,900)
Estate Tax before Credit	$ 256,165
Less Remaining Lifetime Credit ($202,050 − $16,900 applied to	
gift tax in prior years)	185,150
Estate Tax Due	$ 71,015

ESTATE PLANNING

Estate planning is the process whereby an individual plans for the transfer of property to beneficiaries, either during life or at death, in a way that accomplishes a number of objectives, such as the following:

- Providing sufficient availability of assets to meet the individual's lifetime needs
- Minimizing income taxes during the individual's lifetime
- Minimizing estate taxes, both at the time of the individual's death and at the time of beneficiaries' deaths

In the following sections, a number of factors involved in estate planning are briefly discussed.

Transfers During Life

Transfer of assets to beneficiaries during an individual's lifetime may be desirable for several reasons. When the individual's expected future needs are well provided for, lifetime transfers may satisfy personal objectives such as helping one's children to buy a home or start a business. Income tax reductions occur when the recipients are in lower tax brackets than the donor. Savings on gift and estate taxes may also occur but are limited by the cumulative nature of the tax. The $10,000 annual gift tax exclusion permits tax savings where transfers occur in small amounts over a period of time.

One form of transfer during life is **outright gift**, which permanently and irrevocably transfers ownership to the donee. Gifts are typically made to immediate family members, such as spouse or children. For example, if most of a couple's property is acquired and owned by the husband, gifts to his wife reduce the disparity in their estates and may lead to lower total estate taxes.

Another form of transfer during life, which may be permanent or temporary, is the *inter vivos* trust. Various forms of *inter vivos* trusts exist. **Revocable trusts**, sometimes called *living trusts*, exist at the pleasure of the grantor. There are no tax advantages to revocable trusts; the income is taxed to the grantor, and the trust property is included in the grantor's estate. Thus revocable trusts are usually created for nontax reasons, some of which are relevant to estate planning. The trust assets do not go through probate, thereby reducing delays and costs. Also, since wills are public documents when they are brought to probate court, while trust agreements are not, the use of a trust as a "will substitute" results in increased privacy. Trust assets are protected from creditors of the estate and may also be protected from control by a legal guardian should the donor become incapacitated. Finally, the trust, especially if in existence for some time, is less likely than a will to be challenged by heirs. These nontax advantages, which apply to any form of *inter vivos* trust, are often desirable in an estate plan.

Irrevocable trusts are permanent dispositions of property. Once an irrevocable trust is established, the grantor relinquishes control over the property, the income is not taxed to the grantor, except as noted below, and the trust property is excluded from the grantor's estate. Following the Tax Reform Act of 1986, income from property in an irrevocable trust is generally taxable at the *grantor's highest marginal income tax rate* when the income beneficiary is the grantor's dependent child under age 14. Transfer of property to an irrevocable trust constitutes a gift to the trust beneficiaries, and thus a gift tax obligation may be incurred. One advantage of transfer to an irrevocable trust over a direct gift to the beneficiary is that control is provided over the beneficiary's access to the principal. Another is that different income and principal beneficiaries can be named.

Transfers at Death

Transfers of property at time of death are specified in the will. Before these transfers can occur, however, provision for estate taxes must be made. The *marital deduction* is a major factor in reducing estate taxes. Thus estate planning often takes maximum advantage of the marital deduction by leaving much of the estate to the spouse. Note, however, that if the surviving spouse does not remarry, the marital deduction is available only on the death of the first spouse. For this reason, it is necessary to consider how to minimize the estate tax upon the death of the surviving spouse, especially in large estates (those greater than twice the exemption).

One common approach is for the first spouse to leave part of the estate to the surviving spouse, so as to qualify for the marital deduction, and to leave the other part to a trust where the surviving spouse is the income beneficiary but the children are the principal beneficiaries. The amount placed in trust is shielded from the estate tax by the decedent's lifetime credit. In this way, the full amount of the estate is available to provide support for the surviving spouse. And because only part will be included in the surviving spouse's estate, the lifetime credit available to the surviving spouse may be sufficient to shield that part from estate tax as well.

Thus an estate of $1.25 million could use this strategy to avoid federal estate tax completely. The estate plan would call for $625,000 to be left outright to the surviving spouse—tax-free because of the marital deduction—and for $625,000 to be placed in trust. The first spouse's lifetime credit shields the $625,000 placed in trust and the second spouse's lifetime credit shields another $625,000, including whatever is left of the $625,000 inherited outright from the first spouse.

There are some limitations on the use of trusts to minimize estate taxes. So-called *generation-skipping trusts* provide for (1) the children to be income beneficiaries and (2) the grandchildren or subsequent generations to be principal beneficiaries. The *generation-skipping transfer tax* exists to thwart attempts by taxpayers to avoid one or more generations of transfer taxes. This tax is imposed on generation skipping trusts or outright gifts at the highest marginal rate, currently 55%. An exemption of $1,000,000, however, is available to each grantor when generation-skipping is involved.[4]

Joint Ownership

Property owned jointly with right of survivorship automatically passes, upon the death of one owner, to the surviving owners. Although this eliminates the need to provide for disposition of the property in a will, it also limits flexibility in that all owners must agree to any sale of the property. Joint ownership that seems appropriate at one point in time may later prove inappropriate, as in the case of divorce. Jointly owned property is included in each owner's estate in a proportionate manner.

Life Insurance

Life insurance is often a significant part of an estate. Even though the proceeds are paid directly to the beneficiary, the face value of the policy is included in the estate if the decedent owned the policy. Ownership is measured in terms of possession of major rights—**incidents of ownership**—such as the right to cancel the policy or to change the beneficiary. To remove the insurance from the estate, the policy could be permanently transferred as a gift to another individual or to an irrevocable trust. Such action, however, involves loss of control over the cash surrender value and the face value of the policy, both of which may be major assets.

Liquidity

An important aspect of estate planning is the assurance that sufficient cash will be available in the estate to pay expenses, living costs of surviving family members, and estate taxes. Liquidity is a particular problem for individuals whose major asset is a business or a farm. The decedent's desire may have been to leave this asset intact for heirs, but often the asset must be sold to raise necessary cash. Some of the techniques available to ensure availability of cash to the estate are as follows:

- Life insurance is purchased with the estate named as the beneficiary.
- Showing "reasonable cause" may permit payment of the estate tax in installments over several years.
- Certain U.S. Treasury bonds that typically sell at a discount, known as **flower bonds**, can be redeemed at face value in payment of federal estate taxes.

---

[4] Beginning in 1999, this $1,000,000 exemption will be adjusted annually for inflation.

SUMMARY OF ESTATE PLANNING

An estate plan is not fixed or absolute. Once established, it needs regular monitoring and revision as an individual's assets, needs, and circumstances change over time. Because of the complexities involved, estate planning is usually handled by a team of professionals, including accountants, attorneys, tax experts, and perhaps others, such as investment brokers and insurance agents. Insofar as the transfer taxes are concerned, the objective is not simply to minimize their impact but to maximize the aftertax value of property available to beneficiaries.

SUMMARY OF KEY CONCEPTS

Fiduciary accounting relates to entities that exist to hold and manage assets on behalf of others. The **fiduciary** is the individual responsible for managing the assets. **Estates of individuals** and **trusts** are entities to which fiduciary accounting applies.

Legal considerations, especially the distinction between **principal** and **income**, are important in fiduciary accounting.

In **estates of individuals**, a **personal representative**—**executor** or **administrator**—takes charge of the decedent's assets, pays claims against the estate, and makes distributions to beneficiaries. The **charge and discharge statement** details, for both principal and income, the assets under the fiduciary's control and the disposition of those assets.

In the case of **trusts**, accounting and reporting depend on the nature of the trust. Accounting for **personal trusts** is similar to accounting for estates of individuals. A **statement of trust principal** and a **statement of trust income** may be used in lieu of the **charge and discharge statement**.

Estate planning involves consideration of how to transfer assets to beneficiaries, either during lifetime or at death. Minimizing the amount of **estate and gift taxes** is often an important objective in estate planning.

QUESTIONS

QH.1 Legal terminology is important in accounting for estates and trusts. Explain the meaning of the following terms:

1. Executor.
2. Intestate.
3. Administrator.
4. Principal.
5. Receiver.
6. Probate.
7. Residuary devise.
8. Specific devise.

QH.2 When principal assets are sold, are gains and losses resulting from the sale treated as income or as principal items? Can you offer any explanation for such treatment?

QH.3 Does accounting for estates follow cash basis or accrual basis accounting? Discuss your answer.

QH.4 Briefly explain the accounting procedures appropriate to each of the following:

1. Post-inventory discovery of assets (estates).
2. Liabilities existing at date of death (estates).
3. Involuntary conversion of principal assets (trusts).
4. Permanent improvements to principal assets (trusts).
5. Regular maintenance of principal assets (trusts).

QH.5 Complete each of the following statements:

1. An important aspect of fiduciary accounting is the distinction between _____ and _____.
2. The primary financial statement of the estate of a deceased person is known as _____.
3. The list of assets, and their values, owned by an individual at date of death is known in estate accounting as the _____.
4. A trust established by will to be effective at the grantor's death is a _____; a trust that becomes effective during the grantor's lifetime is a _____.

QH.6 At date of death, a decedent owned assets worth $225,000 (tax basis: $110,000) and had liabilities for unpaid income taxes and open charge accounts of $38,000. The inventory prepared by the personal representative includes _____.

EXERCISES

EH.1 Principal and Income Transactions In accounting for estates and trusts, there is a problem of separating the items that should be charged against principal from the items that should be charged against income. State whether each of the following items is charged to principal or to income, assuming the case of a testamentary trust:

1. Taxes on vacant city lots.
2. Interest paid on mortgage on real estate.
3. Depreciation of real estate.
4. Legal fees for collection of rent.
5. Special assessment tax levied on real estate for street improvement.
6. Amortization of premium on bonds which had been purchased by the testator.
7. Loss on sale of trust investments.
   (AICPA adapted)

EH.2 **Principal and Income Transactions** The numbered transactions below pertain to the accounts maintained by the executor of an estate. The decedent died on January 17, 19X0. The will and other documents revealed that the decedent's son was specifically bequeathed the decedent's only rental property and bonds of the MT Corporation ($100,000 par value, 3 percent, due February 28, 19Z5); the decedent's daughter was the beneficiary of a life insurance policy (face amount $150,000), on which the decedent paid the premiums; and his widow was left the remainder of the estate in trust, with full powers to determine the principal beneficiaries.

REQUIRED: For each numbered transaction below, indicate whether the amount in question should be: (a) allocated between principal and income, (b) attributed solely to principal, or (c) attributed solely to income.

1. January 20, 19X0: $3,450 was collected in connection with the redemption of AB Corporation bonds, 3 percent, due January 15, 19X0, par value $3,000.
2. January 20, 19X0: $1,000 was collected from FG Corporation on account of a dividend of $1 per share on common stock declared December 1, 19W9, payable January 15, 19X0, to stockholders of record January 2, 19X0.
3. January 20, 19X0; $3,250.50 was paid to Smith & Company, brokers, for the purchase of income bonds of A.A.R.R., 5 percent, due June 30, 19Y2, face value $3,000.
4. January 21, 19X0: Thirty shares of common stock were received from the DQ Corporation, constituting receipt of a 30 percent common stock dividend declared December 14, 19W9, payable January 20, 19X0, to holders of record January 15, 19X0.
5. February 1, 19X0: $400 quarterly interest was paid on a promissory note due January 31, 19X1.
6. February 1, 19X0: Dr. Mathews, the decedent's physician, was paid $1,000 for professional services rendered during the decedent's final illness.
7. February 1, 19X0: $1,600 was collected from TC Corporation on account of a cash dividend of $.50 per share on common stock, declared January 18, 19X0, payable January 30, 19X0, to holders of record January 27, 19X0.
8. February 1, 19X0: $400 rental income for February was deposited.
9. February 10, 19X0: $500 was paid for real estate taxes covering the period February 1—July 31, 19X0.
10. March 1, 19X0: $1,572 was paid on account of the decedent's state income tax for 19W9.
    (AICPA adapted)

EH.3 **Estate Value and Income** On August 1, 19X3, Kevin Jackson, administrator of Susan Phoenix's will, distributed the following and closed the estate:

Distributed to	Amount	
George Franklin	$ 3,500	
Carol Phoenix	$ 95,000	(gross proceeds from sale of Susan Phoenix's residence)
Darrell Phoenix	$ 48,400	(cash and securities)
Linda Webster	Personal belongings valued at $30,000	

Jackson's term as administrator commenced on December 1, 19X2, immediately after the death of Susan Phoenix. During the period of administration, the following events occurred:

1. Jackson invested some estate cash in securities (Group A).
2. Real estate fees on the sale of the house ($7,500) were paid. There was no mortgage remaining on the house.
3. Dividends on Group B securities (originally purchased by Susan Phoenix) of $1,000 were declared and received. Dividends and interest on Group A securities were received, totaling $2,500.
4. Legal and administrative fees (all charged to principal) of $3,000 were paid.
5. Jackson paid $800 brokerage fees on security transactions during his administration.
6. Group B securities increased in value $1,200.

REQUIRED:

1. Reconstruct the total market value of Susan Phoenix's assets on December 1, 19X2.
2. Calculate the income of the estate during the administration period. What expenses were charged to income?
3. Briefly state the terms of Susan Phoenix's will.

EH.4 **Estate Distributions** During the last few years of Maynard Crowley's life, he underwent expensive surgery and medical treatments. Back taxes and other overdue bills accumulated because Maynard was too ill to manage his financial affairs properly. After Felix Crowley, Maynard's son and executor of the estate, published notice to creditors of Maynard's death, the following bills were received:

Funeral Expenses	$ 2,500
Unpaid Medical Bills, Final Illness	12,000
Taxes Due at Date of Death	10,000
Charges at Local Stores	7,000
Loan from Bank	8,000

Maynard's will contained the following provisions:

1. Bequeathed to Felix Crowley, $30,000 plus residence and automobile (both fully owned by Maynard).
2. Bequeathed to St. Angela's High School, land (fully owned by Maynard) adjoining the school.
3. Bequeathed to Katherine Hutchinson, diamond and emerald brooch.
4. Bequeathed to St. Angela's High School, all property remaining after other distributions are complete.

Executor's fee was $2,000. Felix was also beneficiary of a $40,000 life insurance policy on Maynard's life. The net realizable values of assets at date of death were as follows:

Residence	$ 60,000
Certificates of Deposit	30,000
Land Adjoining St. Angela's High School	15,000
Other Land	10,000
Diamond and Emerald Brooch	4,000
Automobile	1,500

REQUIRED: Prepare a schedule of the assets of Maynard Crowley's estate in the sequence used to satisfy creditors' claims. After showing the appropriate assets used to pay creditors' claims, list the remaining assets to be distributed to Katherine Hutchinson, Felix Crowley and St. Angela's High School.

EH.5 **Trust Journal Entries** When he was 66 years old and his grandson Vincent had just turned 18, Walter Dodson established a trust for Vincent. The principal was composed of 8 percent bonds (face and market value, $80,000) and common stock (market value, $30,000) in several companies. Merchant's Bank agreed to administer the trust for an annual fee of 6 percent of gross trust income. The stocks and bonds were to come under Vincent's control when he reached age 21. Until that time, the yearly net income of the trust was to be paid to Vincent on his birthday. Dividends received on the stock for the three years of the trust were $1,200, $1,800, and $2,000, respectively.

REQUIRED: Record all journal entries made by Merchant's Bank for the trust of Vincent Dodson.

EH.6 **Estate Tax Calculations** Edith Barnes died on July 17, 19X5, leaving one-half of her estate to her husband and one-half to a trust for the benefit of their children. The gross estate amounted to $1,930,000. The estate paid debts, funeral expenses, and administrative costs of $40,000. During her lifetime, Edith made no gifts exceeding the $10,000 exclusion. Assume a $202,050 lifetime credit.

REQUIRED:

1. Calculate the estate tax owed by the estate of Edith Barnes.
2. Calculate the estate tax assuming Edith had left her entire estate to her husband.
3. Calculate the estate tax assuming Edith had left her entire estate to the trust for the benefit of their children.

PROBLEMS

PH.1 **Estate and Trust Accounting** On May 2, 19X2, Theodosia Hale died in a boating accident. The will specified Hale's residence was to be sold and the mortgage settled. Her personal belongings (furniture, jewelry, photographs, and so on) were bequeathed to

Rosenelle Abernathy, Hale's sister and only living relative. Rosenelle Abernathy was also named beneficiary of income from the estate subject to the following limitations:

1. Maximum annual distribution is to be $18,000. Earnings of the estate in excess of that amount are to be added to principal.
2. Minimum annual distribution is to be $10,000. Any deficiency in earnings is to be met by principal.

The will also called for creation of a trust. Income from the trust was to. be distributed to Rosenelle Abernathy, subject to the same limitations established for income from the estate. Upon Abernathy's death, the holdings of the trust were to be given to the United Fund. Kevin Boylston was named as executor of the estate and trustee of the trust.

The following information is available:

1. Residence: estimated fair market value at date of death, $110,000; mortgage payment made on June 1, 19X2, $400, of which $180 was interest; selling price, $108,000; selling and closing expenses, $9,700; payment of remaining mortgage, $25,000; selling date, June 2, 19X2.
2. Personal belongings: estimated fair market value at date of death, $27,000.
3. Estate taxes: $66,000, paid in 19X2; funeral expenses: $3,000, paid in 19X2.
4. Assets other than residence and personal belongings: cash, $20,000; securities, $200,000; undeveloped land, $40,000. Values are stated as of May 2, 19X2.
5. Accrued interest receivable on May 2, 19X2: Security A, $100, and Security B, $900.
6. Creation of the trust: April 30, 19X3.
7. Administrative expenses: May 2, 19X2, to April 30, 19X3, $5,000; May 1, 19X3, to April 30, 19X4, $4,000; divided evenly between principal and income.
8. Security transactions: Security A, interest of $600 received on March 1, 19X3, and March 1, 19X4; Security B, interest of $1,200 received on August 2, 19X2, and August 2, 19X3; dividends and interest on other securities, $16,000 in the first year of administration and $24,000 in the second year; sale of Security W in August 19X3 yielded $42,000 compared to book value of $30,000, with proceeds invested in Security G.
9. All distributions to the beneficiary were made on April 30.
10. Contents of safe deposit box discovered on July 10, 19X2: jewelry worth $9,000 and Security E worth $15,000 (values as of May 2, 19X2).

REQUIRED:

1. Prepare the journal entries made by the fiduciary for the period May 2, 19X2, to April 30, 19X3.
2. Prepare a charge and discharge statement for Kevin Boylston as of April 30, 19X3.
3. Prepare the journal entries made by the fiduciary for the period May 1, 19X3, to April 30, 19X4.
4. Prepare a charge and discharge statement for Kevin Boylston as of April 30, 19X4.

PH.2 Charge and Discharge Statement George Porter died on May 18, 19X3, leaving an estate consisting of the following:

Cash	$ 42,000
Portfolio of Securities	193,000
Automobile	5,000
Household Items	10,000

Debts connected with his final illness were $7,000, and funeral costs were $4,000. Marcia Porter was named executrix of the estate.

The following transactions occurred between date of death and December 31, 19X3:

1. All debts were paid.
2. Dividends received on securities amounted to $23,000.
3. Attorney and accountant fees of $10,000, attributable solely to principal, were paid.
4. Securities were sold as follows:

   ■ Security A sold for $12,000 ($4,000 gain)
   ■ Security B sold for $20,000 ($2,000 loss)
   ■ Security C sold for $26,000 ($5,000 gain)

5. All proceeds of the security sales were reinvested in new securities.
6. The household items were sold at auction, yielding $9,500. The auctioneer received a 10 percent commission.
7. Marcia Porter received a fee as executrix of $6,000, of which 10 percent was attributable to income.
8. A distribution of $10,000 was made to Edith Porter, George's widow. Under terms of the will, Edith is entitled to all income from the estate, distributed at the discretion of the executrix.

REQUIRED: Prepare a charge and discharge statement for the period ending December 31, 19X3.

PH.3 Estate Accounting The will of Albert Brown, deceased, directed that his executor, Charles Dawson, liquidate the entire estate within 2 years of the date of Mr. Brown's death and pay the net proceeds and income, if any, to the Sunnydale Orphanage. Mr. Brown, who was a bachelor, died on February 1, 19X4, after a brief illness.

An inventory of the decedent's property was prepared, and the fair market value of all items was determined. The preliminary inventory, before the computation of any appropriate income accruals on inventory items, follows:

	Fair Market Value
First National Bank Checking Account	$ 6,000
$60,000 City of Laguna School Bonds, Interest Rate 6% Payable January 1 and July 1, Maturity Date July 1, 19X8	59,000
2,000 Shares Jones Corporation Capital Stock	220,000
Term Life Insurance (Beneficiary—Estate of Albert Brown)	20,000
Personal Residence ($45,000) and Furnishings ($5,000)	50,000

During 19X4, the following transactions occurred:

1. The interest on the City of Laguna School bonds was collected. The bonds were sold on July 1 for $59,000, and the proceeds and interest were paid to the orphanage.
2. The Jones Corporation paid cash dividends of $1 per share on March 1 and December 1, as well as a 10 percent stock dividend on July 1. All dividends were declared 45 days before each payment date and were payable to holders of record as of 40 days before each payment date. On September 2, 1,000 shares were sold at $105 per share, and the proceeds were paid to the orphanage.
3. Because of a depressed real estate market, the personal residence was rented furnished at $300 per month commencing April 1. The rent is paid monthly, in advance. Real estate taxes of $900 for the calendar year of 19X4 were paid. The house and furnishings have estimated lives of 45 years and 10 years, respectively. The part-time gardener-handyman was paid 4 months' wages totaling $500 on April 30 for services performed, and he was released.
4. The First National Bank checking account was closed and the balance of $6,000 was transferred to an estate bank account.
5. The term life insurance was paid on March 1 and deposited in the estate bank account.
6. The following disbursements were made:
    a. Funeral expenses, $2,000.
    b. Expenses of final illness, $1,500.
    c. April 15 income tax remittance, $700.
    d. Attorney's and accountant's fees, $12,000.
7. On December 31, the balance of the undistributed income, except for $1,000, was paid to the beneficiary. The balance of the cash on hand derived from the principal of the estate was also paid to the beneficiary on December 31.

REQUIRED: As of December 31, 19X4, the executor resigned and waived all commissions. Prepare a charge and discharge statement separately stated as to principal and income, together with its supporting schedules, on behalf of the executor of the estate of Albert Brown for the period from February 1, 19X4, through December 31, 19X4. *(AICPA adapted)*

PH.4   Estate Accounting   Arthur Taine died in an accident on May 31, 19X2. His will, dated February 28, 19X1, provided that all just debts and expenses be paid and that his property be disposed of as follows:

■ U.S. Treasury bonds and Puritan Company stock—to be placed in trust. All income to go to his wife, Bertha Taine, during her lifetime, with Bertha having the power to appoint the principal beneficiaries upon her death.
■ Seneca Company mortgage notes—bequeathed to Wanda Taine Langer, daughter.
■ Cash—A bequest of $10,000 to David Taine, son.
■ Remainder of estate—to be divided equally between the two children, Wanda Taine Langer and David Taine.

The will further provided that during the administration period Bertha Taine was to be paid $300 a month out of estate income, and estate and inheritance taxes were to be paid out of principal. David Taine was named as executor and trustee.

Bertha and Arthur owned their personal residence jointly with rights of survivorship.

An inventory of the decedent's property was prepared. The fair market value of all items as of the date of death was determined. The preliminary inventory, before the computation of any appropriate income accruals on inventory items, follows:

Personal Residence Property	$ 95,000
Jewelry—Diamond Ring	9,600
York Life Insurance Co.—Term Life Insurance Policy on Life of Arthur Taine, Beneficiary—Bertha Taine, Widow	120,000
Granite Trust Co.—3% Savings Bank Account, Arthur Taine, in Trust for Philip Langer (Grandchild), Interest Credited January 1 and July 1; Balance May 31, 19X2	400
Fidelity National Bank—Checking Account; Balance May 31, 19X2 . .	143,000
$100,000 U.S. Treasury Bonds, 3% (Maturing in 30 Years), Interest Payable March 1 and September 1	100,000
$9,700 Seneca Co. First Mortgage Notes, 6%, due 19X6, Interest Payable May 31 and November 30	9,900
800 Shares Puritan Co. Common Stock	64,000
700 Shares Meta Mfg. Co. Common Stock	70,000

The executor opened an estate bank account to which he transferred the decedent's checking account balance. Other deposits, through July 1, 19X3, were as follows:

Interest Collected on Bonds:	
$100,000 U.S. Treasury	
September 1, 19X2	$ 1,500
March 1, 19X3	1,500
Dividends Received on Stock:	
800 Shares Puritan Co.	
June 15, 19X2, Declared May 7, 19X2, Payable to Holders of Record May 27, 19X2	800
September 15, 19X2	800
December 15, 19X2	1,200
March 15, 19X3	800
June 15, 19X3	800
Net Proceeds of June 19, 19X2, Sale of 700 Shares Meta Mfg. Co. . .	68,810

Payments were made from the estate's checking account through July 1, 19X3, for the following:

Funeral Expenses	$ 2,000
Assessments for Additional 19X0 Federal and State Income Tax ($1,700) plus Interest ($110) to May 31, 19X2	1,810
19X2 Income Taxes of Arthur Taine for the Period January 1, 19X2, through May 31, 19X2, in Excess of Amounts Paid by the Decedent on Declarations of Estimated Tax	9,100
Federal and State Fiduciary Income Taxes, Fiscal Years Ending June 30, 19X2 ($75), and June 30, 19X3 ($1,400)	1,475
Federal and State Estate Taxes	58,000
Monthly Payments to Bertha Taine—13 payments of $300	3,900
Attorney's and Accountant's Fees	25,000

The executor waived his commission. However, he desired to receive his father's diamond ring in lieu of the $10,000 specific legacy. All parties agreed to this in writing, and the court's approval was secured. All other specific legacies were delivered by July 15, 19X2.

REQUIRED: Prepare a charge and discharge statement as to principal and income, together with its supporting schedules, on behalf of the executor of the estate of Arthur Taine for the period from May 31, 19X2, through July 1, 19X3.
(AICPA adapted)

PH.5 Personal Trust Shortly before her death, Theresa Letterman established a $120,000 trust for the daughters of a friend. Emily and Janet Wallace, the beneficiaries of the trust, were each to receive half the income from the trust until their twenty-first birthdays. Upon reaching her majority, Emily was to receive $20,000. Janet (the younger sister) would continue to receive one-half of the trust income with the remainder being added to the principal. On Janet's twenty-first birthday, the remaining trust principal was to be divided equally and distributed to both women. Emily and Janet were 16 and 11 years old at the time Theresa Letterman made the arrangements.

Data concerning earnings and expenses of the trust are as follows:

	Total for First 5 Years	Total for Second 5 Years
Gross Earnings	$ 36,000	$ 43,000
Administrative Expenses (Allocated 60% to Principal and 40% to Income)	2,000	2,500
Gains (Losses) on Sales of Securities	(500)	3,000

REQUIRED:

1. Calculate the distribution of principal on Janet's twenty-first birthday.
2. Calculate the total dollar amount received by Janet from the trust. Calculate the total dollar amount received by Emily from the trust.
3. Calculate the distribution in the third year of the trust, assuming trust investment revenue was $7,000, administrative expenses were $400, and gains on sales of securities were $800 that year.

PH.6 Estate Planning and Taxation At Willa Grove's death, her gross estate amounted to $4,700,000. Expenses of the estate, other than estate taxes, totaled $800,000. Willa's husband had predeceased her by 17 years, and she had not remarried. Willa made two gifts in recent years that exceeded her $10,000 annual gift tax exclusion:

1. A $30,000 gift given fifteen years ago to her daughter, Wanda, for a down payment on a house.
2. A $25,000 sports car given to her son, Wilson, upon completing graduate school twelve years ago.

REQUIRED:

1. Calculate the federal estate tax owed by the estate of Willa Grove, assuming she died in the year 1998.

2. Calculate the federal estate tax owed by the estate of Willa Grove, assuming she died in the year 2006.

3. Because Willa's assets far exceeded what was needed to provide for a comfortable level of support for herself, she had often considered making transfers to her children and grandchildren during her lifetime. However, she never got around to actually doing this. Assume that over the past 17 years (since her husband's death), she had made annual gifts of $10,000 to each of her two children and (since their births) to each of her five grandchildren, who were ages 7, 9, 10, 14, and 18 at the time of her death in 1998. How much estate tax saving would have occurred had these gifts been made? Ignore the time value of money.

INDEX

F

S